Guide to
Networking Essentials
Fifth Edition

Greg Tomsho
Ed Tittel
David Johnson

COURSE TECHNOLOGY
CENGAGE Learning

Australia • Brazil • Japan • Korea • Mexico • Singapore • Spain • United Kingdom • United States

COURSE TECHNOLOGY
CENGAGE Learning™

Guide to Networking Essentials, Fifth Edition
Greg Tomsho, Ed Tittel, David Johnson

Managing Editor: **Will Pitkin III**

Acquisitions Editor: **Nick Lombardi**

Production Editor: Elena Montillo

Technical Editor: **John Freitas**

Editorial Assistant: **Allison Murphy**

Product Managers:

Sarah Santoro

Amy M. Lyon

Robin M. Romer

Developmental Editor: **Lisa M. Lord**

Senior Channel Marketing Manager: **Dennis Williams**

Manufacturing Coordinator:

Susan Carroll

Manuscript Quality Assurance:

Christian Kunciw

John Freitas

Serge Palladino

Cover Design: **Abby Scholz**

Text Design: **GEX Publishing Services**

Compositor: **GEX Publishing Services**

For product information and technology assistance, contact us at
Professional & Career Group Customer Support, 1-800-648-7450

For permission to use material from this text or product, submit all requests online at **www.cengage.com/permissions**
Further permissions questions can be emailed to
permissionrequest@cengage.com

Photo Credits: Cover Image ©2006 Jupiterimages Corporation. Figure 3-4, RJ-45 and RJ-11 connectors, © Gary Herrington Photography. Figure 3-6, patch panels, courtesy of Siemon. Figure 3-9, fiber-optic cable, courtesy of Optical Cable Corporation. Figure 3-10, fiber-optic cable connectors - ST, SC, LC, MTRJ, courtesy of Fiber Connections, Inc. Figure 4-5, CardBus network adapter, courtesy of 3Com Corporation. Figure 4-6, wireless network adapter - WG311, courtesy of NETGEAR.

ISBN-13: 978-1-4188-3718-1

ISBN-10: 1-4188-3718-0

Course Technology Cengage Learning
25 Thomson Place
Boston, MA 02210
USA

Cengage Learning products are represented in Canada by Nelson Education, Ltd.

For your lifelong learning solutions, visit **course.cengage.com**

Visit our corporate website at **www.cengage.com**

Notice to the Reader
Publisher does not warrant or guarantee any of the products described herein or perform any independent analysis in connection with any of the product information contained herein. Publisher does not assume, and expressly disclaims, any obligation to obtain and include information other than that provided to it by the manufacturer. The reader is expressly warned to consider and adopt all safety precautions that might be indicated by the activities described herein and to avoid all potential hazards. By following the instructions contained herein, the reader willingly assumes all risks in connection with such instructions. The publisher makes no representations or warranties of any kind, including but not limited to, the warranties of fitness for particular purpose or merchantability, nor are any such representations implied with respect to the material set forth herein, and the publisher takes no responsibility with respect to such material. The publisher shall not be liable for any special, consequential, or exemplary damages resulting, in whole or part, from the readers' use of, or reliance upon, this material.

Printed in the United States of America
8 9 11 10

Contents

TABLE OF
Contents

CHAPTER THREE
Networking Media   **69**

Preface

This book is intended to serve the needs of information systems professionals and others who are interested in learning more about networking technologies but who might have little or no background in this subject matter. This book's extensive and broad coverage of computer networking technologies gives students a solid networking background to pursue a number of certifications, including Network+, CCNA, MCSA, Linux+, and CNA. With the extensive use of tables that compare important properties of networking technologies, this book also makes an excellent reference.

The fifth edition includes new coverage of network security, small business networking, Windows Vista, Windows XP, Windows Server 2003, and Linux Fedora Core 4. In keeping with the latest trends in networking, this edition has updated coverage on the 802.11 and 802.16 wireless standards, network switches, VPNs, and 10 GB Ethernet. These topics are just a sampling of the many additions and updates to this book, so read on and enjoy.

This edition includes a CD packed with simulations that give visually oriented students an innovative tool to help them grasp difficult networking concepts. The simulations cover topics ranging from baseband versus broadband communications to Network Address Translation (NAT) and Internet e-mail operation.

Intended Audience

Guide to Networking Essentials, Fifth Edition is intended for people who are getting started in computer networking and want to gain a solid understanding of a broad range of networking technologies. This book is ideal for would-be information technology professionals who want to pursue certifications in a variety of computer networking fields as well as for those in a managerial role who want a firm grasp of networking technology concepts. To understand the material in this book, you should have a background in basic computer concepts and have worked with the Windows and/or Linux operating system. This book is ideal for use in a classroom or an instructor-led training environment and is also an effective learning tool for individual self-paced training.

Coping with Change on the Web

Sooner or later, all the specifics on Web-based resources mentioned in this book will become outdated or be replaced by newer information. In some cases, the URLs listed in this book might lead to their replacements; in other cases, they will lead nowhere, resulting in the dreaded 404 error message "File not found."

When that happens, please don't give up! There's always a way to find what you want on the Web, if you're willing to invest some time and energy. Most large or complex Web sites offer a search engine. As long as you can get to the site itself, you can use this tool to help you find what you need. In addition, try using general search tools, such as *www.google.com*, *www.yahoo.com*, or *www.dogpile.com*, to find related information. The bottom line is if you can't find something where the book says it should be, start looking around. It's likely to be somewhere!

Chapter Descriptions

Here's a summary of the topics covered in each chapter of this book:

Chapter 1, "Introduction to Networks and Networking Concepts," introduces many of the computer and networking terms and technologies discussed in detail in later chapters.

In **Chapter 2**, "Network Design Essentials," you learn about network design concepts, network device operation, and networking topologies.

Chapter 3, "Networking Media," covers the cables and connectors required to connect network devices and discusses wireless networking.

In **Chapter 4**, "Network Interface Cards," you learn about the devices that connect computers to local area networks. Bus interfaces, special-purpose cards, and wireless interface cards are also covered.

Chapter 5, "Making Networks Work," discusses the standards and specifications used to build networks, including those related to the OSI model and IEEE 802.

In **Chapter 6**, "Network Communications and Protocols," you learn about the language of networks, including TCP/IP and IPX/SPX. Special emphasis is given to IP addressing and subnetting, and a section on IPv6 is included.

Chapter 7, "Network Architectures," discusses how different network architectures operate. These architectures include Ethernet, token ring, and FDDI as well as broadband technologies such as cable modem. Coverage of 10 GB Ethernet is also included, as is a section on the future of Ethernet operation.

In **Chapter 8**, "Simple Network Operations," you learn about network operating system features and how to install network operating systems. You also learn how to configure network services in Windows and Linux environments.

Chapter 9, "Understanding Complex Networks," discusses integrating multiple operating systems in a complex networking environment, with special attention to integrating Windows, Linux, and NetWare. A section on integrating PDAs into an enterprise network is also included.

In **Chapter 10**, "Introduction to Network Security," you learn about Trojan programs, worms, spammers, denial-of-service attacks, spyware, crackers, backdoors, spoofers, rootkits, and more security concerns. In addition, you learn how to develop a security policy.

Chapter 11, "Supporting a Small Business Network," discusses the unique technology requirements of small businesses to give you more insight into addressing a small business's computer and networking needs.

In **Chapter 12**, "Network Administration and Support," you learn how to create users, develop account policies, monitor network performance, and develop backup strategies.

In **Chapter 13**, "Enterprise and Wide Area Networks," you learn how to expand a network by using switches, routers, and gateways. In addition, you learn how WAN technologies, such as frame relay and ISBN, work and how you can implement these technologies to create networks that can extend across your town or across the country.

Chapter 14, "Solving Network Problems," discusses what you can do to prevent network downtime, data loss, and security breaches. In addition, you learn about the problem-solving process, several different approaches to solving network problems, and the tools for troubleshooting networks.

Appendix A, "Common Networking Standards and Older Technologies," provides information about the standards-making process as it applies to networking. It also covers the most important and influential standards-making bodies in the United States and worldwide. In addition, information about older or obsolete technologies included in earlier editions has been moved to this appendix for reference.

Appendix B, "Planning and Implementing Networks," is an overview of the planning required before designing and installing a network. This planning includes user training requirements and post-sales technical support issues.

Appendix C, "Network Troubleshooting Guide," summarizes advice on how to recognize, isolate, and diagnose trouble on a network, whether it's related to media, hardware, or software.

Appendix D, "Networking Resources, Online and Offline," is a compilation of printed and online resources you can use for additional research into networking essentials.

Features

To help you understand networking concepts thoroughly, this book incorporates many features designed to enhance your learning experience:

- **Chapter Objectives.** Each chapter in this book begins with a detailed list of the concepts to be mastered. This list serves as a quick reference for the chapter's contents and is a useful study aid.

- **Illustrations and Tables.** Numerous illustrations of networking components aid you in visualizing common networking setups, theories, and architectures. In addition, tables provide details and comparisons using both practical and theoretical information. Examples for illustrating concepts and system features encompass Microsoft desktop operating systems, Windows Server, Linux, and Novell NetWare. When client-side functionality is important, desktop operating systems are used for examples; when the focus is on server-side functionality, server operating systems are used. Because most campus labs use Microsoft operating systems, these products have been used for most screen shots and Hands-On Projects.

- **Simulations.** In many chapters, you'll find references to simulations included on the CD that accompanies this book. These simulations provide a visual learning experience, demonstrating concepts such as broadband communications, Ethernet switches, token ring operation, Network Address Translation, Internet e-mail operation, and more.

- **Chapter Summaries.** Each chapter's text is followed by a summary of the concepts introduced in that chapter. These summaries are a helpful way to review the material covered in each chapter.

- **Key Terms.** All terms introduced in the chapter with boldfaced text are gathered into the Key Terms definitions at the end of the chapter. This list gives you an easy way to check your understanding of important terms and provides a useful reference.

- **Review Questions.** End-of-chapter assessment begins with a set of review questions that reinforce the ideas introduced in each chapter. These questions ensure that you have mastered the concepts.

- **Hands-On Projects.** Although understanding the theory behind networking technology is important, nothing can improve on real-world experience. Each chapter includes projects aimed at giving you hands-on experience.

- **Case Projects.** Each chapter closes with a section that proposes certain networking situations. You're asked to evaluate the situation and decide on a course of action to remedy the problems. This valuable tool helps you sharpen decision-making and troubleshooting skills, which are important aspects of network administration.

Text and Graphic Conventions

Additional information and exercises have been added to this book to help you better understand what's being discussed in the chapter. Icons throughout the text alert you to these additional materials:

 The Note icon draws your attention to additional helpful material related to the topic.

 The Tip icon offers extra information based on author experiences about how to approach a problem or what to do in real-world situations.

 The Caution icon identifies important information about potential mistakes or hazards.

 The Hands-On Projects icon precedes each Hands-On Project and a description of the project follows.

 Case Project icons mark case projects, which are scenario-based assignments. In these extensive case examples, you're asked to apply what you have learned.

 Simulation icons refer you to the simulations on the CD that accompanies this book. These simulations reinforce the concepts being discussed in the respective section.

Instructor Support

The following additional materials are available when this book is used in a classroom setting. All supplements available with this book are provided to instructors on a single CD, or you can retrieve them from the Course Technology Web site, *www.course.com*, by going to the page for this book under "Download Instructor Files & Teaching Tools."

Electronic Instructor's Manual. The Instructor's Manual that accompanies this book includes additional instructional material to assist in class preparation, including suggestions for lecture topics, suggested lab activities, tips on setting up a lab for hands-on assignments, and solutions to all end-of-chapter materials.

ExamView®. This book is accompanied by ExamView, a powerful testing software package that instructors can use to create and administer printed, computer (LAN-based), and Internet exams. ExamView includes hundreds of questions that correspond to the topics covered in this book, enabling students to generate detailed study guides with page references for further review. The computer-based and Internet testing components allow students to take exams at their computers, and they save instructors time by grading each exam automatically.

PowerPoint presentations. This book comes with a set of Microsoft PowerPoint slides for each chapter. These slides are meant to be used as a teaching aid for classroom presentations, to be made available to students on the network for chapter review, or to be printed for classroom distribution. Instructors are also at liberty to add their own slides for other topics introduced.

Figure files. All figures and tables in the book are reproduced on the Instructor's Resource CD in bitmap format. Similar to the PowerPoint presentations, they are included as a teaching aid for classroom presentation, to make available to students for review, or to be printed for classroom distribution.

Contact the Author

I would like to hear from you. Please e-mail me with any problems, questions, suggestions, or corrections. I even accept compliments! This book has staying power, so I would not be surprised to see a sixth edition in the future. Your comments and suggestions are invaluable for shaping the content of that next edition. You can contact me at *NetEss@tomsho.com*.

Visit Our World Wide Web Site

Additional materials designed especially for you might be available for your course on the World Wide Web. Go to *www.course.com* and search for this book title periodically for more details.

ACKNOWLEDGMENTS

I would like to thank the team at Course Technology for this opportunity to improve and expand on an already excellent fourth edition of this book. This team includes but is not limited to Robin Romer, Product Manager; Elena Montillo, Production Editor; Nick Lombardi, Acquisitions Editor; the excellent proofreader, Karen Annett; and the Manuscript Quality Assurance folks, Serge Palladino and John Freitas. Thanks also to my developmental editor, Lisa Lord, for her excellent guidance in creating a polished product. Special thanks goes to my beautiful wife, Julie, our daughters, Camille and Sophia, and our newest addition, Michael, whose patience and support made this project successful.

I would also like to thank the following reviewers, who guided me with excellent and helpful feedback on each chapter:

Bill Beaty	Kirkwood Community College
Karl Linderoth	Bay de Noc Community College
Don Mosier	Black Hawk College

Read This Before You Begin

The Hands-On Projects in this book help you to apply what you have learned about computer networking. Although some networking components can be expensive, the projects aim to use widely available and moderately priced hardware and software. The following section lists the minimum hardware and software requirements for completing all the Hands-On Projects in this book. In addition to the following requirements, students must have Administrator privileges on their workstations and (for some projects) on the classroom server as well. Although not necessary, installing virtualization software on student workstations is highly recommended, such as VMware Player or Virtual PC, along with virtual machines for Windows XP, Windows Server 2003, and Linux Fedora Core 4.

Lab Requirements

- **Hardware:**
  - A lab with workstations connected by twisted-pair cable
  - Workstations that can run Windows XP Professional with Service Pack 2
  - One or more servers running Windows Server 2003
  - One or more computers running Linux Fedora Core 4
  - Access to the Internet
  - Small sections of coaxial, fiber optic, and twisted-pair cables and different connectors
  - Networking tools, such as a crimping tool, a wire stripper, and a cable tester
  - One or more basic Ethernet networking hubs or switches (10BaseT or 100BaseT)
  - A network-connected printer
  - One or more computers that can be used to install a new operating system
  - A variety of network interface cards with different bus interfaces and media attachment interfaces

- **Software:**
  - Windows XP Professional for each student workstation
  - Macromedia Flash player installed on each student workstation
  - Linux Fedora Core 4
  - Windows Server 2003 Standard Edition for each server

1

INTRODUCTION TO NETWORKS AND NETWORKING CONCEPTS

After reading this chapter and completing the exercises, you will be able to:

♦ Describe the fundamental reasons for networking

♦ Identify essential network components

♦ Compare different types of networks

♦ Understand the role of a server and describe types of servers

♦ Apply your knowledge when selecting a network type

Networks are vital to the business use of computers, especially for the applications and data that networks can deliver. If a single computer with standard desktop software—such as word processing, spreadsheets, and databases—can make anyone more productive, then interconnecting computers on a network and bringing people and data together improves communications, fosters productivity, and creates opportunities for collaborating and exchanging information quickly and easily.

As a future network administrator, you must understand the fundamental concepts in creating a network and making any network perform correctly. It's also important to understand what's involved in networked communications and which network models are best in different business situations. This knowledge gives you a solid foundation for network design, implementation, and troubleshooting tasks.

WHAT IS NETWORKING?

Networking involves connecting computers and other electronic devices for the purpose of **sharing** information and resources and for communication. Even though the concept of networking is basic, a great deal of technology is required for one device to connect and communicate with another, and many choices for physical connections and related software are possible. In the following sections, you learn about the fundamental concepts that drive all networks to help you understand why networking is so important in the workplace and in people's everyday lives.

Networking Fundamentals

Computer networks represent an important advance from what a single computer can do alone. The most elementary network consists of two computers connected by some kind of transmission medium, such as wire, cable, or air waves, to transmit data from one machine to the other. No matter how many computers are interlinked or what kind of connection is used, all networking derives from this basic description. In fact, when computers communicate, they do so most frequently in pairs—one machine sends information and the other receives that information. Of course, most networks consist of many computers and are usually connected by a networking device, such as a hub, switch, or access point (discussed in Chapter 2).

The primary motivation for networking is the need for people to share data and to communicate quickly and efficiently. Personal computers (PCs) alone are valuable business tools, but without a network, PCs are isolated and can neither share data with other computers nor access network-attached **peripheral devices**, such as printers, scanners, and fax machines. The following uses represent some of the primary benefits of networking:

- Data sharing enables **groups** of **users** to exchange information and route data from one user to another as workflow demands. Data sharing also usually means that master copies of data files reside in a specific place on another computer elsewhere on the network, and users can access the master copy to do their work. When multiple users access the same file simultaneously, their software must be able to merge updates to keep a single master copy consistent and correct.

- Because data sharing makes it possible to circulate messages, documents, and other files among users, it can also improve human communication substantially. Although no company installs a network simply to support **electronic mail (e-mail)**, e-mail remains the most popular networked application in most organizations because it makes communication so easy and efficient.

- Peripheral **device sharing** enables groups of users to take advantage of peripherals, such as printers, scanners, fax machines, and other devices attached directly to a network or to a generally available computer attached to a network. Companies can, therefore, buy fewer peripherals but spend more on each one so that better features and higher levels of service are widely available. For many businesses, this capability alone justifies the costs and efforts of networking.

An old, well-known alternative to networking—passing a disk from machine to machine—is often called a **sneakernet**. Sneakernet doesn't begin to approach the power and convenience of a real network; no group of standalone computers can rival the power and convenience of true networking. Any single computer that's not attached to a network is by definition a **standalone computer**.

If a standalone computer were connected to a number of other computers, as shown in Figure 1-1, that computer could share its data with those other machines and obtain data from them. In addition, all machines could access the printer attached to the same network. In fact, this collection of equipment, plus the medium that links them, is what makes up a network. By extension, sharing resources on a network is called networking. In networking, the material through which information passes from one computer to another is called the medium and can be copper wires, fiber-optic cable, or air waves.

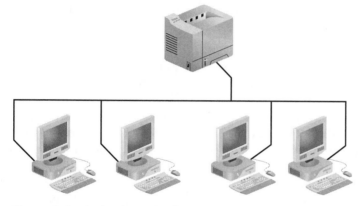

Figure 1-1   A simple network

Local and Wide Area Networks

Originally, networks used expensive and complex technologies, and many of the earliest networks were entirely custom-built. These early networks seldom interconnected more than a dozen computers, nor were they likely to support more than one or two additional peripheral devices. The earliest networking technologies imposed severe restrictions on the number of interconnected machines and the physical span of the networks. For example, one early networking technology could support a maximum of only 30 users on a single network, with a total span of just 607 feet. This setup works well in a small office environment with a limited number of connected machines, where the span from one end of the office to the other—even allowing for characteristic twists and turns—falls within this limitation.

A small network, limited to a single collection of machines and one or more cables and other peripheral equipment, can be called a **local area network (LAN)**. LANs also form the basic building blocks for constructing larger networks called internetworks. An **internetwork** is a network of networks or a networked collection of LANs tied together by devices such as routers (discussed in Chapter 13). For large organizations that occupy more than one floor in an office building or operate in multiple buildings in a campus setting, for example, no single LAN can contain all the computers, cables, and other equipment needed to bring together the entire user community. When the number of computers exceeds 100 and the distance to be spanned is more than 1000 feet, an internetwork is usually needed. The **Internet**, the best example of the largest internetwork in the world, is a vast public wide area internetwork that makes it possible for any computer in the world to communicate with any other computer in the world using standard technologies and protocols.

Because of their limitations, early LANs were unable to meet the networking requirements of large organizations, especially those that operated in multiple locations. The benefits of networking were so great, however, that technology evolved to accommodate larger, geographically dispersed organizations. As the scope of a network expands to encompass multiple groups of users in multiple locations, LANs can grow into **wide area networks (WANs)**. A WAN is an internetwork that spans distances measured in miles and links two or more separate LANs. WANs use the services of third-party communications providers, such as telephone companies, to carry network traffic from one location to another.

Occasionally, you might encounter a network type called a **metropolitan area network (MAN)**. Essentially, MANs use WAN technologies to interconnect LANs in a specific geographic region, such as a county or a city. It's not uncommon to find large, complex networks involving all three network types: LANs for purely local access, MANs for regional or citywide access, and WANs for access to remote sites elsewhere in the country or around the world. MANs have recently received a boost in popularity because of the growing trend in some major cities to implement a citywide wireless network. In these cases, wireless networking is possible in almost any part of the city, allowing users to stay connected whether at home, at work, or at play. Some wireless technologies that make this type of networking possible are discussed in Chapter 3.

Most businesses today use networks to store and share access to all kinds of data and applications and to provide communications for employees and business partners. For these reasons, networks are regarded as critical business tools. Nearly all users in today's workplace use computers to connect to their company networks.

DEVELOPING A NETWORKING LEXICON

As you have likely noticed by now, networking is a subject rich with specialized terminology and technology. Computer networks have spawned a language of their own, and half the challenge of becoming network literate lies in mastering this terminology. To make sense of the upcoming discussion of networking types, you must learn some new vocabulary.

Clients, Peers, and Servers

Fundamentally, any computer on a network plays one of two basic roles: a client or a server. A **server** is a computer that shares its resources across the network, and a **client** is one that accesses shared resources. Another way to understand this relationship is to visualize an information interchange best described as **request–response**. A client requests information, and a server responds by providing the requested information or by denying the request. Figure 1-2 depicts the client/server relationship.

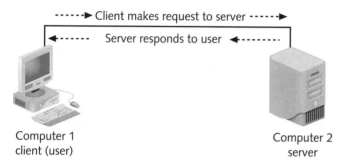

Figure 1-2   Client/server relationship

In **client/server** networking environments, certain computers take specialized roles and function mainly as servers, and ordinary users' machines tend to function mainly as clients. Windows Server 2000/2003, the upcoming server product from Microsoft (code-named Longhorn Server), Linux, and UNIX are operating systems designed for server use. Client/server networking makes it worthwhile to concentrate **central processing unit (CPU)** power and storage capacity in servers because they represent shared resources. The CPU is the collection of circuitry that supplies the "brains" for computers.

In other networking environments, computers can function as clients or servers, as circumstances dictate. For example, a computer can act as a server and provide resources to other machines, or it can request a resource from another computer, thereby acting as a client to that machine. Because all machines on this type of network function at more or less the same level of capability, these machines are called peers. By extension, this type of networking is **peer-to-peer** because peers share and request resources from one another. Typical examples include Microsoft Windows 98 and Windows Me. The Windows desktop operating systems Vista, XP, and 2000 Professional can also operate in peer-to-peer networking environments, as can a number of Linux implementations.

NOTE

For simplicity, when this book refers to Windows 95, Windows 98, and Windows Me, they are referred to collectively as Windows 9x.

Network Medium

To communicate successfully, computers must share access to a common **network medium**. For most networks, the medium takes the form of a physical cable that interconnects the machines the medium services. However, many types of network media exist, including several types of metallic cable (twisted-pair and coaxial are the most common) and fiber-optic cable as well as numerous forms of wireless media.

Whatever medium is used on a network, its job is to carry the signals one computer sends to one or more other computers. To access any network, computers must attach to the network medium by using some kind of physical interface; for PCs, this interface is usually a network interface card (NIC) or network adapter. For large-scale networks, multiple media usually work together (interoperate) across the total networking environment. This flexibility is what makes large, complex networks possible. Network media and network interface cards are discussed in detail in Chapters 3 and 4, but suffice it to say that the media and NICs play a substantial role in determining how a network works. Next, you learn about the software components of a network: protocols, operating systems, and network services.

Network Protocols

When connected to a network through a NIC or another interface, a computer must also be able to use that connection. That is, for two computers on a network to communicate with one another successfully, they must share a common set of rules about how to communicate. At a minimum, these rules must include how to interpret signals, how to identify "oneself" and other computers on a network, how to initiate and end networked communications, and how to manage information exchange across the network medium. These collections of agreed-on rules are **network protocols** or, more simply, protocols.

To communicate successfully, computers must not only share a common network medium, but also have at least one protocol in common so that each can understand what the other is trying to communicate. For example, a Swahili speaker places a call to a French speaker. Unless they have some language in common, it's unlikely they'll be able to communicate, even though they can establish a working connection (in the form of a telephone call). Likewise, for computers to communicate, they must use a common protocol.

NOTE Network protocols are usually referred to by their acronyms, such as TCP/IP, NetBEUI, and IPX/SPX. In Chapter 6, you learn more about these and other network protocols.

Network Software

Even though two computers share a common medium and network protocol, they still might not be able to communicate unless they can actually run programs that access the network. In other words, computers need network software to issue the requests and responses that let them take the roles of clients and servers.

Computers that participate on a network run a **network operating system (NOS)** that determines what services that computer can offer or request. An NOS also controls access to the network services and **network resources** a computer makes available to clients. With today's operating systems, the line between a client and a server has become blurred. Most operating systems can act as both clients and servers, capable of requesting network services (client) and providing network services to clients (server). However, most operating systems have a workstation version and a server version, with the primary difference being the number of services that can be offered and the level of control or security that can be imposed on clients accessing those services. Server versions of operating systems, such as Windows Server 2003 and Red Hat Enterprise Linux, are designed to excel at providing network services securely. Operating systems such as Windows XP, although capable of providing some network services, are designed to access services provided by a server operating system.

 Many Linux operating system implementations don't distinguish between client and server versions. During installation, users have a choice of installing software for Linux to act as a server or a workstation (client).

Network Services

The whole purpose of a network is to allow computers to share resources, such as hard drives and printers, and to allow users to communicate (via e-mail, for example). Sharing resources and communication requires two components: a server component that provides access to the resource and a client component that requests access to the resource. Both components are referred to as a service. The terms "service" or "network service" are generic, so you might hear, for example, that NOSs deliver file and print services, e-mail services, or Web services. In keeping with the client/server model of networking, network servers stand ready to deliver network services to network users who request them. You can liken network services to a telephone call to a company you would like to do business with. You are acting as the client, and the company is acting as the server or service. You establish the call by using the telephone (network media), and you begin a conversation in your native language (protocol). Assuming the person on the other end speaks your language, you can now do business. Next, you must select which service you require: sales, technical support, billing, order fulfillment, and so forth. Each service is handled by a special department, and you might have to be transferred to that department. In the same way, NOSs must be outfitted with the types of services your client operating systems require, whether they are Web servers, e-mail servers, file and print servers, and so on.

In Chapter 6, you learn that network protocols not only define the kinds of messages and communications that computers can exchange with one another, but also define the kinds of services a network can deliver. The success of the Internet stems not from the common protocols it uses, but from the widely used network services those protocols support.

Here's a recap on the layered nature of networked communications: Network applications use an NOS or client networking software to instruct a network protocol to access the network interface; the network interface and its associated software can then address and exchange information with some other computer on a LAN or a WAN. This exchange of information occurs through the network medium. Sometimes these information exchanges call on services that network servers make available to network users. Each layer of software is essential for successful networked communications; each higher layer depends on the one beneath it to perform its specific tasks. In turn, each lower layer provides services to the layer above it to make its own contributions to the networking process, as you can see in Simulation 1-1. Figure 1-3 also depicts this relationship.

Simulation 1-1: Layers of the Networking Process

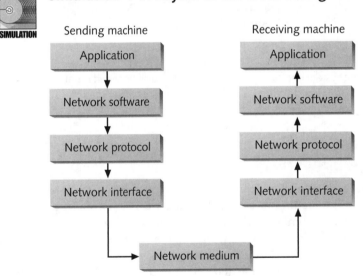

Figure 1-3 Layers of the networking process

UNDERSTANDING NETWORK TYPES

Networks fall into two major types: peer-to-peer and client/server (also called **server-based**). This discussion of network types addresses the role that computers play on the network and how those roles interact, which contrasts with the previous discussion of

LAN versus WAN that focused on the technologies computers use to communicate. Server-based networks are the most typical and represent the primary focus of the discussion here. Understanding both types is essential, especially as they compare with one another.

Peer-to-Peer Networking

As you have learned, computers on a peer-to-peer network can take both a client and a server role. Because all computers on this type of network are peers, these networks impose no centralized control over shared resources, such as files or printers. Any user can share resources on his computer with any other user's computer on the same network, however and whenever he chooses. The peer relationship also means that no single computer has any higher priority to access, or increased responsibility to provide, shared resources on the network. Figure 1-4 shows an example of a typical peer-to-peer network.

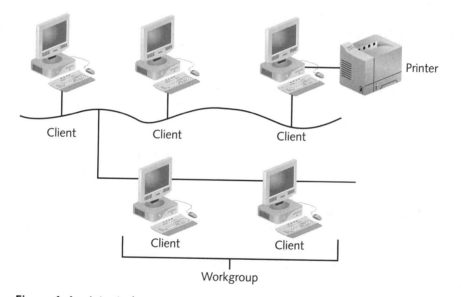

Figure 1-4   A typical peer-to-peer network

In a peer-to-peer network, every user must also act as a **network administrator**, controlling access to the resources on their machines. Users can give everyone else unlimited access to their resources or grant restricted (or no) access to other users on the network. Likewise, users can decide whether other users can access resources simply by requesting them or whether they must supply a password for access requests to succeed. (That is, users with the correct password can access resources, but those who lack the proper password can't.)

Because of this flexibility and individual discretion, institutionalized chaos is the norm for peer-to-peer networks, and security can be a major concern. On a peer-to-peer network, computers can be affiliated into loose federations called workgroups, but no network-wide security can be enforced. Those who know the right passwords can access the resources those passwords guard, and those who don't are denied access.

Although this system can work on small networks, it introduces the possibility that users might have to know, and remember, a different password for every shared resource on a network. As the number of users and resources grows, these networks can become unworkable—not because they don't operate correctly, but because users can't cope with the complexity. This limitation is in contrast to a server-based network, in which security of all resources is administered centrally.

Most peer-to-peer networks consist of collections of typical end-user PCs linked by a common network medium. These machines are not designed to perform as well as network servers. They can bog down easily under increasing loads, as more users try to access resources from a particular machine. The user whose machine is being accessed across the network also has to endure a performance reduction while that machine is busy handling network information requests. For example, if a user's machine has a network-accessible printer attached, the machine slows down every time someone sends a job to that printer. This slowdown is fine for other users but could interrupt the user working at that machine. In addition, if a user restarts the machine not knowing that someone is accessing a resource on it, the network user's access fails or, even worse, data loss can occur.

Another issue that affects peer-to-peer networks is data organization. If every machine can be a server, how can users keep track of what information resides on which machine? If five users are responsible for a collection of documents, any of those users might have to search through files on all five machines to find a document. The decentralized nature of peer-to-peer networks makes locating resources more difficult as the number of peers increases. Likewise, decentralization makes backup considerably trickier: Instead of backing up a single shared repository of data, each machine must be backed up to protect shared data.

Given these issues and complexities, peer-to-peer networks might not seem worth using. However, they offer some powerful advantages, particularly for small organizations (and networks, by extension). Peer-to-peer networks are the easiest and most inexpensive to install. Most peer-to-peer networks require only a suitable operating system (such as Windows 9x or Windows XP) on machines along with network interfaces and a common network medium. After the machines are connected and configured correctly, users can begin to share information and access devices immediately. All nonserver versions of Windows, from Windows 3.11 to Windows Vista, support a special networking model, called the **workgroup model**, that permits groups of machines to work together as peers in the absence of a special-purpose server.

Peer-to-peer networks are uniquely well suited to small organizations, which tend to have small networks and small operating budgets. Peer-to-peer networks are also easy to use and don't require extensive staff training or a dedicated cadre of network administrators. With no centralized control, the loss of a single machine means only the loss of access to the resources on it; otherwise, a peer-to-peer network continues to function when one computer fails. For small businesses, peer-to-peer networks can be an inexpensive, easy, and convenient way to take advantage of the increased productivity and communications that networks provide.

Peer-to-Peer Networking Advantages

The following list summarizes the advantages of peer-to-peer networking:

- A peer-to-peer network is easy to install and configure.
- Machines don't depend on the presence of a dedicated server.
- Users control their own shared resources.
- Peer-to-peer networking is inexpensive to purchase and operate.
- Peer-to-peer networks need no additional equipment or software beyond a suitable operating system.
- No dedicated administrators are needed to run the network.
- A peer-to-peer network works best for networks with 10 or fewer users.

Peer-to-Peer Networking Disadvantages

The following is a summary of the disadvantages of peer-to-peer networking:

- Network security applies to only a single resource at a time.
- Users might be forced to use as many passwords as there are shared resources.
- Each machine must be backed up to protect all shared data.
- Every time a user accesses a shared resource, performance of the machine where the resource resides is reduced.
- There is no centralized organizational scheme to locate or control access to data.
- Access to a shared resource is unavailable if the machine where the resource resides is turned off or crashes.
- A peer-to-peer network doesn't usually work well with more than 10 users.

Server-Based Networks

Although server-based networks can be referred to as client/server, the server is so important to this type of network that NOS vendors, such as Microsoft and Novell, prefer the term "server-based" to emphasize this role. A server is best described as a machine with the sole function of responding to client requests. A server is seldom operated by someone sitting in front of it (and then usually only for installation, configuration, or management tasks); therefore, a server's main role on a network is to be continuously available to handle the many requests for its services that a community of clients can generate. Figure 1-5 shows an example of a server-based network.

Server-based networks provide centralized control over network resources, primarily by instituting network security and control through the server's operating system configuration and setup. The computers used for servers usually have faster CPUs, more memory, larger disk drives, and extra peripherals (such as tape drives and disk storage arrays) compared to

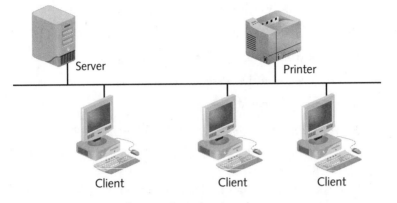

Figure 1-5   A typical server-based network

user machines. Server operating systems are designed to handle multiple requests for shared resources expeditiously. In most cases, servers are **dedicated servers** that handle network requests from their client communities. Because physical security—that is, access to the machine—is a key component of network security, situating servers in controlled-access rooms separate from general work areas is ideal.

Keep in mind that a collection of hardware does not by itself make a computer a server. Although it's true that computers used as servers often have special design features, what makes a computer a server is the operating system that's installed and how the computer is deployed. For example, Novell NetWare, Red Hat Enterprise Linux, and Windows Server 2003 are designed to act as server operating systems, but they can be installed on just about any type of computer hardware.

Server-based networks also provide centralized verification of user accounts and passwords so that one or more **specialized servers** act as sentries, guarding access to the network. Windows Server 2003, for example, uses a **domain model** to manage collections of users, groups, and machines and to control their access to network resources. Before users can access resources on the network, they must identify themselves to a domain controller, which is a server that checks **account names** and **passwords** against a database of information it maintains. This database is known as **Active Directory** for Windows Server 2003 networks.

Only with valid account and password combinations can users access certain resources, and only network administrators can modify security information in the security database. This approach supports centralized security and resource management with varying degrees of control, depending on the resource's importance, sensitivity, or location. In the Novell world, one or more NetWare servers provide similar controls over users and the resources they can access by using **Novell eDirectory** to store and manage the same kind of security information that Windows domain controllers handle. The Linux operating system supports a similar resource directory called **Network Information Service (NIS)**. The rules that govern which resources can be accessed by which accounts are referred to as **access controls**.

Typically, server-based networks also require only a single logon to the network; users don't need to remember a separate password for each resource. Likewise, network resources, such as files and printers, are more accessible because they're located on specific servers, not spread around users' machines across the network. Concentration of resources on fewer servers also makes data resources easier to back up and maintain.

Unlike peer-to-peer networks, server-based networks are easier to scale. Although peer-to-peer networks should be limited to 10 or fewer users, server-based networks can handle anywhere from a handful to thousands of users as networks grow to serve entire organizations or to keep pace with an organization's growth and expansion.

Like peer-to-peer networks, server-based networks have some disadvantages. The most obvious is the additional overhead of operating a server-based network. Server-based networks require one or more high-powered computers to run server software, which adds to the cost of these networks. In addition, these networks usually require at least part-time support from a knowledgeable person. Acquiring the skills to manage a server-based network or hiring a trained network administrator adds significantly to operation costs.

Server-based networks' centralization of resources and control has both negative and positive consequences. Although centralization simplifies access, coordinates control, and aggregates resources, it can also introduce a single point of failure on networks. Without an operational server, a server-based network is no network at all. On networks with more than one server, loss of a single server means loss of all resources associated with that server. In addition, if that lost server is the only source of access control information for a set of users, those users can't access the network either.

Server-Based Networking Advantages

The following list summarizes the advantages of server-based networking:

- Centralized user accounts, security, and access controls simplify network administration.

- More powerful equipment means more efficient access to network resources.

- Server hardware design is generally more robust, providing features such as fault-tolerant hardware and redundant systems.

- A single password for network logon delivers access to network-wide resources as specified in access controls.

- Server-based networking makes the most sense for networks with 10 or more users or any networks where resources are used heavily.

Server-Based Networking Disadvantages

The following list summarizes the disadvantages of server-based networking:

- At the worst, server failure renders a network unusable; at the least, it results in loss of network resources.

- Complex server software requires allocating expert staff, which increases expenses.

- Dedicated hardware and specialized software add to the cost of server-based networking.

Wireless Personal Area Networks (WPANs)

With all the wireless devices people carry and their desire to be connected at all times, it's no wonder that a networking technology designed specifically to connect these devices was developed. The **wireless personal area network (WPAN)** is a short-range networking technology designed to connect personal devices to exchange information. These devices include cell phones, pagers, **personal digital assistants (PDAs)**, global positioning system (GPS) devices, MP3 players, and even watches.

NOTE   A PDA is a handheld computer used for personal organization tasks, such as appointment and address book management.

A WPAN can connect devices you wear or come in close contact with and can transmit to outside devices for a short range, typically within 10 meters or less, by using a secure access method. Devices in a WPAN exchange information; for example, if you wanted to phone Jim Goodfriend, you could speak "Call Jim Goodfriend" into a microphone worn on your body. Your cell phone would then contact your PDA to get the phone number from the address book and make the call. Using a WPAN, you could also transfer information from a device you're carrying to a device another person is carrying. Most devices with built-in WPAN capabilities make it possible to transfer information such as business cards or identity authentication to other devices with the single touch of a button.

The emerging standard for WPANs is the IEEE 802.15 standard (covered in more detail in Chapter 5). This standard covers several areas, including both high and low data-rate transmission. One product using this standard is Bluetooth, which is a short-range wireless technology originally developed by Ericsson and found in a variety of devices, such as PDAs, cell phones, GPS devices, and even MP3 players. A Bluetooth-enabled PDA can be used to synchronize data with and transfer files to a desktop computer or to communicate with a handheld GPS to keep from getting lost while mountain biking, for example.

Understanding the Role of Network Servers

The server is at the heart of any network that's too large for a peer-to-peer configuration. In fact, most large networks with more than a few dozen workstations probably rely on several network servers. Your knowledge of a server's unique hardware requirements and the many roles it can play in a network is essential to being able to design and support today's computer networks.

Server Hardware Requirements

A server's primary function is to handle host computer requests for network resources and other network services. Handling service requests across a network invariably adds to a machine's processing load. The higher that load, the more important it is to purchase computers with additional power to handle demands for network resources. To get an idea of what's involved, review Table 1-1, which compares the minimum (and recommended, shown in parentheses) hardware requirements for Windows XP Professional, Windows Server 2003, and Windows Vista.

Table 1-1   Minimum (and recommended) requirements for Windows operating systems

Item	Windows XP Professional	Windows Server 2003	Windows Vista*
RAM	64 (128+) MB	128 (256+) MB	512 (1024+) MB
Disk type	IDE (EIDE or SATA)	EIDE (SCSI or SATA)	EIDE (SATA)
Disk space	1500 (2000) MB	1.5 (2) GB	N/A
CPU speed	233 (300+) MHz	133 (550+) MHz	1.8 GHz
Number of CPUs	1 (or 2)	1 (2 or 4)	1 (dual core)
NIC type	PCI or PCI-X	PCI or PCI-X	PCI (PCI-X)

*Windows Vista information is preliminary, as Microsoft has not released the product as of this writing.

Table 1-1 has several noteworthy implications. First, it's interesting to see how the Microsoft bare minimum values compare to the industry consensus on recommended values. (Recommended values are shown in parentheses for each entry.) The bare minimum doesn't approach the more realistic requirements of the recommended values, especially for disk space, where the minimum allows room only for the operating system and not much else. (Clearly, this minimum requirement is impractical on a client computer and doubly so on a server.)

The trend worth noting is that the requirements jump appreciably when you compare Windows XP with Windows Vista. Many requirements for Vista are based on the new graphics Microsoft will deploy as part of its new OS. Servers don't usually require fancy 3D graphics, which is why the minimum requirements for Server 2003 are modest in comparison. However, conventional wisdom holds that the best way to deploy a server is to stuff it with the fastest CPUs, add as much **random access memory (RAM)** and disk space as it can hold, and install at least one of the fastest NICs available. That's why Windows Server 2003 was designed to handle up to 64 CPUs and as much as 512 GB of RAM in a single system.

Specialized Servers

Within the broad classification of machines that function as network servers, assigning a variety of specialty roles is possible, depending on the services provided. On large networks in particular, servers with specialized roles are often deployed. In Windows Server 2000/ 2003 and Linux environments, these server types typically include application servers, communication servers, domain controllers/directory servers, fax servers, file and print servers, mail servers, and Web servers.

Application Servers

Application servers supply the server side of client/server applications, and often the data that goes along with them, to network clients. A database server, for instance, not only supplies query-processing and data-analysis functions, but also acts as a repository for the huge amounts of data often stored in a database.

Application servers differ from basic file and print servers by providing processing services as well as handling requests for file or print services. In file and print services, the client does its own file handling and print processing. Generally, clients must run specialized client-side applications (or plug-ins to other applications) to communicate with an application server. For these applications, typically the client side formulates requests and ships them to the application server, which handles all the request's background processing and then delivers the results back to the client side. The client side then formats and displays those results to the user. Microsoft SQL Server delivers complex client/server application support that runs on Windows Server 2000/2003; versions of Oracle with similar capabilities are available for Windows Server 2000/2003, NetWare, and many flavors of UNIX, including Linux. A popular public-license database server called MySQL is available for most versions of Windows, Linux, UNIX, and NetWare, among other operating systems.

Communication Servers

Communication servers provide a mechanism for users outside a network to access that network's resources (inbound communications) and sometimes permit users on that network to access resources outside the network's local scope (outbound communications). Often, installing communication servers on a network enables users who are traveling or working at home to dial in to the network via a modem. Windows Server 2000/2003 includes a powerful communication server, called **Routing and Remote Access Service (RRAS)**, for handling dial-up network connections. Similar add-on products are available for NetWare and Linux, including products from companies such as Citrix.

Domain Controllers/Directory Servers

In general, directory services make it possible for users to locate, store, and secure information about a network and its resources. Windows Server 2000/2003 permits computers, users, groups, and resources to be combined into logical groups called **domains**. Any user belonging to a specific domain can access all resources and information that he or she has permission to use simply by logging on to the domain. The server that handles this logon service and manages the collection of computers, users, and so on in a domain is a **domain controller** or **directory server**. Windows Server 2000/2003 includes all the software needed for a network server to function as a domain controller and/or a directory server, as does Novell NetWare (versions 4.x and above); directory service add-ons for Linux are available from companies such as Netscape Communications Corp., or you can use the built-in NIS.

Fax Servers

Fax servers manage fax traffic for a network. They receive incoming faxes via telephone, distribute them to recipients over the network, and collect outgoing faxes across the network before sending them via telephone. Typically, these servers use one or more fax modem interfaces (often referred to simply as "fax modems") to perform these tasks. As with most communication servers, Windows-, NetWare-, and Linux-based fax servers come from third parties instead of the platform vendors.

File and Print Servers

File and print servers are the mainstay of the server world because they provide basic network file storage, retrieval services, and access to networked printers—functions that define the fundamental uses of most business networks. With these servers, users can run applications locally but keep data files on the server (and print those files when they want hard copies). Any Windows, NetWare, or Linux server can act as a file and print server.

Mail Servers

Mail servers handle e-mail messages for network users; this function might involve simply acting as a clearinghouse for local exchange of messages. However, mail servers also commonly provide "store-and-forward" services, in which the server holds incoming e-mail messages while waiting for users to access them. Likewise, the server can store outgoing messages until a connection to an external mail server is established and then forward messages to their intended destinations. Microsoft Exchange Server is sophisticated mail server software that runs on Windows Server 2000/2003, Novell has its popular GroupWise e-mail system, and Lotus Notes is a mainstay in many organizations.

Web Servers

As companies increasingly turn to software using Transmission Control Protocol/Internet Protocol (TCP/IP, the protocol used on the Internet) to distribute information, no single service has gained popularity as quickly as the **World Wide Web (WWW)**. The World

Wide Web is the most well-known aspect of the Internet, made up of millions of documents that can be interlinked by using hyperlinks. Being able to view and retrieve documents with the click of a mouse makes the resources of the Internet widely available. Windows Server 2000/2003 includes a complete **Web server** called Internet Information Services (IIS) as well as File Transfer Protocol (FTP) services. NetWare includes a Web server as part of its 4.x and 5.x versions; the excellent Apache Web server is available free for Linux and is now part of NetWare 6.5. Many organizational **intranets** (in-house TCP/IP-based networks) that use these operating systems also take advantage of these free Web server packages. In fact, Apache remains the most widely used Web server in the world.

As networks grow larger and more complex, specialization of server roles is increasing. NetWare and Linux operating systems are specifically designed to handle this broad range of needs. Windows Server 2000/2003 is the primary Microsoft operating system that's built to deliver these capabilities and services.

Web-Based Networks

The Internet and the WWW are becoming a part of everyday life, and people increasingly rely on the services of the Web for communication, research, and even entertainment. With new developments in Internet communications and capabilities, this trend will only continue. Most computers today are connected to the Internet, and the latest handheld devices, such as cell phones and PDAs, are connecting through wireless communications.

Until recently, the Web was considered separate from a normal computing environment. Users had to connect through a modem, run their Web browsers to view Web pages, and start their e-mail programs to check e-mail. Today, because of the always-on connections available via DSL and cable modems and high-speed connections at work and at home, the Web is an integral and seamless part of the computing experience. Technologies such as the Microsoft .NET initiative and Web-enabled devices, such as cell phones and PDAs, promise to integrate the Web even further into people's lives.

.NET Computing

The Microsoft .NET computing model uses the Web to deliver applications as well as information and to enable applications on different devices running different operating environments to communicate and share data. This model allows a device with a wireless interface to the Web to download and run applications directly from the Web. It also allows a handheld computer to transfer information to and from a network server or another handheld computer by using the Web as the network. In this communication model, information can be transferred from one place to another easily and conveniently.

Web-Enabled Devices

WPANs allow devices within a person's personal space to communicate. Many devices used in a WPAN are Web-enabled devices that can gather and send information via the Internet. Of course, other devices are becoming Web-enabled. Automobiles can be equipped with a

1

navigation system that tells you not only where you are, but also how to get where you're going. Need to know where the nearest gas station is? A Web-enabled navigation system can download and display a list of nearby service stations.

A host of devices are being created that can access the Web, thus shifting the networking paradigm from clients and servers to Web-enabled and not Web-enabled. The concept of client and server will still exist, but clients will become any Web-enabled device that needs information, and servers will become any Web-enabled device that can provide that information.

SELECTING THE RIGHT TYPE OF NETWORK

You have a number of choices to make when deciding how to design and implement a network. Will a single LAN do, or is an internetwork required? Is a MAN or WAN required? Will peer-to-peer networking suffice, or is a server-based network in order? Or do some functions need to be server-based while others work well as a peer-to-peer network? You have learned enough in this chapter to make some of these decisions, but the following sections offer a brief summary to help in the decision-making process.

Choosing a LAN Versus an Internetwork

Recall that an internetwork is two or more LANs tied together by network devices such as routers. LANs are almost always confined to a specific area or floor of a building, but internetworks are formed when LANs are tied together, whether the distance between the LANs is a few feet, a few hundred yards, or a few hundred miles. The decision to design a LAN or an internetwork is primarily based on how many total computers will participate on the network and whether there's a need to tie groups of computers together with network devices such as routers. The distance the network will span also plays a part in the decision. A simple LAN is usually called for when the following conditions are true:

- The number of computers is fewer than 100.
- Network use and security factors don't require using a router.
- The network is confined to a single building or floor of a building.

If any of these factors isn't true, an internetwork is probably called for. For example, when the number of computers approaches or exceeds 100, the amount of network traffic generated is usually too much for a single LAN to handle efficiently. Breaking the computers into two or more smaller LANs and connecting them with a router is usually the solution to this problem, hence creating an internetwork. In addition, if certain groups of users require a security barrier between their network resources and the rest of the network, a router can provide that extra security.

If two floors on a building or two buildings need to be networked together, or if your network spans multiple sites across town or across the country, each floor, building, or site usually comprises its own LAN, which requires a router to tie them together. With multiple sites, you have not only an internetwork, but also a MAN or a WAN.

Is It a MAN or a WAN?

The only real question in deciding whether your network should be called a MAN or a WAN is the distance the network covers. If you need the services of a communications provider to tie multiple sites together, you have a MAN or WAN. The only real difference is whether the sites are confined to a town or city or whether the sites are located in different cities. Within one town or city, the network is generally referred to as a MAN; if the network spans different cities, it's considered as a WAN.

Choosing a Peer-to-Peer or Server-Based Network

Given the inherent limitations of peer-to-peer networking, there are several easy methods for deciding what type of network is right for a set of circumstances. Choosing peer-to-peer networking exclusively is appropriate *only* when all the following conditions hold:

- The network includes no more than 10 users (preferably no more than five).
- All networked machines are close enough to fit within the span of a single LAN.
- Budget considerations are paramount.
- No specialized servers (for example, communication servers) are needed.

A server-based network, by contrast, makes sense when one or more of the following conditions is true:

- More than 10 users must share network access.
- Centralized control, security, resource management, or backup is desirable.
- Users need access to specialized servers, or they place heavy demands on network resources.
- An internetwork is in use.

Very often, a network starts out small, with modest resource sharing requirements and only a few users. A peer-to-peer network fits these requirements well. Over time, the sophistication of required networked applications increases, as does the number of users. A business finds itself in need of one or more servers to accommodate the additional network use and to run the more sophisticated networked applications. However, some users who have been sharing documents and printers for years in a peer-to-peer arrangement want to continue doing so in the manner to which they're accustomed, and a hybrid network is born. In a **hybrid network,** elements of both a server-based network and a peer-to-peer network are used. Small workgroups share files, printers, and other devices with one another, and all network users log on to and access network-wide resources the servers provide.

CHAPTER SUMMARY

- ❑ The basic elements of all networks include a network medium (cabling) of some kind and a physical interface (network adapter) to that medium for computers seeking access to network resources.

- ❑ In addition to network media and interfaces, computers must have a networking protocol in common to communicate, and they must include networking software that knows how to use the protocol to send and receive information across a network.

- ❑ Networks deliver services such as file sharing, printing, e-mail and messaging services, and more to users.

- ❑ The major types of networks are peer-to-peer, in which any computer can function as a client or a server; server-based, in which users act as clients of dedicated machines that take the server role; and wireless personal area networks, in which the network is limited to a small area around a person.

- ❑ Budget, number of users, types of applications or network services, and requirements for centralized administration and control are the major criteria in deciding which type of network to deploy.

- ❑ Servers require specialized hardware and software and are capable of taking specific roles, acting as file and print servers, fax servers, e-mail servers, application servers, and so on.

KEY TERMS

Because this chapter begins an ongoing dialogue on networking and introduces many terms, there are several key terms to review. Familiarize yourself with these terms to ensure complete understanding of this material, which covers networking fundamentals for hardware, software, and services.

access controls — Methods for imposing controls that allow or deny users access to network resources, usually based on a user's account or a group to which the user belongs.

account names — Strings of letters, numbers, or other characters that identify a user's account on a network.

Active Directory — The directory service environment for Windows Server 2000/2003. Active Directory includes enough information about users, groups, organizational units, and other kinds of management domains to represent a complete digital model of the network.

application server — A specialized network server with the job of providing access to a client/server application and sometimes to the data belonging to that application.

central processing unit (CPU) — The collection of circuitry (a single chip on most PCs) that supplies the "brains" for most computers.

client — A computer on a network that requests resources or services from another computer.

client/server — A model for computing in which some computers (clients) request services and other computers (servers) respond to requests for services. Applications are sometimes divided across the network so that a client-side component runs on the user's machine and supplies request and display services, and a server-side component runs on an application server and handles data processing or other computation-intensive services on the user's behalf.

communication server — A specialized network server that provides access to resources for users not directly attached to the network or enables network users to access external resources not directly attached to the network.

dedicated server — A network server that acts only as a server and is not intended for regular use as a client machine.

device sharing — A primary purpose of networking: permitting users to share access to devices of all kinds, including servers and peripherals such as printers or scanners.

directory server — A specialized server with the job of responding to requests for specific resources, services, users, groups, and so on. This kind of server is more commonly called a domain controller in Windows Server 2000/2003 networking environments.

domain — A uniquely named collection of user accounts and resources that share a common security database.

domain controller — On Windows Server 2000/2003 networks, a directory server that also provides access controls over users, accounts, groups, computers, and other network resources.

domain model — A network based on a Windows server operating system with security and access controls residing in a domain controller.

electronic mail (e-mail) — A networked application that enables users to send and receive text messages, with or without file attachments.

fax server — A specialized network server that can send and receive faxes via phone lines and direct them to users across the network.

file and print server — The most common type of network server (not considered a specialized server). It provides file storage and retrieval services across the network and handles print jobs for users.

groups — Named collections of user accounts, usually created for a specific purpose. For example, the Accounting group might be the only users permitted to use a bookkeeping application.

hybrid network — A network in which elements of a server-based network and a peer-to-peer network are in use. Small workgroups can share files, printers, and other devices with one another in a peer-to-peer fashion, and all network users log on to and access network-wide resources provided by the servers in a server-based arrangement.

Internet — A vast public wide area internetwork that makes it possible for any computer in the world to communicate with any other computer in the world using standard technologies and protocols.

internetwork — A network of networks that consists of two or more physical networks. Unlike a WAN, an internetwork resides in only a single location. Because it includes too many computers or spans too much distance, an internetwork can't fit within the scope of a single LAN.

intranet — An in-house TCP/IP-based network for use within a company.

local area network (LAN) — A collection of computers and other networked devices that fits within the scope of a single physical network and provides a building block for internetworks and WANs.

mail server — A specialized server that manages the flow of e-mail messages for network users.

metropolitan area network (MAN) — A type of network that uses WAN technologies to interconnect LANs within a specific geographic region, such as a county or a city. In most cases, however, a municipality or a communications carrier operates a MAN; organizations must sign up for service and establish connections to use a MAN.

network administrator — The person responsible for installing, configuring, and maintaining a network, usually a server-based network such as Windows Server 2003 or Novell NetWare.

Network Information Service (NIS) — A service available on the Linux operating system that provides a central database for user names and passwords, which controls user access to network resources.

network medium — A term that usually refers to the material (metallic or fiber-optic cable) that links computers on a network. Because wireless networking is possible, it can also describe the type of wireless communications that allow computers to exchange data via a wireless transmission frequency.

network operating system (NOS) — A specialized collection of software that enables a computer to communicate over a network and take advantage of a broad range of networking services. Windows Server 2003, Novell NetWare, and Linux are examples of network operating systems.

network protocols — Sets of rules for communicating across a network. To communicate across a network successfully, computers must share a common protocol.

network resource — Any kind of device, information, or service available across a network. A network resource could be a set of files, an application or a service, or a network-accessible peripheral device.

Novell eDirectory — The centralized database of user, group, and resource information that enables NetWare servers to handle network logins and resource access requests and to manage resource information for an entire network.

passwords — Strings of letters, numbers, and other characters intended to be kept private (and hard to guess) and used to identify a user or to control access to protected resources.

peer-to-peer — A type of networking in which each computer can be a client to other computers and also act as a server.

peripheral device — Any hardware component on a computer that's not the CPU. In a networking context, it usually refers to some kind of device, such as a printer, that users can share across the network.

personal digital assistants (PDAs) — Handheld computers used for personal organization tasks, such as appointment and address book management.

random access memory (RAM) — The memory cards or chips on a PC that provide working space for the CPU to use when running applications, providing network services, and so on. Where RAM on a server is concerned, more is usually better.

Routing and Remote Access Service (RRAS) — A software component bundled in Windows Server 2000/2003 that combines Remote Access Service (RAS) and Multi-Protocol Routing, in addition to packet filtering, demand-dial routing, and support for Open Shortest Path First (OSPF).

request-response — A description of how the client/server relationship works: A request from a client leads to some kind of response from a server. (Usually, the response is the service or data requested, but sometimes it's an error message or a denial of service based on security.)

server — A computer with the job of responding to requests for services or resources from clients on a network.

server-based — A type or model of networking that requires a server to provide services and resources and to manage and control access to those services and resources.

sharing — One of the fundamental justifications for networking. In the Microsoft lexicon, this term refers to the way in which resources are made available to a network.

sneakernet — A metaphorical description of a non-networked data exchange method: A person, presumably wearing sneakers, copies files on a disk at one computer and then hand-carries the disk to another computer.

specialized server — Any special-function server—an application server, a communications server, a directory server or domain controller, a fax server, an e-mail server, or a Web server, among others.

standalone computer — A computer that's not attached to a network.

users — People who use computers as standalone systems or to access a network.

Web server — The combination of hardware and software that stores information accessible over the Internet via the World Wide Web (WWW).

wide area network (WAN) — An internetwork that connects multiple sites; a third-party communications provider, such as a public or private telephone company, that carries network traffic from one location to another.

wireless personal area network (WPAN) — A short-range wireless networking technology used to connect a user's handheld or wearable computing devices.

workgroup model — The Windows name for a peer-to-peer network that includes one or more Windows-based computers.

World Wide Web (WWW) — This most well-known aspect of the Internet is made up of millions of documents that can be interlinked by using hyperlinks. Being able to view and retrieve documents with the click of a mouse makes the Internet's resources available to just about anyone.

REVIEW QUESTIONS

1

1. What is the name for a network that connects two or more local area networks (LANs) across a large geographic area?

    a. peer-to-peer network

    b. wide area network (WAN)

    c. internetwork

    d. intranet

2. Which of the following operating systems supports peer-to-peer networking? (Choose all that apply.)

    a. Windows XP Professional

    b. Windows 9x

    c. Windows 2.0

    d. Windows Server 2003

3. You work for a small company with four users who need network access. The budget is tight, so the network must be as inexpensive as possible. What type of network should you install?

    a. server-based network

    b. peer-to-peer network

    c. WPAN

    d. storage area network

4. The _____ is the cable or communications technology that computers must access to communicate across a network.

    a. medium

    b. protocol

    c. software

    d. connector

5. A _____ is needed to attach a computer to a network.

    a. transceiver

    b. network interface card (NIC)

    c. multistation attachment unit (MSAU)

    d. hub

6. Which of the following characteristics is associated with a peer-to-peer network? (Choose all that apply.)

   a. easy to install

   b. inexpensive

   c. user-managed resources

   d. centralized control

   e. server failure having a drastic effect on the network

7. A server computer shares resources for others to use. True or False?

8. A device interconnects five computers and a printer in a single office so that users can share the printer. This configuration is an example of which of the following?

   a. LAN

   b. MAN

   c. WAN

   d. all of the above

9. The computers in two networks located in offices 1000 miles apart share a set of documents and a common database. This configuration must be which of the following?

   a. LAN

   b. MAN

   c. WAN

   d. WPAN

10. A business occupying two floors of an office building has two groups of 100 computers, with each group tied together by a router. This configuration is an example of which of the following? (Choose the best answer.)

    a. WPAN

    b. MAN

    c. WAN

    d. internetwork

11. At Clairfield Community College, the North and South campuses (two miles apart) have LANs tied together by using the services of the local phone company. This configuration is an example of which of the following? (Choose the best answer.)

    a. MAN

    b. WPAN

    c. WAN

    d. SAN

1

12. A network that permits communication among devices such as cell phones and PDAs but has limited range is which of the following?

    a. MAN

    b. WPAN

    c. SAN

    d. WAN

13. Computers that can act as servers to other machines but can also request network resources are which of the following?

    a. nodes

    b. clients

    c. servers

    d. peers

14. Server-based networks can include which of the following server types? (Choose all that apply.)

    a. fax servers

    b. communication servers

    c. file and print servers

    d. application servers

15. What are the two major types of networks?

    a. client-based

    b. server-based

    c. peer-to-peer

    d. client-peer

16. Any two computers that communicate across a network must share a common language called a _____.

    a. medium

    b. technology

    c. topology

    d. protocol

17. Of the following assertions, which is a true disadvantage of peer-to-peer networking? (Choose all that apply.)

    a. Dedicated hardware and specialized software are required.

    b. Additional staff is needed to maintain the network.

    c. Each resource might have its own unique password.

    d. There is no centralized security.

    e. none of the above

18. The primary reason to install a network is to _____ resources and services.

    a. share

    b. deliver

    c. create

    d. control

19. Some resources shared on a network typically include _____, such as printers, scanners, or tape drives.

    a. protocols

    b. internal devices

    c. peripheral devices

    d. applications

20. A peer-to-peer network always includes at least one dedicated machine called a server. True or False?

21. On a peer-to-peer network, each user must act as _____ for his or her own machine.

    a. administrator

    b. controller

    c. gatekeeper

    d. facilitator

22. Peer-to-peer networks are not suitable if _____.

    a. tight security is required

    b. five or fewer users need network access

    c. budget is the primary consideration

    d. no one uses the network heavily

    e. none of the above

23. Which of the following is the standard model for networks with more than 10 users?

    a. peer-to-peer

    b. workgroup

    c. server-based

    d. server-peer

1

24. Servers that perform specific roles, such as fax servers, application servers, or communication servers, can best be described as which of the following?

   a. specialized servers

   b. custom servers

   c. file and print servers

   d. remote access servers

25. Of the following components, which component need not be as powerful on a server as on a client?

   a. graphics card

   b. operating system

   c. power supply

   d. network interface card

26. Which of the following is considered a directory service? (Choose all that apply.)

   a. eDirectory

   b. NIS

   c. SQL

   d. Active Directory

   e. Linux

27. Which of the following specialized servers is not included with Windows server operating systems?

   a. Web server

   b. communication server

   c. fax server

   d. file and print server

   e. all of the above

HANDS-ON PROJECTS

Numerous networking technologies, but especially those from IBM and Microsoft, have a long association with the enduring application programming interface (API) known as Network Basic Input/Output System (NetBIOS). Originally developed by IBM in the 1970s and adapted for use on the first PCs in the early 1980s, NetBIOS remains a popular networking environment more than 20 years later.

Some observers say it's still around because no usable technology ever disappears entirely; others claim that because NetBIOS is so easy for developers to use, programmers will never let it die. Whatever the case, most Microsoft operating systems with networking capabilities support a series of NetBIOS-based networking capabilities, known as the NET commands, that provide useful information about networks they can access. The following projects give you some exposure to these command-line utilities. As you revisit the commands throughout this book, more of their details should begin to make sense.

All projects in this book that use the Sharing and Security option for folders assume that the Use simple file sharing option has been disabled. To find this option, open Windows Explorer, click Tools, Folder Options from the menu, and click the View tab. The Use simple file sharing option is the last one in the Advanced settings list box. This setting should be cleared.

NOTE

HANDS-ON PROJECTS

Hands-On Project 1-1

In this project, you explore the nuances of the NET HELP utility by following these steps:

For DOS commands in this project and others throughout this book, you can type them in uppercase or lowercase letters. For example, in Step 2 of this project, you can type "NET HELP" or "net help."

TIP

1. In a GUI operating system such as Windows XP, command-line utilities must run in a command prompt window. For Windows XP, this is the sequence: Click **Start**, point to **All Programs**, point to **Accessories**, and then click **Command Prompt**. A variation of this sequence is available in Windows 2000 and Windows 9x. See your instructor if you are using either operating system.

2. At the DOS prompt, type **NET HELP** and press **Enter**. You should see a screen similar to Figure 1-6.

```
Command Prompt

D:\>net help
The syntax of this command is:

NET HELP command
      -or-
NET command /HELP

   Commands available are:

   NET ACCOUNTS              NET HELP              NET SHARE
   NET COMPUTER              NET HELPMSG           NET START
   NET CONFIG                NET LOCALGROUP        NET STATISTICS
   NET CONFIG SERVER         NET NAME              NET STOP
   NET CONFIG WORKSTATION    NET PAUSE             NET TIME
   NET CONTINUE              NET PRINT             NET USE
   NET FILE                  NET SEND              NET USER
   NET GROUP                 NET SESSION           NET VIEW

   NET HELP SERVICES lists the network services you can start.
   NET HELP SYNTAX explains how to read NET HELP syntax lines.
   NET HELP command | MORE displays Help one screen at a time.

D:\>
```

Figure 1-6   The NET HELP command

3. The command you're interested in for this project is VIEW. For information about it, type **NET HELP VIEW** and press **Enter**. You should see a screen similar to Figure 1-7. Read the information on the screen.

```
C:\WINDOWS\System32\cmd.exe                                      _|□|×|
C:\>net help view
The syntax of this command is:

NET VIEW
[\\computername [/CACHE] ! /DOMAIN[:domainname]]
NET VIEW /NETWORK:NW [\\computername]

NET VIEW displays a list of resources being shared on a computer. When used
without options, it displays a list of computers in the current domain or
network.

\\computername           Is a computer whose shared resources you want
                         to view.
/DOMAIN:domainname       Specifies the domain for which you want to
                         view the available computers. If domainname is
                         omitted, displays all domains in the local area
                         network.
/NETWORK:NW              Displays all available servers on a NetWare
                         network. If a computername is  specified, the
                         resources available on that computer in
                         the NetWare network will be displayed.
/CACHE                   Displays the offline client caching settings for
                         the resources on the specified computer

C:\>
```

Figure 1-7   Details on the NET VIEW command

4. The VIEW command offers two levels of information. Type **NET VIEW** and press **Enter** to see the names of all machines on your network (see Figure 1-8). Notice that the command lists the names of machines on the left in the Server Name column with optional "Remark" entries for two of the four machines. You should see something similar for your network, but with different machine names on the left and perhaps no remarks on the right.

```
Command Prompt                                                   _|□|×|
D:\>net view
Server Name              Remark

\\LANW01                 Pentium 166
\\LANW02
\\SRUR1                  486DX4/100 Windows NT 4.0 Server
\\SRUR2
The command completed successfully.

D:\>
```

Figure 1-8   NET VIEW shows registered machines

Depending on your network setup, you might see error or status messages such as "There are no entries in the list" or "Access denied." In this case, you won't be able to perform projects that use the NET VIEW command.

NOTE

The second level of information is displayed when you append the name of a particular machine; for the example in Figure 1-9, the input NET VIEW \\SRVR1 produced the output shown. Pick a computer name from your network (a server name produces the most interesting results), and try using it with NET VIEW. It shows you the names of whatever network shares are available, indicates their type (usually "Disk" or "Print"), indicates whether a drive letter matches a resource (notice that data2 corresponds to the G: drive in Figure 1-9), and might also include a comment field. Figure 1-9 shows resources available on srvr1.

```
Command Prompt                                              _ 8 X

D:\>net view \\srvr1
Shared resources at \\srvr1

486DX4/100 Windows NT 4.0 Server

Share name   Type        Used as  Comment
----------------------------------------------------------------
cdrom        Disk
data2        Disk        G:
HPLJ4        Print                HP LaserJet 4/4M PS
LANW-DATA    Disk
MSOffice     Disk
NETLOGON     Disk                 Logon server share
NTCD         Disk
Server C     Disk
The command completed successfully.

D:\>
```

Figure 1-9   NET VIEW shows resources available on srvr1

5. Close the command prompt window by typing **EXIT** and pressing **Enter** or by clicking the **Close** button in the upper-right corner of the window.

HANDS-ON PROJECTS

Hands-On Project 1-2

Most NOSs support a way of making all or part of a disk drive available to the network. On Microsoft systems, this method is called a file share or sometimes a directory share. The shares shown in Figure 1-9 appear at the left under the heading "Share name." All these shares are available to users on the network who have the correct password or permissions to access them. In this project, you define a share on your own machine that others on the network can access freely by following these steps:

1. Although there are at least three methods for creating shares on Windows XP, the preferred method is to open Windows Explorer. Windows XP users should click **Start**, point to **All Programs**, point to **Accessories**, and click **Windows Explorer**. (A somewhat shorter method that works for all Windows versions is clicking **Start**, **Run**, typing **explorer**, and then clicking **OK**.)

2. First, you create a new folder to share with the network. Begin this process by clicking to select a letter representing the hard drive in the left pane of Windows Explorer. In Figure 1-10, the C: drive has been selected. Right-click somewhere in the right pane, point to **New**, and click **Folder**. Backspace to delete the **New Folder** text next to the folder icon. Type **Temp***machine number*, substituting the computer number your instructor supplies for *machine number*, and then press **Enter**. (If your machine number is 6, for instance, you'd type **Temp6**.)

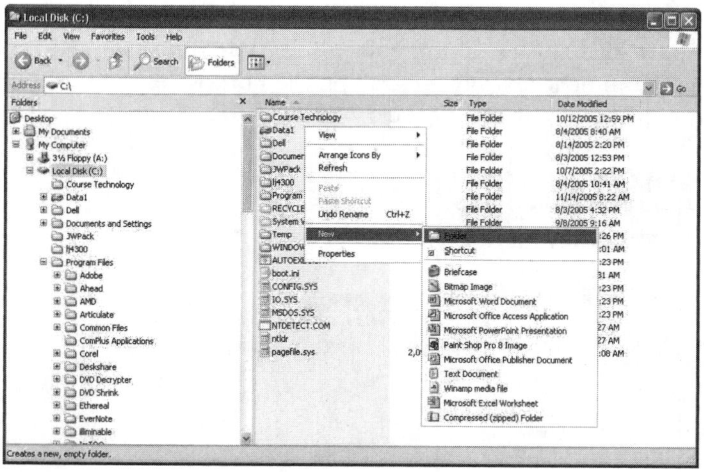

Figure 1-10   Creating a new folder

NOTE

Depending on the settings on your computer and the operating system, your screen might differ from Figures 1-10 and 1-11.

3. Right-click your newly created **Temp** folder, and on the shortcut menu shown in Figure 1-11, click **Sharing and Security**.

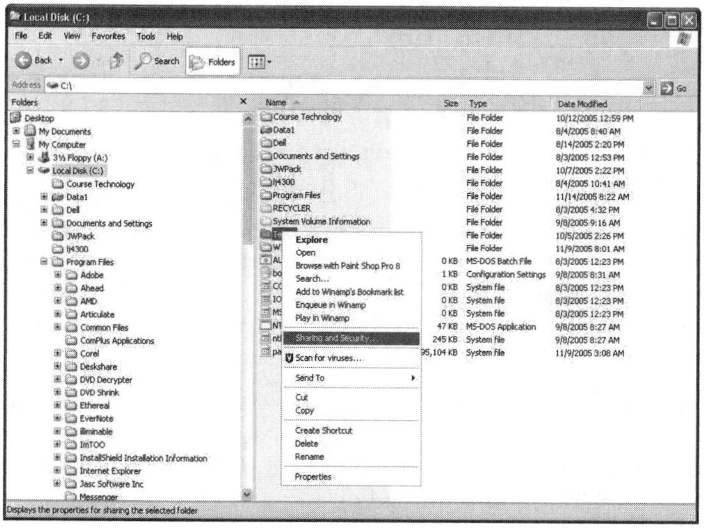

Figure 1-11   The shortcut menu for new folders

4. A Properties dialog box similar to Figure 1-12 opens. If necessary, click the **Sharing** tab. Click the **Share this folder** option button to enable this share, and if you like, add a note in the Comment text box describing the purpose of the share. Then click the **Apply** button in the lower-right corner to turn on the share.

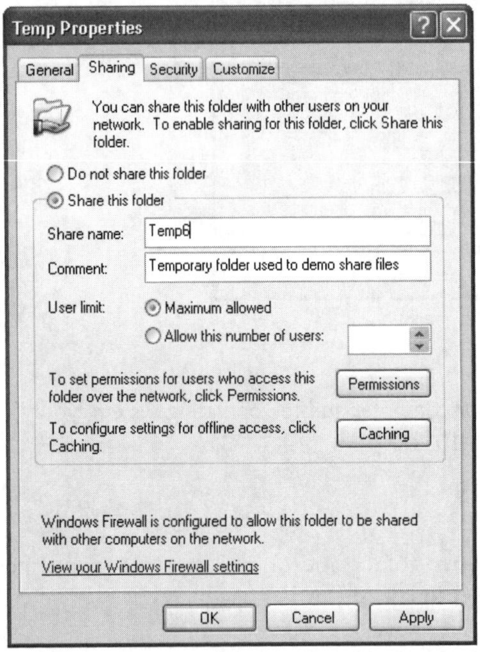

Figure 1-12   Share options in the Sharing tab

5. Click **OK** at the bottom of the dialog box. Your share is now ready for use.

6. To check your work, open a command prompt window. (Reread Step 1 in Hands-On Project 1-1 if you don't remember how to do this.)

7. Type **NET VIEW *your machine name*,** substituting your actual machine name for *your machine name,* and then press **Enter.** (Ask your instructor for your specific machine name; for this example, the input was **NET VIEW \\\\Machine6.**) You should see a screen similar to Figure 1-13. Notice the appearance of the Temp6 share, which confirms that the share was created successfully.

8. To turn off (disable) a share, in Windows Explorer, right-click the folder you just shared, and click the **Sharing and Security** option again. In the Properties dialog box, click the **Do not share this folder** check box, click **Apply** in the lower-right corner, and then click **OK.** You just turned off this share.

9. If you enter **NET VIEW *your machine name*** again, you should no longer see the share.

10. Close the command prompt window and Windows Explorer, if you've left it open.

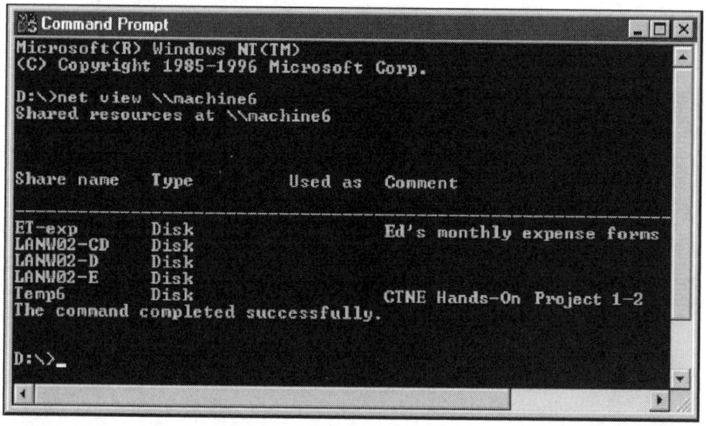

```
Command Prompt                                        _ □ ×
Microsoft(R) Windows NT(TM)
(C) Copyright 1985-1996 Microsoft Corp.

D:\>net view \\machine6
Shared resources at \\machine6


Share name    Type        Used as   Comment
--------------------------------------------------------------
ET-exp        Disk                  Ed's monthly expense forms
LANW02-CD     Disk
LANW02-D      Disk
LANW02-E      Disk
Temp6         Disk                  CTNE Hands-On Project 1-2
The command completed successfully.


D:\>_
```

Figure 1-13   NET VIEW shows the Temp6 folder as a shared resource

Hands-On Project 1-3

Working around networks means learning to swim in a cauldron of alphabet soup. Many of the components and concepts you encounter in this field don't go by their full names—they're known by their acronyms. In this chapter, you have already encountered the following acronyms, among others:

- CPU
- LAN
- MAN
- NIC
- NOS
- WAN
- WPAN
- WWW

That's why this project (which requires Internet access and a Web browser) introduces you to the Acronym Finder tool. Working in a networked environment, you'll find plenty of reasons to add its URL to your bookmarks or favorites list.

1. Start your Web browser.

2. Type **http://www.acronymfinder.com/** in the Address text box, and press **Enter** to go to the Acronym Finder home page (see Figure 1-14).

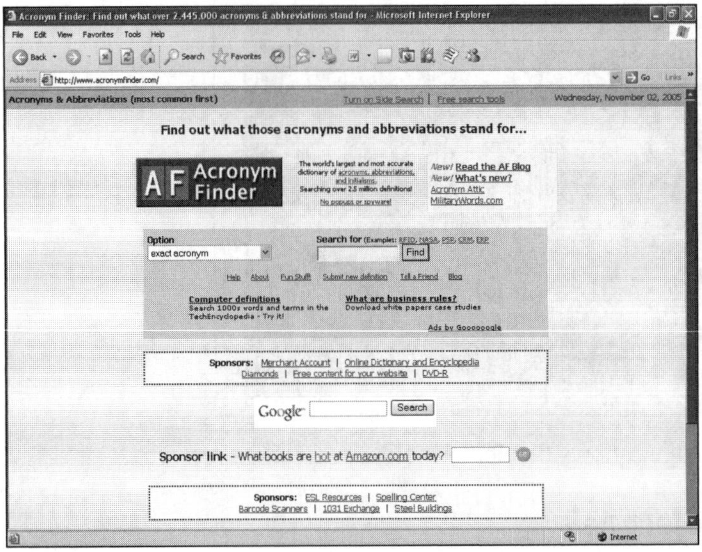

Figure 1-14   The Acronym Finder home page

NOTE

Web locations and Web pages change constantly. Don't worry if the Acronym Finder home page looks a little different from the example—you should still be able to navigate it in much the same way. For tips on how to track down URLs that are no longer "home," see the section "Coping with Change on the Web" in the Introduction.

3. After you've landed on Acronym Finder's home page, you can look up acronyms by typing them into the Search for text box in the middle of the screen. Type the first acronym from the list in this project, **CPU**, and press **Enter** to produce the listing shown in Figure 1-15. As you can see, CPU stands for a number of different things. You must know enough about what a CPU is and does to understand that the first entry, central processing unit, is the right one.

4. Try other entries in the list at the beginning of this project. Without checking the "Key Terms" section in this chapter, try to decide which expansion fits the best. Then check your work by reading through the key terms to see which one is correct.

5. Close your Web browser, unless you plan to go directly to the next project. In that case, skip Step 1 in Hands-On Project 1-4.

HANDS-ON PROJECTS

Hands-On Project 1-4

As any interaction with Acronym Finder shows you, there's nearly always more than one possible expansion for most acronyms. Because you're interested in how this information applies to networking topics, looking up acronym expansions to see what they really mean (and whether a likely looking expansion is indeed the correct one) is often necessary.

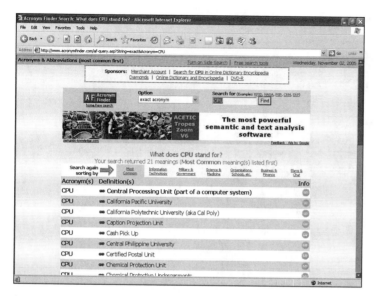

Figure 1-15   Search results for "CPU"

This project (which requires Internet access and a Web browser) introduces some tools you can use to decide which acronym expansion is most likely the correct one. To access networking information online, follow these steps:

1. Start your Web browser.

2. Type **http://www.techweb.com** into the Address text box, and then press **Enter** to go to the TechWeb home page, shown in Figure 1-16.

3. Locate the DEFINE A TERM section. Type **central processing unit** in the text box, and then click the **go** button. Your screen should resemble Figure 1-17. Click the **CPU** link to view a lengthy description.

4. Based on what you wrote for various acronym expansions, try some entries for other acronyms.

5. Close your Web browser.

Hands-On Project 1-5

This project requires some setup by your instructor. You should verify with your instructor that the setup is complete before continuing with this project. In this project, you use a file share that your instructor has created and write a memo to your instructor providing the information specified in the following steps. Then you copy the file you have created to a file share on your instructor's computer (or some other computer your instructor designates). This project assumes you're using Windows XP Professional as your operating system, but you can accomplish the tasks in other operating systems.

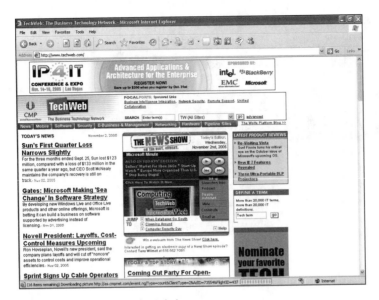

Figure 1-16   The TechWeb home page

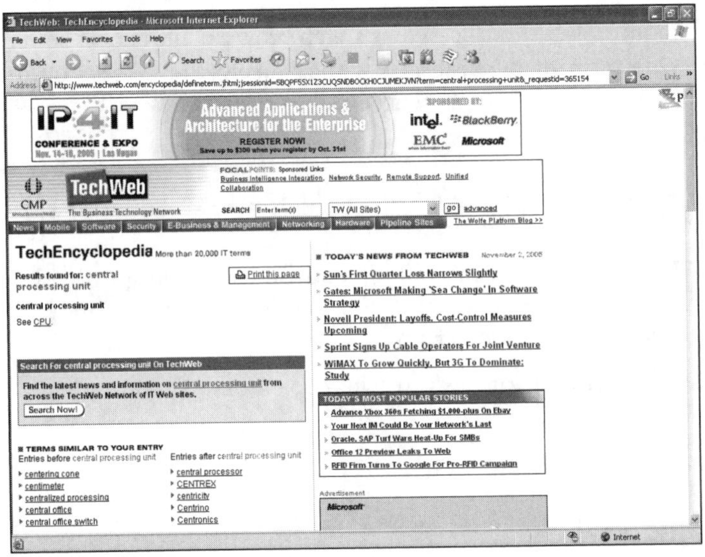

Figure 1-17   Search results for "central processing unit"

1. Log on to your computer, if necessary.

2. Open Microsoft Word or another word processor; even a simple text editor such as Notepad will do. Write a letter to your instructor that includes the following:

   ■ The reason you're taking this class

   ■ What you hope to get out of this class

- How much time you expect to put into this class each week outside of classroom hours

- Whether you expect to take more computer and networking classes

3. Save the document in your **My Documents** folder (or a folder your instructor designates), naming it *yourname*. For example, if your name is Bill Smith, name the document **billsmith**.

Now the networking part of the project: Without a network, you have two ways to get this document to the instructor. One is to print the document and carry the printed page to the instructor. Another is to put the document on a disk or CD, and hand it to the instructor. With a network, however, you can simply copy the document to your instructor's computer by following these steps:

1. Start Windows Explorer and navigate to the folder where you saved the letter. Right-click the document you created, and click **Copy**.

2. To paste the document to a shared folder on another computer, you need to specify the computer name and shared folder name in Windows Explorer or the Run dialog box using this syntax: *computername**sharedfolder*. This syntax is called the Universal Naming Convention (UNC) path. Your instructor will provide the computer name and shared folder name where you should copy the document.

3. Click **Start**, **Run** and type the UNC path your instructor provides (for example: *instructor**share*). Click **OK**. You should see a Windows Explorer window open. (There might be documents in the folder if some of your classmates have already completed the project.) Right-click somewhere on the right side of the window, and click **Paste**. Your document should now be available on your instructor's computer.

4. Close all open windows.

CASE PROJECTS

Case Project 1-1

XYZ Corporation currently employs eight people but plans to hire 10 more in the next four months. Users will work on multiple projects, and only those users assigned to a project should have access to the project files. You're instructed to set up the network to make it easy to manage and back up. Would you choose a peer-to-peer network, a server-based network, or a combination of both? Why?

Case Project 1-2

Widgets Inc. hired you as a productivity consultant. Currently, it employs six people who routinely exchange information via sneakernet. The company wants the most inexpensive solution and only minimal training for employees. Employees must also be able to control resources on their own machines. Would you choose a peer-to-peer network, a server-based network, or a combination of both? Why?

Case Project 1-3

American Tool and Die operates two machine shops, one in Towson, Maryland, and the other in Beltsville, Maryland. The company wants the two locations to share a single database so that managers at each facility can exchange work orders and monitor inventory on demand. Users need some control over resources, but the company also wants network faxing and dial-up services at each location. Would you choose a peer-to-peer network, a server-based network, or a combination of both? Why?

Case Project 1-4

What kind of specialized servers do you need to install at American Tool and Die, based on the information in the previous Case Project?

Case Project 1-5

You want your PDA and cell phone to exchange information, such as addresses and phone numbers, wirelessly. What networking technology might you want as a feature of both your PDA and phone to accomplish this task?

Case Project 1-6

The latest Windows server product (code-named Longhorn Server as of this writing) offers a number of advantages over Windows Server 2003. Research the new features this server product will offer, and write a short explanation of what advantages an organization might realize by upgrading to this operating system.

2

NETWORK DESIGN ESSENTIALS

After reading this chapter and completing the exercises, you will be able to:

♦ Explain the basics of a network layout

♦ Describe the standard networking topologies

♦ Explain the variations on standard networking topologies

♦ Describe the role of hubs and switches in a network topology

♦ Construct a basic network layout

A network's basic design plays an integral part in its operation and performance. The network topology dictates the media used, the type of channel access, and the speed at which the network operates.

Understanding basic network topologies and hybrids of those topologies is important so that you have a firm foundation for designing your network. You can also use this knowledge in subsequent chapters dealing with media, channel access, and network architecture.

EXAMINING THE BASICS OF A NETWORK LAYOUT

In this chapter, you explore the basics of good network design. These basics include analyzing network requirements and selecting a network topology and the equipment to fit that topology. Following that information are pointers on how to map out your design.

Before designing a network layout, understanding some basic networking concepts is important. When you implement a network, you must first decide how to best situate the components in a topology. A network's **topology** refers not only to the physical layout of its computers, cables, and other resources, but also to how those components communicate with each other. (Topology, layout, diagram, and map are some of the many terms used to describe this basic design.)

The arrangement of cabling in a network is considered the network's **physical topology**. The path that data travels between computers on a network is considered the network's **logical topology**. As you'll see, a network can be wired using one physical topology but pass data from machine to machine by using a different logical topology.

A network's topology has a significant effect on its performance and growth potential. In addition, the topology affects decisions such as the type of equipment to purchase and the best approach to network management. When designing a network, you must have a firm grasp on its topologies' uses and limitations. Your design should provide room for growth and meet your defined security requirements. A solid design grows and adapts to the network as needs change, whereas a poor design limits growth potential and must be replaced eventually.

NOTE
Perhaps you have already heard terms such as "Ethernet" and "token ring" and might be wondering where these terms fit into the topology scheme. Ethernet and token ring are two network architectures, sometimes referred to as LAN technologies. These network architectures might be implemented by using one of the topologies discussed in this chapter, but they are distinct concepts and are given full attention in Chapter 7.

UNDERSTANDING STANDARD TOPOLOGIES

All network designs today are based on three simple physical topologies: bus, star, and ring. A bus consists of a series of computers connected along a single cable segment. Computers connected via a central concentration point (hub) are arranged in a star topology. Computers connected to form a loop create a ring. Keep in mind that these topologies describe the physical arrangement of cables. How the data travels along those cables might represent a different logical topology. The logical topologies that dominate LANs include bus, ring, and switching, all of which, as you'll see, are usually implemented as a physical star.

Physical Bus Topology

Also known as a linear bus, the physical **bus** topology, shown in Figure 2-1, is by far the simplest and at one time was the most common method for connecting computers. Inherent in this simplicity, however, is a weakness: A single cable break can halt the entire network. All components of the bus topology connect via a **backbone**, a single cable segment that (theoretically) interconnects all the computers in a straight line. A physical bus topology is no longer a practical choice because technology has moved past this obsolete method of connecting computers, but your understanding of bus communications aids your general understanding of how computers communicate with each other across a network. Two properties inherent on a physical bus are signal propagation and signal bounce. In addition, to understand physical bus topologies fully, you must be familiar with cable termination and what happens when a cable breaks.

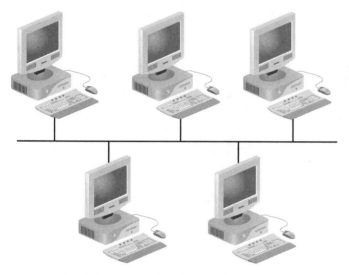

Figure 2-1   A typical bus topology network

Signal Propagation

In any network topology, computers communicate with each other by sending information across the media as a series of signals. When copper wire is the medium, as in a typical physical bus, those signals are sent as electrical pulses. When a computer transmits data as a series of electrical pulses, those signals travel along the length of the cable in all directions. The signals continue to travel along the cable and through any connecting devices until they weaken enough so as not to be detectable or until they encounter a device that absorbs them. This traveling across the medium is called **signal propagation**, which means that even if a signal encounters the end of a cable, it bounces back and travels the other direction.

Signal Bounce

As mentioned, when a signal travels across the network medium, it moves from the point of transmission to both ends of any bus. If allowed to continue unchecked, the signal would travel across the network continuously, bouncing back and forth and preventing other computers from sending data, as shown in Figure 2-2. This is called, fittingly, **signal bounce**. Because of this bouncing phenomenon, a method to ensure that all signals stop when they reach the end of any segment in a bus topology must be devised. Left alone, these bouncing signals render computer communication on a bus network unworkable.

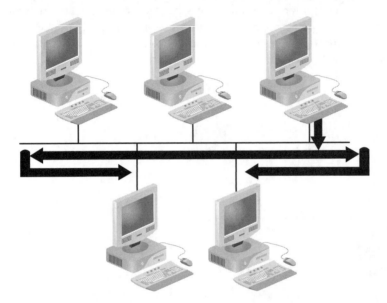

Figure 2-2   Signal bounce on an unterminated network

Cable Termination

A **terminator** attached to each end of a cable prevents signals from bouncing on a physical bus. This terminator absorbs all signals that reach it, thus clearing the network for new communications. On a bus network, each cable segment end must attach to something. Open ends—ends not attached to a computer—must be terminated to prevent signal bounce. Figure 2-3 shows cable terminators absorbing an electronic signal.

Cable Failure

A cable break in a bus network occurs when the cable is physically cut or one end becomes disconnected. When a cable break occurs, that cable is no longer terminated and signals can then bounce, halting all network activity. The computers attached to the bus can still function as standalone systems, but no network communication is possible. Figure 2-4 depicts signal bounce resulting from a cable break.

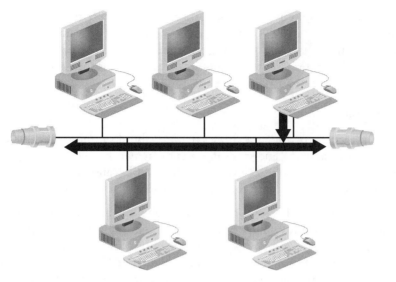

Figure 2-3   A terminated bus network

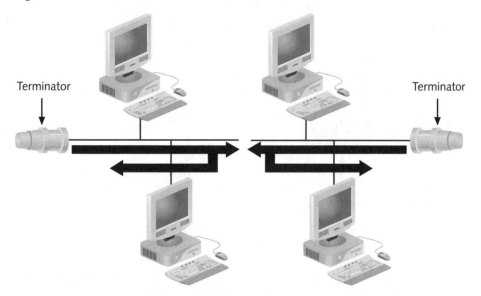

Figure 2-4   A cable break and subsequent signal bounce

Logical Bus Topology

Logical topologies describe the path that data travels from computer to computer. A physical bus topology is almost always implemented as a logical bus as well. As mentioned, technology has moved past the physical bus method of connecting computers. A logical bus topology is still in use, however, on some physical topologies, in particular a star. Regardless of the logical topology, some aspects of computer communication are universally true, and your under-standing of these commonalities helps you understand computer communication in general. All computers, no matter what their topology, communicate in the same way: They address data to one or more computers and then transmit that data across the cable in the form of electronic signals.

Sending the Signal

When a computer has data to send, it addresses that data, breaks it into manageable chunks (discussed in detail in Chapter 5), and sends it across the network as electronic signals. On a logical bus, all connected computers receive them. However, because of the address included in the data, only those computers for which these signals are destined accept the data.

In a logical bus environment, only one computer at a time can send information successfully. Therefore, all network users must share the available amount of transmission time. Because of this limitation, the number of computers attached to a logical bus network can affect network performance. The more computers that are ready to send data at the same time, the longer some computers must wait to send data, which slows overall network performance. Regardless of the physical topology, these concepts are true if the logical topology is a bus.

It's important to note that a bus topology is a **passive topology**. This means that computers on the bus only listen for data being sent; they aren't responsible for moving data from one computer to the next. If one computer fails, it has no effect on the rest of the network. In an **active topology** network, computers and other devices attached to the network regenerate signals and are responsible for moving data through the network.

Physical Ring Topology

When each computer connects directly to the next computer in line, ending at the starting computer, a circle of cable forms to create a physical **ring** topology network (see Figure 2-5). Signals typically travel in only one direction around the ring. Because the circle has no end, termination is not required.

Typically, every computer in a ring is responsible for retransmitting the data, making a ring topology an active topology, as opposed to the passive topology of a bus network. A typical single-ring network can fail if one computer in the ring fails, but a dual-ring network can operate around any such failure. Although a physical ring topology is sometimes used, as in network technologies such as Fiber Distributed Data Interface (FDDI, discussed in Chapter 7), the most common type of ring is a logical ring topology.

Logical Ring Topology

Data in a logical ring topology, as its name suggests, travels from one device, or node, on the network to the next device until the data reaches its destination. **Token passing** is one method for sending data around a ring. A small packet, called a **token**, passes around the ring to each computer in turn. If a computer has information to send, it modifies the token, adds address information and the data, and sends it around the ring. That information travels

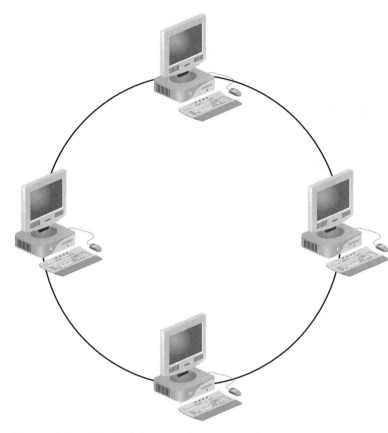

Figure 2-5   A typical ring topology network

around the ring until it reaches its destination or returns to the sender. When the intended destination computer receives the information, it returns a message to the sender to acknowledge its safe arrival. The sender then releases the token and sends it around the ring to begin the process again. This process is covered in more detail in Chapter 7 when specific network architectures are examined.

NOTE   Although a logical ring topology might be implemented as a physical ring, it's much more common for a logical ring to be implemented as a physical star topology.

Modern logical ring topologies use "smart hubs" that recognize a computer's failure and remove the computer from the ring automatically. (This technology is one profound advantage of using a ring topology with star wiring.) Another advantage of the ring topology lies in its capability to share network resources fairly. Each computer has an equal opportunity to send data, so no single computer can monopolize the network. This feature is useful in high-traffic and time-critical applications, in which every device must be able to send data within a given period. A ring topology with token passing guarantees a device's capability to send, whereas a bus topology is a first-come, first-served arrangement in which a single device can monopolize the network medium.

Physical Star Topology

Because of the problems in troubleshooting and managing a physical bus or ring network, and because a single cable failure can bring down the entire network, these topologies have been largely replaced by the physical **star** topology. A star topology, shown in Figure 2-6, describes computers connected by cable segments to a central device. Note that the physical star topology doesn't specify how signals should travel from computer to computer, only that cables connect computers to a central device. In fact, the underlying logical topology in a physical star is likely a bus, a ring, or switching.

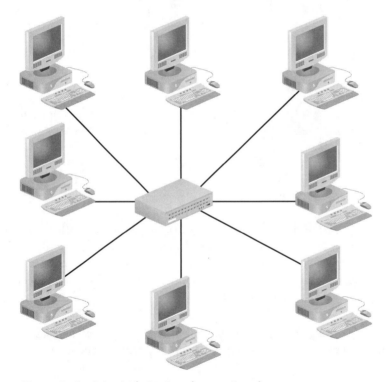

Figure 2-6   A typical star topology network

One benefit of a physical star topology is its inherent centralization of resources. However, because all computers connect at one location, the star topology requires a more involved cable installation. A physical bus simply strings a cable from one computer to the next, but cable installation in a star topology usually involves stringing cable through conduit, under floors, and inside ceilings to get the cable from the computer work area to the connecting device. This installation is usually more labor intensive and requires much more cable.

Another drawback is that the center of the star defines a single point for failure: If the central connecting device fails, all other computers and devices attached to that device lose network access. On the other hand, if one computer or cable fails, it has no effect on the rest of the network (aside from losing the availability of resources that computer might store). This point is important because, unlike in a bus topology, a user can't bring down the entire network simply by disconnecting the cable from his or her computer. Another advantage of the star topology is the relative ease of troubleshooting. Because all computers connect at a central location, an administrator can quickly and easily isolate network problems involving a single device or cable segment without affecting other devices. Furthermore, devices acting as the center of a star topology might be outfitted with special network management and monitoring software that can make network administration much easier.

NOTE   The centralization of resources and management capabilities available on hubs or switches (which form the center of a star) have elevated the star topology to the top choice among networking topologies.

The physical star doesn't really have a logical counterpart; rather, logical topologies implemented as a physical star are often referred to as star bus or star ring, for example, to describe both their physical (star) and logical (bus or ring) topologies. In addition, switching technology uses a device to connect computers in a physical star.

A Logical Bus Implemented as a Physical Star

When the arrangement of cables forms a physical star but data traveling from computer to computer follows a logical bus, the resulting topology is sometimes referred to as a star bus (see Figure 2-7). At the center is a device called a **hub**. When a computer sends a signal, the hub receives it and retransmits it down every other cable segment to all other computers or devices attached to that hub (also called a "node"). All computers hear the signal and check the destination address, but only the computer to which the data is addressed processes the data further. This topology got its start in the early days of mainframe computing when all nodes were attached to a central point, which was a front-end processor attached to the mainframe.

A Logical Ring Implemented as a Physical Star

As with a star bus topology, a star ring topology uses a star's physical cable arrangement, but data travel within the central device is in a ring configuration (see Figure 2-8). The star ring topology is the most common method of implementing a network technology that uses a logical ring for data communication. Keep in mind that the electronics making up this ring are more complicated than what's depicted in the figure, which is intended only to give you a visual reference for how data travels. In addition, although the device at the center of a star bus network is generally called a "hub," the device at the center of a star ring is usually called

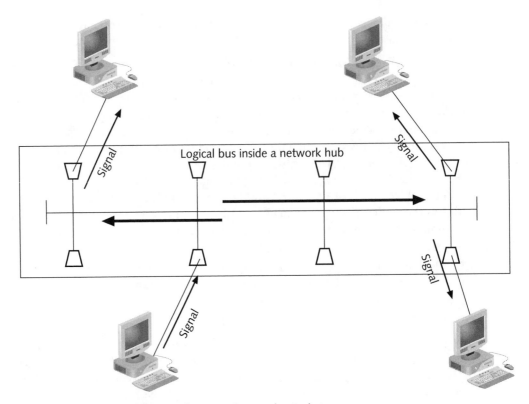

Figure 2-7   A logical bus implemented as a physical star

a concentrator, or multistation access unit (MSAU). The ring-based technologies implemented as a physical star include FDDI and token ring, both token-passing technologies that are discussed in more detail in Chapter 7.

Switching Implemented as a Physical Star

Switching is neither a bus nor a ring logically, but is always implemented as a physical star. When a switch is the central connecting point in a physical star, it takes a signal coming in from a device connected to one of its ports, and then builds a circuit on the fly to forward the signal out of the port where the intended destination computer can be found. This process is called switching because at one moment the circuit between two computers does not exist and the next moment it does, like turning on a switch. This method of data travel from computer to computer is far superior to the other logical topologies discussed because, unlike the bus and ring, multiple computers can communicate simultaneously without affecting each other. In fact, this type of communication is now the dominant method used in almost every LAN design.

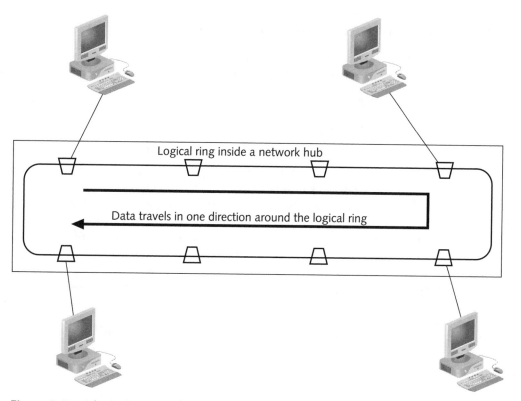

Logical ring inside a network hub

Data travels in one direction around the logical ring

Figure 2-8   A logical ring implemented as a physical star

Wireless Topologies

Wireless networks eliminate the need for a visible physical topology, which is one reason for their growing popularity. There are no cables to run, terminate, and test. However, wireless networking does have a logical topology associated with it and, to a lesser degree, a physical topology. In the simplest wireless configuration, two computers can communicate directly with one another in an **ad hoc topology**, sometimes called a peer-to-peer topology. This type of arrangement is usually used only in small or temporary installations. There's no central device, and data travels from one device to another in a line (more or less), so if you want to describe an ad hoc topology in physical terms, it most resembles a physical and logical bus. In most situations, wireless LANs use a central device, called an **access point (AP)**, to control communications, much like a hub. In this respect, wireless LANs use a star physical topology because all the signals travel through one central device. Because only one wireless device can communicate with an access point at a time, you might call this wireless communication method a logical bus topology as well. When wireless devices are configured to use an access point, they are said to be in **infrastructure mode**.

EXAMINING VARIATIONS OF PHYSICAL TOPOLOGIES

The major physical topologies have three typical variations or combinations: extended star, mesh, and combination star and bus. These combinations can be used to get the most from any network.

Extended Star Topology

The **extended star** topology, shown in Figure 2-9, is the most widely used topology in networks containing more than just a few computers. As the name implies, this topology is a star of stars. A central device, usually a switch, sits in the middle of the topology. Instead of attached computers forming the arms of the star, other switches (or hubs) are connected to the central switch's ports. Computers and peripherals are then attached to these switches or hubs, forming additional stars. The extended star is sometimes referred to as a hierarchical star because there are two or more layers of stars, all connecting back to the central star.

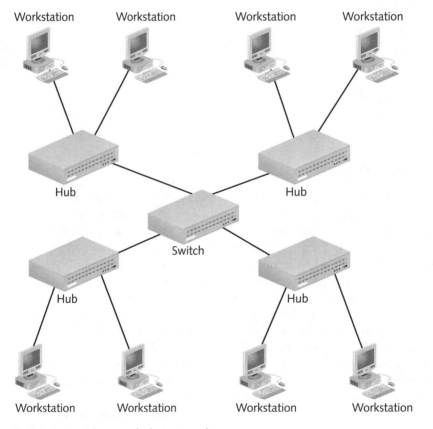

Figure 2-9   An extended star topology

Mesh Topology

A **mesh** network topology is the most fault tolerant but also the most expensive. Connect-ing each device in a network to every other device in the network creates a mesh network topology. Figure 2-10 shows this intricate configuration. Any single cable or device failure in a mesh configuration affects network performance only minimally because of the multiple connections to each device. However, costs increase because more cable and hardware are required. To see how this topology can become expensive and intricate, take a look at the mesh topology formula for determining how many connections are needed for the number of nodes on a network, with n representing the number of nodes on the network:

$n(n-1)/2$

If there are only three nodes, the result is only three connections, which is quite reasonable considering the fault-tolerance advantages. However, with 20 nodes, the number of con-nections required for a full mesh rises to 190! Most often, a mesh topology is used in a WAN to ensure that all sites remain able to communicate, even with one or more cable failures. One of the best examples of a mesh topology is the Internet. Although the entire Internet isn't designed as a mesh, the critical pathways are, providing fault tolerance to the key junction points.

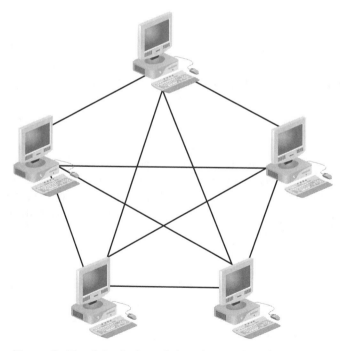

Figure 2-10 A typical mesh topology network

Combination Star Bus Topology

The combination star bus topology, as its name states, combines a star and a bus. For example, a bus backbone interconnecting two or more hubs creates a star bus topology (see Figure 2-11). The star configuration minimizes the effect of any single computer's failure on the network. If a hub fails, the computers attached to it can't communicate, but other hub-computer connections remain intact and communication continues.

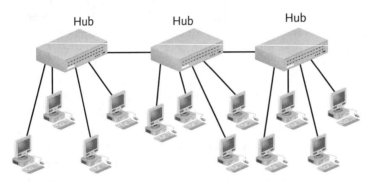

Figure 2-11   A typical combination star bus topology

HUBS AND SWITCHES

As discussed, both hubs and switches can act as the center of a star topology. The basic operation of these types of devices was discussed briefly in the section on topologies, but both devices are so important to your understanding of network design and operation that this section expands on them.

Hubs

In everyday use, a hub is defined as "the center of activity." This definition is quite appropriate in network usage as well. However, in network usage, there are a number of variations on this central theme: active hub, passive hub, repeating hub, and even switching hub. The first two are covered in the following sections. A repeating hub is really just a type of active hub, and switching hubs are covered in the "Switches" section.

Active Hubs

The majority of hubs installed in networks today are **active hubs**. They regenerate, or repeat, the signals as they receive them and send them along. Generally, active hubs have many ports—eight or more—and so are sometimes called multiport repeaters or repeating hubs. A **multiport repeater** is a device that does the following in order:

1. Takes a signal coming in on one port
2. Cleans the signal by filtering out noise and other undesired information

3. Strengthens the signal by regenerating it to original signal levels

4. Sends the regenerated signal out to all other ports

The general concept of this process was shown in Figure 2-7. Because active hubs regenerate signals, they require electrical power to run. One drawback of multiport repeaters is that, like a bus topology, they require sharing the cable bandwidth among all connected stations. For a busy 10 megabits per second (Mbps) Ethernet network using a multiport repeater with 10 devices connected, for example, this bandwidth sharing means that the average effective bandwidth for each computer is only 1 Mbps. Until recently, bandwidth sharing wasn't a big problem because the number and frequency of data transfers in a typical LAN was small, making the actual effective bandwidth much higher than 1 Mbps. However, in today's LANs, where large multimedia data files are frequently transferred, the need for additional dedicated bandwidth has become paramount. The solution to this need is switches, discussed later in this chapter. To see an animation that depicts the operation of a hub, see Simulation 2-1.

Simulation 2-1: Operation of a Hub/Repeater

SIMULATION

For wireless networks, the hub is referred to as an access point (AP). Wireless hubs share bandwidth just as traditional wired hubs do.

NOTE

Passive Hubs

In a **passive hub**, such as a patch panel or punchdown block, the signal passes through the hub without any amplification or regeneration. A passive hub is simply a central connection point and, because no electronic signal modification occurs, requires no power. Passive hubs are used as junction points between a long run of cable (from work area jack to wiring closet patch panel, for example) and between short runs of cable (such as from wiring closet patch panel to a hub or switch). Figure 2-12 illustrates a patch panel used as a passive hub.

Switches

A **switch**, like a hub, is the central connecting point in a star topology network. However, unlike a hub, a switch does more than simply regenerate signals. A switch looks just like a hub, with several ports for connecting workstations in a star topology. However, instead of simply regenerating an incoming signal and repeating that signal to all other ports, a switch actually determines to which port the destination device is connected and forwards the message to only that port. This capability allows a switch to handle several conversations at one time, thereby providing the full network bandwidth to each device rather than requiring bandwidth sharing. Simulation 2-2 shows the operation of a switch.

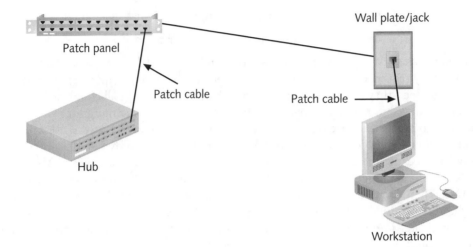

Patch panel

Wall plate/jack

Patch cable

Patch cable

Hub

Workstation

Figure 2-12   Using a patch panel as a passive hub

SIMULATION

Simulation 2-2: Basic Operation of a Switch

The performance advantage of switches has made them the device of choice in corporate networks, at only a marginally higher price than hubs. Because of the popularity of switches and the decrease in their manufacturing costs, switch prices have dropped enough that the improved performance on a LAN justifies the slight additional cost. Most networks today are designed to use switches for connecting computers, servers, and peripheral devices. Although multiport repeaters (hubs) can still be found in the workplace, few new networks are being designed to include these devices, which are quickly becoming obsolete.

NOTE

Chapter 13 covers hubs, switches, and other network devices in more detail.

CONSTRUCTING A NETWORK LAYOUT

Now that you have reviewed the benefits and limitations of major topologies, you're ready to design a simple network. The first step in any network design is to evaluate the underlying requirements. Begin this evaluation process by determining how the network will be used, which often decides the topology you use. Then you must think about the types of devices for interconnecting computers and sites. Finally, the type and usage level of network resources dictate how many servers you need and where to place servers. This section focuses on a fairly small LAN design, in which choices might be limited or foregone conclusions rather than real choices. However, it will get you thinking in the right direction when it's time for you to design a large, complex internetwork with many possible choices.

Selecting a Topology

Not so long ago, there were real choices in deciding on a topology for a LAN. However, technology has marched on, and most new designs come down to only one choice: How fast should the network be? The physical topology will certainly be a star, and the logical topology is almost always switching, with the occasional hub-based bus or ring. Ethernet switches dominate the landscape when it comes to connecting computers on a LAN, but you might consider other logical topologies for the following reasons:

- A ring topology should be considered when legacy equipment using a ring-based architecture, such as token ring or FDDI, would be too difficult or expensive to replace with switching.

- A hub-based bus topology should be considered if a small network (10 or fewer computers) is being constructed and keeping costs down is paramount.

- A hub-based bus topology might be considered if a few computers are being added to an existing network, and the new computers are grouped in a somewhat remote location. An inexpensive hub can be attached to the existing network with a single cable and the new computers attached to the hub with short lengths of cable.

- A wireless topology can always be considered as an add-on to an existing wired network to provide connectivity to mobile users and to reach locations that might be difficult to connect with wires.

- A wireless topology might be the only reasonable topology choice in an environment that's not conducive to running cables, such as warehouses and old or historic buildings.

Creating the Layout

After deciding on the topology, you can start drawing your network layout. The network design and, consequently, the network diagram in a large operation takes a lot of thorough research and knowledge about how the multitude of network technologies work. At this stage of your learning, it's probably enough to understand why you would want to create a network diagram and what factors you should consider in your network design.

A large internetwork running multiple protocols and using different topologies over both LAN and WAN connections can be daunting, especially when problems arise or changes need to be made. Imagine being in charge of a couple of thousand computers and a few dozen servers running different operating systems and different protocols spread out over half a dozen sites. Now add to that multiple WAN technologies and a variety of topologies. When problems come up, a typical network administrator gets a call from a user stating that the network is slow or files are inaccessible. In a small LAN environment, the process usually starts with a few pointed questions to the user. In a large internetwork, however, the first questions that must be answered are Where is the user? and What does the network there look like? For these questions, you consult the network layout or network diagram. Without a map of your network, trying to locate problems or deciding how to upgrade portions of the network are futile exercises.

The previous discussion explains why you need a network layout. Now here's how you go about creating one. Keep in mind that the following questions are only a sampling of what you might ask, and the scope of this fictitious network is limited to a fairly small LAN. It's a starting point, however. The number of questions you would ask and the size of the network you can design will grow along with your knowledge.

Figure 2-13 could be designed as a result of the following questions and their answers:

- How many client computers will be attached? 42
- How many servers will be attached? 2
- Will there be a connection to the Internet? Yes
- How will the building's physical architecture influence decisions, such as whether to use a wired or wireless topology, or both? Two computers require wireless; the rest are wired
- Which topology or topologies will you use? Switching and wireless

After you answer these questions, your next step is to begin sketching a network layout. Starting with a logical depiction of the network is usually best. From there, you can be specific about the location of devices, protocols, and addressing. A diagram similar to the one in Figure 2-13 can be created with a program called SmartDraw, which you can download as a free trial at *www.smartdraw.com*.

You should include enough detail in your network diagram so that anyone can easily understand your network's construction. You might need more than one drawing. For example, the network diagram might include a general view of the overall network, as in Figure 2-13, followed by detailed maps of office layouts, cable numbers, and patch panels. Any technician should be able to take this map and troubleshoot problems. To be effective, a network diagram must be kept up to date. If you don't immediately document changes made to the network, the map becomes worthless.

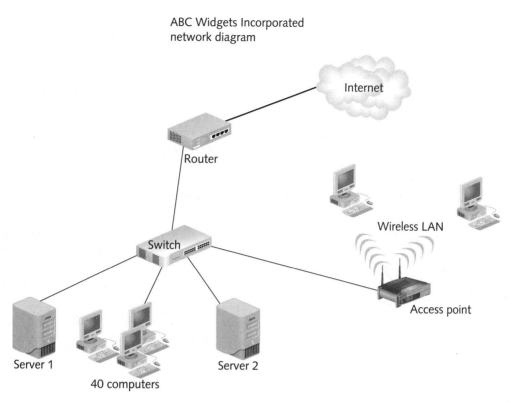

Figure 2-13   A simple network layout diagram

CHAPTER SUMMARY

- All networks build on one of three basic physical topologies: bus, star, or ring. Knowledge of these topologies and their limitations helps ensure informed decisions when designing a network.

- The physical topology of a network describes the physical arrangement of the cables that connect computers. How data travels from computer to computer represents a network's logical topology.

- The physical bus topology, the most basic of the topologies, is easy to install but is an outdated topology that normally shouldn't be used for new installations. The logical bus topology is still used but is almost always implemented as a physical star.

- The physical ring topology connect devices in such a way that the cabling starts and ends with the same computer, forming a circle of sorts. Physical ring topologies are rarely used, except perhaps in technologies such as FDDI. The logical ring topology typically uses token passing to send data around the ring and is normally implemented as a star.

❏ The physical star topology offers centralized management and a higher degree of fault tolerance; a single cable or computer failure does not affect the rest of the network. The star topology is the topology of choice in today's networks.

❏ Wireless networks have their own topology, either ad hoc, which resembles a physical bus in function, or infrastructure mode, which uses a central device that all communications pass through.

❏ Variations on major topologies improve fault tolerance and flexibility. The extended star is the most widely used topology in networks containing more than just a few computers. As the name implies, it's a star of stars. The mesh is the most fault tolerant of all network topologies; it allows every computer to communicate with every other computer. A combination star and bus lends the advantages of a star topology—its centralized management—and the best of the bus topology.

❏ A hub is a central point of concentration for a star network and passes electronic signals to the network. An active hub regenerates the signals; a passive hub simply passes them along. Similar to a hub, a switch provides increased bandwidth and intelligence and offers performance advantages over hubs. Because of these advantages and decreasing prices of switches, they have become the device of choice in corporate star topology networks.

❏ A network layout should be consistent with the existing network and maintained accurately as the network changes. Many third-party tools are available to assist in design and maintenance.

KEY TERMS

access point (AP) — The central device, or hub, through which signals pass in a wireless network.

active hubs — Network devices that regenerate received signals and send them along the network.

active topology — A network topology in which computers are responsible for sending data along the network.

ad hoc topology — A wireless communication scheme by which devices communicate directly with one another without using a central hub.

backbone — A single cable segment used in a bus topology to connect computers in a straight line.

bus — A network topology in which the computers connect to a backbone cable segment to form a straight line.

extended star — Sometimes referred to as a hierarchical star topology, in which devices are connected in a star of stars. A central device, usually a switch, sits in the middle of the topology. Instead of attached computers forming the arms of the star, other switches (or hubs) are connected to the central switch's ports. Computers and peripherals are then attached to these switches or hubs, forming additional stars.

hub — The central point of connection of a star network.

infrastructure mode — The mode of wireless communication in which wireless devices are configured to use an access point.

logical topology — The path that data travels between computers on a network.

mesh — A hybrid network topology in which all computers connect to each other; this topology is used for fault tolerance.

multiport repeater — A device used in a star topology that takes a signal coming in on one port, cleans it up, strengthens it, and then sends the regenerated signal out all other ports. *See also* active hubs.

passive hub — A central connection point through which signals pass without regeneration.

passive topology — A network topology in which computers listen to the data signals being sent but do not participate in network communications.

physical topology — The arrangement of the cabling that interconnects network devices.

ring — A network topology consisting of computers connected in a circle, forming a closed ring.

signal bounce — A phenomenon that occurs when a bus is not terminated and signals continue to traverse the network.

signal propagation — Signals traveling across a medium until they weaken or are absorbed.

star — A network topology in which computers connect through a central connecting point, usually a hub.

switch — A special device that manages connections between any pair of star-wired devices on a network.

terminator — A hardware device used to absorb signals as they reach the end of a bus, thus freeing the network for new communications.

token — A small data packet used in some ring topology networks to ensure fair communications between all computers.

token passing — A method of passing data around a ring network.

topology — The basic physical layout of a network and the way in which network components communicate with each other. *See also* logical topology *and* physical topology.

REVIEW QUESTIONS

1. What term refers to the physical layout of a network's computers, cables, and other resources?

2. Joining the computers in a network at a central point creates a star topology. Which of the following statements is true of a star topology network? (Choose all that apply.)

   a. A cable break can cause all network communications to cease.

   b. A user can disconnect his or her computer cable and cause the entire network to fail.

   c. It requires much more cabling than a bus network.

   d. Its centralized nature makes network management easier.

3. A physical bus topology network requires terminators. True or False?

4. Which of the following statements is true of a ring topology network? (Choose all that apply.)

   a. It requires less cabling than a bus topology network.

   b. It provides equal access to all computers on the network.

   c. It must be terminated at each computer.

   d. A single computer failure does not affect network performance.

5. Which of the following physical topologies is the most fault tolerant?

   a. star

   b. ring

   c. mesh

   d. bus

6. What are two advantages of a star topology network?

7. Which physical topology does switching use?

8. A cable break in a bus network does not affect network communications. True or False?

9. In a bus network, if the ends of the cable aren't terminated, what occurs?

10. Connecting computers to form a straight line creates a _____ topology network.

11. How do switches provide better performance than hubs?

12. Because of its central connection point, a _____ topology network requires a more involved cable installation.

   a. star

   b. ring

   c. mesh

   d. bus

13. What is the central connecting point in a wireless network?

14. What are two disadvantages of a ring topology network?

15. What type of network can use an ad hoc topology?

16. List three reasons to keep a network diagram current.

17. What type of device is usually found at the center of an extended star topology?

    a. token

    b. server

    c. switch

    d. bus

18. What term describes the special packet used in logical ring networks?

    a. token

    b. switch

    c. signal

    d. hub

19. A cable break in a star topology network doesn't affect network communications for the entire network. True or False?

20. FDDI is implemented as which form of logical topology?

21. A ring network is a(n) _____ topology because the computers are responsible for regenerating the signal.

22. Mainframe computers first used the _____ topology.

    a. ring

    b. mesh

    c. bus

    d. star

23. Which device can handle several conversations and provide full network bandwidth to each device?

    a. repeater

    b. switch

    c. multiport repeater

    d. token ring

24. Which device is used as a passive hub?

    a. repeater

    b. switch

    c. patch panel

    d. token ring

25. Which topology is ideal when running cables is impractical?

    a. mesh

    b. wireless

    c. ring

    d. bus

HANDS-ON PROJECTS

Several of the following projects can be enhanced by using a network drawing program. SmartDraw is a simple-to-use program that can be downloaded for evaluation at *www. smartdraw.com* and installed on student workstations.

HANDS-ON PROJECTS

Hands-On Project 2-1

Joe's Brokerage House currently has 25 standalone computers and five laser printers distributed evenly across two floors of a building. A print-sharing device enables users to share the laser printers, but the computers don't connect to each other. Because of good profits, the network administrator plans expansion and upgrades. The company founder, Joe, thinks that all the computers should be able to communicate but doesn't want to spend a lot of money. He does, however, want an easily expandable network design. Wiring closets are available on both floors and have conduit between them. The computers must share sensitive data yet control access to files. Aside from new brokerage software, which runs on the server, the computers will run standard word-processing and spreadsheet programs.

Use the worksheet that follows to evaluate the requirements for this network. After you have completed the worksheet, determine the best network topology or topology combination for the company. On a blank piece of paper, sketch the network design you think best suits Joe's needs.

Network Evaluation Worksheet for Hands-On Project 2-1

Will the network be peer-to-peer or server-based?

_____

If it's server-based, how many servers will be attached to the network?

_____

How many computers will be attached to the network?

_____

What applications will the computers run?

_____

How many printers will be attached to the network?

_____

Hands-On Project 2-2

Old-Tech Corporation has 10 computers in its main office area, which is networked in a star topology using 10 Mbps Ethernet hubs, and wants to add five computers in the manufacturing area. One problem with the existing network is data throughput. Large files are transferred across the network regularly, and it takes quite a while to complete the transfers. In addition, when two or more computers are transferring large files, the network becomes unbearably slow for all the users. Adding the manufacturing computers will only make this problem worse. Adding computers in the manufacturing area presents another problem. Because the ceiling is more than 30 feet high, there's no easy way to run cables to computers, and providing a secure pathway for cables would be next to impossible. Provide a solution to this company's networking problems. As part of your solution, answer the following questions:

1. What changes in equipment are required to bring this company's network up to date to solve the shared-bandwidth problem?

_____

2. What topology and which type of device can be used in the manufacturing area to solve the cabling difficulties?

_____

Hands-On Project 2-3

EBiz.com has 250 networked computers and five servers and uses a star-wired network to reach employees' offices, with a bus interconnecting three floors in its office building. Because of a staggering influx of Internet business, the network administrator's task is to boost network performance and availability as much as possible. The company also wants a network design that's easy to reconfigure and change because workgroups continually form and disband, and their membership also changes regularly. All computers must share sensitive data and control access to customer files and databases. Aside from the customer information and billing databases, which run on all servers, workers' desktop computers must run standard word-processing and spreadsheet programs.

Use the following worksheet to evaluate the requirements for this network. After you complete the worksheet, determine the best network topology or topology combination for the company. On a blank piece of paper, sketch the network design you think best suits EBiz.com's needs. Remember: High performance and easy reconfiguration are your primary design goals!

Network Evaluation Worksheet for Hands-On Project 2-3

What type of topology should be used in this network?

_____

Will the network be peer-to-peer or server-based?

_____

If it's server-based, how many servers will be attached to the network?

_____

How many computers will be attached to the network?

_____

What kind of networking device is easiest to reconfigure? What kind offers the best access to the network medium's bandwidth between pairs of devices?

_____

_____

HANDS-ON PROJECTS

Hands-On Project 2-4

ENormInc has two sites in Pittsburgh that are four miles apart. Each site consists of a large factory with office space for 25 users at the front of the factory and up to 20 workstations in two work cells on each factory floor. All office users need access to an inventory database that runs on a server at the Allegheny Street location; they also need access to a billing application with data residing on a server at the Monongahela site. All factory floor users also need access to the inventory database at the Allegheny Street location.

Office space is permanently finished, but ENormInc must tear down and reconfigure before each new manufacturing run begins. Wiring closets are available in the office space. Nothing but a concrete floor and overhead girders stay the same in the work cell areas. The computers must share sensitive data and control access to files. Aside from the two databases, which run on the two servers, all office computers must run standard word-processing and spreadsheet programs. All work cell machines are used strictly for updating inventory and quality control information for the Allegheny Street inventory database. Workstations in the manufacturing cells are switched on only when they're in use, which might occur during various phases of a manufacturing run. Seldom is a machine in use constantly on the factory floor.

Use the following worksheet to evaluate the requirements for this network. After you complete the worksheet, determine the best network topology, or topology combination, for the company. On a blank piece of paper, sketch the network design you think best suits ENormInc's needs.

Network Evaluation Worksheet for Hands-On Project 2-4

Will the network be peer-to-peer or server-based?

_____

If it's server-based, how many servers will be attached to the network?

_____

How many computers will be attached to the network?

_____

What applications will the office computers run? The factory floor computers?

_____

_____

What topology works best for the offices, given the availability of wiring closets? What topology works best for the factory floor, given its need for constant reconfiguration?

_____

_____

**HANDS-ON
PROJECTS**

Hands-On Project 2-5

In this project, you examine your classroom network and determine what topology, equipment, and cabling are used.

1. Examine your workstation. Find the network connection on the back of the computer and trace the cable to see where it goes. (If you're using wireless, note that when answering the questions in Step 3.) Identify the jack(s), patch cables(s), and other components in the connection. Your instructor will provide a detailed description of how the classroom is wired.

2. If possible, examine the wiring rack where all the cables terminate. (The rack might be in the same room or another room.)

3. Based on your inspections, answer the following questions:

   ■ Which physical topology or topologies are used in the classroom? The campus?

   _____

   ■ Which logical topology or topologies are in use?

   _____

   ■ What type of media is being used?

   _____

- What is the difference between a hub and a switch? Which is being used in the classroom?

_____

_____

CASE PROJECTS

Case Project 2-1

An airline seat reservation system is being designed in a new airport. One problem in the old location is that some fast computers on the network could monopolize the bandwidth, causing agents with slower computers to miss seating opportunities. Which network topology could you use to create a fair environment in which all computers have equal access to the available bandwidth?

Case Project 2-2

The database manager for your company wants to implement a "server farm" (a collection of servers that communicate through a high-speed link) for the database servers. These servers will be replicated; the network must operate reliably and quickly yet still be able to connect to other devices (PCs and so forth). Develop two plans, with different topologies, for implementing this server farm; discuss the advantages and disadvantages of each concept.

Case Project 2-3

Design networks for two classroom environments—a permanent facility and a traveling classroom. They must have connectivity for 20 PCs and a server and be inexpensive and easy to set up. Present both versions of this design to the class, and discuss the benefits of each design.

Case Project 2-4

A law office has just opened its doors in an historic home built in the late 1800s. Eight lawyers and four administrators must be connected to the computer network. The problem is that the walls are made of plaster, and there are no lowered ceilings, which makes cable installation extremely difficult, if not impossible. What type of network can you recommend for this business and why?

3

NETWORKING MEDIA

After reading this chapter and completing the exercises, you will be able to:

♦ Identify general cabling characteristics applied to physical media

♦ Describe the primary cable types used in networking

♦ Identify the components in a structured cabling installation

♦ Describe wireless transmission techniques used in LANs and WANs

Most networks today use cables to interconnect devices. Using a variety of signaling techniques, network cables carry signals between computers, allowing them to communicate with one another. Many kinds of cables, each with its own set of signal-carrying characteristics, can be used to build networks.

Not all computers or networked devices attach to networks by cables, however. A growing portion of the networking population uses wireless technologies because users are mobile or because physical obstructions or distance limitations make cables unsuitable. Wireless technologies are becoming more affordable, and the use of wireless is exploding in the marketplace. This increased use doesn't imply that cable-based networks are waning. On nearly all networks incorporating wireless components, cable-based components continue to play a major role. Wireless technologies offer a way for organizations or users who might otherwise be unable to take advantage of networking's benefits to access the same resources and devices that wired network users can.

In this chapter, you learn about common options for cabled and wireless networking and where these options make sense. You find out about the kinds of transmission technologies for making wireless network links, where the majority of a network might be wired but interconnected by using wireless links. Finally, you discover the transmission technologies that are most appropriate for users and devices that must be constantly on the move—which is what mobile computing is all about.

NETWORK CABLING: TANGIBLE PHYSICAL MEDIA

Regardless of the kind of network media in use, data must be able to enter and leave a computer. Cabling and wireless communication are at the heart of networked communications because these media supply the network's "glue." The interface between a computer and the medium to which it attaches defines the translation from a computer's native digital information into the form needed to send outgoing messages. The process is reversed for incoming messages. Therefore, because all media must support the basic tasks of sending and receiving signals, you can view all networking media as doing the same thing; only the methods vary. Because there are so many different types of media, both wired and wireless, you need to know the physical characteristics and limitations of each kind so that you can make the best use of each type.

Each cabling type comes in a variety of forms, and each has a unique design and usage characteristics with associated cost, performance, and installation criteria. The following sections discuss cable characteristics, transmission types, and bandwidth and then go into more detail on each cabling type.

General Cable Characteristics

All cables share certain fundamental characteristics that you should know to understand their function and appropriate use. Even though wire-based (or conductive) cables differ radically from fiber-optic cables in terms of composition and the types of signals they carry, the following characteristics apply equally to both types of cabling:

- *Bandwidth rating*—Each type of cable can transport only so much data over a given period of time; this characteristic is measured in terms of **bandwidth**, which describes how many bits or bytes of information a cable can carry over a unit of time. Typically, it's measured in number of bits per second (for example, megabits per second, or Mbps).

- *Maximum segment length*—Each type of cable can transport data only so far before its signal begins to weaken beyond where it can be read accurately; this phenomenon is called **attenuation**. When rating maximum cable segment lengths, the **maximum segment length** value falls within a range where signals can be regenerated correctly and retransmitted accurately. So an internetwork can be constructed of several cable segments, as long as the hardware connecting them can capture and regenerate the incoming signal at full strength.

- *Maximum number of segments per internetwork*—Each cable type is also subject to **latency**, which measures the amount of time a signal takes to travel from one end of the cable to another. Most networks are subject to some kind of maximum tolerable delay, after which it's assumed that signals can no longer arrive. A network of networks is, therefore, subject to a maximum number of interconnected segments, simply because of the latency when signals travel from one physical end of the network to another. By arranging cable segments in a hierarchy, a network's span can be quite large, even within these limitations, because the limitations apply to the maximum number of segments between any two network devices.

3

- *Maximum number of devices per segment*—Each time a network device is attached to a cable, a phenomenon called **insertion loss** occurs—each physical connection adds to the attenuation of signals on a cable segment. Therefore, restricting the maximum number of devices is necessary so that the signals traversing it are kept clean and strong enough to remain intelligible to all devices. When calculating maximum legal segment lengths, the real formula for distance equals the rated maximum minus the sum of the insertion losses for all devices attached to that segment:

  true maximum = rated maximum − (insertion losses)

- *Interference susceptibility*—Each type of cable is more or less susceptible to other signals in the environment, where interference can be electromagnetic (called **electromagnetic interference [EMI]**) or result from other broadcast signals (called **radio frequency interference [RFI]**). Motors, transformers, fluorescent lights, and other sources of intense electrical activity can emit both EMI and RFI, but RFI problems are also associated with the proximity of strong broadcast sources in an environment (such as a nearby radio or television station). For the discussion in this chapter, you need to know only four levels of susceptibility: none, low, moderate, and high.

- *Connection hardware*—Every type of cable has connectors that influence the kinds of hardware to which the cable can connect and affect the costs of the resulting network. This chapter also describes whether these connectors are easy to attach, whether attaching them requires specialized equipment, and whether building the cables should be left to professionals.

- *Cable grade*—Building and fire codes include specific cabling requirements, usually aimed at the combustibility and toxicity of the **cladding** (sheath material) and insulation covering most cables. Polyvinyl chloride (PVC) covers the cheapest and most common cables (for example, the 120-volt cord in lamps and other household appliances). Unfortunately, when this material burns, it gives off toxic fumes, which makes it unsuitable for cables strung in ceilings or inside walls.

  The space between a false ceiling and the true ceiling in most office buildings, called the "plenum," is commonly used to aid air circulation for heating and cooling. Any cables in this space must be **plenum-rated**, which typically means they're coated with Teflon because of that material's low combustibility and the relatively nontoxic fumes it produces when burned. These cables can be used in the plenum or within walls without being enclosed in conduit. Although plenum-rated cable is nearly twice as expensive as non-plenum-rated cable, eliminating the need for conduit makes installing plenum-rated network cabling much cheaper. All local fire and building codes must be checked because requirements vary widely.

- *Bend radius*—Although some types of cabling are less prone to damage from bending than others, bending some types beyond a prescribed **bend radius** damages or destroys them. This is particularly true of the most expensive types of cable; for networks, this requirement means primarily that fiber-optic and heavy-duty coaxial cables must be treated with care. Most sensitive cable types can't be bent more than 60 degrees in a one-foot span without sustaining some damage. The key is to understand the cabling's limitations and not bend it past its limits.

■ *Material costs*—Each cable type has a cost per unit length. This factor is a good way to compare cables of the same type to one another. However, it's important to understand that building or fire codes might prohibit using cheaper cables, and the cable's cost is usually less than half the cost of a total installation. Also, note that leaving room to upgrade to faster technologies could mandate buying more expensive cabling; however, reusing existing cable is always cheaper than reinstalling, so it might save money in the long run.

■ *Installation costs*—Labor and auxiliary equipment can easily cost more than the cable when installing a network. That's why it's important to price the design, installation, and troubleshooting of cabling (sometimes called the "cable plant") and to budget for the necessary cabling, connectors, wall plates, patch panels, and other items required for a complete and functioning network. These items are discussed later in "Twisted-Pair Cable."

Now that you know the general characteristics of cabling as well as which characteristics influence selecting a cable type (or collection of cable types for large networks), you can understand the significance of the strengths and weaknesses of cabling types discussed in this chapter. Before you learn the details about coaxial, twisted-pair, and fiber-optic cable, however, you also must understand the two primary techniques for sending signals across a cable: baseband and broadband transmission.

Baseband and Broadband Transmission

Baseband transmission uses a digital encoding scheme at a single fixed frequency, where signals take the form of discrete pulses of electricity or light. In a baseband system, the cable's entire bandwidth is used to transmit a single data signal. That means baseband systems use only one channel on which all devices attached to the cable can communicate. Baseband transmission also limits any single cable strand to half-duplex transmission (where only one sender consumes the entire cable's bandwidth); full-duplex baseband transmissions must, therefore, use two strands of cable—one for sending data and the other for receiving data.

As a signal travels along a network cable, its strength decreases as the distance from the signal transmitter increases. (Recall that this phenomenon is referred to as "attenuation.") Likewise, the degree of distortion increases as the distance from the transmitter increases. The reason each cabling type has a maximum segment length is to ensure that signals on a cable remain intelligible across its entire length. Signal flow on a baseband cable can also be bidirectional so that computers can use a single cable for both transmission and reception. (On a single conductor within the cable, however, only one role at a time can be played.)

Baseband systems—such as Ethernet—can use special devices called **repeaters** that receive incoming signals on one cable segment and refresh them before retransmitting them on another cable segment. That way, they can restore the signal to its original strength and quality before shipping it out on another cable, thereby extending the span a network can cover. As with maximum segment lengths and devices per segment, most cabling is limited by the number of repeaters that can separate any two cable segments on an internetwork. As discussed in Chapter 2, the use of repeaters has decreased in recent years, giving way to the superior technology of switching, which is not subject to many of the limitations imposed by repeaters.

Broadband transmission systems use a different kind of signaling to transmit information across a cable. Instead of digital pulses, broadband systems use **analog** techniques to encode binary 1s and 0s across a continuous range of values. Broadband signals move across the medium in the form of continuous electromagnetic or optical waves rather than discrete pulses. On broadband systems, signal flow at a particular frequency is one-way only, which makes two channels necessary for computers to send and receive data. (This arrangement also makes full-duplex communications much easier to set up on broadband systems.)

When the cabling supports sufficient bandwidth, multiple analog transmission channels can operate on a single broadband cable. This capability permits your cable television company to send many channels across a single wire. When multiple channels are used, however, the sending and receiving equipment must be able to "tune in" the correct channel to permit senders and receivers to communicate with one another.

Because of the differences between analog and digital signaling technologies, broadband cable segments are interlinked with devices called **amplifiers** that detect weak signals, strengthen those signals, and then rebroadcast them. Because two channels are needed for computers to send and receive data on broadband cabling, there are two primary approaches to supporting two-way broadband communications (see Simulation 3-1):

- **Mid-split broadband** uses a single cable but divides the bandwidth into two channels, each on a different frequency. One channel transmits, and the other receives network communications.

- **Dual-cable broadband** uses two cables; each computer or networked device must connect to both cables simultaneously. One cable transmits, and the other receives network communications. (This approach works for broadband the same way it does for baseband when full-duplex communications must occur.)

Simulation 3-1: Baseband Versus Broadband Communication

SIMULATION

Traditionally, broadband systems offered higher bandwidths than baseband systems. For example, original Ethernet cable supports 10 Mbps, but ordinary TV cable supports the equivalent of 250 Mbps or more. Today, higher-speed networking alternatives for both technologies blur this distinction, but generally, broadband systems remain more expensive than baseband systems (of comparable bandwidth) because of the broadband system's need for multiple cables or channels and for tuners and amplifiers for each channel.

The Importance of Bandwidth

Anyone who's spent time online knows that the faster the connection, the better. Because accessing information and services is the name of the game in networking, and faster access is clearly better than slower access, overstating the importance of bandwidth in making any kind of network connection is impossible.

The trend in networking is to offer more complex, comprehensive, and powerful services—including services such as real-time video teleconferencing, voice-only networking services, streaming video and audio, and other high-bandwidth applications. Although these services enable users to get more from their networks than ever before, they also require much higher bandwidth to deliver an acceptable quality of service. Therefore, the trends in networking are for technologists to deliver ever-higher amounts of bandwidth and for application developers to build software requiring more bandwidth to operate. Users demand access to these applications and have increased their use of existing networked applications, consuming still more bandwidth.

As you make your way through this chapter, notice that newer networking technologies are invariably faster and often more powerful than older ones. At the same time, technologists keep finding ways to stretch the bandwidth limits of existing technologies—especially networking media—so that older, difficult-to-replace networking components (such as cabling) can still remain yet support higher bandwidth than originally rated. Now that you understand basic cabling characteristics and the primary transmission systems, you're ready for the details of cabling types.

PRIMARY CABLE TYPES

Despite the many types available, all forms of cabling are similar, in that they provide a medium across which network information can travel in the form of a physical signal, whether it's a type of electrical transmission or some sequence of light pulses. Although many types of cable are available in today's marketplace, you need to be familiar with only three, which represent the majority of cabling types used to interconnect networks:

- Coaxial cable
- Twisted-pair cable, in unshielded and shielded varieties
- Fiber-optic cable

NOTE
As you investigate the network cabling schemes in the following sections, pay special attention to the tables summarizing each type's basic cost, performance characteristics, and device and distance limitations. All these factors play a role when you choose cabling for your own networks.

Coaxial Cable

For many years, **coaxial cable**—often called "coax" for short—was the predominant form of network cabling. Relatively inexpensive and reasonably easy to install, coaxial cable was the networker's choice. Improvements in electronics and signaling technologies conspired to knock coax off its pedestal, however, as the next section describes.

TIP
Coaxial cable in LAN installations is obsolete. The majority of coaxial cable used today is for carrying broadband signals for cable TV or from a home satellite dish to the satellite receiver. The information in this section about the properties of coax refers to all types of coaxial cabling. Information on the use of coaxial cable for a LAN is offered for historical purposes only. Keep in mind that this type of cabling should not be used in new LAN installations.

Simply put, coaxial cable consists of a single conductor at the core, surrounded by an insulating layer, braided metal shielding (called braiding), and an outer cover (usually called the **sheath** or jacket), as shown in Figure 3-1. The networking signals carried by the coax cable travel over the central conductor; the remaining elements protect coax cable from external electrical, mechanical, or environmental influences.

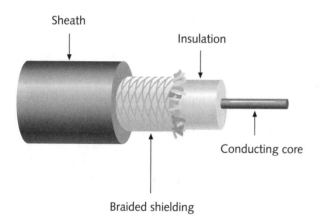

Sheath
Insulation
Conducting core
Braided shielding

Figure 3-1   Coaxial cable

Shielding refers to any protective layers wrapped around a cable to protect it from external interference (EMI or RFI). Shielding increases the viability of signals passing through a cable by absorbing stray electronic signals or fields so that they don't affect data the conductor in the cable must carry. Shielding works like a form of built-in **conduit**, a type of metal or plastic pipe built specifically to contain cabling. In a sense, conduit represents the ultimate form of shielding.

Coaxial cable is less susceptible to interference and attenuation than twisted-pair cabling but more susceptible than fiber-optic cable, partly because of the beneficial influence of coax cable's shielding. This shielding absorbs environmental interference and diminishes its impact on coax cable's capability to transport information. Nevertheless, when coax cable must pass through especially noisy environments—near transformers or large electrical motors, for example—running cable through metal conduit for extra shielding is wise.

The Use of Coaxial Cable for Ethernet

Ethernet's beginnings are in coaxial cable. It's a testament to this flexible and scalable technology that Ethernet could go through several transformations in media type, connectors, and bandwidth upgrades and still be essentially the same technology that it was more than 30 years ago.

For years, Ethernet was run only over coaxial cable. First, it was run on a very thick, rigid cable, usually yellow, referred to as thick Ethernet (also known as **thicknet** or thickwire). Later, a more manageable coaxial cable called thin Ethernet (also known as **thinnet**, thinwire, or cheapernet) was used. The **Institute of Electrical and Electronics Engineers (IEEE)** designates these cable types as **10Base5** and **10Base2**, respectively. This notation indicates the following information:

- *Total bandwidth for the technology*—In this case, 10 means 10 megabits per second (Mbps) and applies to both thin and thick varieties.

- *Base*—The network uses baseband signaling for both types of cable.

- *2 or 5*—Roughly indicates the maximum segment length measured in hundreds of meters. Thinwire (10Base2) originally supported 200 meters but was reduced to a maximum segment length of 185 meters to compensate for patch cables; thickwire (10Base5) supports a maximum segment length of 500 meters.

NOTE Because these coaxial versions of Ethernet are obsolete for new installations and rarely seen in existing installations, the details of these two cable types have been relegated to Appendix A.

Coaxial Cable in Cable Modem Applications

Coaxial cable's use as the primary medium in LAN applications has become obsolete, but its use to access the Internet is exploding. The standard cable (75 ohm, RG-6; RG stands for "radio grade") that delivers cable television (CATV) to millions of homes nationwide is also being used for Internet access.

A typical configuration for a home Internet connection using a **cable modem** is depicted in Figure 3-2. Cable modem Internet access uses broadband technology to carry Internet data signals and cable television channels on the same medium. Typical cable modem connections provide bandwidth from 256 Kbps to more than 1 Mbps for home users, but the technology is capable of carrying data at much higher rates. Because a cable modem uses a shared medium, the bandwidth on any one connection depends on the number of active connections in a neighborhood. The more active connections on a cable segment, the less total bandwidth available on any one modem.

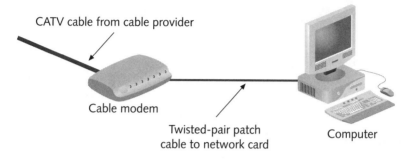

Figure 3-2   A typical cable modem connection

Other Coaxial Cable Types

Coaxial cable works for other types of networks besides Ethernet and CATV. Other applications for coax include ARCnet and computer terminal attachments to mainframes and minicomputers. **Attached resource computing network (ARCnet)** is an older networking technology developed at DataPoint Corporation in the late 1970s. It supports a bandwidth of only 2.5 Mbps, which probably explains why it has faded from use on modern networks. ARCnet implementations that use fiber-optic and twisted-pair cable are available but are usually limited to specialized applications that require properties unique to ARCnet, such as deterministic communication and low overhead.

Twisted-Pair Cable

The most basic form of **twisted-pair (TP)** wiring consists of one or more pairs of insulated strands of copper wire twisted around one another. These twists are important because they cause the magnetic fields that form around a conducting wire to wrap around one another and improve TP's resistance to interference. They also limit the influence of signals traveling on one wire over another (called **crosstalk**). In fact, the more twists per unit length, the better these characteristics become. It's safe to say, therefore, that more expensive TP wire is usually more twisted than less expensive kinds.

There are two primary types of TP cable: **unshielded twisted-pair (UTP)**, which simply contains one or more pairs of insulated wires within an enclosing insulating sheath, and **shielded twisted-pair (STP)**, which encloses each pair of wires within a foil shield as well as an enclosing insulating sheath. Figure 3-3 depicts both types of wire. TP wiring, whether shielded or unshielded, comes in many forms. Many networks commonly use one-, two-, four-, six-, and eight-pair wiring; some forms of TP wiring bundle as many as 50 or 100 pairs within a single cable.

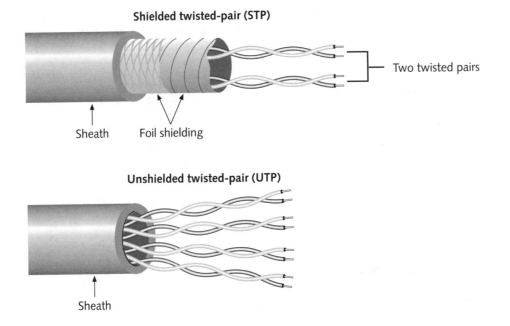

Figure 3-3   STP and UTP cable

Unshielded Twisted-Pair (UTP)

Another version of the IEEE Ethernet specification is called **10BaseT**; the "T" stands for UTP and represents another type of cabling. In fact, UTP is now the most popular form of LAN cabling, even though the maximum length of a 10BaseT segment is 100 meters (328 feet).

The UTP cable used for networking usually includes one or more pairs of insulated wires. UTP specifications govern the number of twists per foot (or per meter), depending on the cable's intended use. Because it's the type of cable used for telephone systems, UTP is common in most office buildings and other work environments. Voice telephony is much less demanding than networking in terms of bandwidth and signal quality, however. Therefore, even though turning unused telephone wiring into network connections might be tempting, it's not worth attempting unless a cable technician tests those lines and pronounces them fit for network use.

UTP Cabling Categories

UTP cabling is rated according to a number of categories devised by the **Telecommunications Industries Association (TIA)** and the **Electronic Industries Alliance (EIA)**; since 1991, the **American National Standards Institute (ANSI)** has also endorsed these standards. The ANSI/TIA/EIA 568 Commercial Building Wiring Standard defines standards that apply to the kinds of wiring used in commercial environments. This set of standards helps ensure consistent performance from wiring products that adhere to its requirements. Currently, the ANSI/TIA/EIA 568 standard includes seven categories for UTP wiring:

- *Category 1*—Applies to traditional UTP telephone cabling, which is designed to carry voice but not data. This cabling is, therefore, labeled as **voicegrade**. Most UTP installed before 1982 falls into this category.

- *Category 2*—Certifies UTP cabling for bandwidth up to 4 Mbps and consists of four pairs of wire. Because 4 Mbps is slower than most current networking technologies (except for original token ring installations and ARCnet), Category 2 is rarely seen in networking environments.

- *Category 3*—Certifies UTP cabling for bandwidth up to 10 Mbps with signaling rates up to 16 MHz. This category includes most conventional networking technologies, such as 10BaseT Ethernet, 4 Mbps token ring, ARCnet, and more. Category 3 consists of four pairs, each pair having a minimum of three twists per foot (10 twists per meter). 100VG-AnyLAN is also rated to work on Category 3 cable, but testing is recommended for older installations. Cat 3 remains in use in many older networks but should be replaced when the networks are upgraded. Most networks are migrating toward 100 Mbps speeds, for which Cat 3 isn't suitable.

- *Category 4*—Certifies UTP cabling for bandwidth up to 16 Mbps with signaling rates up to 20 MHz. This category includes primarily 10BaseT Ethernet and 16 Mbps token ring and is the first ANSI/TIA/EIA designation that labels the cables as **datagrade** (meaning they're capable of carrying data) rather than voicegrade. Category 4 consists of four pairs.

- *Category 5*—Certifies UTP cabling for bandwidth up to 100 Mbps with signaling rates up to 100 MHz. This category includes 100BaseX, Asynchronous Transfer Mode (ATM) networking technologies at 25 and 155 Mbps, plus Fiber Distributed Data Interface (FDDI) at 100 Mbps, as governed by the Twisted-Pair, Physical Media Dependent (TP-PMD) specification. Some experimental implementations of Gigabit Ethernet use Category 5 cable, but standards for this technology haven't been defined. Category 5 also uses four pairs.

- *Category 5e*—Category 5 Enhanced UTP cabling, as the name suggests, is an enhancement to Category 5 UTP. It differs primarily in the tests it must undergo and was designed to correct some shortcomings in Category 5 cabling, particularly in Gigabit Ethernet and full-duplex operation. Category 5e is an acceptable cable type for Gigabit Ethernet, but the newer Category 6 should be considered for new installations. Category 5e is rated for 100 MHz signaling rates.

- *Category 6*—This standard, published in June 2002 by the TIA/EIA, is the recommended UTP cabling standard for Ethernet applications over copper media at speeds up to 1 gigabit. Category 6 cabling uses the same type of modular jack as lower categories and is backward compatible with Category 5 and Category 5e cable plants. Category 6 cabling is specified to operate at signaling rates of 200

MHz. Some Category 6 cabling includes a spline, or separator, in the jacket for additional separation between pairs of wires. However, this separator is not a requirement.

An additional category is not yet a TIA/EIA standard and might never be in the United States. However, Europe has accepted the Category 7 standard, which specifies a fully shielded twisted-pair cable (each wire pair is shielded, as is the outer sheath) with performance characteristics well above earlier cabling standards. Signaling rates are specified at up to 600 MHz, more than doubling the data transfer rate of Category 6 cable. Because of a different connecting hardware design, Category 7 cable and connectors will not likely be backward compatible.

Of these categories of UTP cabling, Categories 5, 5e, and 6 are by far the most popular types. Their huge install base guarantees that developers of new high-speed networking technologies will strive to make their technologies compatible with these categories of UTP cable; for example, Category 5 cable, originally designed for 10 Mbps Ethernet, is capable of running at speeds up to 1 gigabit. UTP is particularly prone to crosstalk, and the shielding for STP is designed specifically to mitigate this problem.

Shielded Twisted-Pair (STP)

As its name indicates, STP includes shielding to reduce crosstalk and limit the effects of external interference. For most STP cables, that means the wiring includes a wire braid inside the cladding or sheath material as well as a foil wrap around each wire pair. This shielding improves the cable's transmission and interference characteristics, which in turn support higher bandwidth over longer distances than UTP. Unfortunately, no set of standards for STP corresponds to the ANSI/TIA/EIA 568 Standard for UTP, yet it's not unusual to find STP cables rated according to those standards. STP uses two pairs of 150 ohm wire, as defined by the IBM cabling system, and was not designed to be used in Ethernet applications, but it can be adapted to do so by using special adapters.

NOTE Another type of STP cabling is screened twisted pair (ScTP) or foil twisted pair (FTP). Both use 100 ohm, four-pair cabling, just like UTP. The cabling is wrapped in a metal foil or screen. This type of cabling can be used in place of UTP in electrically noisy environments.

Whether STP or UTP, twisted-pair network cabling most commonly uses **registered jack 45 (RJ-45)** telephone connectors to plug into computer network interfaces or other networked devices. This connector looks much like the **RJ-11** connector on modular telephone jacks, except that it's larger and contains eight wire traces rather than the four housed in an RJ-11. Figure 3-4 shows an RJ-45 connector and an RJ-11 connector.

Figure 3-4 RJ-45 (left) and RJ-11 (right) connectors

The longevity of phone wire management systems and components, and the fact that twisted-pair networks can use the same kinds of equipment, help explain the burgeoning popularity of twisted-pair network cabling schemes of all kinds. Typically, these systems include the following elements, often in a **wiring center**:

- Distribution racks and modular shelving help organize cables and can be arranged vertically to conserve floor space. In many companies, phone closets are used for both telephone and network wire management.

- Modular **patch panels** permit varied arrangements of network connections. They can accommodate different types of fiber-optic connections and connections for UTP cabling. Many patch panels for bandwidth up to 100, and even 155, Mbps are available today. The increasing use of Gigabit Ethernet (1000 Mbps) promises even higher-bandwidth solutions for this kind of equipment.

- **Wall plates** are special built-in receptacles used in many offices. Like electrical outlets, these plates supply access to voice and network connections and sometimes even to fiber-optic or private broadcast video outlets. Modular wall plates make it easier to wire offices and provide a single point of access for all kinds of communications (such as voice and data), as shown in Figure 3-5.

- **Jack couplers** are special RJ-45-terminated TP cables that permit modular cables to stretch between wall plates (where built-in wiring terminates) and equipment (where the cables span the gap from wall to network interface).

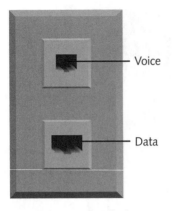

Figure 3-5   A wall plate providing both voice and data connections

All this specialized technology keeps unsightly wiring out of the way and lets network configuration be handled behind the scenes in wiring closets at patch panels (shown in Figure 3-6) without requiring cables to be rerouted. In fact, many organizations choose to run lots of unused wiring pairs to allow for easy growth.

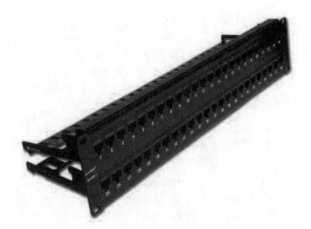

Figure 3-6   Patch panel

Twisted-pair cabling is usually a common choice for a network cabling scheme. Most office environments include a place for TP wiring schemes, if only as a way to bring network connections to workspaces, even when coax or fiber backbones interlink vast internetworks behind the scenes. Normally, the only reasons that twisted-pair wouldn't play at least some role in a network is if bandwidth or distance requirements rule out TP or if TP's high susceptibility to interference renders it unsuitable for networking use in signal-rich environments (such as power plants or factory floors). For easy reference, Table 3-1 summarizes common characteristics of Category 5, 5e, and 6 UTP cabling, the most prevalent in today's networks.

Table 3-1   Category 5, 5e, and 6 UTP cabling characteristics

Characteristic	Value
Maximum cable length	100 m (328 ft.)
Bandwidth	Up to 1000 Mbps
Bend radius	Minimum four times the cable diameter or 1 inch
Installation and maintenance	Easy to install, no need to reroute; the most flexible
Cost	Least expensive of all cabling options
Connector type	RJ-45 for device and wall-plate connections
Security	Moderately susceptible to eavesdropping
Signaling rates	100 MHz for Cat 5 and 5e; 200 MHz for Cat 6
Interference rating	Low; most susceptible of all electrical cable types

Making Twisted-Pair Cable Connections

One of the skills required of a network technician is making a twisted-pair patch cable. A **patch cable** is used to connect a computer's network interface card to a jack in the work area or to connect from a patch panel to a hub or switch in the wiring closet. To do this, a technician needs the following tools:

- Wire cutters or electrician's scissors
- Wire stripper
- Crimp tool
- RJ-45 plugs

Hands-On Project 3-2 walks you through the process of making a patch cable. One of the most important aspects of making a cable or terminating a cable at a jack or patch panel is to get the colored wires arranged in the correct order. There are two competing standards for the arrangement of wires: TIA/EIA 568A and TIA/EIA 568B. Either standard is okay to follow as long as you stick to one throughout your network. The arrangement of wires for both standards is shown in Figures 3-7 and 3-8. Two wires are used for transmitting and two wires are used for receiving, labeled transmit+/transmit- and receive+/receive-, respectively. The plus and minus symbols indicate that the wires carry a positive (+) or negative (-) signal. This **differential signal** mitigates the effects of crosstalk and noise that might be encountered on the cable.

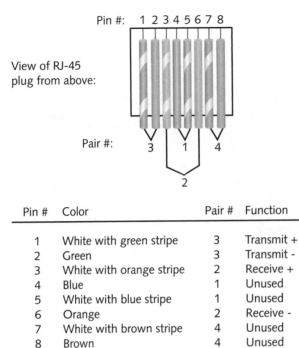

Pin #:   1 2 3 4 5 6 7 8

View of RJ-45
plug from above:

Pair #:   3   1   4

                2

Pin #	Color	Pair #	Function
1	White with green stripe	3	Transmit +
2	Green	3	Transmit -
3	White with orange stripe	2	Receive +
4	Blue	1	Unused
5	White with blue stripe	1	Unused
6	Orange	2	Receive -
7	White with brown stripe	4	Unused
8	Brown	4	Unused

Figure 3-7   TIA/EIA 568A cable pinouts

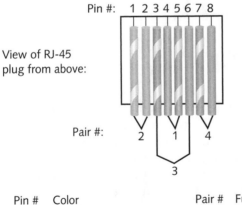

Pin #:   1 2 3 4 5 6 7 8

View of RJ-45
plug from above:

Pair #:   2   1   4

                3

Pin #	Color	Pair #	Function
1	White with orange stripe	2	Transmit +
2	Orange	2	Transmit -
3	White with green stripe	3	Receive +
4	Blue	1	Unused
5	White with blue stripe	1	Unused
6	Green	3	Receive -
7	White with brown stripe	4	Unused
8	Brown	4	Unused

Figure 3-8   TIA/EIA 568B cable pinouts

Fiber-optic Cable

Fiber-optic cable trades electrical pulses for their optical equivalents, which are pulses of light. Because no electrical signals ever pass through the cable, fiber-optic media is as immune to interference as any medium can get. This characteristic also makes fiber-optic cables highly secure. They emit no external signals that might be detected, unlike electrical or broadcast media, thereby eliminating the possibility of **electronic eavesdropping**. In particular, fiber-optic cable is a good medium for high-bandwidth, high-speed, long-distance data transmissions because of its lower attenuation characteristics and vastly higher bandwidth. Today, commercial implementations at 10 Gbps are in use.

Figure 3-9 shows a picture of a typical fiber-optic cable. Fiber-optic cable consists of five components: a slender cylinder of glass fiber called the core, surrounded by a concentric layer of glass called the cladding. The fiber is then jacketed in a thin transparent plastic material called the buffer. These three components make up what's referred to as the optical fiber in Figure 3-9. The fiber is optionally surrounded by a jacket made of colored plastic, shown as the inner jacket in the figure. A strengthening material, usually made of Kevlar, comes next, followed by an outer jacket. Sometimes the core consists of plastic rather than glass fibers; plastic is more flexible and less sensitive to damage than glass but more vulnerable to attenuation. In addition, it can't span the enormous distances that glass fiber-based cables can.

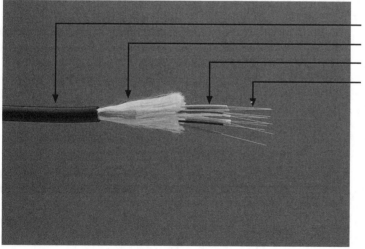

Figure 3-9   Fiber-optic cable

In any fiber-optic cable, each light-conducting core can pass signals in only one direction (so that one end is always the sender and the other always the receiver). That means most fiber-optic connections consist of two or more strands, each within a separate inner sheath; however, these cables can be enclosed within a single sheath (or jacket) or can be two separate cables, each with its own sheath. In most forms of fiber-optic cable, an insulating layer of plastic or glass surrounds the light-conducting fibers at the core for reinforcement and to maintain a consistent diameter. Kevlar fibers are used as a strengthening material because they are extremely strong and resist shearing.

Some testing has shown that glass fibers can carry as much as 200 Gbps. Best of all, the maximum segment length for fiber is measured in miles (or kilometers), as shown in Table 3-2.

Table 3-2   Fiber-optic cable characteristics

Characteristic	Value
Maximum cable length	2 km (6562 ft.) to 100 km (62.14 miles)
Bandwidth	10 Gbps and up
Bend radius	30 degrees per foot
Installation and maintenance	Difficult to install and reroute, sensitive to strain and bending
Cost	Most expensive of all cabling options
Connector type	Several types (see bulleted list later in this section)
Security	Not susceptible to eavesdropping
Interference rating	None; least susceptible of all cable types

A wide variety of connectors can be used with fiber-optic media. The number of options is related to the number of different kinds of light-emitting sources used to generate, and the corresponding light-detecting sensors used to detect, light pulses traveling across the medium. Several of the connectors described in the following list are shown in Figure 3-10:

- *Straight tip (ST)*—ST connectors join fibers at interconnects or to optical devices. They appear most often in Ethernet networks that use fiber-optic cable as backbones. An ST connector locks onto the jack when twisted.

- *Straight connection (SC)*—SC connectors push on, which makes them easy to install and requires less space for an attachment. SC connectors make a strong connection and can be used when splicing fiber-optic cables. An SC connector is a one-piece component, with two receptacles for sending and receiving fibers. A notch in its jacket ensures the correct orientation when inserted.

- *Locking connection (LC)*—LC connectors push on and pull off using an RJ-45 style latching mechanism. They are about half the size of SC connectors, which makes them good for high-density applications.

- ***Medium interface connector (MIC)***—MIC connectors are used for Fiber Distributed Data Interface (FDDI). Like SC connectors, MIC connectors are one-piece constructions.

- ***Subminiature type A (SMA)***—The company Amphenol originally designed SMA connectors for microwave use and later modified them for fiber-optic use. Two SMA versions are widely available: The 905 uses a straight ferrule, which is a metal sleeve used to strengthen the connector; the 906 uses a stepped ferrule with a plastic sleeve to ensure precise alignment of the fibers. Like ST connectors, SMAs use two connectors for each fiber strand.

- ***Mechanical transfer registered jack (MT-RJ)***—The MT-RJ connector looks a little like an RJ-45 connector. It provides a high-density fiber-optic connection using two fiber-optic cables. Compared to other connector types, MT-RJ connectors take only half the space for the same number of cable terminations. Besides saving space, MT-RJ advantages include ease of installation and the requirement of only one connector for a two-fiber termination.

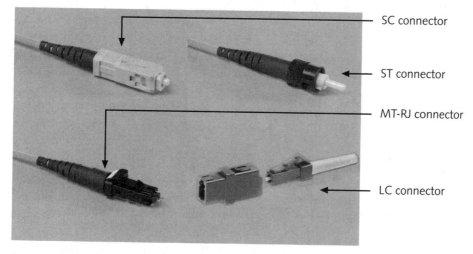

Figure 3-10   Fiber-optic connectors

Installation of fiber-optic networks is somewhat more difficult and time-consuming than copper media installation, but advances in connector technology have made field termination of fiber-optic cables almost as fast and easy as copper terminations. The connectors and test equipment required for proper termination are still considerably more expensive than their copper counterparts, but the trend toward easier, more affordable fiber-optic networks continues. Fiber-optic cable to the desktop could possibly be a feasible option for more companies.

Fiber-optic cables come in two primary types: single-mode cables, which include only one glass fiber at the core, and multimode cables, which incorporate two or more glass fibers at the core. Single-mode cable costs more and generally works with laser-based emitters but spans the longest distances; multimode cables cost less and work with **light emitting diodes (LEDs)** but span shorter distances.

Historically, fiber-optic cable's high cost and difficult installation meant that it was used only when a network required extremely high bandwidth or needed to span long distances between individually wired network segments. However, because of the falling costs of fiber and the inherent advantages of this medium in interference immunity, high bandwidth capability, and increased security, fiber-optic cable is being used almost exclusively for all network backbone connections. Likewise, it's the medium of choice for cable-based, long-haul telecommunications, where large amounts of voice and data traffic are routinely aggregated.

Cable Selection Criteria

Given so many different kinds of networking cable from which to choose, making a selection might seem daunting. As you consider the following criteria for any network installation, however, the corresponding choices become clear:

- *Bandwidth*—How fast must the network be? Higher bandwidth means more expensive cable and higher installation costs. The higher the bandwidth requirements, the more likely you are to use a less flexible, more heavily shielded, if not fiber-optic, cable.

- *Budget*—How much money can you spend on cabling? Can the network be deployed piecemeal? Sometimes, budget alone dictates a choice. Because all the cabling types have been ranked by cost, it should be easy to tell what your budget dictates.

- *Capacity*—How much traffic must the network carry? How will the traffic flow? Planning a network layout to separate light-to-moderate users from heavy users and to separate backbone traffic from local user traffic is generally a good idea. These considerations can also affect cable choices and equipment requirements.

- *Environmental considerations*—How noisy is the deployment environment? How important is data security? Sometimes signal-rich environments or security requirements can dictate cable choices, regardless of other factors. The higher either factor weighs, the more likely it becomes that you choose fiber-optic cable.

- *Placement*—Where will the cables run? How tight are the spaces? Requirements for cable flexibility, access, and routing also weigh heavily on cable selection, particularly where there are tight spaces or it's necessary to avoid obstacles. With a high need for sharp bends or increased flexibility, TP cable is a more likely selection.

- *Span*—What kind of distance must the network span? Longer spans need more expensive, higher-bandwidth cables, if not more exotic options. (This chapter covers more exotic options later in "Wireless Extended LAN Technologies.") Strategic placement of small hubs for use with TP wiring, interlinked by coax cable, gives TP surprising reach in many office environments where workers tend to cluster in groups, even if those groups are widely scattered.

- *Local requirement*—Local building and fire code officials must approve any new installation and should be consulted before making installation decisions.

- *Existing cable plant*—The **cable plant** is the combination of installed network cables, connectors, patch panels, wall jacks, and other media components. For a new installation, only the previously listed criteria need to be considered, but for an upgrade, the existing cable plant must be considered. For example, if some of the existing cable is to remain, is it compatible with the speeds and new equipment that are planned?

At one extreme, when money is no object and the need for speed or long spans is great, fiber-optic cable is an obvious choice. At the other end of the spectrum, when quick, cheap, and easy networking is desirable, UTP with a small inexpensive hub does the job. Networks combining fiber-optic and UTP cabling are also common, with fiber-optic cables providing a backbone that ties together clusters of devices networked with UTP cable through hubs and wiring centers. Table 3-3 condenses the most important cabling information for the cable types covered so far in this chapter.

Table 3-3   Comparison of general cable characteristics

Type	Maximum Cable Length	Bandwidth	Installation	Interference	Cost
UTP	100 m	10–1000 Mbps	Easy	High	Cheapest
STP	100 m	16–1000 Mbps	Moderate	Moderate	Moderate
10Base2	185 m	10 Mbps	Easy	Moderate	Cheap
10Base5	500 m	10 Mbps	Hard	Low	Expensive
Fiber-optic	2–100 km	100 Mbps–10 Gbps	Moderate	None	Most expensive

MANAGING AND INSTALLING THE CABLE PLANT

Entire books are written on cable installation and management, and the full details are beyond the scope of this book. However, understanding some of the basic methods and terminology of cable management will give you a good foundation. As mentioned earlier, the TIA/EIA developed the document "568 Commercial Building Wiring Standard," which specifies how network media should be installed to maximize performance and efficiency. This standard defines what's often referred to as structured cabling.

Structured Cabling

Structured cabling specifies how cabling should be organized, regardless of the type of media or network architectures. Although a variety of logical topologies can be used, structured cabling relies on an extended star physical topology. TIA/EIA 568 can be applied to any size network and divides the details of a cable plant into six separate components. A small LAN in a 10-computer business might need only two or three of these components, but large networks typically use most or all of the following six components:

- Work area
- Horizontal wiring
- Telecommunications closets
- Equipment rooms
- Backbone or vertical wiring
- Entrance facilities

Network cabling standards are designed to ensure that limitations on media and standards for equipment rooms and wiring closets are adhered to, which helps limit the number of possible reasons for network failure or poor performance. If the network cable plant is in good working order and meets standards, a network administrator's job is easier. Structured cabling facilitates troubleshooting as well as network upgrades and expansion.

Work Area

The **work area**, as the name suggests, is where computer workstations and other user devices are located—in short, the place where people work. Faceplates and wall jacks are installed in the work area, and patch cables connect computers and printers to wall jacks, which are in turn connected to a nearby telecommunications closet. Patch cables in the work area should be limited to less than 6 meters long (about 20 feet). The TIA/EIA 568 standard calls for at least one voice and one data outlet on each faceplate in each work area. The connection between wall jack and telecommunications closet is made with horizontal wiring.

Horizontal Wiring

Horizontal wiring runs from the work area's wall jack to the telecommunications closet and is usually terminated at a patch panel. Acceptable horizontal wiring types include four-pair UTP (Category 5e or 6 is the current recommended UTP standard) or two fiber-optic cables. Horizontal wiring from the wall jack to the patch panel should be no longer than 90 meters. The total maximum distance for horizontal wiring is up to 100 meters; patch cables in the work area and in the telecommunications closet can total up to 10 meters.

Telecommunications Closet

The **telecommunications closet (TC)** provides connectivity to computer equipment in the nearby work area. In small installations, the TC can also serve as the entrance facility. Typical equipment includes patch panels to terminate horizontal wiring runs, hubs and switches to provide network connectivity, and patch cables to connect from patch panels to hubs and switches. In smaller installations, network servers can be housed in the TC. Larger installations usually have connections from the TC to an equipment room. Figure 3-11 shows the relationship and connections between the work area, horizontal wiring, and telecommunications closet.

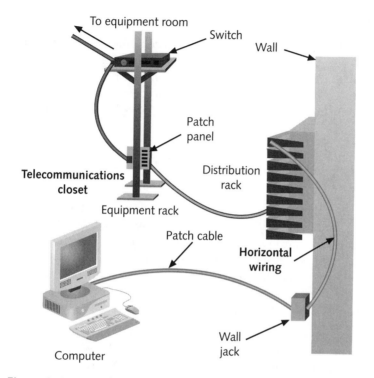

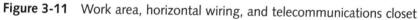

Figure 3-11   Work area, horizontal wiring, and telecommunications closet

Equipment Rooms

The **equipment room** houses servers, routers, switches, and other major network equipment and serves as a connection point for backbone cabling running between TCs. An equipment room can be the main cross-connect of backbone cabling for the entire network, or it might serve as the connecting point for backbone cabling between buildings. In multibuilding installations, each building often has its own equipment room.

Backbone Cabling

Backbone cabling (or vertical cabling) interconnects TCs and equipment rooms. This cabling runs between floors or wings of a building and between buildings to carry network traffic destined for devices outside the work area. Backbone cabling is frequently fiber-optic cable but can also be UTP if the distance between rooms is less than 90 meters. When it connects buildings, backbone cabling is almost always fiber-optic. Multimode fiber-optic cable can extend up to 2000 meters, whereas single-mode fiber can reach distances up to 3000 meters when used as backbone cabling between the main cross-connect and TCs. Between equipment rooms and TCs, the distance is limited to 500 meters for both fiber-optic cable types; from the main cross-connect to equipment rooms, fiber-optic cable can run up to 1500 meters.

Entrance Facilities

An **entrance facility** is the location of the cabling and equipment that connects a corporate network to a third-party telecommunications provider. It can also serve as an equipment room and the main cross-connect for all backbone cabling. This location is also where a connection to a WAN is made and the point where corporate LAN equipment ends and a third-party provider's equipment and cabling begins—also known as the "demarcation point."

WIRELESS NETWORKING: INTANGIBLE MEDIA

Wireless technologies continue to play an increasing role in all kinds of networks. Since 1990, especially, the number of wireless options has increased, and the cost of these technologies continues to decrease. As wireless networking has become more affordable, demand has increased, and as demand increases, so does production of wireless equipment, which brings prices down even further. For this reason, wireless networks can now be found in most towns and cities in the form of hot spots, and more home users have turned to wireless networks so that their computers are no longer tethered to a network cable.

The adjective "wireless" might lead you to believe that wireless networks have no cabling of any kind. Nothing is further from the truth, however. Wireless networks are often used with wired networks to interconnect geographically dispersed LANs or groups of mobile users with stationary servers and resources on a wired LAN. Microsoft calls networks that include both wired and wireless components hybrid networks.

The Wireless World

Wireless networking has considerable appeal in many circumstances and can offer the following capabilities:

- Create temporary connections to existing wired networks.
- Establish backup or contingency connectivity for existing wired networks.
- Extend a network's span beyond the reach of wire-based or fiber-optic cabling, especially in older buildings where rewiring might be too expensive.
- Enable users to roam with their machines within certain limits (referred to as "mobile networking").

Each capability supports uses that extend the benefits of networking beyond conventional limits. Although wireless networking is invariably more expensive than cable-based alternatives, sometimes these benefits can more than offset the extra costs. Today, common applications for wireless networking technologies include the following:

- Ready access to data for mobile professionals, such as doctors or nurses in hospitals or delivery personnel. For instance, United Parcel Service (UPS) drivers maintain connections to a server at the home office; their handheld computers send and receive delivery updates and status information to a network server over a wireless telephone connection.

- Delivery of network access into isolated facilities or disaster-stricken areas. For example, the Federal Emergency Management Agency (FEMA) uses battery-powered wireless technologies to install field networks in areas where power and connections might be unavailable.

- Access in environments where layout and settings change constantly. For instance, film studios often include wireless network components on the set so that information is always available, no matter how the stage configuration changes.

- Improved customer services in busy areas, such as check-in or reception centers. For example, Hertz employees use handheld units to check in returned rental vehicles right in the parking lot.

- Network connectivity in structures, such as historical buildings, where in-wall wiring would be impossible to install or prohibitively expensive.

- Home networks where the installation of cables is inconvenient. More people who own multiple computers are installing inexpensive wireless networks to share Internet connections and files between family members. Figure 3-12 shows an example of using wireless in a home network.

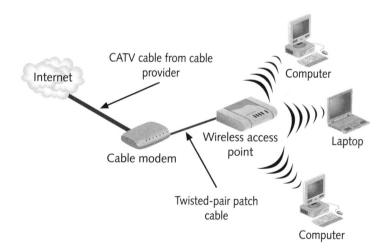

Figure 3-12 A typical home wireless network

In fact, as wireless technologies decrease in cost, their number of uses grows correspondingly. See Simulation 3-2 to get an idea of how wireless networks operate.

Simulation 3-2: Wireless LAN Operation

SIMULATION

Types of Wireless Networks

Depending on the role that wireless components play in a network, wireless networks can be subdivided into three main categories:

- *Local area networks (LANs)*—In LANs, wireless components act as part of an ordinary LAN, usually to provide connectivity for mobile users or changing environments or perhaps across areas that might not otherwise be networkable. Examples include older buildings where installing wiring would be impractical or areas that encompass public or common property where cabling might not be permitted.

- *Extended LANs*—In **extended LANs**, an organization might use wireless components to increase a LAN's span beyond normal distance limitations for wire-based or fiber-optic cables.

- *Mobile computing*—With **mobile computing**, users communicate by using a wireless networking medium, such as radio or cell phone frequencies, that enable them to move while remaining attached to a network.

An easy way to differentiate among these uses is to distinguish in-house from carrier-based facilities. Both LAN and extended LAN wireless networking involve equipment that an organization owns and controls. However, mobile computing typically involves a third party that supplies transmission and reception devices to link the mobile part of a network with the wired part. Most often, the company providing these services is a **communications carrier** (such as MCI or AT&T) that offers wireless communications for data and voice to its customers.

Wireless LAN Components

The wireless components of most LANs behave like their wired counterparts, except for the media and related hardware. The operational principles are much the same: Attaching a network interface of some kind to a computer is still necessary, but the interface attaches to an **antenna** and an emitter rather than to a cable. Users can still access the network just as though cable connects them to it.

Another item of equipment is required to link wireless users with wired users or resources. At some point on a cabled network, a transmitter/receiver device, called a **transceiver** or an access point, must be installed to translate between the wired and wireless networks. This device broadcasts messages in wireless format that must be directed to wireless users and relays messages sent by wireless users to resources or users on the wired side of its connection. An **access point device** includes an antenna and a transmitter to send and receive wireless traffic but also connects to the wired side of the network. This connection permits the device to shuttle traffic back and forth between a network's wired and wireless sides.

Some wireless LANs use small transceivers, which can be wall mounted or freestanding, to attach computers or devices to a wired network. This setup permits some limited mobility with an unobstructed view of the transceiver for devices. Although these attachments are indeed wireless, some experts contend that this approach doesn't represent wireless networking because each component has its own separate wireless connection. Regardless, you might still see these technologies advertised as "wireless LANs."

Wireless LAN Transmission

All wireless communications depend on sending and receiving signals broadcast through the atmosphere to carry information between network devices. These signals take the form of waves in the electromagnetic spectrum. The frequency of the wave forms used for communication is measured in cycles per second usually expressed as **hertz (Hz)**, in honor of Heinrich Hertz, one of the inventors of radio. The spectrum starts with low-frequency waves, such as those used for electrical power (60 Hz in the United States) and telephone (0 to 3 kilohertz [KHz] for traditional voice systems) and goes all the way through the spectra associated with visible light to the highest frequencies in existence, at which gamma rays and other high-energy particles operate.

In wireless communications, frequency affects the amount and speed of data transmission. The transmission's strength or power determines the distance that broadcast data can travel and still remain intelligible. In general, however, the principles governing wireless transmissions dictate that lower-frequency transmissions can carry less data more slowly over longer distances, and higher-frequency transmissions can carry more data faster over shorter distances.

The middle part of the electromagnetic spectrum is commonly divided into several named frequency ranges, or bands. These are the most commonly used frequencies for wireless data communications:

- *Radio*—10 KHz (kilohertz) to 1 GHz (gigahertz)
- *Microwave*—1 GHz to 500 GHz
- *Infrared*—500 GHz to 1 THz (terahertz)

The important principles to remember about a broadcast medium are the inverse relationship between frequency and distance and the direct relationship between frequency and data transfer rate and bandwidth. It's also important to understand that higher-frequency technologies often use tight-beam broadcasts and require a clear line of sight between sender and receiver to ensure correct delivery.

Wireless LANs make use of four primary technologies for transmitting and receiving data, discussed in the following sections:

- Infrared
- Laser
- Narrowband (single-frequency) radio
- Spread-spectrum radio

Infrared LAN Technologies

Infrared wireless networks use infrared light beams to send signals between pairs of devices. These devices typically generate reasonably strong signals to prevent interference from light sources in most office environments. Infrared works well for LAN applications because of its high bandwidth, which makes 10 to 100 Mbps transmission rates easy to deliver. The four main kinds of infrared LANs include the following:

- **Line-of-sight networks** require an unobstructed view, or a clear line of sight, between the transmitter and receiver.
- **Reflective wireless networks** broadcast signals from optical transceivers near devices to a central hub, which then forwards signals to their intended recipients.
- **Scatter infrared networks** bounce transmissions off walls and ceilings to deliver signals from sender to receiver. This approach limits maximum reception distances to approximately 30 meters (100 feet). Because bounce technologies introduce signal delays, scatter infrared results in less bandwidth than line of sight.
- **Broadband optical telepoint networks** provide broadband services. This technology offers high speed and wide bandwidth, can handle high-end multimedia traffic, and matches the capabilities of most modern wired networks.

Infrared transmissions are being used increasingly for **virtual docking** connections that enable portable computing devices to communicate with wired computers or peripheral devices, such as printers. Even though infrared offers reasonable networking speeds and convenience, infrared LANs are hampered by the typical 100-foot distance limitation. Because infrared light is close in frequency to visible light (and most visible light sources emit strongly in infrared frequencies), infrared is prone to interference problems in most work environments. These devices are often called **IrDA devices**, named after the Infrared Device Association, a trade association for designers and manufacturers of infrared equipment.

Laser-Based LAN Technologies

Laser-based transmissions also require a clear line of sight between sender and receiver. Any solid object or person blocking a beam blocks data transmissions. To protect people from injury and avoid excess radiation, laser-based LAN devices are subject to many of the same limitations as infrared but aren't as susceptible to interference from visible light sources.

Narrowband Radio LAN Technologies

Narrowband radio (also called "single-frequency radio") LANs use low-powered, two-way radio communications, much like those used in taxis, police communications, and other private radio systems. Receiver and transmitter must be tuned to the same frequency to handle incoming and outgoing data. Unlike light-based communications, such as infrared or laser, narrowband radio requires no line of sight between sender and receiver, as long as both parties stay within the broadcast range of these devices—typically, a maximum range of approximately 70 meters (230 feet).

In the United States, government agencies, such as the **Federal Communications Commission (FCC)**, regulate nearly all radio frequencies. Organizations that want to obtain frequencies for their exclusive use in specific locales must complete a time-consuming, expensive application process before being granted the right to use them. Because of the difficulty in securing exclusive use, the FCC sets aside certain frequencies for unregulated use. (They include the frequencies at which cell phones and remote-control toys operate, for instance.) As wireless networking and other forms of wireless communications become more popular, crowding of these frequencies could become a problem.

Depending on the frequency, walls or other solid barriers can block signals and prevent transmission and reception. Interference from other radio sources is also possible, particularly if the devices broadcast in the unregulated frequency ranges, as do most wireless LAN technologies. As with any broadcast technology, anyone who comes within range of the network devices could eavesdrop on networked communications. For narrowband radio technologies, this range is quite short. Table 3-4 summarizes the characteristics of narrowband wireless LAN technologies.

Table 3-4   Narrowband wireless LAN characteristics

Characteristic	Value
Frequency ranges	Unregulated: 902–928 MHz, 2.4 GHz, 5.72–5.85 GHz
Maximum distance	50–70 m (164–230 ft.)
Bandwidth	1–10 Mbps
Installation and maintenance	Easy to install and maintain
Interference	Highly susceptible
Cost	Moderate
Security	Highly susceptible to eavesdropping within range

Other single-frequency LAN technologies operate at higher power ratings. Networks of this type can usually transmit as far as the horizon and even farther by using repeater towers or signal-bouncing techniques. This kind of technology is well suited for communicating with mobile users but much more expensive than lower-powered alternatives. Likewise, transmission equipment is more expensive and usually requires FCC licensing. Most users of this technology, even in the largest organizations, choose to purchase this service from a communications carrier, such as AT&T or GTE, instead of operating their own facilities.

Security can be a profound concern with this kind of networking technology. Anyone with the correct receiver can eavesdrop on these communications, which explains why encryption of traffic is common for networks operating at these frequencies. Table 3-5 summarizes the characteristics of high-powered single-frequency radio networks.

Table 3-5   High-powered single-frequency LAN characteristics

Characteristic	Value
Frequency ranges	Unregulated: 902–928 MHz, 2.4 GHz, 5.72–5.85 GHz
Maximum distance	Line of sight, unless extension technologies are used
Bandwidth	1–10 Mbps
Installation and maintenance	Difficult, highly technical, requires licensing
Interference	Highly susceptible
Cost	Expensive to very expensive
Security	Highly susceptible to eavesdropping

Spread-Spectrum LAN Technologies

Spread-spectrum radio addresses several weaknesses of single-frequency communications, whether high or low power. Instead of using a single frequency, spread-spectrum uses multiple frequencies simultaneously, thereby improving reliability and reducing susceptibility to interference. Also, using multiple frequencies makes eavesdropping more difficult.

The two main kinds of spread-spectrum communications are frequency hopping and direct-sequence modulation. **Frequency hopping** switches data among multiple frequencies at regular intervals. Transmitter and receiver must be tightly synchronized to keep communications ongoing. The hardware handles the timing of hops and chooses the next frequency without sending any information about this activity, so eavesdropping is nearly impossible. Because frequency-hopping technologies use only one frequency at a time, however, their effective bandwidth is usually 1 Mbps or less and seldom exceeds 2 Mbps.

Direct-sequence modulation breaks data into fixed-size segments called **chips** and transmits the data on several different frequencies at the same time. The receiving equipment knows what frequencies to monitor and how to reassemble the arriving chips into the correct sequences of data. It's even possible to transmit dummy data on one or more channels, along with real data on other channels, to make it more difficult for eavesdroppers to re-create the original data. Typically, direct-sequence networks operate in unregulated frequencies and provide bandwidths from 2 to 6 Mbps, depending on the number of dummy channels used. Table 3-6 summarizes the characteristics of spread-spectrum LAN technologies.

Table 3-6   Spread-spectrum LAN characteristics

Characteristic	Value
Frequency ranges	Unregulated: 902–928 MHz or 2.4 GHz
Maximum distance	Limited to cell boundaries but often extends over several miles
Bandwidth	1–2 Mbps for frequency hopping, 2–6 Mbps for direct-sequence modulation
Installation and maintenance	Depends on equipment; ranges from easy to difficult
Interference	Moderately resistant
Cost	Inexpensive to moderate
Security	Not very susceptible to eavesdropping

802.11 Wireless Networking

The 1997 **802.11 Wireless Networking Standard**, also referred to as **Wireless Fidelity (Wi-Fi)**, has continued to undergo development. With it, manufacturers of wireless networking devices have brought inexpensive, reliable, wireless LANs to homes and businesses. The current standards include 802.11b and 802.11g running at a 2.4 GHz frequency with speeds of 11 Mbps and 54 Mbps, respectively, and 802.11a, which specifies a bandwidth of 54 Mbps at a 5 GHz frequency.

Of these competing standards, 802.11b is the most prevalent as of this writing and has been in use the longest. Of the two higher-speed standards, 802.11g is backward compatible with 802.11b and, therefore, offers a convenient bandwidth upgrade path. On the other hand, 802.11a, because of its higher frequency, presents problems for upgrades from 802.11b but provides more reliable and flexible transmission. Many manufacturers are building wireless access points that support two of the standards, thereby accommodating the older 802.11b standard yet offering an upgrade path to one of the faster standards.

NOTE   Just to complicate matters, a newer technology, dubbed "MIMO" for multiple-in, multiple-out, is available in some wireless products. This technology uses multiple antennas that boost transfer rates to 108 Mbps and beyond. As you can see, there's no end in sight for the speed upgrades of wireless LANs.

Essentially, 802.11 wireless is an extension to Ethernet using airwaves as the medium. In fact, most 802.11 networks incorporate some wired Ethernet segments. The 802.11 networks can extend from several feet to several hundred feet, depending on environmental factors, such as obstructions and radio frequency interference. The prevalence of people with 802.11-enabled laptops and PDAs has spawned a new mode for accessing the Internet. Many businesses are setting up Wi-Fi **hot spots**, which are localized wireless access areas. You can sit outside your favorite coffee shop, for example, and be able to use a wireless Internet connection with your laptop, PDA, or even cell phone. College campuses, too, are using hot spots so that students can sit in a campus courtyard between classes and access the campus network and the Internet with their Wi-Fi-enabled laptops.

For a wealth of information on the 802.11 standards, see *www.wi-fiplanet.com*.

TIP

Wireless Extended LAN Technologies

Certain kinds of wireless networking equipment extend LANs beyond their normal cable-based distance limitations or provide connectivity across areas where cables are not allowed (or able) to traverse. For instance, **wireless bridges** can connect networks up to three miles (4.4 km) apart. These LAN bridges permit linking locations by using line-of-sight or broadcast transmissions. LAN bridges can also make it unnecessary to route dedicated digital communications lines from one site to another through a communications carrier. Normally, upfront expenses for this technology are as much as 10 times higher, but it eliminates recurring monthly service charges from a carrier. That savings can quickly make up for (and exceed) the initial expense. Spread-spectrum radio, infrared, and laser-based equipment are readily available on the commercial market.

Longer-range wireless bridges are also available, including spread-spectrum solutions that work with Ethernet or token ring over distances up to 25 miles. As with shorter-range wireless bridges, the communications cost savings over time can justify the cost of a long-range wireless bridge. When it's connected correctly, this equipment (in long- and short-range varieties) can transport both voice and data traffic. Table 3-7 summarizes the characteristics of wireless extended LAN technologies.

Table 3-7   Wireless extended LAN characteristics

Characteristic	Value
Frequency ranges	Spread-spectrum, infrared, laser
Maximum distance	1–3 miles for short-range, up to 25 miles for long-range
Bandwidth	1–6 Mbps for spread-spectrum, 2–100 Mbps for infrared and laser
Installation and maintenance	Depends on equipment; ranges from easy to difficult
Interference	Highly resistant
Cost	Inexpensive to moderate
Security	Not very susceptible to eavesdropping

Wireless bridges always appear in pairs, and both devices function together as a repeater—whatever comes in on the wired side of one device is transmitted out the wired side of the other. These devices are sometimes called "half-repeaters," a reference to the frequency ranges they use. Therefore, you sometimes hear this equipment called "optical half-repeaters" (for laser or infrared versions) or "radio half-repeaters" for their spread-spectrum counterparts.

NOTE

Wireless MAN: The 802.16 Standard

One of the latest wireless standards, 802.16 **Worldwide Interoperability for Microwave Access (WiMax)**, comes in two flavors: 802.16-2004 (previously named 802.16a), or fixed WiMax, and 802.16e, or mobile WiMax. These standards promise wireless broadband to outlying and rural areas, where last-mile wired connections (the connections between service provider and homes or businesses) are too expensive or impractical because of rough terrain, and to mobile users so that they can maintain a high-speed connection while on the road. WiMax delivers up to 70 Mbps of bandwidth at distances up to 30 miles. It operates in a wide frequency range, from 2 to 66 GHz, although some products currently operate only in the lower end of that range.

Fixed WiMax: 802.16-2004

Besides providing wireless network service to outlying areas, fixed WiMax is being used to deliver wireless Internet access to entire metropolitan areas rather than the limited-area hot spots available with 802.11. Fixed WiMax can blanket an area up to a mile in radius, compared to just a few hundred feet for 802.11. Already, the city of Los Angeles has begun implementing fixed WiMax in an area of downtown that encompasses a 10-mile radius.

Mobile WiMax: 802.16e

Mobile WiMax promises to bring broadband Internet roaming to the public. Although fixed WiMax can create a wider hot spot than 802.11 wireless networks, network users are still confined to the coverage area. After a user leaves the coverage area of a transmitting station, his or her connection is dropped. Mobile WiMax promises to allow users to roam from area to area without losing the connection, which offers mobility much like cell phone users enjoy. Fixed WiMax is being implemented now, but the mobile WiMax standard is not yet finalized. However, that standard is expected to be approved in late 2005 or early 2006. Many experts agree that fixed WiMax will be the dominant technology for the next several years, but mobile WiMax will win out in the end.

Microwave Networking Technologies

Microwave systems deliver higher transmission rates than radio-based systems do, but because the frequencies are so high, transmitters and receivers must share a common clear line of sight. Microwave communications usually require FCC approval and licensing and are more expensive than radio systems. Experts distinguish between two types of microwave systems: terrestrial and satellite.

Terrestrial refers to line-of-sight transmissions between special microwave towers or between transmitters and receivers mounted on tall buildings, mountaintops, or other locations with long, clear lines of sight to desirable locations. **Terrestrial microwave** systems use tight-beam, high-frequency signals to link sender and receiver. By using relay towers, microwave systems can extend a signal across continental-scale distances.

In fact, many communications carriers use microwave towers to send traffic across sparsely populated areas where traffic is moderate and distances make laying cable expensive. The tight-beam nature of microwave systems means that transmitters and receivers must align precisely for best results. Some low-powered microwave systems are available for short-range LAN use, but they, too, require a clear line of sight between transmitters and receivers. Table 3-8 summarizes the characteristics of terrestrial microwave networks.

Table 3-8   Terrestrial microwave LAN/WAN characteristics

Characteristic	Value
Frequency ranges	4–6 GHz or 21–23 GHz
Maximum distance	Typically 1–50 miles
Bandwidth	1–10 Mbps
Installation and maintenance	Difficult
Interference	Varies depending on power and distance; longer distances are more prone to weather disturbances
Cost	Expensive
Security	Highly susceptible, but signals are usually encrypted

The other main alternative for microwave transmission is satellite. Instead of aiming at transmitters or receivers within a clear line of sight on the ground, **satellite microwave** systems send and receive data from **geosynchronous** satellites that maintain fixed positions in the sky. This is how television signals and some long-distance telephone signals travel from one side of the world to another: The sender beams the signal to a satellite visible on the horizon, the satellite relays the signal to one or more satellites until it comes onto the receiver's horizon, and then the satellite redirects the signal to the receiver.

NOTE   Geosynchronous satellites orbit 50,000 km (23,000 miles) above Earth. The distances are great enough to incur measurable transmission delays (called "propagation delays") that vary between 0.5 and 5 seconds, depending on the number of hops (jumps across network segments) between sender and receiver.

Most organizations can't fund launching satellites, so most satellite microwave systems must lease frequencies on satellites operated by global communications carriers. Because this approach is prohibitively expensive, even multinational companies with legitimate needs to send data around the globe typically choose to pay for their communications time rather than exclusive use of their own frequency.

Even more than terrestrial microwave, satellite communications cover a broad area and can be received by anyone with the right reception equipment. That's why microwave transmissions are routinely encrypted—to make sure only their intended recipients can access their contents. Table 3-9 summarizes the characteristics of satellite microwave communications.

Table 3-9 Satellite microwave WAN characteristics

Characteristic	Value
Frequency ranges	11–14 GHz
Maximum distance	Global reach
Bandwidth	1–10 Mbps
Installation and maintenance	Prohibitively difficult
Interference	Prone to EM interference, jamming, atmospheric disturbances
Cost	Prohibitive
Security	Not very susceptible to eavesdropping

For extending the reach of a network to its ultimate dimensions, microwave technologies currently offer the broadest reach. That's why they are labeled LAN/WAN (terrestrial) or WAN (satellite) technologies.

CHAPTER SUMMARY

❑ Working with network media—whether wired or wireless—requires careful attention to user requirements and consideration of budget, distance, bandwidth, and environmental factors. Choosing an appropriate technology depends on weighing all these factors, meeting immediate needs, and leaving room for growth and change.

❑ Cabled networks typically use one of two transmission schemes: broadband or baseband. Broadband transmissions use analog signals to carry multiple channels on a single cable, where one channel is required to send and another to receive signals on most networks. Baseband transmission uses only a single channel to send digital signals that occupy the cable's entire carrying capacity.

❑ For wired networks, the primary choices are twisted-pair and fiber-optic cables. Coaxial cable is obsolete for new LAN installations but is still the medium of choice for delivering cable television and broadband Internet over cable to homes.

❑ Twisted-pair cable comes in unshielded (UTP) and shielded (STP) varieties. UTP is commonly rated according to the ANSI/EIA/TIA 568 standard in seven categories; Categories 5, 5e, and 6 are the most commonly used in modern networks. STP has no similar rating scheme, but its shielding supports higher bandwidth and longer network spans than UTP. Category 6 cabling is the recommended cabling standard for Gigabit Ethernet. Category 7, if the standard is accepted in the United States, lacks backward compatibility with older standards and will likely be used only in special situations.

❑ Fiber-optic cable supports the highest bandwidth and offers the best security and resistance to interference of any type of cable, but it's also the most expensive. Fiber-optic cable is more sensitive to stress and bending and requires considerable expertise to attach connectors and install. Connector types include ST, SC, and a newer type called MT-RJ.

❑ Structured cabling facilitates troubleshooting, modifying, and expanding a network cable plant. Defined in TIA/EIA 568A, structured cabling consists of six components: work area, horizontal cabling, telecommunications closet, equipment room, backbone cabling, and entrance facility.

❑ Wireless networking is assuming an increasing portion of the networking load. Wireless technologies work well to provide cable-free LAN access, to extend the span of LANs (called extended LANs), to provide WAN links, and to support mobile computing needs.

❑ A typical wireless network acts like its wired counterpart—that is, a network adapter transfers communications across the networking medium, except that wires aren't needed to carry the signals. Otherwise, users communicate as they would on any other network.

❑ Wireless networks use a variety of electromagnetic frequency ranges, including narrowband and spread-spectrum radio, microwave, infrared, and laser transmission techniques. A pair of devices called a wireless bridge can also extend LANs. Short-range wireless bridges can span distances up to three miles; long-range wireless bridges can span up to 25 miles.

❑ The 802.11b wireless standard and its higher-speed successors promise to make wireless networking commonplace in homes and the corporate environment. The 802.11b standard specifies bandwidth of 11 Mbps; the 802.11a and 802.11g standards specify bandwidth up to 54 Mbps.

❑ An emerging wireless standard, 802.16, provides up to 70 Mbps of bandwidth over long distances (30 miles) and can be used to create MANs and provide broadband wireless access to outlying areas. The two versions of this standard are fixed WiMax (802.16-2004) and mobile WiMax (802.16e).

❑ Mobile computing involves using broadcast frequencies and communications carriers to transmit and receive signals with cellular or satellite communications techniques. Wireless networking appears poised to grab an increasing share of networking installations, as newer and more powerful technologies and standards start to come online.

KEY TERMS

10Base2 — A designation for 802.3 Ethernet thin coaxial cable (also called thinnet, thinwire, or cheapernet). The 10 indicates a bandwidth of 10 Mbps, the Base indicates it's a baseband transmission technology, and the 2 indicates a maximum segment length of 185 meters (originally 200, hence the "2") for this cable type.

10Base5 — A designation for 802.3 Ethernet thick coaxial cable (also called thicknet or thickwire). The 10 indicates a bandwidth of 10 Mbps, the Base indicates it's a baseband transmission technology, and the 5 indicates a maximum segment length of 500 meters for this cable type.

10BaseT — A designation for 802.3 Ethernet twisted-pair cable. The 10 indicates a bandwidth of 10 Mbps, the Base indicates it's a baseband transmission technology, and the T indicates that the medium is twisted-pair. (Maximum segment length is around 100 meters, or 328 feet, but the precise measurement depends on the manufacturer's testing results for the cable.)

802.11 Wireless Networking Standard — An IEEE standard for wireless networking. A version of the 802.11 standard appeared late in 1997.

access point device — The device that bridges wireless networking components and a wired network. It moves traffic between the wired and wireless sides as needed.

American National Standards Institute (ANSI) — The U.S. representative in the International Organization for Standardization (ISO), a worldwide standards-making body. ANSI creates and publishes standards for networking, communications, and programming languages.

amplifiers — Hardware devices that increase the power of electrical signals to maintain their original strength when transmitted across a large network.

analog — The method of signal transmission used on broadband networks. Creating analog waveforms from computer-based digital data requires a special device called a digital-to-analog (d-to-a) converter; reversing the conversion requires an analog-to-digital (a-to-d) converter. Broadband networking equipment must include both kinds of devices to work.

antenna — A tuned electromagnetic device that can send and receive broadcast signals at particular frequencies. In wireless networking devices, an antenna is an important part of a device's sending and receiving circuitry.

attached resource computing network (ARCnet) — A 2.5 Mbps LAN technology created by DataPoint Corporation in the late 1970s. ARCnet uses token-based networking technology and runs over several kinds of coaxial cable, twisted-pair, and fiber-optic cable.

attenuation — The weakening of a signal as it travels the length of a medium, which eventually causes the signal to be unreadable.

backbone cabling — The part of the cable plant that interconnects telecommunications closets and equipment rooms. Backbone cabling runs between floors or wings of a building and between buildings to carry network traffic destined for devices outside the work area.

bandwidth — The range of frequencies that a communications medium can carry. For baseband networking media, the bandwidth also indicates the theoretical maximum amount of data that the medium can transfer. For broadband networking media, the bandwidth is measured by the variations that any single carrier frequency can carry, minus the analog-to-digital conversion overhead.

baseband transmission — A technology that uses digital signals sent over a cable without modulation. It sends binary values (0s and 1s) as pulses of different voltage levels.

bend radius — For network cabling, the maximum arc that a segment of cable can be bent over some unit length (typically, one foot or one meter) without incurring damage.

broadband optical telepoint networks — An implementation of infrared wireless networking that supports broadband services equal to those a cabled network provides.

broadband transmission — An analog transmission technique that can use multiple communication channels simultaneously. Each data channel is represented by modulation on a particular frequency band, and sending or receiving equipment must be tuned to that band.

cable modem — A special-purpose networking device that permits a computer to send and receive networking signals, primarily for Internet access, by using two data channels on a broadband CATV network (one to send outgoing data, the other to receive incoming data). Cable modems can support bandwidth up to 1.544 Mbps, but upstream traffic (from computer to network) between 100 and 300 Kbps and downstream traffic (from network to computer) between 300 and 600 Kbps are more typical.

cable plant — The combination of installed network cables, connectors, patch panels, wall jacks, and other media components.

chips — Fixed-sized elements of data broadcast over a single frequency by using direct-sequence modulation. *See also* direct-sequence modulation.

cladding — A nontransparent layer of plastic or glass material inside fiber-optic cable; cladding surrounds the inner core of glass or plastic fibers. Cladding provides rigidity, strength, and a manageable outer diameter for fiber-optic cables.

coaxial cable — A type of cable that uses a center conductor, wrapped by an insulating layer and surrounded by a braided wire mesh and an outer jacket or sheath, to carry high-bandwidth signals, such as network traffic or broadcast television frequencies. "Coax" is often used as a shortened form of "coaxial cable."

communications carrier — A company that provides communications services for other organizations, such as a local phone company and long-distance telephone carriers. Most mobile computing technologies rely on the services of a communications carrier to handle wireless traffic from mobile units to a centralized wired network.

conduit — Plastic or metal pipe laid specifically to provide a protected enclosure for cabling of any kind.

crosstalk — A phenomenon that occurs when two wires lay against each other in parallel. Signals traveling down one wire can interfere with signals traveling down the other, and vice versa.

datagrade — A designation for cabling of any kind; datagrade indicates that cabling is suitable for transporting digital data. When applied to twisted-pair cabling, "datagrade" indicates that the cable is suitable for voice or data traffic.

differential signal — The use of two wires to carry a signal, where one wire carries a positive voltage signal and the other carries a negative voltage signal. Differential signals help mitigate the effects of noise and crosstalk. *See also* electromagnetic interference (EMI) *and* crosstalk.

direct-sequence modulation — The form of spread-spectrum data transmission that breaks data into fixed-length segments called chips and transmits the data on multiple frequencies.

dual-cable broadband — A broadband technique in which two cables are used; one is for transmitting, and one is for receiving.

electromagnetic interference (EMI) — A form of interference, also referred to as "noise," caused by emissions from external devices, such as transformers or electrical motors, that can disrupt network transmissions over an electrical medium.

electronic eavesdropping — The capability to "listen" to signals passing through a communications media by detecting its emissions. Eavesdropping on many wireless networking technologies is especially easy because they broadcast data into the atmosphere.

Electronic Industries Alliance (EIA) — An industry trade group of electronics and networking manufacturers that collaborates on standards for wiring, connectors, and other common components.

entrance facility — The location of the cabling and equipment that connects a corporate network to a third-party telecommunications provider.

equipment room — An area that serves as a connection point for backbone cabling running between telecommunications closets; also houses servers, routers, switches, and other major network equipment.

extended LANs — Microsoft's name for the networks resulting from certain wireless bridges' capability to expand the span of a LAN up to 25 miles.

Federal Communications Commission (FCC) — Among other responsibilities, the FCC regulates access to broadcast frequencies throughout the electromagnetic spectrum, including those used for mobile computing and microwave transmissions. When these signals cover any distance (more than half a mile) and require exclusive use of a frequency, FCC requires a broadcast license. Many wireless networking technologies make use of unregulated frequencies set aside by the FCC. These frequencies don't require licensing, but they must be shared with others.

fiber-optic — A cabling technology that uses pulses of light sent along a light-conducting fiber at the heart of the cable to transfer information from sender to receiver. Fiber-optic cable can send data in only one direction, so two cables are required to permit network devices to exchange data in both directions.

frequency hopping — The type of spread-spectrum data transmission that switches data across a range of frequencies over time. Frequency-hopping transmitters and receivers must be synchronized to hop at the same time to the same frequencies.

geosynchronous — An orbital position relative to Earth where a satellite orbits at the same speed as Earth rotates. This orbit permits satellites to maintain a constant fixed position in relation to Earth stations and represents the positioning technique used for microwave satellites.

hertz (Hz) — A measure of broadcast frequencies in cycles per second; named after Heinrich Hertz, one of the inventors of radio communications.

horizontal wiring — Network cabling that runs from the work area's wall jack to the telecommunications closet and is usually terminated at a patch panel.

hot spots — A term used in wireless networking for areas in which wireless access to a network or the Internet is possible. Often these areas are in nontraditional locations, such as outside cafes or college campus courtyards.

infrared — The portion of the electromagnetic spectrum immediately below visible light. Infrared frequencies are popular for short- to medium-range (10 m to 40 m) point-to-point network connections.

insertion loss — The weakening of signals that occurs on a cable segment each time a network device is attached. Necessary restrictions on the maximum number of devices keep the signals that traverse the network clean and strong enough to remain intelligible to all devices.

Institute of Electrical and Electronics Engineers (IEEE) — An engineering organization that issues standards for electrical and electronic devices, including network interfaces, cabling, and connectors.

IrDA devices — Devices that are compliant with the Infrared Device Association's specifications for infrared components and devices.

jack couplers — The female receptacles into which modular TP cables plug.

latency — The amount of time a signal takes to travel from one end of a cable to the other.

light-emitting diodes (LEDs) — A lower-powered alternative for emitting data at optical frequencies. LEDs are sometimes used for wireless LANs and for short-haul, fiber-optic-based data transmissions.

line-of-sight networks — Networks that require an unobstructed view, or clear line of sight, between the transmitter and receiver. Narrowband tight-beam transmitters and receivers must have an unobstructed path between them.

locking connection (LC) — A type of fiber-optic connector that pushes on and pulls off using an RJ-45 style latching mechanism.

maximum segment length — The longest cable segment that a particular networking technology permits. This limitation helps network designers and installers make sure the entire network can send and receive signals properly.

mechanical transfer registered jack (MT-RJ) — A fiber-optic connector that provides a high-density connection using two fiber-optic cables.

medium interface connector (MIC) — One of a number of fiber-optic cable connector types. MIC connectors feature a separate physical connector for each cable in a typical fiber-optic cable pair.

mid-split broadband — A broadband technique in which two channels on different frequencies are used to transmit and receive signals via a single cable.

mobile computing — A form of wireless networking that uses common carrier frequencies to permit networked devices to be moved freely within the broadcast coverage area yet remain connected to the network.

narrowband radio — A type of broadcast-based networking technology that uses a single specific radio frequency to send and receive data. Low-powered, narrowband implementations don't usually require FCC approval but are limited to a 250-foot or so range; high-powered narrowband implementations do require FCC approval and licensing. Also called "single-frequency radio."

patch cable — A short length (1 to 20 feet) of network cable used to connect a computer's network interface card to a jack in the work area or to connect from a patch panel to a hub or switch in the wiring closet.

patch panels — Elements of a wiring center in which separate cable runs are brought together. By making connections between any two points on the patch panel, the physical path of wires can be controlled and the sequence of wires managed.

plenum-rated — Cable that has been burn-tested to make sure it doesn't emit toxic fumes or large amounts of smoke when incinerated. Most building and fire codes require this designation for any cable to be run in plenum space.

radio frequency interference (RFI) — Any interference caused by signals operating in the radio frequency range. This term has become generic for interference caused by broadcast signals of any kind.

reflective wireless networks — An infrared wireless networking technology that uses a central optical transceiver to relay signals between end stations. All network devices must have an unobstructed view of this central transceiver, which explains why they're usually mounted on the ceiling.

registered jack 45 (RJ-45) — The eight-wire modular jack used for TP networking cables and PBX-based telephone systems.

3

repeaters — Networking devices used to strengthen a signal suffering from attenuation. *See also* attenuation.

RJ-11 — The four-wire modular jack commonly used for home telephone handsets.

satellite microwave — A microwave transmission system that uses geosynchronous satellites to send and relay signals between sender and receiver. Most companies that use satellite microwave lease access to the satellites for an exorbitant fee. *See also* geosynchronous.

scatter infrared networks — An infrared LAN technology that uses flat reflective surfaces, such as walls and ceilings, to bounce wireless transmissions between sender and receiver. Because bouncing introduces delays and attenuation, this variety of wireless LAN is the slowest and supports the narrowest bandwidth of any infrared technology.

sheath — The outer layer of coating on a cable; sometimes also called a jacket.

shielded twisted-pair (STP) — A variety of TP cable in which a foil wrap encloses each of one or more pairs of wires for additional shielding, and a wire braid or an additional layer of foil might enclose the entire cable for further shielding.

shielding — Any layer of material included in cable to mitigate the effects of interference on the signal-carrying cables it encloses.

spread-spectrum radio — A form of wireless networking technology that passes data by using multiple frequencies simultaneously.

straight connection (SC) — A type of one-piece fiber-optic connector that's pushed on yet makes a strong and solid contact with emitters and sensors.

straight tip (ST) — The most common type of fiber-optic connector used in Ethernet networks with fiber backbones. These connectors come in pairs, one for each fiber-optic cable.

structured cabling — A specification for how network media should be installed to maximize performance and efficiency.

subminiature type A (SMA) — Another fiber-optic connector that twists on and comes in pairs.

telecommunications closet (TC) — A small room or area housing equipment (such as patch panels, hubs, and switches) that provides connectivity to computer equipment in the nearby work area.

Telecommunications Industries Association (TIA) — An industry consortium of telephone equipment, cabling, and communications companies that formulates hardware standards for equipment, cabling, and connectors used in phone systems and on networks.

terrestrial microwave — A wireless microwave networking technology that uses line-of-sight communications between pairs of Earth-based transmitters and receivers to relay information. The large distances the signals must extend requires positioning microwave transmitters and receivers well above ground level on towers, on mountaintops, or atop tall buildings. This equipment is usually expensive.

thicknet — A form of coaxial Ethernet that uses a rigid cable about 0.4 inches in diameter. Because of its common jacket color and its rigidity, this cable is sometimes called "frozen yellow garden hose." Also known as thickwire and 10Base5.

thinnet — A form of coaxial Ethernet that uses a thin, flexible cable about 0.2 inches in diameter. Also known as thinwire, 10Base2, and cheapernet.

transceiver — A compound word made from the words "transmitter" and "receiver" to describe a device that combines the functions of a transmitter and a receiver and integrates into a single device the circuitry needed to emit and receive signals on a medium.

twisted-pair (TP) — A type of cabling in which two copper wires, each enclosed in some kind of sheath, are wrapped around each other. The twisting permits narrow-gauge wire, otherwise extraordinarily sensitive to crosstalk and interference, to carry higher-bandwidth signals over longer distances than is traditionally possible with straight wires. TP cabling is used for voice telephone circuits as well as networking.

unshielded twisted-pair (UTP) — A form of TP cable that includes no additional shielding material in the cable composition. This cable encloses one or more pairs of twisted wires inside an outer jacket.

virtual docking — One of numerous point-to-point wireless infrared technologies that enable portable computing devices to exchange data with desktop machines or allow data exchange between a computer and a handheld device or a printer. The "virtual" term is used because this capability replaces a cable between the two devices.

voicegrade — A designation for cable (usually TP) that indicates it's rated to carry only telephone traffic. Voicegrade cable is not recommended for network use.

wall plates — A modular plate used to accommodate numerous outlets used for networking and voice applications.

wireless — A network connection that depends on transmission at an electromagnetic frequency through the atmosphere to carry data transmissions from one networked device to another.

wireless bridges — A pair of devices, typically narrowband and tight beam, that relay network traffic from one location to another. Wireless bridges that use spread-spectrum radio, infrared, and laser technologies are available and can span distances from hundreds of meters up to 25 miles.

Wireless Fidelity (Wi-Fi) — A term used to indicate wireless networking, usually using one of the 802.11 wireless networking standards.

wiring center — A set of racks with associated equipment that generally includes hubs, patch panels, backbone access units, and other network-management equipment, which brings TP-wired network cables together for routing, management, and control.

work area — The space in a facility or office where computer workstations and other user devices are located.

Worldwide Interoperability for Microwave Access (WiMax) — A wireless technology designed for wireless metropolitan area networks defined in standards 802.16-2004 and 802.16e.

REVIEW QUESTIONS

1. Of the following cabling elements, which does not commonly occur in coaxial cable?

   a. wire braid

   b. center conductor

   c. outer sheath

   d. cladding

2. Which of the following is a common media characteristic? (Choose all that apply.)

   a. bandwidth rating

   b. interference susceptibility

   c. broadband rating

   d. maximum segment length

3. What surrounds the center conductor in a coaxial cable to separate it from the wire braid?

   a. a vacuum

   b. conductive mesh

   c. piezoelectric material

   d. insulating layer

4. Which of the following types of fiber-optic connectors provides high density and requires only one connector for two cables?

   a. SC

   b. ST

   c. MT-RJ

   d. RJ-45

5. The condition that requires cables not to exceed a recommended maximum length is called _____ .

   a. diminution

   b. resistance

   c. carrying capacity

   d. attenuation

6. Which of the following is not a wireless networking standard?

   a. 802.11a

   b. 802.11b

   c. 802.16e

   d. 802.17b

7. The space between a false ceiling and the true ceiling where heating and cooling air circulates is called the _____ .

   a. duct-equivalent airspace

   b. conduit

   c. return air

   d. plenum

8. Cable sheathed with _____ material should not be routed in the plenum or walls.

   a. Teflon

   b. Kevlar

   c. foil

   d. PVC (polyvinyl chloride)

9. The fire-resistant cable specified by fire and building codes is rated as which of the following?

   a. fire-resistant

   b. fire-retardant

   c. inflammable

   d. plenum-rated

10. To build the network in your New York City headquarters, you must run a cable through the elevator shaft from the customer service center on the second floor all the way up to the corporate offices on the 37th floor. The distance is 550 meters. What type of cable must you use?

    a. unshielded twisted-pair (UTP)

    b. thinwire coax (10Base2)

    c. thickwire coax (10Base5)

    d. fiber-optic cable

11. Which of the following cables is not suitable for network use of any kind?

    a. Category 1

    b. Category 2

    c. Category 3

    d. Category 4

12. What type of connector is used most commonly with TP network wiring?

    a. RJ-11

    b. RJ-45

    c. BNC

    d. MT-RJ

13. Both Category 3 and Category 5 cable can be used for 100 Mbps Ethernet. True or False?

14. You have been hired to install a network at a large government agency that wants to reduce the likelihood of electronic eavesdropping on its network. What kind of cable should you use?

    a. UTP

    b. STP

    c. coaxial

    d. fiber-optic

15. You're preparing to install a conventional Ethernet network in your new office building, but your boss tells you to be ready to handle a switchover to 1 Gbps Ethernet next year. What two types of cable could you install? (Choose two answers.)

    a. thinwire

    b. fiber-optic

    c. Category 4

    d. Category 6

    e. Category 3

16. When two cables run side by side, signals traveling down one wire might interfere with signals traveling on the other wire. What is this phenomenon called?

    a. RFI

    b. attenuation

    c. impedance

    d. crosstalk

17. What characteristic of twisted-pair cabling helps mitigate the effects of crosstalk?

    a. differential signals

    b. copper conductors

    c. four pairs of wires

    d. 100 ohm impedance

18. Which of the following cabling elements does not occur in fiber-optic cable?

    a. glass or plastic fiber core

    b. glass or plastic cladding

    c. wire braid

    d. Kevlar sheathing

    e. plastic or Teflon jacket

19. What benefits does shielding confer on shielded twisted-pair cable? (Choose all that apply.)
    a. improves flexibility
    b. lowers susceptibility to interference
    c. supports higher bandwidth over longer distances
    d. decreases cost

20. If you want to share an Internet connection among three home computers but find it difficult to run cables, what type of network should you use?
    a. 802.3
    b. 10Base2
    c. 802.12b
    d. 802.11b

21. Currently, you're using 802.11b wireless in your LAN but are considering an upgrade to 54 Mbps speed. For best compatibility, which wireless standard should you choose for this higher bandwidth?
    a. 802.11g
    b. 802.11a
    c. 802.11b
    d. 802.11c

22. Baseband transmission sends signals in which of the following forms?
    a. analog
    b. digital
    c. spread-spectrum
    d. frequency-hopping

23. Broadband transmission sends signals in which of the following forms?
    a. analog
    b. digital
    c. spread-spectrum
    d. frequency-hopping

24. What are the devices used to manage transmission and reception of data between a wired LAN and wireless components?
    a. access points
    b. gateways
    c. wireless interfaces
    d. antennae

25. What is the wireless device used to link buildings without cable?

    a. hub

    b. router

    c. gateway

    d. bridge

26. Which of the following technologies might be used in wireless communications? (Choose all that apply.)

    a. narrowband radio

    b. microwave transmission

    c. infrared

    d. laser

27. Which of the following is a wiring standard for twisted-pair cable connections? (Choose all that apply.)

    a. IEEE 802.3

    b. TIA/EIA 568A

    c. IEEE 802.5

    d. TIA/EIA 568B

28. Which of the following wireless technologies isn't appropriate for linking two buildings? (Choose all that apply.)

    a. reflective infrared

    b. point-to-point infrared

    c. spread-spectrum radio

    d. terrestrial microwave

    e. low-power single-frequency radio

29. Which new wireless standard can be used in place of a wired last mile?

    a. point-to-point infrared

    b. 802.16-2004 WiMax

    c. 802.11b Wi-Fi

    d. 802.11g

30. What is the distance limitation for Category 5e UTP running 100 Mbps Ethernet?

    a. 100 m

    b. 10 km

    c. 1000 m

    d. 10 m

HANDS-ON PROJECTS

When working with networking media, being able to distinguish among as many types of media—and the connectors that go with them—as possible is important. The first Hands-On Project consists of a demonstration from your instructor, giving you an opportunity to touch and examine several different types of networking media. The second Hands-On Project walks you through the steps required to create a patch cable. The remaining Hands-On Projects ask you to consider a variety of methods for combining networking media using pencil and paper rather than the real thing.

Hands-On Project 3-1

For this project, your instructor will pass around several different types of networking media, along with the connectors that go with each kind. Examine each one closely, and learn to recognize each by its shape and size. Write a short description of each media type and connector you examine and be prepared to identify these components when your instructor asks. Here are some hints to help you:

- The RJ-45 connector used with twisted-pair Ethernet looks just like a conventional telephone jack, only slightly larger. Close examination reveals that it incorporates eight wire traces, whereas the RJ-11 jacks for regular telephone handsets incorporate only four traces.

- The BNC connectors and coaxial cable used for thinwire Ethernet are relatively small. The cable is flexible and often looks insubstantial. Examine the cable's outer sheath. You should see some kind of code printed at regular intervals, such as "20 AWG CL2 RG-58A/U E111378A (UL)."

- The connectors for fiber-optic cable might be of several configurations. The ST connector is round, and the SC connector is more square—both connectors can accommodate only one strand of fiber. The MT-RJ connector has a similar look to an RJ-45 and can accommodate two strands of fiber.

Remember that you must be able to recognize and distinguish among these types of cables and connectors. Also, be aware that the kind of coaxial cable used for thinwire closely resembles cable TV. That's why learning to read the jacket codes is important: This knowledge might keep you from using the wrong medium on a network connection. Always check the jacket codes!

Hands-On Project 3-2

In this project, you practice making a Category 5/5e or Category 6 UTP patch cable. You need the following tools and materials to complete this project:

- Wire cutter and stripper
- RJ-45 crimp tool
- 3 to 4 feet of Category 5/5e or Category 6 cable

3

❏ Two RJ-45 plugs

❏ Patch cable checker (optional)

1. Strip approximately two inches of the outer jacket off one end of the cable. Be careful not to nick the inner wires.

2. Untwist the four pairs of wires.

3. Here comes the tricky part: Arrange the wires from left to right (as you're looking down on them) so that the wires are in the following order: white with orange stripes, orange, white with green stripes, blue, white with blue stripes, green, white with brown stripes, brown. (This order of wires adheres to the 568B wiring standard. Another commonly used wiring standard, 568A, switches the orange and green wires.)

4. Clip the eight wires so that about 3/4 inch of wire extends beyond the outer jacket.

5. While holding the RJ-45 connector in one hand with the key facing away from you, insert the eight wires into the connector, being sure that the tops of the wires extend to the front of the connector and the cable jacket goes far enough into the connector so that the jacket will be caught by the crimp bar (see Figure 3-13).

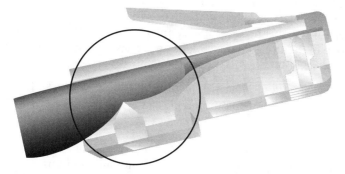

Figure 3-13   Correct RJ-45 plug installation

6. Now insert the RJ-45 connector into the crimping tool while making sure the wires don't slip. Close the handle on the crimp tool firmly.

7. Repeat the process for the other side of the cable, and test with a patch-cable tester, if available. Congratulations! You have made a network patch cable.

Hands-On Projects 3-3 Through 3-7

During the design of most real-world networks, you'll discover that using more than one type of networking medium is common. The usual reasons for needing more than one type of medium include the following:

- Two or more areas must be interconnected, and the distance separating them is greater than the maximum segment length for the type of medium used in (or best suited for) each area.

- A connection must pass through a high-interference environment (across some large transformers, near heavy-duty electrical motors, and so on). Failure to use a different type of medium increases the risk of impeding data flow. This is an especially popular reason for using thickwire or fiber-optic cable in many networks, especially when connecting floors in an office building and the only available pathway is the elevator shaft.

- Certain parts of a network of networks (also known as an internetwork) might have to carry more traffic than other parts. Typically, the segment where traffic aggregates is the backbone, a common cable segment that interconnects two or more subsidiary networks. (Think of a tree trunk as the backbone and the major branches as cable segments.) Often, a higher-capacity cable is used for a backbone (for example, fiber-optic cable or Category 6 cable rated for Gigabit Ethernet), along with a higher-speed networking technology for attachments to the backbone. This arrangement means that outlying segments might use conventional 10 or 100 Mbps Ethernet, and the backbone uses 1 Gbps or 10 Gbps Ethernet.

Using this information, suggest solutions that involve at least two types, if possible, of networking media to address the following projects.

Hands-On Project 3-3

XYZ Corp. is planning a new network. Engineers in the design shop must have connections to accountants and salespeople in the front office, but all routes between the two areas must traverse the shop floor, where arc welders and metal-stamping equipment create potent amounts of EMI and RFI. Given that both the engineering and the front office areas use 10BaseT (twisted-pair Ethernet), how might you interconnect those two areas? What medium guarantees immunity from the interference?

Hands-On Project 3-4

After the front office network at XYZ Corp. is set up, an accountant realizes that if the loading dock connects to the network, the dock workers could log incoming and outgoing shipments and keep the inventory more current. Even though the loading dock is nowhere near the shop floor, the dock is 1100 feet from the front office. What kinds of cable will work to make this connection? What kind would you choose and why?

3

Hands-On Project 3-5

ABC Company occupies three floors in a 10-story building, where the elevator shaft provides the only path to all three floors. In addition, users on the ninth and tenth floors must access a collection of servers on the eighth floor. Explain what kind of connections would work in the elevator shaft. If more than one choice is possible, pick the best option and explain the reasons for your choice. Assuming that interfloor connections might someday need to run at much higher speeds, reevaluate your choice. What is the best type of medium for open-ended bandwidth needs? Explain your answer.

Hands-On Project 3-6

Very Big ISP Corporation (VBISP) wants to increase the bandwidth it can access at its downtown location in New York City. The distance between locations is about 20 miles, and the desired bandwidth between locations is at least 50 Mbps. What media types could work to provide this connection?

Hands-On Project 3-7

Following a year of major sales increases in the Pacific Rim, MarTexCo decides to open a second plant in Malaysia. The company wants the new plant to be able to access the headquarters database in Des Moines, Iowa, in real time, but long-haul telephone connections aren't possible, owing to the lack of communications infrastructure at the Malaysia location. What kind of wireless networking alternative makes the most sense when considering network links that span an appreciable portion of the globe? Explain why laying cable might not be feasible.

Case Projects

Case Project 3-1

XYZ Corp.'s Nashua, NH, facilities are two office buildings 400 feet apart, each with its own LAN. To connect the two networks, you plan to dig a trench and lay cable in conduit between the two buildings. You want to use fiber-optic cable, but your budget-conscious facilities manager wants to use 100 Mbps Ethernet over twisted-pair. What reasons can you use to justify fiber-optic cable in this case?

  a. Twisted-pair will not span a 400-foot distance.

  b. Fiber-optic cable is cheaper and easier to work with than twisted-pair.

  c. Twisted-pair is a conductive cable and can, therefore, carry current based on the difference in ground potential between the two buildings.

  d. Fiber-optic leaves more room for growth and future needs for increased bandwidth than twisted-pair does.

Case Project 3-2

TVBCA is moving to new facilities. Its new campus includes three buildings, each no more than 100 meters apart from the others. The network should link all the buildings. Each building is to be remodeled, so there's plenty of space to run cable and put the network together.

Required result: The network must support speeds of up to 100 Mbps.

Optional desired results: The network should be as secure as possible from electronic eavesdropping. To stay within TVBCA's budget, the network should also be as inexpensive as possible.

Proposed solution: The network staff suggests using a fiber-optic backbone to link all three buildings. Which results does this solution deliver? Why?

    a. The proposed solution delivers the required result and both optional desired results.

    b. The proposed solution delivers the required result and only one of the two optional desired results.

    c. The proposed solution delivers the required result but neither optional desired result.

    d. The proposed solution does not deliver the required result.

Case Project 3-3

An advertising firm decides to install a network to link all employees' computers. The company plans to introduce some video teleconferencing software across the board and plans heavy use of e-mail and database applications. Because of the anticipated load, you want the network to be as fast as possible.

Required result: The network must operate at speeds up to 1 Gbps.

Optional desired result: You want the cabling to handle an upgrade in speed to 10 Gbps several years down the road.

Proposed solution: You suggest using Category 6 UTP to connect all workstations. Which results does this proposed solution produce? Explain your answer.

    a. The proposed solution delivers the required result and the optional desired result.

    b. The proposed solution delivers the required result but not the optional desired result.

    c. The proposed solution does not deliver the required result.

Case Project 3-4

XYZ Corp. decides to set up mobile computing for its field engineers. Each field engineer is to be supplied with a laptop, a portable fax/printer, and some kind of wireless transmission device.

Required result: Field engineers must be able to send and receive e-mail with employees at the headquarters.

Optional desired results: The wireless technology should be as inexpensive as possible. It should also be secure from electronic eavesdropping.

Proposed solution: The network manager recommends leasing a cellular link from GTE MobilNet for $2500 a month plus air-time charges and encryption fees. Which results does this solution deliver? Explain your answer.

a. The proposed solution delivers the required result and both optional desired results.

b. The proposed solution delivers the required result and only one of the two optional desired results.

c. The proposed solution delivers the required result but neither optional desired result.

d. The proposed solution does not deliver the required result.

Case Project 3-5

TVBCA has just occupied an old historic building in downtown Pittsburgh in which 15 employees will work. Because of historic building codes, TVBCA is not permitted to run cables inside walls or ceilings.

Required result: Employees must be able to share files and printers as in a typical LAN environment without the use of cables.

Optional desired results: Employees must be able to use their laptops and move freely throughout the office while maintaining a network connection. Because of the size of some computer-aided design (CAD) files employees use frequently, data transfer speeds should be more than 20 Mbps.

Proposed solution: Install an 802.11a wireless access point and configure each computer and laptop with a wireless network card. Which results does the proposed solution deliver? Explain your answer.

a. The proposed solution delivers the required result and both optional desired results.

b. The proposed solution delivers the required result and only one of the two optional desired results.

c. The proposed solution delivers the required result but neither optional desired result.

d. The proposed solution does not deliver the required result.

4

NETWORK INTERFACE CARDS

After reading this chapter and completing the exercises, you will be able to:

♦ Describe a network interface card's function and configurable options

♦ List important factors for selecting network adapters

♦ Describe types of special-purpose network interface cards

♦ Explain the role of driver software in network adapters

Attaching a computer to a network requires a physical interface between the computer and the networking medium. For most PCs, this interface is in a network interface card (NIC), also known as a network adapter or a network card, that plugs into an adapter slot inside the computer's case. Laptops and other computers might include built-in interfaces or use special modular interfaces to accommodate a network adapter. In any case, special hardware to mediate the connection between a computer and the networking medium—the focus of this chapter—is necessary.

As a network administrator, you must understand what a network interface does and how it works. It's also important to understand what's involved in installing and configuring this hardware because network adapters are key ingredients in assembling a network. Therefore, you need to know how to install and configure PC adapters and how to select the right adapter for your situation. This knowledge is critical to your ability to manage any network.

Network Interface Card (NIC) Basics

For any computer, a **network interface card (NIC)** performs two crucial tasks:

- Establishes and manages the computer's network connection
- Translates digital computer data into signals (appropriate for the networking medium) for outgoing messages and translates signals into digital computer data for incoming messages

In other words, the NIC establishes a link between a computer and a network, and then manages that link on the computer's behalf.

From Parallel to Serial and Vice Versa

Because of the nature of the connection between most NICs and the computers to which they're attached, NICs also manage transformations in network data's form. Most computers use a series of parallel data lines, called a **computer bus** (or simply "bus"), that link components inside a computer to send data between the CPU and network adapters. A bus allows the computer and adapters to exchange data in chunks equal to the number of lines extending between them. Because data travels along multiple lines at the same time, and those lines run parallel, this type of data transmission is called **parallel transmission**.

However, for nearly all forms of networking media, signals traversing the media consist of a linear sequence of information that corresponds to a linear sequence of bits of data. Because these bits of data follow one another in a straight line, or a series, this type of transmission is called **serial transmission**. Therefore, one of the most important jobs a NIC performs is to take outgoing transmissions from the CPU in parallel form and recast them into their serial equivalents. For incoming messages, the process reverses: The NIC grabs an incoming series of signals, translates them into bits, and distributes those bits across the parallel lines that communicate with the CPU. Figure 4-1 depicts this process.

To help clarify the difference between parallel and serial forms of data, you can think of parallel transmission as working like a multilane highway: Each lane carries part of a stream of traffic—information between sender and receiver—at the same time. The more lanes, the more traffic—or information—the highway can carry at any given moment.

Using the same analogy, serial transmission resembles a single-lane road. A NIC must take data coming in from the media serially (single lane) and redistribute that data to the parallel lines (multilane) and vice versa. Consequently, one of the most important components on a network adapter is memory, which acts as a **buffer**, a staging area to hold data. Outgoing parallel data is stored in the buffer until the network media is ready to serially transmit the data, and incoming data is stored in the buffer in parallel chunks until the computer's CPU is ready to process it.

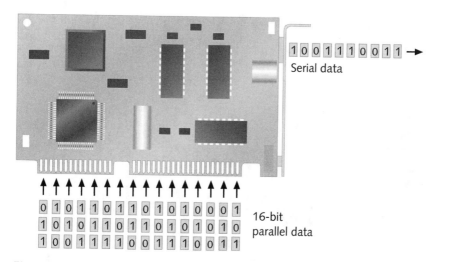

Serial data

16-bit
parallel data

Figure 4-1 NICs mediate communication between a computer and the network cable

The process of translating data bits that a computer generates into a suitable form for the network medium is called encoding. Encoding is covered in more detail in Chapter 5.

NOTE

When data moves from one component to another, it moves along the bus. Most of the early-generation PCs used 8-bit buses; they used eight lines for data in parallel and could move 8 bits of data in a single bus transfer. The number of parallel lines in a computer bus is called its **bus width**. For example, a bus with 16 parallel lines has a 16–bit bus width.

One significant improvement in the original IBM PC was its 16-bit bus. This bus became so prevalent that it's called the **Industry Standard Architecture (ISA)** bus. For years, it was the primary bus in PCs. Today, you would be hard-pressed to find a new computer with an ISA adapter slot. An **adapter slot** is a socket built into PC motherboards that are designed to accommodate add-on cards, such as NICs. In the late 1980s to early 1990s, 32-bit buses were introduced, and the 64-bit-capable **Peripheral Component Interconnect (PCI)** and its variations are the fastest and most popular in use today. These bus types are explained later in the "PC Buses" section.

To transmit data across the network medium, a NIC must include or access a device called a transceiver designed specifically for the medium in use. For common networking technologies, such as Ethernet, that work over a variety of media, multiway NICs that can be configured to use one of several media attachments built into the card are common.

Figure 4-2 shows an Ethernet NIC that includes a female BNC connector, where the base of the T-connector attaches for a thinnet network; a 15-pin AUI connector for fiber-optic or other selected media; and an RJ-45 connector for 10BaseT. With the appropriate setting chosen, the NIC can be configured to use a particular attachment and the correct circuitry. For both thinnet and 10BaseT, these NICs include a built-in on-board transceiver; for fiber-optic, an external transceiver must be connected to the card through the AUI port on the back. Most contemporary cards support only one type of media connector.

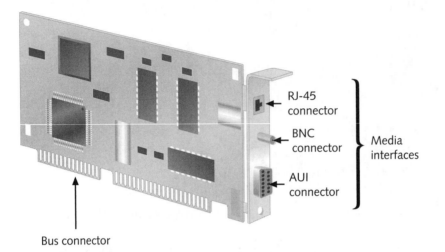

Bus connector

Figure 4-2   An Ethernet NIC with interfaces for 10BaseT (RJ-45), thinnet (BNC), and fiber-optic (AUI)

Additional Functions of a NIC

NICs also handle important data-packaging functions as they serialize outgoing parallel data streams from the CPU and translate incoming serial data streams from the network medium into parallel data. The NIC packages all the bits into orderly collections called frames, and then transmits each frame serially onto the network medium. For incoming messages, the NIC creates frames of data from incoming signals, and then extracts each frame's contents for parallel translation and delivery to the CPU. Frames are the fundamental unit of data for network transmission and reception. Much of the important processing that network adapters perform involves creating, sending, and receiving frames as well as dealing with frame-level errors and incomplete or unintelligible frame structures.

The term "packet" is often used to describe the unit of information sent between network devices, but "frame" is more accurate when discussing the unit of information the NIC handles.

NOTE

Other important roles a NIC plays are packaging and preparing data for transmission across the medium and managing access to the medium to know when to send data. NICs examine incoming network frames and check the frame's destination address to see whether it matches the adapter's address. The NIC acts as a gatekeeper and permits inbound communications aimed only at its computer to pass through the interface and on to the CPU. In addition, a NIC permits inbound communications when the frame's destination address is a broadcast address, indicating that all computers should process the data. Some NICs can operate in what's called "promiscuous mode"—essentially, this mode turns off the gatekeeper functions and enables the NIC to forward any frames it sees to the computer. This mode is important when the NIC interacts with network scanning or sniffing software that analyzes overall traffic flow or permits detailed inspection of frames. For typical users, however, it isn't usually necessary.

The NIC's role as gatekeeper points to another important function network adapters provide. Each card has a unique identifier, called a **Media Access Control (MAC) address**, in the form of data programmed on to read-only memory (ROM) on the interface. When a NIC receives a frame, it checks the frame's destination address and compares it to the MAC address burned into the NIC to determine whether the frame should be processed. The IEEE sponsors a manufacturers' committee that designed an addressing scheme for NICs and assigns unique blocks of addresses to NIC manufacturers. Each new NIC has a unique, identifiable address encoded on it, guaranteeing that each computer has its own network address. The gatekeeper function simply looks for an address bit string in the decoded frame that matches its own address or corresponds to a valid "general delivery" address, or broadcast.

NOTE   The address on a NIC is called the MAC address because the NIC's Media Access Control functions handle it. These addresses take the form of six two-digit **hexadecimal** numbers separated by colons—for example, 00:60:97:33:90:A3 is a MAC address. The first three numbers identify the manufacturer; the second three numbers define a unique address assigned to the NIC.

By now, it should be clear that a NIC is essential to managing and controlling network access, and its role goes beyond creating a physical link between a computer and a network medium. A NIC also handles data transfers to and from the network and CPU and translates which forms data can take between parallel and serial representations. In addition, a NIC interacts with the medium to determine when data transmission is allowed.

PC Buses

When PCs were introduced, only a single bus design existed: an 8-bit bus of limited speed and capability. As the technology evolved, however, other buses came along (and some have already left the scene). Today, a couple of bus types, also known as bus architectures, dominate modern PCs. Each bus differs in its layout and configuration; therefore, any network adapter you want to use *must* match a bus type supported by the computer's motherboard. The following list explains the major PC bus architectures:

- *Peripheral Component Interconnect (PCI)*—Several local bus standards appeared in the early 1990s as computers became faster, but by 1995, Intel's PCI bus became the default 32-bit bus standard. PCI is also widely available in a 64-bit version. PCI 2.x moved PCI from being a local bus tied to the CPU to a microprocessor-independent bus that can be used with any CPU. PCI operates at 33 MHz and

66 MHz with a maximum data transfer rate of about 533 megabytes per second (MBps). PCI supports bus mastering and was the first bus to accommodate the Microsoft Plug and Play architecture. Finally, PCI supports interrupt sharing on a PC, so any PCI adapters can share a single **interrupt request (IRQ) line** without requiring a unique IRQ for each adapter. (Therefore, only a single free IRQ is required for all PCI cards on a PC.) Most computer systems today come with two to six PCI (or PCI-X) slots and, more frequently, one or more PCI Express slots.

- *PCI-X*—A newer PCI specification, PCI-X 2.x is backward compatible with PCI but supports speeds from 66 MHz to 533 MHz, providing data transfers from 500 MBps to more than 4 gigabytes per second (GBps). The original PCI-X 1.0 specification topped out at 133 MHz with a transfer rate of 1066 MBps. Like PCI, PCI-X supports 32-bit or 64-bit bus widths. These tremendous speeds essentially eliminate the system bus as a performance bottleneck and accommodate developments in network cards (such as Gigabit and 10 Gigabit Ethernet) and disk controllers (such as Ultra3 SCSI and 10Gb Fibre Channel). As of this writing, both PCI and PCI-X NICs support Gigabit Ethernet running on fiber-optic or Cat 5, 5e, and 6 cabling. Figure 4-3 shows a PCI/PCI-X bus NIC.

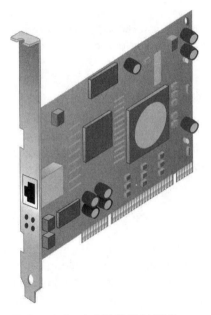

Figure 4-3   A PCI/PCI-X NIC

- *PCI Express*—PCI Express, or PCIe (formerly named 3GIO), uses a high-speed serial communication protocol of one or more lines or lanes; each one can operate at 250 MBps in each direction. Because PCI Express can be set up in lanes, several lanes can be combined, resulting in tremendous transfer speeds up to 8 GBps. Future implementations promise to double this data transfer rate. Although PCI-X bus slots are backward compatible with existing PCI boards, PCI Express hardware maintains backward compatibility with PCI only in board design; the expansion slot required for PCI Express is vastly different from PCI. Because PCIe can be arranged in lanes, PCIe boards are specified with notations such as x1, x4, x8, and x16. The number following the x is the number of lanes. The more lanes, the higher the bandwidth. For example, a PCIe x1 board supports data transfer rates up to 512 MBps, whereas a PCIe x16 board supports transfer rates up to 8 GBps. This technology promises to replace most existing bus types. Figure 4-4 depicts a PCIe x1 NIC.

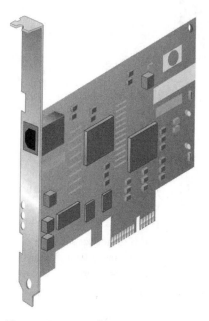

Figure 4-4   A PCIe x1 NIC

- *PCMCIA cards*—PCMCIA cards are credit-card-size expansion cards used primarily to add functionality to laptop computers. Two primary standards are in common use: **Cardbus** and **ExpressCard**. Cardbus is the more mature standard, having been around since the mid-1990s. Cardbus operates at 33 MHz and supports a 32-bit bus providing up to 132 MBps data transfer rates. ExpressCard was developed as computer users' thirst for faster data transfer speeds continued to grow. ExpressCard uses PCI Express technology to provide data transfer rates up to 500 MBps, with future versions reaching 4 GBps. A variety of NICs are available in these formats, including wireless NICs. Figure 4-5 shows a Cardbus NIC with an RJ-45 connector.

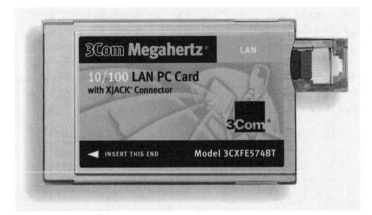

Figure 4-5   A Cardbus NIC

- *Industry Standard Architecture (ISA)*—The ISA bus originally appeared in the first PCs in an 8-bit form. With the introduction of the IBM PC/AT in 1984, the bus size doubled to 16 bits. Even so, the top end of rated bus speed for ISA remains a leisurely (by today's standards) 10 MHz, resulting in an uninspiring 20 MBps transfer rate. Although you might find ISA bus slots in a PC manufactured before 2002, this bus is no longer used on newer PCs.

NOTE   Although it's important to understand the characteristics and capabilities of these PC buses, memorizing their chronology or the companies that introduced them isn't necessary. Note that EISA and MCA (both obsolete) are included in the following table for historical reasons.

Table 4-1 is a quick reference of several bus types used for networking.

Table 4-1   Common bus types

Bus Type	Maximum Transfer Rate	Bus Size	Use
ISA	16 MBps	8 or 16 bits	Only in PCs built before 2002
Extended ISA (EISA)	33 MBps	16 or 32 bits	Obsolete
Micro Channel Architecture (MCA)	264 MBps	16 or 32 bits	Obsolete
PCI	533 MBps	32 and 64 bits	Standard
PCI-X	4 GBps	32 and 64 bits	Servers, high-end workstations
PCI Express (PCIe)	8 GBps	1 to 16 serial lanes	Servers, high-end workstations
PCMCIA	132 MBps	32 bits	Laptops

When working with PC buses, the most important requirement is that the adapter you install in a PC—whether a network interface or another peripheral device—must match the socket in the PC where you want to put it. As you become more familiar with what's inside PCs, you'll see that most incorporate slots for more than one bus type. At the time of this writing, current computer ads show that the most popular buses for desktop machines and network servers are PCI, PCIe, and PCI-X.

TIP For network servers, where fast network access is a key component in network performance, use 64-bit PCI-X or PCIe NICs when possible. Because traffic aggregates at the server, spending extra money on a faster NIC pays for itself quickly.

Other PC Interfaces Used for Networking

Although the following interface technologies don't replace the buses in most typical PCs, they do offer other ways to attach computers to networks. As with bus types, a computer must be equipped to accommodate devices built for a specific interface so that the interface can be attached successfully. Typically, these interfaces can be added to a PC by inserting an adapter card for that interface into a bus. The interface is then made available on the back of the adapter card and communicates with the PC through the bus connector on the adapter card. Today, these are the two most common interfaces:

- *Universal Serial Bus (USB)*—USB comes in two versions: USB 1.0 and USB 2.0. USB 1.0 is a relatively low-speed serial interface that operates at a maximum bandwidth of 12 Mbps. It's used primarily for low-speed peripheral devices, such as mouses, keyboards, or joysticks, but can also be used to attach printers, scanners, telephones, or some video devices to a computer. USB is now a standard interface on both PCs and Macintoshes for these uses. In networking, USB is usually used as an interface for wireless network adapters or as the attachment for cable or DSL modems. USB 2.0 can operate at up to 480 Mbps—40 times faster than USB 1.0. This interface is used for external hard drives, CD/DVD burners, flash memory card readers, high-speed scanners, wireless network adapters, and digital cameras.

- *FireWire (also known as IEEE 1394)*—FireWire is a high-speed serial bus, developed jointly by Apple Computer and Texas Instruments, that operates at bandwidths up to 400 Mbps. A newer version of the governing IEEE standard, 1394b, supports transfer rates up to 3200 Mbps. FireWire is used for high-bandwidth multimedia applications and can reserve guaranteed bandwidth for streaming video and multimedia. It's also used for networking and to attach digital cameras and video devices to computers. The popularity of FireWire and the USB 2.0 standard has prompted many manufacturers to offer combo cards with both interfaces.

Principles of NIC Configuration

After you match a network adapter to a slot in a PC or plug it into a serial bus, the next step is to configure it to work with your computer. In a perfect world, this might mean opening the PC, seating (positioning) the network adapter in a bus slot, closing the PC case, and turning on the system. Alternatively, it might require simply plugging an external network interface into a serial bus port (handy for laptops). As soon as the computer starts, the network would be available. Unfortunately, the task isn't always this easy.

In an effort to make this task easier, Microsoft introduced **Plug and Play (PnP)** architecture with Windows 95. PnP attempts to define a set of configuration protocols so that a computer can communicate with its peripherals during the **power-on self test (POST)** sequence and negotiate a working configuration without requiring user intervention. In other words, you plug it in, and it works. If the motherboard, OS, and all adapters support PnP, this procedure works well. If some devices don't support PnP (referred to as "legacy devices"), or if any device fails to conform precisely to PnP requirements, user intervention is required, however. For computer systems that don't fit the PnP model precisely or for PCs running OSs that don't support PnP, manual configuration is essential to make any NIC work correctly.

Typically, NIC configuration involves working with three types of PC settings:

- Interrupt request line (IRQ)
- Base I/O port
- Base memory address

NOTE

Today's operating systems and PCI-bus PnP NIC cards make manual configuration largely unnecessary. However, older NICs or OSs might require manual configuration from time to time. For more details on expansion card configuration, see the A+ *Guide to Managing and Maintaining Your PC, 5th Edition* (Course Technology, ISBN 1-4188-3557-9).

Integrated NICs

With all this discussion about bus types, NIC configuration, and PnP, it's easy to overlook one other network interface option: the **on-board NIC**. Because a network connection is almost an assumed function of today's computers, most PC motherboard and laptop computer manufacturers integrate the network interface directly on to the motherboard. This integration means you don't need to purchase and install this common add-on card unless the network interface doesn't meet your needs. An on-board NIC might not meet a user's needs for the following reasons: wrong media (a wireless or fiber-optic interface is needed), wrong speed (the integrated interface runs at 100 Mbps, but the user requires

Gigabit Ethernet), or wrong architecture (the user requires token ring but the on-board device is Ethernet, for example). That being said, most on-board NICs are suitable for most users' requirements. However, as a computer or network technician, you will undoubtedly be required to select, purchase, and install more than a few NICs in your lifetime.

Making the Network Attachment

4

Network adapters perform several vital roles to coordinate communications between a computer and a network, including the following:

- Establishing a physical link to the networking medium
- Generating signals that traverse the networking medium
- Receiving incoming signals
- Implementing controls for when to transmit signals to or receive signals from the network medium

Because the network medium attaches directly to the network adapter, or through a transceiver attached to the adapter, matching the adapter you choose with the medium it must attach to is essential. Every networking medium has its own physical characteristics that the adapter must accommodate. That's why NICs are built to accept certain kinds of connectors that match the media.

For common networking technology—for example, Ethernet—a network adapter usually supports twisted-pair cabling using an RJ-45 jack, a fiber-optic connection, or a wireless connection. Some adapters do support multiple media types, and configuration is usually automatic or done through software. When you encounter this type of card, read the manual to get the information you need to configure the card correctly.

CHOOSING NETWORK ADAPTERS FOR BEST PERFORMANCE

As the focus of network traffic on workstations and of large volumes of traffic on network servers (even those with more than one network interface), NICs can have a major influence on network performance. If a NIC is slow, it can limit network performance. Particularly on networks with shared media, slow NICs anywhere on the network can decrease performance for all users.

When selecting a network adapter, first identify the physical characteristics the card must match. They include the type of bus the card will connect with (PCI or PCMCIA, for example), the type of network technology in use, and the kind of connector or physical attachment the adapter must accommodate. After you determine these basic characteristics, it's equally important to consider purchasing other options that can seriously affect a card's speed and data-handling capabilities. Some of these options suit servers better, whereas others work equally well for servers and clients; all help improve overall network performance. These hardware-enhancement options include the following:

- **Direct memory access (DMA)** allows an adapter to transfer data directly from its on-board buffers into the computer's memory, without requiring the CPU to coordinate memory access.

- **Shared adapter memory** means the adapter's buffers map directly into RAM on the computer. A computer actually writes to buffers on the NIC instead of writing to its own memory. In this instance, the computer treats adapter RAM as its own RAM.

- **Shared system memory** means a NIC's on-board processor selects a region of RAM on the computer and writes to it as though it were buffer space on the adapter. In this instance, the adapter treats computer RAM as its own RAM.

- **Bus mastering** permits a network adapter to take control of the computer's bus to initiate and manage data transfers to and from the computer's memory, independent of the CPU. This feature lets the CPU concentrate on other tasks and can improve network performance 20% to 70%. These cards are more expensive than other NICs but are worth the price, especially for servers.

- **RAM buffering** means a NIC includes additional memory to provide temporary storage for incoming and outgoing data that arrives at the NIC faster than it can be shipped out. This option speeds overall performance because it lets the NIC process data as quickly as it can, without having to pause occasionally to grab (or send) more data.

- **On-board co-processors** included on some NICs permit the card to process incoming and outgoing network data without requiring service from the CPU. Today, most NICs include these processors to speed network operations.

- Security features are available on some high-end NICs. They permit the card to handle several protocol functions, including IP Security (IPSec) and other encryption services related to authentication and payload protection. IPSec is a secure transport mechanism that protects network traffic from unwanted snooping.

- **Traffic management** might also be available on some high-end NICs. These services include improved capabilities to guarantee network access to support remote management software and services and more. These improved capabilities are called **Quality of Service (QoS)** when applied to streaming video or multimedia or other applications requiring bandwidth guarantees.

- **Automatic link aggregation** allows you to install multiple NICs in one computer and aggregate the bandwidth so that, for example, you can install two 1 Gbps NICs and have a total bandwidth of 2 Gbps to and from that computer. This feature is found most commonly on NICs designed for servers.

- Improved **fault tolerance**, in the form of redundant NICs with failover capabilities, is available on some high-end NICs. By installing a second NIC in a PC, failure of the primary NIC shifts network traffic to the second NIC instead of cutting off the PC from the network. Hot-plug-capable NICs are also an option for fault tolerance because a NIC can be installed or removed without turning off the server. NICs with dual ports provide added bandwidth and fault tolerance. These NICs have two media connectors, both of which can be active, providing double the bandwidth and fault tolerance if one media connection fails.

- Improved management is possible with features such as wake-on-LAN, which allows an administrator to power on a PC remotely by accessing the NIC through the network. This feature is useful for maintenance tasks. In addition, Simple Network Management Protocol (SNMP) is built in on some NICs, allowing remote configuration and management.

When you select additional options for a network interface, you should weigh how much network traffic the adapter must handle and how important its continued functioning is. The more traffic, the bigger the payback speed-up options can provide. For servers, this means buying the fastest network interface you can find (or afford), usually 64-bit, bus-mastering PCI-X or PCIe NICs with shared memory and substantial on-board buffer space. For workstations, slower cards might be acceptable for light network use, but any machine that accesses the network heavily for demanding applications, such as database management systems (DBMSs) or computer-aided design (CAD), benefits from any speed-up options a quality NIC can provide. Increased availability, reliability, and manageability have obvious payoffs for servers that might not apply to workstations. The following is a checklist for purchasing NICs:

- *Bus width*—Higher is better; pick PCI or PCI-X at 32 or 64 bits.

- *Bus type*—Choose 64-bit PCI-X or PCIe for servers when possible.

- *Memory transfer*—Shared memory outpaces I/O or DMA.

- *Special features*—You need security, management, protocol-handling, and hot-plug capabilities.

- *Bus mastering*—This feature is important for servers.

- *Vendor factors*—Look for quality, reliability, staying power, and reputation.

SPECIAL-PURPOSE NICs

In addition to straightforward network adapters, several types of cards deliver specialized capabilities. They include interfaces for wireless networks as well as a feature for so-called diskless workstations (also called "thin clients"), which must access the network to load an OS when they boot. For that reason, these cards are said to support remote booting or remote initial program load.

Wireless Adapters

Wireless network adapters usually include more gear than conventional cabled NICs. Nevertheless, wireless NICs are available for all major network operating systems, including Windows Vista, Windows XP/2000, Windows Server 2000/2003, Linux, and NetWare, among others. In fact, wireless is such an important part of today's network environment that Windows Vista includes a Wireless Network Setup Wizard to help guide you through the process of connecting to a wireless network. Wireless interfaces usually incorporate some or all of the following components:

- Indoor antenna and antenna cable
- Software to enable the adapter to work with a particular network environment
- **Diagnostic software** to check initial installation or to troubleshoot later
- Installation software

Although it's unusual, these adapters can be used to build entirely wireless LANs (WLANs). More commonly, they are used with a wireless access point device to add wireless elements to an existing wired network. A typical wireless NIC is shown in Figure 4-6.

The choices you must make when selecting a wireless adapter depend on the data transfer speed you want. The most common choices today are 11 Mbps or 54 Mbps, but wireless can operate at speeds faster than 100 Mbps by using the MIMO (IEEE 802.11n) technology mentioned in Chapter 3. Then you have to choose the right wireless standard, which can depend on the type of wireless access point you're connecting to. More than likely, your choices will boil down to 802.11b, 802.11a, 802.11g, and, in the future, 802.11n. From there, you might have additional choices for the type of wireless security you want to use. Two older Wi-Fi security standards are Wired Equivalent Privacy (WEP) and Wi-Fi Protected Access (WPA). The WEP standard has substantial security weaknesses and was superseded by the superior WPA. The IEEE has since ratified a more robust wireless security standard based on WPA called 802.11i. Chapter 10 covers more details on wireless security.

Remote Boot Adapters

In some situations, organizations want to use workstations without disk drives for security reasons, to set up kiosks, or for other public-access uses. It's not surprising that these computers are often called **diskless workstations**. However, because most computers start themselves (in a process called **boot up**) by reading information from a disk, the network must be the source of access to the programs needed to start a diskless workstation.

For these uses, some network adapters include a chip socket for a special bit of circuitry called a **Boot PROM** (programmable read-only memory), which is referred to as preboot execution environment (PXE) compliant. The Boot PROM contains just enough hard-wired code (usually 0.5 MB or less) to allow the NIC to obtain initial configuration information and access the network to download an OS and other software that enables the machine to perform its assigned tasks. After a diskless workstation finishes booting, it can use

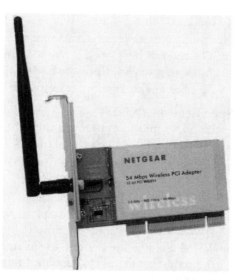

Figure 4-6   A PCI bus wireless NIC

the network to read and write any additional needed data. Most manufacturers also offer bootable floppy disks to support this type of diskless environment.

Remote boot adapters offer several advantages. First, there is cost savings because no hard drive is required, which also improves reliability because hard drives are a common source of problems in PCs. Second, security is increased. Without a hard drive, no sensitive data can be stored on the computer. In addition, virus attacks are useless on a diskless workstation because the virus has no place to reside or files to infect. For these reasons, diskless workstations using remote boot adapters are useful when the workstation doesn't need to maintain long-term local data storage.

DRIVER SOFTWARE

At first, a network adapter appears to be entirely physical. It's a piece of hardware that connects to a networking medium and provides the signaling circuitry necessary to use that medium for sending and receiving information across a network. Before a network adapter can become more than an inert hunk of metal, plastic, and silicon, a software driver—more formally, a **device driver**—for the card must be installed on your computer. A device driver is a small, specialized program that represents a device to an OS and manages communications between the OS and network adapter. Incorrect drivers or poorly written drivers can have a detrimental impact on a network's overall performance or even prevent a PC from booting. The proper installation of correct drivers is extremely important.

In the earliest days of networks, each NIC vendor custom-built its own drivers. It quickly became apparent, however, that tracking every software change and hardware revision was a difficult (and thankless) task. Consequently, OS vendors developed a way to define device drivers to permit their operating systems to communicate with hardware devices installed in a computer. You should become familiar with these major vendor standards for drivers:

- **Network Device Interface Specification (NDIS)**—This standard defines a communications interface (called the NDIS interface) between the MAC sublayer and the NIC driver. The main benefit of NDIS is that it allows NICs to use multiple protocols simultaneously. All Windows operating systems in common use today, including Windows 9x, Server 2000/2003, XP, and Vista, use the NDIS interface.

- **Win32 Driver Model (WDM)**—This standard defines a complete NIC driver interface for PCs that run 32-bit Windows operating systems (which means versions since Windows 98). The WDM architecture divides drivers into bus and device classes by function, enabling generic-class drivers to handle common details for the adapter bus and the type of device it attaches to (such as Ethernet card, token ring card, printer, and scanner). Therefore, developers who create device drivers can concentrate on writing only the most device-specific portion of the driver code. This feature improves overall driver quality because it subjects class drivers to intense scrutiny and testing and allows manufacturers to concentrate on writing code specific to the devices they want to sell. The WDM also interfaces with the PnP manager in Windows, allowing maximum automation for most devices and their drivers.

- **Open Data-link Interface (ODI)**—Apple Computer and Novell defined the ODI standard to allow a NIC to use multiple protocols and to simplify driver development for NIC manufacturers. Therefore, ODI is quite similar to NDIS (but different enough to require a separate driver architecture).

These standards apply to more than network interfaces. Printers need printer drivers, tape drives need tape drivers, disk controllers need controller drivers, and so on. In short, the driver mediates between an OS and an attached device. As a result, the OS can communicate with that device without implementing all the specifics of sending and receiving data from a piece of hardware.

Installing a driver for a network adapter is usually easy. Many OSs ship with drivers for a broad range of devices—including many NICs—as part of their release packages. Also, most NICs include disks with drivers for the most widely available OSs, including the current Windows and Linux OSs. Although the details of installing a driver are operating system specific, most installation programs have a graphical interface with built-in help to make the job as easy as possible. For example, Windows provides a wizard for creating a new connection. Figure 4-7 shows the New Connection Wizard in Windows Vista. To get to this window, click Start, Control Panel, Network and Internet, Network Connections, and, finally, click the Create a new connection option.

4

Figure 4-7 The New Connection Wizard in Windows Vista

NOTE Although driver installation for NICs on modern OSs is fairly straightforward, it hasn't always been. Windows NT, for example, provides limited support for NICs during installation and often doesn't recognize a NIC. This limitation can cause problems for novice installers of NT. Having the NIC drivers available on disk during NT installation is essential.

During the driver installation, you might be prompted to supply configuration information, which usually includes the card's IRQ and its base I/O port ID, at a minimum. Usually, this configuration information is necessary only with legacy NICs because of resource conflicts. Most PnP NICs install and use available computer resources without any user intervention.

NIC driver software evolves continually. When you plan to install a NIC, try to determine whether newer software is available. Good places to check for this information are the NIC's manual, the vendor's Web site and its technical support line, or the Web site of the OS vendor. NIC and OS vendor Web sites are also good places to find troubleshooting information for NIC installation and operation. Large vendors have a searchable database of problems and their solutions in a **knowledge base**, where you can enter a keyword or an error code to search for information.

You should also check these resources from time to time just to see whether drivers have changed since your installation. If so, updating a NIC driver is usually as easy as installing one—all you need is a copy of the latest driver. In fact, easy driver upgrades are often touted as yet another benefit of modern operating systems, which treat drivers as independent software components that you can change at any time. If the driver were built into the OS, you'd have to wait for the OS to change before the driver could change.

NIC Driver Configuration

After a NIC is installed along with its driver, usually there's little left to do; the system should be ready to connect on the network. However, sometimes you need to configure options that are different from the default settings. The options for configuring NIC drivers are as varied as NIC vendors, so options discussed here may or may not be available with your NIC. Most of the configurable options for a NIC can be found in the Advanced tab of the NIC's Properties dialog box (see Figure 4-8).

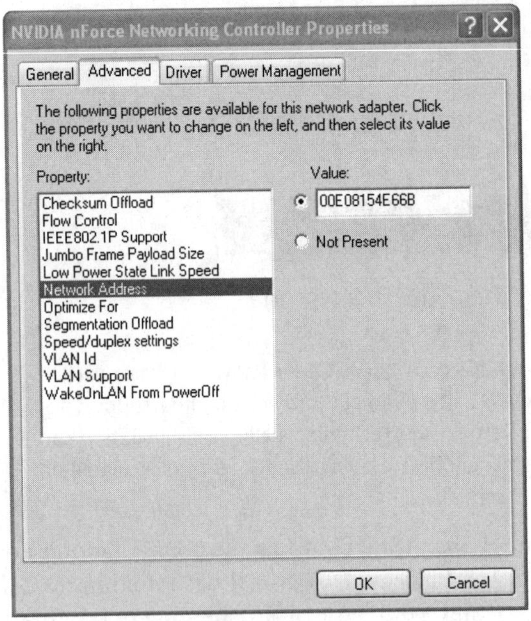

Figure 4-8   The Advanced tab of the NIC's Properties dialog box

This NIC driver has a number of options, many of which are beyond the scope of this discussion. Two fairly common options are Network Address and Speed/duplex settings (shown in the Property list box on the left in Figure 4-8). You use the Network Address option to change the burned-in MAC address of your network card. Normally, you don't need to change your MAC address, but you might in some situations. For example, some ISPs register your MAC address when you connect via cable modem or DSL. If you change your NIC, your MAC address changes, and you might lose connectivity to your ISP. To avoid a call to technical support, you could simply change your new MAC address to be the same as your old one, and then you're good to go.

The Speed/duplex settings option forces your card to operate in a particular mode, such as half duplex at 100 Mbps or full duplex at 1 Gbps. Typically, the driver is set for a mode called **autonegotiation**, which lets the driver work out the optimal connection type with the device the NIC is connected to. In rare cases, however, autonegotiation doesn't work, and a manual setting is called for.

Another tab in the NIC Properties dialog box bears mention. The Driver tab, shown in Figure 4-9, displays details about the driver version and vendor and has several buttons for driver management. Use the Driver Details button to view more information about the driver, such as the file names of each file in the driver. The Update Driver button starts the Hardware Update Wizard for installing a new driver version. The Roll Back Driver button essentially undoes the action of the Update Driver button. If a newly installed driver fails to work, you can use this button to go back to the previous version. Finally, you can use the Uninstall button to remove the driver from the system.

Figure 4-9   The Driver tab of the NIC's Properties dialog box

Wireless NIC Configuration

Configuring a wireless NIC requires a few more steps before a successful connection can be made. Figure 4-10 shows the Status and Properties dialog boxes for a wireless NIC. As you can see, this NIC is connected at 54 Mbps to a network called CNT-APG. As you might have gathered, wireless networks are assigned a name so that WLANs in the same area can be distinguished from one another. The name assigned to a WLAN is called the **service set identifier (SSID)**. A client on a wireless network might need to know this SSID, unless the network administrator configured the access point to broadcast the SSID. In addition, the wireless client will probably need to enter a network key, or encryption **keycode**, which acts like a password to allow entry to the wireless network. When security is enabled on a WLAN, communications are encrypted so that unauthorized parties can't connect. The keycode serves as a decryption key, allowing a client to access the wireless network. Figure 4-11 shows a client connecting to the CNT-APG network and entering the required keycode.

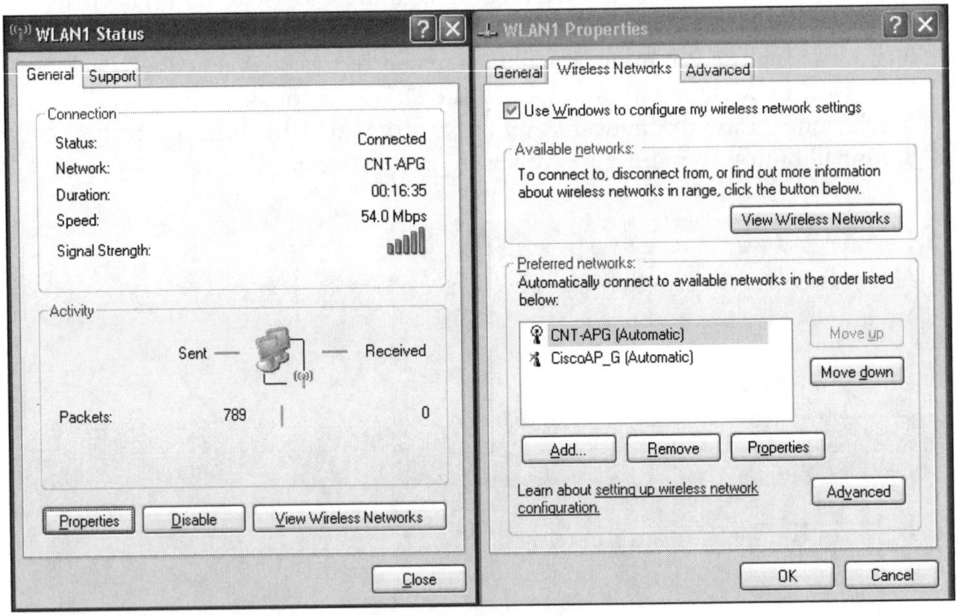

Figure 4-10 The Status and Properties dialog boxes for a wireless NIC

As you can see, NIC driver configuration can be as easy as plugging it in and having it work, or it might involve more steps to make a successful connection, particularly with a wireless connection.

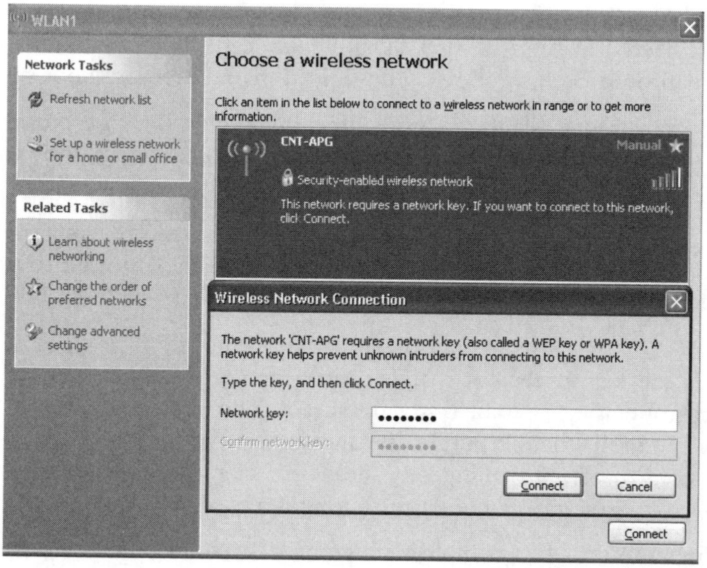

Figure 4-11   A wireless client connecting to a wireless network

CHAPTER SUMMARY

- Network interface cards (NICs) supply the interface between a computer and the networking medium. They also prepare, send, and control data flow across the network.

- When sending data, a NIC must reformat outgoing data from the parallel form that arrives through the computer's bus to the serial form used over most networking media; to receive data, this process is reversed. Each NIC incorporates a unique hardware network address (called the MAC address) to distinguish it from other NICs on a network.

- NICs include configurable options that must be set correctly for an adapter to make a working network connection; these options are usually selected automatically by Plug and Play, but sometimes they require specifying a unique interrupt request line (IRQ), base I/O port, and base memory address.

- For compatibility, the NIC's edge connector must match the PC slot into which it plugs; likewise, the NIC's media attachment must match the network medium and connector type to which it will connect.

- Many motherboards today have integrated, or on-board, NICs because computers are so often part of a network. If an integrated NIC's features meet your needs, there's no need to install a NIC.

- Network adapters can have a profound effect on overall network performance. Numerous performance-improving options, including direct memory access (DMA), shared adapter or system memory, and bus mastering, can enhance NIC capabilities. Other useful enhancements include RAM buffering or incorporating an on-board co-processor to offload data-handling chores from the computer's CPU. Network adapters can even incorporate specialized capabilities, such as hot-plug capability, dual ports, security settings, management interfaces, wireless communications, and remote boot support.

▢ When purchasing a network adapter, consider the following checklist: bus width, bus type, memory transfer, special features (such as security), bus mastering, and vendor factors (such as support).

▢ When purchasing a wireless NIC, keep in mind the Wi-Fi standard you want to use: 802.11a, 802.11b, or 802.11g. Also, consider the type of security you want to use for the wireless network and whether the adapter supports the security standard (WEP, WPA, and, in the future, 802.11i).

▢ Driver software is the key ingredient that permits a network adapter to communicate with a computer's operating system. Ensuring that a valid driver is available for your operating system is essential before purchasing an adapter; even better, always obtain the latest driver versions before installing any network adapter. Making regular driver upgrades part of your network maintenance routine is also a good idea.

▢ NIC driver configuration can be as simple as plugging it in and having it work, or it might require setting some options. Additional configuration, such as entering an SSID and a network keycode, is often needed with wireless NICs.

Key Terms

adapter slot —The sockets built into a PC motherboard that are designed to accommodate add-on cards, such as NICs. *See also* Industry Standard Architecture (ISA) and Peripheral Component Interface (PCI). (Both are specific types of adapter slots.)

automatic link aggregation — A feature of some NICs that adds the bandwidth of two installed NICs together, resulting in a higher aggregate bandwidth.

autonegotiation — The process by which a NIC driver automatically selects an operating mode (speed and duplex mode). To make this selection, the NIC driver negotiates the optimal connection type with the device the NIC is connected to.

Boot PROM — A special programmable chip that includes enough software to permit a computer to boot sufficiently and access the network. From there, it can download an operating system to finish the boot process. Also known as PXE compliant.

boot up — The process a computer goes through when starting; also called booting.

buffer — A temporary storage area that a device uses to contain incoming data before it can be processed for input or to contain outgoing data before it can be sent as output.

bus mastering — The capability of an adapter card's circuitry to take possession of a computer's bus and coordinate data transfers without requiring any service from the computer's CPU.

bus width — The number of parallel lines that make up a type of bus. For example, ISA supports 8- and 16-bit bus widths, and PCI supports 32- and 64-bit bus widths.

Cardbus — A credit-card-size expansion card used primarily to add functionality to laptop computers. Cardbus provides data transfer rates up to 132 MBps. *See also* ExpressCard.

4

computer bus — A specialized collection of parallel lines in a PC used to transfer data between the CPU and peripheral devices and occasionally from one peripheral device to another.

device driver — A software program that mediates communication between an operating system and a device for the purpose of sending and receiving input and output from that device. These drivers are operating system dependent. They also need to be kept up to date per information on the manufacturer's Web site.

diagnostic software — Specialized programs that can probe and monitor a system (or system component) to determine whether it works and, if not, try to establish the cause of the problem.

direct memory access (DMA) — A technique for addressing memory on some other device as though it were local memory directly available to the device accessing that memory. This technique lets a CPU gain immediate access to the buffers on any NIC that supports DMA.

diskless workstations — Network computers that require a special type of ROM because they have no built-in disk drives.

ExpressCard — A credit-card-size expansion card used primarily to add functionality to laptop computers. ExpressCard provides data transfer rates up to 500 MBps. *See also* Cardbus.

fault tolerance — A feature that allows a system to continue working after an unexpected hardware or software failure.

FireWire — A high-speed, external serial bus that supports bandwidths up to 400 Mbps and can connect up to 63 devices; also known as IEEE 1394. FireWire is used for streaming video and multimedia, networking, and attaching video devices to computers.

hexadecimal — A mathematical notation for representing numbers in base 16. The numbers 10 through 15 are expressed as A through F; 10h or 0x10 (both notations indicate the number is hexadecimal) equals 16.

Industry Standard Architecture (ISA) — Originally an 8-bit PC bus architecture, but upgraded to 16-bit with the introduction of the IBM PC/AT in 1984.

interrupt request (IRQ) line — Any of 16 unique signal lines between the CPU and bus slots on a PC. IRQs define the mechanism whereby a peripheral device of any kind, including a network adapter, can stake a claim on a PC's attention. This claim is called an "interrupt," so the lines carrying this information are called "interrupt request lines."

keycode — A string of characters that a user must supply to wireless NIC software so that the computer can decrypt communications on a wireless LAN, therefore allowing the client to access the LAN.

knowledge base — A searchable online database containing problems and errors, along with their solutions, related to a manufacturer's product.

Media Access Control (MAC) address — The number that identifies the physical address of a network computer. This address is burned into the computer's NIC in the form of data programmed on to the interface's ROM.

Network Device Interface Specification (NDIS) — A driver standard for providing an interface between a network interface card and the network medium; this standard enables a NIC to use multiple protocols.

network interface card (NIC) — The hardware device that mediates communication between a computer and the networking medium.

on-board co-processor — A special- or general-purpose microprocessor on an adapter card, usually for offloading data from a computer's CPU. Typically, NICs with on-board co-processors use the special-purpose variety.

on-board NIC — The electronics that make up a network interface integrated directly onto a computer motherboard.

Open Data-link Interface (ODI) — A specification developed by Apple Computer and Novell that simplifies driver development and enables a single NIC to use multiple protocols.

parallel transmission — The technique of spreading bits of data across multiple parallel data lines to transmit them simultaneously, instead of according to an ordinal and temporal sequence.

PCI Express — A high-speed bus standard that relies on serial communications arranged in lanes to provide communications up to 8 GBps.

PCI-X — A high-speed bus standard that supports 64 bits at 66 MHz up to 533 MHz for .5 GBps to more than 4 GBps data transfer rates.

PCMCIA cards — Credit-card-size expansion cards used primarily to add functionality to laptop computers. Two standards are in common use: *See also* Cardbus and ExpressCard.

Peripheral Component Interconnect (PCI) — The 32- and 64-bit PC bus architecture that currently prevails as the best and fastest of all available bus types, operating at 33 and 66 MHz.

Plug and Play (PnP) — The Microsoft requirements for PC motherboards, buses, adapter cards, and operating systems that enable a PC to detect and configure hardware on a system automatically. For PnP to work, all system components must conform rigorously to its specifications; currently, Windows 9x, 2000, XP, 2003, and Vista support this architecture.

power-on self test (POST) — The set of internal diagnostic and status-checking routines a PC and its peripheral devices run each time the computer is powered on.

Quality of Service (QoS) — A networking term that specifies a guaranteed level of service when applied to applications requiring high bandwidth.

RAM buffering — A memory-access technique that permits an adapter to use a computer's main memory as though it were local buffer space.

serial transmission — A technique for transmitting data signals that sends each bit's worth of data (or its analog equivalent) one at a time, one after another, in sequence.

service set identifier (SSID) — The name assigned to a wireless LAN.

shared adapter memory — A technique for a computer's CPU to address memory on an adapter as though it were the computer's own main memory.

shared system memory — A technique for an adapter to address a computer's main memory as though it resided on the adapter.

traffic management — In terms of NICs, features that improve network accessibility for remote users, especially those using applications that require higher bandwidth, such as streaming video or multimedia.

Universal Serial Bus (USB) — A hot-pluggable Plug and Play serial interface; USB ports support peripheral devices, such as mouses and keyboards, in addition to some printers, scanners, telephony equipment, and monitors. USB 1.0 operates at a maximum data transfer rate of 12 Mbps; USB 2.0 supports up to 480 Mbps.

Win32 Driver Model (WDM) — A unified driver standard that allows a single driver to be written for any 32-bit version of Windows (those since Windows 98).

4

REVIEW QUESTIONS

1. Of the following PC bus types, which supports 32-bit data transmission? (Choose all that apply.)

   a. PCI-X

   b. PCI

   c. PCI Express

   d. ISA

2. Which of the following statements is true?

   a. A driver is a small program that mediates between the computer's operating system and a hardware device.

   b. A driver is a user application.

   c. Only one driver is needed to handle communications between the computer's operating system and all peripheral devices.

   d. Operating systems usually include all the drivers you need to install for any NIC.

   e. You need a driver only if the NIC does not support Plug and Play.

3. When installing a NIC driver, the driver supplied by the card manufacturer is always the most up to date. True or False?

4. A network adapter card converts serial data from the computer into parallel data for transmission and reverses that process on reception. True or False?

5. Which of the following lists the most common PC bus widths?

   a. 16-bit and 24-bit

   b. 24-bit and 48-bit

   c. 8-bit and 32-bit

   d. 32-bit and 64-bit

6. The PCI-X bus standard pushes data transfer rates to _____ .

7. Where is temporary data stored on a network adapter to act as a buffer for excess input or output?

   a. transceiver

   b. physical attachment

   c. on-board co-processor

   d. on-board RAM

8. To work correctly, which characteristics of a network adapter must match those of the network medium? (Choose all that apply.)

   a. network technology

   b. connector type

   c. transmission speed

   d. media type

9. Which standard provides a more robust security protocol for a wireless LAN and is based on WPA?

   a. 802.11b

   b. 802.11n

   c. 802.11i

   d. WEP

10. Which of the following is a common type of wireless protocol? (Choose all that apply.)

    a. 802.11a

    b. 802.12a

    c. 802.11b

    d. 802.12g

11. Which of the following PC buses was commonly seen on new PCs until around 2002?

    a. ISA

    b. EISA

    c. MCA

    d. PCI

12. Plug and Play provides which service?

    a. automatic operating system installation without user intervention

    b. automatic detection and configuration of new hardware devices

    c. automatic connection to a wireless LAN

    d. automatic configuration of network settings

13. A PCI NIC works with which type of motherboard slot? (Choose all that apply.)

    a. PCI-X

    b. EISA

    c. PCIe

    d. PCI

14. Which of the following NIC performance enhancements is recommended for use in a server? (Choose all that apply.)

    a. hot-plug capability

    b. automatic link aggregation

    c. Cardbus interface

    d. PCI-X bus

15. Which of the following is a type of security for wireless LANs? (Choose all that apply.)

    a. WSC

    b. WEP

    c. WAP

    d. WPA

    e. 802.11i

16. The NIC device that translates digital data into signals for transmission and translates signals into digital data on receipt is called a(n) _____ .

17. Which of the following roles does a network adapter play in connecting a computer to a networking medium? (Choose all that apply.)

    a. formats outgoing data into frames for transmission on to the media

    b. provides a physical link to the network medium

    c. enforces password authentication for incoming frames

    d. converts data from one network protocol to another, if necessary

    e. provides a unique hardware-level network address

18. Which of the following factors contributed to the development of new data buses in PCs? (Choose all that apply.)

    a. Networks got faster, so buses did too.

    b. Increased CPU speeds demanded faster, wider buses.

    c. Standalone computers are used more frequently.

    d. Network protocols required faster buses.

    e. Bigger operating systems bred bigger buses.

19. The POST sequence is intended to perform which of the following tasks?

    a. Check the CPU, motherboard, and peripherals at PC boot time.

    b. Provide built-in operating system diagnostics when errors occur.

    c. Support Microsoft Plug and Play functionality.

    d. Develop an ongoing set of performance and operations data for PCs.

20. Which of the following driver architectures is supported only in Microsoft operating systems since Windows 98?

    a. Plug and Play

    b. WDM

    c. NDIS

    d. ODI

21. A special circuitry device that can be inserted into some NICs to support booting the system across the network is called which of the following?

    a. bootstrap loader

    b. boot chip

    c. Boot PROM

    d. Bootable IC

22. Which of the following buses or serial interfaces supports the highest bandwidth? (*Hint:* To calculate bandwidth, multiply maximum speed in MHz by bus width.)

    a. ISA

    b. USB

    c. PCI

    d. PCI-X

    e. FireWire

23. Which serial standard improves on the older version by up to 40 times the existing data transfer rate?

    a. 1394

    b. PCI-X

    c. 3GIO

    d. USB 2.0

24. Which serial bus technology brings data transfer rates up to 8 GBps?

25. The address burned into ROM on a NIC is called the _____ .

26. Advantages of a remote boot adapter include which of the following? (Choose all that apply.)

   a. increased reliability

   b. better security

   c. higher performance

   d. virus protection

27. Which two vendors defined the ODI driver standard?

28. The name given to a wireless LAN is called a(n) _____ .

29. The type of connector used for a 10BaseT network is the _____ .

30. Which of the following connector types is used for a fiber-optic network?

   a. MT-RJ

   b. transceiver

   c. RJ-45

   d. BNC

HANDS-ON PROJECTS

Installing a NIC in today's PCs is fairly simple. Selecting the right NIC for your environment and configuring postinstallation settings are usually more difficult. The following projects help you identify NICs for different buses and media and allow you to explore some features and configuration options for NICs.

Hands-On Project 4-1

Your instructor will gather a variety of NICs with different bus types that accommodate different cabling. Each NIC is labeled with a number. The instructor will also collect several labeled types of network cable without connectors installed.

1. Examine each NIC, being careful to note which type of cable each NIC supports and the bus type for each NIC. Examine each cable, note what type of media it is, and determine the type of connector that can be installed on the cable.

2. Fill out Table 4-2. Match the NIC with the cable, using the label numbers fixed to each. The first entry is filled out as an example. The type of label your instructor uses for the NIC and cable might vary from the example.

Table 4-2 NIC and media matching

NIC Label	Cable Type	Cable Label	Bus Type	Connector Type
Z	10Base2	9	ISA	BNC

3. Based on your experience and reading, what type of connector, cable, and NIC bus type are the most common in today's LANs?

HANDS-ON
PROJECTS

Hands-On Project 4-2

In this project, you examine some of the advanced configuration options for a NIC in the Windows environment. This project uses Windows XP but can be adapted to Windows Vista, Windows 2000, or Windows 9x with some adjustments. For information on those adjustments, see your instructor.

1. From the Windows XP desktop, click **Start**, **Control Panel**, click **Network and Internet Connections**, and then click **Network Connections**.

2. Right-click **Local Area Connection** and click **Properties**. (If you don't have a connection labeled "Local Area Connection," ask your instructor for the name of another connection.)

3. In the Connect using section, you'll see the name of an interface. Write down the name of this interface:

_____

4. Click the **Configure** button in this section, and then click the **Advanced** tab.

5. Depending on the NIC you have installed, you'll see one or more selections in the Property list box. Select each property and explore the options for that property in the Value list box. List the available properties and their options:

_____

_____

_____

6. Next, click the **Resources** tab. List the resource types and their associated settings:

_____

_____

_____

7. Click the **Driver** tab. What options are available for driver installation and configuration?

_____

_____

8. Close the Properties dialog box by clicking **Cancel**. Close the Network Connections dialog box.

HANDS-ON PROJECTS

Hands-On Project 4-3

In this project, you research some of the latest advances in NIC technology by visiting the Web site of a large NIC manufacturer (3Com) and browsing through the products available to support high-speed networking. This project assumes you have an Internet connection.

1. Start your Web browser, type **www.3com.com/index2.html** in the Address text box, and press **Enter**.

2. In the Products & Services drop-down list, click **Network Interface Cards & LOMs**. Click **Gigabit Ethernet**, and then click **3Com Gigabit Server NIC**.

3. Using the Features and Benefits page, write down some of the features you think help make this NIC ideally suited to server systems:

_____

_____

_____

_____

4. Click **Product Specifications**. Write down the following information—media, connector, bus, and operating distance:

_____

_____

_____

_____

5. Click the **Back** button two times, and then click **3Com Gigabit Fiber-SX Server NIC**.

6. Click **Product Specifications** and write down the same information you wrote in Step 4 for the other NIC:

_____

_____

_____

_____

7. Explain the major differences you found between these NICs and why you think these differences exist:

_____

_____

_____

Hands-On Project 4-4

In this project, you use some common networking diagnostic tools in Windows XP.

1. Open a command prompt window by clicking **Start**, **Run**, typing **cmd**, and then clicking **OK**.

2. To find the NIC MAC address, type the simple command **getmac** and press **Enter**. This command displays the MAC address for each NIC installed on your computer.

3. Another method of displaying the MAC address is to use the ipconfig command. At the command prompt, type **ipconfig /all** and press **Enter**. Notice that the MAC address is listed as the "Physical Address."

4. One way to see the MAC address of other computers is to view the Address Resolution Protocol (ARP) cache (covered in Chapter 6). Your first step in viewing the cache is to get a list of other computers on your network by typing **net view** and pressing **Enter**.

5. You should see several computer names listed, each preceded by a double backslash (\\). The first one in the list is usually your own. Pick one of the other computer names and ping it by typing **ping computername** and pressing **Enter**. (Substitute one of the listed computers for *computername*.) You should see the IP address of the computer you just pinged.

The Ping command sends a message to the computer specified in the command. If the computer receives the message, a reply is returned. The output of the Ping command tells you whether the reply was received and how long it took for the response.

6. To view that computer's MAC address, type **arp –a** and press **Enter**. The MAC address is listed next to the IP address of each computer with which your computer has communicated recently.

7. Close the command prompt window by typing **exit** and pressing **Enter**.

Hands-On Project 4-5

In this project, you configure your LAN connection status to show as an icon in the taskbar and perform some troubleshooting tasks.

1. Click **Start**, **Control Panel**, click **Network and Internet Connections**, and then click **Network Connections**.

2. Right-click **Local Area Connection** and click **Properties**. (If you don't have a connection labeled "Local Area Connection," ask your instructor for the name of another connection.)

3. Make sure both check boxes at the bottom of the dialog box are selected, as shown in Figure 4-12.

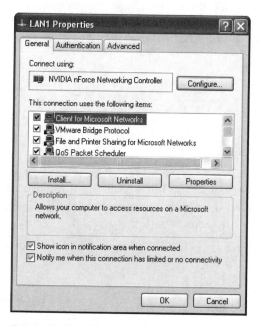

Figure 4-12 The Properties dialog box for a network connection

4. Selecting the Show icon in notification area when connected check box displays an icon in the taskbar that looks like two monitors side by side (assuming your NIC is currently connected to a network). This icon is referred to as the network connection status icon. Place your mouse pointer over this icon in the taskbar, and write down the message shown in the yellow pop-up box:

5. Now find the cable that goes into your NIC. (If you're using wireless, you can't do this step or the next one.) You should see an LED lit up next to where the cable plugs in. Pull out the cable, and you should see the LED go out. The LED is often referred to as the "link light." When there's a proper network connection, the link light is on.

6. Place your mouse pointer over the network connection status icon in the taskbar. What does the yellow pop-up box tell you about your connection? Reconnect your network cable.

7. Right-click the network connection status icon. Note the options you have for managing the connection. Click the **Status** option. List the information in the Status dialog box:

_____

_____

_____

8. Click the **Support** tab in the Status dialog box. Click the **Details** button to view details about your IP address settings, and then click **Close**. If your computer can't connect to the network, you can click the Repair button to attempt to retrieve new IP address settings and flush the DNS and ARP caches.

9. Click **Close** to close the Status dialog box.

CASE PROJECTS

CASE PROJECTS

Case Project 4-1

Your company just decided to install a network for the first time. Your manager asks you to specify configurations for 120 clients. Because of heavy data load anticipated on the network, it's essential that the servers keep up with high amounts of traffic. Your manager asks you to put together a "killer server" to keep up with the demand.

Required result: The server must be able to handle all the network traffic it receives "with a reasonable response time."

Optional desired results: Because some network segments are busy and others are relatively idle, you must keep the hardware costs to a minimum. You also need to make sure the server won't slow down the network.

Proposed solution: Because of high demand on one segment, you get approval to buy 64-bit bus-mastering PCI-X NICs with additional RAM for all segments. Which result does the proposed solution produce? Why?

    a. The required result and both optional desired results

    b. The required result, but only one optional desired result

c. The required result but neither optional desired result

d. The proposed solution does not produce the required result.

Case Project 4-2

On an Ethernet 10BaseT network, all computers are connected with a hub. Recently, a network-intensive application has been installed, and users are complaining that response times are quite slow on the network. You decide you need to upgrade the network to a faster speed—100BaseT. You have checked the cabling and verified that it's Category 5 and terminated correctly. What else must you check for to complete an upgrade to 100BaseT?

Case Project 4-3

You are in the process of purchasing new computers for a new wing of your building. You want these machines to be as management friendly as possible—and that includes the network interface cards. You know that new features are available to meet this goal. What features might you look for on NICs for these new computers?

Case Project 4-4

You are in the process of choosing an enterprise server for your organization. Major requirements for this server include high availability, fault tolerance, and high performance. List some features to look for on the NIC you select for this server. Do some research on the Internet by checking a few major NIC manufacturers to see what features are available. To start, try *www.3com.com*, *www.intel.com*, and *www.transition.com* for some ideas. Write a report describing some key features that meet this server's requirements.

5

MAKING NETWORKS WORK

**After reading this chapter and completing the
exercises, you will be able to:**

- Explain the OSI reference model layers and their relationship to hard-ware and software
- Describe the function and creation of a data frame
- Explain the IEEE 802 networking model and related standards

This chapter discusses two different but complementary models for what networks are and how they work. The Open Systems Interconnection (OSI) reference model for networking explains how networks behave within an orderly, seven-layered model for networked communications. Many of the networking hardware components discussed in this book can be identified as working within one or more of the OSI model layers. The IEEE 802 networking model and its accompanying standards are formal specifications of how networking technologies should be implemented. This model has layers of its own and can be compared with the OSI model.

UNDERSTANDING THE OSI AND 802 NETWORKING MODELS

The concept of networking is almost as important as the real thing. Several models sought to create an intellectual framework to clarify network concepts and activities, but none has been as successful as the **Open Systems Interconnection (OSI)** reference model proposed by the **International Organization for Standardization (ISO)**. This model is sometimes referred to as the ISO/OSI reference model.

ISO is not an acronym; it comes from the Greek prefix iso, which means "equal" or "the same." The ISO, based in Geneva, Switzerland, is a network of national standard institutes from 140 countries. The expanded name differs from language to language. For example, in France the organization is the Organisation Internationale de Normalisation. The term ISO gives the network of institutes a common name.

The OSI reference model has become a key part of networking, in large part because it's a common framework for developers and students of networking to work with and learn from. The attempt to develop a working set of protocols and technologies based on the OSI model and put those efforts into common use never materialized, in part because existing protocols, such as TCP/IP and IPX/SPX, were already entrenched in the marketplace. However, the OSI reference model has an unrivaled place in networking as a model and teaching tool. This chapter covers the model's organization and its capabilities.

The set of protocols that was developed to conform to the OSI model is called ISO. You can view the fruits of those labors at *www.protocols.com/pbook/iso.htm*.

This chapter also describes the IEEE 802 networking model, which provides detailed implementation specifications for a number of networking technologies. This model is one of the most influential sets of networking standards in use anywhere. In fact, the 802 specification encompasses most types of networking and is open ended, allowing the addition of new types of networks (such as 10 Gigabit Ethernet) as necessary.

Role of a Reference Model

You might wonder why a reference model for networking is needed and why the layer concept in particular is so valuable. To see the value of this layered model, consider the process of purchasing mobile telephone service. The functions of each option and feature in mobile phone service can be divided into layers. At the most basic level or layer is the type of communication, such as analog or digital. From there, you can decide on calling features, such as forwarding, conferencing, and instant messaging. Then you can focus on the phone's features, such as whether it includes a digital camera. After you choose a phone, you can select the level of service you need, such as the number of minutes in your plan and whether your minutes are local, regional, or nationwide.

Many details of how mobile phone service works might be unclear to you, but you know what it can do for you and the basics of using it. You also know that even though there are many mobile telephone services, you can communicate with users of other services. Furthermore, even if you travel outside your service area, you can usually continue using your phone. If you want a phone with the latest styles and features, you can probably just purchase a new phone without changing your service. All this interoperability among layers is possible because of reference models and standards.

The process of buying a mobile phone can be confusing because so many options are available, but after you break it down into steps or layers, the process becomes clearer and easier to understand. Also, because you know that mobile services are generally compatible, you don't have to focus on the details of how the service works. All you have to do is pick the mobile phone package that best meets your communication requirements.

Like mobile phone service, computer networking, computer compatibility, and networking features and functions can be daunting concepts to grasp. However, they would be more difficult to comprehend if networking weren't built on a common framework with the process separated into layers. The OSI model and its seven-layer approach to networking provides this common framework.

OSI Reference Model

In the late 1970s, the ISO drafted a theoretical model for networks of all kinds that became known as the **OSI reference model**. By 1983, the draft became ISO Standard 7498. The real value of the OSI reference model is that it offers a useful way to describe—and think about—networking.

One word—**layers**—conveys the essence of the OSI reference model. Essentially, this model's foundation rests on the idea that networking can be separated into a series of related tasks; each task can be conceptualized as a single aspect, or layer, of the communication process. This approach reduces the complexity of networked communications, from applications to hardware, into a series of interconnected tasks and activities. Even though the relationship among these tasks and activities persists, each task or activity can be handled separately and its issues solved independently. Computer scientists like to call this approach "divide and conquer" because it creates a method for solving big problems by deconstructing them into a series of smaller problems with separate solutions.

Understanding Layers

Chapter 1 discussed layers of the networking process and included a simulation of a chat session. Now is a good time to review the related concepts that were shown in Simulation 1-1 and Figure 1-3. To help you understand the layered communication process, consider the following analogy of creating and delivering a letter through the U.S. mail:

1. Tom, who lives in New York, writes a letter to Cindy, who lives in San Francisco. When the letter is finished, it's ready for Cindy to read, but Tom needs to get the letter to Cindy, so he decides to use the U.S. mail.

2. Tom folds the letter and places it in an envelope, which is the container prescribed by the U.S. mail letter-sending protocols. Tom can't send the letter yet, however; first he must address the envelope.

3. Tom addresses the envelope by putting Cindy's name and address in the middle of the front of the envelope, which is where the post office expects to find the destination address. Tom also puts his return address in the envelope's upper-left corner.

4. Before Tom can send the envelope, per post office protocol, he must place a stamp in the envelope's upper-right corner.

5. Tom then walks to the post office and drops the letter in the mailbox. At this point, Tom's job is done; it's up to the post office (the next layer) to take care of getting the letter to its destination.

6. The mail carrier picks up the mail in the mailbox at the prescribed time and brings it to the central office for sorting. The mail carrier's job is done, and now it's up to other post office workers (the next layer) to get the letter to its destination.

7. The mail is sorted according to ZIP code, which identifies for which part of the country the mail is destined. After sorting, the letter goes into the pile headed for the West Coast of the United States. The mail is put on a plane, and the job of the post office worker in New York is completed.

8. After the mail arrives in San Francisco, it's sorted by ZIP code to determine the area of San Francisco to which it should be delivered. After the letter has been sorted, a mail carrier takes it on his or her route.

9. The mail carrier uses the street address to determine which house to deliver the letter to, and he or she leaves the letter in Cindy's mailbox. At this point, the mail carrier's job is done.

10. Cindy receives the letter, opens the envelope, and now has exactly what Tom had in his hand before he placed the letter in the envelope. Mission accomplished.

As you can see, a number of tasks had to be completed to deliver this message. All were separate tasks, but for one task to be completed, the previous task (or layer) had to be completed correctly:

- The letter had to be addressed in the correct format.

- The local post office in New York had to sort the letter correctly and get it on the right plane to San Francisco.

- The post office in San Francisco had to sort the letter correctly for the right part of town.

- The local carrier had to deliver the letter to the correct house.

The OSI reference model for networking clarifies many communications activities and related tasks and requirements to help in understanding what networks are and how they work. For the letter delivery, several activities (for example, placing the letter in an envelope and addressing and sorting the letter) happened well before the letter's delivery. The structure of the OSI reference model breaks down all the events that must occur for data to be addressed and formatted correctly before it can actually be delivered to its final recipient. To further exemplify the value of layers in this analogy, consider the effect on the process of having the mail carrier switch from walking the mail route to driving a delivery truck. In fact, the only step that's affected is the mail carrier's job—his or her job gets done faster. Addressing the envelope is still done in the same way, and post office workers still follow the same procedure to sort the mail. In short, people involved in those steps don't even have to know that the mail carrier is using a truck to get from house to house. As you can see, with a layered approach, one part of the process can change, sometimes drastically, while the rest of the process remains unchanged.

Structure of the OSI Reference Model

The OSI reference model divides networked communications into seven layers. The names and order of these layers are shown in Figure 5-1.

TIP   Here are two good mnemonics to remember the seven layers of the OSI reference model. From the bottom up, starting with the Physical layer, the acronym is "Programmers Do Not Throw Sausage Pizza Away." From the top down, starting with the Application layer, it's "All People Seem To Need Data Processing."

At the top, the Application layer provides a set of interfaces that permit networked applications—such as Windows Explorer, an e-mail package, or a Web browser—to access network services. Applications are not part of the reference model, but communicate with its top layer. At the bottom of the reference model, the Physical layer is where the networking medium and the signals traversing it reside. All the activities needed to handle networked communications occur between the top and bottom layers.

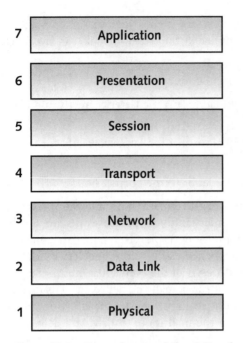

7	Application
6	Presentation
5	Session
4	Transport
3	Network
2	Data Link
1	Physical

Figure 5-1 Seven layers of the OSI reference model

To comprehend the model's function, you need to understand how it behaves as a whole and how computers carry out the services and functions within the model. At the outset, any computer that can access a network must have a protocol stack (also known as a **protocol suite** because it consists of a collection of related software elements and services that correspond to the layers of the OSI model, instead of a single massive program). Protocol stacks provide the software that enables computers to communicate across a network. Currently, the most common protocol stacks include the following:

- Transmission Control Protocol/Internet Protocol (TCP/IP) is the protocol suite used on the Internet and is the default protocol for Windows, Linux, and Novell NetWare 5.0 and later.

- Internetwork Packet Exchange/Sequenced Packet Exchange (IPX/SPX) is the protocol suite most commonly used with Novell NetWare 4.x and earlier.

- NetBIOS Extended User Interface (NetBEUI) is a protocol suite developed by IBM for PC networking and is traditionally used in IBM and Windows products, such as Windows NT, Windows 9x, and Windows for Workgroups. This protocol suite is no longer available to install on Windows Vista, XP, and Server 2003.

- AppleTalk is the protocol suite Apple developed for its Macintosh computers and is still used sometimes in Macintosh-based networks.

TCP/IP is by far the most commonly used protocol suite. It's likely that IPX/SPX, NetBEUI, and AppleTalk will soon be discussed only in a historical context. Protocol suites, combined with drivers for network devices attached to a computer, are the crucial software link that enables applications to communicate with a network. Taken as a whole, protocols plus drivers equal network access.

Looking further into the model helps explain the activities and functions involved and shows why layering is a powerful concept for software developers and model builders. Each layer in the OSI model has its own set of well-defined functions, and the functions of each layer communicate and interact with the layers immediately above and below it. For example, the Transport layer works with the Network layer below it and the Session layer above it. (The Physical layer, where transmission of outgoing signals to the networking medium or decoding of incoming signals constitutes its lower-layer handoff, is an exception.)

In the broadest sense, Layers 1 and 2 (Physical and Data Link) define a network's physical media and the signaling characteristics needed to send and receive information across the network medium and to request access to the medium for transmission. Layers 3 and 4 (Network and Transport) move information from sender to receiver and handle the data to be sent or received. Layers 5 through 7 (Session, Presentation, and Application) manage "conversations," or ongoing communications, across a network and deal with how data is represented and interpreted for use in applications or for delivery across the network.

Figure 5-2 shows these layers in an operating system context. The properties of a computer's network connection contain components representing layers of the OSI model. The Ethernet adapter shown in the Connect using section represents the two bottom layers of the model: Physical and Data Link. Internet Protocol (TCP/IP) represents the next two layers: Network and Transport. The Client for Microsoft Networks and File and Printer Sharing for Microsoft Networks options represent the top three layers: Session, Presentation, and Application. All these components (layers) are required for Windows network communication to work, but any component can be replaced with a suitable substitute (for example, replacing the NIC and its driver with a different NIC and driver) without affecting the other components.

Rigidly defined boundaries called "interfaces" separate layers in the OSI reference model. Any request from one layer to another must pass through the interface. Each layer builds on the capabilities and activities of the layers below it and acts to support the layers above, and any layer can communicate directly with its adjacent layers.

In general, the purpose of any layer in the model is to provide services to the next higher layer but also shield that higher layer from the details of how its services are carried out. In the OSI model, layer construction follows a concept called "peer layers"—that is, each layer on one computer behaves as though it were communicating with its twin on the other computer. This behavior is sometimes called logical, or virtual, communication between peer layers, as shown in Figure 5-3.

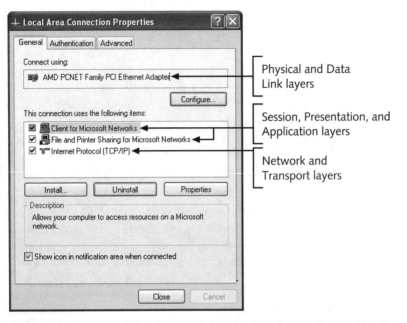

Figure 5-2 Layers of the OSI model in the Local Area Connection Properties dialog box

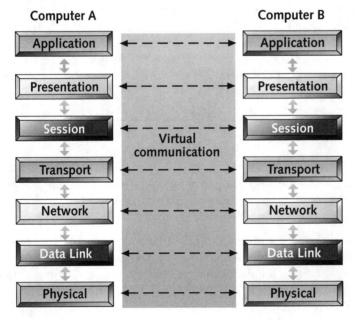

Figure 5-3 Peer communication among OSI layers

5

In reality, communications pass up and down the protocol stacks on both machines. Operations that occur on the way down the stack on the transmitting machine are largely reversed on the way up the stack on the receiving machine, so data on one layer of the sender is nearly identical to data arriving on that layer for the receiver. That's why it seems as though peer layers communicate directly, but at each layer, software provides specialized network functions defined by the set of protocols in use.

On its way down the stack, as data gets passed from one layer to the next, it's divided into data units appropriate for the layer. Each unit of information is called a **protocol data unit (PDU)**, which is passed as a self-contained data structure from one layer to another on its way up or down the protocol stack. In the preceding discussion, it's more accurate to say that an outgoing PDU for the sender at any layer should agree with the incoming version of that PDU on the receiver. At each layer in the stack, the software adds its own formatting or addressing to the PDU to allow successful delivery of its payload across the network. This special formatting or addressing added to the PDU is referred to as a "header," and the process of adding this header is called **encapsulation**. Remember the mail delivery analogy in which the sender must put the letter (data) into an envelope (encapsulation) and address the envelope.

When data arrives at the receiving end, the packet travels up the stack from the Physical layer through the Application layer. At each layer, the software reads its PDU data and performs any additional processing that's required. It then strips its header information from the PDU (a process called **decapsulation**) and passes the PDU to the next higher layer. When the packet leaves the Application layer, the data is in a form that the receiving application can read and has been stripped of all the network addressing and packaging instructions needed to move the data from sender to receiver. Again, using the mail delivery analogy, the decapsulation process is analogous to the letter recipient reading the envelope and verifying the address before opening and discarding the envelope to finally read the letter.

No layer can pass information directly to its counterpart on another computer except for the Physical layer. Therefore, if the Network layer includes addressing information in its PDU components for transmission across the network—that data must pass down through the Data Link and Physical layers on the transmitting computer, across the network medium, and back through the Physical and Data Link layers on the receiving computer before that machine can "read" the address information the sender has supplied.

Simulation 5-1 shows how data generated from an application travels down through the OSI model layers, with encapsulations added where necessary, and how the process is reversed on the receiving computer.

Simulation 5-1: OSI Model, Peer Communications, and Encapsulation

SIMULATION

The following sections describe the layers of the OSI reference model and the services each one provides for its adjacent layers. After reading this material, you should have a good idea of the functions of each layer in the model, how they interact with adjacent layers, and some problems that can occur at each layer.

Application Layer

The **Application layer** (Layer 7) provides a set of interfaces for applications to access networked services, such as networked file transfer, message handling, and database query processing. The Application layer also handles general network access, movement of data from sender to receiver, and error recovery for applications, when applicable. The PDU at this layer (and the Presentation and Session layers) is referred to simply as "data." Generally, components at the Application layer have both a client component and a server component. An example of this client/server pairing is a Web browser (client component) that accesses a Web server (server component), both of which provide access to the Application layer protocol Hypertext Transfer Protocol (HTTP). Another example is Client for Microsoft Networks, which is used to access Windows network services, such as File and Print Sharing, or the UNIX/Linux Network File System (NFS) client, which provides access to NFS server resources. Possible problems at this layer include missing or misconfigured client or server software and incompatible or obsolete commands used to communicate between a client and a server.

Presentation Layer

The **Presentation layer** (Layer 6) handles data-formatting information for network communications. For outgoing messages, it converts data into a generic format that can survive the rigors of network transmission; for incoming messages, it converts data from its generic networked representation into a format that makes sense to the receiving application. The Presentation layer also handles protocol conversion, data encryption or decryption, character set issues, and graphics commands.

In some cases, data managed by the Presentation layer is compressed to reduce the volume of data to be transmitted. (This process requires decompression on the receiving end to restore data to its original form.) A software component known as a **redirector** operates at this layer. The redirector intercepts requests for service from the computer; requests that can't be handled locally are redirected across the network to a networked resource that can handle the request. Software components operating at this layer are usually built into the Application layer component. These components include FTP clients and servers, HTTP clients and servers, and operating-system-specific clients. The Presentation layer deals with the details of data presentation; an example of functionality at this level is a Web browser displaying graphics files embedded in a Web page. In this situation, the Presentation layer component informs the Application layer what type of data or graphics format to display.

Another job of the Presentation layer might involve character conversion. For example, PCs represent the carriage return/line feed combination in text files differently than Linux and UNIX systems do. A text file created on a Linux system looks like one long string of sentences when read by Notepad on a PC if no conversion takes place. However, if the file is transferred from Linux to a PC using a file transfer program that can convert the codes, the Presentation layer component of the file transfer program handles the conversion.

Session Layer

Layer 5, the **Session layer**, permits two parties to hold ongoing communications—called a "session"—across a network, so applications on either end of the session can exchange data for as long as the session lasts. The Session layer handles session setup, data or message exchanges, and teardown when the session ends. It also monitors session identification so that only designated parties can participate and monitors security services to control access to session information (or to permit only authorized parties to establish sessions). Some common network functions this layer handles include name lookup and user logon and logoff. Therefore, Domain Name System (DNS) and NetBIOS name resolution both work in part at this layer, as does the logon and logoff function built into most client software, such as FTP, Client for Microsoft Networks, and NFS.

In keeping with its role of managing ongoing communications over time, the Session layer also provides synchronization services between tasks on both ends of a connection. It can place checkpoints in the data stream so that if communications fail at some point, only data after the most recent checkpoint needs retransmission. The Session layer also manages the mechanics of any ongoing conversation, such as identifying which side can transmit data when and for how long and maintaining a connection by transmitting keep-alive messages that prevent inactivity from shutting down an open connection.

Transport Layer

The **Transport layer** (Layer 4) manages the transfer of data from one application to another across a network. It segments long data streams into chunks that match the maximum packet size for the networking medium, includes error checks to ensure error-free delivery, and handles resequencing chunks into the original data on receipt. The Transport layer also handles **flow control**, which ensures that the recipient of transmitted data isn't overwhelmed with more data than it can handle. The PDU at this layer is called a segment (see Figure 5-4). The components working at this layer include TCP from the TCP/IP protocol suite and SPX from IPX/SPX. Problems that can occur at this layer include a corrupt protocol stack and segments that are too large for the medium between the source and destination networks. This situation forces the Network layer to fragment the segments, which causes performance degradation. Specific Transport layer protocols are discussed more thoroughly in Chapter 6.

Network Layer

Layer 3, the **Network layer**, handles addressing messages for delivery and translates logical network addresses into their physical counterparts, known as Media Access Control (MAC) addresses (discussed in Chapter 4). The Network layer also determines how to route transmissions from sender to receiver, based on factors such as network conditions, Quality of Service (QoS) information, cost of alternate routes, and delivery priorities. This layer is also the traffic cop for network activity and handles routing and access control. **Routing** is the process whereby a device (usually a router) receives a packet destined for another network, determines the best way to get the packet to its destination, and then forwards the

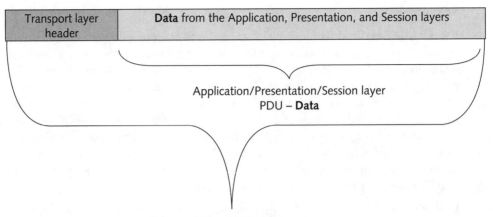

Transport layer PDU – **Segment**

Figure 5-4   The Transport layer PDU: a segment

packet out of one of its other network interfaces. **Access control** is handled at the Network layer during the routing process; the router consults a list of rules before forwarding an incoming packet to determine whether a packet meeting certain criteria (such as source and destination address) should be permitted to reach the intended destination.

NOTE
The Network layer is the first layer discussed so far that addresses the operation of a networking device. Routers and some advanced switches with built-in routing functions operate at this layer.

The PDU at the Network layer is referred to as a packet, as shown in Figure 5-5. The software components working at the Network layer include IP from TCP/IP and IPX from IPX/SPX. Many problems can occur at the Network layer and often include incorrect IP addresses or subnet masks (discussed in Chapter 6), incorrect router configuration, and router operation errors.

Data Link Layer

Layer 2, the **Data Link layer**, sends PDUs from the Network layer to the Physical layer. On the receiving side, the Data Link layer packages raw data from the Physical layer into frames for delivery to the Network layer.

The PDU at the Data Link layer is called a data frame or, more simply, a frame (see "Function of Data Frames in Network Communication" later in this chapter). As shown in Figure 5-6, it consists of both a header and a trailer component. The trailer component labeled as "FCS" (frame check sequence) contains an error-checking value called a **Cyclical Redundancy Check (CRC)**. The CRC value is the result of a mathematical function based on data in the frame and is recalculated on the receiving end. If the recalculated and sent values agree, the assumption is that the data wasn't altered during transmission.

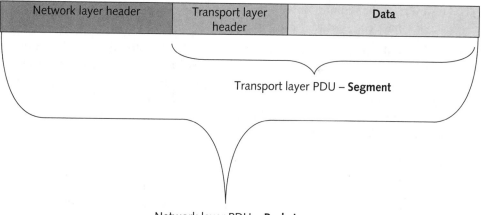

Figure 5-5   The Network layer PDU: a packet

The Data Link header contains fields for source and destination addresses. The destination address is the hardware address of the computer to which the frame should be delivered or of an intermediate device, such as a router; the source address is the hardware address of the sending computer or device and tells the recipient where to send a reply.

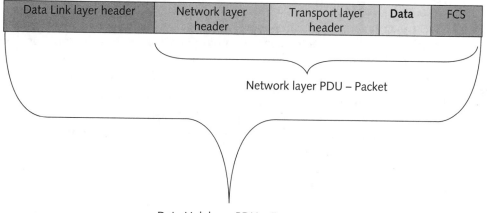

Figure 5-6   The Data Link layer PDU: a frame

The Data Link layer handles delivery of frames from sender to receiver through the Physical layer (and across the network medium). After receiving a frame and verifying the address in the frame header and the CRC, the Data Link layer strips its header and trailer information from the frame and sends the resulting packet up to the Network layer for further processing. In most networking technologies, the Data Link layer is also responsible for detecting errors in frame transmission and discarding frames that arrive containing errors.

However, it's the responsibility of the upper layers (usually the Transport layer) to retransmit data that has been discarded because of errors.

The software component operating at this layer is the NIC driver. The hardware components at this layer include the NIC and switches. Problems occurring in the Data Link layer include collisions and invalid frames, which are often caused by collisions, poor network design, line noise, or NIC driver problems. Another problem that can occur at this layer results from trying to use incompatible network architectures, such as token ring and Ethernet, on the same LAN.

Physical Layer

Layer 1 is the **Physical layer**; its job is to convert bits into signals for outgoing messages and signals into bits for incoming messages. The type of signals generated depend on the medium; for example, wire media, such as twisted-pair cable, use electrical pulses, fiber-optic media use pulses of light, and wireless uses radio waves. At this layer, details for creating a network connection are also specified, such as how the medium attaches to (or communicates with) the NIC. The Physical layer also governs the type of connector used and regulates the transmission technique for sending signals across the network medium.

Ultimately, the Physical layer handles the intricacies of transmitting the pattern of bits representing a frame from the sending to the receiving computer. The Physical layer attempts to guarantee that the pattern of bits translated into signals at the sending end matches the pattern of bits those signals translate into at the receiving end. It specifies how to encode 1s and 0s, the timing and interpretation of signals sent across the medium, and the form those signals must take. **Encoding** is the representation of 0s and 1s as a physical signal, such as electrical voltage or a light pulse. For example, a 1 bit might be represented on a copper wire as a 5-volt signal, whereas a 0 bit might be represented as a signal less than 2 volts.

The network components working at the Physical layer include all the cables and connectors used on the medium plus repeaters and hubs. Problems that occur here are often related to improper media termination, electrical noise that scrambles the signals, and NICs and hubs that are misconfigured or don't work correctly.

Summary of the OSI Layers

The OSI reference model is a helpful way to categorize and compartmentalize networking activities, and most discussions of protocol suites and networking software use its terminology. Table 5-1 summarizes the actions occurring at each layer. Even though most protocol suites don't adhere strictly to this model (perhaps because so many of them were already implemented in some form before the model's development), they still incorporate its outlook on networking.

Although not all networking protocols adhere to the OSI model, a network administrator's clear understanding of the functions at each layer is essential in troubleshooting networks and network equipment and in understanding how network devices operate. Many network devices are described in terms of the OSI model. For example, you might hear the term "Layer 3 switch."

5

Table 5-1   Actions for each layer of the OSI reference model

OSI Layer	Function
Application	Provides programs with access to network services. The PDU is called data.
Presentation	Handles data representation to the application and data conversions, ensures that data is readable by the receiving system, and handles encryption/decryption. The PDU is called data.
Session	Establishes, maintains, and coordinates communication between applications. The PDU is called data.
Transport	Ensures reliable delivery of data, breaks data into segments, handles sequencing and acknowledgements, and provides flow control. The PDU is called a segment.
Network	Handles packet routing, logical addressing, and access control through packet inspection. A router is a Network layer device, and the PDU is called a packet.
Data Link	Provides physical device addressing, device-to-device delivery of frames, media access control, and MAC addresses. NICs and switches are Data Link layer devices, and the PDU is called a frame.
Physical	Manages hardware connections, handles sending and receiving binary signals, and handles encoding of bits; components include network media, connectors, repeaters, and hubs.

No protocol suite developed after the OSI reference model was introduced has been free of its influence. In Chapter 6, you learn how the most popular protocol suites stack up against the OSI model.

The OSI model helps explain how data is formatted and moves from one computer to another. Another network communication concept that must be understood is the data frame, including its structure and how it's created. This concept is explained in the following section.

FUNCTION OF DATA FRAMES IN NETWORK COMMUNICATIONS

Computer communications usually involve transmitting messages that contain a considerable amount of data. Because networks have difficulty handling large chunks of data, network protocols reformat the data into smaller, more manageable pieces called data frames (or simply frames) before sending the data on to the medium. A **frame** is the basic unit for network traffic as it travels across the medium.

NOTE

You often hear the term "packet" used instead of frame, but because this discussion focuses on the unit of data sent on to the medium, the appropriate term is "frame."

Networks split data into small pieces for two reasons. First, large units of data sent across a network hamper effective communications by saturating the network. If a sender and receiver use all the available bandwidth, other computers can't readily communicate. Transmitting smaller chunks of data allows other computers to send data during the slight pause between each chunk other computers are sending. This process can be compared to the conversation stream of a group of people. If one person talks nonstop for minutes on end, nobody else is able to join the conversation. However, if the speaker is polite and pauses occasionally between sentences, other people have an opportunity to speak.

The second reason for breaking large amounts of data into smaller chunks is that networks can sometimes be unreliable. If errors occur during transmission of a large amount of data, all the data must be sent again. If that data is split into many smaller chunks that are subsequently packaged into frames, only those frames in which errors occur need to be sent again. With data split into chunks, communication is faster and more efficient, which allows more computers to use the network. When data frames reach their destination, the receiving computer collects them, strips off the header and trailer information, and reassembles them into the correct order to re-create the original data. If some frames have been lost or were received with errors, the missing data can be sent again without having to resend all the data.

Examining the Structure of a Data Frame

All data frames have three basic parts, shown in Figure 5-7: header, data, and trailer. The **frame header** usually contains the address of the sender (source) and the address of the receiver (destination), information indicating the frame's size or content, an alert signal to indicate data transmission, and clocking information to synchronize the transmission.

The **data section** of a frame (also known as the "payload") consists of the actual data being sent along with the headers of other PDUs in the frame. Although the headers aren't actually part of the data, within the frame, they are considered part of the data section. The size of this section can vary from less than 50 bytes to 16 KB, depending on the network type.

The **frame trailer** contains information to verify the contents' validity. This information usually involves a CRC value. As discussed earlier, the sending computer calculates this value and adds it to the trailer. When the receiving computer gets the frame, it recalculates the CRC independently and compares its calculated value to the CRC value embedded in the trailer. If the two CRCs match, the receiver accepts the frame as undamaged. If the CRCs don't match, the receiving computer discards the frame.

	Frame header			Data		Frame trailer

Figure 5-7   Typical data frame structure

Creating a Data Frame

As data moves through the OSI model, first down through the sender's layers and then up through the receiver's layers, each layer adds or removes its header or trailer information, as shown in Figure 5-8. (Simulation 5-1 showed an animated version of the process.) For example, information added at the Transport layer on the sending computer is read in the Transport layer on the receiving computer.

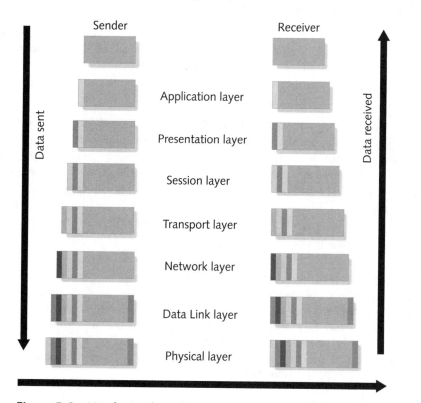

Figure 5-8   Header/trailer information is added or removed as data passes from layer to layer

When an outgoing data stream is passed from the Application layer down to the lower layers, it's a complete message. The Transport layer then splits it into segments. The protocol used by the sending and receiving computers defines that transport segment structure. As the Transport layer splits the data into segments, it includes sequence information that allows the Transport layer on the receiving computer to put those segments back together in the right order. When the segment reaches the Network layer, the Network layer adds its own header information, and the segment becomes a packet. At the Data Link layer, a header and trailer are added, and the packet becomes a frame. When the frame reaches the Physical layer, it includes information from the other six layers, and the frame is transmitted across the medium as bits.

Most protocols, such as TCP/IP, add header information only at the Transport, Network, and Data Link layers.

NOTE

Understanding Types of Data Frames

As mentioned earlier, a frame's header information includes the source and destination addresses. A frame is usually addressed to only one computer and is called a **unicast frame**. Network adapters (NICs) in computers see all frames as they pass through the network on a shared medium. However, adapters read the frames and pass them to higher layers only if the destination address in the frame header matches their own address.

In some cases, special frames called **broadcast frames** are created for all computers on a network. In this case, the frame's destination address is a value of all binary 1s, which indicates that every computer must read and process the frame. Likewise, **multicast frames** are created for any computers on a network that "listen" to a shared network address. This approach works particularly well for traditional broadcast applications on a network, such as video or audio broadcasts, in which a single sender emits data streams to multiple receivers. Again, a special kind of address allows any receiver interested in listening to the broadcast to read these multicast data streams.

The types of frames discussed in this section, unicast, broadcast, and multicast, can also refer to the Network layer PDU (packets). Packets have their own header information containing source and destination addresses that can also be unicast, broadcast, or multicast. The difference is that the packet header contains logical addresses, such as TCP/IP addresses, assigned to the computer manually, whereas the frame header contains the computer's physical address (MAC address) burned into the NIC.

NOTE

UNDERSTANDING THE IEEE 802 NETWORKING SPECIFICATIONS

By the late 1970s, it was clear that local area networks (LANs) would have an important place in business computing environments. Spurred by this realization, the Institute of Electrical and Electronics Engineers (IEEE) defined a set of LAN standards to ensure that network interfaces and cabling from multiple manufacturers would be compatible as long as they adhered to the same IEEE specification. This effort was called **Project 802** to indicate the year (1980) and month (February) of its inception. Since then, the IEEE 802 specifications have taken firm root in the networking world. Because the OSI reference model was not standardized until 1983–1984, the IEEE 802 standards predate the model. Nevertheless, the two were developed in collaboration and are compatible with one another. (The IEEE is one of the U.S. participants in ISO.)

NOTE For more information on the IEEE and its standards, visit *www.ieee.org*.

5

Project 802 concentrates its efforts on standards that describe a network's physical elements, including NICs, cables, connectors, signaling technologies, media access control, and the like. Most of these elements reside in the lower two layers of the OSI model, the Data Link and Physical layers. In particular, the 802 specification describes how NICs can access and transfer data across a variety of networking media and what's involved in attaching, managing, and detaching these devices in a networked environment.

IEEE 802 Specifications

IEEE codified the various efforts undertaken as part of Project 802 in several standards categories numbered 802.1 through 802.20, described in Table 5-2. For the purposes of this book, standards 802.1 through 802.5 are of the most interest, with some attention devoted to 802.11, 802.12, 802.15, and 802.16. These categories, which encompass a large body of standards, are the focus of ongoing development and extension efforts at the IEEE through its working groups.

Table 5-2   IEEE 802 standards

Standard	Name	Explanation
802.1	Internetworking	Covers routing, bridging, and inter-network communications
802.2	Logical Link Control	Covers error control and flow control over data frames
802.3	Ethernet LAN	Covers all forms of Ethernet media and interfaces, from 10 Mbps to 10 Gbps (10 Gigabit Ethernet)
802.4	Token Bus LAN	Covers all forms of token bus media and interfaces
802.5	Token Ring LAN	Covers all forms of token ring media and interfaces
802.6	Metropolitan Area Network	Covers MAN technologies, addressing, and services
802.7	Broadband Technical Advisory Group	Covers broadband networking media, interfaces, and other equipment

Table 5-2 IEEE 802 standards (continued)

Standard	Name	Explanation
802.8	Fiber-Optic Technical Advisory Group	Covers use of fiber-optic media and technologies for various networking types
802.9	Integrated Voice/Data Networks	Covers integration of voice and data traffic over a single network medium
802.10	Network Security	Covers network access controls, encryption, certification, and other security topics
802.11	Wireless Networks	Sets standards for wireless networking for many different broadcast frequencies and techniques
802.12	High-Speed Networking	Covers a variety of 100 Mbps-plus technologies, including 100VG-AnyLAN
802.13		Unused standard number
802.14	Defunct working group	Specifies data transports over cable TV
802.15	Wireless PAN	Covers the standards for wireless personal area networks
802.16	Wireless MAN	Covers wireless metropolitan area networks
802.17	Resilient Packet Ring	Covers emerging standards for very high-speed, ring-based LANs and MANs
802.18	Wireless Advisory Group	A technical advisory group that monitors radio-based wireless standards
802.19	Coexistence Advisory Group	A group that addresses issues of coexistence with current and developing standards
802.20	Mobile Broadband Wireless	A group working to enable always-on multivendor mobile broadband wireless access

IEEE 802 Extensions to the OSI Reference Model

The two lowest layers of the OSI model—the Physical and Data Link layers—define how computers attach to specific network media and specify how more than one computer can access the network without causing interference with other computers on the network. Project 802 took this work further to create the specifications (primarily 802.1 through 802.5) that define the most successful LAN technologies, including Ethernet and token ring, which together dominate the LAN world.

The IEEE 802 specification expanded the OSI reference model at the Physical and Data Link layers. Figure 5-9 shows how the 802 standards provide more detail by separating the Data Link layer into the following sublayers:

- Logical Link Control (LLC) for error recovery and flow control
- Media Access Control (MAC) for access control

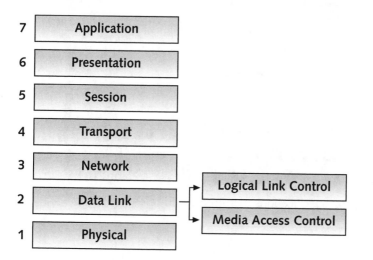

5

Figure 5-9 The IEEE 802 standard divides the OSI Data Link layer into two sublayers

The **Logical Link Control (LLC)** sublayer (defined by 802.2) controls data-link communication and defines the use of logical interface points, called **Service Access Points (SAPs)**, that other computers can use to transfer information from the LLC sublayer to the upper OSI layers. The LLC is also responsible for error recovery in some situations and is the sublayer that communicates with the Network layer. There are several modes of LLC operation; some modes require the LLC to detect and recover from errors in transmission. This function is largely carried out in hardware on the NIC.

The **Media Access Control (MAC)** sublayer manages access to the physical medium and, therefore, communicates with the Physical layer. It communicates directly with a computer's NIC and is responsible for physical addressing. The physical address burned into every NIC is called a MAC address because it operates at this sublayer of the 802.2 specification.

Figure 5-10 shows how the IEEE 802 specifications map to the LLC and MAC sublayers. The MAC sublayer describes various networking architectures or technologies, such as Ethernet, token bus, token ring, and demand priority. These networking technologies are discussed in Chapter 7.

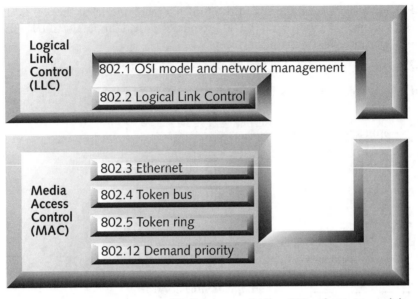

Figure 5-10   IEEE 802.x specifications map to the OSI reference model

CHAPTER SUMMARY

- The OSI reference model and IEEE Project 802 define a frame of reference for networking and specify the lower-layer behaviors for most networks in use today. Together, these models describe the complex processes and operations involved in sending and receiving information across a network.

- The OSI reference model separates networking into seven layers, each with its own purposes and activities. From the bottom up, the layers are Physical, Data Link, Network, Transport, Session, Presentation, and Application. This reference model explains most networks, even those that predate its introduction. Most network products and technologies are also specified in terms of the layers they occupy; the layers help describe the features and functions the products and technologies deliver.

- Data frames consist of three parts: frame header, data section, and frame trailer. They can be classified as unicast, multicast, or broadcast frames.

- The IEEE 802 project elaborates on the functions of a network's Physical and Data Link layers by dividing the Data Link layer into two sublayers: Logical Link Control (LLC) and Media Access Control (MAC). Together, these sublayers handle media access, addressing, and control (through the MAC sublayer) and provide reliable, error-free delivery of data frames from one computer to another.

KEY TERMS

802.2 — The IEEE specification in Project 802 for the Logical Link Control (LLC) sublayer of the OSI model's Data Link layer.

802.3 — The IEEE specification in Project 802 for Carrier Sense Multiple Access/Collision Detection (CSMA/CD) networks (more commonly called "Ethernet"). Ethernet users can attempt to access the medium any time it's perceived as "quiet," but they must back off and try to transmit again if they detect any collisions after transmission begins.

802.5 — The IEEE specification in Project 802 for token ring LANs, which map a circulating ring structure onto a physical star and circulate a token to control access to the medium.

802.11 — The IEEE specification in Project 802 for wireless networks.

802.15 — The IEEE specification that covers emerging standards for wireless personal area networks (PANs).

802.16 — The IEEE specification that covers wireless metropolitan area networks (MANs).

access control — In the context of the Network layer and routing, the process whereby a router consults a list of rules before forwarding an incoming packet. The rules determine whether a packet meeting certain criteria (such as source and destination address) should be permitted to reach the intended destination.

Application layer — Layer 7 in the OSI reference model provides interfaces that enable applications to request and receive network services. *See also* OSI reference model.

broadcast frames — Data frames with destination addresses that specify that all computers on a network must read and process these frames.

Cyclical Redundancy Check (CRC) — A mathematical recipe that generates a specific value, called a checksum, based on a frame's contents. The CRC is calculated before frame transmission and then included with the frame; on receipt, the CRC is recalculated and compared to the sent value. If the two agree, it's assumed that the data frame was delivered intact; if they disagree, the frame must be retransmitted.

Data Link layer — Layer 2 in the OSI reference model is responsible for managing access to the networking medium and ensuring error-free delivery of data frames from sender to receiver. *See also* OSI reference model.

data section — The frame component that's the actual data being sent across a network. The size of this section can vary from less than 50 bytes to 16 KB, depending on the network type.

decapsulation — The process of stripping the header from a PDU as it makes its way up the communication layers before being passed to the next higher layer. *See also* protocol data unit (PDU).

encapsulation — The process of adding header information to a PDU as it makes its way down the communication layers before being passed to the next lower layer. *See also* protocol data unit (PDU).

encoding — The representation of 0s and 1s as a physical signal, such as electrical voltage or a light pulse.

flow control — A process designed to regulate information transfer between a sender and a receiver. Flow control is often necessary when there's a speed differential between sender and receiver.

frame — The basic unit for network traffic as it travels across the medium. Data is broken into these smaller, more manageable pieces for faster, more efficient delivery.

frame header — Information added to the beginning of data being sent, which contains, among other things, addressing and sequencing information.

frame trailer — Information added to the end of the data being sent in a frame; it generally contains error-checking information, such as the CRC.

International Organization for Standardization (ISO) — The international standards-setting body based in Geneva, Switzerland, that sets worldwide technology standards.

layers — The functional subdivisions of the OSI reference model. *See also* OSI reference model.

Logical Link Control (LLC) — The upper sublayer of the IEEE Project 802 model for the Data Link layer of the OSI model. It handles error-free delivery and controls the flow of frames between sender and receiver across a network.

Media Access Control (MAC) — The lower sublayer of the IEEE Project 802 model for the Data Link layer of the OSI model. It handles access to network media and mapping between logical and physical network addresses for NICs.

multicast frames — Frames that use a special destination address so that any computer listening for this address can read and process the frame's data.

Network layer — Layer 3 of the OSI reference model handles addressing and routing PDUs across internetworks in which sender and receiver must traverse multiple networks. *See also* protocol data unit (PDU) *and* OSI reference model.

Open Systems Interconnection (OSI) — The family of ISO standards developed in the 1970s to facilitate functionality of networking services among dissimilar computers on a global scale. The OSI initiative was unsuccessful, owing to a fatal combination of an all-inclusive standards-setting effort and a failure to develop standard protocol interfaces to help developers implement its manifold requirements.

OSI reference model — ISO Standard 7498 defines a frame of reference for understanding networks by dividing the process of network communication into seven layers. Each layer is defined in terms of the services and data it handles on behalf of the layer directly above it and the services and data it needs from the layer directly below it. The OSI reference model remains the OSI initiative's most enduring legacy.

Physical layer — Layer 1, the bottom layer of the OSI reference model, transmits and receives signals and specifies the physical details of cables, adapter cards, connectors, and hardware behavior. *See also* OSI reference model.

Presentation layer — At Layer 6 of the OSI reference model, data can be encrypted and/or compressed to facilitate delivery. Platform-specific application formats are translated into generic data formats for transmission or from generic data formats into platform-specific application formats for delivery to the Application layer. *See also* OSI reference model.

Project 802 — The IEEE effort that produced the collection of 802 networking specifications and standards.

protocol data unit (PDU) — A unit of information passed as a self-contained data structure from one layer to another on its way up or down the network protocol stack.

protocol suite — A family of related protocols in which higher-layer protocols provide application services and request handling facilities, and lower-layer protocols manage the intricacies of Layers 1 to 4 in the OSI reference model.

redirector — A software component that intercepts requests for service from a computer and redirects requests that can't be handled locally across the network to a networked resource that can handle the request.

5

routing — A Network-layer service that determines how to deliver an outgoing packet of data from sender to receiver. Routing entails several methods for managing delivery and requires error and status reporting so that senders can determine whether packets are reaching the receivers.

Service Access Points (SAPs) — Logical interface points used to transfer information from the LLC sublayer to the upper OSI layers. *See also* Logical Link Control (LLC).

Session layer — Layer 5 of the OSI reference model is responsible for setting up, maintaining, and ending ongoing sequences of communications (called sessions) across a network. *See also* OSI reference model.

Transport layer — Layer 4 of the OSI reference model is responsible for fragmenting large PDUs from the Session layer for delivery across the network, inserting integrity controls, and managing delivery mechanisms to allow for error-free reassembly on the receiving end of a network transmission. *See also* OSI reference model *and* protocol data unit (PDU).

unicast frame — A data frame addressed to a single recipient.

REVIEW QUESTIONS

1. The OSI reference model divides networking activity into how many layers?
   a. four
   b. five
   c. seven
   d. eight

2. The addition of information to a PDU as it's passed from one layer to the next is called which of the following?
   a. headlining
   b. encapsulation
   c. decapsulation
   d. converting

3. Layers that act as though they communicate directly with each other across the network are called which of the following?

   a. partners

   b. synchronous

   c. interchangeable

   d. peers

4. Write the corresponding number for each of the following OSI layers (for example, 7 is the top layer, and 1 is the bottom layer).

   a. Presentation

   b. Data Link

   c. Session

   d. Physical

5. The _____ layer handles the creation of frames.

6. Which layer handles flow control, data segmentation, and error recovery?

   a. Application

   b. Physical

   c. Transport

   d. Data Link

7. The _____ layer governs how a NIC must be attached to the network medium.

8. Which layer determines the route a packet takes from sender to receiver?

   a. Application

   b. Physical

   c. Network

   d. Data Link

9. The _____ layer handles converting data from platform-specific application formats to a generic, network-ready representation (and vice versa).

10. Which layer is responsible for setting up, maintaining, and ending ongoing information exchanges across a network?

    a. Application

    b. Presentation

    c. Session

    d. Transport

11. The _____ layer handles segmentation of large amounts of data for transmission and reassembly of segmented data on receipt.

12. Which of the following elements might occur within a frame? (Choose all that apply.)
    a. physical addresses
    b. logical addresses
    c. data
    d. CRC

13. CRC is an acronym for which of the following?
    a. Circular Redundant Checksum
    b. Cyclical Redundancy Check
    c. Convex Recalculation Check
    d. Computed Recursive Count

14. How many times is a CRC calculated?
    a. once before transmission
    b. once after receipt
    c. twice; once before transmission and again on receipt
    d. three times; once before transmission, once on receipt, and a third time during transmission

15. Of the following Project 802 specifications, which belongs at the LLC sublayer?
    a. 802.1
    b. 802.2
    c. 802.3
    d. 802.4
    e. 802.5
    f. 802.12

16. Which layer of the OSI reference model does Project 802 divide into two sublayers?
    a. Physical
    b. Data Link
    c. Network
    d. Session

17. What are the names of the two sublayers specified as part of Project 802? (Choose two answers.)

    a. Data Link Control (DLC)

    b. Logical Link Control (LLC)

    c. Carrier Sense Multiple Access/Collision Detection (CSMA/CD)

    d. Media Access Control (MAC)

18. Which term refers to stripping header information as a PDU is passed from one layer to a higher layer?

    a. decapsulation

    b. encapsulation

    c. PDU stripping

    d. packetization

19. Which IEEE 802 standard applies to Ethernet?

    a. 802.2

    b. 802.3

    c. 802.4

    d. 802.5

    e. 802.11

20. Which IEEE 802 standard applies to token ring?

    a. 802.2

    b. 802.3

    c. 802.4

    d. 802.5

    e. 802.11

21. Which IEEE 802 standard applies to wireless PANs?

    a. 802.3

    b. 802.12

    c. 802.16

    d. 802.15

    e. 802.11

22. Which IEEE 802 standard applies to wireless LANs?

    a. 802.2

    b. 802.3

c. 802.4

d. 802.5

e. 802.11

23. What is the name of the PDU at the Transport layer?

a. bit

b. packet

c. segment

d. data

24. Which of the following definitions best describes a redirector?

a. a software service that handles only network access requests

b. a software service that handles only local resource access requests, determines the correct driver to load, and calls the associated API to complete the request

c. a software service that handles resource requests, passes on local requests for local service, and redirects network access requests to the correct network server or service

d. none of the above

25. Which of the following is an example of software found at the Application layer? (Choose all that apply.)

a. FTP

b. TCP

c. HTTP

d. IPX

26. At which Data Link sublayer does the network address burned into every NIC reside?

a. Media Access Control (MAC)

b. Logical Link Control (LLC)

c. Data Access Control (DAC)

d. Network Access Control (NAC)

27. Which of the following problems can occur at the Physical layer? (Choose all that apply.)

a. NIC driver problems

b. incorrect IP addresses

c. signal errors caused by noise

d. incorrect segment size

HANDS-ON PROJECTS

Unfortunately, you can't do much in the lab to observe the OSI model and IEEE 802 specifications at work. However, the Hands-On Projects in this chapter show you how to take advantage of the standardization of unique IDs programmed into firmware on NICs.

Hands-On Project 5-1

Microsoft includes the Ipconfig command-line utility to display a machine's TCP/IP configuration. In this project, you run this command to produce a listing that includes your computer's MAC address.

1. To open a command prompt window, click **Start**, point to **All Programs**, point to **Accessories**, and click **Command Prompt**.

2. At the command prompt, type **ipconfig /all** and press **Enter**. Your output will look similar to Figure 5-11.

```
Command Prompt
(C) Copyright 1985-2001 Microsoft Corp.

C:\Documents and Settings\Administrator>ipconfig /all

Windows IP Configuration

        Host Name . . . . . . . . . . . . : winxp-01
        Primary Dns Suffix  . . . . . . . :
        Node Type . . . . . . . . . . . . : Hybrid
        IP Routing Enabled. . . . . . . . : No
        WINS Proxy Enabled. . . . . . . . : No

Ethernet adapter Local Area Connection:

        Connection-specific DNS Suffix  . : gtomsho.com
        Description . . . . . . . . . . . : AMD PCNET Family PCI Ethernet Adapter
        Physical Address. . . . . . . . . : 00-0C-29-6A-2A-9C
        Dhcp Enabled. . . . . . . . . . . : No
        IP Address. . . . . . . . . . . . : 172.31.209.23
        Subnet Mask . . . . . . . . . . . : 255.255.0.0
        Default Gateway . . . . . . . . . : 172.31.1.250
        DNS Servers . . . . . . . . . . . : 172.31.209.22

C:\Documents and Settings\Administrator>
```

Figure 5-11   Output of the ipconfig /all command

3. Look for a line beginning with "Physical Address," and then write down the first three sets of numbers in the corresponding value to the right. In Figure 5-11, those numbers are 00-0C-29.

4. Type **exit** and press **Enter** to exit the command prompt window.

Hands-On Project 5-2

This project uses the Linux operating system to obtain your NIC's MAC address.

1. Start Linux and log in as **root**.

2. If you're running the Linux GUI, open a terminal window to get to a command-line prompt. At the prompt, type **ifconfig eth0** and press **Enter**. Eth0 is the name of the first Ethernet card installed on your computer.

3. The first line of the output should be similar to "Link encap: Ethernet HWaddr 00:60:59:32:44:31". The numbers separated by colons after "HWaddr" are your hardware MAC address. Write down the first three numbers for use in the next project:

_____

4. Log out of Linux.

Hands-On Project 5-3

The IEEE operates a Web page for collecting Organizational Unique IDs (OUIs) that it maintains. In this project, you visit that page, and try to locate the NIC manufacturer's OUI. Not all OUIs are made public, but you should be able to find them for most commercially available NICs.

1. Start your Web browser.

2. Type **http://standards.ieee.org/regauth/oui/index.shtml** in the Address text box and press **Enter** to go to the Web page shown in Figure 5-12.

3. Click in the Search for text box, and then type the three sets of numbers you wrote down in Hands-On Project 5-1 or 5-2, including the hyphens. (If you're using the Linux address, replace the colons with hyphens.) Click the **Search!** button.

4. Write down the name of the manufacturer from the search results:

_____

5. Close your Web browser.

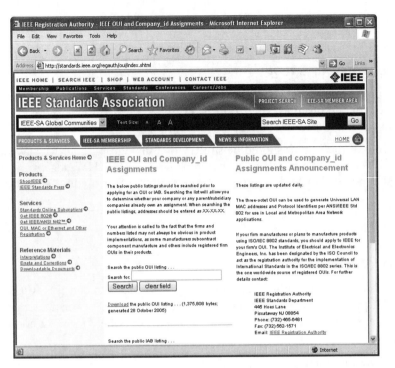

Figure 5-12   The IEEE OUI and Company_id Assignments Web page

CASE PROJECTS

CASE
PROJECTS

Case Project 5-1

As the chapter discusses, the OSI model is a useful tool in troubleshooting a network, allowing you to isolate a problem to a particular software module or piece of hardware. In this project, after reading the description of a problem, you identify the OSI model layer or layers that are most likely involved.

1. A computer won't connect to the network. After some investigation, you find that the patch cable isn't terminated properly.

2. A computer can access resources on the local LAN but not on a different subnet. You find that the computer's default gateway isn't configured correctly.

3. You can ping a computer that you are trying to transfer files to via FTP, but you can't communicate using FTP.

4. All computers connected to a particular hub have lost network connectivity. You determine that the hub is the problem.

   _____

5. You receive an encrypted text file, but when you open it, the text is unreadable. You determine that decryption did not take place as it should have.

   _____

6. You check some statistics generated by a network-monitoring program and discover that an abnormally high number of CRC errors were detected.

   _____

7. One of your servers has been exhibiting sluggish network performance. You use a network-monitoring program to try to evaluate the problem. You find considerable TCP retries occurring because the server is being overwhelmed by data and packets are being discarded.

   _____

8. A user is trying to connect to another computer, but the logon attempt is continually rejected.

   _____

9. You try to access a Linux server to share files using NFS. You can communicate with the server, but the shared files don't appear to be available.

   _____

10. You inspect a computer that isn't able to communicate with other computers. You find that IPX/SPX instead of TCP/IP is installed on that computer.

   _____

Case Project 5-2

You have learned plenty about the OSI model but haven't seen a networking protocol that actually contains components at all seven layers. However, after doing some research at *www.protocols.com*, you discover a protocol with components at each layer—the ISO protocol suite. Research this protocol and make a table showing which ISO components are found at each OSI model layer. You can find details on the ISO protocol at *www.protocols.com/pbook/iso.htm*. (*Hint*: This is an excellent Web site for researching protocols of all types.)

Case Project 5-3

Your instructor might want you to organize in groups for this project. This chapter presented a few real-world examples that use a layered approach to describing a process. See whether you can come up with another process that can be described in layers. You should give a presentation to the class with a detailed description of the layered process you decide on.

Case Project 5-4

You want to transfer a document from one computer to another, and *you want the document to be encrypted*. The destination computer is on another network, so you know *the data will have to travel through one or more routers*. The network technology used on *your network is Ethernet, but the technology on the destination network is token ring*. From what you have learned about networking, should this document transfer work? Why or why not? Which layers of the OSI model are involved in the italicized parts of this description?

Case Project 5-5

The original commercial version of Ethernet supported 10 Mbps bandwidth; a newer version introduced in the early 1990s supports 100 Mbps; in 1998 a 1000 Mbps (1 Gbps) version called Gigabit Ethernet was introduced. All versions use the same data frame formats, with the same maximum PDU sizes, so they can interoperate freely. Furthermore, networks can upgrade from one technology to another by making changes to only the layers in which Ethernet operates. No changes to networking protocol suites or applications are necessary. Given this information, which of the following statements is true? (Choose all that apply.)

    a. Ethernet works at the Data Link and Physical layers of the OSI model, and upgrades to newer and faster versions of Ethernet can be made by changing only the components that work at those layers.

    b. Ethernet spans several layers and requires a completely new protocol stack to upgrade to new versions.

    c. Changes in technology at one layer of the OSI model don't affect the operation of other layers.

    d. Ethernet is not considered a scalable technology.

6

NETWORK COMMUNICATIONS AND PROTOCOLS

After reading this chapter and completing the exercises, you will be able to:

♦ Explain the function of protocols in a network

♦ Describe common protocol suites

For effective communication across a network, computers must be capable of transmitting data completely and safely. To design and troubleshoot a network, you need to understand how this communication takes place. The components involved in this communication are data frames, protocols, and channel access methods. This chapter covers the function of protocols and common protocol suites, and Chapter 7 covers channel access methods.

PROTOCOLS

Strictly speaking, **protocols** are the rules and procedures for communicating. When people travel to other countries, they must be familiar with the proper way to meet, greet, and communicate with the locals. This need to adapt applies to computers as well. For two computers to communicate, they must speak the same language and agree on the rules of communication.

The Function of Protocols

Computers use many protocols today; although every protocol provides basic communications, each one has a different purpose and function. As protocols serve their functions in the OSI model, they might work at one or many layers. The higher the layer at which a protocol operates in the OSI model, the more sophisticated that protocol is.

When a set of protocols works cooperatively, it's called a **protocol stack** or protocol suite. The most common protocol stack is **Transmission Control Protocol/Internet Protocol (TCP/IP)**, the Internet protocol suite. Another protocol suite, IPX/SPX, used in older versions of Novell NetWare, is disappearing as companies upgrade to newer versions of NetWare. Within any protocol stack, the different levels map, or correspond, to their functions in the OSI model. Together, these related collections of protocols constitute a complete communications method.

Connectionless Versus Connection-Oriented Protocols

There are two methods for delivering data across a network: connectionless and connection oriented. Protocols that use **connectionless** delivery place the data on the network and assume it will get through, in much the same way people rely on the U.S. Postal Service to deliver their mail when they drop it in a mailbox. However, much like the Postal Service, delivery is not always guaranteed, so connectionless protocols aren't entirely reliable. However, connectionless protocols are fast because they require little overhead and don't waste time establishing, managing, and tearing down connections. When a connectionless protocol transports data across a network, higher layers handle packet sequencing and sorting, thereby allowing faster communication.

Connection-oriented protocols are more reliable and, consequently, slower. When a connection-oriented protocol is used, two computers establish a connection before data transfer begins. With the connection established, the data is sent in an orderly fashion. As each packet or group of packets reaches the destination, its receipt is acknowledged. This type of communication can be compared with using certified delivery for a U.S. Postal Service letter. When the package or letter is received, it's signed for and acknowledgement of that receipt is returned to the sender. If errors occur during transmission, the packet is sent again. After the communication is completed, the connection terminates. This procedure ensures that all data is received and is accurate or that suitable error messages are generated when successful communications don't occur within a reasonable time. With these assurances, upper-layer protocols can rely on connection-oriented delivery to handle matters of sequencing, data integrity, and delivery timeouts. On the Internet and most LANs, connection-oriented protocols are used for the majority of data transfers.

Routable Versus Nonroutable Protocols

As mentioned in Chapter 5, the Network layer of the OSI model is responsible for moving data across multiple networks. Devices called routers are responsible for this process, called routing. However, not all protocol suites operate at the Network layer. Protocol suites that do function at the Network layer are called **routable** or routed protocols, whereas protocol suites that don't are called **nonroutable**. Because routing operates at the Network layer, the routable/nonroutable attribute applies primarily to protocols that operate this layer.

A protocol suite's capability to be routed (or not) has a major impact on its effectiveness in any network that requires a router's services, such as internetworks, MANs, and WANs. TCP/IP and IPX/SPX are routable protocols well suited for these types of networks. An older and nearly obsolete protocol, NetBEUI, is a nonroutable protocol that works well in small networks, but its performance drops considerably as a network grows. When choosing the protocol suite for your network, consider the network's current size and possibilities for future expansion.

Protocols in a Layered Architecture

Most protocols can be explained or positioned in terms of the OSI model's layers, even though they might not map exactly to that model layer for layer. Because each protocol performs a specific function and has its own rules, a protocol stack often has a different protocol for each layer. Figure 6-1 recaps the functions of each layer of the OSI model. Figure 6-2 shows how the tasks required for network communication combine to form three major protocol types—application, transport, and network.

Network Protocols

Network protocols provide addressing and routing information, error checking, retransmission requests, and rules for communicating in a networking environment. These services are called link services. Some popular network protocols, discussed in detail later in this chapter, include:

- *Internet Protocol version 4 (IPv4)*—This TCP/IP network protocol provides addressing and routing information. Frequently, it's referred to simply as IP, but as you'll see, a new version of IP called IPv6 is beginning to take hold and is covered later in this chapter.

- *Internetwork Packet Exchange (IPX)*—Novell's protocol for packet routing and forwarding. In the IPX/SPX protocol suite, IPX serves many of the same functions as IP in the TCP/IP suite.

- *Internet Protocol version 6 (IPv6)*—A new version of Internet Protocol that's being implemented on many current networking devices and operating systems. This new version addresses some weaknesses of IPv4.

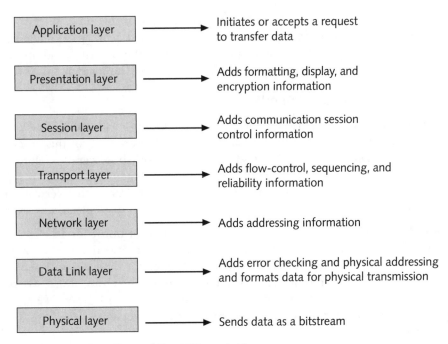

Figure 6-1   Functions of the OSI model layers

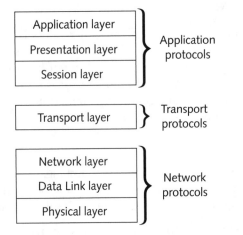

Figure 6-2   Three main protocol types

Transport Protocols

Transport protocols handle data delivery between computers. Recall that connection-oriented transport protocols ensure reliable delivery, whereas connectionless transport protocols provide only best-effort delivery. These are some of the most widely used transport protocols:

- *Transmission Control Protocol (TCP)*—The TCP/IP protocol responsible for reliable delivery of data.

- *Sequential Packet Exchange (SPX)*—Novell's connection-oriented protocol used to guarantee data delivery.

- *NetBIOS/NetBEUI*—NetBIOS establishes and manages communications between computers and provides naming services; NetBEUI provides data transport services for these communications.

NOTE

NetBIOS also runs over TCP/IP and IPX/SPX, so using NetBIOS doesn't require using NetBEUI.

Application Protocols

Application protocols operate at the upper layers of the OSI model and provide services to client applications, such as Web browsers and e-mail programs, and to server applications, such as Web and e-mail servers. Some of the more prevalent application protocols include the following:

- *Simple Mail Transport Protocol (SMTP)*—A member of the TCP/IP protocol suite responsible for transferring e-mail

- *File Transfer Protocol (FTP)*—Another member of the TCP/IP protocol suite used to provide file transfer services

- ***Simple Network Management Protocol (SNMP)***—The TCP/IP protocol used to manage and monitor network devices

- ***NetWare Core Protocol (NCP)***—Novell's client shells and redirectors

- ***AppleTalk File Protocol (AFP)***—Apple's remote file-management protocol

COMMON PROTOCOL SUITES

Because most protocols contain a combination of components to make communications work correctly, these components are usually bundled as a protocol suite. Many protocols are available for communication, and each has its own strengths and weaknesses. These are the most common protocol suites:

- TCP/IP
- IPX/SPX
- NetBIOS/NetBEUI
- AppleTalk

Each protocol suite has had an important role to play in the history of networking but only one dominates the networking arena to the point of making most of the other suites nearly obsolete. That protocol suite is TCP/IP.

Transmission Control Protocol/Internet Protocol (TCP/IP)

The TCP/IP suite is the most commonly used protocol suite in the networking world. TCP/IP enables easy communications across platforms and provides the basis for the global Internet. For that reason, it's discussed in more detail than the other suites.

NOTE

This section discusses the most prevalent version of IP, which is IPv4. IPv6 is discussed separately in the section "Internet Protocol Version 6 (IPv6)."

Internet development began in 1969 as part of the U.S. Department of Defense's Advanced Research Projects Agency (ARPA, which later became DARPA) to provide internetwork communications. TCP/IP gained popularity when UNIX adopted it as the protocol for its systems. TCP/IP's scalability and superior functionality over WANs made it the standard for connecting different types of computers and networks. Because of its wide acceptance, TCP/IP is the default protocol in Novell NetWare (starting with version 5.0); Windows Vista, XP, and Server 2000/2003; all UNIX/Linux variations; and even Mac OS X. On (usually older) operating systems in which TCP/IP is not the default, it's usually available as an option. Although the TCP/IP suite predates the OSI model by nearly a decade, its protocols and functions are quite similar. Figure 6-3 shows TCP/IP's relation to the OSI model.

More than any other protocol suite, TCP/IP uses highly compartmentalized and specialized protocols. The following sections discuss some of the many constituent protocols of TCP/IP. Then you see how some of these protocols work together during a typical communication session.

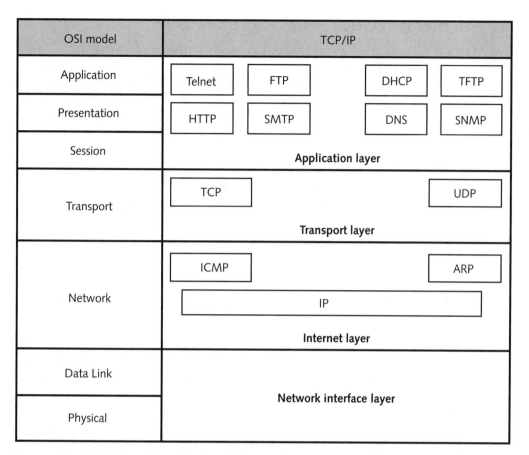

Figure 6-3 TCP/IP compared to the OSI model

TCP/IP Network Layer Protocols

Internet Protocol version 4 (IPv4), or just IP, is a Network layer protocol that provides source and destination addressing and routing for the TCP/IP suite. IP is a connectionless protocol, so it's fast but unreliable. Note that unreliable doesn't mean it fails often. Unreliable in this sense simply means that IP has no method for ensuring that data is delivered to the destination. IP assumes that the Transport or Application layer will provide reliable data delivery in applications that require it.

Internet Control Message Protocol (ICMP) is a Network layer protocol used to send error and control messages between systems or devices. The Ping utility uses ICMP to request a response from a remote host to verify whether it's available for communication. The response, if received, indicates not only that the remote host is reachable but also how long it took for the message to make the round trip from sender to receiver. To see how Ping works with ICMP, take a look at Simulation 6-1.

Simulation 6-1: How PING Works Using ICMP

Address Resolution Protocol (ARP) is another Network layer protocol used to resolve a logical (IP) address to a physical (MAC) address. When a system begins a conversation with a host for which it lacks a MAC address, it sends an ARP broadcast frame requesting the MAC address that corresponds to the host's IP address. When a computer is assigned the specified IP address, it responds with an ARP reply containing its MAC address. Then the Data Link layer can send the frame correctly through the network.

> **NOTE** Communication using ARP can occur only between two systems on the same network; holding a conversation with a host that must be reached through a router requires sending the frame to the router, which forwards it to its final destination.

IP, ICMP, and ARP in Action

Now that you have a basic description of the Network layer protocols—IP, ICMP, and ARP—you can see these protocols work together to accomplish communication between two computers. Take a look at the sample network in Figure 6-4. Before computer A can send a message to computer B, computer A must have two addresses: computer B's IP address and MAC address. The MAC address is necessary because when a computer receives a frame, the NIC checks the destination MAC address in the frame header and verifies it against the MAC address burned into the NIC. If they match, the NIC driver reads the frame, the frame header is removed, and the packet is passed from the Data Link layer up to the Network layer for further processing. At the Network layer, another check is made. The Network layer verifies that the IP address in the packet header's destination field matches the IP address assigned to the computer. If they match, the packet header is removed, and processing of the packet continues.

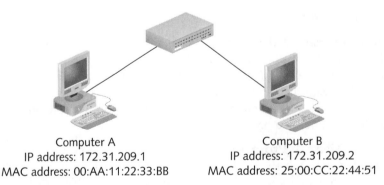

Computer A
IP address: 172.31.209.1
MAC address: 00:AA:11:22:33:BB

Computer B
IP address: 172.31.209.2
MAC address: 25:00:CC:22:44:51

Figure 6-4 A sample computer network

To better understand the need for two addresses, go back to the mail analogy used in Chapter 5. The street address of your home doesn't change, and it's the address the post office uses to deliver your mail. The street address can be compared to the MAC address. However, the name of the person living in that house can change, and the name to whom mail is addressed can be compared to the IP address. Typically, both "addresses" (the street address and the name of the person for whom the mail is intended) are used when addressing an envelope or letter. Mail reaches your home because the street address on the envelope matches your home's street address (MAC address), but when that mail is picked up at the home's mailbox (sent from the Data Link layer to the Network Layer), the name on the envelope (IP address) is verified by the homeowner (Network layer) before it's opened. So just like mail delivery, data delivery in an IP network uses two addresses: one address that stays the same (MAC address) and one that can change fairly easily (IP address). If you have ever moved into a house that had a previous owner, you know it's quite possible to get a letter at your house that wasn't intended for you.

If you want to send mail to another person, often you have that person's name, but you might not have the street address (unless you have written it down in an address book). To solve this problem, typically you look up the address in a phone book. Addressing messages in a network is similar. Often you have the IP address (or name) of the computer you want to send a message to, but you don't have its MAC address. Because there's no phone book mapping IP addresses to MAC addresses, IP networks use another method, which is where ARP comes in. Again, referring to Figure 6-4, if computer A wants to Ping computer B, a command such as Ping 172.31.209.2 is entered at the command line. To finish addressing the frame, the Network layer needs the MAC address that belongs to IP address 172.31. 209.2. To get that address, the Network layer on computer A sends out an ARP broadcast message requesting that the computer with IP address 172.31.209.2 respond with its MAC address. When computer B receives the ARP request, it responds by sending a frame containing its MAC address back to computer A. The frame can then be addressed with both a destination IP address and MAC address. Simulation 6-2 helps you visualize this process. Figure 6-5 shows you the progression of building a frame, from an ICMP message to an IP packet to a data frame. Note that although the example described here uses an ICMP message, the process is much the same for any type of IP message.

Simulation 6-2: How ARP Works

TCP/IP Transport Layer Protocols

Transmission Control Protocol (TCP) is the primary Internet transport protocol. It accepts messages of any length from an upper-layer protocol and provides transportation to a TCP peer on another network station. TCP is connection oriented, so it provides more reliable delivery than IP alone. TCP establishes a connection by using a process called a three-way handshake, whereby the computer initiating a conversation sends a special packet to the intended destination indicating its desire to create a connection with a certain network service on the destination computer. The destination computer responds with a positive acknowledgement if the requested service is available. The initiator then sends its own acknowledgement, and a connection is established. When a connection is established, a TCP port address determines for which connection a packet is destined. TCP is

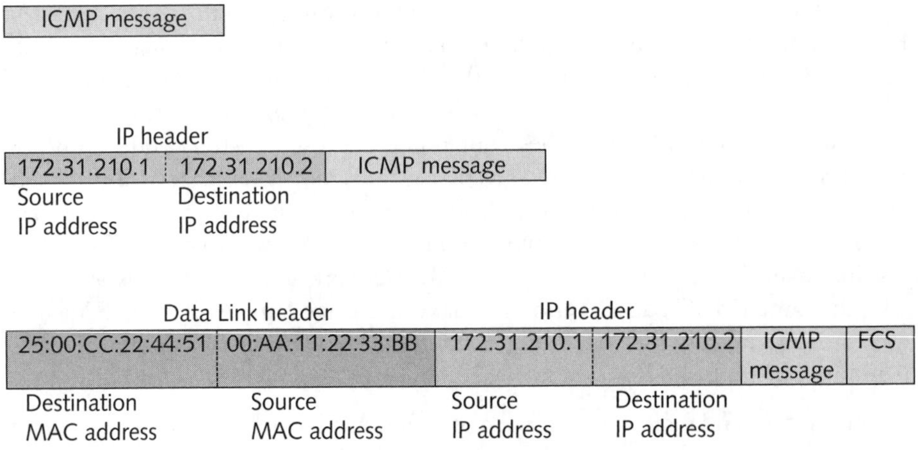

ICMP message

IP header
| 172.31.210.1 | 172.31.210.2 | ICMP message |
| Source IP address | Destination IP address | |

Data Link header   IP header
| 25:00:CC:22:44:51 | 00:AA:11:22:33:BB | 172.31.210.1 | 172.31.210.2 | ICMP message | FCS |
| Destination MAC address | Source MAC address | Source IP address | Destination IP address | | |

Figure 6-5   From ICMP message to data frame

responsible for message fragmentation and reassembly. It fragments large messages into segments and uses a sequencing function to ensure that received segments are reassembled in the correct order. In addition, TCP uses acknowledgements to ensure that all data was received and to provide flow control. Note that TCP is a Transport layer protocol and relies on IP to handle message addressing and routing; IP, in turn, relies on the Data Link layer for physical addressing and preparing the message to be sent to the physical medium. Most Application layer TCP/IP services (such as FTP, Telnet, and HTTP) use TCP as their transport protocol.

User Datagram Protocol (UDP) is a connectionless Transport layer protocol. Its reduced overhead makes it generally faster, although less reliable, than TCP. Because it's connection-less, there is no initial three-way handshake to start a communication session. In addition, UDP doesn't provide a way to break large chunks of data into smaller chunks or to resequence packets that arrive out of order. Also, UDP doesn't use acknowledgements to ensure that all the data arrived; it relies on the application to detect whether data is missing or arrives out of order. The usual remedy for missing data or data that arrives out of order is for the application to resend the entire file or message. Only a few higher-level layer TCP/IP services use UDP as their transport protocol, such as Network File System (NFS) and Domain Name System (DNS).

TCP/IP Application Layer Protocols

Domain Name System (DNS) is a name-to-address resolution protocol that functionally operates at the Session layer of the OSI model. In the TCP/IP model, however, the Application layer encompasses the Session layer, so DNS is referred to as an Application layer protocol in the TCP/IP model. A DNS server keeps a list of systems' names and their associated IP addresses. Through a correctly configured workstation, a user can use a remote system's logical name—for instance, microsoft.com rather than a numerical address, such as 207.46.134.189—to communicate with that remote system. For example, when you type www.course.com into your Web browser's address box, the Web browser contacts the DNS function on your computer. The DNS function contacts the DNS server specified in your IP configuration requesting that www.course.com be resolved to an IP address. The DNS server responds with the IP address assigned to the computer named www at the course. com domain. From there, using the IP address returned, your Web browser application can contact the Web server to request a Web page.

Hypertext Transport Protocol (HTTP) is used to transfer Web pages from a Web server to a Web browser. The acronym HTTP should be familiar to anyone who uses a Web browser; it's part of the URL used to specify a Web page.

File Transfer Protocol (FTP) provides services for file transfer as well as directory and file manipulation functions. It also provides a method for logging on to an FTP server, which is functionally a Session layer service. FTP can also handle data translation (for example, converting Windows text files to Linux text files, and vice versa), which is a Presentation layer function.

Telnet is a remote terminal emulation protocol that operates at all three upper layers (Session, Presentation, and Application) and is used mostly to provide connectivity between dissimilar systems (for example, a PC connection to a router for configuration and monitoring purposes). Through Telnet, remote equipment (such as routers and switches) can be monitored and configured and remote systems can be managed.

Simple Mail Transport Protocol (SMTP) is another protocol that operates at all three upper layers. As its name implies, SMTP provides messaging services to the TCP/IP suite and is the basis for most e-mail that travels across the Internet.

A number of other protocols are part of the TCP/IP protocol suite. A category of specialized protocols, called routing protocols, work at the Network layer. Many of these specialized routing protocols are discussed in Chapter 13, but a key part of the Network layer is IP addressing. No network administrator can truly be called an expert on TCP/IP unless he or she fully understands the ins and outs of IP addressing, discussed in the next section.

IP Addressing

As you learned earlier, IP is responsible for addressing and routing in the TCP/IP environment. IP addresses are logical addresses that are 32 bits (4 bytes) long. Each byte of the address is represented as a decimal number from 0 to 255, and these decimal numbers are called octets. An **octet** ("oct" means eight) is a grouping of eight binary digits or bits usually expressed as a decimal number. The four decimal numbers are separated by periods in a notation referred to as **dotted decimal**. For example, 172.24.208.192 is a dotted decimal IP address.

An IP address is divided into two distinct parts. One part of the IP address assigned to a computer designates which logical network the computer is a part of; the remainder of the address represents the host ID for that computer on that particular network. For example, a computer with the address 172.24.208.192 resides on the 172.24 network with a host ID of

208.192. In this case, the complete network address is 172.24.0.0, with the trailing zeros indicating a network address. The computer next to it might have the address 172.24.18.26; both computers are on the same network because they share the same network address (172.24), even though their host IDs are quite different.

IP addresses are categorized into ranges referred to as Classes A, B, C, D, or E. Only IP addresses in the A, B, and C classes are available for assigning an address to a host. Although the IP address class system has been somewhat superseded by a more flexible way to manage IP addresses, called Classless Interdomain Routing (CIDR, discussed later in this chapter), the class system provides a basis for determining which part of an IP address is the network designator and which part is the host ID. The first octet of an address denotes its class. Note the following facts about IP address classes:

- Class A addresses are intended for use by large corporations and governments. An IP address registry assigns the first octet, leaving the last three octets for network administrators to assign to hosts. This allows for 16,777,214 hosts per network address. The value of the first octet for Class A addresses is between 1 and 126.

- Class B addresses begin with network IDs between 128 and 191 and are intended for use in medium-size networks. An IP address registry assigns the first two octets, leaving the third and fourth octets available for administrators to assign as host addresses. Having two octets in the host ID allows for 65,534 hosts per network address.

- Class C addresses are intended for small networks. An IP address registry assigns the first three octets, ranging from 192 to 223. These networks are limited to 254 hosts per network.

- Class D addresses are reserved for multicasting, in which a packet is addressed so that more than one destination can receive it. Applications that use this feature include videoconferencing and streaming media. In a Class D address, the first octet is in the range 224 to 239. Class D addresses can't be used to assign IP addresses to host computers.

- Class E addresses have a first-octet value in the range 240 to 255. This range of addresses is reserved for experimental use and cannot be used for address assignment.

Notice that a few addresses are missing. These addresses are used for special services. For example, the network beginning with 127 is called the **loopback address**. The loopback address always refers to the local computer and is used to test the functionality of TCP/IP. A packet sent to any host address starting with 127 is sent to the local device without reaching the media. Likewise, the reserved name **localhost** always corresponds to the IP address 127.0.0.1 so that a local machine can always be referenced using this name.

Because of the popularity of TCP/IP and the Internet, IP addresses are rapidly becoming scarce. To help alleviate this problem, TCP/IP's technical governing body reserved a series of addresses for private networks—that is, networks that don't have hosts that are accessible directly on the Internet. This governing body, the Internet Engineering Task Force (IETF), is public, nonprofit, and responsible for TCP/IP standards and characteristics. The reserved addresses are as follows:

- Class A addresses beginning with 10 (one Class A network address)
- Class B addresses from 172.16 to 172.31 (16 Class B network addresses)
- Class C addresses from 192.168.0 to 192.168.255 (256 Class C network addresses)

The addresses in these ranges can't be routed across the Internet, which is why any organization can use them to assign IP addresses to their internal hosts. If access to the Internet is necessary, a process called Network Address Translation (NAT) is used, as explained later in this chapter.

IPv6 eliminates the need for private addressing because it provides a 128-bit address space compared to IPv4's mere 32 bits. More information on IPv6 is provided later in this chapter in "Internet Protocol Version 6 (IPv6)."

NOTE A number of public and private companies around the world, known as IP address registries, cooperatively manage the total collection of valid IP addresses. This activity occurs under the control of the Internet Assigned Numbers Authority (IANA), a public nonprofit agency responsible for Internet addressing and address management.

Classless Interdomain Routing (CIDR)

As mentioned earlier, addressing by class has been superseded by a more flexible addressing method. To use all available addresses more efficiently, the Internet now uses a different addressing scheme called **Classless Interdomain Routing (CIDR)**. With this scheme, when an address is assigned, the network and host demarcation isn't always made on octet boundaries according to the IP address class; instead, it can be made with any specific number of bits from the beginning of the address.

For example, a Class C address's network section is 24 bits. Using CIDR, an address registry can assign an address with a network section of 26 bits. Because this technique involves "borrowing" bits from the host portion of the address to create two or more network numbers, it's called **subnetting**. Subnetting is the process of dividing a single network address into two or more subnetwork addresses, each with fewer available host IDs than the original network address. Subnetting provides fewer hosts on each network but uses more networks overall.

When CIDR addresses are assigned, a slash denotes the number of bits in the network section. For example, if your company requires only 30 host addresses to assign to computers that will be attached to the Internet, your ISP might give you a network address of 192.203.187.0/27. The slash is referred to as CIDR notation. In a 32-bit IP address, the /27 means that the first 27 bits of the IP address designate the network number, and the last 5 bits designate the host ID. This example results in host IP addresses in the range 192.203.187.1 through 192.203.187.30. How you arrive at this range is discussed in more detail in upcoming sections.

Why Subnet?

An IP network or subnetwork can be defined as a group of computers and devices that share the same network portion of their assigned IP address and don't have to go through a router to communicate with one another. Another term for an IP network is broadcast domain, explained later in this section. Dividing IP networks into smaller subnetworks is done for a number of reasons:

- Subnetting usually makes more efficient use of the available IP addresses. For example, in the older class-based system of determining the network number and host ID, the smallest network, using a Class C address, consisted of 254 hosts. If an organization requires only 30 host addresses, it can be assigned a portion of a Class C address, leaving most of the remaining addresses available for assignment on other networks.

- Subnetting allows a company to divide its network into logical groups. When one large network is divided into two or more smaller subnetworks, a router is needed to allow hosts on one subnetwork to communicate with hosts on another subnetwork. A router provides a natural security barrier between the two subnetworks because access control lists can be configured on a router to restrict the type of network traffic traveling from one subnet to another. Being able to restrict access enables network administrators to, for example, place the Payroll Department computers and servers on their own subnet and disallow computers from other subnets to access any resources in the Payroll Department.

- Subnetting can make network communication more efficient. For example, suppose you're in a large room containing 100 people with varying interests. Rules of communication have been set up so that when one person speaks, all others must listen and, if appropriate, respond. You might grow frustrated after a time because you might not be interested in what some people have to say, and, if you do find a common interest with others, you would have to shout out your conversation for all others to hear. This form of communication would prove quite inefficient. A better arrangement is for all people of a common interest to be grouped together so that they could talk among themselves, with no interference from other groups. Ten groups of 10 people, for example, would result in a far better experience. If a person from one group had to periodically communicate with someone from another group, that could be arranged by using some type of message-passing system. This segmenting of the communication process is the idea behind subnetting.

Recall that not all network frames are addressed to a single destination. Broadcast frames specify a destination address consisting of all binary 1s. When a broadcast frame is sent to the network, all computers on the same IP network that the frame reaches are required to process the message in the frame. Hubs and switches forward all broadcast frames to each network cable segment to which they have a connection. However, when a broadcast frame reaches a router, a router doesn't forward the frame onto other subnets, thereby keeping other subnets from having to process the broadcast frame. The extent to which a broadcast frame is forwarded from device to device without going through a router is called a **broadcast domain**.

The fact that broadcasts aren't forwarded by routers becomes important in large networks and networks connected to the Internet. Imagine if you use a Class B network to assign an IP address to 10,000 computers in a network with no routers. Every broadcast that a computer sends on the network would be forwarded to all 10,000 computers. Broadcast messages are a common type of message in networking. You have already seen one example of broadcasts used with ARP. Broadcasts are also used for other protocols, such as DHCP (explained later in this chapter). The number of broadcasts generated (and, therefore, processed) by these 10,000 computers would make network communication exceedingly inefficient. However, if you subnet the network into 50 smaller networks of 200 computers each, with each subnet separated by a router, broadcast traffic is generated and processed only by the 200 computers in each subnet.

Subnet Masks

As already mentioned, an IP address consists of two sections: one that defines on which network a computer is located, and one that defines the host ID for a computer. IP uses an address's **subnet mask** to determine which part of the address denotes the network portion and which part denotes the host. The subnet mask is a 32-bit number that's always assigned to a host when the IP address is assigned. In a subnet mask, a binary 1 signifies that the corresponding bit in the IP address belongs to the network portion, and a binary 0 signifies that the corresponding bit in the IP address belongs to the host portion.

Each of the three main address classes has a default subnet mask that uses the decimal number 255 for each octet in the address that corresponds to the network portion of the IP address. (The number 255 is 11111111 in binary and fills all 8-bit positions in an IP address octet.) Therefore, the default Class A subnet mask is 255.0.0.0, the default Class B subnet mask is 255.255.0.0, and the default Class C subnet mask is 255.255.255.0.

For example, if a computer has an IP address of 153.92.100.10 and a subnet mask of 255.255.0.0 (a Class B mask), the network portion of the address is 153.92 and the host portion is 100.10. However, if the computer uses the address 192.92.100.10 and the subnet mask is 255.255.255.0 (a Class C mask), the network portion is 192.92.100 and the host portion is 10.

NOTE

All devices on a single logical network (where each device can communicate with another device without going through a router; sometimes called a network segment) must share the same network address and, therefore, must also use the same subnet mask.

Some Simple Binary Arithmetic

Working with IP addresses, especially for subnetting and supernetting (covered later in this section), is a lot easier if you understand the basics of binary arithmetic. For the purposes of this book, you need to master four kinds of binary calculations:

- Converting between binary and decimal
- Converting between decimal and binary
- Understanding how setting high-order bits (the leftmost bits in a binary string or the most significant bits) to the value of 1 in 8-bit binary numbers corresponds to specific decimal numbers
- Recognizing the decimal values for numbers that correspond to low-order bits when they're set to the value of 1

Before you tackle these calculations, you need to be sure you understand how the decimal number system works. The decimal number system is based on 10s (which is where the word "decimal" comes from, with dec meaning "ten"). Ten different symbols, 0 through 9, are used to represent any possible number. Each place in a decimal number can have one of ten different possible values, again 0 through 9. Furthermore, each place in a decimal number can be expressed as a power of 10. The ones place can be expressed as a number, 0 thru 9, multiplied by 10 raised to the 0 power, or 10^0 (any number raised to the 0 power equals 1). The tens place can be expressed as a number multiplied by 10 to the 1 power, or 10^1. The hundreds place can be expressed as a number times 10^2, and so on. For example, the number 249 can be expressed as either of the following:

```
2 * 10² + 4 * 10¹ + 9 * 10⁰
2 * 100 + 4 * 10 + 9 * 1
```

When you see the number 249, you don't think of it in those terms because you grew up using the decimal number system, and the recognition of the hundreds place, tens place, and ones place happens without conscious effort, as does the multiplication and addition that occurs. However, take a look at this number:

```
379420841645
```

A little more thought has to go into recognizing that the 3 represents 300 billion, the 7 represents 70 billion, and so forth. The binary number system works the same way, except everything is governed by twos. Two digits, 0 and 1, represent every possible number, and each place in a binary number is either 0 or 1 multiplied times a power of 2. So instead of having the ones place, the tens place, the hundreds place, and so on, you have the ones place, the twos place, the fours place, and so on, based on $2^0, 2^1, 2^2$, and so forth. For example, using the same method you used to solve the decimal example, you can express the binary number 101 as either of the following:

```
1 * 2² + 0 * 2¹ + 1 * 2⁰
1 * 4 + 0 * 2 + 1 * 1 = 5
```

Converting Decimal to Binary: The preceding calculation is easy, if you don't mind thinking mathematically. If you find this approach too challenging, try a different method, which has the advantage of working for any number. With this method, you divide the decimal number by 2, write down the remainder (which must be 0 or 1), write down the dividend, and repeat until the dividend is 0.

The decimal number 125 is converted to binary in the following example:

125 divided by 2 equals 62, remainder 1

62 divided by 2 equals 31, remainder 0

31 divided by 2 equals 15, remainder 1

15 divided by 2 equals 7, remainder 1

7 divided by 2 equals 3, remainder 1

3 divided by 2 equals 1, remainder 1

1 divided by 2 equals 0, remainder 1

To produce the binary number corresponding to 125, you must then write the digits starting from the bottom of the remainder column and work your way up: 1111101. Now check the work involved. Because you have only 7 binary digits and want to have 8 total, you pad with zeros on the left, leaving you with 01111101. The exponential expansion of 01111101 is $0*2^7 + 1*2^6 + 1*2^5 + 1*2^4 + 1*2^3 + 1*2^2 + 0*2^1 + 1*2^0$.

Another way to convert from decimal to binary is shown in Table 6-1. The first two rows are the binary and exponent values of each bit position of an 8-bit number. You use 8 bits because in subnetting, the majority of work can be done 8 bits at time. The third row is what you complete to determine the decimal number's binary representation.

Table 6-1 Decimal-to-binary conversion table

128	64	32	16	8	4	2	1
2^7	2^6	2^5	2^4	2^3	2^2	2^1	2^0
0	1	1	1	1	1	0	1

This approach is sometimes referred to as a step function. You start with the number you're trying to convert to binary, in this case 125, which is referred to as the test number. You compare the test number to the leftmost number in the preceding table (128). If it's equal to or greater than that number, you place a 1 in the column and subtract the number in the column from your test number; otherwise, place a 0 in the column. Remember: 8 binary places or 8 bits can represent only a value up to 255. If you're converting a number greater than 255, simply extend the table to the left until the leftmost column has a value greater than or equal to the test number (256, 512, and so on). Here is the sequence of steps:

1. 125 is less than 128, so you place a **0** in the column under the 128.

2. 125 is greater than 64, so you place a **1** in the column under the 64 and subtract 64 from 125, leaving your new test number as 61.

3. 61 is greater than 32, so you place a **1** in the column under the 32 and subtract 32 from 61, leaving your new test number as 29.

4. 29 is greater than 16, so you place a **1** in the column under the 16 and subtract 16 from 29, leaving your new test number as 13.

5. 13 is greater than 8, so you place a **1** in the column under the 8 and subtract 8 from 13, leaving your new test number as 5.

6. 5 is greater than 4, so you place a **1** in the column under the 4 and subtract 4 from 5, leaving your new test number as 1.

7. 1 is less than 2, so you place a **0** in the column under the 2.

8. 1 is equal to 1, so you place a **1** in the column under the 1 and subtract 1 from 1, leaving your new test number as 0. When your test number is 0, you're done.

Now try this with 199, 221, and 24. You should get the following results:

```
199 = 11000111
221 = 11011101
24  = 00011000
```

Converting Binary to Decimal: Using 11010011 as the example, here are the steps:

1. Count the total number of digits in the number (11010011 has eight digits).

2. Subtract one from the total (8 - 1 = 7).

3. That number (7) is the power of 2 to associate with the highest exponent for two in the number.

4. Convert to exponential notation, using all the digits as multipliers.

5. 11010011, therefore, converts to:

$$11010011 = 1*2^7+1*2^6+0*2^5+1*2^4+0*2^3+0*2^2+1*2^1+1*2^0$$
$$= 128+64+0+16+0+0+2+1 = 211$$

Another way to do this is to use the same Table 6-1 you used for the decimal-to-binary conversion. Of course, if your binary number is more than 8 bits, you can simply extend the table to the left as many places as necessary. Here's how to do it: Write your binary number in the third row of the table. For every column that has a 1 bit, write down the corresponding decimal number from the first row. For columns that have a 0 bit, you can simply skip them or write down a 0. Using the binary number 11010011, you have 1 bits in the 128, 64, 16, 2, and 1 columns. Add those values together, and you get 211. Choose some numbers and practice to make sure you understand how to do this.

High-Order Bit Patterns: Subnet masks always consist of consecutive 1s and 0s. You never have, for example, a subnet mask that looks like 10110001 in binary (177 in decimal). Each octet in a subnet mask always consists of a series of zero or more 1s, followed by a series of zero or more 0s, as Table 6-2 shows.

Table 6-2 High-order bit patterns

Binary	Decimal
00000000	0
10000000	128
11000000	192
11100000	224
11110000	240
11111000	248
11111100	252
11111110	254
11111111	255

Work on memorizing these correlations so that you can deal with subnet masking problems when you see them later in this chapter.

Low-Order Bit Patterns: In Table 6-3, you stand the previous example on its head and start counting up through the 8-bit numbers from right to left, adding 1s as you increment. If you memorize the values of the powers of 2, from 0 through 7, you can calculate this table quickly.

Table 6-3 Low-order bit patterns

Binary	Decimal	Calculation
00000001	1	2^0
00000011	3	2^1+2^0
00000111	7	$2^2+2^1+2^0$
00001111	15	$2^3+2^2+2^1+2^0$
00011111	31	$2^4+2^3+2^2+2^1+2^0$
00111111	63	$2^5+2^4+2^3+2^2+2^1+2^0$
01111111	127	$2^6+2^5+2^4+2^3+2^2+2^1+2^0$
11111111	255	$2^7+2^6+2^5+2^4+2^3+2^2+2^1+2^0$

Memorize these numbers, or how to calculate them, so that you can work out subnet masking problems when you see them later in this section. These numbers are easy enough to calculate. Now you're ready to tackle the intricacies of IP subnetting and, later, supernetting, explained in the following sections.

Calculating a Subnet Mask: To decide how to build a subnet mask, you must follow this procedure:

1. Decide how many subnets you need. This number is usually derived as a result of a network design document. You can figure out the number of subnets needed for a network by seeing how many network cable segments are connected to router interfaces. Each cable segment indicates a required subnet.

2. Next, decide how many bits you need to meet or exceed the number of required subnets. To figure this value, use the formula 2^n, with n representing the number of bits you must add to the starting subnet mask (and, therefore, "borrow" from the host portion of the subnet mask). For example, if your network number is a Class C address, such as 200.10.10.0, which has a default subnet mask of 255.255.255.0, this subnet mask is your starting point.

3. Borrow bits from the top of the host portion of the address down (that is, from the left side).

4. You must also ensure that you have enough host bits available to assign to computers on each subnet. To figure out the number of host addresses available, use the formula 2^n-2, with n representing the number of host (0) bits in the subnet mask.

Here's an example to help you put this formula to work:

1. ABC Inc. wants 12 subnets for its Class C address: 200.10.10.0. No subnet needs more than 14 host addresses.

2. The nearest power of 2 is 16, which equals 2^4. This means you must borrow 4 bits from the host portion of the original subnet mask (255.255.255.0) and make those 4 bits subnet bits.

3. Borrowing 4 bits, starting from the left of the host portion, creates a subnet mask with the pattern 11110000. The decimal value for this number is 128+64+32+16, or 240. This borrowing of bits changes the default subnet mask for the Class C address from 255.255.255.0 to 255.255.255.240.

4. To calculate the number of host addresses for each subnet, reverse the logic from the subnet mask. In other words, any bit used for the subnet mask can't be used for host addresses. Count the number of 0s remaining in the subnet mask to determine the number of bits left for the host address. In this case, that number is 4. Remember, the formula to determine the number of host addresses is 2^n-2, so you have $2^4-2=14$. This number of host addresses works for this network example because the requirement was for no more than 14 hosts per subnet.

Here's a quick summary of what you just did: Based on the requirement for 12 subnets in a Class C address, with no subnet needing more than 14 host addresses, you calculated that a 4-bit subnet mask is required. Because the corresponding bit pattern, 11110000, equates to 240 in binary, the default subnet mask for Class C, 255.255.255.0, must be changed to borrow those 4 bits from the host portion of the address. Therefore, the new subnet mask becomes 255.255.255.240. Because the remaining 4 bits for the host portion allow up to 14 host addresses per subnet, and the requirements call for no more than 14 addresses per subnet, the design works as intended.

Now that you have an appropriate subnet mask, you need to determine what network numbers can be derived from using that subnet mask. The way to determine that information is to take the borrowed 4 bits, place them in the network number, and cycle the 4 bits through the possible combinations of values they represent. In Table 6-4, the subnetwork numbers resulting from the preceding steps are shown with the last octet written in binary on the left and the resulting subnetwork address written in decimal shown on the right. The bits shown in bold are the 4 bits used to create the subnets.

Table 6-4 Subnetwork numbers and addresses

Subnetwork Number in Binary	Subnetwork Address
200.10.10.**0000**0000	200.10.10.0
200.10.10.**0001**0000	200.10.10.16
200.10.10.**0010**0000	200.10.10.32
200.10.10.**0011**0000	200.10.10.48
200.10.10.**0100**0000	200.10.10.64
200.10.10.**0101**0000	200.10.10.80
200.10.10.**0110**0000	200.10.10.96
200.10.10.**0111**0000	200.10.10.112
200.10.10.**1000**0000	200.10.10.128
200.10.10.**1001**0000	200.10.10.144
200.10.10.**1010**0000	200.10.10.160
200.10.10.**1011**0000	200.10.10.176
200.10.10.**1100**0000	200.10.10.192
200.10.10.**1101**0000	200.10.10.208
200.10.10.**1110**0000	200.10.10.224
200.10.10.**1111**0000	200.10.10.240

Similarly, the host addresses in each subnet can be determined by cycling through the 4 host bits. Therefore, the subnetwork 200.10.10.32 would have host addresses from 200.10.10.33 through 200.10.10.47. However, you can't use the IP address in which all host bits are 1s because it's the broadcast address for that network, so your actual range is 200.10.10.33 through 200.10.10.46, giving you 14 host addresses.

Another Subnet Mask Example: In Figure 6-6, the network number is 172.31.0.0, which is a Class B network address with a default subnet mask of 255.255.0.0.

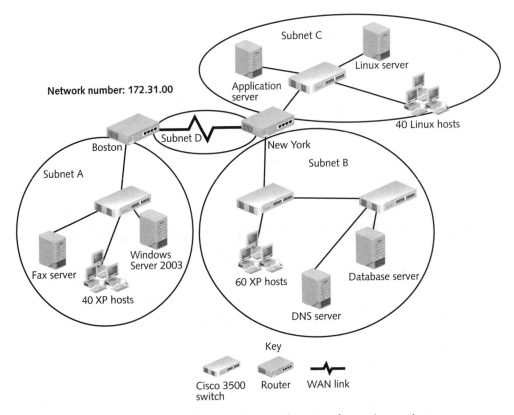

Figure 6-6 A sample network for calculating subnet mask requirements

The following steps show how to calculate a new subnet mask:

1. In this example, you can see that four cable segments are connected to router interfaces. The WAN cable segment between the two routers counts as a single cable segment and, therefore, a single subnet. You have to account for the WAN subnet even if the network has no hosts because the router interfaces require an IP address. As you can see, there are four subnetworks: Subnet A requires 43 IP addresses (40 for the XP hosts, 2 for the servers, and 1 for the router interface). Subnet B requires 63 IP addresses, subnet C requires 43 IP addresses, and subnet D requires only 2 IP addresses.

2. You need a power of 2 that's equal to or greater than 4. Because $2^2 = 4$, you need to borrow 2 bits.

3. Borrowing 2 bits from the leftmost part of the host portion of the original subnet mask (255.255.0.0) gives the last two octets of your new subnet mask the bit pattern 11000000.00000000. Converting to decimal and putting the entire subnet mask together yields 255.255.192.0. The 192 in the third octet is derived from adding the 128 place and the 64 place together because they are the only two bits that are 1 in the third octet.

4. To be sure that you have enough host bits per subnet, count the number of 0 bits in the new subnet mask and raise two to that power, giving $2^{14} = 16,384$. That number of host addresses far exceeds your requirement of a maximum of only 63 hosts per subnet, but that's fine. If you were doing this for a real network, you might borrow more bits than you need for creating subnets, which would allow more subnets to be added to the network later.

TIP If you want to read more about this topic and try an outstanding tutorial to help you calculate subnets (and supernets, for that matter), point your Web browser to *www.learntosubnet.com*.

6

Calculating Supernets: The act of **supernetting** "borrows" bits from the network portion of an IP address to "lend" those bits to the host portion. Supernets permit multiple consecutive IP network addresses to be combined and make them function as a single logical network. Here's how it works:

1. Say you have four Class C network addresses, 192.168.0.0, 192.168.1.0, 192.168.2.0, and 192.168.3.0, available for your network design. You have a total of 900 hosts on your proposed network. You don't have four router interfaces that can use the four different network numbers, however. You can combine the four networks into one by borrowing 2 bits ($2^2=4$) from the network portion of the address and adding them to the host portion. You then have a network address of 192.168.0.0 with a subnet mask of 255.255.252.0. The 252 in the third octet is derived from setting the last 2 bits of the original Class C subnet mask (255.255.255.0) to 0, thereby making them part of the host portion.

2. Instead of supporting only 8 bits for the host address portion, the supernet now supports 10 bits (8 + 2) for host addresses. This number of bits provides 2^{10} - 2 host addresses on this supernet, or 1022, which satisfies your requirement for 900 hosts and allows you to assign all host addresses in a single network.

Combining two or more small networks into one larger network is only one reason to supernet. In any network that uses routers, the routers maintain a table of networks, called a routing table, which allows the router to select the interface a network packet should be routed to so that it gets to the intended destination. This routing table might not be a big deal for most corporate networks, but routers on the Internet can have enormous routing tables. The larger the routing table, the more work the router must do to determine where to send a packet. Supernetting can combine multiple routing table entries into a single entry, which can drastically decrease the table's size on Internet routers. This reduction in routing table size increases the speed and efficiency of Internet routers. The next section discusses a service that helps network administrators manage IP address allocation.

Network Address Translation (NAT)

Although subnetting and supernetting can help alleviate the IP address shortage problem, they simply make more efficient use of existing addresses. **Network Address Translation (NAT)** helps considerably more by allowing an organization to use private IP addresses while connected to the Internet.

Using NAT, an organization can, for example, assign all its workstations' addresses in the 10.x.x.x private network. Assume that an organization has 1000 workstations. Although these addresses can't be used on the Internet, the NAT process translates a workstation address as it leaves the corporate network into a valid Internet address. When data returns to the workstation, the address is translated back to the original 10.x.x.x address. NAT is usually handled by a network device that connects the organization to the Internet, such as a router. Figure 6-7 depicts this process.

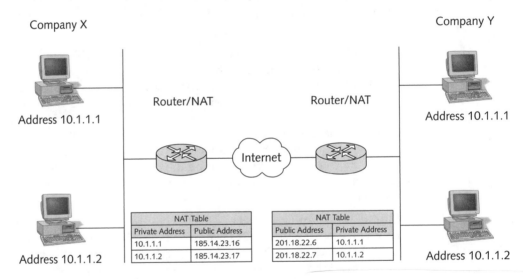

Figure 6-7 NAT in action

Notice that workstations in Company X are assigned the same IP addresses as workstations in Company Y. These addresses in the 10.x.x.x network are used within the corporate network, but as soon as a workstation attempts to access the Internet, the address is translated into a valid public Internet address. This process allows any number of companies to use private IP addresses within their own network but requires a public IP address only when a workstation attempts to access the Internet. This process reduces the number of public IP addresses required because a public address is required only if a workstation accesses the Internet. An extension of NAT, called Port Address Translation (PAT), allows several hundred workstations to access the Internet with a single public Internet address. This process relies on each packet containing not only a source and destination IP address, but also a source and destination TCP or UDP port number. With PAT, the address is translated into a single public IP address for all workstations, but a different source port number (which can be any value from 1024 to 65535) is used for each communication session, allowing a NAT device to differentiate between workstations. In Simulation 6-3, you can see how NAT and PAT work; both go a long way toward extending the life of IPv4 addresses.

Simulation 6-3: Network Address/Port Address Translation

For an excellent tutorial on NAT, see *www.howstuffworks.com/nat.htm*.

TIP

6

Dynamic Host Configuration Protocol (DHCP)

Some drawbacks to using TCP/IP in a large network include the detailed configuration of devices, keeping track of assigned addresses and to which machine they were assigned, and so forth. To make this process easier, **Dynamic Host Configuration Protocol (DHCP)** was developed.

To use DHCP, a server must be configured with a block of available IP addresses and their subnet masks. To receive its address from the server, each computer must then be configured to request its address configuration. A computer requests IP address information from the DHCP server in the form of a broadcast message each time the operating system boots when TCP/IP is started. Each time a computer requests an address, the server assigns one until it has no more addresses to assign.

The computer only leases the address the server assigns to it. The network administrator defines the lease time when the DHCP server is configured. This time can be as little as a few minutes to an infinite period, in which case the lease never expires. A typical lease time is one day or a few days. When 50% of the lease time has elapsed, the computer attempts to renew the lease from the same DHCP server that responded to the initial DHCP request. If no response is received, the computer waits until 87.5% of the lease time has elapsed; at that point, a broadcast DHCP renewal request is sent. If no response is received, at lease expiration the computer broadcasts a DHCP request (the same type of request sent at system boot) for a new IP address. If no DHCP server responds, one of two things happens: TCP/IP stops functioning, or, in an APIPA-enabled operating system, the computer assigns itself an address from the special range of addresses that begin with 169.254.

This special range of addresses is reserved for **automatic private IP addressing (APIPA)**. APIPA is used by the Windows operating system, starting with Windows 98. An address in the APIPA range is automatically assigned to a Windows 98 or later computer when DHCP is enabled but no DHCP server responds to the DHCP request. The use of APIPA rather than a DHCP server is recommended only for small, nonrouted networks.

One major benefit of using DHCP is the ease with which computers can be moved. When a computer is moved to a new network segment and turned on, it requests its configuration from a DHCP server on that segment. This type of address assignment should not be used for systems that require a static address, such as Web servers, DNS servers, and DHCP servers, because computers with these network services are usually expected to always have the same IP address.

NOTE

All major operating systems today include a DHCP client service, and most server operating systems include the DHCP server component.

Internet Protocol Version 6 (IPv6)

Internet Protocol version 6 (IPv6) is the network community's answer to resolving some of the problems in IPv4. These problems include a somewhat limiting 32-bit address space, lack of built-in security, a sometimes complicated setup, and a lack of built-in QoS.

An IPv6 address is 128 bits compared to the 32 bits in an IPv4 address. This length increases the number of possible addresses from about 4 billion in IPv4 to 3.4×10^{38} addresses (that's 34 followed by 37 zeros!) in IPv6. Unless IP addresses are assigned to every star in the universe, it's safe to say enough IPv6 addresses will be available.

IPv6 incorporates the IP Security (IPSec) protocol that must be added to an existing IPv4 network. IPSec provides authentication and encryption. Authentication ensures that the sender and receiver of data packets are known to each other and have permission to send and receive data. Encryption makes the underlying data in packets unreadable except to the computers involved in the transmission.

IPv6 is autoconfiguring, which means there is no IP address to assign and no subnet mask to determine. Two types of autoconfiguration are available in IPv6:

- Stateless autoconfiguration is the simplest. When a workstation boots, it listens for information broadcast by a local router and assigns itself an address based on the network configuration broadcast by the router and the station's MAC address.

- Stateful address configuration relies on a DHCP server, as with IPv4. This configuration type requires setting up and configuring a DHCPv6 server. Of the two autoconfiguration types, stateless autoconfiguration is usually the most common.

As mentioned in Chapter 4, Quality of Service (QoS) is a term that describes a network's capability to prioritize data packets, based on the type of information they contain (for example, voice, video, or file data) or the urgency of the information. QoS headers in IPv6 packets can identify packets that require special or priority handling, making applications such as streaming audio and video much easier to implement.

IPv6 Addresses

Unlike IPv4 addresses, which are specified in decimal format in 8-bit sections separated by a dot, IPv6 addresses are specified in hexadecimal format in 16-bit sections separated by a colon. An example of an IPv6 address looks like the following:

```
2001:1b20:302:442a:110:2fea:ac4:2b
```

Note that if one of the 16-bit numbers doesn't require four hexadecimal digits, the leading 0s are omitted. Furthermore, some IPv6 addresses contain consecutive 0s in two or more 16-bit sections. A shorthand notation is used to eliminate consecutive 0 values. Two colons replace two or more consecutive 0 values, as the following example shows:

6

- Longhand notation: 2001:260:0:0:0:2ed3:340:ab
- Shorthand notation: 2001:260::2ed3:340:ab

There's actually some order to these seemingly cumbersome IPv6 addresses. Within the IPv6 address space, an addressing hierarchy of three parts is used: a public topology, a site topology, and an interface identifier. In short, the first three 16-bit sections (totaling 48 bits) of an IPv6 address represent the public topology, which could represent an Internet backbone service provider, for example. The next 16 bits represent the site topology, such as a business or a local ISP, and the last 64 bits (four 16-bit sections) represent the interface identifier, which is derived from the MAC address on the host's NIC. The interface identifier is the unique host address.

This hierarchical address scheme will enable faster and more efficient location of Internet resources after IPv6 is commonplace. It will also eliminate the need for problem-prone IPv4 processes, such as NAT and complicated subnetting and supernetting.

Other Protocol Suites

Although TCP/IP is the dominant network protocol suite, other protocol suites are sometimes used on older networks, where the need to change to TCP/IP is not warranted, or in environments suited to the suite's features. The three protocol suites discussed in this section are NetBIOS/NetBEUI, which is used primarily on older Windows networks; IPX/SPX, which was designed for use on NetWare networks; and AppleTalk, which is used almost exclusively on Macintosh networks.

NetBIOS and NetBEUI

In the early 1980s, IBM hired a third-party company named Sytek to build a simple, basic set of network programming interfaces. The result became **Network Basic Input/ Output System (NetBIOS)**. This interface persisted much longer than anyone expected and remains in broad use today. Its initial deployment occurred in a basic networking product that IBM called PC-Net and that Microsoft later remarketed as MS-Net.

By the mid-1980s, Microsoft, 3Com, and IBM together developed a protocol suite for use with OS/2 and LAN Manager. Using NetBIOS to provide Application-layer capabilities, this consortium developed a lower-layer protocol known as **NetBIOS Extended User Interface (NetBEUI)** that spans Layers 2, 3, and 4 of the OSI model. From their inception, NetBIOS and NetBEUI were designed to work in small to medium networks of 2 to 250 computers. NetBIOS used with TCP/IP or IPX/SPX is still around, but Microsoft has discontinued support for NetBEUI starting with Windows XP.

Although NetBIOS and NetBEUI work closely together and are often confused with each other, they are neither inseparable nor the same. Figure 6-8 shows the Microsoft protocol suite and its relationship to the OSI model. As shown, the Microsoft protocol suite defines four components above the Data Link layer. For this reason, Microsoft protocols can run on any network card or physical medium.

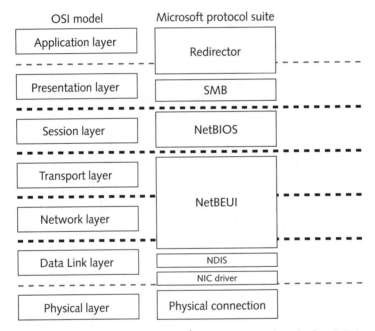

Figure 6-8   Microsoft protocol suite compared with the OSI model

The redirector interprets requests from the computer and determines whether requests are local or remote. The redirector passes a local request to the local operating system and passes a request for remote network service to the protocol below, in this case **Server Message Block (SMB)**. SMB is the message format that DOS and Windows use to share files, directories, and devices. SMB file sharing is also supported by most Linux and UNIX systems. The SMB passes information between networked computers. The redirector is responsible for repackaging SMB requests for transmission to other devices for processing.

As mentioned in Chapter 5, the Session layer is responsible for managing communications between two computers. NetBIOS works at this layer to establish and maintain those connections. NetBEUI works at the Transport layer to manage communications between two computers. Figure 6-8 shows NetBEUI operating at the Network layer, but it's actually a nonroutable protocol and skips this layer. A NetBEUI packet has no fields for source or destination network information.

NetBIOS operates at the Session layer to provide peer-to-peer network application support. A unique 15-character name identifies each computer in a NetBIOS network. A NetBIOS broadcast advertises a computer's name. Periodically, a computer broadcasts its NetBIOS name so that other computers can communicate with it. All computers on the network keep a cache of names and hardware addresses of computers from which they received broadcasts. If a computer wants to communicate with a computer whose name is not in its cache, it sends a broadcast requesting the hardware address for that computer.

NetBIOS is a connection-oriented protocol responsible for establishing, maintaining, and terminating network connections. Also, NetBIOS can use connectionless communications, if necessary. Although closely related to NetBEUI, NetBIOS can use a number of other lower-layer protocols, including TCP/IP and IPX/SPX, for transport and lower-layer services. NetBIOS is a nonroutable protocol, but it can be routed when using a routable protocol for transport.

NetBEUI is a small, fast, nonroutable Transport and Data Link layer protocol designed for use with NetBIOS on small networks. NetBEUI 3.0 is the Microsoft improvement on IBM's version of NetBEUI (and, therefore, works only on Microsoft networks). Its low overhead makes NetBEUI ideal for DOS-based computers that require network connectivity. NetBEUI's speed and size also make it a good choice for slow serial links. Because NetBEUI is not routable, its use is typically limited to small networks. However, because TCP/IP is the protocol of choice and NetBEUI is not routable, Microsoft no longer includes support for NetBEUI, starting with Windows XP.

IPX/SPX

Internetwork Packet Exchange/Sequenced Packet Exchange (IPX/SPX) is the original protocol suite developed for use with the Novell NetWare network operating system. Novell continues to support this protocol suite, even in its latest version of NetWare (version 6.5 as of this writing) but does so primarily for backward compatibility with older NetWare implementations. Currently, TCP/IP is the protocol suite of choice for networking, even in NetWare.

NWLink is the Microsoft implementation of the IPX/SPX protocol suite. Figure 6-9 shows the protocols that compose the NWLink suite and their corresponding layers in the OSI model. In Windows 98, Microsoft changed its terminology for the IPX/SPX protocols from NWLink to Novell IPX ODI Protocol (Windows 98, Release 2) or IPX/SPX-Compatible Protocol (Windows 98, Release 1).

Windows Server 2000/2003 and Windows XP include NWLink, mostly to support connections to older NetWare servers. However, NWLink can also provide transport for NetBIOS. Because it's a routable protocol suite, network expansion is easier with NWLink than with NetBEUI.

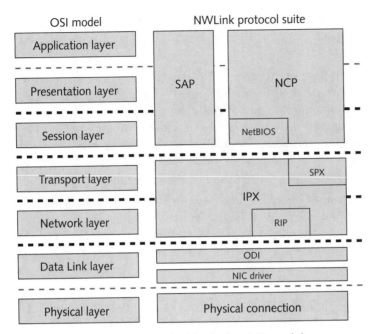

Figure 6-9   NWLink compared with the OSI model

One major consideration when using IPX/SPX or NWLink is which Ethernet frame type to use. (A frame type defines the format of the Data Link layer protocol data unit.) Chapter 7 discusses Ethernet frame types and their applications. For now, remember that all computers on a network must use the same frame type to communicate successfully. If computers on a network use IPX/SPX and communication does not occur, verify that all computers use the same frame type. Because use of IPX/SPX is waning in today's networks, details on it have been moved to Appendix A.

For more information about IPX/SPX and Novell NetWare, you can visit *www.protocols.com/pbook/novel.htm*.

NOTE

AppleTalk

Although the AppleTalk standard defines physical transport in Apple Macintosh networks, it also establishes a suite of protocols those computers use to communicate. Apple created AppleTalk Phase II to allow connectivity outside the Macintosh world. Rather than define networks, AppleTalk divides computers into zones. AppleTalk zones allow a network administrator to logically group computers and other resources that have frequent communication, in a manner similar to subnetting.

For more information on these protocols and others, see *www.protocols.com*.

Implementing and Removing Protocols

In most operating systems, adding or removing protocols is relatively easy. For example, in Windows Professional and Server machines and in most versions of UNIX, TCP/IP loads automatically when the operating system is installed. More protocols, such as IPX/SPX or IPv6, can be added during installation. Also, they can be added or removed later using the Local Area Connection Properties dialog box in Windows Vista or XP, as shown in Figure 6-10, or using a similar utility in other operating systems.

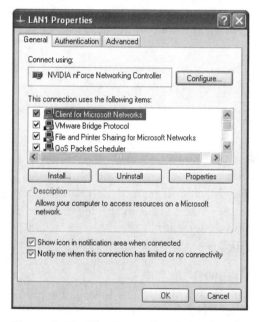

Figure 6-10   The Properties dialog box for a network connection in Windows XP

Although installing several protocols on a machine to ensure interoperability with any operating system might be tempting, adding unnecessary protocols can have a detrimental effect on network performance. Furthermore, when multiple protocols are installed, the operating system must be configured carefully to prioritize the use of each protocol. This priority is referred to as the protocol binding order. Typically, the most frequently used protocol should be first in the binding order.

CHAPTER SUMMARY

❑ Many protocols are available for network communications, each with its own strengths and weaknesses. A protocol suite or stack allows a number of protocols to work cooperatively to achieve maximum performance. The major protocol suites are TCP/IP, IPX/SPX, AppleTalk, and NetBEUI. Each smaller protocol within a suite has its own network function.

❑ The TCP/IP protocol suite dominates network communication in part because of its use on the Internet.

❑ IP addressing involves several concepts, including address classes, subnetting, supernetting, and subnet masks. The current method for Internet addressing, called Classless Interdomain Routing (CIDR), uses all available addresses more efficiently. Other IP addressing concepts include Dynamic Host Configuration Protocol (DHCP), which is a method for assigning and managing IP addresses automatically, and Network Address Translation (NAT), which allows companies using private IP addresses to access the Internet and use public IP addresses more efficiently.

❑ IPv6 will eventually replace IPv4 because it offers several advantages: 128-bit address space, autoconfiguration, built-in security, and Quality of Service.

KEY TERMS

Address Resolution Protocol (ARP) — A protocol in the TCP/IP suite used to resolve logical IP addresses to physical MAC addresses.

AppleTalk File Protocol (AFP) — The Macintosh remote file-management protocol.

application protocol — A type of protocol that works in the upper layers of the OSI model to provide application-to-application interaction.

automatic private IP addressing (APIPA) — A special range of addresses that starts with 169.254 and is used by a computer when no DHCP server responds to a DHCP request. *See also* Dynamic Host Configuration Protocol (DHCP).

broadcast domain — The extent to which a broadcast frame is forwarded from device to device without going through a router. An IP network or subnet is also referred to as a broadcast domain.

Classless Interdomain Routing (CIDR) — An IP addressing method in which address classes no longer dictate the part of an IP address designated as the network portion. With CIDR, a network administrator can assign however many bits are appropriate to the network design.

connectionless — A type of protocol that sends data across the network to its destination without guaranteeing receipt.

connection-oriented — A type of protocol that establishes a formal connection between two computers, guaranteeing that data will reach its destination.

Domain Name System (DNS) — A TCP/IP protocol used to associate a computer's IP address with a name.

dotted decimal — The format of an IP address, expressed as four decimal numbers separated by a period.

Dynamic Host Configuration Protocol (DHCP) — A TCP/IP protocol that allows automatic IP address and subnet mask assignment.

File Transfer Protocol (FTP) — A TCP/IP protocol used for file transfer and manipulation services.

Hypertext Transfer Protocol (HTTP) — The protocol used to transfer Web pages from a Web server to a Web browser.

Internet Control Message Protocol (ICMP) — A TCP/IP protocol used to send information and error messages.

Internet Protocol version 4 (IPv4) — TCP/IP's primary network protocol; it provides addressing and routing information.

Internet Protocol version 6 (IPv6) — An updated version of IPv4 created to solve some problems inherent in that protocol, such as a somewhat limiting 32-bit address space, lack of built-in security, a sometimes complicated setup, and a lack of built-in Quality of Service.

Internetwork Packet Exchange/Sequenced Packet Exchange (IPX/SPX) — IPX is Novell's protocol for packet routing and forwarding. In this protocol suite, IPX serves many of the same functions that IP does in the TCP/IP suite. SPX is Novell's connection-oriented protocol that supplements IPX by providing reliable transport.

localhost — A special DNS host name that refers to whatever IP address is assigned to the machine where this name is referenced. (Think of it as a special way to access the current IP address on any computer.)

loopback address — A special DNS host name that refers to the reserved Class A address 127.0.0.1, used to confirm that a computer's IP configuration works.

NetBIOS Extended User Interface (NetBEUI) — A network protocol developed by IBM and Microsoft specifically to provide transport services for NetBIOS. NetBEUI is not routable. In addition, it's nearly obsolete and is no longer supported on current Windows operating systems.

NetWare Core Protocol (NCP) — Novell's upper-layer protocol that provides all client/server functions.

Network Address Translation (NAT) — A process by which an organization can assign private IP addresses to workstations; those addresses are translated to public IP addresses when accessing the Internet.

Network Basic Input/Output System (NetBIOS) — A protocol that establishes and manages communications between computers and provides naming services.

nonroutable — A protocol that doesn't include Network layer or network address information.

NWLink — The Microsoft implementation of the IPX/SPX protocol suite. *See also* Internetwork Packet Exchange/Sequenced Packet Exchange (IPX/SPX).

octet — A grouping of eight binary digits or bits ("oct" means eight), usually expressed as a decimal number. An octet is one of the four decimal values that make up an IP address.

protocols — The rules and procedures for communicating.

protocol stack — An ordered collection of networking protocols that together provide end-to-end networked communications between a sender and a receiver.

routable — A protocol that includes Network layer information and can be forwarded by a router.

Server Message Block (SMB) — The message format used by DOS and Windows to share files, directories, and devices. SMB file sharing is also supported by most Linux and UNIX operating systems.

Simple Mail Transport Protocol (SMTP) — A TCP/IP protocol used to send mail messages across a network. SMTP is the basis for e-mail on the Internet.

Simple Network Management Protocol (SNMP) — A TCP/IP protocol used to monitor and manage network devices.

subnet mask — A 32-bit dotted decimal number used to signify which part of an IP address is the network portion and which part is the host portion. The subnet mask consists of a string of binary 1s followed by a string of binary 0s. The binary 0s mask the host portion of an IP address. A binary 1 signifies that the corresponding bit in the IP address belongs to the network portion of the IP address, and a binary 0 signifies that the corresponding bit in the IP address belongs to the host portion.

subnetting — The process whereby a single network address is divided into two or more subnetwork addresses, each with fewer available host IDs than the original network address.

supernetting — The operation of "borrowing" bits from the network portion of an IP address to combine a group of contiguous IP addresses. For supernetting to work, the group of IP addresses must be contiguous.

Telnet — A TCP/IP protocol that provides remote terminal emulation.

Transmission Control Protocol (TCP) — The core of the TCP/IP suite. TCP is a connection-oriented protocol responsible for reformatting data into packets and reliably delivering those packets.

Transmission Control Protocol/Internet Protocol (TCP/IP) — A protocol suite that supports communication between heterogeneous systems. TCP/IP has become the standard communications protocol for the Internet.

transport protocol — A protocol type responsible for providing reliable communication sessions between two computers.

User Datagram Protocol (UDP) — A connectionless TCP/IP protocol that provides fast data transport.

REVIEW QUESTIONS

1. The IPX/SPX protocol was used primarily in which operating system?

   a. Linux

   b. NetWare

   c. DOS

   d. Mac OS

2. An IPv6 address is made up of how many bits?

   a. 32

   b. 48

   c. 64

   d. 128

   e. 256

3. The subnet mask of an IP address does which of the following?

   a. provides encryption in a TCP/IP network

   b. allows automated IP address configuration

   c. defines which part of the address specifies the network portion and which part specifies the host portion

   d. allows users to use a computer's given name rather than its address

4. A nonroutable protocol does not operate in which layer of the OSI model?

   a. Presentation

   b. Data Link

   c. Transport

   d. Physical

   e. Network

5. Which of the following is a private IP address and can't be routed across the Internet?

   a. 192.156.90.100

   b. 172.19.243.254

   c. 11.200.99.180

   d. 221.24.250.207

   e. 12.12.12.12

6

6. As data travels through the OSI model, the _____ layer is responsible for splitting data into segments.

7. Which of the following is a reason to subnet? (Choose all that apply.)

   a. Networks can be divided into logical groups.

   b. Subnetting increases network bandwidth.

   c. Subnetting can decrease the size of broadcast domains.

   d. There's no need to assign static IP addresses to each computer.

8. NetBEUI is well suited for large enterprise networks because it's very fast. True or False?

9. Which Transport layer protocol reduces overhead?

   a. UDP

   b. TCP

   c. IP

   d. DNS

10. Which of the following protocols resolves logical addresses to physical addresses?

   a. DHCP

   b. TCP

   c. IP

   d. DNS

   e. ARP

11. Which of the following protocols provides connectionless service? (Choose all that apply.)

   a. IP

   b. UDP

   c. TCP

   d. SMTP

   e. NetBIOS

12. Which of the following does TCP use to establish a connection?

   a. sequence numbers

   b. segments

   c. three-way handshake

   d. port numbers

13. A(n) _____ is a grouping of 8 binary digits expressed as a decimal number.

14. Which of the following represents a valid IPv6 address?
    a. 2001:345:abcd:0:230:44
    b. 2001:345:abcd::230:44
    c. 2001:345::abcd:0:79f::230:44
    d. 2001:345:abcd:0:FEED:230:44

15. When using TCP/IP, computers on the same network segment must have the same _____ . (Choose all that apply.)
    a. network number
    b. host ID
    c. subnet mask
    d. computer name

16. A connection-oriented protocol provides fast but unreliable service. True or False?

17. Which are enhancements of IPv6 compared to IPv4? (Choose all that apply.)
    a. larger address space
    b. more cumbersome configuration
    c. built-in security
    d. hierarchical addressing

18. Which protocol can configure a computer's IP address and subnet mask automatically?
    a. TCP
    b. IP
    c. ARP
    d. DNS
    e. DHCP

19. For the Class C network address 192.168.10.0, which of the following subnet masks provides 32 subnets?
    a. 255.255.255.252
    b. 255.255.255.248
    c. 255.255.255.240
    d. 255.255.255.224

20. For the Class C subnet mask for 192.168.10.0 described in the previous question, how many host addresses are available on each resulting subnet?

    a. 2

    b. 6

    c. 14

    d. 30

21. For the Class C network address 192.168.220.0, what subnet mask supports up to 16 subnets?

    a. 255.255.255.252

    b. 255.255.255.248

    c. 255.255.255.240

    d. 255.255.255.224

22. For the Class C subnet mask for 192.168.220.0 described in the previous question, how many hosts are available per subnet?

    a. 2

    b. 6

    c. 14

    d. 30

23. If you create a supernetted subnet mask for seven contiguous Class C IP addresses, how many bits worth of additional address space for host addresses do you create?

    a. 2

    b. 3

    c. 4

    d. 5

24. Which IP addressing scheme permits workstations to use private IP addresses to access the Internet?

    a. supernetting

    b. NAT

    c. DHCP

    d. subnetting

25. When a Windows 98 or later computer is configured to use DHCP but no DHCP server is available, what type of address is configured automatically for that computer?

    a. subnetted

    b. APIPA

    c. NAT

    d. static

HANDS-ON PROJECTS

Adding, configuring, and removing protocols in a Windows environment is handled by a variety of means. For these projects, you view the properties for TCP/IP and add and remove other protocols. You learn about several command-line utilities, including Ping and Netstat, that help you examine your local TCP/IP networking environment. Finally, you discover an easy tool available on the Internet for calculating IP subnets.

Hands-On Project 6-1

6

Follow these steps to view a Windows XP TCP/IP configuration:

1. Right-click the **My Network Places** desktop icon, and click **Properties**. If My Network Places is not on the desktop, click **Start**, **Control Panel**, and then (assuming Control Panel is in Category view) click **Network and Internet Connections** and click **Network Connections** at the bottom.

2. Double-click the **Local Area Connection** icon in the Network Connections window.

3. In the Local Area Connection Status dialog box, click the **Properties** button.

4. In the Local Area Connection Properties dialog box, click the **Internet Protocol (TCP/IP)** entry in the This connection uses the following items list box, and then click the **Properties** button.

5. A pair of option buttons controls the top section. You can decide to obtain an IP address from a DHCP server or elect to use a static IP address. If the second option button is selected, you can assign an IP address, a subnet mask, and gateway information to the computer. Another pair of option buttons controls the lower section. You can decide to obtain a DNS server address automatically or elect to define one or more static DNS server addresses. If you select the second option button, you can define IP addresses for a preferred and an alternate DNS server.

6. If you click the Advanced button in this dialog box, the Advanced TCP/IP Settings dialog box opens. It contains four tabs: one for IP settings, one each for DNS and WINS settings, and a fourth (Options) for managing TCP/IP filtering settings.

   The DNS tab contains DNS server information, such as the addresses of DNS servers on the network and the domain suffixes appended to host names during resolution.

   Use the WINS Address tab to configure a WINS server for name resolution. This tab includes an option for adding WINS server addresses in order of use, options to enable LMHOSTS lookup, and an option to enable or disable NetBIOS over TCP/IP. (This option should be disabled only in a network that includes Windows 2000 or Windows XP machines.)

7. Click the **Cancel** or **Close** button four times to ensure that you don't change the existing configuration, and then close the Network Connections window. Leave your system running for the next project.

Hands-On Project 6-2

To add the IPv6 protocol in Windows XP, follow these steps:

1. Right-click the **My Network Places** desktop icon, and click **Properties**. If My Network Places is not on the desktop, click **Start**, **Control Panel**, and then (assuming Control Panel is in Category view) click **Network and Internet Connections** and click **Network Connections** at the bottom.

2. Double-click the **Local Area Connection** icon in the Network Connections window.

3. In the Local Area Connection Status dialog box, click the **Properties** button.

4. In the Local Area Connection Properties dialog box, click **Install**. In the Select Network Component Type dialog box, click **Protocol**, and then click **Add**.

5. In the Select Network Protocol dialog box, click **Microsoft TCP/IP version 6** and click **OK**. Notice that the protocol has been added to the Local Area Connection Properties dialog box. No properties are available for configuration because IPv6 is self-configuring. Close the Local Area Connection Properties dialog box, the Status dialog box, and the Network Connections window.

6. Open a command prompt window and type **ipconfig**. (If you can't remember how to open this window, check the Hands-On Projects in Chapter 1.) You should be able to see IPv6 configuration information. Close the command prompt window, and leave your system running for the next project.

Hands-On Project 6-3

To remove the IPv6 protocol from your computer's configuration, follow these steps:

1. Right-click the **My Network Places** desktop icon, and click **Properties**.

2. Double-click the **Local Area Connection** icon in the Network Connections window.

3. In the Local Area Connection Status dialog box, click the **Properties** button.

4. In the Local Area Connection Properties dialog box, click **Microsoft TCP/IP version 6** and click **Uninstall**. Click **Yes** to confirm the deletion. When prompted to restart your computer, click **Yes**.

5. Close any open windows, and leave your system running for the next project.

Hands-On Project 6-4

Start this project by opening a command prompt window. Then follow these steps to use the Ping utility to check your computer's IP configuration:

1. Type **ping loopback** and press **Enter**. This command shows you the output for the special IP address 127.0.0.1, as shown in Figure 6-11, and confirms that your IP stack is configured correctly.

Figure 6-11 Ping loopback results

2. Type **ipconfig** and press **Enter**. Write down the IP address for your local machine:

   _____

3. Type **ping** *xx.xx.xx.xx* and press **Enter** on the command line (substituting your local machine's IP address for *xx.xx.xx.xx*). The output should be similar to Figure 6-12, except that it displays your computer's current IP address.

Figure 6-12 Ping results for the local IP address

4. Repeat Step 2 to obtain your computer's default IP gateway address (or get the IP gateway address from your instructor), and write it down:

   _____

5. Then type **ping** *yy.yy.yy.yy* and press **Enter** (substituting the gateway address you wrote down for *yy.yy.yy.yy*). The output should resemble what's shown in Figure 6-13. If it executes properly, ping *yy.yy.yy.yy* confirms that you can access your default IP gateway (and, therefore, send packets outside your local cable segment).

6. Type **exit** and press **Enter** to close the command prompt window. (If you plan to continue to Hands-On Project 6-5, omit this step.)

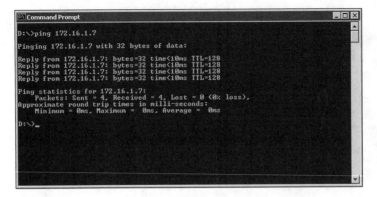

Figure 6-13 Ping results for the gateway IP address

Hands-On Project 6-5

To use the Netstat utility to observe your computer's IP communications statistics, follow these steps:

1. Unless you're continuing from the preceding project, open a command prompt window. Type **netstat /?** and press **Enter** to see the online help file for this command. Read the file so that you understand the commands you're entering in the next three steps. Remember that your output from these commands will differ from what's shown in the figures.

2. Type **netstat –a** and press **Enter**. Your output should look similar to Figure 6-14.

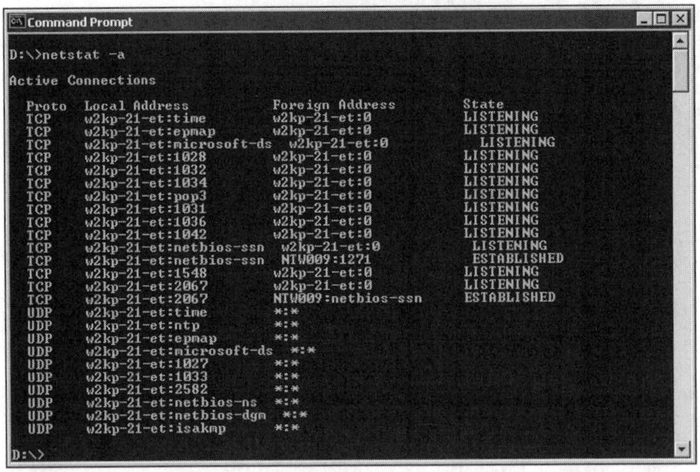

Figure 6-14 Netstat -a results

3. *Note*: If you're not using Ethernet in your computer lab, your instructor will tell you to skip this step. If you are, however, type **netstat –e** and press **Enter** to see output similar to Figure 6-15.

Figure 6-15   Netstat -e results

4. Type **netstat –s** and press **Enter**. This command displays output similar to Figure 6-16.

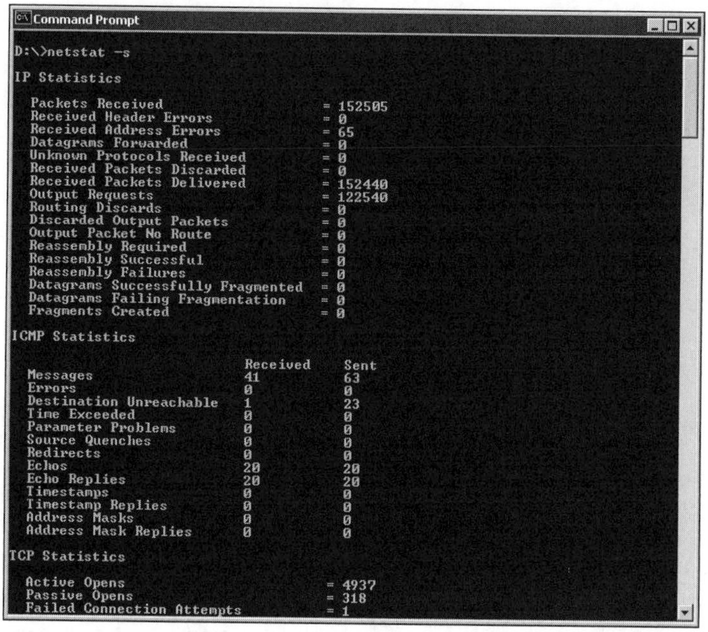

Figure 6-16   Netstat -s results

5. Type **exit** and press **Enter** to close the command prompt window. Leave your system running for the next project.

6

Hands-On Project 6-6

This chapter teaches you to calculate IP subnets by hand, should you ever need to do so. If you have access to the Internet, however, you can take advantage of the subnet calculator software tool. To access a subnet calculator on the Internet, follow these steps in Windows XP:

1. Start your Web browser and enter **www.wildpackets.com/products/ipsubnetcalculator** in the Address text box.

2. Click the **Free Download** link and follow the instructions to download and install the IP Subnet Calculator software. (Your instructor might provide other instructions, especially if the software has already been downloaded and is available from a local server or on your local machine.)

3. Click **Start**, point to **All Programs**, and click **WildPackets IP Subnet Calculator**. WildPacket's IP Subnet Calculator includes numerous handy tools to calculate subnet masks and the resulting number of hosts and subnets.

4. Click the **Subnet Info** tab in the IP Subnet Calculator window. Investigate how selecting a value for the Max Subnets field controls the Max Hosts per Subnet field, and vice versa.

5. Type the IP address **192.168.10.0** in the IP Address text box, and then click the **Subnets/Hosts** tab to see how it displays usable host addresses within subnets.

6. Click the **CIDR** tab and explore how varying the number in the Mask Bits field changes the Supernet Mask, Max Supernets, and Max Addresses fields.

7. Click the **Close** button in the upper-right corner of the IP Subnet Calculator window to exit the application.

CASE PROJECTS

Case Project 6-1

As the network administrator for a growing ISP, you want to make efficient use of your network addresses. One of the network addresses IANA assigned to you is a Class C network of 197.14.88.0. You have decided that you will use the addresses in this Class C network to satisfy the IP address requirements of 16 corporate customers who require between 10 and 14 addresses each. Without using a subnet calculator, calculate a subnet mask that will fulfill this requirement. List the subnet mask and the first four subnetwork addresses that the mask will create:

_____

_____

_____

Case Project 6-2

You work at a help desk and have just received a call from an employee who says she can't access network resources. You want the employee to view her IP address configuration. Write down the command-line program you should ask her to use. After following your instructions, the employee tells you that her IP address is 169.254.14.11 with a subnet mask of 255.255.0.0. What conclusion can you make from this information?

_____

_____

_____

6

Case Project 6-3

You have been contracted by a small company to expand its network of 100 Windows 98 computers to more than 200 computers. The company wants you to leave Windows 98 on the existing 100 computers. Windows XP should be the OS installed on the new computers. You have decided that to make the most efficient use of bandwidth, you should break the network into two broadcast domains. You examine a number of computers and find that the protocol in use is NetBEUI. Write a short paper explaining what issues are involved in completing this task, including any new hardware and configuration requirements.

Case Project 6-4

You must install 125 computers for a new business that wants to run TCP/IP and have access to the Internet. The ISP in town will assign you only four public IP addresses, so you decide to assign the computers addresses in the range 172.16.1.1/16 through 172.16.1.125/16. What else must you do to allow these computers to access the Internet?

NETWORK ARCHITECTURES

After reading this chapter and completing the exercises, you will be able to:

♦ Compare and contrast media access methods used in network architectures

♦ Describe the operation of Ethernet

♦ Differentiate between Ethernet standards and speeds

♦ Explain the four Ethernet frame types and how they are used

♦ Describe the token ring architecture and its components

♦ Describe the AppleTalk network architecture

♦ Explain the function of Fiber Distributed Data Interface

♦ Describe other LAN and WAN architectures and their role in today's networks

A network's architecture generally refers to its overall structure, including topology, physical media, and channel access method. This chapter explains channel access methods, network architectures, and the specifics of different network architecture standards, including Ethernet, token ring, Apple-Talk, Fiber Distributed Data Interface (FDDI), and Asynchronous Transfer Mode (ATM). Understanding these topics is essential to assessing requirements for implementing network technology.

Putting Data on the Cable: Access Methods

Given that network architectures communicate in a number of different ways, some factors in network communications must be considered, including how computers put data on the cable and how they ensure that the data reaches its destination undamaged.

Function of Access Methods

When multiple computers are attached to a network, the way those computers share the cable must be defined. When computers have data to send, they transmit it across the network. However, when two computers send data at the same time, a data **collision** can occur, requiring both computers to resend the data. A collision is the result of two or more devices sending a signal along the same channel at the same time. Splitting data into smaller chunks is one way to ensure that it reaches its destination, but often this method is not enough.

In addition to reformatting data into segments, packets, and frames, computers must have a way to ensure that data they send is not corrupted. A number of rules have been defined to prevent collisions. These rules, called **channel access methods**, specify when computers can access the cable or data channel. Channel access methods ensure that data reaches its destination by preventing two or more computers from sending messages that might collide on the cable. Allowing only one computer at a time to send data, or preventing collisions in some other way, gives data a better chance of reaching its destination intact.

As with all other network communication parameters, every computer on a network must use the same access method. If not, data is not received and, depending on the method, all network communications might be interrupted.

Major Access Methods

Channel access is handled at the MAC sublayer of the Data Link layer in the OSI model. There are five major types of channel access:

- Contention
- Switching
- Token passing
- Demand priority
- Polling

Contention

Have you ever attended a meeting without a moderator? Effective communication is difficult because everyone talks at the same time. In early networks based on **contention**, computers sent data whenever they had data to send. This method might work well in a small environment where computers send little data along the cable. As more computers send data, however, outgoing messages collide more frequently, must be sent again, and then collide again. The network becomes a useless jumble of electronic signals. To organize contention-based networks, two carrier access methods were created: Carrier Sense Multiple Access with Collision Detection and Carrier Sense Multiple Access with Collision Avoidance.

Carrier Sense Multiple Access with Collision Detection (CSMA/CD) is one of the most popular ways to regulate network traffic. Used by Ethernet, this access method prevents collisions by listening to the channel to see whether another computer is sending data, as shown in Figure 7-1. This process is also demonstrated later in this chapter in Simulation 7-1 when the operation of Ethernet is discussed.

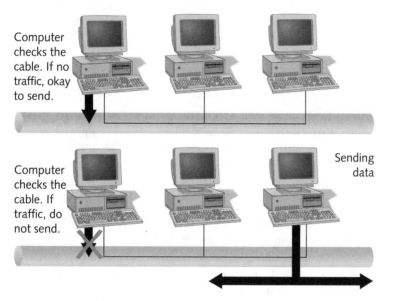

Figure 7-1   With CSMA/CD, computers check for cable traffic

If the computer senses no data on the line, it sends its message. If another computer is using the channel, the computer waits a random amount of time and then checks again. This process continues until the channel is free and the computer can send its data. If two or more stations do send data simultaneously, a collision occurs. The sending stations involved in the collision then send a jamming signal to alert all stations to the collision. The stations involved in the collision wait a random period of time before attempting to resend their data. If 16 collisions occur in a row involving the same station, that station then "gives up," and the upper-layer protocols are sent an error message. It's the responsibility of the upper layers to try the transmission again.

CSMA/CD doesn't allow traffic from a server to take precedence over traffic from a workstation. All computers on the network have an equal chance to control the channel.

NOTE

Although this method might seem like a good way to prevent collisions, it has the following limitations:

- CSMA/CD is not effective when too many network hubs separate host computers, which causes delays in signal transmission.

- The more computers on a network, the more collisions are likely to occur. Adding computers places higher demands on the network, increases the likelihood of collisions, and requires retransmitting data, which can slow network transmissions dramatically.

- Computers don't have guaranteed access to network media within a certain time period. A computer with large amounts of data to send monopolizes the network channel, slowing transmission for all other computers on the network.

Carrier Sense Multiple Access with Collision Avoidance (CSMA/CA) is another channel access method that uses Carrier Sense Multiple Access. However, it uses collision avoidance rather than detection to prevent collisions. With CSMA/CA, when the computer senses that no other computer is using the network, it signals its intent to transmit data. Any other computers with data to send must wait when they receive the "intent-to-transmit" signal and can send their intent-to-transmit signals only when they see that the channel is free.

Although this method avoids collisions more reliably than CSMA/CD, the additional overhead created by intent-to-transmit packets reduces network speed significantly. Therefore, CSMA/CA is not used nearly as much as CSMA/CD. A form of CSMA/CA is, however, used in wireless LANs with an access point. Because one wireless device might not be able to detect another's transmission (because of obstacles or distance, known as the hidden node problem), a wireless device must inform the access point of its intent to transmit. Because the access point hears transmissions from all devices, it can determine whether it's okay to transmit.

Switching

When networks interconnect nodes through a special device called a switch, the switch is what controls access to the media. This method of channel access control is called **switching**. Contention occurs on a switch only when two or more senders ask to reach the same receiver simultaneously or when the number of simultaneous transmission requests exceed the switch's capability to handle multiple connections.

Except in these special circumstances, contention is not a problem for a network switch because it can interconnect any pair of nodes that want to exchange data on demand. Furthermore, because each connection between two machines that want to exchange data is reserved for their exclusive use, that connection can use the entire available bandwidth for whatever networking technology is in use.

Switching has many advantages. First, it's fairer than strict contention-based technologies. Switches permit multiple simultaneous conversations. Therefore, a computer need not wait to access the media, as is required in contention-based methods, and no single computer can monopolize the network medium. Second, switching supports centralized management, and certain computers (routers or servers, for example) can receive priority over other computers; they can get preferential access to a channel because of priority settings or because of Quality of Service (QoS) guarantees (which offer access to minimum guaranteed bandwidth for time-sensitive network services, such as video or audio streams). Third, a switch can have connection ports that operate at different speeds, so, for example, all client stations can be attached to 100 Mbps Ethernet ports, and servers can be attached to 1 Gbps ports.

One drawback to switching is the somewhat higher cost (particularly for the switch). Despite the slight additional cost of a switch compared to a hub, almost all new network designs use the switching method.

Token Passing

Chapter 2 discussed token passing as a function of the ring topology. Using this channel access method, a special frame called the token passes from one computer to the next. Only the computer holding the token can send data. A computer can keep the token for only a specific amount of time. If the computer with the token has no data to send, it passes the token to the next computer. Figure 7-2 and Simulation 7-2 (in the section on token ring later in this chapter) show communication in a token-passing network.

Because only the computer with the token can transmit data, this method prevents collisions. Computers no longer spend time waiting for collisions to be resolved, as they do in a contention-based environment. All computers have equal access to the media, which makes token-passing networks best suited for time-sensitive environments, such as banking transactions and databases that require precise timestamps. Also, because traffic moves in a specific "direction" around a ring topology, faster access methods (such as 16 Mbps token ring) can circulate two tokens at the same time without fear of collision. (By keeping the two sets of messages from overlapping, both tokens can circulate in order.) However, token passing has two disadvantages:

- Even if only one computer on the network has data to send, it must wait to receive the token. If its data is large enough to warrant two or more "turns" at the token, the computer must wait until the token makes a complete circuit before starting its second transmission.

- The complicated process of creating and passing the token requires more expensive equipment than that used by contention-based networks.

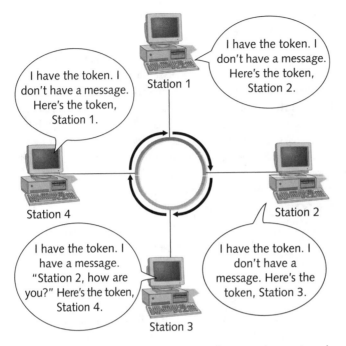

Figure 7-2 Communications in a token-passing network

Demand Priority

Demand priority is a channel access method used solely by the 100VG-AnyLAN 100 Mbps Ethernet standard (IEEE 802.12). 100VG-AnyLAN runs on a star bus topology. In demand priority, intelligent hubs control access to the network. The hub searches all connections in a round-robin fashion. When an end node—a computer, bridge, router, or switch—has data to send, it transmits a **demand signal** to the hub. The hub then sends an acknowledgement that the computer can start transmitting its data.

The major disadvantage of demand priority is price. To work, this access method requires special hubs and other equipment. The 100VG-AnyLAN standard, although it's promising technology, lost out to the more pervasive and less expensive Ethernet and is now considered obsolete.

Polling

Polling is one of the oldest ways to control access to the network. A central controller, often referred to as the primary device, asks each computer (the secondary device) on the network if it has data to send. If so, the computer can send up to a certain amount of data; then it's the next computer's turn, as shown in Figure 7-3.

Polling has many advantages. First, like token passing, it allows all computers equal access to the channel; no single computer monopolizes the medium. The central controller allows centralized management, and certain computers (such as file servers) can receive priority

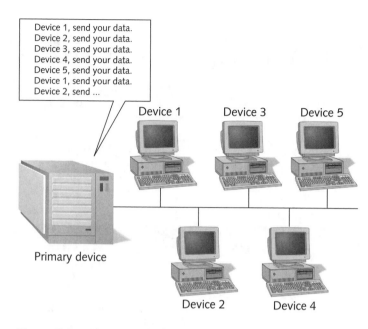

Device 1, send your data.
Device 2, send your data.
Device 3, send your data.
Device 4, send your data.
Device 5, send your data.
Device 1, send your data.
Device 2, send ...

Figure 7-3   The primary device controls polling

over other computers; they can be polled more often or be allowed to send for a longer time than the remaining computers.

Like token passing, however, polling does not make efficient use of network media. Another major drawback is that if the primary device fails, the network fails. For this reason, finding networks today that use this method, other than IBM Systems Network Architecture (SNA) networks, is difficult.

Choosing an Access Method

The access method is an integral part of your network. The biggest factor in choosing access methods is the network topology. For example, a ring topology network generally uses the token-passing channel access method. Switching is an exception to the topology constraint because switches support nearly arbitrary node groupings and can manage traffic circulation when necessary. Switches can emulate all the common networking topologies (and sometimes even combine them within a single device). Tables 7-1 through 7-5 outline the advantages, disadvantages, and typical network architectures of each channel access method.

Table 7-1   Summary of the contention access method

Typical Network Architecture	Advantages	Disadvantages
Ethernet (CSMA/CD)	Inexpensive to implement	Slow in a large network with high traffic
LocalTalk (CSMA/CA)	Fast in a small network with low traffic	Does not support priority; a single computer can monopolize the network
Wireless (CSMA/CA)	Solves hidden node problem	Increased overhead because of handshaking with access point

Table 7-2   Summary of the switching access method

Typical Network Architecture	Advantages	Disadvantages
Ethernet (from 10 Mbps to 1 Gbps)	Higher levels of access for all users	Slightly more expensive equipment
Token ring (4 Kbps, 16 Kbps)	Support for guaranteed bandwidth (QoS)	Configuration and setup often time consuming and difficult
Other architectures, including Asynchronous Transfer Mode (ATM), voice and data traffic, and so forth	Provides highest bandwidth interconnections between senders and receivers	

Table 7-3   Summary of the token-passing access method

Typical Network Architecture	Advantages	Disadvantages
Token ring	Guaranteed equal access for all computers on the network	Slow in low-traffic environments
Fiber Distributed Data Interface (FDDI)	Fast and reliable; suited to critical campus backbones	Very expensive because more sophisticated equipment is required

Table 7-4   Summary of the demand priority access method

Typical Network Architecture	Advantages	Disadvantages
100VG-AnyLAN	Very fast in high- and low-traffic environments; provides guaranteed channel access; allows certain computers to be given higher priority over others on the same network	Expensive because special equipment is required; now obsolete

Table 7-5   Summary of the polling access method

Typical Network Architecture	Advantages	Disadvantages
IBM SNA	Guaranteed access for all computers; supports priority assignment	Inefficient use of network media

THE ETHERNET ARCHITECTURE

During the late 1960s and early 1970s, many organizations worked on methods to connect computers and share their data. One of these projects was the ALOHA network at the University of Hawaii. From this research, Robert Metcalf and David Boggs, researchers at Xerox's Palo Alto Research Center (PARC), developed an early version of Ethernet in 1972. PARC released the first commercial version in 1975, which allowed users to transmit data at approximately 3 Mbps to up to 100 computers with a maximum of 1 km of total cable.

Xerox teamed with Intel Corporation and Digital Equipment Corporation in the industry group DIX (Digital, Intel, Xerox) to develop a standard based on Xerox Ethernet and raised the transfer rate to 10 Mbps. In 1990, the IEEE used this version of Ethernet as the basis for its 802.3 specification, which defines how Ethernet networks operate at the Physical and Data Link layers of the OSI model.

Overview of Ethernet

Ethernet is the most popular network architecture. Its many advantages include ease of installation, scalability, media support, and low cost. Ethernet supports a broad range of transmission speeds from 10 Mbps to 10 Gbps.

All Ethernet standards use the NIC's MAC address to address frames. As explained in Chapter 4, a unique address is burned into the card's ROM when it's created. When a frame is sent, the hardware (MAC) addresses of both the source and destination computers are added to the frame header.

Although there are many variations of Ethernet, all forms are similar in their basic operation and frame formatting. What differs among the variations is the cabling, speed of transmission, and method by which bits are encoded on the medium. Because the frame formatting is the same, however, Ethernet variations are compatible with one another. That's why you often see NICs and Ethernet hubs and switches described as 10/100 or 10/100/1000 devices. These devices can support multiple Ethernet speeds because the underlying technology remains the same, regardless of speed. Note that although the frame formatting between Ethernet speeds can be the same, as you see in the "Ethernet Frame Types" section, different Network layer protocols can use different frame formats.

7

NOTE 10 Gbps Ethernet imposes some exceptions to the compatibility of Ethernet variations, as discussed later in this chapter in "10 Gigabit Ethernet: 10 Gbps IEEE 802.3ae Standard."

Ethernet Operation

Ethernet is considered a best-effort delivery system, meaning that when a frame is sent, there's no acknowledgement or verification that the frame arrived at its intended destination. Like all network architectures, Ethernet works at the Data Link layer of the OSI model. It relies on the upper-layer protocols to ensure reliable delivery of data. To fully understand how Ethernet operates and make good decisions when designing an Ethernet network, understanding the following concepts is important:

- How Ethernet accesses network media
- Collisions and collision domains
- How Ethernet handles errors
- Half-duplex and full-duplex communications

Accessing Network Media

The media access method Ethernet uses in a shared-media environment (a logical bus) is CSMA/CD, as discussed earlier in this chapter. CSMA/CD requires that an Ethernet device listens for a signal or carrier (carrier sense) on the medium first. If no signal is present, no other device is using the medium, so a frame can be sent. However, two or more devices listening simultaneously might discover no carrier present, and each one could send a frame (multiple access) at the same time, which causes a collision. Ethernet devices have circuitry that detects collisions and automatically resends the frame that was involved in the collision.

Collisions and Collision Domains

Collisions can occur only in an Ethernet shared-media environment, which means a logical bus topology is in use. In this environment, all devices interconnected by one or more hubs or coaxial cable segments hear all signals generated by all other devices. The signals are propagated from hub to hub until there are no more devices or until a device is encountered that doesn't simply forward all signals, such as a switch or a router. The extent to which signals in an Ethernet network are propagated is called a **collision domain**. Figure 7-4 shows a network diagram with five collision domains, each denoted by a circle. All devices in a collision domain are subject to the possibility that whenever a device sends a frame, a collision might occur with another device sending a frame at the same time. This fact has serious implications for the number of computers that can reasonably be installed within a single collision domain. The more computers, the more likely it is that collisions occur. The more collisions, the slower network performance is.

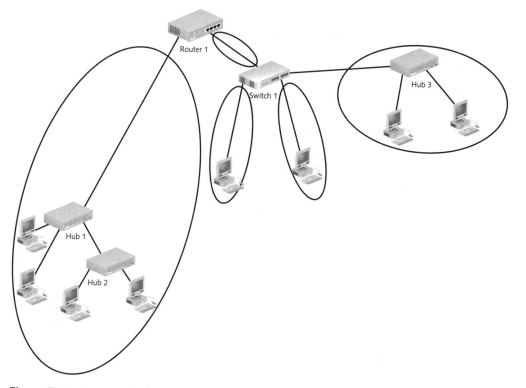

Figure 7-4   A network diagram showing five collision domains (circled)

Ethernet Error Handling

Collisions are the only type of error for which Ethernet automatically attempts to resend the data involved in the collision. Another type of error that can occur happens when data is altered as it travels across the medium. This error is usually caused by noise or faulty media connections. As explained in Chapter 5, an Ethernet frame trailer consists of the frame check sequence (FCS) field, which contains the Cyclical Redundancy Check (CRC) value. When the destination computer receives a frame, the CRC is recalculated and compared against the CRC value in the FCS. If the two values match, the data is assumed to be okay. If the values don't match, the data was corrupted. In the event of a CRC error, the destination computer discards the frame. No notice is given to the sender that this error has occurred. It's up to the upper-layer protocols, primarily TCP if the TCP/IP protocol suite is used, to detect that not all the data that was sent actually arrived at its destination and to resend that data.

Half-Duplex Versus Full-Duplex Communications

When Ethernet is implemented in a logical bus topology, only one computer at a time can send data. Furthermore, while a station is receiving data, it's not possible for that station to try to send data. No station can send and receive data at the same time. This type of communication is called **half-duplex communication**. When half-duplex communication is used with Ethernet, CSMA/CD must also be used. However, using a switched topology, a computer (and even several computers at the same time) can send and receive data simultaneously, which is called **full-duplex communication**. In a full-duplex environment, the collision detection circuitry is turned off because collisions aren't possible. Full-duplex communication results in a considerable performance advantage over half-duplex communication, which is another reason that switching has become the dominant technology in today's networks.

NOTE

Full-duplex communication is possible only when the medium includes data pathways for both the transmit and receive signals. Twisted-pair cabling provides both transmit and receive pathways, as does fiber-optic cable when two strands of fiber are used. Coaxial cable and current wireless implementations do not.

ETHERNET STANDARDS

As mentioned previously, each Ethernet variation is associated with an IEEE standard. The following sections discuss many of the standards, some of which are obsolete or had limited use. Keep in mind while reading about these standards that Ethernet over UTP cabling has been the dominant technology since the early 1990s and will likely to continue to be for the foreseeable future.

100 Mbps IEEE Standards

The most widely accepted Ethernet standard today is 100BaseT, which is also called **fast Ethernet**. Almost all implementations of 100 Mbps Ethernet are derived from this standard. The current IEEE standard for 100BaseT is 802.3u. Three subcategories of this standard define the type of cable used:

- *100BaseTX*—Two-pair Category 5 or higher UTP
- *100BaseT4*—Four-pair Category 3 or higher UTP
- *100BaseFX*—Two-strand fiber-optic cable

NOTE

Common use of the term 100BaseT typically implies 100BaseTX, where two pairs of wire are used over Category 5 or higher cabling.

The naming scheme of these standards works as follows: The "100" in all these standards indicates the speed of transmission: 100 Mbps. The "Base" indicates a baseband signaling method, which was discussed in Chapter 3. The last part of the name specifies the type of cable, with "T4" standing for twisted-pair using four pairs of wires, "TX" meaning two-pairs of wires, and "FX" indicating two strands of fiber-optic cable.

This technology is well suited for networking applications of all types and, because of its widespread use, the cable and equipment in fast Ethernet are inexpensive. Although faster technologies are available today, as you'll see, the low cost of 100 Mbps Ethernet and its continued suitability for typical network applications makes it the architecture of choice for all but heavily used servers and multimedia applications.

NOTE Another 100 Mbps Ethernet standard was 100VG-AnyLAN. It was a promising technology, but short-lived. For more information on this technology, see Appendix A.

7

100BaseTX

100BaseTX is the standard that's usually in mind when discussing 100 Mbps Ethernet. It requires two of the four pairs bundled in a Category 5 twisted-pair cable. Although three cable types are available for 100BaseT, 100BaseTX is the most widely accepted and, therefore, is the standard generally referred to as fast Ethernet.

100BaseT4

As the name implies, **100BaseT4** Ethernet uses all four pairs of wires bundled in a UTP cable. The one advantage that 100BaseT4 has over 100BaseTX is the capability to run over Category 3 cable. When 100 Mbps speeds became available, many companies wanted to take advantage of the higher bandwidth. However, if the cable plant consisted of only Category 3 cable, there were just two choices: Replace the cabling with higher-grade Category 5 cabling so that 100BaseTX could be used, or use 100BaseT4 Ethernet. One of the biggest expenses of building a network is cable installation, so many organizations chose to get the higher speed with the existing cable plant by using 100BaseT4.

100BaseFX

In environments that aren't conducive to using copper wiring to carry network data (such as electrically noisy settings), the only real choice in a wired network is to use fiber optics. In addition, fiber-optic cable can span much greater distances between devices than can twisted-pair cabling. For these reasons, **100BaseFX**, which uses two strands of fiber-optic cable, might be the best choice of network architecture. Fiber-optic cable installation is still far more expensive than twisted-pair, but its advantages of being impervious to electrical noise and electronic eavesdropping and of supporting longer segment lengths are worth it if the network requires these properties. 100BaseFX is rarely used as a complete replacement for 100BaseTX; rather, it's typically used as backbone cabling between hubs or switches and to connect wiring closets between floors or buildings. It's also used to connect client or server computers to the network when immunity to noise and eavesdropping is required.

100BaseT Design Considerations

An important consideration when designing a 100BaseT network is the total number of hubs allowed between end stations. There are two types of 100BaseT hubs: class I and class II. Class I hubs can have only one hub between communicating devices, whereas class II hubs can have a maximum of two hubs between devices. This limitation is designed to ensure that when a collision occurs on a hub-based network, all stations in the collision domain have enough time to hear the collision and respond appropriately. Typical 100BaseT networks use switches to interconnect multiple hubs, as shown in Figure 7-5, to avoid this limitation. Table 7-6 summarizes the 100BaseT Ethernet standard.

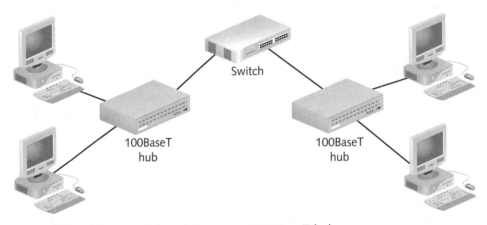

Figure 7-5   Using a switch to interconnect 100BaseT hubs

Table 7-6   100BaseT Ethernet summary

Category	Summary
IEEE specification	802.3u
Advantages	Fast; easy to configure and troubleshoot
Disadvantages	High cost; limited distance
Topology	Star
Cable type	Category 3 or higher UTP for 100BaseT4 Category 5 or higher UTP for 100BaseTX Fiber-optic for 100BaseFX
Channel access method	CSMA/CD
Transceiver location	On NIC
Maximum cable segment length	100 m (328 ft.) for 100BaseT4 and 100BaseTX; 2000 m (6561 ft.) for 100BaseFX
Maximum number of segments	1024
Maximum devices per segment	1
Maximum devices per network	1024
Transmission speed	100 Mbps

10 Mbps IEEE Standards

There are four major implementations of 10 Mbps Ethernet:

- *10Base5*—Ethernet using thicknet coaxial cable
- *10Base2*—Ethernet using thinnet coaxial cable
- *10BaseT*—Ethernet over UTP cable
- *10BaseF*—Ethernet over fiber-optic cable

Of these 10 Mbps standards, only 10BaseT and 10BaseF are seen today; the older 10Base2 and 10Base5 standards are essentially obsolete. For this reason, the discussion of 10Base2 and 10Base5 has been moved to Appendix A so that you can focus on 10BaseT and 10BaseF.

7

10BaseT

10BaseT Ethernet uses Category 3 or higher UTP cable but can also transmit with shielded twisted-pair (STP) cable. However, most cable plants installed after the early 1990s use Category 5, 5e, or 6 UTP, which supports up to 1 Gbps Ethernet. Like 100BaseTX Ethernet, 10BaseT is wired in a star topology using a logical bus or switching to move data from computer to computer.

100BaseTX networks are limited to only one or two hubs between end stations, but 10BaseT is somewhat more forgiving in its timing requirements. The rule for expanding a 10BaseT network states that no more than five cabling segments and no more than four hubs can be placed between two communicating workstations. This rule ensures that all stations on the network can detect a collision. Because of the delays inherent in repeaters, if more than four repeaters/hubs exist between end stations, a collision on one end of the collision domain might not be detected by stations on the other side of the collision domain in time for them to react properly.

The IEEE 802.3 specification allows a total of 1024 computers on a 10BaseT network connected with multiple hubs. This limitation of 1024 computers is caused by the collision detection algorithm used. When a collision occurs, the algorithm attempts to ensure that no two stations attempt to retransmit at the same time, thereby causing another collision. More than 1024 computers on a network would increase the likelihood of multiple collisions.

The biggest limitation of twisted-pair Ethernet networks is distance. The maximum cable segment length is only 100 meters for any twisted-pair cable segment. Networks that require a longer distance between hubs or stations can use fiber-optic connections, additional repeaters, or perhaps even a 10Base2 connection between hubs. Simulation 7-1 shows 10BaseT Ethernet in operation, and Table 7-7 outlines the 10BaseT Ethernet specifications.

Simulation 7-1: 10BaseT Ethernet Operation

Table 7-7 10BaseT Ethernet summary

Category	Summary
IEEE specification	802.3
Advantages	Very inexpensive; easy to install and troubleshoot
Disadvantages	Small maximum cable segment length
Topology	Star
Cable type	Category 3 or higher UTP, but typically Cat 5e or 6 today
Channel access method	CSMA/CD
Transceiver location	On NIC
Maximum cable segment length	100 m (328 ft.)
Minimum distance between devices	N/A
Maximum number of segments	1024
Maximum devices per segment	2
Maximum devices per network	1024
Transmission speed	10 Mbps

10BaseF

The IEEE specification for running 10 Mbps Ethernet over fiber-optic cable is **10BaseF** and is generally divided into three subcategories:

- 10BaseFL is used to link computers in a LAN environment (fiber to the desktop).

- 10BaseFP is used to link computers with passive hubs rather than repeaters. This category has a maximum cable segment length of 500 meters.

- 10BaseFB uses fiber-optic cable as a backbone between hubs.

All 10BaseF implementations use a star topology. Like 10BaseT, the specification lists 1024 as the maximum number of nodes on a single network connected by repeaters. Because faster speeds over fiber-optic cable are available, such as 100BaseFX, and cost essentially the same, 10BaseF isn't likely to be used in new network designs. Table 7–8 summarizes 10BaseF Ethernet.

Table 7-8 10BaseF Ethernet summary

Category	Summary
IEEE specification	802.3
Advantages	Long distance
Disadvantages	Higher cost; more difficult installation
Topology	Star
Cable type	Fiber-optic
Channel access method	CSMA/CD

Table 7-8   10BaseF Ethernet summary (continued)

Category	Summary
Transceiver location	On NIC
Maximum cable segment length	2000 m (6561 ft.), except for 10BaseFP at 500 m (1635 ft.)
Maximum number of segments	1024
Maximum devices per segment	2
Maximum devices per network	1024
Transmission speed	10 Mbps

Gigabit Ethernet: IEEE 802.3ab and 802.3z Standards

7

Gigabit Ethernet can be divided into two implementations, discussed in more detail in the following sections: 1000BaseX, which defines Gigabit Ethernet over fiber-optic cable and copper jumper cables, and 1000BaseT, which defines Gigabit Ethernet over twisted-pair cables. Two extensions to the IEEE 802.3 specification cover 1000BaseX and 1000BaseT:

- 802.3z-1998 covers 1000BaseX specifications, including the L (long wavelength laser/fiber-optic), S (short wavelength laser/fiber-optic), and C (copper jumper cables) discussed in the following sections.

- 802.3ab-1999 covers 1000BaseT specifications, which require four pairs of 100 ohm Category 5 or higher cable.

1000BaseT

1000BaseT, released as the 802.3ab standard in June 1999, supports Gigabit Ethernet over 100-meter segments of balanced Category 5 copper cabling and requires four pairs of wires. The 1 Gbps data rate results from sending and receiving data simultaneously (in full-duplex mode) at 250 Mbps in each direction over each of the four pairs of wires in Category 5 cable. Therefore, each wire pair can send and receive data at the same time at 250 Mbps, which results in a bandwidth of 1000 Mbps (or 1 Gbps) in each direction in full-duplex mode. 1000BaseT uses equipment called hybrids and cancellers (to combine multiple signals and to cancel interference) to support full-duplex transmission over a single pair of wires. So if the link operates in half-duplex mode, the channel speed is 1000 Mbps (250 Mbps times 4 wire pairs). When operating in full-duplex mode, 1000BaseT actually delivers 2 Gbps total bandwidth.

Unlike 10BaseT and 100BaseT Ethernet, 1000BaseT Ethernet does not dedicate a wire pair to transmitting or receiving. Each wire pair is capable of transmitting and receiving data simultaneously, thereby making the 1000 Mbps data rate possible in both half-duplex and full-duplex modes. Similarly to 100BaseT, 1000BaseT allows only one hub or repeater between end stations when using half-duplex communications. Most installations use switches that detect the speed of the connected device automatically, whether it's 10 Mbps, 100 Mbps, or 1000 Mbps. Therefore, the one-repeater limitation is unlikely to be a problem for most organizations.

1000BaseT Ethernet is gaining wide acceptance in corporate data centers to connect servers to the corporate backbone and as the primary connection type for storage area networks (SANs). Because 1000BaseT works over standard Category 5 cable, the upgrade path for companies currently running 100BaseT should be fairly simple. NICs and hubs or switches must be replaced, but the cabling infrastructure doesn't need to be replaced. Although Category 5 cable is the minimum requirement, 1000BaseT also works over Category 5e and 6 cable. Table 7-9 summarizes 1000BaseT Ethernet.

Table 7-9   1000BaseT Ethernet summary

Category	Summary
IEEE specification	802.3ab
Advantages	Fast; supports full-duplex communications
Disadvantages	High cost; short-haul cable segments only
Topology	Star
Cable type	Four-pair, balanced Category 5 cable; 100-ohm impedance
Channel access method	CSMA/CD or switching
Transceiver location	On NIC
Maximum cable segment length	Half-duplex: 100 m (328 ft.) Full-duplex: 100 m (328 ft.)
Maximum number of segments	1024
Maximum devices per segment	2
Maximum devices per network	1024
Transmission speed	1000 Mbps; 2000 Mbps in full-duplex mode

1000BaseLX

1000BaseLX uses fiber-optic media; the "L" stands for "long wavelength," the kind of laser used to send signals across the medium. These lasers operate at wavelengths between 1270 to 1355 nanometers and work with single-mode fiber (SMF) and multimode fiber (MMF). Long wavelength lasers cost more than short wavelength lasers but can transmit their signals over longer lengths of cable. Table 7-10 summarizes 1000BaseLX Ethernet.

Table 7-10   1000BaseLX Ethernet summary

Category	Summary
IEEE specification	802.3z
Advantages	Fast; supports full-duplex communications
Disadvantages	High cost; hard to deploy and install
Topology	Star

Table 7-10 1000BaseLX Ethernet summary (continued)

Category	Summary
Cable type	Two strands of fiber-optic cable per connection MMF: 62.5/125 μm or 50/125 μm (μm means micrometer) cable SMF: 10 micron cable
Channel access method	Switching
Transceiver location	On NIC
Maximum cable segment length	Half-duplex MMF and SMF: 316 m (1036 ft.) Full-duplex MMF: 550 m (1804 ft.) Full-duplex SMF: 5000 m (16,404 ft.)
Maximum number of segments	1024
Maximum devices per segment	2
Maximum devices per network	1024
Transmission speed	1000 Mbps (uses 8B/10B encoding); 2000 Mbps in full-duplex mode

Although the 1000BaseLX standard specifies a maximum cable segment length of 5000 meters, some manufacturers have extended that distance by using specialized and proprietary optical transceivers. Cisco Systems, for example, offers a product called 1000BaseLH ("LH" stands for "long haul") that provides a maximum cable segment length of 10,000 meters over single-mode fiber. For extremely long-distance Gigabit communications, a product called 1000BaseZX is capable of distances up to 100,000 meters over single-mode fiber. These long-range Gigabit products clearly have important implications for high-speed MANs and ISP connections to the Internet backbone.

1000BaseSX

1000BaseSX uses fiber-optic media; the "S" stands for "short wavelength" laser. These lasers operate at wavelengths between 770 to 860 nanometers and work only with MMF cable. Short wavelength lasers can't cover as much distance as long wavelength lasers, but they are less expensive (and use cheaper MMF cable). Table 7-11 summarizes the 1000BaseSX standard.

Table 7-11 1000BaseSX Ethernet summary

Category	Summary
IEEE specification	802.3z
Advantages	Fast; supports full-duplex communications
Disadvantages	High cost; hard to deploy and install
Topology	Star
Cable type	Two strands of fiber-optic cable per connection MMF: 62.5/125 μm or 50/125 μm cable

Table 7-11   1000BaseSX Ethernet summary (continued)

Category	Summary
Channel access method	Switching
Transceiver location	On NIC
Maximum cable segment length	Half-duplex 62.5 MMF: 275 m (902 ft.) Half-duplex 50 MMF: 316 m (1036 ft.) Full-duplex 62.5 MMF: 275 m (902 ft.) Full-duplex MMF: 550 m (1804 ft.)
Maximum number of segments	1024
Maximum devices per segment	2
Maximum devices per network	1024
Transmission speed	1000 Mbps (uses 8B/10B encoding); 2000 Mbps in full-duplex mode

1000BaseCX

1000BaseCX uses specially shielded, balanced, copper jumper cables; the "C" stands for "copper," the kind of electrical signaling used. Jumper cables are normally used for interconnections between devices or to link virtual LANs (VLANs) on a switch; these jumper cables might also be called twinax or short-haul copper cables. Segment lengths for 1000BaseCX cables top out at 25 meters, which means they're used primarily in wiring closets or equipment racks. Table 7-12 summarizes 1000BaseCX Ethernet.

Table 7-12   1000BaseCX Ethernet summary

Category	Summary
IEEE specification	802.3z
Advantages	Fast; supports full-duplex communications
Disadvantages	High cost; short-haul only
Topology	Star
Cable type	Two strands of copper cable (twinax), sold in prefabricated lengths only
Channel access method	Switching
Transceiver location	On NIC or switch
Maximum cable segment length	Half-duplex: 25 m (82 ft.) Full-duplex: 25 m (82 ft.)
Maximum number of segments	1024 (normally far fewer are used)

Table 7-12   1000BaseCX Ethernet summary (continued)

Category	Summary
Maximum devices per segment	2
Maximum devices per network	1024
Transmission speed	1000 Mbps (uses 8B/10B encoding); 2000 Mbps in full-duplex mode

10 Gigabit Ethernet: 10 Gbps IEEE 802.3ae Standard

The 802.3ae standard that governs 10 Gigabit Ethernet was adopted in June 2002. This Ethernet version is much like the other, slower Ethernet versions in frame formats and media access method, but it's faster. However, it does have some important technical differences. It's defined to run only on fiber optic cabling, both SMF and MMF, but the 10 Gbps Ethernet standard specifies a maximum distance of 40 km, compared with just 5 km for Gigabit Ethernet over fiber optic. This distance has important implications for WANs and MANs because although most WAN and MAN technologies can be measured in megabits, 10 Gbps Ethernet provides bandwidth that can transform how WAN speeds are thought of. Another design difference is that 10 Gbps Ethernet runs in full-duplex mode only, so the CSMA/CD method required in other Ethernet standards is not necessary.

The primary use of 10 Gigabit Ethernet is as the network backbone, interconnecting servers and network segments running 100 Mbps and 1000 Mbps Ethernet technologies. However, it also has its place in storage area networks (SANs) and will eventually be the interface for enterprise-level servers.

As this technology matures, a number of implementations have been and are being developed. They are divided into two basic groups: 10GBASE-R for LAN applications and 10GBASE-W for WAN applications. The W group of standards uses SONET framing over OC-192 links. (SONET and OC standards are explained in "ATM and SONET Signaling Rates" later in this chapter.) Both groups have short (S) range, long (L) range, and extended (E) range implementations, which include the following:

- *10GBASE-SR*—Runs over short lengths (between 26 and 82 meters) over MMF. Applications are likely to include connections to high-speed servers, interconnecting switches, and SANs.

- *10GBASE-LR*—Runs up to 10 km on SMF and is used for campus backbones and MANs.

- *10GBASE-ER*—Runs up to 40 km over SMF. Primary applications are for MANs.

- *10GBASE-SW*—Uses MMF for distances up to 300 meters.

- *10GBASE-LW*—Uses SMF for distances up to 10 km.

- *10GBASE-EW*—Uses SMF for distances up to 40 km.

As you can see, Ethernet has come a long way since Xerox transmitted at 3 Mbps over coaxial cable, and the journey from 3 Mbps to 10 Gbps is not yet over.

What's Next for Ethernet?

The future of Ethernet is bright and fast. Implementations of 40 Gbps Ethernet are underway. Estimations are that Ethernet could increase tenfold every four to six years, with 100 Gbps Ethernet available by 2006 to 2008, terabit Ethernet (1000 Gbps) by 2011, and 10 terabit Ethernet by 2015. In October 2005, Lucent Technologies demonstrated for the first time the transmission of Ethernet over fiber-optic cable at 100 Gbps. This kind of mind-boggling speed will be able to transfer data across the city faster than today's CPUs can transfer data to memory. When Internet providers begin using this level of bandwidth to connect to the Internet backbone, and when homes and businesses can tap into that bandwidth, extraordinary amounts of information will be at your fingertips. This level of speed has major implications for the entertainment industry and many other aspects of both business and pleasure. The Ethernet train is revving up, and it promises to be an exhilarating ride.

ETHERNET FRAME TYPES

One major distinction between Ethernet and other network architectures is that Ethernet can structure data several different ways before placing it on the network medium. As discussed in Chapter 5, a computer places data on the network in frames, which define the data's structure. Ethernet supports four unique **frame types**, and these frame types don't work with each other. For communication to take place between Ethernet devices, their frame type settings must match. These are the Ethernet frame types, discussed in more detail in the following sections:

- Ethernet 802.3 is generally used by IPX/SPX on Novell NetWare 2.x and 3.x networks.

- Ethernet 802.2 is the default frame type used by IPX/SPX on Novell NetWare 3.12 and 4.x networks. It's also the native frame type supported by default when Microsoft NWLink is installed.

- Ethernet SNAP is used in EtherTalk and mainframe environments.

- Ethernet II is used by TCP/IP.

All Ethernet frame types support a packet size between 64 and 1518 bytes and can be used by all network architectures mentioned previously. In most cases, a network requires only one frame type, but occasionally devices, such as file or database servers, must support multiple frame types (for instance, when some clients use one frame type, but other clients use another).

When running a protocol that can use more than one frame type, such as IPX/SPX, there must be a method to select the frame type. In Windows, this selection is made in the Properties dialog box for the local area connection. Windows defaults to auto-detection of the frame type, but this setting could cause undesirable results because non-server versions of Windows support only the first frame type detected. If resources on the network use different frame types, some resources won't be available to workstations that auto-detect a different frame type. Therefore, ensuring that only a single frame type is used or that all workstations have been set to a common frame type is essential for allowing access to resources.

NOTE   Always remember that mismatched frame types prevent network communication.

Ethernet 802.3

Sometimes called Ethernet raw, the **Ethernet 802.3** frame type was developed before completion of the IEEE 802.3 specification. Therefore, the 802.3 frame does not completely comply with the 802.3 specification, despite its name. Generally, Ethernet 802.3 frames occur only on Novell NetWare 2.x or 3.x networks.

The Ethernet 802.3 frame shown in Figure 7-6 begins with a preamble and a **start frame delimiter (SFD)** statement, which indicates the beginning of the frame. The frame's destination and source addresses follow. Because Ethernet supports variable length frames (64 to 1518 bytes), the next field specifies the length of the frame's data section. Then a 4-byte CRC follows to verify that the data reached its destination undamaged.

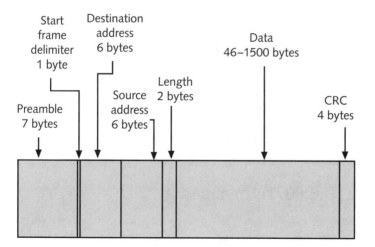

Figure 7-6 An Ethernet 802.3 frame

Ethernet 802.2

Ethernet 802.2 frames comply completely with the Ethernet 802.3 standard. The IEEE 802.2 group didn't address Ethernet, only the Logical Link Control (LLC) sublayer of the OSI model's Data Link layer. However, because Novell had already decided to use the term Ethernet 802.3 to describe Ethernet raw, it's generally accepted that Ethernet 802.2 means a fully 802.3- and 802.2-compliant Ethernet frame. Ethernet 802.2 frames contain similar fields to 802.3, with three additional LLC fields.

Ethernet SNAP

Ethernet SubNetwork Address Protocol (SNAP) is generally used on the AppleTalk Phase 2 networks discussed later in "The AppleTalk Environment." It contains enhancements to the 802.2 frame, including a **protocol type field**, which indicates the network protocol used in the frame's data section.

Ethernet II

Ethernet II frames are used in TCP/IP networks. As Figure 7-7 shows, Ethernet II frames differ only slightly from 802.3 frames. Instead of a separate SFD field, the preamble includes that data. The type field replaces the length field and is used in much the same way as in Ethernet SNAP—to identify which network protocol is in the frame's data section.

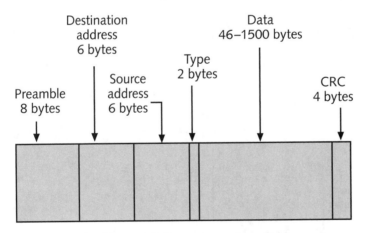

Figure 7-7 An Ethernet II frame uses a type field.

Wireless Ethernet: IEEE 802.11b, a, and g

Understanding how wireless networking differs from traditional wired networks is important so that you know how to install and support wireless technologies. The 802.11b/a/g technologies use an access point (AP) that serves as the center of a star topology network. Workstations equipped with wireless NICs send packets to the AP, which then sends the packets to the destination workstation.

You have learned about CSMA/CD as the access method in wired forms of Ethernet, but wireless networks have a special problem with this access method. CSMA/CD requires that all stations can hear each other so that each station knows when another station is sending data. This requirement is reasonable, but if two stations try to send at exactly the same time, a collision can occur. Fortunately, in a wired network, the sending stations hear the collision and attempt to resend the data. However, 802.11b/a/g stations can't send and receive at the same time, so if a collision does occur, the sending stations wouldn't detect it. For this reason, 802.11b/a/g specify the CSMA/CA access method, in which an acknowledgement is required for every packet sent. With this requirement, if a collision occurs, the sending stations know the packet didn't arrive safely because there's no acknowledgement.

7

Another problem exists in wireless networks that doesn't happen in wired networks. It's quite possible that in a three-station wireless network, all workstations can communicate with the AP—workstation A can hear workstation B and workstation B can hear workstation C, but workstation A can't hear workstation C, perhaps because the two are out of range. This situation is called the hidden node problem. CSMA/CA doesn't work because workstation A never knows whether workstation C is sending, and vice versa. To counteract this problem, the 802.11b/a/g standards specify another feature that uses handshaking before transmission. In this implementation, a station must send the AP a ready to send (RTS) packet requesting transmission. If it's okay to transmit, the AP sends a clear to send (CTS) message, and the workstation starts its communication. All other devices communicating with the AP hear the exchange of RTS and CTS messages, thus informing them that another device has control of the medium.

The 802.11b standard specifies a transmission rate of 11 Mbps, but this value is not absolute. Environmental conditions could prevent transmission at that speed. Therefore, transmission speeds might be dropped incrementally from 11 Mbps to 5.5 Mbps to 2 Mbps and, finally, to 1 Mbps to make a reliable connection. In addition, there's no fixed segment length for wireless networks because reliable communication relies heavily on the environment—for example, the number of walls between stations and the AP. The 802.11a and 802.11g standards behave in a similar fashion.

In general, an 802.11 network has a maximum distance of 300 feet with no obstructions. However, this distance can be extended by using large, high-quality antennas. Keep in mind that the data rate might suffer as the distance and number of obstructions increase.

NOTE

For an excellent tutorial on wireless networking and 802.11b, visit *www.networkcomputing.com/1115/1115ws22.html*.

THE TOKEN RING ARCHITECTURE

Developed by IBM in the mid-1980s, the **token ring** network architecture provides fast, reliable transport. Based on the IEEE 802.5 standard, token ring networks are cabled in a physical star topology but function as a logical ring, as shown in Figure 7-8. The token-passing channel access method, rather than the network's physical layout, gives token ring its name. The original version of token ring operated at 4 Mbps, but newer versions have increased that speed to 16 Mbps.

NOTE

If a 4 Mbps NIC is used in any workstation in an otherwise 16 Mbps token ring network, the entire network operates at 4 Mbps.

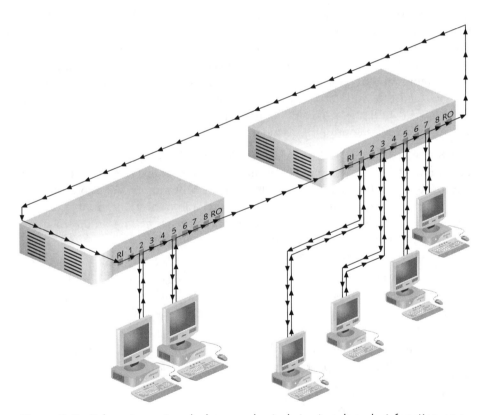

Figure 7-8   Token ring networks have a physical star topology but function as a logical ring

Token Ring Function

By using the token-passing access method, token ring networks ensure that all computers get equal time on the network. As described in Chapter 2, a small frame, called the token, passes around the ring. A computer receives the token from its **Nearest Active Upstream Neighbor (NAUN)**. If the token is not in use at the time—no nearby computer is sending data—and the computer has data to send, it attaches its data to the token and sends it to its **Nearest Active Downstream Neighbor (NADN)**. Each computer thereafter receives the token, determines that the token is in use, and verifies that it's not the data's destination station. If not, the computer re-creates the token and the data exactly as it received them and sends them to its NADN.

When data reaches its destination, the receiving computer sends the data to the upper-layer protocols (the Network, Transport, Session, Presentation, and Application layers) for processing. Then the receiving computer toggles two bits in the data packet to indicate it received the data and sends the token and data along the network to its NADN. Eventually, both token and data reach the original sender; the sender sees that the data was received successfully, frees the token, and then passes it along. To see a simulation of token ring operation, run Simulation 7-2.

Simulation 7-2: Token Ring Operation

SIMULATION

Beaconing

One unique aspect of the token ring network architecture is its capability to isolate faults automatically by using a process called **beaconing**. The first computer powered on in a token ring network is assigned the responsibility of ensuring that data can travel along the ring. This computer, the **active monitor**, manages the beaconing process. All other computers on the network are **standby monitors**.

Every seven seconds, the active monitor sends a special packet to its NADN announcing the address of the active monitor and the fact that it's the upstream neighbor. The station examines the packet and passes it along to its NADN, changing the upstream address. The third station then has a packet listing the active monitor's address and the address of its upstream neighbor. The third station repeats the process, sending to its NADN a packet containing the active monitor's address and its own address. When the active monitor receives the packet, it knows that the packet has navigated the ring successfully and the ring is intact. In addition, all stations know the address of their upstream neighbor.

Like Ethernet, token ring addresses are burned into the NIC when it's created.

NOTE

As shown in Figure 7-9, if a station does not hear from its upstream neighbor in seven seconds, it sends a packet down the ring containing its address, the address of its NAUN (from which it received no packet), and a beacon type. As the other computers in the network receive this packet, they check their configurations. If the NAUN does not answer, the ring can reconfigure itself to avoid the problem area. Beaconing allows some level of automatic fault tolerance in the token ring network, something many other network architectures lack.

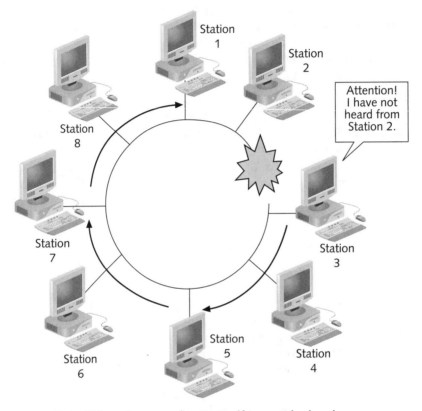

Figure 7-9   Token ring reconfigures itself to avoid a break

Although this process seems laborious, it's fairly efficient. Unlike Ethernet, there are no collisions, so data seldom has to be sent again, and much larger data packets can be sent—between 4000 and 17,800 bytes. Because all computers on the network have equal access to the token, traffic is consistent, and token ring handles increases in network size and bandwidth utilization efficiently.

Hardware Components

In a token ring network, a hub can be referred to as a **multistation access unit (MSAU)** or **smart multistation access unit (SMAU)**. IBM's implementation of token ring is the most popular adaptation of the IEEE 802.5 standard. Although there are some minor differences, such as the maximum number of computers on an STP ring, between IBM and IEEE specifications, they are very similar. When discussing hardware components of the token ring architecture, IBM equipment is most often used.

A typical IBM token ring hub, such as the 8228 MSAU, has 10 connection ports, eight of which can be used for connecting computers. As previously shown in Figure 7-8, the other two ports are used to connect the hubs in a ring. The Ring Out (RO) port on one hub connects to the Ring In (RI) port on the next hub, and so on to form a ring among the hubs. New hubs must also be added to the ring in this manner. IBM's implementation of token ring allows connecting 33 hubs in this fashion. The original token ring hubs provided a total of 260 stations per network. However, newer hubs that allow 16 computers per hub double this number.

Cabling in a Token Ring Environment

In 1984, IBM defined a comprehensive cabling system that specified cable types, connectors, and all other components required for computer networking. This cabling system categorizes cables based on the American Wire Gauge (AWG) standards that specify wire diameters. When token ring was introduced, it followed these standards for cabling and equipment. Table 7-13 shows the cable types included in the IBM system and used by token ring.

Table 7-13   IBM/token ring cabling

Cable Type	Description
Type 1	STP with two pairs of 22-AWG solid copper wire surrounded by a braided shield and casing. This cable is used to connect computers to MSAUs and can be run through conduit or inside walls.
Type 2	STP with two pairs of 22-AWG solid copper wire for data and four pairs of 26-AWG wire for voice. This cable is used to connect both data and voice without running two cables.
Type 3	UTP voicegrade cable with 22-AWG or 24-AWG, each pair twisted twice every 3.6 m (12 ft.). It's a cheaper alternative to Type 1 but limited to 4 Mbps.
Type 5	Fiber-optic cable, 62.5- or 100-micron diameter; used for linking MSAUs over distance.
Type 6	STP cable with two twisted pairs of 26-AWG stranded wire surrounded by braided shield and casing. Similar to Type 1, except that the stranded wire allows more flexibility but less distance (two thirds that of Type 1). This cable is generally used as a patch cable or for extensions in wiring closets.
Type 8	STP cable for use under carpets. It's similar to Type 6 but is flat.
Type 9	Plenum-rated Type 6 cable.

NOTE   AWG numbers are inversely related to the cable's diameter—larger AWG numbers indicate smaller diameters. For example, standard telephone wire has a thickness of 22 AWG, whereas thicknet cable is 12 AWG.

Table 7-14 summarizes the token ring network architecture.

Table 7-14 Token ring summary

Category	Summary
IEEE specification	802.5
Advantages	Fast and reliable
Disadvantages	More expensive than Ethernet; difficult to troubleshoot
Topology	Ring; cabled as star
Channel access method	Token passing
Maximum cable segment length	45 m (150 ft.) for UTP; 101 m (330 ft.) for STP
Maximum number of segments	33 hubs
Maximum devices per segment	Depends on hub
Maximum devices per network	72 with UTP, 260 with STP
Transmission speed	4 Mbps or 16 Mbps

THE APPLETALK ENVIRONMENT

Apple Computer, Inc., designed the AppleTalk architecture for use in its Macintosh networks. AppleTalk can run over a variety of other physical architectures, including Apple's own LocalTalk, Ethernet, and token ring. Because of Ethernet's superior speed and large installation base, AppleTalk is most commonly run over Ethernet, sometimes referred to as EtherTalk.

First introduced in 1983, AppleTalk is a simple, easy-to-implement network architecture designed for use with Apple Macintosh computers. Because all Macintoshes have a built-in network interface, implementing AppleTalk is as easy as attaching all the computers with cable. Therefore, AppleTalk networks were popular in early Macintosh environments.

NOTE At its introduction, "AppleTalk" referred to the networking protocols and the hardware used to connect computers. In 1989, Apple changed AppleTalk's definition to refer to the overall architecture of the network and added the term "LocalTalk" to refer to the cabling system.

Unlike Ethernet and token ring, which use the NIC's address, AppleTalk applies a dynamic scheme to determine a device's address. When the computer is powered on, it chooses a numeric address—generally, the last address it used. It then broadcasts this address to the network to determine whether the address is available. If the address is not taken, the computer starts transmitting from that address. If, however, another device on the network is using the address, the computer chooses another address randomly and broadcasts it to the network. This process continues until the computer finds an unused address.

The original version of AppleTalk, now called AppleTalk Phase 1, supported only 32 computers per network, and those computers could use only LocalTalk cabling. Including hubs and repeaters increased the number of computers to 254. When Apple introduced

AppleTalk Phase 2 in 1989, it also introduced EtherTalk and TokenTalk, which allow AppleTalk protocols to operate over Ethernet and token ring networks, respectively. These architectures increased the number of computers that an AppleTalk network can include to more than 16 million. In practice, standards governing AppleTalk networks, token ring, or Ethernet limit the number of computers to well below 16 million. It's important to remember, however, that for a Macintosh running AppleTalk Phase 2 over a LocalTalk network, the maximum number of computers is still 254.

NOTE   To put it simply, the underlying network architecture sets the maximum number of computers on an AppleTalk Phase 2 network—254 for LocalTalk, 1024 for EtherTalk, 72 for TokenTalk over UTP, and 260 for TokenTalk over STP. Most newer Macintoshes (manufactured in 1996 or later) support Ethernet interfaces in addition to LocalTalk. For obvious reasons, the Ethernet option is currently selected far more often than LocalTalk.

LocalTalk

Apple Computer, Inc., designed the **LocalTalk** network architecture, which uses STP in a bus topology, to allow users to share peripherals and data in a small home or office environment. LocalTalk uses the CSMA/CA channel access method. This method avoids more collisions, but it's cumbersome. Imagine if every time you sent a letter, you had to mail a postcard first announcing that you were sending a letter.

The maximum transmission speed of a LocalTalk network is only 230.4 Kbps. When compared to other network architectures' speeds (10, 100, 1000 Mbps, and even 10,000 Mbps for Ethernet and 4 or 16 Mbps for token ring), it's easy to see why this architecture was used primarily in small, Macintosh-only environments.

NOTE   Starting with Mac OS X, LocalTalk hardware is no longer supported. However, if a LocalTalk network is required, purchasing a third-party adapter to convert from Ethernet to LocalTalk might be possible.

EtherTalk and TokenTalk

In an effort to overcome LocalTalk's speed limitation, Apple created EtherTalk and TokenTalk. **EtherTalk** is the AppleTalk protocol running over a 10 Mbps IEEE 802.3 Ethernet network. **TokenTalk** is principally the same thing—the AppleTalk protocol running over a 4 or 16 Mbps IEEE 802.5 token ring network.

Both implementations require using a different NIC on the computer. These NICs include all drivers and protocols needed to run EtherTalk or TokenTalk. With extra software, each protocol can be used to connect Macintosh computers to a PC Ethernet or token ring environment. Since 1996, Apple Computer has offered systems with built-in Ethernet interfaces or with options to add Ethernet or token ring to its systems at a low cost. Note that a Macintosh running Mac OS X with an Ethernet interface can freely participate in a Windows-based network, accessing Windows file and printer shares and allowing Windows clients access to Macintosh file and printer shares.

THE FIBER DISTRIBUTED DATA INTERFACE (FDDI) ARCHITECTURE

Fiber Distributed Data Interface (FDDI) uses the token-passing channel access method and dual counter-rotating rings for redundancy, as shown in Figure 7-10. The rings in an FDDI network are usually a physical ring of fiber-optic cable. FDDI transmits at 100 Mbps and can include up to 500 nodes over a distance of 100 km (60 miles). FDDI full-duplex technology, an extension to standard FDDI, can support up to 200 Mbps. Like token ring, FDDI uses token passing; however, FDDI networks are often wired as a physical ring, not as a star. An FDDI network has no hubs; devices generally connect directly to each other. However, devices called **concentrators** can serve as a central connection point for buildings or sites in a campus setting.

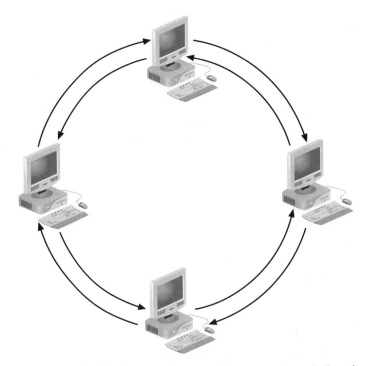

Figure 7-10 FDDI networks operate two counter-rotating rings

An FDDI network handles token passing differently from token ring. As in token ring, an FDDI token passes around the ring. However, unlike token ring, when the computer possessing the token has more than one frame to send, it can send the next frame before the initial frame fully circles the ring. This transmission is possible because the sender possesses the token, so no other senders can become active. The computer can avoid data collisions by calculating the network latency and waiting an appropriate interval before sending the next packet. This process transmits data more quickly around the network. Also, after a computer finishes sending its data, it can immediately pass the token along without waiting for confirmation of the data's receipt; the data doesn't need to make a complete circuit of the ring before the token can be passed on. Unlike token ring, FDDI supports assigning a priority level to a station or type of data. For example, a server can receive higher priority than workstations, and video or time-sensitive data can receive even higher priority.

As mentioned, FDDI uses two physical rings operating in different directions to avoid cable problems. In a token ring network, beaconing and network reconfiguration resolve cable breaks. In an FDDI network, all data transmission occurs along the **primary ring**, and the **secondary ring** circumvents a cable break. When a computer determines it can't communicate with its downstream neighbor, it sends the data along the secondary ring. When the data reaches the other end of the ring where the cable break is located, the data is transferred to the primary ring where it continues its journey.

An FDDI uses two types of NICs: **dual attachment station (DAS)** and **single attachment station (SAS)**. DASs attached to both rings are intended for use in servers, concentrators, and other devices that require full reliability. SASs connected to only one ring are intended for workstations attached to concentrators. These stations still benefit from the reliability of the dual rings in FDDI because the concentrators to which they are attached are usually also attached to both rings. Table 7-15 outlines the FDDI architecture.

Table 7-15   FDDI summary

Category	Summary
IEEE specification	No IEEE; ANSI X3T9.1
Advantages	Very fast; reliable; long distance; highly secure
Disadvantages	Expensive; difficult to install
Topology	Ring
Cable type	Fiber optic
Channel access method	Token passing
Maximum total network length	100 km (60 miles)
Maximum number of devices per network	500
Transmission speed	100 Mbps

NETWORKING ALTERNATIVES

Many other network architectures are available. Some are good for specialized applications, and others are emerging as new standards.

Broadband Technologies

The earlier discussion of the IEEE naming convention briefly mentioned broadband as a signal transmission type. Chapter 3 described the two techniques for sending data along a cable: baseband and broadband. Baseband systems use a digital encoding scheme at a single fixed frequency, where signals take the form of discrete pulses of electricity or light. In baseband systems, the cable's entire bandwidth transmits a single data signal, so these systems use only one channel on which all devices attached to the cable communicate.

However, broadband systems use analog techniques to encode information across a continuous range of values, instead of using binary 0s and 1s that characterize digital data in a baseband environment. Broadband signals move across the medium in the form of continuous electromagnetic or optical waves rather than discrete pulses. On broadband systems, data flows one way only, so two channels are necessary for computers to send and receive data. When trying to conceptualize broadband, think of your cable television connection. A single cable delivers dozens or hundreds of channels. This delivery is possible because each channel uses a different frequency, and the television tuner is used to capture only the data traveling on the channel that's currently set. Historically, broadband technology was limited to special applications. However, the Internet's rapid growth pushed broadband to the forefront again. New networking products use broadband transmission for extremely high-speed, reliable connectivity.

Cable Modem Technology

Cable modem networking is a broadband technology used to deliver Internet access to homes and businesses over standard cable television (CATV) coaxial cable. Because it's a broadband technology, data delivered to a cable modem shares the same cable as the television channels delivered to your TV set. In fact, Internet data simply travels on a television channel that's not used by the cable company to deliver television video. The official standard governing cable modem operation is called **Data Over Cable Service Interface Specification (DOCSIS)**. Although cable modems are considerably more complicated than dial-up modems, they are true modems in the sense that they modulate and demodulate signals.

Cable modem networks share some properties of traditional 10Base2 Ethernet. They are shared-media, bus topology networks at the point where data is delivered to a home. Other parts of a cable modem network use high-speed WAN technologies, such as ATM or SONET (discussed later in this chapter), as shown in Figure 7-11.

Cable modems have exploded in popularity because of the high speeds that Internet data can be delivered to homes and businesses. Internet data can be delivered at up to 27 Mbps, but most providers limit the data rate to between .5 Mbps and 2.5 Mbps. Cable modem uses an asymmetrical communication scheme—data rates going to the home (downstream rates) are different from data rates coming from the home to the cable provider (upstream rates). Upstream data rates can be as much as 10 Mbps but are usually limited to between 256 Kbps

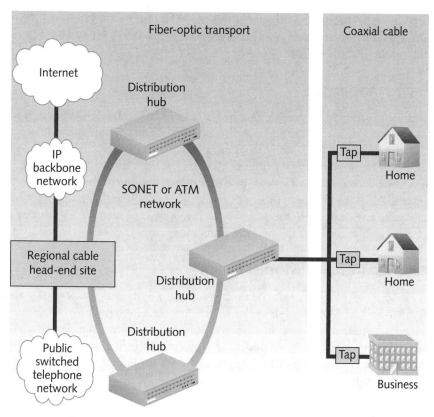

Figure 7-11   A typical cable modem network

and 1 Mbps. You can find additional information on cable modem and other modem technologies in the Chapter 13 discussion of enterprise and distributed networks.

For a wealth of information on cable modem technologies, see *www.cablemodem.com* and *www.cable-modem.net/tt/primer.html*.

NOTE

Digital Subscriber Line (DSL)

Digital subscriber line (DSL) bears special mention in this section, as it competes with cable modem technologies for Internet access. DSL is a broadband technology that uses existing phone lines to carry voice and data simultaneously. Many variations of DSL are available; the most prominent one for home Internet access is Asymmetric DSL (ADSL), named because the download and upload speeds differ significantly, so the data rates aren't symmetrical. ADSL splits the phone line into two frequency ranges: Frequencies below 4 KHz are used for voice transmission, and frequencies above 4 KHz are used to transmit data.

Typical connection speeds for downloading data range from 256 Kbps to 8 Mbps; upload speeds are typically much slower, in the range of 16 Kbps to 640 Kbps. Chapter 13 discusses DSL technology in more detail.

Broadcast Technologies

By definition, broadcast technologies are one-way transmissions. However, the advent of the Internet changed this, too, particularly in Internet access by satellite television systems. These systems work on the principle that most traffic a user generates is to receive files, text, and graphics. The average user's computer sends very little traffic. A user taking advantage of satellite service connects to a service provider through a regular modem. Then the service provider sends data by satellite to the user's home at speeds up to 400 Kbps. This method can be a more efficient way to use the available technology. One satellite TV vendor that offers Internet access via its broadcast network is DirectTV, through its DirectPC add-on products.

Asynchronous Transfer Mode (ATM)

Unlike the rest of the network architectures covered in this chapter, **Asynchronous Transfer Mode (ATM)** is a high-speed network technology designed for both LAN and WAN use. ATM uses connection-oriented switches to allow senders and receivers to communicate over a network. A **dedicated circuit**, which is an ongoing (but possibly transient) link between two end systems, must be set up before communication between those systems can begin.

In an ATM environment, data travels in short, 53-byte cells; 5 bytes contain header information and 48 bytes contain the data payload. All ATM transmissions consist of these cells, so a final cell in the data stream is padded with empty payload bytes when there are fewer than 48 bytes of payload to send. Fixed-length cells enable ATM to work at extremely high speeds because no single transmission is ever larger (or smaller) than the required cell size.

ATM works with network switches, which enables ATM cells to transit switches quickly and efficiently. Fixed-cell sizes help make traffic flow predictable because transfer time is a strict function of the amount of data to be transferred and the bandwidth available for its transfer. This predictability also enables ATM to guarantee QoS and deliver time-sensitive information, such as multimedia, audio, and videoconferencing, within a specified delay period. QoS features in ATM also permit certain types of network traffic to receive priority; time-sensitive data is always processed and forwarded before less time-sensitive traffic.

ATM originated as a telephone company technology and is used quite heavily for the backbone and infrastructure in large communications companies, such as AT&T, World-Com, and the Regional Bell Operating Companies. Since the mid-1990s, there has been a strong impetus to use ATM for both voice and data traffic and to make lower-speed ATM implementations available for LAN use as well. To a certain extent, the delivery and broad acceptance of Gigabit Ethernet somewhat blunted this initiative because Gigabit Ethernet retains the same basic frame structure and packet-level characteristics as slower forms of

Ethernet. As a result, it integrates more easily with existing LANs (most of which already use Ethernet). ATM's cell structure and its connection-oriented switching requirements mean that some form of LAN emulation (LANE) is required to use ATM for LAN applications. Likewise, these characteristics mean that using ATM for WAN backbones with conventional LAN technologies requires a special-purpose gateway device (or router interface) to permit ATM to send LAN traffic from one location to another.

Because of Gigabit Ethernet's popularity, ATM is best suited for LAN applications in situations where voice, data, and time-sensitive information (video, audio, multimedia, and so forth) travel on the same media. Also, ATM is the overwhelming choice for long-haul, high-bandwidth applications of just about any kind.

ATM and SONET Signaling Rates

ATM bandwidths are rated in terms of an optical carrier (OC) level that takes the form OC-*x*, with *x* representing a multiplier of the basic OC-1 carrier rate of 51.840 Mbps. The Exchange Carriers Standards Association (ECSA), working under the American National Standards Institute (ANSI), originally defined this rate for **Synchronous Optical Network (SONET)**. SONET is a high-speed, baseband digital networking standard that specifies incrementally increasing data rates across fiber-optic links. Because ECSA is a consortium of communications carriers—primarily long-distance telephone companies—ATM and SONET have strong roots in the telephone company community. ATM (the underlying signaling technology and transmission medium) and SONET (the overlying communications standards) represent state-of-the-art, all-digital, high-bandwidth communications designed to mix and match data, voice, and all kinds of time-sensitive information through a single high-capacity networking technology.

The signaling rates associated with SONET are the same as those for ATM. Table 7-16 lists common SONET optical carrier rates, which range from OC-1 (51.840 Mbps) to OC-3072 (159.2 Gbps). Typical ATM signaling rates currently range from OC-3 to OC-12, but both slower and faster implementations are available.

Table 7-16 Optical carrier signaling rates from OC-1 to OC-3072

Optical Carrier Designation	Signaling Rate
OC-1	51.84 Mbps
OC-3	155.52 Mbps
OC-9	466.56 Mbps
OC-12	622.08 Mbps
OC-24	1.244 Gbps
OC-36	1.866 Gbps
OC-48	2.488 Gbps
OC-96	4.976 Gbps
OC-192	9.953 Gbps
OC-255	13.271 Gbps
OC-768	39.813 Gbps

Table 7-16   Optical carrier signaling rates from OC-1 to OC-3072 (continued)

Optical Carrier Designation	Signaling Rate
OC-1536	79.6 Gbps
OC-3072	159.2 Gbps

As of early 2004, Internet backbone segments were being built that operated fiber-optic links at OC-768, and devices that supported OC-1536 were coming on the market. Other implementations on the horizon include striping OC-768 links to create aggregate bandwidth of hundreds of Gbps.

High Performance Parallel Interface (HIPPI)

Developed in the late 1980s, **High Performance Parallel Interface (HIPPI)** is a high-speed communication interface originally developed to serve supercomputers and high-end workstations. Serial HIPPI is a fiber-optic version of the original HIPPI, which uses a series of point-to-point optical links to provide network bandwidth up to 800 Mbps. In the early 1990s, 800 Mbps was blazingly fast, and HIPPI enjoyed some popularity as a network backbone and for interconnecting supercomputers. HIPPI networking products are still available in the form of NICs and switches, but with the advent of Gigabit Ethernet, interest in HIPPI as a LAN backbone decreased. In 1998, HIPPI extension HIPPI-6400 was developed, which provides up to 6.4 Gbps data transfer rates. HIPPI-6400 is now known as Gigabyte System Network (GSN). Although these speeds are impressive, HIPPI and GSN are considered exotic networking products and aren't often found in typical corporate networks. For more about HIPPI and GSN, point your Web browser to *www.hnf.org*.

CHAPTER SUMMARY

❑ Cable access methods determine how a network architecture gains access to the network medium (or data channel) to transmit data onto a network.

❑ A network's architecture defines how data is placed on the network, how that data is transmitted and at what speed, and how problems in the network are handled.

❑ Digital, Intel, and Xerox teamed to introduce Ethernet, which later became the IEEE 802.3 standard, transmitting data at 10 Mbps. This standard originally defined the standards for transmission over thicknet cable (10Base5). Later revisions to the standard included thinnet (10Base2), twisted-pair (10BaseT), and fiber-optic (10BaseF) cables. 100 Mbps Ethernet standards, most notably 802.3u, have been developed using the existing 802.3 standard. These standards encompass two cable types—twisted-pair and fiber-optic—and two twisted-pair cable configurations.

❑ Gigabit Ethernet is defined by two standards: 802.3z and 802.3ab. 802.3z defines 1000BaseX, which includes 1000BaseLX, 1000BaseSX, and 1000BaseCX, for specifying Gigabit Ethernet on different media types ranging from single-mode fiber-optic cable to twinax copper cable. 802.3ab defines 1000BaseT, which is Gigabit Ethernet running on Category 5 twisted-pair cable.

❏ 10 Gigabit Ethernet runs only over fiber-optic cable and only in full-duplex mode. A series of 10 Gigabit standards has been developed that specifies the type of fiber-optic cable and the distance limitations for various forms of 10 Gigabit Ethernet. These 10GBASE standards are divided into LAN and WAN implementations.

❏ Developed by IBM in the early 1980s, token ring networks are reliable, fast, and efficient. Capable of transmitting at 4 Mbps or 16 Mbps, token ring networks reconfigure themselves automatically to avoid cabling problems. Although wired as a physical star, the token ring architecture operates as a logical ring. One of the biggest benefits of token ring is that all computers have equal access to the network, which enables the network to grow easily and efficiently.

❏ Macintosh computers use AppleTalk to communicate over a network. AppleTalk Phase 2 includes the capability to use Ethernet and token ring networks for transporting Apple-Talk instead of the older and slower LocalTalk cabling system developed by Apple.

❏ FDDI is an extremely reliable, fast network architecture that uses dual counter-rotating rings in a token-passing environment. The dual rings enable FDDI to route traffic around problems in the network. However, it's an expensive network architecture usually reserved for installations where speed and security are paramount.

❏ Cable modem technology delivers high-speed Internet access to homes and businesses over existing CATV cable. Data rates typically range from 256 Kbps to 2.5 Mbps.

❏ ATM, a high-speed network technology designed both for LANs and WANs, uses connection-oriented switches to allow senders and receivers to communicate over a network. A dedicated circuit between two end systems must be set up before communication between those systems can begin. ATM is best suited for long-haul, high-bandwidth applications, although Gigabit Ethernet is still more popular because of the ease of incorporating it into existing Ethernet networks.

KEY TERMS

10BaseF — The 10 Mbps Ethernet standard that defines Ethernet over fiber-optic cable.

100BaseFX — 100 Mbps Ethernet over two-strand fiber-optic cable.

100BaseT4 — 100 Mbps Ethernet over four-pair Category 3 or higher UTP.

100BaseTX — 100 Mbps Ethernet over two-pair Category 5 or higher UTP.

1000BaseT — 1000 Mbps Ethernet (1 Gbps) over twisted-pair cabling; defined by IEEE Standard 802.3ab.

active monitor — A computer in a token ring network responsible for guaranteeing the network's status.

Asynchronous Transfer Mode (ATM) — A high-speed network technology designed for both LAN and WAN use. ATM uses connection-oriented switches to allow senders and receivers to communicate over a network.

beaconing — The signal transmitted on a token ring network to inform networked computers that token passing has stopped because of an error.

Carrier Sense Multiple Access with Collision Avoidance (CSMA/CA) — A contention-based channel access method in which computers avoid collisions by broadcasting their intent to send data.

Carrier Sense Multiple Access with Collision Detection (CSMA/CD) — A contention-based channel access method in which computers avoid collisions by listening to the network before sending data. If a computer senses data on the network, it waits and tries to send its data later.

channel access methods — Rules that determine when a computer can access the cable or data channel for the purposes of sending data.

collision — The result of two or more devices sending a signal along the same channel at the same time.

collision domain — The extent to which signals are propagated on an Ethernet network.

concentrators — Devices used in an FDDI network to connect computers at a central point. Most concentrators connect to both available rings.

contention — A channel access method in which computers vie for time on the network.

Data Over Cable Service Interface Specification (DOCSIS) — The official standard governing cable modem operation.

dedicated circuit — An ongoing (but possibly transient) link between two end systems.

demand priority — A high-speed channel access method used by 100VG-AnyLAN in a star hub topology.

demand signal — A signal sent by a computer in a demand priority network that informs the controlling hub it has data to send.

digital subscriber line (DSL) — A broadband-based technology that delivers Internet data over existing phone lines.

dual attachment station (DAS) — A type of NIC connected to both rings in an FDDI network.

Ethernet — A network architecture developed by Digital, Intel, and Xerox that uses CSMA/CD as its channel access method.

Ethernet 802.2 — An Ethernet frame type used by IPX/SPX on Novell NetWare 3.12 and 4.x networks.

Ethernet 802.3 — An Ethernet frame type generally used by IPX/SPX on Novell NetWare 2.x and 3.x networks; also called Ethernet raw.

Ethernet II — An Ethernet frame type used by TCP/IP.

Ethernet SubNetwork Address Protocol (SNAP) — An Ethernet frame type used in Apple's EtherTalk environment.

EtherTalk — The standard for sending AppleTalk over Ethernet cabling.

fast Ethernet — The 100 Mbps implementation of standard Ethernet, also called 100BaseT.

Fiber Distributed Data Interface (FDDI) — A networking architecture that uses a token-passing channel access method and is defined to run at 100 Mbps over fiber-optic cable.

frame types — A standard that defines the structure of an Ethernet packet: Ethernet 802.3, Ethernet 802.2, Ethernet SNAP, or Ethernet II.

full-duplex communication — In this type of communication, a computer can send and receive data simultaneously.

Gigabit Ethernet — An IEEE standard (802.3z) that allows for 1000 Mbps transmission using CSMA/CD and Ethernet frames.

half-duplex communication — In this type of communication, a computer can send data and receive data, but can't send and receive simultaneously.

High Performance Parallel Interface (HIPPI) — A high-speed parallel communication interface originally developed to serve supercomputers and high-end workstations.

LocalTalk — The cabling system used by Macintosh computers. Support for LocalTalk is built into every Macintosh.

multistation access unit (MSAU) — An active hub in a token ring network.

Nearest Active Downstream Neighbor (NADN) —The computer in a token ring environment to which another computer sends the token.

Nearest Active Upstream Neighbor (NAUN) —The computer in a token ring environment from which a computer receives the token.

polling — A channel access method in which a primary device asks secondary devices in sequence whether they have data to send.

primary ring — The FDDI ring around which data is transmitted.

protocol type field — A field used in the Ethernet SNAP and Ethernet II frames to indicate the network protocol being used.

secondary ring — An FDDI ring used for the sole purpose of handling traffic in the event of a cable failure.

single attachment station (SAS) — A type of NIC that's connected only to the primary ring in an FDDI network.

smart multistation access unit (SMAU) — An active hub in a token ring network.

standby monitors — Computers in a token ring network that monitor the network status and wait for a signal from the active monitor. *See also* active monitor.

start frame delimiter (SFD) — A field in the Ethernet 802.3 frame that defines the beginning of the packet.

switching — A media access method whereby all devices connect to a network switch, and the switch controls access to the medium. With switching, each device connected to the switch has access to the full media bandwidth.

Synchronous Optical Network (SONET) — A high-speed, baseband digital networking standard that specifies incrementally increasing data rates across fiber-optic links.

token ring — A network architecture developed by IBM that's physically wired as a star but uses token passing in a logical ring topology.

TokenTalk — The standard for sending AppleTalk over token ring cabling.

7

REVIEW QUESTIONS

1. Which access control method uses a device to check each potential sender to see whether it wants to transmit data?

   a. token ring

   b. Ethernet

   c. polling

   d. demand priority

   e. switching

2. Which access control method circulates special transmission packets to control media access?

   a. token passing

   b. Ethernet

   c. polling

   d. demand priority

   e. switching

3. Which access control method provides the highest bandwidth to the senders and receivers it connects?

   a. token passing

   b. Ethernet

   c. polling

   d. demand priority

   e. switching

4. Which of the following channel access methods is used in Ethernet networks?

   a. CSMA/CD

   b. polling

   c. demand priority

   d. CSMA/CA

   e. token passing

5. Which of the following is an advantage of polling? (Choose all that apply.)

   a. price

   b. equal access to the medium for all computers on the network

   c. efficient use of network media

   d. allows priority assignment

6. What are the different implementations of 100 Mbps Ethernet? (Choose all that apply.)

   a. 100BaseT4

   b. 100BaseTX

   c. 100BaseFX

   d. 100BaseSX

7. How many rings exist in an FDDI network?

   a. one

   b. two

   c. three

   d. four

8. Which Ethernet frame type does TCP/IP use?

   a. Ethernet 802.2

   b. Ethernet II

   c. Ethernet 802.3

   d. Ethernet SNAP

9. What is the function of the active monitor in a token ring network?

10. How many hubs can exist between two communicating hosts in an Ethernet hub-based network?

11. What channel access method does 802.11b use?

    a. polling

    b. CSMA/CD

    c. CSMA/CA

    d. token passing

12. Which of the following is common to all Ethernet implementations?

    a. speed

    b. encoding method

    c. frame formats

    d. media type

13. What is the function of the CRC in Ethernet?

14. What device serves as the central point of connection in an FDDI network?

    a. hub

    b. router

    c. concentrator

    d. bridge

7

15. What is the maximum bandwidth you can achieve when running Gigabit Ethernet in full-duplex mode?

    a. 2000 Mbps

    b. 1 Gbps

    c. 500 Mbps

    d. 5000 Mbps

16. What minimum grade of cable is required for 1000BaseT?

    a. Category 3

    b. Category 4

    c. Category 5

    d. Category 6

17. How many rings are used in a token ring environment?

    a. one

    b. two

    c. three

    d. four

18. The _____ problem requires 802.11b hosts to send a CTS frame before transmitting data.

19. What type of cable does 10GBASE-SR use?

20. Which 100 Mbps Ethernet standard can use Category 3 cable?

    a. 100Base2

    b. 100Base5

    c. 100BaseFX

    d. 100BaseT4

21. Which of the following is a transmission speed for token ring?

    a. 10 Mbps

    b. 100 Mbps

    c. 14 Mbps

    d. 16 Mbps

22. Which network architecture can automatically correct for cable failures? (Choose all that apply.)

    a. ARCnet

    b. Ethernet

    c. token ring

    d. FDDI

23. Data is sent on the _____ ring in an FDDI network.

24. What is a hub in a token ring network called?

    a. transceiver

    b. MSAU

    c. AUI

    d. DIX

25. Which channel access method does LocalTalk use?

    a. polling

    b. CSMA/CD

    c. CSMA/CA

    d. token passing

26. What kind of connections does ATM establish before starting network communications?

    a. dedicated circuit

    b. temporary circuit

    c. short circuit

    d. connection-oriented circuit

27. Which of the following IEEE specifications applies to 1000BaseX?

    a. 802.3

    b. 802.3z

    c. 802.3ab

    d. 802.3ac

28. Which of the following capabilities does ATM's fixed-length (53-byte) cell structure enable? (Choose all that apply.)

    a. By making all traffic elements the same size, it makes traffic flow more predictable.

    b. It makes it possible to offer QoS guarantees for time-sensitive data.

    c. It helps make traffic prioritization possible.

    d. It makes cell-switching fast and efficient.

    e. It is required to support connection-oriented services, such as phone calls.

29. What is the standard for 10 Gbps Ethernet?

    a. 802.3g

    b. 802.11b

    c. 802.3ae

    d. 802.5

30. The document governing cable modem standards is _____ .

31. The maximum number of class I fast Ethernet repeaters allowed between stations is
_____ .

   a. four

   b. three

   c. two

   d. one

HANDS-ON PROJECTS

The rate of change in networking technology is truly amazing. In the mid-1990s, networking at 100 Mbps was considered astonishingly fast; today, 10/100 Ethernet NICs and devices are the most commonly purchased networking components. Currently, Gigabit Ethernet is becoming increasingly affordable, and 10 Gbps is in use for backbone connections.

This set of projects helps you learn how to locate current information about networking architectures and technologies. As you work through them, be aware that learning how to search for information is as important as understanding the information you find. Likewise, identifying what's worth your time and effort amid the many sources of information a search engine returns is an essential skill. (In fact, you can find information more quickly and easily if you work with the best possible sources.)

HANDS-ON PROJECTS

Hands-On Project 7-1

This project requires a computer with a Web browser and Internet access. You access the IEEE Web site to download an IEEE 802 standard. Feel free to spend some time exploring the site after you complete the steps.

1. Open your Web browser, type **standards.ieee.org/getieee802/portfolio.html** in the Address text box, and then press **Enter**.

2. Click the **IEEE 802.11 TM: Wireless** link.

3. Next, click the **IEEE 802.11b-1999** link.

4. Click the **USER TYPE** list arrow, and then click one of the available options. Read the license agreement, and click the **ACCEPT/BEGIN DOWNLOAD** button if you want to download the document. You can follow these directions to download any of the listed 802 documents.

5. Close your Internet connection, unless you plan to continue to the next project.

HANDS-ON PROJECTS

Hands-On Project 7-2

This project requires a computer with a Web browser and Internet access. You access the SmartDraw Web site to download diagramming software, which you can use for a 30-day trial in this project.

1. Open your Web browser, type **www.smartdraw.com** in the Address text box, and then press **Enter**.

2. Click the **Download** button at the upper left, and then click the **Free Download!** button.

3. Make sure the **Save to Disk** option button is selected, and then click **OK**.

4. While the file is downloading, read the installation instructions, and then install SmartDraw after it has finished downloading.

5. Close your Internet connection, and leave your system running for the next project.

**HANDS-ON
PROJECTS**

Hands-On Project 7-3

7

This project requires a network connection. Follow these steps to display the status of your network connection and view its current speed:

1. Right-click the **My Network Places** desktop icon, and click **Properties**. (If My Network Places is not on the desktop, click **Start**, right-click **My Network Places**, and click **Show on Desktop**.)

2. In the Network Connections window, right-click the **Local Area Connection** icon, and click **Properties** to open the Local Area Connection Properties dialog box.

3. In the Connect using section, note the type of NIC installed for this connection. At the bottom of the dialog box, click to select the **Show icon in notification area when connected** check box.

4. Click **OK** and then close the Network Connections window. An information box showing the connection speed is displayed in the lower-right corner of your desktop.

5. Now look at the network connection status icon in the taskbar, which you learned about in Hands-On Project 4-5. Place your mouse pointer over this icon, and write down the speed displayed in the yellow pop-up box:

_____

6. Click this icon to open the Local Area Connection Status dialog box, which shows the connection status (connected, disconnected, or disabled) and the duration and speed of the connection. Write down these values:

_____

_____

7. Close the Local Area Connection Status dialog box, and leave your system running for the next project.

Hands-On Project 7-4

This project requires a computer with a Web browser and Internet access. Follow these steps to access a Web-based encyclopedia to look for information about FDDI:

1. Open your Web browser, type **webopedia.internet.com** in the Address text box, and then press **Enter**.

2. In the SEARCH section, type **FDDI** in the Enter a word for a definition text box, and then click **Go!**

3. Scroll to the LINKS section near the bottom of the page, and click the **Fiber Distributed Data Interface** link. You see another page that includes several links. Browse through these links to learn more about FDDI.

4. Close your Internet connection, unless you plan to continue to the next project.

NOTE   Start your search for technical information at a site that specializes in explaining that content, such as TechFest, Webopedia, and CMP's TechWeb (*www. techweb.com*). These sites help you find the information you need much faster than a conventional search engine. Building your own list of these resources is recommended, and you should skip general-purpose search engines except when specialized tools don't help you find what you need.

Hands-On Project 7-5

This project shows you how to select the correct frame type in an IPX/SPX environment.

1. Right-click the **My Network Places** desktop icon, and click **Properties**.

2. In the Network Connections window, right-click the **Local Area Connection** icon, and click **Properties**.

NOTE   This project assumes that the NWLink IPX/SPX protocol is not already installed on your computer. If it is, skip to Step 5.

3. Click the **Install** button. In the Select Network Component Type dialog box, click **Protocol**, and then click the **Add** button.

4. Click **NWLink IPX/SPX/NetBIOS Compatible Transport Protocol**, and then click **OK**.

5. In the Local Area Connection Properties dialog box, find and click the **NWLink IPX/SPX/NetBIOS Compatible Transport Protocol**. (Do not click the check box next to the protocol description.) Click the **Properties** button.

6. In the Adapter section of the Properties dialog box, find the Frame type drop-down list. What is the current frame type selected?

_____

7. Click the **Frame type** list arrow to see the available frame type selections, and list them here. When you're finished, click **Cancel**.

_____

_____

_____

_____

7

8. Click **Close** and close the Network Connections window.

CASE PROJECTS

If you downloaded and installed SmartDraw in Hands-On Project 7-2, you can use it for some of these case projects.

CASE PROJECTS

Case Project 7-1

Handy Widgets, Inc., operates in an office park in three buildings that aren't currently connected to each other. Each building has four floors and is occupied by 50 to 60 Handy employees, all of whom have computers. Each floor has four printers that all employees on that floor use. The cabling closet on each floor of each building is centrally located, with no desktop run past 50 meters. You're hired to design a new network that must support high-speed connections between the buildings, which are 500 to 700 meters apart, with some fault tolerance.

Two of the buildings (buildings 1 and 3) are prewired to the desktop with Category 5 UTP. Currently, they run in a workgroup environment. Building 2 is new, ready for cabling to your specifications. The Information Technology (IT) steering committee wants the network to be able to move easily from 10 Mbps to 100 Mbps and asks you to design the network with this requirement in mind. Building 3 houses all servers in a computer control center, which occupies the entire second floor; speed and fault tolerance are imperative there, too.

Outline the specifications you'll use to design this network, including the network architectures, transmission speeds, cabling changes, and so forth. Draw the network you design, including media types, distances, numbers of hubs, locations, and so forth. Your drawing might resemble Figure 7-12.

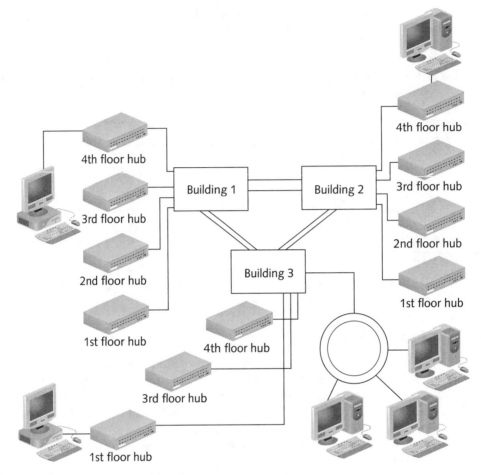

Figure 7-12   One possible solution

Case Project 7-2

As administrator for your group's Macintosh network (still running Apple's proprietary LocalTalk), you're asked to help upgrade and connect the network to the existing PC network. Your department has grown rapidly, raising concerns about whether the network can handle the expansion. With these considerations in mind, develop a plan to upgrade and connect the networks. Outline the specifications you will use to design this network, including the network architectures, protocols, transmission speeds, cabling changes, and so forth. Draw the network you design.

Case Project 7-3

Your company expanded recently to include two new buildings for a total of three, roughly arranged in a triangle with each building about 500 meters apart. Previously, these buildings were wired with Category 3 UTP running 10BaseT Ethernet. The IT director mandates that your company be among the first to use 1000 Mbps Ethernet to the desktop. Define a comprehensive network architecture that fulfills the director's requirements and allows for future growth.

Case Project 7-4

You're asked to design a network for use in a training environment. It should be mobile, easy to set up, and simple to tear down. Speed is not an issue. Develop a network design that accommodates these requirements and keeps costs down.

7

CHAPTER

8

SIMPLE NETWORK OPERATIONS

After reading this chapter and completing the exercises, you will be able to:

♦ Explain the operation fundamentals of network operating systems

♦ Describe networking software components

♦ Describe the basic steps of network operating system installation

♦ Configure network services

♦ Explain network application installation and configuration concepts

The subject of network operations spans many aspects of network computing, including the types of applications and services, how an administrator installs or enables these services for access by users, and how the network is managed. Before anything occurs on a network, however, a few prerequisites must be satisfied. First, a network operating system (NOS) must be installed; then the network must offer some type of resource or service, such as network applications or shared files and peripherals. This chapter also discusses the issues in installing an NOS, connecting network printers, sharing files and directories, and accessing network applications.

NETWORK OPERATING SYSTEMS

A network operating system (NOS) is a computer operating system with functions that facilitate network communication, allow computer resources to be shared on a network, and provide management functions to control access to those resources. Whereas the cables, devices, and protocols discussed in previous chapters provide the infrastructure for networks, the NOS serves as an interface for users and applications to access the network and its resources.

The addition of NOSs to the personal computing world occurred during the mid-1980s. Initially, the capability to communicate over a network was added to existing operating systems by installing drivers, network protocols, and network client software. Therefore, early networks did not use an NOS at all; they used standalone operating systems, such as DOS or Windows 2.x, with additional, usually third-party, software that allowed them to communicate on the network. Both the main OS and NOS extensions had to be installed on a single computer before it could communicate over the network.

True NOSs quickly replaced this solution. These systems handle standalone computer activities as well as communication over the network. The most notable examples of these NOSs include Novell NetWare, Windows Server 2000/2003, UNIX, and Linux.

Basic Functions of an Operating System

Not so long ago, networks consisted of client operating systems and server operating systems. A client OS ran on a computer that sat on a user's desktop, and its main job was to run productivity applications, such as word processors and spreadsheets, and access network resources on a server. A server operating system or NOS ran on a computer that sat in an equipment room, and its job was to share files and printers and provide access to other shared resources. The NOS needed special capabilities to handle multiple network requests and provide a variety of services simultaneously. Two features unique to an NOS were multitasking and time slicing. Now, however, most operating systems can be considered an NOS because they can access and provide network services and manage access to those services. In addition, every contemporary OS includes the functions of multitasking and time slicing—two functions critical to your understanding of how operating systems work.

A computer's OS directs the activities of that computer's hardware components. It controls memory, CPU, storage devices, and peripherals (such as printers). Without an OS, a computer is a nonfunctional pile of expensive metal and plastic. The OS coordinates interaction between software applications and computer hardware. Although applications can sometimes operate on multiple versions of an OS (such as Windows XP and Windows Vista or Red Hat Linux and SUSE Linux), most applications are written so that they can be used only with a particular OS family. For example, the Apache Web server written for Linux does not function on a computer running Windows without changes being made to the software.

Multitasking is the capability of an OS to support numerous processes at one time. A process can be a running application, such as a Web browser, or a service that runs behind the scenes, such as a virus scanner. Support for a process includes managing the memory space a process uses, providing access to hardware, and providing CPU time for the process to run. Most multitasking gives the illusion that multiple applications can run simultaneously. For example, you can be surfing on the Internet while your virus scanner is busy checking files downloaded to and accessed on your computer. In reality, unless you have more than one CPU, the multitasking function is quickly switching control of the CPU from one application or service to another. This switching can occur so fast that you don't realize it's happening.

NOTE   Many of today's CPUs have the capability to act as multiple CPUs through the use of hyperthreading technology or dual-core CPU design, thus allowing these CPUs to process more than one instruction at a time.

8

Time slicing occurs when the CPU's computing cycles (of which there are billions per second) are divided between more than one task. Each task receives a limited number of process cycles before the CPU halts it and activates the next task. This activity repeats until each task is completed. This activity is perceived as many applications operating simultaneously because each time slice is a very small amount of time, on the order of 1/50th of a second. Human inability to distinguish instances of this brief time period creates the illusion of multitasking. There are two types of multitasking:

- *Preemptive multitasking*—The OS controls which process gets access to the CPU and for how long; when the assigned time slice expires, the current process halts, and the next process gets its computing time.

- *Cooperative multitasking*—The OS cannot stop a process; when a process receives control of the CPU, it maintains control until it satisfies its computing needs. No other process can access the CPU until the current process releases it.

A true high-performance NOS must be a preemptive multitasking system. Otherwise, it couldn't complete many time-dependent tasks and would repeatedly fail to complete tasks. All contemporary operating systems are designed to use preemptive multitasking.

Although it's true that today's operating systems include many of the features once reserved for an NOS, a number of features and functions, discussed in the following section, are still reserved for OSs designed to be installed on a server computer versus OSs designed to work on a desktop computer.

SOFTWARE COMPONENTS OF NETWORKING

A true NOS is an operating system that has built-in capabilities to both manage the local computer's activities and provide a network environment within which all computers on a network can operate. Some of these capabilities include the following:

- Organize all machines and peripherals on a network into an interactive whole
- Coordinate and control the functions of machines and peripherals across the network
- Support security and privacy for both the network and users
- Control access to resources by user authentication
- Advertise and manage resources from a centralized directory
- Provide access to shared resources, such as printers, files, and the Internet

These capabilities are made possible through a number of NOS components, such as naming services, directory services, and client and server software, discussed in the following sections.

Naming Services

On most networks, a name is necessary to identify and access resources of all kinds. Because humans recognize symbolic names more easily than numeric names, modern networks generally include one or more naming services to translate symbolic names (such as "AccountingServer") into corresponding network addresses (such as 172.16.12.23). In the NetBIOS discussion in Chapter 6, you learned some functions of NetBIOS names on a Microsoft network or on a Linux network using Samba. This chapter explains the relationship between how Microsoft uses NetBIOS names and how the TCP/IP-based Domain Name System uses domain names.

NetBIOS Names

Until the release of Windows 2000, Microsoft networking depended almost completely on using NetBIOS names to identify computers, shared drives and directories, printers, and other network resources. Recall that the NetBIOS name is the name assigned to a Windows computer during OS installation. Correct use of NetBIOS names depends on understanding the following rules for their construction:

- NetBIOS names can be no longer than 15 characters.
- Certain characters, listed in Table 8-1, can't appear anywhere in a valid NetBIOS name.

■ Ending a NetBIOS name with a dollar sign ($) prevents that name from appearing in the NetBIOS browse list. You use this character to hide computer and share names. Windows Server 2000/2003, XP, and Vista use this technique to create administrative drive shares by default; any administrator can access the share by adding a dollar sign after the drive letter. (For example, \\Ntw009\C$ accesses the C: drive on the machine named Ntw009.) However, only an administrator can access the share, and it must be accessed with the Universal Naming Convention path rather than through a My Network Places browse list.

Table 8-1   Invalid characters in a NetBIOS name

Symbol	Description	Symbol	Description
/	Right slash	\	Left slash
<	Left angle bracket	>	Right angle bracket
[	Left square bracket	]	Right square bracket
+	Plus sign	=	Equal sign
"	Double quotation mark	'	Apostrophe/single quotation mark
,	Comma	?	Question mark
:	Colon	*	Asterisk
;	Semicolon	|	Vertical slash
)	Close (right) parenthesis	(	Open (left) parenthesis

Universal Naming Convention

Drive mapping is the process of associating a network storage resource with a local drive letter. However, it's not the only way to access network resources. Windows and Linux (running Samba) operating systems and most other modern NOSs recognize **Universal Naming Convention (UNC)** paths, a standard method for specifying network resources. UNC paths usually take the form *servername**sharename*; for example, the Accounting share on the FINANCE server is \\FINANCE\Accounting. In UNC-aware applications and many command-line activities, a UNC path can be used instead of a drive letter to access a network resource. A quick way to try UNC paths is to click Start, Run, and type *computername* (replacing *computername* with the name of another computer on the network or even your own computer name). If the computer is found, a Windows Explorer window opens, showing the shared resources available on that computer.

Domain Names and DNS

In Chapter 6, you learned about the IP-based Domain Name System (DNS), which makes it possible to translate symbolic domain names, such as *microsoft.com*, into numeric IP addresses, such as 207.46.131.30. The NetBIOS-based naming services Microsoft uses enable users to access resources and services through symbolic names on a Microsoft network. In much the same way, DNS permits users to access resources and services by using symbolic domain names on the Internet (and other TCP/IP-based networks where DNS is available).

NOTE Beginning with Windows 2000 Server, Microsoft included support for the Dynamic DNS (DDNS) naming service, which largely replaces the NetBIOS-based naming service in Microsoft networks. However, NetBIOS naming is still configured by default for backward compatibility.

A DNS server maintains a database of computer name and IP address pairs. At least one DNS server is maintained for every domain. A domain is a named logical grouping of network resources, usually representing a company or a department within a company. For example, *course.com* is the domain name of this book's publisher, and *www* specifies the Web server maintained at Course Technology. For someone inside the *course.com* domain, the Web server can probably be accessed by using just the name *www*. To access that server from outside the domain, however, you must specify its name and domain in the format *www.course.com*. When a network request for *www.course.com* is made, the request is sent to the DNS server responsible for the *course.com* domain. That DNS server responds with the IP address of the computer hosting Web services at Course Technology. In this way, DNS servers help provide a centralized way to organize and access computers in a network.

Directory Services

The disadvantage of name services, such as DNS, is that you must know—or guess—a name before you can ask for a resource or browse a list of available resources by network and node. A better approach to handling network names, especially for resources, is to take advantage of a directory service. A **directory service** is a network service that manages information about other network services, resources, users, groups, and other objects so that users can access resources and services by browsing for them or asking for them by type. In addition, a directory service manages and controls access to network resources. A directory service works for a network much like the yellow pages in a phone book. You look up companies by name (if you know the name), but you can also look them up by type of service or resource (such as "electricians" or "plumbers"). Users can request services or resources in a generic way—such as "printer" or "e-mail server"—and let the underlying directory server figure out which printer is closest to their desk (or give users directions on how to find the printer) or which server they should use for file services, Internet access, remote access, and so forth. However, typically users don't care which server they use, as long as they get the services they request as soon as possible!

Windows 2000 Server is the first Microsoft NOS that included Active Directory, a comprehensive directory service, just as NetWare (starting with version 4.0) includes Novell eDirectory (formerly Novell Directory Services [NDS]). Both services use a "tree and forest" metaphor to organize directory contents. Network resources are displayed in some kind of container (such as a subdirectory in Windows Explorer) in which all resources are organized and listed for easy inspection and access. Most Linux versions include a directory service of sorts called Network Information System (NIS). This service primarily handles centralized logon and file sharing. Add-on directory services with enhanced capabilities are also available from Sun Microsystems and Novell.

Better still, the servers that store directory information—directory servers—do so in a database that lists the shared resources available over the network, and users or programs can make queries to this database. Therefore, if a user or program wants to use a color laser printer, for example, a quick query to the directory server determines whether the server can fulfill that request and whether the user is allowed to use the color laser printer. The server redirects the print job without requiring further user or program action.

In addition, directory servers store access control information about services and resources as part of the database record that represents these devices to the directory. Therefore, directory services can prevent users from seeing resources or services they're not allowed to access. In fact, most directory services perform routine access control checks as a part of granting access to the services and resources that users are allowed to see. In this way, directory services help centralize security information for a network as well as coordinate and advertise the network's available resources and services.

Both Novell eDirectory and Microsoft Active Directory were patterned after a vendor-independent directory service called **X.500** that's built around the OSI protocol stack. Because X.500 has considerable overhead, another directory service, Lightweight Directory Access Protocol (LDAP), was developed. LDAP is similar to X.500 but is far easier to implement. LDAP runs on TCP/IP and is making inroads as a directory service for Linux and for Internet resources. With the addition of LDAP, many remote devices, such as handheld PDAs, can access the NOS directory without running the NOS locally. Directory services are becoming more critical in today's information-intensive computing environments; their importance will only increase in the future.

NOTE

The following section covers software components that operate on the client side to make networking possible. Strictly speaking, naming and directory services are server services, but because they are so important to the functioning of modern networks, they have been discussed before other software components.

Client Network Software

Client network software is a portion of the NOS installed on computers that's used to access network services or network resources. From the user's point of view, an NOS simply offers a wider range of resources to access. However, a lot more goes on inside an NOS client than inside a non-network-enabled OS. The most important of these software components is a redirector.

As mentioned in Chapter 5, a redirector is a software component operating at the OSI model's Presentation layer and is found on both client and server NOSs. Whenever a user or an application requests a resource—such as a printer or a data file—a redirector intercepts that request. Then the redirector examines the request to determine whether the resource is local (on the computer) or remote (on the network). If the resource is local, the redirector sends the request to the local software component for immediate processing. If the resource is remote, the redirector sends the request over the network to the server of that resource.

Although Microsoft documentation uses the term "redirector," Novell uses the term "requester." In Linux (and some other OSs), the term "shell" sometimes refers to this component.

Redirectors route resource requests to computers or directly to a peripheral device. Redirector resource routing most commonly occurs when the local printer port, LPT1, is mapped to a network printer instead of to a locally attached printer. In these cases, the redirector intercepts the print request, recognizes that the LPT1 port is mapped to a network peripheral instead of being assigned locally, and then routes that request to the server hosting the network printer.

The advantage of a redirector is its capability to hide from users the complicated tasks involved in accessing network resources. After a network resource is defined, users never have to think about its location; access to network resources works the same as access to local resources.

A **designator** is another NOS software component that aids in network resource interaction. A designator keeps track of the drive letters assigned locally to remote or shared drives. (A shared drive is known as a **share**.) When a drive is mapped, the designator notes the drive letter assigned to each network resource. When a user or an application attempts to access the assigned drive letter, the designator substitutes the resource's real network address before letting the request go to the redirector.

Redirectors and designators make up the client portion of a client/server OS used in a network environment for file and print sharing. Today, because use of the Internet and TCP/IP is commonplace, client software can refer to a Web browser, an e-mail program, an FTP client, or other Internet access applications. In addition, new forms of client software are being developed for the exploding handheld OS market to meet the unique requirements of these devices.

Server Network Software

Server network software, a component integral to an NOS, handles resources and services to be distributed to clients. This type of networking software is called a server because it's the networking system component that "serves" resources—in other words, makes them available to users. Although a client computer can function with only a redirector, server computer components are more complex. The purpose of a server is to allow sharing resources, as shown in Figure 8-1.

Part of resource sharing is the capability to restrict access to resources by using access controls. Access controls are security features that determine which resources users are permitted to access, what type of access they are allowed, and how many simultaneous users can access a resource at the same time. They ensure data privacy and protection and help maintain a productive computing environment.

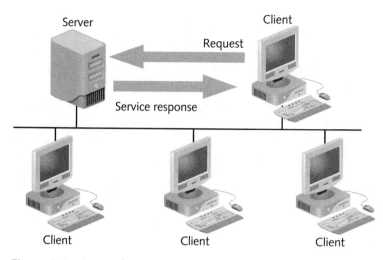

Figure 8-1 Server functions

The following example demonstrates why access controls are important. A shared folder on a network contains an organization's financial statement. Users in the Finance Department have full control over that report, so they can change, replace, or delete it. Users in the Sales Department have read-only access to the report, so they can only examine its contents. Users in the Data Entry Department have no access to the report, so they can't even open the file. Only authorized users have access to the confidential data in this report, and this authorized access can be fine-tuned further if needed.

In addition to protecting and delivering resources, server software usually has other responsibilities, such as:

- Management of users and groups
- Logon authentication of users
- Management, control, and auditing tools to administer the network
- Fault tolerance to protect the integrity of the network and the data it supports

In addition to these features, most server operating systems contain or support the same features found in client OSs, including redirectors, designators, and UNC name support. Servers use these features to host and offer resources to clients and to access resources from other servers elsewhere on the network.

Client and Server Capabilities

Many NOSs, such as Windows Server 2003, XP, and Vista, include client and server capabilities in both the server versions and the versions intended for desktop computers, such as the Professional and Home Edition versions of XP. Having both capabilities enables servers and desktop computers to host and use network resources. Generally, the desktop version of the NOS is not as powerful or robust as the server version. For example, Windows Server 2003 can host the Active Directory service and DNS and allows fault-tolerant disk configurations, but Windows XP and Vista don't have these capabilities. An important resource located on a computer running the desktop OS version can still be shared with the rest of the network, however.

Unlike Windows, Novell NetWare is strictly a server NOS, so there's no desktop version of NetWare. A desktop computer, whether it's running Windows, Linux, or Mac OS, can become a NetWare client by installing the appropriate client software. In Linux, the choice between a desktop or server installation is usually made during installation. Desktop installations generally have far fewer network services installed; server installations usually offer a wide variety of network services. So with Linux, you can choose how you want the computer to behave—more like a desktop computer or more like a server computer. In addition, by simply adding the appropriate services, you can transform a Linux desktop computer into a server, if need be.

NOTE

If a single PC hosts more than two heavily accessed resources, you should consider transferring these resources to a real server because accessing them can reduce performance on a PC running a desktop OS.

Installing a Network Operating System

Installing an NOS is not much different from installing a standard desktop OS. It requires only a few additional steps focused on configuring the network and the server services. Later sections in this chapter review the major steps in installing Windows Server 2003, Linux Fedora Core 4, and Novell NetWare 6.5. Before installation of an NOS can begin, however, you must complete a few preparatory steps.

Installation Preparation

Before you begin an NOS installation, you need to understand the following network aspects, discussed in more detail in the following sections:

- Size of the network
- Job requirements of the server
- Organization of storage devices
- File systems to be used
- Identification or naming convention
- Network adapter configuration

- Protocol selection
- Hardware compatibility

Size of the Network

The size of a network can affect which services you decide to configure, how many servers you need, and the number of connection licenses you require, among other things. A small LAN with fewer than 10 users who require only file and printer sharing can probably function fine with a peer-to-peer network without a dedicated server. In this case, Windows XP or Vista could serve as the OS. However, with more users or more advanced networking service requirements, a dedicated server with an NOS designed for servers is definitely in order.

Server Job Requirements

The services and resources a server hosts often determine what components or add-ons are installed. Knowing a machine's job requirements before installing the NOS is important. This information can simplify installation and guide configuration later by having the correct components active on the system. Some services you might evaluate and install include DNS, Dynamic Host Configuration Protocol (DHCP), Web services, and remote access services, among others.

A server's responsibilities don't end with the services and resources it hosts. You must resolve many other server-related issues. In the world of Windows networking, you can configure a server as a domain controller or a member server. A domain controller, as mentioned in Chapter 1, authenticates users and maintains directory services and the security database for a domain. A **member server** simply hosts a service or resource and doesn't participate in maintaining the directory and security database. In general, installing at least two domain controllers in a domain is a good idea so that if one server fails, the other continues to provide access to the directory and security database. An additional domain controller provides built-in data redundancy to avoid loss of access to a key data resource for a Windows domain.

NetWare servers require that you decide whether to install the server into an existing eDirectory tree (typically the choice for all servers except the first one installed in the organization) or create a new tree (typically the choice when it's the first NetWare server installed in the organization).

When installing Linux on a server, you can choose which networking services you require, such as DNS, DHCP, Web servers, and more. Most Linux installations have an option to install Linux as a server, in which case most essential networking services are installed automatically. Linux can also be installed as a workstation or desktop OS, in which case client software is primarily installed. Another option is a custom installation, which allows you to choose each service you want to install.

Storage Device Organization

The organization of storage devices is crucial to a network's success when accessibility, performance, and fault tolerance are essential. The most important organization decision about storage devices is how to organize the drive containing or hosting the NOS, especially deciding whether partitions are used. A **partition** is a logical organization of disk space, in which each portion (partition) appears as a separate logical drive. There are four schools of thought on the best way to organize an NOS host drive:

- *Multiple-boot*—A multiple-boot configuration enables you to select among many OSs and NOSs at startup. Although multiboot systems are good for testing and learning purposes, they can compromise security in networks that are in actual business use.

- *Single-partition, single-NOS*—A single-partition, single-NOS configuration is a drive that has a single primary partition reserved for the NOS. This configuration is the most secure.

- *Multiple-partition, single-NOS*—A multiple partition, single-NOS configuration is a drive with two or more partitions, one partition for the NOS and the other partitions for data storage. This configuration is useful for separating data from OS files on large drives but increases the level of drive activity and can degrade the life of the drive more quickly.

- *Fault-tolerant storage*—Most server computers today come equipped with two or more drives that can be configured for fault tolerance. The simplest form of fault tolerance is disk mirroring, which requires two identical disk partitions on two separate drives. Although most NOSs include fault-tolerant disk configuration, computers designed as servers often come equipped with disk controllers called redundant array of independent disks (RAID) controllers that provide fault tolerance in hardware. However it's done, the fault-tolerant configuration of your storage systems is a critical part of the NOS installation. For more information on RAID and levels of RAID, go to *www.acnc.com/04_01_00.html*.

The organizational method you choose for storage devices should reflect and support your security needs as well as your hardware availability.

File Systems

A second important issue of storage organization is the file system. A **file system** is the method by which an OS stores, organizes, and manages access to files on a mass storage device, such as a hard drive. File systems differ in how they allocate space for files, how files are located on the disk, what level of fault tolerance is built into the system, and how access to files is secured. Some fault-tolerant features of a file system include backup copies of the file allocation table (FAT) and journaling, in which file transactions are kept in a digital journal so that incomplete or corrupt transactions can be undone if needed. File systems such as FAT and FAT32, a more advanced version, are fairly simple and ensure compatibility across operating systems and OS versions but do not provide any folder- or file-level security. This lack of built-in security means that anyone who logs on to the system can access all files on the hard drive. FAT was used in the original DOS, and FAT32, which allows larger hard drive partitions, came about in the second release of Windows 95. More advanced file systems, such as New Technology File System (NTFS, used in Windows NT/2000/XP/2003/Vista) and ext3 (used in Linux) provide folder- and file-level security as well as some fault-tolerant features. When building a server, it's best to use the most secure file system available for the OS you're installing.

Naming Conventions

A **naming convention** is a predetermined method of creating names for use on a network or standalone computer. A good naming convention incorporates a scheme for user accounts, computers, directories, network shares, printers, and servers. In addition, these names should be descriptive enough so that anyone can determine which names correspond to which objects. This requirement applies equally to Windows, Novell, and Linux servers because regardless of the server in use, names provide a way for users to identify and access resources.

Using a formal naming convention might seem pointless for a single computer or small networks. However, small networks seldom stay small. In fact, most networks expand at an alarming rate. If you begin naming server resources randomly, you soon forget which name corresponds to which resource. Even with excellent management tools, without a standard way to name items, you can quickly lose track of important resources.

The naming convention your organization chooses doesn't matter, as long as it creates useful names for new resources. These common naming schemes give you an idea of how naming conventions work:

- Construct user names from the user's first and last names, plus a code identifying his or her job title or department, such as BobSmithVP.

- Construct group names from resource types, department names, location names, project names, and combinations of all four. Adding the word "group" or an abbreviation to the end of the group name is a good idea. For example, to identify a group of users allowed to use Printer1, you could name the group Printer1-Group, or to identify users in the Accounting Department at the Phoenix location, you could name the group AcctPhx-Grp.

- Construct computer names for servers and clients from their department, location, and an identifying number, such as SalesTexas01.

No matter what naming convention you use, it must meet the following requirements:

- Be consistent across all objects

- Be easy to use and understand

- Be able to identify object types clearly

Therefore, before you install a new server, you must create its name. Identifying a server's name (and a corresponding network address) are key steps in any server's installation.

Network Adapter Configuration

The network interface card (NIC) is the primary communication device between a computer and the rest of the network. A computer purchased as a server already has a NIC installed, but verifying the NIC manufacturer and model number is important so that you can ensure compatibility and update device drivers as necessary. Most of today's NICs are plug-and-play-compatible with the OS, so NIC configuration isn't usually necessary. However, you should verify compatibility with the OS version you are using and have a driver disk ready in case the OS doesn't recognize the NIC.

Protocol Selection

Selecting and configuring a protocol are key to NOS installation. All computers on a network must communicate by using the same protocol. Each protocol usually has configuration options that should be determined before NOS installation. The protocol and its configuration options must be compatible for computers to communicate. For example, TCP/IP—the most commonly used network protocol suite—requires the following pieces of information before NOS installation begins:

- *IP address*—This value is a 32-bit address used to identify each computer on the network.

- *Subnet mask*—This value is entered along with the IP address that specifies which part of the IP address is the network number.

- *Default gateway*—Because computers communicate only with other computers in the same subnet without additional help, the default gateway is the IP address of a device, such as a router, that gives access to other computers in other subnets.

- *DNS*—This server-based service resolves host names, such as *www.course.com*, into IP addresses. Internet access usually requires the IP address for a DNS server.

- *WINS*—The Windows Internet Naming Service (WINS) is a server-based service that resolves NetBIOS names into IP addresses. Large intranets often require the IP address of a WINS server. WINS applies only to Windows networks that use NetBIOS names. Linux-based networks, except when Samba is used, do not require NetBIOS names and WINS.

- *DHCP*—When DHCP is the selected option for TCP/IP configuration, the host configures the IP address, subnet mask, and default gateway for the workstation, along with DNS and WINS server addresses, using information passed to it from the DHCP server. The computer simply broadcasts a DHCP request to the network. A DHCP server (which must be configured first) responds with an IP address and subnet mask and, optionally, a default gateway, WINS server address, and DNS server address. The workstation then uses these values for its TCP/IP settings.

Other protocols require different configuration options. For example, IPX/SPX might require specifying a frame type and network number, but the computer's address is derived from its MAC address. (Frame types were discussed in Chapter 7.)

Hardware Compatibility

For an NOS to operate, the hardware components of the computer on which it's installed must be compatible with the NOS. Most NOS vendors publish lists of compatible hardware that they have tested with their software. If you use incompatible hardware, the vendor might not provide technical support. Always double-check that your computer's hardware components are fully compatible with the NOS to prevent possible problems. Microsoft publishes the Windows Catalog for Windows 2000 and later, which lists the hardware tested as compatible with Windows. The Windows Catalog was formerly called the Hardware Compatibility List (HCL). Linux distributors publish a similar list for the various Linux versions. Novell typically certifies whole systems as NetWare compatible.

Installing Microsoft Windows Servers

Windows server versions are not much more difficult to install than Windows XP or Vista. With the proper preparation—as described in the previous sections—the Setup Wizard makes the installation process as simple as entering a few key data items. You need not know every detailed step in the setup process, especially because you're studying networking essentials, not NOS specifics. However, the major steps or sections of the installation included here give you insight into the architecture and simplicity of the Windows server line of operating systems.

Beginning the Installation

The first step is to choose the installation method, which includes the following:

- *Complete baseline installation or use existing OS?* New computers without an existing OS require drive partitioning and a fully compatible CD-ROM. An existing OS might require no new partitioning and can use an unsupported CD-ROM. (These devices are seldom encountered now.)

- *Network or local installation?* You can store the Windows distribution files on a network-shared CD or directory; however, this method requires that the computer have a network-compatible OS already running. A local installation forces the distribution files to be pulled from a local CD-ROM drive or copied to a local hard drive.

No matter which installation method you use, both options require running Winnt.exe (or Winnt32.exe if you're starting the installation from Windows 95 or later) to start the setup process. (When installing from a CD, the correct program is usually started automatically.) After running Winnt or Winnt32, the installation begins with a text-based phase. Figure 8-2 shows the text-based screen of a Windows Server 2003 installation.

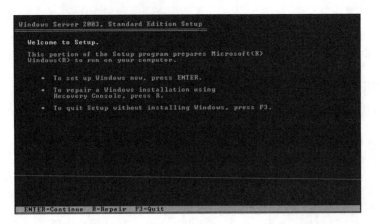

Figure 8-2 Windows Server 2003 text-based setup screen

Text-Based Phase

You perform the initial phase of Windows Server 2003 setup in a text-only mode. During this phase, you configure hard drives, format file systems, confirm the license agreement, and define the name of the system directory. Figure 8-3 shows the hard drive configuration screen. After this phase has been completed, the distribution files are copied into a temporary directory on the destination partition. The computer then restarts in the graphical user interface (GUI) phase of setup.

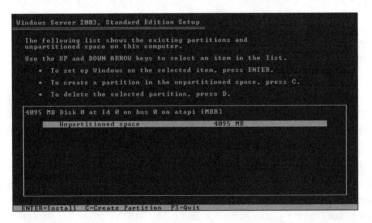

Figure 8-3 Windows Server 2003 hard drive configuration screen

GUI Phase

In the GUI phase, you use a mouse or keyboard to enter items or make selections. During this phase, you define the computer and domain names, enter the identification key from the installation CD, select the server type as a domain controller or a member server, assign a password to the Administrator account, and select environment and desktop components.

Setup copies some files from the temporary folder to the destination folder and then moves into the network setup phase.

Network Setup Phase

The next phase installs and configures the network communication components. During the network setup phase, you install drivers for the NIC, select and configure protocols, and review bindings. After this phase is completed, setup copies files to the final destination folder (the system folder) and deletes the temporary folder.

After files are moved to the system folder, you define the time zone and display settings. Then the computer restarts, the Administrator logs on, and the Configure Server Wizard starts. This phase of the setup allows the server to be configured as a domain controller, member server, or standalone server. If the server is to act as a domain controller, Active Directory is installed and configured.

8

Installing Novell NetWare 6.5

Installing NetWare is not too different from installing Windows Server 2003. In fact, installation of any NOS involves similar steps. You can install NetWare by using one of two methods:

- *Over the network*—If a NetWare server is already online on your network and a network-enabled OS is already on the current machine, you can perform the NetWare installation across the network.

- *From a CD*—You can start most NetWare installations from a CD; this method usually involves a CD-ROM-enabled OS or a bootable disk with the correct drivers.

No matter which installation method you use, the primary install utility is INSTALL.NLM. After you start this utility (it's started automatically if you boot from the installation CD), the text-based setup screen appears. Select the Simple installation method; it requests only a few specific configuration items, and the process proceeds quickly.

Like Windows, NetWare is installed in two phases—text mode and then GUI mode. During the text-mode phase, you create partitions, accept the license agreement, copy files, install storage device drivers, and select drivers for the NIC. During the GUI phase, you assign the server name, set up protocols (such as TCP/IP or IPX), and install eDirectory. After these tasks are finished, the machine restarts, and the NetWare installation is completed.

Installing Linux

Installing Linux is similar to other NOS installations. You can install most Linux distributions easily from CD; this method usually involves a CD-ROM-enabled OS or a bootable disk with the correct drivers. The installation details and screen shots differ depending on the distribution of Linux. This book uses Linux Fedora Core 4 to demonstrate the process.

The Linux Fedora Core 4 CD-ROM distribution comes on four CDs. Additional CDs are available but aren't required for installation. To begin the installation, start the computer with CD 1 inserted. The text-based setup screen appears. Two installation modes are available: text and graphical. Graphical is the default mode and is started by pressing Enter. To use text mode, type "linux text" at the boot prompt.

Although the Linux installation contains many of the same steps as a Windows or NetWare server installation, there are important differences. When installing Linux, you can choose one of four modes: Personal Desktop, Workstation, Server, or Custom, as shown in Figure 8-4. Based on your choice, the installation program installs the most appropriate services and applications for that mode.

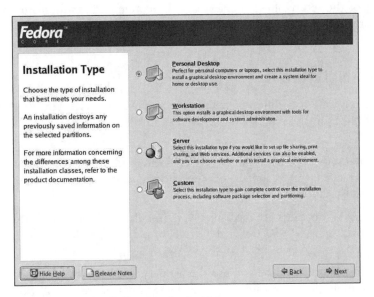

Figure 8-4   Installation modes in Linux

The Linux installation includes a step for the boot loader choice (see Figure 8-5), an option you don't find in a Windows or NetWare installation. A boot loader is a small program that runs when the computer first starts, allowing you to choose which OS to load or to change the default manner in which Linux starts.

Linux developers have always been concerned about security, so they developed a built-in firewall for the Linux OS. During installation of Linux, you can select the level of security you want and customize the firewall's operation, as shown in Figure 8-6.

Most other Linux installation tasks are similar to those in Windows and NetWare and include disk partitioning, network configuration, administrator password assignment, and selection of optional operating components.

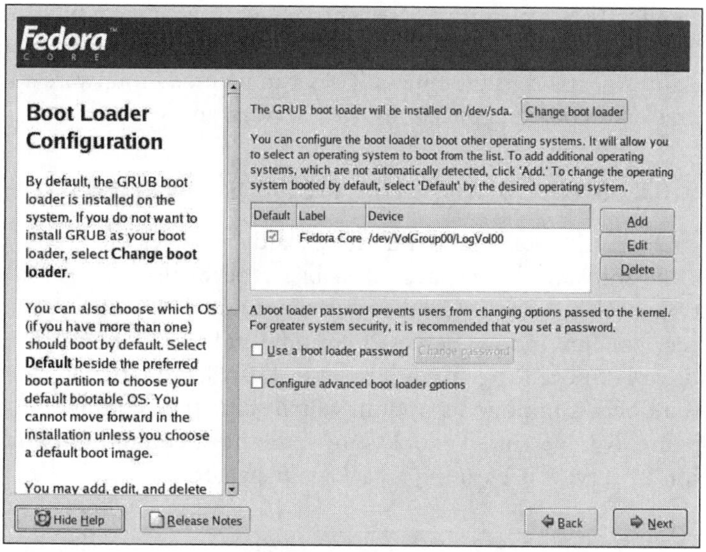

Figure 8-5   Selecting a boot loader in Linux

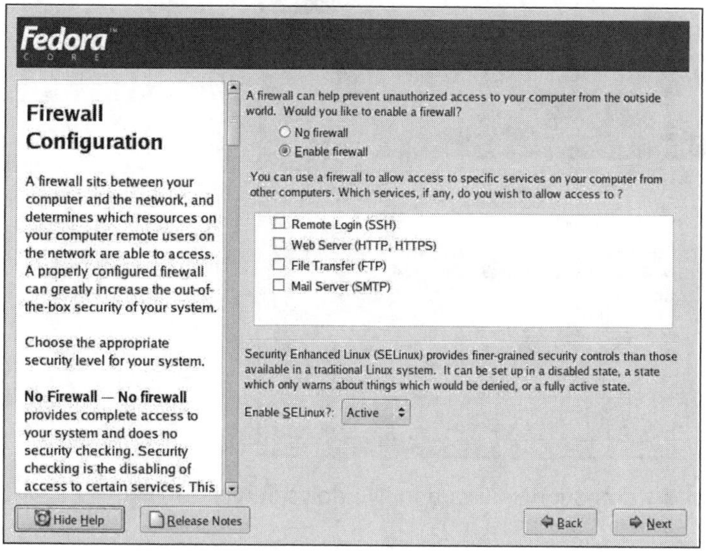

Figure 8-6   Linux firewall configuration

CONFIGURING NETWORK SERVICES

Network services, the basic resources on all networks, are the foundation of network applications. Without these basic services, networks cannot exist. Earlier chapters defined a network's central purpose: to share resources. The two most basic shared network resources (that is, network services) are printers and file folders or directories.

A network is not limited to these two primary services; in fact, the range of possible network services is broad. You can add numerous capabilities, resources, and delivery methods to a default NOS installation to extend its usefulness. They can include groupware applications, e-mail packages, shared whiteboard applications, Web servers, and so forth.

Installing, Removing, and Configuring Network Services

Setting up network services is similar to configuring hardware device drivers. In a way, a network service (or the software that creates or enables a network service) is a driver for software or the network itself. Most NOSs have an administrative tool for installing and removing network services. In Windows Server 2003 and Windows XP, network services are installed by using Add or Remove Programs from Control Panel. From this applet, you select the Add/Remove Windows Components option, which starts the Windows Components Wizard shown in Figure 8-7. In Linux Fedora Core 4, the most common way to install or remove an application or service is by using a package manager.

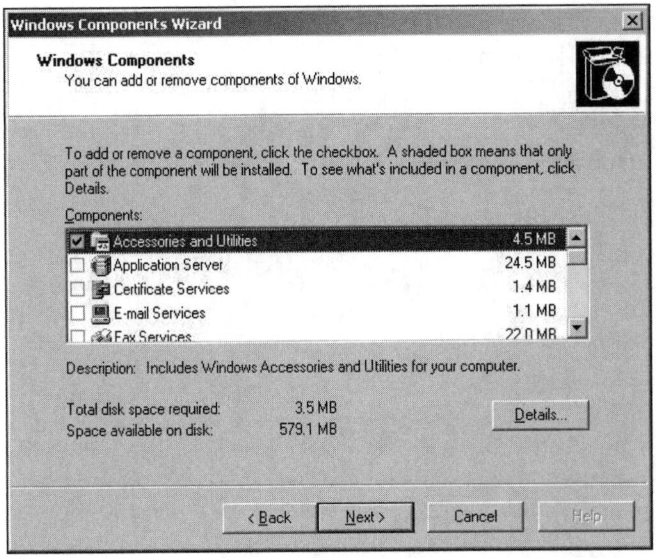

Figure 8-7   Windows Components Wizard in Windows Server 2003

After a network service has been added in Windows, you can control its operation parameters in one of two ways. The first is through a global services administrative tool, such as the Services applet in Control Panel, where you can start and stop all active network services and modify basic operational parameters. The second method uses a specific administrative tool for some services, such as Routing and Remote Access Service (RRAS) for Windows Server 2000/2003. These tools are added as "snap-ins" via the Microsoft Management Console (MMC). Hands-On Project 8-5 walks you through the steps of configuring an MMC snap-in.

Installation of a network service in Linux usually involves editing one or more configuration files and/or installing a new package containing the service. Linux services and applications are often distributed in a file format called a package. If a service isn't installed on Linux, an administrator can use the package manager to install it. For example, if you want your Linux installation to be able to access Windows NetBIOS shares, you should install the Samba package. You learn more about this process in Hands-On Project 8-4 at the end of this chapter.

Network Bindings

Another issue related to network services and the general operation of a network is **binding**, the process of linking network components from various levels of the network architecture to enable communication between those components. Bindings associate upper-layer services and protocols to lower-layer network adapter drivers. Many NOSs enable all valid bindings by default, but this option often results in some performance degradation.

Your binding order should enhance the computer's use of the network. For example, if your network has both TCP/IP and IPX/SPX installed (most network devices use TCP/IP), you should set bindings to access TCP/IP first and IPX/SPX second. In other words, you should bind the most frequently used protocol, service, or adapter first to speed network connections. A timeout period must elapse after each unsuccessful connection attempt before trying the next possible connection; these delays add up and slow system performance.

Network Printing

Network printing, one of the two essential network services, makes it possible for a client located anywhere on the network to access and use a printer hosted by a server (if that user has the correct access permission). The redirector plays a major role in network printing by intercepting print requests and forwarding them to the right print servers or network-connected printers.

Network printing consists of three components: the print server, the print queue, and the printer. It begins with installing a printer on a server (or installing a workstation to act as a server for the printer) or as a direct network-connected device. After you install the printer and it's functioning, the printer's logical representation in the NOS can be shared. The process of sharing on a network is what enables remote access of a local resource. When a printer is shared on the network, the computer sharing the printer plays the role of the print server. The print queue is a storage location, usually on the print server's hard drive, that accepts print jobs from network clients and stores the print job until the printer is available to print it.

NOTE User access, security, and auditing are discussed in Chapters 9 and 10. You address these issues simply by taking additional steps in the share-establishment process for printers and folders or directories.

In some cases, a workstation or client computer must have local printer drivers installed; in other cases, a workstation can access printer drivers from the print server. In either case, a new logical printer that points to the printer share, as shown in Figure 8-8, is installed. After this logical device is constructed, users send print jobs to the printer simply by directing any application to print to the defined redirected port. The redirector handles all the complicated network communications involved in transferring the print job to the remote printer.

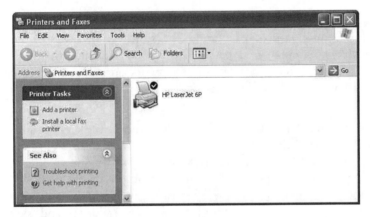

Figure 8-8 Windows XP printer share

Printer Management

On most networks, you manage printers from local direct access or through the network printer share. Windows XP/2003/Vista also enables you to manage printers via your Web browser by using the Internet Printing Protocol (IPP). Obviously, management and administration can be performed only when the correct level of access is granted to a user, but this is the only limitation to printer share management. Printer management covers a wide range of activities, including:

- Granting and restricting user access to printers
- Monitoring the print queue for proper functioning, including stopping, restarting, reordering, and deleting print jobs

- Limiting access by time frame, department, or priority

- Updating local and remote printer drivers

- Maintaining printers

- Managing printers remotely

This list encompasses just a few responsibilities of printer management; many other tasks are NOS specific as well.

Sharing Fax Modems

Just as printers can be shared across the network, so can fax modems. Although this feature is not often a default component in an NOS, many third-party vendors offer add-on products, such as RightFax, to share a fax modem over a network. With these add-on products, clients can fax documents from the desktop. You can manage and administer fax shares just like printer shares. Usually, additional client-installed software is needed to connect to a fax share, but this requirement simply means that the drivers and setup utility aren't native to the NOS. After the correct drivers are installed, there's no major difference between using a printer share and a fax share.

File Shares

A file share, sometimes referred to as a directory share, is the second primary network service. File shares make it possible for clients to access and interact with storage devices anywhere on the network. Figure 8-9, for example, shows three shared folders, indicated by the "offering hand" icon. Again, the redirector and the designator play major roles in the file-sharing service. You can access a file share (also called a "network share" or just "share") in three ways:

- By mapping an unused local drive letter to the share

- By using a UNC name to reference the share

- By selecting the share from a list

Like a printer share, you can manage a file share by granting and restricting user access levels.

Sharing files and folders in Linux is usually done by using the Network File System (NFS) or Samba. NFS is usually used in an all-Linux or UNIX environment, although add-on NFS products for Windows can be installed. Samba emulates Windows file and print sharing, making it fairly simple to integrate Linux servers into a primarily Windows environment. These two services are discussed in more detail in Chapter 9.

Figure 8-9 Windows XP folder shares

NETWORK APPLICATIONS

Most computer applications were originally electronic versions of existing data-management tools, such as typewriters and calculators. You have probably worked with many of these applications. However, most of these software tools are designed for a single user on a single computer. **Network applications** are designed for multiple simultaneous users on numerous computers connected over a network. Initially, single-user applications were enhanced to accommodate multiple users. Soon, completely new applications were developed specifically for use as network applications. Three types of network applications, discussed in more detail in the following sections, are essential tools on any network:

- E-mail or messaging
- Scheduling or calendaring
- Groupware

The benefits of network applications go beyond improved communication. Network applications are much easier to administer than their standalone counterparts, especially on large networks. They simplify the headache of version control because a single server-based software update brings the entire network up to date. Network applications also save money. Standalone software requires purchasing a complete version for each user, whereas a network application can host multiple users with a single installation of the software through user licenses. However, even with these benefits, network applications do have drawbacks. Poor network performance or limited bandwidth degrades application performance. Also, when the network is down, the application is often unusable. Another service, called clustering, is available to correct the problem of network applications being unavailable, but it also requires advanced hardware and administrative skills. Even with these drawbacks, network applications offer previously unachievable communication solutions.

Not all network applications operate in the same manner. There are at least three types of architectures for network applications:

- *Centralized*—The application operates exclusively on a server. All clients interact with the central application through a simple terminal interface.

- *File-system sharing*—The application resides on each client, but all clients share a common database file or storage directory.

- *True client/server*—Some aspects of the application reside on the server and some on the client. This setup enables processing group activities on the server separately from local processing.

E-Mail or Messaging

E-mail, the most popular network application, distributes messages from one person to others on the same network or across the Internet. E-mail is fast and asynchronous and can contain graphics and multimedia in addition to plain text. Most e-mail applications have similar capabilities, such as deleting messages, storing messages in folders, and replying to messages. This easy-to-use communication tool has many powerful and sophisticated features, including attaching files, filtering, and using distribution lists.

In addition to message delivery, many e-mail software products offer a versatile address book to store names, addresses, phone numbers, and more for each contact you maintain. Also, if the e-mail application is based on the Internet standards SMTP, POP3, and/or IMAP, communication outside the local network over the Internet is possible.

There's more to e-mail than just typing a message, attaching a file, and sending it to a colleague. E-mail is based on a common protocol and standards for communication. You need to be familiar with only a few of the many e-mail communication protocols:

- **Post Office Protocol version 3 (POP3)**—E-mail clients use this protocol to download incoming messages from an e-mail server to their local desktops. POP3 clients must manage messages locally (not on the server, as they can using IMAP).

- *Simple Mail Transport Protocol (SMTP)*—This protocol is the current (as of this writing) standard protocol for sending Internet and other TCP/IP-based e-mail. Whereas POP3 is used to retrieve e-mail, SMTP is used to send e-mail.

- **Internet Message Access Protocol (IMAP)**—This standard might replace POP3 on the Internet in the future. It has advanced message controls, including the capability to manage messages locally yet store them on a server, plus numerous fault-tolerance features.

- **X.400**—This message-handling protocol is hardware and software independent.

- *X.500*—This improved message-handling protocol is closely linked to the X.400 standard but offers improved directory services. The X.500 protocol communicates across networks and maintains a global database of addresses.

- *Message Handling System (MHS)*—This Novell-developed standard is similar to X.400.

Sending an Internet e-mail message involves a series of steps. After a message has been written and the user clicks the Send button, the e-mail client software contacts an SMTP server. The SMTP server's address is part of the e-mail client's configuration. The SMTP server receives the message, looks up the domain of the destination address, and contacts an SMTP server at the destination domain. The destination SMTP server sends the message to the POP3 server containing the recipient's mailbox. The POP3 server deposits the message into the recipient's mailbox, where it sits until the mailbox owner instructs the e-mail client software to retrieve messages. To view a simulation of this process, open Simulation 8-1.

SIMULATION

Simulation 8-1: Internet E-mail Operation

Scheduling or Calendaring

A network scheduler (sometimes known as a calendar) is an electronic form of an appointment book and to-do lists. The real benefit of this application is easy coordination of meetings, appointments, and contact details. Most schedulers offer private and public calendars, appointment books, task lists, and contact/address books. In addition to recording information, the network scheduler can notify users about an upcoming meeting, warn about overlapped schedules, and offer reminders of special events or the need to contact someone.

Most scheduler programs offer integration into e-mail programs and office-productivity suites. This integration simplifies exchanging information with commonly used applications on a user's desktop. To supplement or replace a paper-based personal information manager, daily, weekly, monthly, and yearly schedules can be printed in a variety of layouts and styles.

Groupware

Groupware enables multiple users to interact simultaneously with a single file, document, or project. Using groupware, an entire department can contribute to a document's production and watch as the groupware combines everyone's input into a single document. Some examples of groupware include multiuser multimedia authoring tools, Lotus Notes, Novell Virtual Office, and HP's TeamLinks.

Groupware products make good use of networking's inherent capabilities to keep users synchronized and to coordinate distributed data and activities. Today, many companies focus their research and development activities on creating technologies that enable them to take advantage of groupware features across the Web, thereby making it possible to collaborate across the Internet (with appropriate access controls, of course).

Probably the biggest explosion in groupware products is integrating PDAs with corporate networks. More users are carrying their calendars, e-mail, and important documents with them and later synchronizing changes with network applications. This trend adds yet another task to overburdened network administrators' plates, as they must support multiple PDA implementations, maintain security for the synchronization process, and keep groupware applications running.

Chapter Summary

- A network operating system (NOS) is software that controls the operations of a computer, including local hardware activity as well as communication over network media. Because NOSs must support both local and remote activities, they are multitasking systems.

- An NOS also enables sharing resources, managing peripherals, maintaining security, supporting privacy, and controlling user access. Naming services on networks provide a way for users to identify services and resources by name. On Microsoft networks, UNC names serve as a standard method of naming a shared resource; on TCP/IP-based networks, domain names and well-known port addresses provide much the same service. Modern NOSs—especially Windows Server 2003 and NetWare (version 4.0 and later)—include built-in directory services that do the work of locating and providing access to resources and services when users request them.

- Client network software on workstations allows users to take advantage of network resources. Two components—redirectors and designators—simplify network access and hide details of the process from users. A redirector intercepts a request for resources, interprets the request, and then guides the request to local devices or network shares. A designator is associated with drive mappings of network directory shares. It replaces a local drive letter with the corresponding network share name. The designator acts on behalf of, or in coordination with, the redirector.

- Client software doesn't always mean redirectors and designators. Many Internet services have separate client software components, such as Web browsers, e-mail clients, and FTP clients that access server services without using a redirector and designator.

- Server network software on server computers is designed to host resources so that multiple clients can access them. Part of a server's responsibility in hosting resources is controlling access to those resources, managing users and groups, administering the network, and protecting data integrity.

❏ Installing an NOS is similar to installing any OS. However, because a network is more complicated than a standalone computer, you must specify additional items and have a more thorough understanding of the server's role in your network than you might require for installing a desktop OS. Issues you must be aware of include size of the network, job requirements of the server, storage device organization, naming conventions, NIC and protocol selection and configuration, and hardware compatibility.

❏ The steps for installing Windows Server 2000/2003, Novell NetWare, and Linux are similar. Proper preparation and a clear understanding of the required data items, such as system requirements, are essential to a successful installation.

❏ There are two fundamental network services—sharing printers and sharing files. However, networks are not limited to just these two services; networked applications, such as groupware and e-mail, extend network capabilities.

❏ Some standalone applications have been revised to function as cross-network applications. A network application offers many benefits to networks, including improved communication, simplified application maintenance, and lower storage requirements. Some examples of network applications include e-mail, schedulers, and groupware.

Key Terms

binding — The OS-level association of NICs, protocols, and services to fine-tune network operation and performance.

client network software — A type of software designed for workstations that enables the use of network resources.

cooperative multitasking — A form of multitasking in which each process controls the length of time it maintains exclusive control over the CPU.

designator — This NOS software component aids in network resource interaction and drive mapping. Working in coordination with a redirector, it exchanges the locally mapped drive letter with the correct network address of a directory share inside a resource request.

directory service — A comprehensive network service that manages information about network services, resources, users, groups, and other objects, so that users can access resources and services by browsing for them, or asking for them by type, along with maintaining and enforcing access control information for directory objects.

drive mapping — The convention of associating a local drive letter with a network directory share to simplify access to the remote resource.

file system — The method by which an operating system stores, organizes, and manages access to files on a mass storage device, such as a hard drive.

groupware — A type of network application in which multiple users can simultaneously interact with each other and with data files.

Internet Message Access Protocol (IMAP) — An Internet e-mail standard that might replace POP3 because of its advanced message controls and fault-tolerance features. The appeal of IMAP (a more modern client message transfer protocol) is that it permits clients to read and manage messages locally while leaving them stored on the server.

member server — Any server on a Windows NT or Server 2000/2003 network that's not responsible for user authentication.

Message Handling System (MHS) — A Novell-developed standard that's similar to X.400.

multitasking — A mode of CPU operation in which a computer processes more than one task at a time. In most instances, multitasking is an illusion created through the use of time slicing.

naming convention — A predetermined schema for naming objects within network space. It simplifies the location and identification of objects.

network applications — Enhanced software programs made possible through the communication system of a network. Examples include e-mail, scheduling, and groupware.

network services — Resources offered by a network that aren't normally found in a standalone OS.

partition — A logical separation of disk space that is viewed as a separate logical drive.

Post Office Protocol version 3 (POP3) — An Internet message transfer protocol that e-mail clients use to copy messages from an e-mail server to a client machine to be read and managed on the local desktop.

preemptive multitasking — A form of multitasking in which the NOS or OS retains control over the length of time each process can maintain exclusive use of the CPU.

server network software — A type of software designed for a server computer; this software enables the hosting of resources for clients to access.

share — A network resource made available for remote access by clients.

time slicing — A method of granting CPU cycles to different processes by limiting the amount of time each process has exclusive use of the CPU.

Universal Naming Convention (UNC) — A standard method for naming network resources; it takes the form \\servername\sharename.

X.400 — A hardware- and software-independent message-handling protocol.

X.500 — An improved message-handling protocol that can communicate across networks and maintain a global database of addresses.

8

REVIEW QUESTIONS

1. NOSs were originally add-ons to standalone operating systems. True or False?

2. In Windows Server 2003, what is the most important aspect of a server's responsibilities or purpose that must be decided before installation?

   a. the names of clients in the network it supports

   b. whether it serves as a domain controller or member server

   c. the number of users it will support

   d. whether to allow remote access

3. Which of the following is an example of a true NOS? (Choose all that apply.)
    a. Windows XP Professional
    b. Windows 98
    c. Microsoft LAN Manager
    d. Linux
    e. Windows Server 2003

4. Which of the following storage device organizational schemes is the most secure?
    a. multiple-boot
    b. single-partition, single-NOS
    c. multiple-partition, single-NOS
    d. single-partition, multiple-NOS

5. Multitasking is _____ .
    a. the installation of more than one protocol
    b. the computing method whereby multiple processes seemingly operate simultaneously by sharing the CPU
    c. the act of binding two or more services to a single protocol
    d. the activity of accessing a directory share over a network link

6. Preemptive multitasking is the method of computing in which the NOS/OS maintains control of the CPU by assigning specific time slices to processes. True or False?

7. Cooperative multitasking is the method of computing in which the NOS/OS maintains control of the CPU by assigning specific time slices to processes. True or False?

8. If TCP/IP is one of the protocols installed on your network, which of the following items is important to define before installation? (Choose all that apply.)
    a. IP address
    b. e-mail address
    c. subnet mask
    d. Web server name

9. Which of the following is a feature of an NOS?
    a. maintains a directory of resources and services available on the network
    b. coordinates and controls the functions of machines and peripherals across the network
    c. supports security and privacy for both the network and users
    d. controls access to resources via user authentication
    e. all of the above

10. Verifying hardware compatibility before NOS installation is important for which of the following reasons?

    a. Not all hardware is supported by the high-performance requirements of an NOS.

    b. Server hardware is rarely plug-and-play.

    c. High-speed CPUs do not support some protocols.

    d. all of the above

11. Client network software has the primary purpose of _____ .

    a. supporting local resources

    b. distributing graphics files to other users in the network

    c. accessing network resources

    d. offering local resources to other users

12. Which of the following installation methods might you choose if you had 10 servers to install and only one copy of the installation CDs?

    a. CD-ROM based

    b. over the network

    c. floppy-based

    d. remote boot

13. What is the function of a redirector?

    a. maintain a group appointment list

    b. map directory shares to local drive letters

    c. associate protocols, NICs, and services in order of priority

    d. forward requests to local or remote resource hosts depending on the target of the request

14. What is the benefit of having an existing operating system on a computer when you're planning to install an NOS?

    a. It enables a boot floppy disk to function correctly.

    b. It removes the need to decide which file system to use.

    c. It provides an alternative boot OS for security purposes.

    d. It can provide access to installation files over a network.

15. Which of the following is a component of client network software? (Choose all that apply.)

    a. redirector

    b. resource-hosting protocols

    c. designator

    d. DNS server

8

16. Which of the following installation tasks happens in a Linux installation but not in a Windows or NetWare server installation?

    a. boot loader selection

    b. network configuration

    c. disk partitioning

    d. administrator password assignment

17. Which of the following is the correct format for a UNC name?

    a. *(sharename)->servername*

    b. *\\servername\sharename*

    c. *sharename://servername/path*

    d. *servername, sharename*

18. Printer shares and file shares are considered which of the following?

    a. network applications

    b. groupware

    c. network services

    d. network protocols

19. What is a common feature in server network software for managing resources?

    a. access controls

    b. user authentication

    c. auditing tools

    d. all of the above

20. What is the name of the Linux file-sharing service?

    a. FTP

    b. MHS

    c. NFS

    d. SMB

21. Which of the following is not an e-mail protocol?

    a. POP3

    b. TCP

    c. IMAP

    d. MHS

    e. SMTP

22. Which of the following is important to address before initiating the setup of an NOS? (Choose all that apply.)

    a. job requirements of the server

    b. OSI model protocol installation

    c. naming conventions

    d. server manufacturer

    e. organization of storage devices

23. Windows file shares can be mapped to local drive letters. True or False?

24. To hide a NetBIOS name, you must end that name with which of the following characters?

    a. #

    b. $

    c. @

    d. &

25. Which of the following is considered a directory service?

    a. eDirectory

    b. Active Directory

    c. LDAP

    d. all of the above

Hands-On Projects

HANDS-ON PROJECTS

Hands-On Project 8-1

This project walks you through creating a shared folder in Windows XP. Before starting, make sure the option Use simple file sharing has been disabled in Windows Explorer. To check, click Tools, Folder Options from the Windows Explorer menu, click the View tab, and scroll down to this option.

1. Log on to Windows XP.

2. Open Windows Explorer by clicking **Start**, **Run** and typing **explorer** in the Open text box. Click **OK**.

3. In the left pane, click the **My Documents** folder, if it's not already selected.

4. From the menu, click **File**, point to **New**, and click **Folder**. A folder named New-Folder is displayed in the lower-right pane.

5. Press **Backspace**, type **MyShare**, and press **Enter** to rename the new folder.

6. Right-click the **MyShare** folder you just created and click **Sharing and Security**.

7. To share this folder, click the **Share this folder** option button, as shown in Figure 8-10. At this point, you can change the name of the share so that users on the network see this folder with a different name. For the purposes of this project, you can leave the name as is.

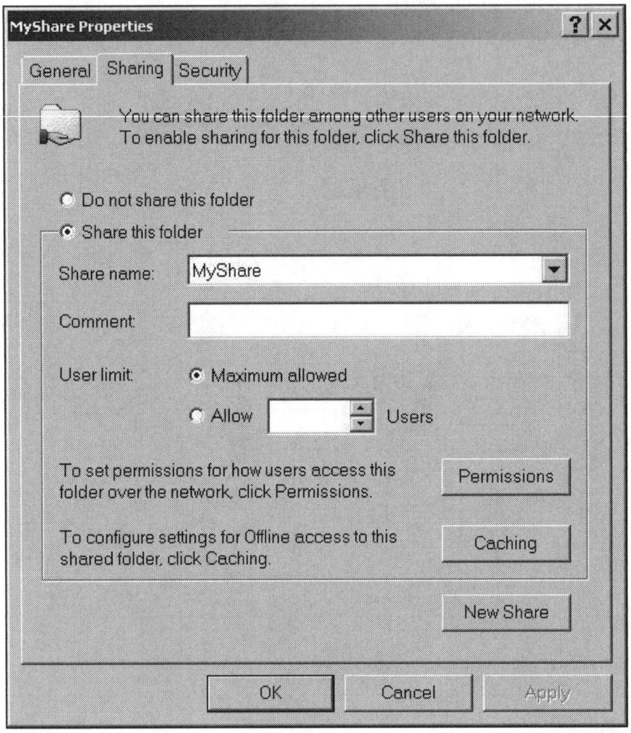

Figure 8-10 The Sharing tab of a folder's Properties dialog box

8. Click **OK**.

9. Look for the folder in Windows Explorer. An offering hand icon has been added to the folder icon, which indicates that the folder is ready for access from the network. Close Windows Explorer. The next projects show you how to access shared resources.

Hands-On Project 8-2

> **NOTE**
>
> This project assumes that a network printer share has been created and named "HP LaserJet 5L."

To connect to a printer share, follow these steps:

1. Log on to Windows XP.

2. Click **Start**, **Printers and Faxes**.

3. Click the **Add a printer** link under the Printer Tasks heading to start the Add Printer Wizard.

4. Click **Next**. In the Local or Network Printer window shown in Figure 8-11, click to select the **A network printer, or a printer attached to another computer** option button, if it's not already selected.

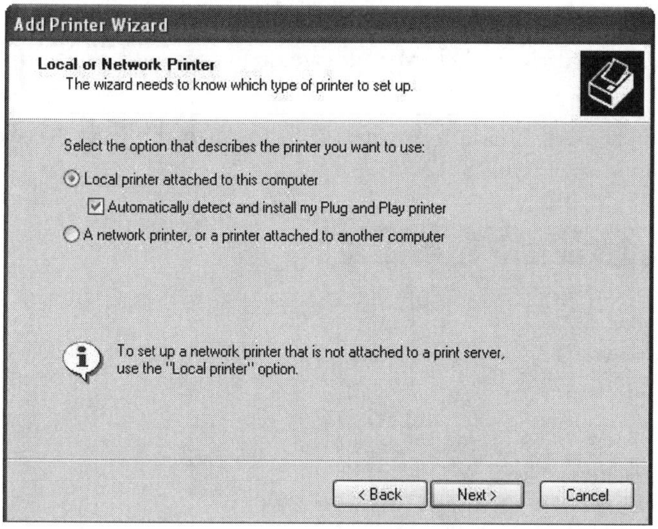

Figure 8-11   The Windows XP Add Printer Wizard

5. Click **Next**. In the Specify a Printer window, click **Next** to make Windows XP browse the network for UNC names of shared printers.

6. Click to select the printer share **HP LaserJet 5L** (or the printer specified by your instructor) in the Shared printers list, and then click **Next**. If necessary, click **Yes** in the Connect to Printer dialog box to install the printer driver on your computer.

7. Click **No** to the inquiry about setting this printer as the default.

8. Click **Next**, and then click **Finish**.

9. The new logical printer should be displayed in the Printers and Faxes folder. If not, press **F5** or click **View**, **Refresh** from the menu to update the display. Close the Printers and Faxes window.

NOTE

To remove a network printer, highlight it in the Printers folder, right-click and click Delete, and then click Yes to confirm the deletion.

HANDS-ON PROJECTS

Hands-On Project 8-3

NOTE

This project assumes that a folder share named Users has been created by the instructor and is available for student access.

1. Log on to Windows XP.

2. Double-click the **My Network Places** desktop icon. (If My Network Places is not on the desktop, click **Start**, right-click **My Network Places**, and click **Show on Desktop**.)

3. Click **Tools**, **Map Network Drive** from the menu to open the Map Network Drive dialog box shown in Figure 8-12.

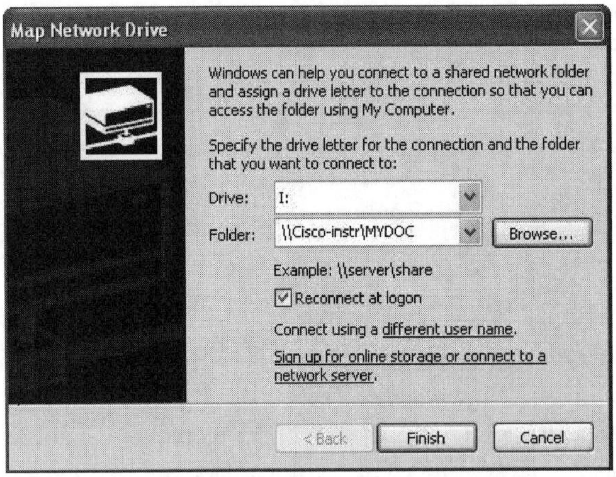

Figure 8-12 The Map Network Drive dialog box in Windows XP

4. In the Drive drop-down list box, click **I:** (or a drive specified by your instructor).

5. Click the **Browse** button to open the Browse For Folder window, and ask your instructor to help you navigate to the Users share.

6. After you have selected the folder, click **OK**. The UNC name of the folder is displayed in the Folder text box shown in Figure 8-12.

7. Click **Finish**. Windows Explorer opens, displaying the share's contents. If you open My Computer on your desktop, you see a new drive listed that represents the drive mapping you just completed. Close all open windows.

Hands-On Project 8-4

In this project, you install a new network service on a Fedora Core 4 Linux computer. This project assumes that the Samba service has not yet been installed, as would be the case on a typical workstation or personal desktop. (Your instructor might do this project as a demonstration if enough Linux computers aren't available.) The Samba service allows Windows users to access Linux-shared directories and Linux users to access Windows-shared folders.

1. Start the computer with Linux installed and log on as the **root** user.

2. If the X-Window graphical environment isn't already running, type **startx** at the Linux command prompt and press **Enter**.

3. From the menu, click the **Fedora** icon, **System Settings**, **Add/Remove Applications** to start the Package Management program.

4. Scroll down in the Package Management window, and under the Servers section, click to select the **Windows File Server** check box.

5. Click the **Update** button at the lower right of the Package Management window.

6. In the Completed System Preparation message box, click the **Continue** button.

7. When prompted, insert the Fedora Core 4 CD 1 in the CD-ROM drive and click **OK**.

8. Click **No** if you're asked whether you want to run /mnt/cdrom/autorun.

9. Click **OK** in the Update Complete dialog box.

10. Click **Quit** to close the Package Management program.

11. Congratulations! You have just installed the Samba service on Linux. In a project in Chapter 9, you use Samba to access a Windows share. For now, you can log off Linux.

Hands-On Project 8-5

In this project, you create a custom Microsoft Management Console (MMC). MMCs are used to manage most aspects of a Windows operating system.

1. From your Windows XP desktop, click **Start**, **Run**. Type **mmc** in the Open text box, and click **OK**.

2. In the Console1 window shown in Figure 8-13, click **File**, **Add/Remove Snap-in** from the menu. Click the **Add** button to open the Add Standalone Snap-in dialog box (see Figure 8-14).

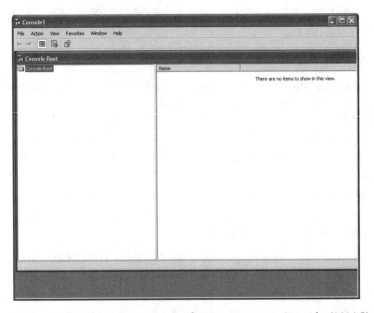

Figure 8-13   The main Microsoft Management Console (MMC) window

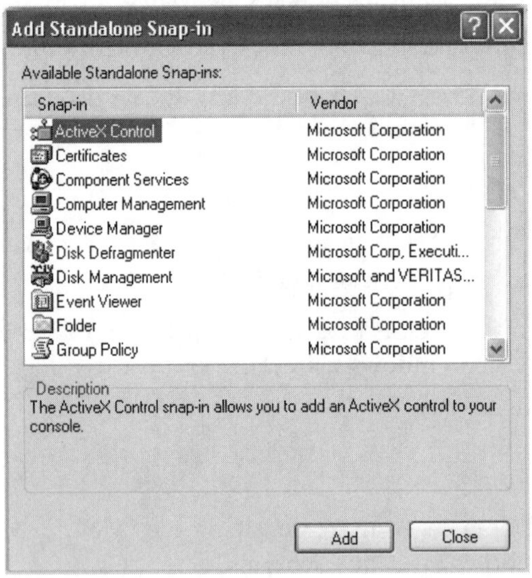

Figure 8-14   Adding a snap-in to the MMC

3. Scroll down and click the **Services** snap-in and click **Add**. Then click **Finish** and click **Close**.

4. Click **OK**. The Services snap-in is then added to the Console1 window under the Console Root folder.

5. Click **Services (Local)** and you see a list of available Windows services in the right pane. Scroll down the list of services until you find the Server service. What is its description and status?

_____

_____

6. To save this console for easy retrieval, click **File**, **Save As** from the menu. In the Save in drop-down list box, click **Desktop**, and in the File name text box, type **Services.msc**. Click **Save**.

7. Close the Services MMC you just created. You should see the Services MMC icon on your desktop.

8

Hands-On Project 8-6

NOTE

This project assumes you have access to a Web browser and an Internet connection.

Part of preparing to install any NOS on a PC is a step often called "prequalifying the hardware." It consists of two tasks:

❑ Record a complete list of the PC's components—motherboard make and model; CPU make and model; RAM size and make; hard disk(s) manufacturer, model, and size; and so forth. You can usually find this information on the sales receipt and documentation you received when you purchased your PC. If you don't have this documentation or if it doesn't contain the information, you have to open the computer case and start hunting; sometimes you have to unplug or dismount components to obtain this information. Make sure you know how to put things back together before you start taking them apart!

❑ For each component, check a hardware qualification list of some kind to see whether it works with the NOS you want to install. For this project, you use the Windows Marketplace Tested Products List (formerly the Hardware Compatibility List) on the Microsoft Web site.

To use the Windows Marketplace Tested Products List, follow these steps:

1. Start your Web browser.

2. In the Address text box, type **http://testedproducts.windowsmarketplace.com/**, and then press **Enter** to access the home page for the Windows Marketplace Tested Products List.

3. For each item in Table 8-2, select the appropriate category from the hardware testing status column. This project walks you through the first item: Creative Labs Vibra 128 PCI.

4. Click the **Components** link under the hardware testing status column.

5. Under By category at the left, click **Sound Cards**. Next, click **Creative Technology, LTD** under the By company column.

6. In the list that appears, find and click **Creative Labs Vibra 128 PCI**.

7. The next page shows the Windows versions that are certified compatible. To get back to the main page, click **Home** at the upper left. Repeat this process for each item. Determine whether the entire machine is compatible with Windows XP.

Table 8-2   System compatibility lookup items

Category	Manufacturer	Make/Model	Notations
Sound cards	Creative Technology, Ltd.	Creative Labs Vibra 128 PCI	
CPU	AMD	Athlon XP 2100	
Video	ATI	Rage 128 Pro Ultra	
Storage/IDE	Promise	PDC 20262	
Network/Ethernet	3Com	3C905B Ethernet	
Storage/SCSI controller	Adaptec	29160LP Ultra 160 Controller	

CASE PROJECTS

Case Project 8-1

You work for a small consulting firm. When you introduce the idea of implementing a client/server network, your manager says she's wary of using a server because she heard they are vulnerable to crashes. What could you tell your manager about modern networking technologies and NOS features that might alleviate her fears?

Case Project 8-2

You are a consultant who's been asked to install a new server for a small business. Before you begin the installation process, prepare a checklist of information you should obtain before beginning the installation. Much of the information you need will come from the owner of the business or someone in charge of computing at the company. In addition, prepare a list of questions you might ask that will help you fill out the checklist.

Case Project 8-3

As a follow-up to Case Project 8-2, you must decide what network applications and services should be available on the server. List the network applications and services you have learned about and write a brief description of each one. Explain under what circumstances the application or service should be installed.

Case Project 8-4

As you learned in this chapter, TCP/IP-based e-mail clients use either POP3 or IMAP to read and manage e-mail messages. XYZ Company's salespeople are out of the office three days a week on average, during which time they access e-mail from their laptops. The two days a week they're in the office, they access e-mail on desktop machines. Select the client e-mail protocol (POP3 or IMAP) most appropriate for these circumstances, and justify your selection.

Case Project 8-5

Compare the feature sets of Windows Server 2003, Fedora Core 4 Linux, and Novell NetWare 6.5. Information about these products can be found at the following sites:

- *www.microsoft.com/windowsserver2003/default.mspx*
- *http://fedora.redhat.com/docs/release-notes/fc4/*
- *www.novell.com/products/netware/*

Also use periodicals and reviews that might give you a more objective view. For instance, you can check sites such as the following:

- *www.itarchitect.com/*
- *www.networkcomputing.com/*
- *www.zdnet.com/*
- *www.internetweek.com/*

Present your findings to the class. Cover features such as server management, security, reliability, storage management, directory services, and networking services (including file and print sharing, Web services, database support, groupware support, and remote access). In addition, research costs for these network operating systems, including license pricing for each client connection.

9

UNDERSTANDING COMPLEX NETWORKS

After reading this chapter and completing the exercises, you will be able to:

♦ Explain how to implement a multivendor network environment

♦ Discuss the differences between centralized and client/server computing

♦ Define the client/server networking environment

♦ Discuss the basics of Web-based computing environments

This chapter examines aspects of complex network environments from the standpoint of clients and servers. In this chapter, you explore the issues in getting various vendors' products to interoperate and the differences between centralized and distributed client/server computing.

IMPLEMENTING MULTIVENDOR SOLUTIONS

Typically, in today's networking environments, you must connect computers and networks from different vendors and provide remote as well as local network access. This section discusses networking vendors and includes suggestions that should help you overcome typical interconnectivity challenges.

One of the biggest trials of a network administrator's job involves connecting systems that use different vendors' network operating systems (NOSs). To make a multivendor environment work effectively, the server's operating system, the clients' operating systems, and the redirectors must be compatible. A good example is an environment in which one computer runs Windows XP or Windows Vista with the client for Microsoft networks, one computer runs Linux with Samba, one client runs Mac OS, and the server runs Windows Server 2003. In this environment, the computer running Windows Server 2003 can support all clients on the network.

Operating systems from different vendors use different methods to access files across a network. Windows OSs use the **Common Internet File System (CIFS)**, which is just a newer version of the SMB protocol discussed in Chapter 6. Native to Linux and UNIX is the Network File System (NFS). The native Macintosh protocol for accessing network files, which is part of the AppleTalk protocol suite, is AppleTalk Filing Protocol (AFP), and Novell NetWare uses NetWare Core Protocol (NCP).

There are two basic ways to get the file systems from different OSs to communicate: from the client end and from the server end. The solution you choose depends on which vendors' products you want to interconnect.

Client-Based Solutions

As discussed in Chapter 8, it's the job of the client's redirector to intercept messages from the client and forward those messages to the correct server if a request can't be fulfilled locally. In a multivendor environment, multiple redirectors can be loaded on to a single client to facilitate connections to different vendors' servers. This setup is called a **client-based multivendor solution**. Figure 9-1 shows the Local Area Connection Properties of a Windows XP client that has both the Client Service for NetWare and the Client for Microsoft Networks installed.

For example, if a Windows XP client requires access to Windows Server 2003 and a Novell NetWare server, you can load a redirector for each OS on to that client. Each redirector redirects a request to the appropriate server, as shown in Figure 9-2.

When multiple client redirectors are installed on a single OS, adjusting the bindings of those redirectors might be necessary to ensure that the network protocols used with each redirector are appropriate and arranged in priority order. For example, if TCP/IP is the only protocol used for accessing Microsoft servers, unbinding the NWLink protocol from the Client for Microsoft Networks might be necessary. Binding and unbinding client redirectors

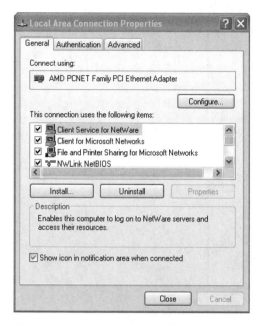

Figure 9-1   Windows XP with clients for NetWare and Microsoft installed

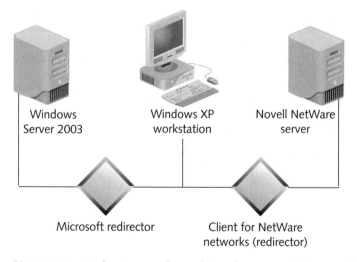

Figure 9-2   Redirectors make multivendor connectivity possible

to protocols is done in the Advanced Settings dialog box via Control Panel's Network Connections window, as shown in Figure 9-3. Redirectors can also be arranged in priority order by using the Provider Order tab in this same dialog box, thereby allowing you to ensure that the client of the most frequently used resources (Microsoft or NetWare) is accessed first. Prioritizing client software speeds access to network resources.

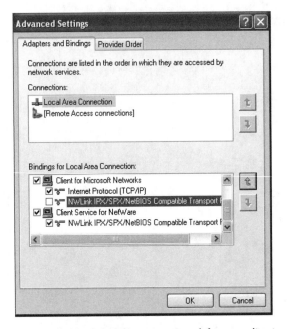

Figure 9-3 Unbinding a protocol from a client redirector

In a network with both Windows and Linux servers and clients, a similar solution is required. The native Linux file-sharing protocol is called NFS. For a Windows client OS to access NFS resources on a Linux server, NFS client software must be installed on the Windows OS. Windows installation CDs don't come with the necessary software, but it can be downloaded free from the Microsoft Web site in a package called Windows Services for Unix. Similarly, for a Linux client computer to access Windows server resources, Windows-compatible client software must be installed and configured on the Linux computer. The client software that allows Linux computers to access Windows file and printer shares is called Samba. In Hands-On Project 9-3, you install and use the Linux Samba client and server software.

As you see in the next section, installing multiple clients on computers is not the only way to implement multivendor solutions. Installing appropriate server software on your network servers to accommodate a variety of clients is another multivendor option.

Server-Based Solutions

To implement a **server-based multivendor solution**, software must be loaded on the server to provide services for a particular client. For example, if a Windows Server 2003 network includes Macintosh computers, the administrator can add Services for Macintosh to any of the Windows server operating systems. Windows Server 2003 NOSs include this service, which supplies a simple solution for Macintosh connectivity. (You practice installing server services in the Hands-On Projects at the end of this chapter.)

With Services for Macintosh installed on a Windows server, Macintosh clients can connect to resources on the Windows server. This service also converts files to Macintosh format automatically when retrieving them from the server. This automatic conversion enables Macintosh users to share files with any other user connected to the Windows server where Services for Macintosh is installed. Another benefit of using Services for Macintosh is that Macintosh users can access resources on a Windows server in the same way they access resources on a Macintosh server. This feature, which allows easy transition from a Macintosh-only network, is also available in other Windows server services, such as Gateway (and Client) Services for NetWare.

Similarly, Windows servers can be outfitted with Windows Services for Unix, which can provide NFS server functionality on a Windows computer, and Samba can be configured to allow Windows-compatible file and printer sharing.

Vendor Options

Many NOSs are available from vendors such as Sun, SCO, and IBM. This chapter focuses on the four most popular PC operating system product vendors: Microsoft, Linux, Novell, and Apple.

NOTE

Throughout this chapter, Linux is referred to as a "vendor" for ease of explanation, but Linux is actually an open-source OS available in many different versions from a variety of vendors.

In an effort to ease connectivity between different NOSs, these companies include utilities in their OSs to allow simple connectivity between clients and servers from different vendors. The following sections outline these interconnectivity options.

Microsoft Redirector

All Windows OSs, starting with Windows for Workgroups, include the Microsoft redirector, Client for Microsoft Networks. The Microsoft redirector is designed to access CIFS or SMB-based file systems across a network. Installing the OS installs the Microsoft redirector automatically. The installation process loads all required drivers and edits the startup files so that when the computer restarts, the redirector is in place, ready for immediate use.

In addition, the server component, called File and Printer Sharing for Microsoft Networks, used for sharing files and printers via CIFS or the older SMB, is installed on Windows OSs automatically, allowing users of Windows computers to share their own files and printers with other network users easily. The automatic installation of both client and server software on Windows desktop OSs, such as Windows XP and Vista, and Windows server versions makes peer-to-peer networking exceedingly convenient.

Microsoft in a Novell Network

To connect a Windows Vista or Windows XP Professional client to a Novell NetWare network running the IPX/SPX protocol, NWLink and the Microsoft version of the NetWare requester, Client Service for NetWare (CSNW), must be loaded on that Windows machine. Recall that NWLink is the Microsoft implementation of the IPX/SPX protocol suite. When connecting a Windows Server 2003 system to a NetWare network, NWLink as well as Gateway Service for NetWare (GSNW) must be loaded on the Windows server. GSNW allows Windows clients running Client for Microsoft Networks to access NetWare resources by using the Windows server as an intermediary. In this arrangement, the Windows server running GSNW establishes a connection with a NetWare server. The administrator of the Windows server creates share points that are pointers to file folders on a NetWare server. Microsoft clients can access those share points as though they were normal shared folders on the Windows server. In reality, however, the Windows server retrieves data from the NetWare server when access to a share point is requested.

NOTE The NetWare client that comes with Windows OSs connects only to NetWare servers running IPX/SPX. If a NetWare 5.x or 6.x server is running only the default protocol of TCP/IP, you must install Novell Client (available from the Novell Web site) on Windows PCs. Novell Client is also required to run Novell management utilities, such as ConsoleOne and iManager.

MS-DOS Clients

MS-DOS has no built-in network capabilities, but each NOS vendor offers utilities to allow MS-DOS clients to connect to servers of all four types—Microsoft, Novell, Linux, and Apple. Also, each utility can coexist with other utilities to provide MS-DOS client connections to all servers.

In an Apple Macintosh network, MS-DOS clients must have AppleShare PC software to use file and print services offered by Apple servers. A LocalTalk card, which includes firmware that controls the link between the AppleTalk network and the PC, can also be installed on a PC to allow the computer to communicate on a LocalTalk network.

In a Linux-based network, an MS-DOS client typically uses some kind of UNIX-derived client software, such as Sun Microsystem's PC-NFS. In this case, PCs participate in a TCP/IP-based network as though they were a "junior version" of Linux or UNIX. On many networks where PC clients need to access Linux servers, particularly when these PCs run some form of DOS or Windows, the popular add-on Linux server called Samba can be installed. It makes Linux servers look and act like Windows servers instead. In that case, a native Microsoft networking client can be used. (The "Linux/UNIX Networks" section later in this chapter explains Samba in more detail.)

Novell Networks

The Novell NetWare NOS provides file and print services for the client OSs discussed in this chapter. Windows clients can install Microsoft Client for NetWare or download and install Novell Client to access NetWare volumes and network printers. NetWare does not use the concept of shared folders, as CIFS and NFS do. Rather, NetWare servers have volumes that represent disk partitions. Each volume on a NetWare server is available to the network, as long as the user accessing the volume has appropriate rights. Any file or folder on a NetWare volume that a user has rights to can be accessed by using the Novell Client software, so there's no need to share specific folders—only to assign rights to folders for the users you want to have access to files contained in the folders. Macintosh clients can also access NetWare servers by installing the Novell Client for Mac OS, and, if necessary, NetWare servers can support the AppleTalk protocol as well.

With Novell Native File Access Pack (NFAP), Windows CIFS and SMB clients (Client for Microsoft Networks), UNIX/Linux NFS clients, and Macintosh clients using AFP can have network file access to NetWare resources. NFAP allows Windows, UNIX/Linux, and Mac OS clients to operate seamlessly in a Novell NetWare environment without having to install any additional client software on computers running those client OSs. In essence, a NetWare server with NFAP installed appears to be a Windows server to a Windows client, an NFS server to a UNIX/Linux client, and a Macintosh server to a Mac OS client.

9

NetWare 6.5 also includes a platform-independent method for accessing file and print services. Novell NetStorage provides access to a NetWare network's resources through any Web browser, so users can log on and access their files and printers, regardless of the client OS they're running and without the need for a NetWare redirector. Figure 9-4 shows the NetStorage service allowing users to access files remotely. This type of Web-based access to traditional file and print services is growing in popularity and extends to handheld computing devices as workforces become increasingly mobile.

Linux/UNIX Networks

Nearly every distribution of Linux includes a wealth of network services. These services include an implementation of **Network File System (NFS)**, which is a distributed file system native to UNIX and Linux systems. NFS permits networked machines to export portions of their local file systems and make them available to authorized users elsewhere on the network.

After an exported NFS portion, known as an **NFS volume**, is published on the network, authorized users with NFS client capability can install, or mount, the volume in their local file systems into a local directory on their hard disk. The directory into which the NFS volume is mounted is referred to as the **mount point**. To these users, this networked NFS volume becomes an extension of their local file systems, accessible the same way as local files. NFS also supports printer sharing, but its file and print services appear most commonly in multivendor networks where PCs are in the minority and the UNIX or Linux OS predominates.

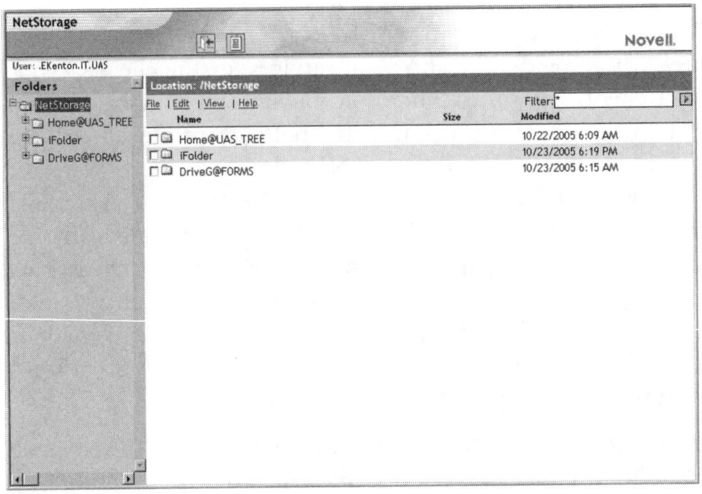

Figure 9-4   Accessing files remotely via NetStorage

Because enabling PC clients to access NFS requires adding software to those clients, many Linux administrators prefer to add the Samba service to their Linux servers instead. **Samba** is named after the Server Message Block (SMB) services it adds to a UNIX or Linux host. Using Samba to allow DOS or Windows machines to access Linux- or UNIX-based file systems and services makes sense for three reasons:

- Because Samba is a server-based solution, software and services need to be installed only on a fairly small number of servers rather than a large number of clients.

- Because Samba is an **open source** software product, you can download it free from the Internet and install and use it without charge.

- Because Samba allows a Linux or UNIX machine to masquerade as a native Microsoft network server, Windows clients need no extra software to access its services. Samba-based resources appear in a Windows browse list along with other network nodes and their file and print shares.

For these reasons, Samba is the preferred service to interconnect Windows clients with UNIX or Linux hosts. Samba also permits Linux hosts to connect to Windows shared folders. Users simply create a directory on their Linux drive and then connect that directory to the Windows network share by using the smbmount command-line utility.

Apple Macintosh

Included in every Macintosh are the OS files and the hardware required to communicate in an AppleTalk network. The AppleShare networking software automatically provides file sharing and includes a print server that allows computers to share printers.

Mac OS X

Mac OS X is a major departure from previous Mac OS versions. This Mac OS includes network client software to run in a Macintosh, Windows, or UNIX environment. In short, OS X negates the need for Windows servers to install special services for Macintosh computers or AppleTalk protocols because it provides support for native Windows file sharing through SMB services. In addition, because Mac OS X is built on a UNIX core, it's right at home in a UNIX environment. Backward-compatible support is available for traditional Macintosh file sharing through other Macs or through Windows or NetWare servers providing Macintosh services.

Handheld Computing Environment

The handheld computing market is somewhat fragmented—there's no clear hardware or software standard on which users can rely. The lack of compatibility between competing manufacturers presents a challenge for network administrators who must integrate these devices into the corporate computing environment.

 NOTE The OSs leading the way in the handheld arena are Palm OS, by PalmSource, and Microsoft PocketPC or Windows Mobile.

A key challenge of managing handheld computers on a LAN is that, unlike desktop computers, handheld computers are rarely connected to the corporate LAN. In addition, although most handheld devices offer some type of Ethernet connection, other options for connecting include modem, infrared communications, USB, Wi-Fi, Bluetooth, and serial links. Maintaining a working environment for these handhelds, while maintaining security and data integrity, is the latest challenge for network administrators.

Desktop computers connect to the corporate network to access shared resources on a continuous basis, but the normal operating mode of a handheld computer is disconnected and mobile. Therefore, the primary reason for connecting to the corporate LAN is to synchronize data between the network and the handheld device. This synchronization is often accomplished with a software program loaded on a user's desktop computer. The handheld device is then connected to a cradle that has a connection to the desktop. Other methods for synchronizing handhelds include through a USB port, a Wi-Fi connection, or a Bluetooth connection.

In recognition that handheld computing is here to stay and is integral to the corporate computing environment, enterprise software companies have developed server-based software that handles synchronization, backup, and even application loading for all handheld computers in a company. This sector of the computing industry is growing rapidly as the technology matures, and before long, managing and configuring handheld computers will be just another trick in a network administrator's bag of magic.

Integrating PDAs into a Corporate Network

Advances in PDA capabilities, including processor speed, RAM capacity, OS enhancements, and wireless interfaces, have transformed the PDA from an electronic scheduler and address book to a full-fledged computing device. PDAs are running Web browsers, e-mail clients, and several other client applications. The majority of PDAs come equipped with a Wi-Fi connection, allowing these devices to synchronize data with the user's desktop computer and access corporate data and the Internet directly through a Wi-Fi access point. This new use of networks brings flexibility to mobile users and headaches to network administrators.

In past years, administrators' only worry was how users would synchronize their PDAs with their desktop computers. Now administrators are asked to set up wireless access points and special Web content, and even write new applications to accommodate PDA capabilities. Security is also a concern. An unsecured wireless network can be infiltrated by a hacker with a wireless device and some free software, so it's critical for network administrators to enforce the use of wireless security protocols on all wireless devices, including PDAs and notebook computers. The older Wired Equivalent Privacy (WEP) standard might suffice for a small network that's not as security conscious, but for more robust security, Wi-Fi Protected Access (WPA) or the newer 802.11i standard should be used.

CENTRALIZED VERSUS CLIENT/SERVER COMPUTING

The client/server model for computing evolved from the centralized computing environment. In **centralized computing**, mainframes perform all processing, and "dumb" terminals connect directly to the mainframe. PCs and so-called "thin clients" attached to a terminal server of some kind can also access a mainframe. In essence, all these approaches behave much the same: The terminal requests information from the mainframe, and the mainframe retrieves and displays the information on the terminal. Generally character-based, these applications require little input from the PC, thin client, or terminal.

When a central computer performs processing in a network environment, traffic increases greatly because for every keystroke a user makes, a packet is sent across the network to the mainframe. Then the mainframe sends a response, which can be quite large. This type of network generates a lot of data and doesn't use the PC's power efficiently. As a result, client/server computing is used instead of centralized computing applications.

Understanding Terminal Services

Halfway through the Windows NT Server product cycle and with the release of Windows 2000 Server, Microsoft included a software subsystem called **Terminal Services**. Essentially, Terminal Services provides support for a specialized kind of network processing that's quite useful under certain circumstances.

Terminal Services makes it possible for older, less capable PCs, thin clients, or narrow-bandwidth remote users to run large or complex Windows applications by transferring the burden of client processing to the server. A **thin client** is a bare-bones PC that includes little more than a local keyboard, display device, network interface, and enough memory and processing power to access the network to connect to a server running Terminal Services. For each user, the server running Terminal Services runs a software-based "virtual PC" that actually runs services or applications on the user's behalf. The client runs a small program that intercepts keystrokes and mouse activity on the local machine, and then sends that information to the virtual PC running on the server, where all real processing takes place. The server then sends only screen updates to the client machine in response to user input.

Because the only processing that the local client handles is user input and displaying program output, the client doesn't require much power or capability. This explains how older PCs, thin clients, and remote users on slow connections can operate like fully functional, heavily loaded modern PCs—the virtual PCs that work on their behalf do indeed deliver state-of-the-art capabilities.

Terminal Services is well suited for certain uses, including the following:

- Providing access to modern Windows applications on older PCs or thin clients that otherwise might not be able to run those applications.

- Providing access to centralized applications or services that otherwise would have to be installed on client machines.

- Allowing remote clients using narrow bandwidth connections (usually dial-up to the Internet or a private network) to access powerful Windows applications without imposing bandwidth-related performance delays.

- Remotely administering computers. For remote administration and remote control of computers, Microsoft has renamed Terminal Services as Remote Desktop Connection, starting with Windows XP. Administrators can run a Remote Desktop Connection session on a Windows desktop OS, such as Windows XP or Vista, and remotely control a Windows server computer or any other Windows computer that supports Remote Desktop. An example is shown in Figure 9-5, where a Remote Desktop Connection to a Windows Server 2003 computer is being established from a Windows Vista computer.

NOTE

Virtual Network Computing (VNC) provides remote control and administration of computers across Windows and Linux platforms. It can be downloaded free from *www.realvnc.com* and installed on Windows and Linux machines.

Of course, servers running Terminal Services must be heavily configured with large amounts of RAM and disk space and one or more (but usually four or more) powerful CPUs to provide the power required to create and operate multiple virtual PCs. However, sometimes companies must support older PCs (for embedded systems on a factory floor, for instance, where removing and replacing machines is often difficult). Using special-purpose, single-use applications, such as point of sale (cash register) or data entry stations, doesn't usually require the power and flexibility of a general-purpose PC. In these instances, it often makes sense to

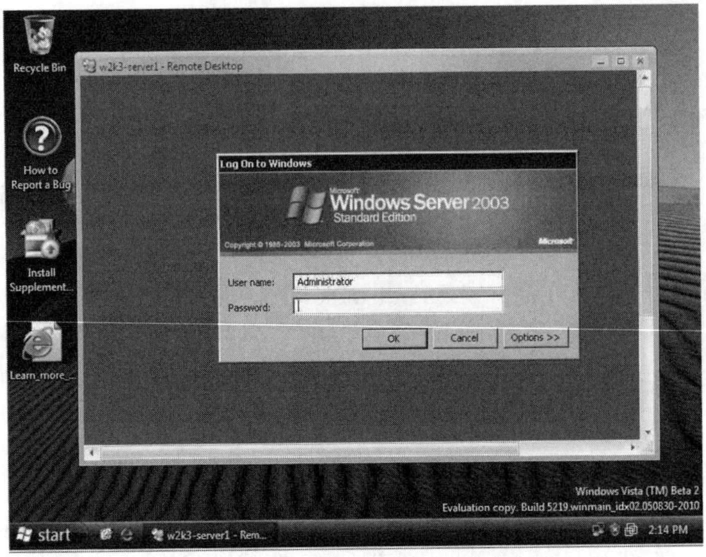

Figure 9-5 A Remote Desktop Connection session

use a thin client computer, which can be more reliable and secure than a full-blown PC. Finally, when remote users must communicate through low-bandwidth connections, putting as much processing activity and power on the client or remote side of the connection as possible is more effective. Doing so limits the amount of traffic that must travel across the remote connection. In all these cases, Terminal Services offers a useful solution for these computing needs.

In addition to Microsoft Terminal Services, which supports PCs that run DOS or some form of Windows, other vendors offer terminal server products. Some, such as those from Citrix (the WinFrame and MetaFrame products), support multiple-client OSs and can make sense when UNIX/Linux and Macintosh machines along with Microsoft-based PCs require terminal servers. In addition, Linux includes support for Telnet services and X-Window System graphical clients, so any TCP/IP-based computer can obtain the same services that Terminal Services provides, except access to Windows-based applications.

Thin-Client Computing

Some OSs include capabilities for thin clients to connect to the server, access resources, and run applications, all with considerably fewer resources than a typical desktop computer. Thin clients add the following benefits to the computing environment:

- *No removable storage*—Without a floppy drive or other removable storage disk, employees can't copy sensitive files from the corporate server to take home. In addition, viruses can't be brought into the corporate LAN via these media types.

- *No hard drive*—Without a hard drive, few configuration tasks are necessary on the local thin-client computer. So when the OS or applications must be upgraded, they need to be upgraded only at the server, which decreases problems caused by old or incompatible software. Not having a hard disk saves money and improves reliability. The lack of a hard disk also means that viruses have no place to live on the machine.

- *Lower total cost of ownership*—Thin clients typically cost less than a full-blown desktop PC. In addition, because these computers can be managed completely from a centralized server, support costs are dramatically lower. Therefore, the total cost of ownership of thin clients is considerably less than desktop PCs.

Back to the Future: The Mainframe Environment

As you have learned, the mainframe computers introduced to users in the late 1950s and early 1960s also introduced the centralized computing model, which is the basis of terminal services. Even today, certain transaction-intensive applications—such as large-scale airline, hotel, and rental car applications—work well with mainframes and terminals (or terminal emulation, which temporarily transforms a fully functional PC into a simple terminal). Although computing currently comes in many forms, the centralized mainframe, with huge numbers of terminals accessing its large-scale, heavily trafficked data collections, remains a viable processing model for applications. Despite many predictions of their demise, mainframes continue to be important computing resources today and for the foreseeable future.

CLIENT/SERVER ENVIRONMENT

The client/server method of network communications is currently the most popular. Its ease of implementation and scalability make it a good choice in many different networking environments. A client is a computer that requests access to shared network resources from a server, a computer that provides shared resources (files and directories, printers, databases, and so on) in response to client requests. **Client/server computing** generally refers to a network structure in which the client computer and server computer share processing requirements.

Note that some services provided by file servers are often not considered client/server. One such service is shared-file storage. For example, many popular e-mail programs, such as Microsoft Exchange Server, Outlook, or Eudora, use the file server as a central location to store messages. When users access the e-mail program, they retrieve data from a specific directory on the server. Many other programs, such as scheduling programs, database management systems, and personal information managers, use this kind of data retrieval.

A shared-file network configuration makes better use of the PC's power but doesn't make full use of a server's potential. This configuration also does not solve the problem of network traffic. Unlike a terminal-based application that sends each keystroke, client-side applications on the PC retrieve large amounts of data across the network. These applications then process that data locally (on the client machine) before sending updated data files back to the server.

One of the most prominent uses of the client/server model is the World Wide Web. When you type the name of a Web site in the Address text box of your Web browser, your computer sends a request to the server that's responsible for that site. That server processes your request and returns the corresponding page. Your browser receives the file, formats it for your screen, determines whether any other data, such as graphics, is required, and displays the page. At this point, the server is no longer responsible for communication. If you use a hyperlink to jump to another page, click a graphic to view it, or click a link to send e-mail, your computer sends the request to the server (the same server or another), and the process begins again.

Client/Server Model in a Database Environment

Database management systems (DBMSs) are another example of efficient use of the client/server model. The client in a DBMS environment uses **Structured Query Language (SQL)** to translate what the user sees into a request that the database can understand. IBM designed SQL as a fairly simple way to manipulate data by using language based on English rather than a cryptic programming language. Its ease of use prompted many database vendors to adopt SQL as their query language as well, and it's now a de facto standard for database queries in general. These are the two major components in a client/server SQL environment:

- The application, often referred to as the **front end** or client
- The database server, also referred to as the **back end** or server

Requesting data from a server in SQL is a six-step process:

1. The user requests the data.
2. The client software translates that request into SQL.
3. The SQL request is sent across the network to the server.
4. The server processes the request.
5. The results are sent back across the network to the client software.
6. The results are presented to the user.

In this type of DBMS environment, the server doesn't contain user interface software. The client software is responsible for presenting data in a usable form via user interfaces and report writing. It accepts instructions from the user, formats them for the server, and sends its requests to the server.

The server in this environment is usually dedicated to storing and managing data, so most database functions occur on the server. The server receives requests from clients, processes them, and returns information to the client. The back-end processing that takes place to fulfill a user's request includes sorting data and extracting requested data from the database.

Advantages of Working in a Client/Server Environment

The client/server networking environment has many advantages over centralized computing. It uses client and server computers more efficiently and makes better utilization of network bandwidth.

By using the server's superior processing power for functions such as database queries, the client computer's configuration can be less complex. It can have a smaller processor and less RAM than the server because it doesn't have to search for data. Drive space on the client can be reserved for local applications instead of for storing large amounts of database information. In addition, network bandwidth is conserved because the only data transferred across the network is the database query command (from client to server) and the results of the query (returned from the server to the client). This comparatively small amount of data transfer is in contrast to a shared-file database application, in which entire database files must be transferred from the server to the client, where the query is performed locally.

One additional benefit of the client/server environment is centralized location. Because all file services and data reside on servers, the servers are easy to secure and maintain in one location. Centralization also simplifies the backup process and ensures that security can be maintained for all users across all servers.

9

WEB-BASED COMPUTING ENVIRONMENTS

Having a connection to the Internet once was considered a luxury; today it's a necessity, and Internet connections can be found almost anywhere: work, home, the library, hotels, the airport, and coffee shops. Because Internet connections are now so ubiquitous, many traditional OSs make file and print services available over a standard Web browser. Novell offers this capability in NetWare with its NetStorage application. Another technology called WebDAV (short for Web Distributed Authoring and Versioning) attempts to go one step further by providing a single framework that can be used on all client and server computing platforms.

WebDAV is an extension to HTTP (the protocol used for transferring Web pages) that allows a Web browser to carry out traditional file system tasks, including file reads, file writes, file locking, and version control. Initially, applications for WebDAV included document collaboration and Web publishing, but its potential is limitless. For instance, e-mail, calendaring, and a host of other applications can be accomplished with a single client. Because WebDAV capabilities are expandable, it might be possible in the future to do away with traditional redirectors, FTP, and e-mail clients in favor of a single client/server technology based on the WebDAV protocol. WebDAV has risen in popularity, as evidenced by the WebDAV client software built into both Mac OS X and Windows XP and Vista. WebDAV clients can mount shared folders or volumes on a WebDAV-enabled Web server so that files on that server can be accessed as though they were local. Whether WebDAV lives up to its promise, it's clear that client/server networking is taking the direction of making simple-to-use, vendor-independent access to networking resources possible. For more information on WebDAV, see *www.webdav.org.*

Extending the idea of using a Web browser as the primary client interface, one Internet business segment that's exploding is **application service providers (ASPs)**. ASPs offer businesses access to their tools and applications through a Web browser. Customers pay as they go for using the application, typically on a subscription or per-use basis. ASPs provide access to applications ranging from simple (file sharing) to complex (accounting and order management) through standard Internet technologies, such as Java and Extensible Markup Language (XML). The move by some organizations to using ASPs reduces their reliance on in-house IT staff, thereby decreasing overhead and the total cost of ownership of their IT assets.

You might be thinking that moving applications and file access to standard Web-based technology starts to erode the necessity of multivendor support in a network, and you would be right. Although the necessity for supporting multiple OSs and file access protocols on both the client side and the server side is far from being a thing of the past, many people can envision a day when standardized protocols for accessing files and applications will homogenize the networking environment. The TCP/IP protocol suite and its Application-layer protocols, such as WebDAV and extensions to HTTP, are already stepping in that direction.

Chapter Summary

- Interconnectivity between multiple-vendor operating systems is often necessary in networking. There are two ways to connect multivendor environments: client-based and server-based.

- A client-based multivendor network environment relies on the client computer's redirectors to decide which server should be sent the request. For example, a computer that requires connections to both a NetWare server and a Windows Server 2003 server loads software to connect to both servers.

- In a server-based solution, the server supports multiple client types. For example, a server running Windows Server 2003 or Novell NetWare can support Microsoft, Novell, Linux/UNIX, and Apple clients.

- Using the processing power of a mainframe computer creates a centralized computer environment. This type of computing can generate large amounts of network traffic and doesn't fully utilize the power available in PCs today. It's not well suited for typical user productivity applications, such as word processing, spreadsheets, e-mail, and so forth. Mainframes still play a valid role in modern networks, especially for large-scale, transaction-oriented applications, such as airline, hotel, and rental car reservation systems and financial trading applications.

- Server-based terminal services can provide useful access to networks and centralized server-based resources for remote users away from the network or for single-use workstations (such as point of sale or data entry terminals).

- The handheld computing environment is growing in leaps and bounds. The nonstandardized hardware and software used for these devices poses challenges for network administrators. To complicate matters, many PDAs are shipped with Wi-Fi interfaces, allowing these devices to maintain a live connection with the corporate LAN, making handheld computing convenient but also a security challenge.

- In a client/server computing environment, the PC and server share processing and use the resources of both machines more efficiently. The World Wide Web is a good example of a client/server networking environment. When you ask for a Web page, your browser (the client) asks the server to send you the page. This type of computing environment reduces network traffic.

- Most database management systems use SQL as their query language. The database application resides on the client, or front end, while the server, or back end, stores and maintains the data.

- The trend in today's networking environment is to remove the obstacles and incompatibilities of working in a multivendor environment. To that end, companies are turning to Web-based computing, in which access to data and applications can be carried out through a standard Web browser, regardless of the platform on which the browser runs.

9

KEY TERMS

application service providers (ASPs) — Companies that specialize in providing customers with access to applications and file services through a Web browser over the Internet.

back end — A server in a client/server networking environment.

centralized computing — A computing environment in which all processing takes place on a mainframe or central computer.

client-based multivendor solution — In this environment, when multiple redirectors are loaded on a client, the client can communicate with servers from different vendors.

client/server computing — A computing environment in which processing is divided between the client and server.

Common Internet File System (CIFS) — The Windows method of accessing files across a network; this method is a newer version of Server Message Block.

database management systems (DBMSs) — Client/server computing environments that use SQL to retrieve data from the server. *See also* Structured Query Language (SQL).

front end — A client in a client/server networking environment.

mount point — The local directory in a UNIX or Linux file system in which an NFS volume is made accessible. *See also* Network File System (NFS).

Network File System (NFS) — A distributed file system originally developed at Sun Microsystems. It supports network-based file and printer sharing using TCP/IP-based network protocols and is the native file-sharing protocol for Linux/UNIX systems.

NFS volume — A portion of a UNIX or Linux file system that has been exported and made available to NFS clients.

open source — A term describing software that's always available at no charge, even after modifications to its source code.

Samba — An open-source software suite that makes Linux servers look and act like Windows servers. It permits DOS or Windows clients to access Linux- or UNIX-based file systems and services without special software on the client end.

server-based multivendor solution — A server, such as one running Windows Server 2003, that can readily communicate with clients from multiple vendors.

Structured Query Language (SQL) — The standard database query language designed by IBM.

Terminal Services — A software subsystem for Windows NT and Windows 2000 Server that permits clients to run large or complex applications on computers with minimal processing power by transferring the burden of client processing to the server.

thin client — A networked computer with a keyboard, a pointing device (mouse), a display device, a network interface, and enough processing power to access terminal services or a mainframe, where the real application processing occurs.

REVIEW QUESTIONS

1. The software component that intercepts a client request for a network resource and forwards it to the correct server is the _____ .

    a. server

    b. DLL

    c. redirector

    d. interceptor

2. Which of the following is the native file-sharing service in UNIX/Linux environments?

    a. NFS

    b. NDS

    c. PCS

    d. IPX

3. A _____ -based multivendor solution provides connectivity by loading multiple redirectors.

    a. client

    b. server

    c. workstation

    d. peer

4. NetWare 6.5 includes the _____ application to enable users to access network resources with a Web browser.

    a. AFP

    b. NetWare Core Protocol

    c. NetStorage

    d. Network File System

5. Which of the following is the native file access protocol in Windows networks?

    a. AFP

    b. CIFS

    c. NFS

    d. NCP

6. In a DBMS environment, which of the following has become a standard for making queries?

    a. NFS

    b. SQL

    c. WebDAV

    d. Samba

7. In a client/server environment, the client is usually a dumb terminal and requires no processing power. True or False?

8. What is the directory in a Linux file system, where remote NFS files are accessed as though the files were local, called?

    a. file

    b. volume

    c. server

    d. mount point

9. Instead of shared folders, NetWare has _____ , which can be accessed by network users who have the appropriate rights.

10. _____ is the default Microsoft implementation of a NetWare requester.

11. Which of the following is an advantage of thin-client computing? (Choose all that apply.)

    a. No removable storage improves security.

    b. No CPU necessary means reduced cost.

    c. No hard drive means fewer configuration problems.

    d. The total cost of ownership is higher.

12. Mac OS X provides client software capable of accessing server resources in a Windows, Macintosh, or UNIX environment. True or False?

13. A(n) _____ computer accesses shared resources on a network.

    a. client

    b. server

    c. standalone

    d. application

14. By using a _____ –based multivendor solution, different clients are easily connected to a server without having to install special software on clients.

    a. client

    b. server

    c. network

    d. WAN

15. In a DBMS environment, the application is sometimes called the

    _____ .

16. Which service allows a Linux computer to access natively shared Windows folders?

    a. NFS

    b. Client for Microsoft Networks

    c. Samba

    d. WebDAV

17. For remote administration and control, Terminal Services was renamed as _____ in Windows XP.

18. Internet companies that provide remote access to applications for businesses are called which of the following?

    a. ISPs

    b. ASPs

    c. APSs

    d. IPSs

19. The World Wide Web is an example of a(n) _____ computing environment.

    a. workstation

    b. client/server

    c. peer-to-peer

    d. all of the above

20. Terminal Services allows clients to run applications locally and access data remotely. True or False?

21. Which of the following types of clients is most likely to benefit from terminal services? (Choose all that apply.)

    a. older, less capable PCs

    b. thin clients

    c. network-attached PCs with high-bandwidth connections

    d. remotely attached PCs with narrow-bandwidth connections

    e. none of the above

22. When sharing files and printers on a Linux machine with Windows clients, the best solution is _____ .

    a. Services for Macintosh

    b. PC-NFS

    c. Samba

    d. Client Service for NetWare

23. What does the acronym NFS stand for?

    a. Network File Sharing

    b. New File System

    c. Novell File System

    d. Network File System

24. Which of the following security protocols is preferred on PDAs that access network resources using Wi-Fi?

    a. WPA

    b. WAP

    c. WEP

    d. WPE

25. An NFS volume is _____ .

    a. an exported file system portion

    b. an imported directory

    c. an SMB shared folder

    d. the native NetWare file-sharing protocol

HANDS-ON PROJECTS

Hands-On Project 9-1

To install, view, and remove File Services for Macintosh and Print Services for Macintosh on a Windows Server 2003, Standard Edition, computer, follow these steps:

1. Click **Start**, **Control Pannel**, right-click **Network Connections**, and click **Open** to open the Network Connections window (see Figure 9-6).

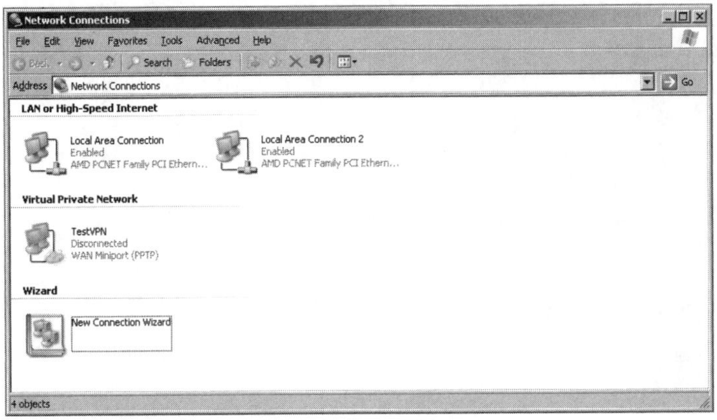

Figure 9-6   The Network Connections window in Windows Server 2003

2. Click **Advanced**, **Optional Networking Components** from the menu to start the Windows Optional Networking Components Wizard (see Figure 9-7).

3. Click the **Other Network File and Print Services** item in the Components list.

4. Click the **Details** button to open the Other Network File and Print Services dialog box.

5. Click the **File Services for Macintosh** and **Print Services for Macintosh** check boxes (see Figure 9-8). If necessary, click to clear the **Print Services for Unix** check box.

6. Click **OK**, and then click **Next**.

7. Wait while Windows installs the necessary files for these networking components. If necessary, insert the Windows installation CD. If it's not already installed, AppleTalk is installed automatically along with the Macintosh network services.

8. Restarting is usually not necessary. However, if prompted, restart your system.

9. If the Network Connections window is not open, open it by right-clicking the **My Network Places** desktop icon and clicking **Properties**.

10. Right-click the **Local Area Connection** icon that Macintosh clients will use, and click **Properties**.

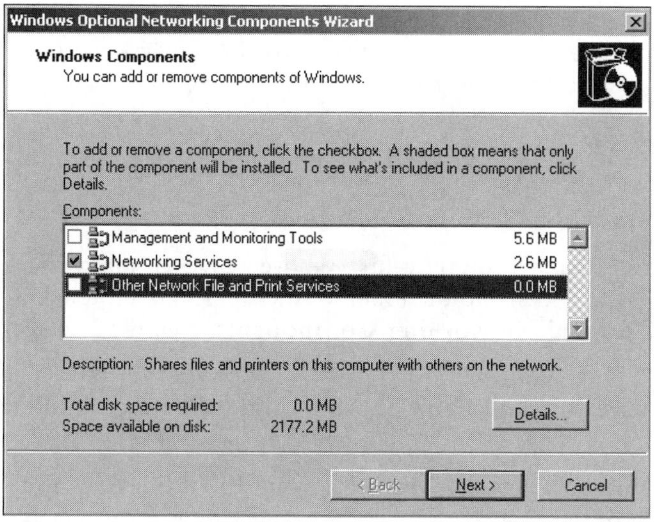

Figure 9-7   The Windows Optional Networking Components Wizard in Windows Server 2003

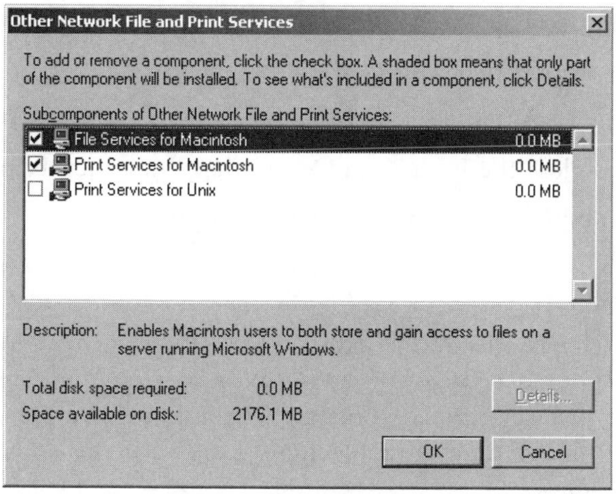

Figure 9-8   The File Services for Macintosh and Print Services for Macintosh subcomponents

11. Click the **AppleTalk Protocol** in the Local Area Connection Properties dialog box.

12. Click the **Properties** button to open the AppleTalk Protocol Properties dialog box, where you can select the AppleTalk zone in which this system will appear.

NOTE

The Macintosh systems connected to the network segment define the selections in this drop-down list. Windows does not define or control AppleTalk zones; it can only join or communicate with an existing zone.

13. Click **OK** to close this dialog box.

14. Click **Close** to return to the Network Connections window.

15. To remove Macintosh support, you must first remove all Macintosh services (File Services and/or Print Services) and then remove the AppleTalk protocol. To do this, click **Advanced, Optional Networking Components** from the Network Connections menu.

16. Click **Other Network File and Print Services** in the Components list, and click the **Details** button.

17. Click to clear the **File Services for Macintosh** and **Print Services for Macintosh** check boxes.

18. Click **OK**, and then click **Next**. Windows removes the networking components.

19. Right-click the **Local Area Connection** icon that Macintosh clients use, and click **Properties**.

20. Click **AppleTalk Protocol**, and click **Uninstall**.

21. Click **Yes** to confirm removal. Windows removes the protocol.

22. Click **Close** or **Cancel** to close the Local Area Connection Properties dialog box.

23. Click **Yes** to restart the computer if you're prompted to do so.

HANDS-ON PROJECTS

Hands-On Project 9-2

Microsoft includes NetWare Client software that coexists with Client for Microsoft Networks installed by default on all modern Windows OSs—Windows 9x, Windows XP, and Windows Vista. In this project, you step through installing Client Service for NetWare on a Windows XP workstation and then removing the client:

1. Click **Start, Control Panel**. (If necessary, click **Switch to Category View**.) Click **Network and Internet Connections**, and then click **Network Connections**.

2. Right-click the **Local Area Connection** icon, and then click **Properties**. (If you have more than one Local Area Connection icon, ask your instructor which one to select.)

3. Click the **Install** button in the Local Area Connection Properties dialog box, and then make sure the Client entry in the Select Network Component Type section is selected. (If not, click it once to select it.) Click the **Add** button.

4. In the Select Network Client window, click to select **Client Service for NetWare**, and then click **OK**.

5. You might be prompted for a path to the installation files. (If so, you should get this information from your instructor.) After the files are loaded and installed, you're prompted to restart your computer. Click **Yes** in the Local Network window to restart your computer. (This is one of the few situations in which you must restart a Windows XP computer for configuration changes to take effect.)

6. Before the restart is finished, you're asked to supply information in the Select Net-Ware Logon window. Ordinarily, you use this window to supply a preferred NetWare server for bindery-based NetWare networks, to designate a default eDirectory tree and context, and to indicate whether login scripts should run at login. In this case, type **Server1** (or another NetWare server name supplied by your instructor) in the Preferred Server text box, and then click **OK**. Unless the server is on your local network, Windows XP can't locate it and asks whether you want to use it as your preferred server. Click **Yes** to close this window and continue restarting.

7. After the computer restarts, the Network Connections window should open. (If it doesn't, open it by following the instructions in Step 1.) Right-click the **Local Area Connection** icon, and then click **Properties**.

8. When the Local Area Connection Properties dialog box opens, the Client Service for NetWare check box should be selected and the item highlighted. Notice that you can't access any properties (the button is grayed out) unless you actually establish a connection to a real NetWare server on your network.

9. Click the **Uninstall** button to remove Client Service for NetWare, and then click **Yes** in the removal confirmation dialog box.

10. Click **Yes** to allow Windows XP to restart your machine and remove the NetWare client code from your system. When your machine finishes restarting, you've completed this project.

Hands-On Project 9-3

Samba, an open-source implementation of an SMB server for Linux and UNIX, permits hosts to masquerade as Windows servers on a Microsoft network. Samba has the undeniable advantages of no cost and no required changes to modern Windows clients to allow access to file and print shares. In Hands-On Project 8-4, you installed the Samba package on your Linux computer. In this project, you create a Samba user, start the Samba service, and access a shared Samba directory from a Windows computer. This project assumes you have a Linux computer and Windows XP computer set up on the same network and that you completed Hands-On Project 8-4 on your Linux computer.

1. Start Linux and log in as **root**. If you are in X-Window, open a terminal window.

2. From the Linux console prompt, create a new Linux user by typing **useradd samba1** and pressing **Enter**.

3. Create a password for the user you just created by typing **passwd samba1** and pressing **Enter**. When prompted, type the password **smbpass1** and press **Enter**. Enter the password again when prompted.

4. Next, to create a Samba user with the same name and password, type **smbpasswd –a samba1** and press **Enter**. When prompted, type the password **smbpass1** and press **Enter**. Enter it again to confirm.

5. To start the Samba service, type **/etc/init.d/smb start** at the Linux console prompt and press **Enter**. (*Note*: Be sure to include a space after smb and start.) You should see output confirming that the Samba service started.

6. To verify that Samba is running, you can access Samba shares from the local Linux computer. At the command prompt, type **smbclient //localhost/samba1 –U samba1** and press **Enter**. When prompted, type the password **smbpass1** and press **Enter**. You are successful if you get the smbclient prompt, which looks like this: smb: \>. Type **exit** and press **Enter** to quit smbclient.

7. Next, you access the Samba server from a Windows computer. In Windows, click **Start**, **Run**, type **\\linuxcomputername** (replacing *linuxcomputername* with the name of the Linux computer), and click **OK**. You could also type the IP address of the Linux computer instead of the name.

8. Next, type **samba1** for the user name, press **Enter**, type **smbpass1** for the password, and press **Enter**. You should see a shared folder in Windows Explorer with the name samba1. From here, you can access the shared folder like any folder in a Windows system.

Hands-On Project 9-4

Samba is a Linux solution for making Linux operate by using the Windows file-sharing system (SMB) so that Linux can access Windows shares and vice versa. Another way to integrate Windows and Linux is by using Telnet. In this project, you use the Telnet client on any Windows computer to access a Linux computer. (This Linux computer must be set up already with the Telnet service running.)

1. Start Windows XP and log on. Open a command prompt window by clicking **Start**, **Run**, typing **cmd**, and clicking **OK**.

2. To connect to the Linux computer, type **telnet *IPaddress***.

3. When prompted for a user name, enter a user name supplied by your instructor, and then enter the password. If you're accessing the Linux computer you used in Hands-On Project 9-3, you can use the user name and password you created in that project.

4. You receive a Linux prompt. To see which directory you are in, type **pwd** and press **Enter**. (*Hint*: "pwd" means print working directory.)

5. Explore some Linux commands: Type **ls –a** and press **Enter** to view a file listing of all files in the current directory.

6. Type **ps –A** and press **Enter** to view a listing of all running processes.

7. To see who is currently logged on, type **who** and press **Enter**.

8. To see how to get information about the ls command, type **man ls** and press **Enter**. You can use the up and down arrows to navigate through the help file. Type **q** and press **Enter** to quit. (Note that you can get help on most Linux commands by typing man followed by the command name; "man" is short for manual.)

9. To exit Telnet, type **exit** and press **Enter**.

Hands-On Project 9-5

This project walks you through the process of enabling Remote Desktop on Windows Server 2003, Standard Edition, for the purposes of remote administration. To install and configure Remote Desktop, follow these steps:

1. Log on to Windows Server 2003.

2. Right-click the **My Computer** desktop icon, and click **Properties**.

If there's no My Computer icon on your desktop, click **Start**, right-click **My Computer**, and click **Properties**.

NOTE

3. In the System Properties dialog box, click the **Remote** tab.

4. In the Remote Desktop section, click to select the **Allow users to connect remotely to this computer** check box. Click **OK** if the Remote Sessions message box is displayed.

5. By default, all members of the Administrators group can access Remote Desktop. If other users should be allowed to access the server using Remote Desktop, click the **Select Remote Users** button and add users as appropriate.

6. Click **OK** to close the System Properties dialog box. In the next project, you access the Windows Server 2003 computer using Remote Desktop.

Hands-On Project 9-6

This project walks you through connecting to a Windows Server 2003 computer by using Remote Desktop in Windows XP Professional. Your instructor will provide the server name, user name, and password needed to connect if you don't have this information. To connect to a Windows Server 2003 computer using Remote Desktop, follow these steps:

1. Log onto a Windows XP Professional computer. To open a remote desktop connection, click **Start**, point to **All Programs**, point to **Accessories**, point to **Communications**, and click **Remote Desktop Connection**.

2. When the Remote Desktop Connection dialog box opens, type the server name in the Computer text box, and click **Connect**.

3. When prompted for a user name and password, type the user name and password provided by your instructor, and then click **OK**. You are now connected to the server desktop through Remote Desktop.

4. To close the connection, in the Remote Desktop window, click **Start**, **Log Off**. Click **Log Off** to close the Remote Desktop window.

CASE PROJECTS

Case Project 9-1

You are the network administrator for a small college. The Engineering Department has been running its own network for years with a Novell NetWare server using the IPX/SPX protocol. All 25 client computers are running Windows XP Professional. This network is running a hub-based Ethernet 10BaseT implementation that is physically separate from the campus network. You have been asked to bring this department into the main campus network with as little disruption as possible to its current operation. The campus network runs Windows Server 2003 servers in a domain configuration and Windows XP Professional client computers using TCP/IP.

Develop a plan that allows clients from the Engineering Department network to access resources on the main campus network. Discuss any questions you must address before proceeding, and list any software that must be changed or added to clients and/or servers.

Case Project 9-2

Three departments in your company—Accounting, Advertising, and Engineering—have been running in their own workgroup environments for a number of years. Engineering runs a Linux Fedora Core 4 network with 10 Linux computers. The Advertising Department uses LocalTalk, which is built into its Macintosh computers. Accounting uses Windows XP to share its files and printers. Your task is to connect these three workgroups and purchase a server, if necessary. Develop a solution that allows these three departments to share resources easily.

Case Project 9-3

We've Got Parts Inc. distributes industrial machine replacement parts to its clients worldwide. The company's network includes 40 workstations and a single server. The president wants all employees to access a new order/inventory database that will interface with the accounting database currently residing on its server. Choose a client/server or a client-based computing model, and explain your choice. How could the company improve the availability and fault tolerance of its network?

Case Project 9-4

At XYZ Corp., the sales staff carries laptops and sometimes requires access to the corporate network to read e-mail, access a customer contact database, place orders, and check order status. In most cases, salespeople dial in with 56Kbps modems. They complain that it takes an inordinately long time to access the customer contacts database and interact with the order-handling system. What kind of remote access could they use instead of Dial-up Networking, if they go through a correctly configured Windows Server 2003 server, that would speed their access? Explain how this performance improvement is achieved.

Case Project 9-5

BlueSkies Inc., a regional airline based in Des Moines, decided to go nationwide, open at least two reservation counters in every U.S. city with a population over 800,000, and create a Web site where customers can make reservations online. The company expects to handle more than 200,000 transactions per day. Select a terminal services or mainframe-based architecture for the airline's solution, and defend your choice. Be sure to explain why your solution is superior to the other architecture.

9

10

INTRODUCTION TO NETWORK SECURITY

> **After reading this chapter and completing the exercises, you will be able to:**
>
> ♦ Develop a network security policy
>
> ♦ Secure physical access to network equipment
>
> ♦ Secure network data
>
> ♦ Use tools to find network security weaknesses

You have learned about network media and topologies. You can make wise choices about which network architectures to use and decide on the ideal networking protocol for your network, and you have a good handle on what operating systems are available and how to integrate them into a cohesive network. Your work as a network administrator is almost done, right? Wrong. You have plenty to do before you can bring your network online because of all the security risks that can make your network fail: Trojan programs, worms, spammers, denial-of-service attacks, spyware, network attackers, backdoors, spoofers, and on and on. Understanding and preventing attacks that can infiltrate or disrupt your network is what network security is all about. This chapter strives to give you a solid foundation of knowledge and tools to protect your network and its users.

NETWORK SECURITY OVERVIEW AND POLICIES

Network security can mean different things to different people. To network users, network security is sometimes thought of as a necessary evil that takes the form of hard-to-remember passwords that must be changed frequently and cryptic terms, such as "VPN" and "IPSec," to describe methods they must use to access the network. To other users, network security means the comfort of knowing that if they erase their hard drives accidentally, the friendly network administrator will gladly restore all their data from the most recent system backup.

Perceptions about network security also vary depending on the industry a person is in or the job a person does. A chemical engineer might perceive network security to mean that the compound he has just developed is safe from the competition's eyes. A lawyer might describe network security as a means of safeguarding against illegal activities, such as unlawful distribution of copyrighted materials. To a network engineer, network security might simply mean that she can get a good night's sleep, secure in the knowledge that the network is safe against the latest threats—at least until tomorrow. To a chief information officer (CIO), however, network security means more than job-specific tasks. A CIO knows that the goal of network security is to protect the organization and its users, customers, and business partners from any threat to the integrity of information passing through or residing on the corporate network.

Ideally, network security should be as unobtrusive as possible, allowing network users to concentrate on the tasks they want to accomplish rather than how to get to the data they need to perform those tasks. Achieving that goal permits an organization to go about its business confidently and efficiently. In today's security-conscious world, a company that can demonstrate its information systems are secure is more likely to attract customers, partners, and investors.

Developing a Network Security Policy

The lofty goal of good, unobtrusive security encompasses many dimensions, so where do you start? With a security policy that reflects the attitude of your organization. A network security policy is a document that describes the rules governing access to a company's information resources, the enforcement of those rules, and the steps taken if rules are breached. The document should describe not only who can have access to which resources, but also the permissible use of those resources after they're accessed. In addition, it should follow these basic guidelines:

- A security policy should be easy for ordinary users to understand and reasonably easy to comply with. If you make the policy too difficult to understand or follow, users resist adhering to it. A policy that requires users to change their passwords every week, for example, is too difficult to follow. Users who must change their passwords too frequently often select easy-to-remember passwords that are based on common words and, therefore, are easy to crack.

- A security policy should be enforceable. A rule that can't be reasonably enforced will almost always be broken. For example, you shouldn't prohibit use of the Internet during certain hours of the day unless you have a method of monitoring or restricting this use.

- A security policy should clearly state the objective of each policy so that everyone understands its purpose. For example, a policy that states "Misuse of the network is forbidden" doesn't define misuse, making this policy useless because of its lack of specificity.

The preceding guidelines explain how a security policy should be written. Now you need to know what information should be included in a security policy.

Determining Elements of a Network Security Policy

Explaining all the elements of a security policy is beyond the scope of this book, but the following items give you a solid start:

- *Privacy policy*—Describes what staff, customers, and business partners can expect for monitoring and reporting network use.

- *Acceptable use policy*—Explains for what purposes network resources can be used.

- *Authentication policy*—Describes how users identify themselves to gain access to network resources. Logon names, password conventions, and authentication methods should be described.

- *Internet use policy*—Explains what constitutes proper or improper use of Internet resources.

- *Access policy*—Specifies how and when users are allowed to access network resources. Policies should exist for both on-site and remote access to the network.

- *Auditing policy*—Explains the manner in which security compliance or violations can be verified and the consequences for violations.

- *Data protection*—Outlines the policies for backup procedures, virus protection, and disaster recovery.

 To learn more about security policies, refer to RFC 2196 at *http://rfc.net/rfc2196.html*.
TIP

Your security policy might have other elements, depending on the type of organization it's being created for and the level of security required, but the preceding list is usually the minimum for most networks. Keep in mind that a well-thought-out security policy also protects the organization legally. If no policy exists, disciplining or prosecuting people who misuse or intrude on the network is more difficult. Unfortunately, after you create a security policy, your work is not done. A security policy should be a continual work in progress, with modifications made as needed to reflect changing technology and business practices.

Understanding Levels of Security

Before starting to design a network security policy, you need to be aware of the relationship between the level of security imposed on a network and the cost and difficulty required to support that network. Security doesn't come without a cost. If you're the network administrator for the security department of a government office, price is likely no object in determining the extent of security measures. However, if you're setting up a network for a small manufacturer of household items, you might need to scale back on security measures. Before determining what level of security your network requires, answer these questions:

- What must be protected? Is there information on the network that would compromise the viability of the company or its customers if it fell into the wrong hands?

- From whom should data be protected? Is the biggest threat from people inside or outside the company?

- What costs are associated with security being breached and data being lost or stolen?

- How likely is it that a threat will actually occur? Do you have a high-profile business, or do you have known competitors who are likely to want to sabotage your business or steal trade secrets?

- Are the costs to implement security and train personnel to use a secure network outweighed by the need to provide an efficient, user-friendly environment?

Depending on your answers, you will likely decide to implement one of these levels of security or some combination of them: highly restrictive, moderately restrictive, and open.

Highly Restrictive Security Policies

Highly restrictive security policies usually include features such as data encryption, complex password requirements, detailed auditing and monitoring of computer and network access, intricate authentication methods, and policies that govern use of the Internet and e-mail. Some features needed for this type of policy might require third-party hardware and software. The high expense of implementing these restrictive policies comes in the form of high design and configuration costs for software and hardware, staffing to support the security policies, and lost productivity caused by a high learning curve for users. However, if you need highly restrictive security, it's probably because the cost of a security breach would be more expensive than implementing the security policy.

Moderately Restrictive Security Policies

Most organizations can probably opt for a moderately restrictive security policy. These policies require passwords for each user but not overly complex passwords. Auditing is geared toward detecting unauthorized logon attempts, misuse of network resources, and network attacker activity. Most network OSs contain satisfactory authentication, monitoring, and auditing features to implement the required policies. The network infrastructure can be secured with moderately priced off-the-shelf hardware and software, such as firewalls and access control lists. The costs of moderate security policies are primarily in initial configuration and support. This type of policy is used in a typical business setting, in which users have personal files that require moderate security and users in some departments are responsible for files that might need additional security measures, such as payroll or personnel files.

Open Security Policies

A company that uses an open network security policy might have simple or no passwords, unrestricted access to resources, and probably no monitoring and auditing. This type of policy might make sense for a small company with the primary goal of making access to network resources easy. The company might not want to spend additional funds for the employee training often required for more restrictive policies.

In an open security environment, Internet access should probably not be possible via the company LAN because it invites too many possibilities for outside mischief or inside abuse. If Internet access is available company-wide, a more restrictive policy is probably warranted. In an open security environment, sensitive data, if it exists, might be kept on individual workstations that are backed up regularly and are physically inaccessible to other employees.

10

Common Elements of Security Policies

No matter which type of security policy your company uses, some common elements should be present. Virus protection for servers and desktop computers is a must for every computing environment, and there should be policies aimed at preventing viruses from being downloaded or spread. Backup procedures for all data that can't be reproduced easily should be in place, and a disaster recovery procedure must be devised. Remember: Security is aimed not only at preventing improper use of or access to network resources, but also at safeguarding the company's information, which today is often more valuable than its physical assets. Before you turn to methods and practices for securing data, however, one often neglected aspect of security must be discussed: the physical security of servers and network devices.

SECURING PHYSICAL ACCESS TO THE NETWORK

A common guideline in discussing network security is "If there is physical access to the equipment, there is no security." This guideline applies to servers, desktop computers, network devices such as routers and switches, and even network media. No matter how strong your logon name and password schemes are, if a person has physical access to a device, access to data is not far behind.

There are numerous ways to break into an unprotected computer or networking device. A computer left alone with a user logged on is particularly vulnerable. A person walking by could access all the files the currently logged-on user has access to. If the computer is a server and an administrator account is logged on, a person has full reign of the network and can even give his or her account administrator control. Even if no user is logged on, people could log on to the computer with their own accounts and access files to which they wouldn't normally have access. Failing that, the computer could be restarted and booted from removable media, thereby bypassing the normal OS security. Last, if a person is desperate, the entire computer or its hard drives could be stolen and later cracked. The following sections describe best practices for preventing a physical assault on your network.

Physical Security Best Practices

The following list is an overview of best practices to secure your network from physical assault:

- When planning your network, ensure that rooms are available to house servers and equipment. These rooms should have locks to prevent unauthorized access and be suitable for the equipment being housed, including having enough power receptacles, adequate cooling measures, and an environment clear of electromagnetic interference (EMI) sources. In addition, rooms should be inaccessible through false ceilings.

- If a suitable room isn't available, locking cabinets, freestanding or wall mounted, can be purchased to house servers and equipment in public areas. Wall-mounted cabinets are particularly useful for hubs, switches, and patch panels. You must be certain cabinets have suitable ventilation for the devices they're housing.

- Wiring from workstations to wiring cabinets should be inaccessible to eavesdropping equipment. Wiring that's not concealed in floors or ceilings should be concealed in raceways or other channeling devices to discourage access.

- Your physical security plan should include procedures for recovery from natural disasters, such as fire or flood.

Physical Security of Servers

Securing servers from physical access should be a high priority in any security plan. This goal can be accomplished in a number of ways, and sometimes a combination of methods works best, depending on your environment. Many servers are stashed away in a lockable wiring closet along with the switch to which the server is connected. This setup is fine as long as the environment is suitable for the server, and the same people who have authority to access wiring and hubs also have authority to access the servers, although this isn't always the case.

Servers often require more tightly controlled environmental conditions than do patch panels, hubs, and switches. Servers can generate a substantial amount of heat and, therefore, need adequate cooling. The lack of cooling can damage hard drives, cause CPUs to shut down or malfunction, and damage power supplies, among other things.

In addition to adequate cooling, server rooms should be equipped with power that's preferably on a circuit separate from other electrical devices. Enough power outlets should be installed to eliminate the need for extension cords. Because you will be putting servers on uninterruptible power supplies (UPSs), you need to verify power requirements for UPSs. Some UPSs require special twist-lock outlet plugs rated for high currents. Nothing is more frustrating than getting a brand-new UPS and preparing to plug in your servers, only to find that the power outlets are incompatible with the UPS requirements.

Sometimes putting your servers in a place that's accessible to people who should *not* have physical access to servers is unavoidable. For example, you might have different teams maintaining internetworking equipment and servers, and you don't want internetworking maintenance teams to have access to servers. If you don't have the facilities to separate the two types of equipment physically, however, you can still take some steps to provide a measure of physical security. Many servers come with locking cabinets to prevent access to the inside of the case. Some also have lockable covers that protect the drives and power buttons from unauthorized access (or these components can be removed altogether). You can also place the keyboard, mouse, and monitor in an area separate from the actual server by using long-distance cable extenders. Last, you can place the server in a freestanding locking cabinet.

If you're forced to place servers in a public access area, locking cabinets are a must. Even if no users have malicious intentions, someone is sure to kick the server, spill coffee on it, unplug it, or inflict some sort of accidental damage. You can purchase rack-mountable servers, which are designed to bolt to a standard 19-inch equipment rack. To conserve space, you can purchase a freestanding cabinet with a built-in 19-inch rack, allowing you to store several servers. Be sure that the cabinet you purchase is well ventilated or permits you to add fans for ventilation. These cabinets typically start at about $1000. Like everything else, security comes with a price.

Security of Internetworking Devices

Routers and switches contain critical configuration information and perform tasks that are essential to your network's operation. A user with physical access to these devices needs only a laptop or handheld computer and a few easily discovered keystrokes to get into the router or switch, change the passwords, and view or change the device's configuration. In addition, a person who has access to a hub or switch port can attach a laptop with a protocol analyzer installed. From that point, it's simply a matter of waiting for the right data to be captured to gain access to critical or sensitive information.

Clearly, internetworking devices such as hubs, switches, and routers should be given as much attention in terms of physical security as servers. These devices give potential network infiltrators access to the network and an opportunity to wreak havoc. Configuration changes made to routers, switches, and even hubs can have disastrous consequences. In addition, access to routers can reveal network topology information that you might not want everyone to know. The more troublemakers know about a network's configuration, the more tools they have to break into the network or otherwise cause problems on it.

A room with a lock is the best place for internetworking devices, but a wall-mounted enclosure with a lock is the next best thing. These cabinets are usually heavy-duty units with doors that swing out and built-in 19-inch racks. Wall-mounted cabinets are expensive, so budget between $300 and $1000 for them, depending on the features and size you need. Some cabinets come with a built-in fan or have a mounting hole for a fan. The racks also come with convenient channels to run wiring.

Securing Access to Data

Physically securing your network assets is only one part of the security puzzle. Networks are designed to give users operating from remote locations access to data, whether the remote location is the next room or the other side of the world. Securing data on a network has many facets, some of which are discussed in more detail in the following sections:

- *Authentication and authorization*—Identifying who is permitted to access which network resources

- *Encryption/decryption*—Making data unusable to anyone except authorized users

- *Virtual private networks (VPNs)*—Allowing authorized remote access to a private network via the public Internet

- *Firewalls*—Installing software or a hardware device that protects a computer or network from unauthorized access and attacks designed to cripple network or computer performance

- *Virus and worm protection*—Securing data from software designed to destroy data or make the computer or network operate inefficiently

- *Spyware protection*—Securing computers from inadvertently downloading and running programs that gather personal information and report on users' Web browsing and computing habits

- *Wireless security*—Implementing unique measures for protecting data and authorizing access to the wireless network

The following sections discuss these areas of security and explore some features on network OSs that help secure a network.

Implementing Secure Authentication and Authorization

Authentication and **authorization** are security features that allow administrators to control who has access to the network (authentication) and what users can do after they are logged on to the network (authorization). Network OSs include tools that enable administrators to specify a number of options and restrictions on how and when users can log on to the network. There are options for password complexity requirements, logon hours, logon locations, and remote logons, among others. After a user is logged on, file system access controls and user permission settings determine what a user can access on a network and what actions a user can perform (such as shutting down a system) on the network.

Configuring Password Requirements in a Windows Environment

Administrators can specify whether a password is required for all users, how many characters a password must be, and whether the password should meet certain complexity requirements. Windows XP allows passwords up to 128 characters, but a minimum of five to eight characters is typical. A password minimum length of zero means that blank passwords are allowed, a setting that might be adequate for networks with open security policies but should never be used for networks requiring more security. A password policy with complexity requirements means that user passwords must have three of these four characteristics: lowercase letters, uppercase letters, numbers, and special (nonalphanumeric) characters.

Other password options include Maximum password age, Minimum password age, and Enforce password history. The Maximum password age setting specifies, in days, how often users must change their passwords. The Minimum password age setting specifies the minimum number of days that must pass before users can change their passwords. The Enforce password history setting determines how many different passwords must be used before a password can be used again. One word of caution: Don't make your password requirements so stringent that well-meaning users feel forced to write their passwords down so that they can remember them. Password policies should make it difficult for would-be attackers to gain access to the system, but not so difficult that your users have trouble adhering to the policies.

When a user fails to enter a correct password, a policy can be set to lock the user account, preventing that account from logging on. This account lockout option, used to prevent intruders from guessing a password, can be enabled or disabled. If it's enabled, the administrator can specify how many times an incorrect password can be entered before the account is locked. After it's locked, the administrator can require manual unlocking or automatic unlocking of the account after a certain amount of time has expired.

Password policies for a single Windows XP/Vista or Windows Server 2003 computer can be set in the Local Security Settings MMC found in the Administrative Tools section of Control Panel. Figure 10-1 shows the Local Security Settings MMC with the Password Policy settings selected. In a domain environment, password policies can be set by using group policies on a domain controller. Password policies take effect immediately for all existing and new user accounts.

Configuring Password Requirements in a Linux Environment

Like Windows, Linux has a number of password options that can be configured. Whereas Windows password policies are set globally and affect all users, Linux password configuration can be done globally or on a user-by-user basis. Password options in a standard Linux Fedora Core 4 environment include the maximum password age, minimum password age, and number of days' warning a user has before the password expires.

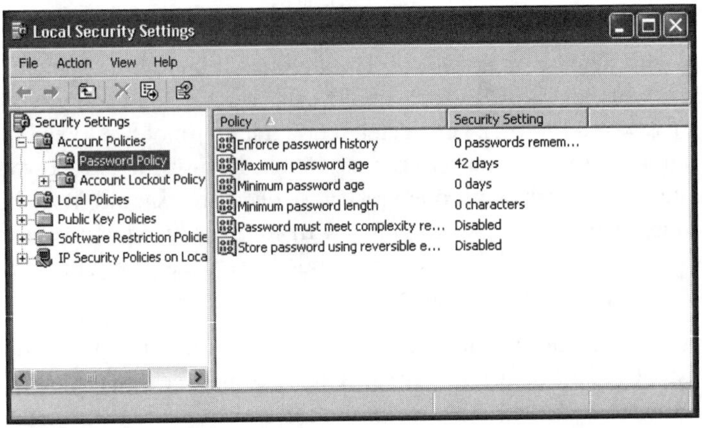

Figure 10-1   Password Policy settings in Windows

For these password options to be available, the Linux system must be using **shadow passwords**, a secure method of storing user passwords on a Linux system. The passwords are stored in an encrypted format in the shadow file located in the /etc directory; this file is accessible only by the root system user. Most Linux installations use shadow passwords by default. Password options can be set by editing the /etc/login.defs configuration file. Only accounts created after the login.defs file has been edited are affected.

A number of other password options can be configured, including account lockout and password history, by using **Pluggable Authentication Modules (PAM)**. PAM is the standard software service on many Linux distributions for authenticating users. One standard feature of PAM authentication is a password complexity test. When a new password is created for a user account, a database of common dictionary words is searched. If the password is found, the user is informed that the password is not complex enough to be considered secure. The default configuration allows weak passwords to be used, but this feature can be configured to disallow a weak password.

Reviewing Password Dos and Don'ts

Some general rules for creating passwords include the following:

- Do use a combination of uppercase letters, lowercase letters, and numbers.

- Do include one or more special characters, such as periods, dollar signs, exclamation points, and question marks.

- Do consider using a phrase, such as NetW@rk1ng !s C00l. Phrases are easy to remember but generally difficult to crack, especially if you mix in special characters and numbers.

- Don't use passwords based on your logon name, your family member's names, or even your pet's name. Users often use these types of passwords, but unfortunately, they're easy to guess after attackers discover personal information about users.

- Don't use common dictionary words unless they are part of a phrase, and substitute special characters and numbers for letters.

- Don't make your password so complex that you forget it or need to write it down somewhere.

Restricting Logon Hours and Logon Location

Some network administrators allow users to log on any time of the day and any day of the week, but if your security policy states otherwise, both Windows and Linux have solutions to restrict logon by time of day, day of the week, and location.

In a Windows domain environment, allowed logon times can be set for each user account, as shown in Figure 10-2. The default settings allow logon 24 hours per day, seven days a week. A common use of restricting logon hours is to disallow logon during system backup, which usually takes place in the middle of the night. In Figure 10-2, the dark boxes indicate times that the user can log on, and the white boxes indicate hours the user can't log on. In this example, logging on from 2 a.m. to 4 a.m. is not allowed. Note that the logon hours option is available only in a Windows domain environment.

10

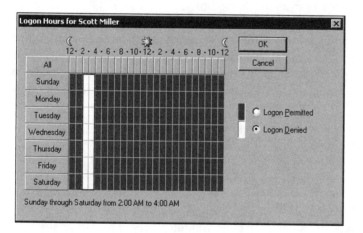

Figure 10-2   Setting logon hours for a user

Sometimes users log on to the network from computers that aren't their regular workstations. This practice might be allowed in your environment, but extending this option to users who have access to sensitive data can be dangerous. If a user logs on at a workstation in a coworker's office and then walks away from that machine, the coworker now has access to the sensitive data. To prevent this problem, users can be restricted to logging on only from particular workstations. Figure 10-3 shows the Windows user account settings for logon location; the user can log on only to the computers named smiller01 and engineering. As with logon hours, this option is available only in a Windows domain environment.

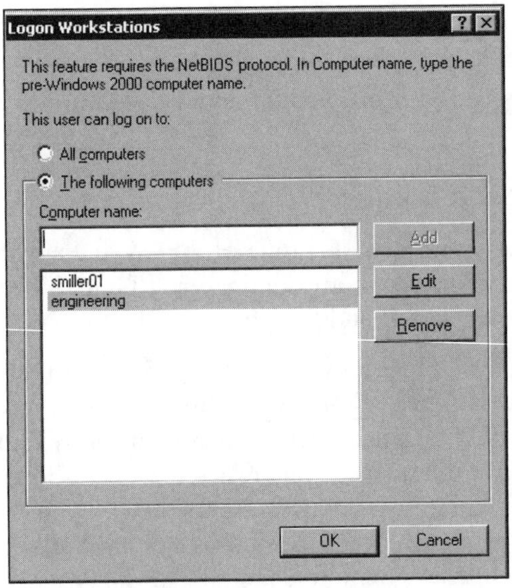

Figure 10-3   The Logon Workstations dialog box

The Linux OS offers similar features for logon restrictions using the PAM authentication service discussed earlier. In general, standard Linux distributions don't include a GUI to configure these settings. Typically, text configuration files must be edited to enable and configure logon restrictions, and those details are beyond the scope of this book.

NOTE

In Novell NetWare, an administrator can configure all the logon settings discussed previously in ConsoleOne, iManager, or NetWare Administrator.

Authorizing Access to Files and Folders

After users have logged on to a network or computer, they must be authorized to access network resources. A common network resource is shared files, which are controlled by the OS file system security. File system security allows administrators to assign file and folder permissions to users or groups of users.

Windows OSs have two options for file security: sharing permissions and NTFS permissions. **Sharing permissions** are applied to folders (and only folders) shared over the network. The files in a shared folder inherit the same permissions applied to the parent folder. Sharing permissions don't apply to files or folders if a user is logged on locally; they restrict only users accessing files across the network. Sharing permissions are the only file security option available in a FAT or FAT32 file system. In other words, if a user is logged on locally to a Windows system formatted with FAT or FAT32, that user has full access to all files on all drives.

NTFS permissions are considerably more sophisticated than sharing permissions. With NTFS permissions, administrators can assign permissions to files as well as folders, so one level of permission can be assigned to a folder but a different level of permission assigned to files in the folder, if needed. Additionally, NTFS permissions apply not only to access over the network, but also to file access by a locally logged-on user. With NTFS permissions, administrators can assign permissions to user accounts and group accounts. Six standard permissions are available for folders, ranging from Read to Full Control, and 14 special permissions, such as Take Ownership, Write Attributes, and Traverse Folder, enable you to fine-tune file and folder permissions. Details on these special permissions are beyond the scope of this book, but you can get a quick overview by searching for "special permissions for files and folders" in the Windows help system.

To set Windows NTFS permissions on a folder, right-click the folder, click Sharing and Security, and then click the Security tab in the Properties dialog box (see Figure 10-4).

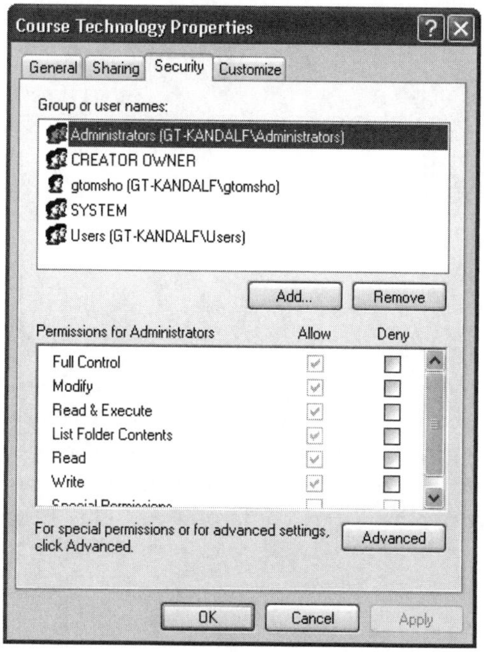

Figure 10-4   Setting NTFS folder permissions

The Linux OS also supports file and folder security. Linux permissions are fairly simple, however, compared with the multitude of configuration options in Windows NTFS permissions. Linux permissions are divided into three categories: owner, group, and others. For each category, three permissions can be set: read, write, and execute. The owner category specifies permissions for the owner of the file, which is usually the user who created the file. The group category specifies the group account assigned to the file. By default, the group account assigned to a file or folder is the owner's primary group membership. The others category specifies all users. The read permission allows a user to read the contents of a file or folder, the write permission allows a user to change a file's contents or create files in a folder, and the execute permission allows running a program file or script. Figure 10-5 shows the Permissions tab of a folder's Properties dialog box on a Linux Fedora Core 4 system.

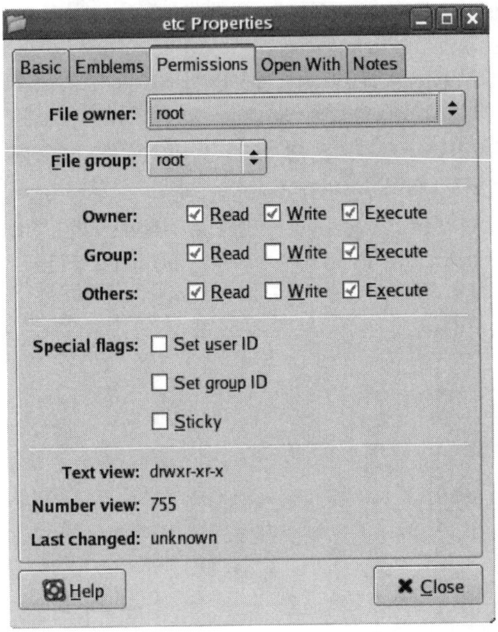

Figure 10-5   Setting folder permissions in Linux

File and folder permissions are a necessary tool administrators use to make network resources secure and still give users appropriate access to the resources they are permitted to use. However, permissions don't protect data traversing the network media, nor do they protect data in files if file system security has been compromised. This is where data encryption comes in.

Securing Data with Encryption

Many network administrators use **encryption** technologies to safeguard data as it travels across the Internet and even within the company network. This security measure prevents somebody using eavesdropping technology, such as a packet sniffer, from capturing packets and using data in the packets for malicious purposes. Data stored on disks can also be secured with encryption to prevent someone who has gained physical access to the computer from being able to use the data.

Using IPSec to Secure Network Data

The most popular method for encrypting data as it travels network media is to use an extension to the IP protocol called **IP Security (IPSec)**. IPSec works by establishing an association between two communicating devices. An association is formed by two devices authenticating their identities via a preshared key, Kerberos authentication, or digital certificates.

A preshared key is a series of letters, numbers, and special characters, much like a password, that both communicating devices use to authenticate each other's identity. A network administrator must enter the same preshared key in the IPSec configuration settings on both devices. Kerberos authentication is used in a Windows domain environment or on a Linux system to authenticate users and computers. Kerberos authentication also uses keys, but the OS generates the keys, which makes this method more secure than having an administrator enter keys. Digital certificates involve a third party called a certification authority (CA). Someone wanting to send encrypted data must apply for a digital certificate from a CA, which is responsible for verifying the applicant's authenticity. When an IPSec communication session begins, the communicating parties exchange certificates, and each party sends the certificate to the CA electronically to verify its authenticity.

After the communicating parties are authenticated, encrypted communication can commence. Data sent across the network, even if it's captured by an eavesdropper, will be unreadable to all but the intended recipient. Only the message recipient has the information needed to decrypt the message.

IPSec is configured on a Windows Vista, Windows XP, or Windows Server 2003 computer in the IP Security Policies MMC shown in Figure 10-6. Three standard IPSec policies are available: Client (Respond Only), Server (Request Security), and Secure Server (Require Security). These policies are intended as models for administrators to create their own policies suitable for their networks, but they can be used as is or edited. The Client (Respond Only) policy is intended primarily for client computers that need to access secure resources. With this policy, the computer uses encrypted communications only if the device it's communicating with requests secure communications. If the Server (Request Security) policy is set, the computer requests IPSec-encrypted communication but allows unencrypted communication if the other device doesn't support IPSec. The Secure Server (Require Security) policy should be used when all communication of the type specified in the policy must be secure. A computer with this policy set rejects attempts to communicate if encryption is not used.

An IPSec policy must be assigned before IPSec can be enabled on a computer. To assign an IPSec policy, you simply right-click the policy and select Assign. Only one IPSec policy can be assigned per computer.

In a Linux Fedora Core 4 environment, IPSec is configured with the Network Configuration tool, shown in Figure 10-7. This Linux distribution includes no default IPSec configurations, so to start using IPSec, a new IPSec configuration must be created.

10

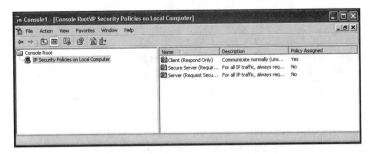

Figure 10-6   Viewing IPSec policies in Windows XP

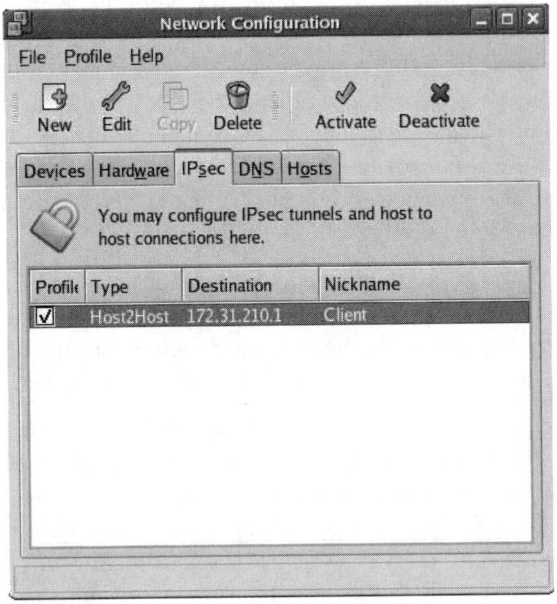

Figure 10-7   The IPsec tab in Network Configuration

Although IPSec is an excellent way to secure data as it travels across a network, it doesn't secure data on disk drives if someone gains unauthorized access to the computer. Other security methods, discussed in the following section, are available for addressing this possibility.

Securing Data on Disk Drives

Sometimes file system permissions aren't enough to stop an attacker who is bound and determined to gain access to data on your system. If someone gains access to the hard disk on which sensitive data is stored or otherwise compromises system security, your data could be vulnerable. Data stored on a computer's disk drive can be encrypted, however, so that only the person who created the encrypted file can read the data, even if the hard disk is read sector by sector, therefore bypassing the file system security.

In Windows XP, Vista, and Server 2003, **Encrypting File System (EFS)** is a standard feature available on NTFS-formatted disks. To encrypt a file or the files in a folder, you simply select the Encrypt contents to secure data option in the Advanced Attributes dialog box (see Figure 10-8), which is accessible from a file or folder's Properties dialog box.

Figure 10-8   Configuring encryption settings in Windows XP

After a file is encrypted, Windows Explorer displays the file name in green text so that it's recognizable as an encrypted file. By default, only the creator of the file and the designated Data Recovery Agent for the system can decrypt the file. The Data Recovery Agent is usually the Administrator account in a domain system. To give additional users authority to open the encrypted file, click the Details button in the Advanced Attributes dialog box. EFS decrypts the file automatically when an authorized user attempts to open it, so the decryption process is transparent—that is, not noticeable to users.

On Linux systems, a simple method to encrypt files involves using a command-line program called gpg (Gnu Privacy Guard). This program uses a password entered by the user to encrypt the file specified as an argument to the gpg command, which then creates a new file with the encrypted contents of the specified file. The original file can then be deleted, and the only way to decrypt the data is to use the gpg command and supply the correct password.

Securing Communication with Virtual Private Networks

Virtual private networks (VPNs) are temporary or permanent connections across a public network—such as the Internet—that use encryption technology to transmit and receive data. VPNs are meant to make packets secure as they are transmitted across a public network. Therefore, the connection between sender and receiver is private, even though it uses a link across a public network to carry information. This ability to use public resources privately on demand gives a VPN its name. (In other words, a VPN makes something public behave as though it were private.) Figure 10-9 depicts a typical VPN connection in which a "tunnel" carries data securely from the VPN client to the VPN server through the Internet. The tunnel is really a special encapsulation of the IP protocol, in which it appears to the client as though a direct point-to-point connection exists between client and server.

CORPORATE NETWORK

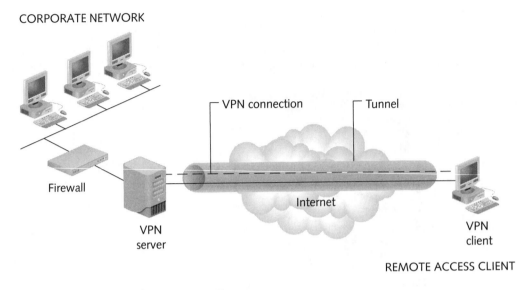

Figure 10-9 A typical VPN connection

VPN servers can be configured on network OSs, such as Windows Server 2003 and Linux. VPN servers can also be in the form of a dedicated device with the sole purpose of handling VPN connections or as a software add-on solution to some routers. Whatever solution is used, the VPN server must have at least two network interfaces: one for the internal or company network and one that connects to the external or public network.

VPNs in a Windows Environment

Windows OSs support a special TCP/IP protocol called Point-to-Point Tunneling Protocol (PPTP). With PPTP, a user running a Windows OS can dial up a Windows server when it's running Routing and Remote Access Service (RRAS). It supports the equivalent of a private, encrypted dial-up session across the Internet. Similarly, a VPN could be established permanently across the Internet by leasing dedicated lines to an ISP at each end of a two-way link and maintaining ongoing PPTP-based communications across that dedicated link.

Starting with Windows 2000, Windows supports a more secure VPN protocol called Layer 2 Tunneling Protocol (L2TP). Working in tandem with IPSec, these Windows OSs can use PPTP or L2TP to create safe, secure VPN connections through a private carrier or across the Internet. L2TP supports advanced authentication and encryption technologies; however, it requires Windows machines on both sides of any remote connection.

VPNs in Other OS Environments

Windows OSs are not the only ones supporting VPNs. Linux OSs also support VPN client and VPN server applications. Linux implementations of VPNs typically use PPTP or IPSec, and an L2TP implementation is now available. One of the most popular VPN solutions for Linux is a free downloadable package called OpenSwan. OpenSwan uses IPSec as the encryption protocol and is becoming the default in many Linux versions, including Fedora Core 4. The Linux OpenSwan package can be found at *www.openswan.org*, and documentation is included in the downloadable software.

Novell NetWare (along with BorderManager, the Novell firewall) provides VPN server connections to corporate networks for VPN clients. In addition, corporate LANs can be tied together over VPN connections through the Internet to form a VPN WAN.

Mac OS 9 and later supports VPN client connections to Windows servers by using PPTP or IPSec. Mac OS X Server has a VPN server service that allows Mac OS X, Windows, and UNIX/Linux clients to connect to a corporate LAN through the Mac OS X VPN server, using PPTP or L2TP.

One method of providing VPN services to connect remote sites is to use routers with VPN capability to form a router-to-router VPN connection. This type of VPN connection uses the Internet to connect remote sites with corporate headquarters or to connect corporate partners to form an extranet. In this arrangement, the VPN software resides on the router rather than on client systems and is considerably less expensive than using leased or dedicated lines to connect remote networks.

10

VPN Benefits

VPNs enable organizations to use the Internet as a private dial-up or broadband service for users with machines running a VPN-supported OS. Organizations can also interconnect multiple LANs across the Internet—one pair of networks at a time. Using VPNs to connect users to a company network has clear advantages:

- Installing several modems on an RRAS server so that users can dial up the server directly isn't necessary; instead, users can dial up any ISP. As long as the VPN server has an Internet connection, a private connection can be established. This method saves money on hardware and systems management.

- Remote users can usually access an RRAS server by making only a local phone call, no matter where they might be, as long as they can access a local ISP. Distance from the RRAS server no longer matters; this feature saves money on long-distance telephone charges.

- When broadband connectivity to the Internet is available, such as DSL or cable modem, remote users can connect to the corporate network at high speed, making remote computing sessions more productive than dial-up connections.

A VPN is not limited to dial-up connections. Anywhere a user has a connection to the Internet, whether through dial-up, cable modem, or a corporate LAN, a VPN can be used.

Cost savings notwithstanding, the greatest benefit of a VPN—whether it uses PPTP, L2TP, or another equivalent protocol—is that it extends the reach of private networks across public ones both easily and transparently. Used more today for on-demand, dial-up connections, dedicated PPTP or L2TP connections are also increasingly used to connect LANs across the Internet.

Protecting Networks with Firewalls

A **firewall** is a hardware device or software program that inspects packets going into or out of a network or computer and then discards or forwards those packets based on a set of rules. A hardware firewall is configured with two or more network interfaces typically placed between a corporate LAN and the WAN connection. The WAN link can connect to an ISP, another corporate LAN in another city, or even the network of a partner organization. The type of firewall you use and how it's configured are determined by what lies at the other end of the WAN link. For example, you might want to allow a remote sales office to access the corporate database, but you would want to deny this access to Internet users and perhaps restrict it for users in a partner network. A software firewall is installed on a computer or server and simply inspects all packets coming into or leaving the computer. Based on predefined rules, the packets are then discarded or forwarded to the OS.

Today, a network administrator is courting disaster if a firewall is not installed between the corporate network and the Internet. Firewalls protect against outside attempts to access unauthorized resources, and they protect against malicious network packets intended to disable or cripple a corporate network and its resources. A second use of firewalls placed between the Internet and the corporate network is to restrict corporate users' access to Internet resources. This type of restriction is usually intended to prevent users from accessing offensive Web sites or bandwidth-intensive content, such as streaming audio or video, which might not be the best use of an employee's time or the network's bandwidth.

Firewalls installed on the corporate network are usually dedicated devices that have preinstalled software that must be configured by a knowledgeable administrator. This type of firewall, however, is usually not suitable for home Internet users trying to protect their computers from would-be attackers. Because of the availability of fast, always-on Internet connections for home users, personal firewalls were developed to guard a single workstation against Internet attacks. These software firewalls are programs you install on your computer. They guard your computer from attempts to access your computer's resources and services through the Internet. Personal firewalls are not just for the home, however. Because many attacks occur inside corporate networks, these lightweight firewalls can also be used in the office to prevent other users from infiltrating your workstation or to prevent the spread of network-aware worms. Most Linux distributions have included a preconfigured firewall for years, and Microsoft followed suit with Service Pack 2 (SP2) of Windows XP.

Firewall devices from different vendors vary quite a bit in configuration details, but they are all based on one premise: Rules are created to determine what type of traffic is allowed to enter and exit the network. A firewall, by default, is usually a closed device. After the firewall is installed and the interfaces are configured, the firewall stops all incoming packets (and sometimes all outgoing packets, depending on the firewall). To configure a firewall, the network administrator must build rules that allow only certain packets to enter or exit the network. The rules are based on a variety of properties of the incoming and outgoing packets, including source and destination address; protocols such as IP, ICMP, TCP, HTTP, SMTP, and FTP; and sometimes even the context of a packet.

The source and destination addresses can be examined to determine whether the packet is coming from an approved network to an approved network. For example, a corporate network might have a restricted segment where no traffic from the outside world is permitted. The firewall can examine all incoming packets and discard packets with a destination address of the network's restricted segment. The protocol in the packet can be examined to ensure that it's a type that should be permitted into the network. For example, you might want to deny certain ICMP packets from entering the network. (ICMP packets are generated by the Ping command, among other applications, and can be used to saturate a network's bandwidth or tie up a network server, thereby denying legitimate users access to the network. This is a denial-of-service [DoS] attack.) Firewalls can also attempt to determine the context of a packet; this process is called **stateful packet inspection (SPI)**. SPI helps ensure that a packet is denied if it's not part of an ongoing legitimate conversation. Attackers can insert rogue packets into a data stream in an attempt to hijack a legitimate connection or tie up network services. Examining packet context can reduce the success of these attacks.

NOTE

Firewalls perform other functions not mentioned here, but the functions discussed in this section are typically universal of all firewalls.

Using a Router as a Firewall

Conceptually, a firewall is just a router with specialized software that facilitates creating rules to permit or deny packets. Many routers have capabilities similar to firewalls but with one key difference: Routers, by default, are open systems. After a router is first configured, by default, all packets are permitted both into and out of the network. Therefore, a network administrator must create rules, called **access control lists**, that deny certain types of packets. Typically, an administrator builds access control lists so that all packets are denied, and then creates rules that make exceptions. Access control lists can examine many of the same packet properties that firewalls can.

Using Intrusion Detection Systems

An **intrusion detection system (IDS)** usually works with a firewall or router with access control lists. A firewall protects a network from potential break-ins or DoS attacks, but an IDS must detect an attempted security breach and notify the network administrator. In some cases, an IDS can take countermeasures if an attack is in progress. These countermeasures include resetting the connection between source and destination devices or even disabling the link between inside and outside networks. An IDS is an invaluable tool to help administrators know how often their network is under attack and devise security policies aimed at thwarting threats before they have a chance to succeed.

Using Network Address Translation to Improve Security

Network Address Translation (NAT) was discussed in Chapter 6 in the context of alleviating the IP address shortage. An additional benefit of NAT is that the real address of an internal network resource is hidden and inaccessible to the outside world. Because most networks use NAT with private IP addresses, those devices configured with private addresses can't be accessed directly from outside the network. In fact, when NAT is used, the only way an outside device can send a message to a device in the internal network is in response to a message from the internal device. That is, an external device can't initiate a network conversation with an internal device, thus limiting an attacker's options to cause mischief. NAT is usually an integral part of the operation of a network firewall positioned between the network and the Internet or another outside network.

Protecting a Network from Worms, Viruses, and Rootkits

In today's Internet-connected networks, virus and worm attacks are a constant threat. Users download programs, bring disks from home, and open e-mail attachments. All these actions are normal computing activities, but they can also bring viruses into the network. A **virus** is a program that spreads by replicating itself into other programs or documents. Its sole purpose is to disrupt computer or network operation by deleting or corrupting files, formatting disks, or using large amounts of computer resources. A **worm** is similar to a virus in that it's self-replicating, but a worm doesn't attach itself to another program; rather, it's a self-contained program. Worms are now more common than viruses because with the Internet and widespread network connectivity in general, worms don't need help to spread. Whereas a virus requires a user to run the program containing the virus to operate, and then copy that file to spread, a worm can do its work without any help and can spread through an available network connection. Some insidious actions a worm can perpetrate include using large amounts of network bandwidth, deleting files, sending e-mails, and creating backdoors into computers. A **backdoor** is a program installed on a computer that permits access to the computer, bypassing the normal authentication process. A common use of backdoors created by worms is to allow spammers to send e-mail from the computer on which the backdoor is installed, thereby hiding the spammer's true identity.

Viruses, worms, and rootkits are part of a broader category of software called **malware**, which is any software designed to cause harm or disruption to a computer system or perform activities on a computer without the consent of the computer's owner. To help prevent the spread of viruses and worms, every desktop and server should have virus-scanning software running. Most virus-protection software is also designed to detect and prevent worms. A virus scanner that's resident in memory should be used so that every program file or document that's accessed is scanned. Documents should be scanned if the document type might contain macros, and servers should run virus-scanning software that scans every file read or written to and from server drives. If a server file accessed by other users on the network gets infected, the virus can spread through the network in a matter of seconds.

Viruses and worms that spread through e-mail attachments have been commonplace for years. They are simple to avoid; just don't open any e-mail attachments sent by someone from whom you're not expecting a message. Even if you know the sender, beware; malware programs can use an e-mail program's address book to send messages, causing you to believe the message is safe. Most virus scanners actually detect a virus or worm contained in an e-mail message and often delete the attachment before it ever reaches your inbox, but if the virus is very new, it might not be detected.

Another type of malware that's not technically a virus because it's usually not self-replicating is a **Trojan program**, which appears to be something useful, such as a free utility, but in reality contains some type of malware. What's unfortunate about a Trojan program is that users willingly run the software and don't even know it's causing problems on their systems.

Rootkits are a form of Trojan programs that can monitor traffic to and from a computer, monitor keystrokes, and capture passwords. They are the ultimate backdoor into a system and are among the most insidious form of Trojan software because they can mask that the system has been compromised by altering system files and drivers required for normal computer operation. Rootkits aren't specific to an OS and can be found for Windows, Linux, and various forms of UNIX. They are notoriously difficult to detect because they hide themselves so well and integrate into the OS they have infected. Typically, detection requires restarting the system and booting to another medium, such as CD-ROM or a flash drive, with tools that can scan for and detect the presence of a rootkit. Removal is even more difficult because rootkits often alter system files and drivers on which the system depends to run normally. Many experts agree that the time and effort required to remove a rootkit is better spent backing up critical data files, reformatting the disk, and reinstalling the OS.

The **hoax virus** is one of the worst kinds of virus. With a hoax virus, someone sends an e-mail proclaiming that Microsoft, the government, or another well-known entity has just discovered a new virus that formats your hard drive or performs some other nefarious deed. Usually, the warning is that the virus will appear in an e-mail message. The hoax message goes on to say that you should send this message immediately to everyone you know to inform them of this terrible virus. The flood of e-mail from people actually falling for this hoax *is* the virus! This type of hoax clogs e-mail servers, decreases productivity, and generally wastes time. If you're concerned that the warning might be real, check the Web site of the organization the message references or the Web site of your antivirus software. (You do have antivirus software installed, don't you?) If the supposed virus isn't mentioned at these sites, stop this type of virus in its tracks and delete the e-mail without forwarding it to innocent friends and acquaintances.

In the Computer section of the *www.snopes.com* site, you can find a list of real and hoax viruses.

TIP

Virus and worm protection can be expensive, although many quite capable freeware or shareware packages are available. However, the loss of data and productivity that can occur when a network becomes infected is much more costly. Remember that virus software must be updated because developers of virus and worm software are always looking for new and clever ways to wreak havoc on your network.

Protecting a Network from Spyware and Spam

Spyware and spam aren't that similar in their function, but both are an affront to your privacy, and their primary goal is to get you to buy something or get taken by a fraud. **Spyware** is a type of malware that monitors or in some way controls part of your computer at the expense of your privacy and to the gain of some third party. The result of spyware is usually a decrease in computer performance and an increase in pop-up Internet messages and spam. These afflictions occur because one goal of spyware is to monitor your Internet activity, such as which Web sites you visit and how often you visit. The data the spyware gathers is then used by advertisers, spammers, and perhaps even more malicious third parties for the sole purpose of extracting money from your wallet.

Unlike a virus or worm, spyware is not usually self-replicating. Spyware usually gets installed on a system when a user installs some legitimate software or is too quick to click OK when a message pops up on a Web site offering to install a program. Many free peer-to-peer file-sharing applications, such as Kazaa and LimeWire, install spyware on your computer as a condition of being free. Nonetheless, millions of users install the software (*and* the spyware) because the prospect of being able to download free music and software is just too compelling.

Many anti-spyware programs are available, and some are bundled with popular antivirus programs. Microsoft offers a free download of a beta version of Windows AntiSpyWare, which it acquired from another company. This product will be repackaged as Windows Defender and be available in mid-2006. Anti-spyware programs scan your computer for known spyware and remove it, and some can provide real-time protection, stopping spyware from being installed in the first place. Take note, however, that some freeware programs installed on your computer might stop working if the spyware that came packaged with them is removed.

Spam, like spyware, is more a nuisance than a threat to your computer system. Spam is simply unsolicited e-mail. Although it doesn't delete files or format disks, spam is a thief of e-mail storage space, network bandwidth, and, most important, people's time. For those naive enough to click where spam leads, it can also be a thief of your hard-earned cash if you end up purchasing the products it advertises or fall for frauds it might solicit. Like spyware and virus protection, spam detection and prevention is an uphill battle because for every rule or filter anti-spam software places on your e-mail account, spammers find a way to get around them.

Probably one of the best ways to avoid spam is to not give your e-mail address to anyone but trusted parties. If you must register on a Web site using an e-mail address, use one from a free e-mail service that you never use for personal mail. That way, you can simply log on to the free e-mail Web site periodically and delete all the messages. Unfortunately, this method still doesn't guarantee your protection from spam, as even legitimate organizations with whom you communicate regularly can sell their e-mail lists or have them stolen. In addition, worms and spyware can use the address books of people you know to get access to your e-mail address.

It should be clear by now that the Internet, with its wealth of information and its avenues of entertainment and business, is also a dangerous place. The best advice, in lieu of pulling the plug on your Internet connection, is to be dutiful in keeping anti-everything software up to date, and use common sense when opening e-mails or responding to Web-based solicitations. Network security is effective only when users understand the risks of installing and using certain types of software and have a solid understanding of the organization's security policies. A well-educated workforce is a safe workforce.

Implementing Wireless Security

The explosion of wireless networking devices creates a new problem for network administrators. Because wireless signals aren't bound by physical cables, an attacker need not have physical access to your network cabling system to compromise the network. Anyone with a wireless scanner and some software who gets within range of your wireless network's signals can intercept data or access your wireless devices. What's worse, because most wireless networks eventually tie into a wired network, an attacker potentially has access to your entire network infrastructure while sitting in a car outside your building. Attackers who drive around looking for wireless LANs to intercept are called **wardrivers**.

To foil would-be wireless attackers, wireless security must be enabled on all your networking devices by using one or more of the following methods:

- *Service set identifier (SSID)*—An SSID is an alphanumeric label configured on the access point that identifies one wireless LAN (WLAN) from another. Each client must configure its wireless NIC for that SSID to connect to the access point. A private WLAN should set the SSID to a value that's not too easy to guess, and the SSID should not be set to broadcast. When an SSID is broadcast, wireless software can scan the network to look for available SSIDs and be set automatically, allowing an attacker to gain the first piece of information required to access your WLAN. Setting an SSID correctly doesn't stop a seasoned wardriver, but it can at least discourage casual or inexperienced attackers.

- *Wired Equivalency Protocol*—This option must be set at the access point and on the wireless client. **Wired Equivalency Protocol (WEP)** provides data encryption so that a casual attacker who gains access to your wireless signals sees only encrypted gibberish. However, WEP has its flaws, and a determined attacker can eventually crack the encryption code. Nonetheless, WEP has the advantage of being available in just about all wireless equipment, so you can have some security without buying anything new.

- *Wi-Fi Protected Access*—**Wi-Fi Protected Access (WPA)**, the successor to WEP, has enhancements that make it much more difficult to crack the encryption code. WEP uses a static encryption key, but WPA alters the key periodically and automatically, so even if an attacker does determine the key, the key soon changes and the attacker must start over. WPA also uses an enhanced authentication method, with a centralized server maintaining the database of users permitted to access the wireless network.

■ *802.11i*—The **802.11i** standard, an extension to 802.11, was ratified in 2004 and is the latest standard that defines wireless security. 802.11i is sometimes referred to as WPA2 because it incorporates much of what composed the WPA standard. Its advantage over WPA, however, is that it uses more advanced encryption standards and a more secure method of handling encryption keys.

■ *MAC address filtering*—If your wireless network is fairly small and only specific computers are to have access to the network, you can use the **MAC address filtering** feature on access points that restrict network access to computers with specific MAC addresses. This security measure is not viable in a large or nonstatic network where new laptops and PDAs access the network frequently.

A final word about wireless networking security: Implementing a strong encryption protocol doesn't mean you are completely safe—determined attackers can and will get into any network if they want to. With that in mind, you should use some policies that further protect your network:

■ Do a site survey and try to position your access points so that only the required areas are covered by the signal; limit signal access outside the building whenever possible.

■ If you're using WEP, manually change the encryption key on a regular basis.

■ When possible, use access points that can filter MAC addresses, allowing only known addresses access to the network.

Remember, the joy of a wireless network is easy, anywhere access to the corporate LAN, but that access also applies to attackers wanting to harm your network.

USING A CRACKER'S TOOLS TO STOP NETWORK ATTACKS

If you want to design a good, solid, network infrastructure, hire a security consultant who knows the tools of the cracker's trade. Sometimes confused with hacker, a **cracker** is someone who attempts to compromise a network or computer system for the purposes of personal gain or to cause harm. Contrast this with the term hacker, which has had a number of meanings throughout the years. **Hacker** is sometimes a derogatory term to describe an unskilled or undisciplined programmer. It can also mean someone who is highly skilled with computer systems and programs and is able to use some of the same tools crackers use to poke around networks or systems, but not for evil purposes. These two terms, cracker and hacker, are also sometimes called black hats and white hats, respectively. A black hat is, as the analogy implies, the bad guy, and a white hat is the good guy. White hats often use the term **penetration tester** for their consulting services. In fact, a new certification has been developed for the white hat hacker called Certified Ethical Hacker (CEH; *www.eccouncil.org*). This section approaches the subject of network security from the white hat's perspective. The goal is to see what type of holes exist in a network's security for the purpose of closing those holes.

Discovering Network Resources

Before attackers can gain access to or cause problems with your network, they must get information about the network configuration and available resources. Some tools they use are command-line utilities such as Ping, Traceroute, Finger, and Nslookup. These commands can help you find out which devices are available, identify name information for those devices, and possibly learn user information. Ping, as you have learned, can be used to determine whether a particular computer is responding on the network. Because you can ping a computer by name and have its IP address returned, the command can also be used to resolve a computer name to an IP address. The Traceroute utility provides information about the route a packet takes from one computer to another. The information Traceroute supplies can help determine a network's topology. The Finger utility allows you to query a computer and determine who is logged on to the computer and the address of the computer from which they are connected. The Nslookup utility is used to query DNS servers. Depending on how well a DNS server is secured, Nslookup could retrieve a list of all computer names and mail servers on a domain.

Other tools of the trade include ping scanners and port scanners. A **ping scanner** is an automated method for pinging a range of IP addresses. A **port scanner** determines which TCP and UDP ports are available on a particular computer or device.

With a ping scanner, a network address can be entered into the scanner, and the program queries all IP addresses in that network (or a range of IP addresses). Many ping scanners also look up the DNS name of any computer that provides a response. Attackers use this information to see what computers are available on a network, and the DNS name can provide useful information because most network administrators name their devices to describe their purpose or location, such as naming a database server SQL-Server or a router Router-3rdFloor. Figure 10-10 shows the results of a ping scan.

A port scanner, by determining which ports are active, can tell you what services are enabled on a computer. Figure 10-11 shows a program that ran a port scan on a computer with IP address 172.31.1.200. Most of the services are closed, but several are open. A network administrator should use this information to be sure the ports listed as open are necessary for the operation of that computer. Any unnecessary ports should be closed. Closing a port usually involves stopping a service or application from running.

Whois is a handy utility for discovering information about an Internet domain. You can find the name and address of the domain name owner, contact information for the domain, and the DNS servers that manage the domain (see Figure 10-12). The information that can be gleaned from a Whois query includes IP address information and names and addresses of DNS servers used by that domain. DNS servers can be further queried to determine names and addresses of computers in that domain.

Protocol analyzers are also useful for resource discovery because they allow you to capture packets and determine which protocols services are running. They require access to the network media and are, therefore, effective tools only if the attacker is an internal user or has gained access to the internal network.

10

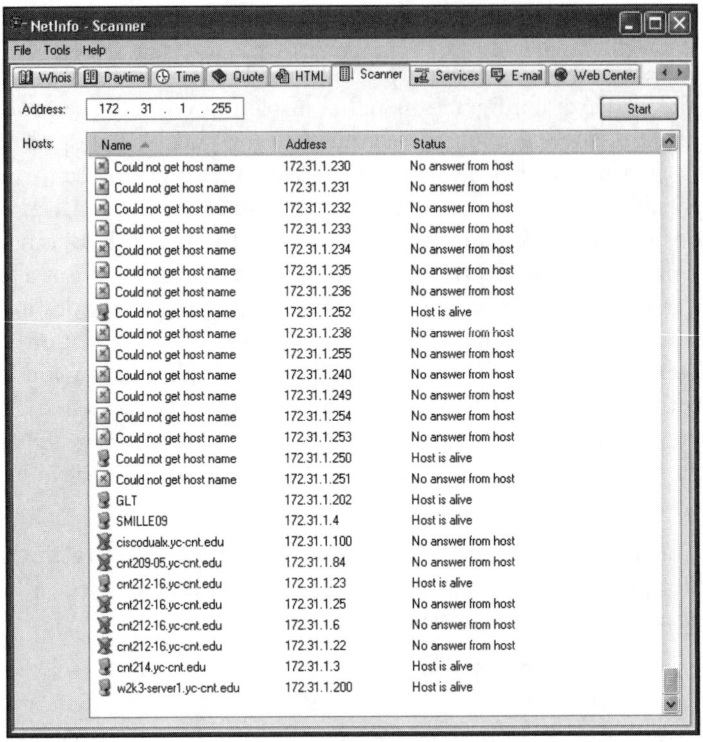

Figure 10-10   The results of a ping scan on a computer

To protect your network from some of these utilities, you can take a variety of actions. Some utilities, such as Finger, can be rendered useless if they are turned off on all devices that support them. Some Linux and UNIX systems as well as some routers often leave the Finger service on by default. A port scan should be run on all network devices to see which services are on, and then services that aren't necessary should be turned off. This process is a white hat use of a port scanner.

Access lists on routers and firewalls, including personal firewalls, can block pings to prevent the use of ping scanners. To protect the network from internal users of protocol analyzers, all hubs and switches should be secured to prevent an unauthorized user from hooking up a laptop or other device to the network.

Gaining Access to Network Resources

After an attacker has discovered the resources available on a network, the next step might be gaining access to those resources for the purposes of viewing, stealing, or destroying data. One of the easiest resources to open is one in which no password is set. Believe it or not, this situation happens more often than you think, and often numerous routers and switches are

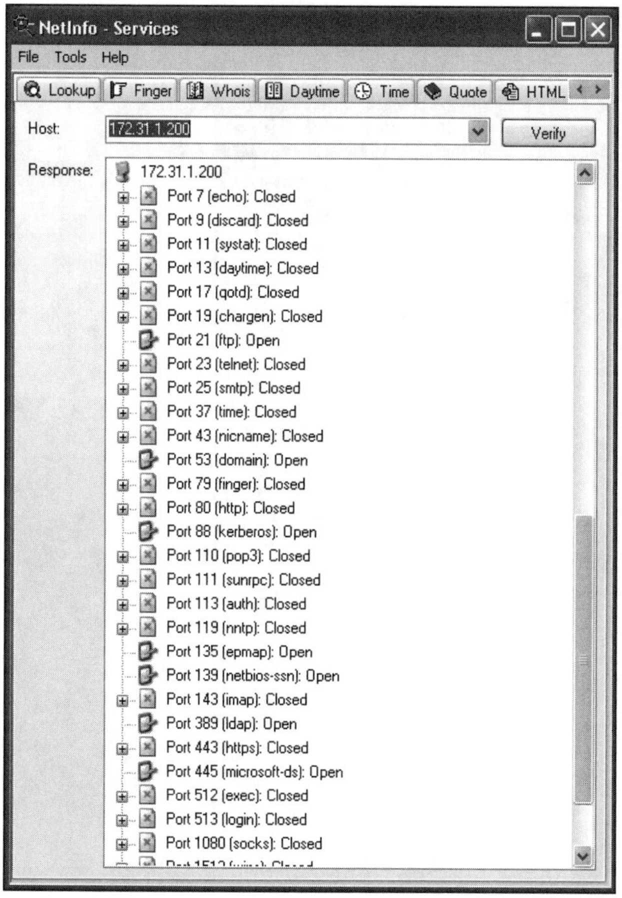

Figure 10-11 The results of a port scan on a computer

found to be available through the Internet or on a company network that have had no passwords set. The remedy to this problem is, of course, to check all devices that support Telnet, FTP, e-mail, and Web services. Verify that passwords are set on all devices and disable any unnecessary services.

Often an attacker runs into a resource that requires a user name and password. Finger can be used in some cases to discover user names. Linux, NetWare, and Windows servers have default administrator names that are often left unchanged—a fact that an attacker with a password-cracking tool can easily exploit. Some of these tools use a systematic method of guessing passwords from a dictionary of words or from an algorithm that uses all combinations of letters, numbers, and symbols. This type of cracking tool can be extremely time and CPU intensive. If passwords are strong, these tools are often impractical because guessing very complex passwords could take days. Using a password-cracking tool on your own system is recommended to see whether your passwords are complex enough.

Figure 10-12   Results returned from a Whois query

NOTE

For a complete list of security and hacking tools, including password crackers, visit *www.securiteam.com/tools/archive.html*.

Disabling Network Resources

A **denial-of-service (DoS) attack** is an attacker's attempt to tie up network bandwidth or network services so that it renders those resources useless to legitimate users. Some attackers launch a DoS attack for fun; others do it to satisfy a grudge. Three common types of DoS attacks focus on tying up a server or network service: packet storms, half-open SYN attacks, and ping floods. Programs that can create these attacks are readily available for download.

Packet storms typically use the UDP protocol because it's not connection oriented. One packet storm program called Pepsi5 sends a stream of UDP packets that have spoofed host addresses, causing the host to be unavailable to respond to other packets. A **spoofed address** is a source address inserted into the packet that isn't the actual address of the sending station.

Half-open SYN attacks use the TCP three-way handshake to tie up a server with invalid TCP sessions, thereby preventing real sessions from being created. The attacker sends a series of packets with a valid port number, requesting to start a conversation. These packets, called SYN packets, cause the server to respond. The original SYN packet contains a spoofed source address, resulting in the server waiting for the final packet in the three-way handshake until it times out. If enough SYN packets are sent, the server uses all available connections and is unable to respond to legitimate attempts to a make a connection. A number of programs that create this type of attack are commonly available.

A ping flood is exactly what it sounds like. A program sends a large number of ping packets to a host. They cause the host to reply, tying up CPU cycles and bandwidth. A variation is the smurf attack, in which pings are sent to a broadcast address. All the requests contain the spoofed source address of the host to be smurfed. When computers respond to the broadcast ping, they send their replies to the single host whose address is spoofed. The host is then flooded with ping responses, causing it to slow down or even freeze up while it processes all the packets.

There's no end to the methods available to wreak havoc on a network. Becoming familiar with the tools and methods that can be used against your network is essential so that you can prepare defenses against network attacks. You can also use these tools to test the integrity of your network security. Firewalls, access lists, virus scanners, and strong OS security are some ways to prevent these attacks or reduce their effects. In addition, the use of an IDS helps you analyze attempts to breach network security and track down and close potential holes in your security measures. Regardless of your tools, you should always start by devising a sound security policy that maps out your overall network security plan and contains provisions for auditing and revising the policy as your needs and technology change. Implementing your policies and using the tools available to protect your network keep your data safe and keep you sleeping well at night.

CHAPTER SUMMARY

- A network security policy is a document that describes the rules governing access to a company's information resources. A security policy should be easy to understand and enforce and should state each policy objective clearly.

- A security policy should contain these types of policies: privacy policy, acceptable use policy, authentication policy, Internet use policy, auditing policy, and data protection policy.

❏ Securing physical access to network resources is paramount. Separate rooms or locking cabinets should be available to house network servers and equipment. Wiring should be inaccessible to eavesdroppers. Physical security includes procedures to recover from natural disasters.

❏ Securing access to data includes authentication and authorization, encryption/ decryption, VPNs, firewalls, virus and worm protection, spyware protection, and wireless security.

❏ VPNs are an important aspect of network security because they provide secure remote access to a private network via the Internet.

❏ Firewalls, a key component of any network security plan, filter packets and permit or deny packets based on a set of defined rules.

❏ Malware encompasses viruses, worms, Trojan programs, and rootkits. Malware protection should be a required element of every computer and network design.

❏ Wireless security involves attention to configuring a wireless network's SSID correctly and configuring and using one of several wireless security protocols, such as WEP, WPA, or 802.11i.

❏ Tools that crackers use to compromise a network can also be used to determine whether a network is secure. Ping scanners, port scanners, and protocol analyzers are a few tools used to verify network security.

❏ Denial of service is one method attackers use to disrupt network operation. Three types of DoS attacks include half-open SYN attacks, ping floods, and packet storms.

KEY TERMS

802.11i — A security extension to 802.11 and a successor to Wi-Fi Protected Access that is the currently accepted best security protocol for wireless networks.

access control lists — Sets of rules defined by an administrator that determine which packets should be allowed and which should be denied.

authentication — A security feature that allows an administrator to control who has access to the network.

authorization — A security feature that allows an administrator to control what a user can do and which resources can be accessed after the user is authenticated to the network.

backdoor — A program installed on a computer that permits access to the computer, thus bypassing the normal authentication process.

cracker — Someone who attempts to compromise a network or computer system for the purposes of personal gain or to cause harm.

denial-of-service (DoS) attack — An attempt to tie up network bandwidth or services so that network resources are rendered useless to legitimate users.

Encrypting File System (EFS) — A feature available on Windows operating systems that allows file contents to be encrypted on the disk. These files can be opened only by the file creator or designated agents.

encryption — A technology used to make data unusable and unreadable to anybody except authorized users of the data.

firewall — A hardware device or software program that inspects packets going into or out of a network or computer and then discards or forwards those packets based on a set of rules.

hacker — Sometimes a derogatory term to describe an unskilled or undisciplined programmer. Hacker can also mean someone who is highly skilled with computer systems and programs and is able to use some of the same tools crackers use to poke around networks or systems, but not for evil purposes.

hoax virus — A type of virus that's not really a virus but simply an e-mail announcement of a made-up virus. Its harm lies in people believing the announcement and forwarding the message on to others.

intrusion detection system (IDS) — Usually a component of a firewall, an IDS detects an attempted security breach and notifies the network administrator. An IDS can also take countermeasures to stop an attack in progress.

IP Security (IPSec) — An extension to the IP protocol suite that creates an encrypted and secure conversation between two hosts.

MAC address filtering — A security method often used in wireless networks, whereby only devices with MAC addresses specified by the administrator can gain access to the wireless network.

malware — Any software designed to cause harm or disruption to a computer system or otherwise perform activities on a computer without the consent of the computer's owner.

NTFS permissions — Permissions assigned to files or folders on an NTFS-formatted volume in a Windows system. NTFS permissions affect user access to resources whether the user is logged on locally or over the network.

penetration tester — A term used to describe a security consultant who is able to detect holes in a system's security for the purpose of correcting these vulnerabilities.

ping scanner — An automated method for pinging a range of IP addresses.

Pluggable Authentication Modules (PAM) — A software service used on many Linux distributions for authenticating users. PAM is extensible so that new authentication features can be added as needed.

port scanner — Software that determines which TCP and UDP ports are available on a computer or device.

protocol analyzers — Programs or devices that can capture packets traversing a network and display packet contents in a form useful to the user.

rootkits — Forms of Trojan programs that can monitor traffic to and from a computer, monitor keystrokes, and capture passwords. They are among the most insidious form of Trojan software because they can mask that the system has been compromised by altering system files and drivers required for normal computer operation.

shadow passwords — A secure method of storing user passwords on a Linux system.

sharing permissions — A list of permissions that can be assigned to users and groups and applied to Windows shared folders. Sharing permissions don't affect access to files and folders by users logged on locally to the system hosting the files.

10

spam — Unsolicited e-mail. The harm in spam is the loss of productivity when people receive dozens or hundreds of spam messages daily and the use of resources to receive and store spam on e-mail servers.

spoofed address — A source address inserted into a packet that is not the actual address of the sending station.

spyware — A type of malware that monitors or in some way controls part of your computer at the expense of your privacy and to the gain of some third party.

stateful packet inspection (SPI) — A filtering method used in a firewall, whereby packets are not simply filtered based on packet properties but also the context in which packets are being transmitted. If a packet is not part of a legitimate, ongoing data conversation, it's denied.

Trojan program — A program that appears to be something useful, such as a free utility you can use on your computer, but in reality contains some type of malware.

virtual private networks (VPNs) — Temporary or permanent connections across a public network that use encryption technology to transmit and receive data.

virus — A malicious program that spreads by replicating itself into other programs or documents. A virus usually aims to disrupt computer or network functions by deleting and corrupting files.

wardrivers — Attackers who drive around with a laptop or PDA looking for wireless LANs to access.

Wi-Fi Protected Access (WPA) — A wireless security protocol that is the successor to Wired Equivalency Protocol. WPA has enhancements that make cracking the encryption code more difficult.

Wired Equivalency Protocol (WEP) — A form of wireless security that encrypts data so that unauthorized people receiving wireless network signals can't interpret the data easily.

worm — A self-replicating program, similar to a virus, that uses network services such as e-mail to spread to other systems.

REVIEW QUESTIONS

1. Your friend creates a shared folder on her computer for several coworkers to use. She assigns the password "0OxqH}ml2-wO" to the folder. Is it an example of a good password or a bad password? Explain.

2. List at least three techniques you could use to help secure a wireless network.

3. Which of these protocols is used for VPNs? (Choose all that apply.)

   a. PPTP

   b. PPP

   c. VPNP

   d. L2TP

   e. UDP

4. How do VPNs accomplish the *private* part of a virtual private network?

5. Which of the following terms refers to attacking an Internet server by forcing it to respond to a flood of ping packets so that the server can't respond to normal traffic?

    a. DDR

    b. ICMP

    c. DoS

    d. worm

6. Which of the following is a guideline for creating a security policy?

    a. A security policy should be cryptic to prevent attackers from understanding it.

    b. A security policy should be vague enough so that rules can be added as needed.

    c. A security policy should be enforceable.

    d. A security policy should have different provisions depending on the user.

7. Which of the following is a component of a security policy? (Choose all that apply.)

    a. authentication policy

    b. privacy policy

    c. network configuration policy

    d. computer specification policy

8. List two questions that must be answered before determining what level of security a network requires.

9. Which of the following should be a common element in any level of security policies? (Choose all that apply.)

    a. complex passwords

    b. backup procedures

    c. data encryption

    d. virus protection

10. Choose two words from the following list that best complete this sentence: If there is _____ access to the equipment, there is no _____ .

    a. physical

    b. network

    c. data

    d. security

11. Which of the following is a requirement for rooms housing network servers?

    a. separate heating system

    b. adequate cooling

    c. false ceilings

    d. shared electrical circuit

10

12. The resources users can access and the tasks they can perform on a network are referred to as which of the following?

    a. authentication

    b. auditing

    c. authorization

    d. logon

13. If you want to allow a blank password in a Windows XP system, you set the password minimum length to _____ .

    a. blank

    b. 0

    c. –1

    d. nothing

14. If you want to prevent password guessing to foil intruders, you should enable which of the following?

    a. account lockout

    b. password expiration

    c. password disabling

    d. account policies

15. Which of the following is a secure method of storing passwords on a Linux system?

    a. PAM

    b. login.defs

    c. shadow passwords

    d. reverse encryption passwords

16. Which of the following is a good password?

    a. astronomical

    b. FluffEE

    c. L0sT!n@Z

    d. BillSmithJr

17. Which of the following is a method used by IPSec to authenticate the identity of communicating devices? (Choose all that apply.)

    a. multishared key

    b. Kerberos

    c. PAM

    d. digital certificates

18. To encrypt data stored on a hard drive on a Windows Server 2003 computer, you should use which of the following?

   a. EFS

   b. DFS

   c. NTFS permissions

   d. gpg

19. Firewalls can filter packets based on which of the following? (Choose all that apply.)

   a. source address

   b. protocol

   c. operating system

   d. context

20. If network administrators want to be informed when an attempt has been made to compromise the network, they should use a(n) _____ .

10

HANDS-ON PROJECTS

HANDS-ON PROJECTS

Hands-On Project 10-1

In this project, you download a utility that includes a port scanner and then find information about another classroom computer. This project requires a program for unzipping the downloaded file.

1. Start your Web browser and go to **www.download.com**.

2. In the SEARCH FOR text box, type **netinfo**, and then click the **SEARCH** button.

3. In the search results box, click the green **Download** button.

4. When prompted, save the file to your desktop or some other location your instructor specifies.

5. Open the downloaded file and double-click the **NetInfo.msi** file. The installation process should begin. Follow the prompts to install the NetInfo program.

6. To find out about other computers on your network, open a command prompt window by clicking **Start**, **Run**, typing **cmd**, and clicking **OK**.

7. At the command prompt, type **net view** and press **Enter**. Write the list of computer names this command returns:

_____

_____

8. Choose one of the computers you wrote down in Step 7. Type **ping** *computername* (replacing *computername* with the name of the computer you chose) and press **Enter**.

9. Write down the IP address of the computer returned by the Ping command:

   _____

10. Open the NetInfo program by clicking **Start**, pointing to **All Programs**, pointing to **NetInfo**, and clicking **NetInfo**. If you haven't registered your copy of NetInfo, click the **I Agree** button to continue. In addition, if the Tip of the Day dialog box opens, click to clear the **Show tips at startup** check box, and then click **Close**.

11. Click the **Services** tab. In the Host text box, type the IP address you wrote down in Step 9.

12. Find ports that show a status of Open, and write the name and number of those ports:

   _____

   _____

13. You'll use the information from Step 12 in a Case Project. For now, close NetInfo.

Hands-On Project 10-2

In this project, you find IP addresses that are active for a particular network. This project assumes you downloaded the NetInfo program in Hands-On Project 10-1.

1. Open NetInfo, and click the **Scanner** tab.

2. In the Address text box, type the first three octets of the IP address you used in Step 9 of Hands-On Project 10-1, followed by a 0 for the last octet. For example, if the address you used was 192.168.1.55, you would type 192.168.1.0. This setting scans all addresses from 192.168.1.0 through 192.168.1.255.

3. Write down the name and address of the first three computers for which NetInfo indicated the status "Host is alive":

   _____

   _____

   _____

4. In the Name column, right-click one of the computers, point to **Send To**, and then click **Services**. In the Services tab, click **Verify** to see a list of services provided by that computer.

5. Write a short explanation of how NetInfo's Scanner and Services features could help an attacker:

   _____

   _____

6. Close NetInfo.

HANDS-ON
PROJECTS

Hands-On Project 10-3

In this project, you explore some settings and features of Windows Firewall with a partner. You must have Windows XP SP2 or later and be able to enable Windows Firewall. Administrator access is necessary.

1. Open the Windows Security Center by clicking **Start**, **Control Panel** and double-clicking **Security Center**.

2. The Windows Security Center shows the status of your firewall, Windows updates, and virus protection. Under the heading Manage security settings for, click **Windows Firewall**.

3. If Windows Firewall is not enabled, enable it now. Click the **Exceptions** tab. If the File and Printer Sharing check box is not selected, click to enable it. If it's already selected, go to the next step.

4. With File and Printer Sharing highlighted, click **Edit**. Write down the four ports associated with the File and Printer Sharing service:

   _____

   _____

5. Click **OK**, and then click **OK** again to close the Windows Firewall dialog box.

6. Ask your partner for the IP address of his or her computer, and write it down:

   _____

7. Open NetInfo and click the **Services** tab. Type your partner's IP address in the Host text box, and then click **Verify**. After a few moments, a list of services should be displayed. Note that ports 139 and 445 are indicated as Open. (By default, NetInfo doesn't scan UDP ports 137 and 138, so they aren't listed here.)

8. After you and your partner have verified that ports 139 and 445 are open, close NetInfo and open the Windows Firewall dialog box again.

9. Click to clear the **File and Printer Sharing** check box, and then click **OK**.

10. After your partner has completed Step 9, open NetInfo and click the **Services** tab. Type your partner's IP address in the Host text box, and then click **Verify**. When the list of services is displayed, note that ports 139 and 445 are indicated as Closed. Windows Firewall is stopping access to those ports.

11. After your partner has completed Step 10, close NetInfo.

12. If File and Printer Sharing was selected when you started this project, open the Windows Firewall dialog box again and click to select the **File and Printer Sharing** check box. Click **OK**, and then close the Windows Security Center and all other open windows.

10

Hands-On Project 10-4

This project shows you how to use the Local Security Policy MMC in Windows XP. You must be logged on with an account that has Administrator access. In this project, you set a password policy that specifies the following:

◻ Users must use 10 different passwords before reusing a password.

◻ Users must change their password every 30 days.

◻ Users can't change their password more often than every seven days.

◻ The minimum password length is five characters.

◻ The password must contain three of these characteristics: uppercase letters, lowercase letters, numbers, or special nonalphanumeric characters.

1. Click **Start**, **Control Panel**, double-click **Administrative Tools**, and double-click **Local Security Policy**. The Local Security Settings window opens.

2. Under Account Policies, click **Password Policy**. Note the current settings, as you might want to change them back to their original values after this project.

3. In the right pane, double-click **Enforce password history**. Set the value to **10** passwords remembered, and then click **OK**.

4. Double-click **Maximum password age**, set the value to **30**, and click **OK**.

5. Double-click **Minimum password age**, set the value to **7**, and click **OK**.

6. Double-click **Minimum password length**, set the value to **5**, and click **OK**.

7. Double-click **Password must meet complexity requirements**, click the **Enabled** option button, and click **OK**. The Local Security Settings window should look similar to Figure 10-13 when you're finished.

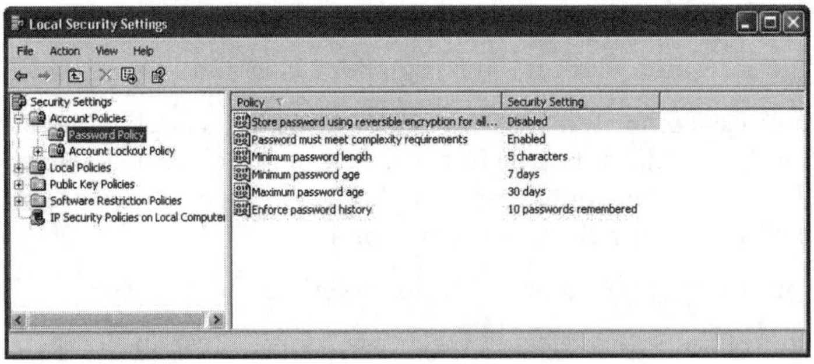

Policy	Security Setting
Store password using reversible encryption for all...	Disabled
Password must meet complexity requirements	Enabled
Minimum password length	5 characters
Minimum password age	7 days
Maximum password age	30 days
Enforce password history	10 passwords remembered

Figure 10-13 Configuring password policies

8. If necessary, change the values back to their original settings. Close the Local Security Settings window.

Hands-On Project 10-5

This project shows you how to set an account lockout policy that accomplishes the following:

- ◘ User accounts are locked out after three invalid logon attempts.
- ◘ Locked accounts are unlocked automatically after 60 minutes.
- ◘ The counter is reset 15 minutes after each invalid logon attempt.

1. Click **Start**, **Control Panel**, double-click **Administrative Tools**, and double-click **Local Security Policy**. The Local Security Settings window opens.

2. Under Account Policies, click **Account Lockout Policy**. Note the current settings, as you might want to change them back to their original values after the project.

3. In the right pane, double-click **Account lockout threshold**, set the value to **3**, click **OK**, and then click **OK** again. Windows automatically fills in the other policies with default values.

4. Double-click **Account lockout duration**, set the value to **60** minutes, and click **OK**.

5. Double-click **Reset account lockout counter after**, set the value to **15** minutes, and click **OK**. The Local Security Settings window should look similar to Figure 10-14 when you're finished.

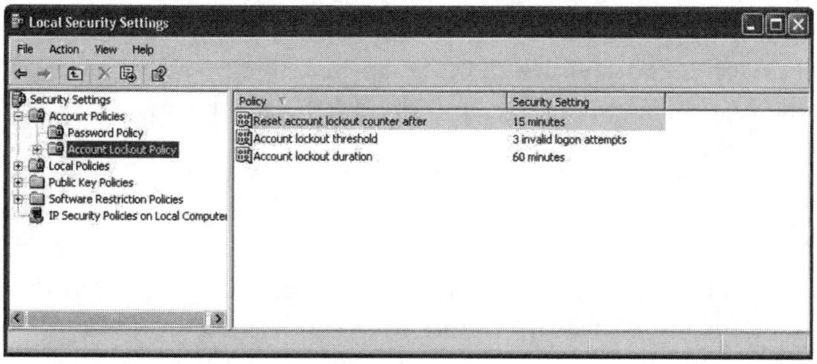

10

Figure 10-14   Configuring account lockout policies

6. If necessary, change the values back to their original settings. Close the Local Security Settings window.

Hands-On Project 10-6

In this project, you connect to a Web site to run a free Internet vulnerability test.

1. Start your Web browser and go to **www.grc.com**. Click the **Shields UP!!** graphic or wait until you're redirected to the page.

2. Scroll down and click the **ShieldsUP!** link.

3. Read the information on that page, and then click the **Proceed** button. (Click **Continue** if prompted.)

4.   In the ShieldsUP!! Services box, click **File Sharing**. ShieldsUP displays your IP address or the translated IP address, and then attempts to connect to your computer. Port 139 should not be available; if it is, tell your instructor to contact your network administrator immediately. This open port is a serious security problem.

5.   Next, click **Common Ports** and see whether any other ports are available through the Internet.

6.   Continue clicking available ShieldsUP options and write a summary of your findings on the following lines. If ShieldsUP finds any security vulnerabilities, report them to your instructor.

   _____

   _____

   _____

7.   Close your Web browser.

CASE PROJECTS

Case Project 10-1

Denial-of-service (DoS) attacks are one of the easier attacks to perpetrate on a network, so they are quite popular with people who have a grudge against a company or are out to commit acts of vandalism. To read about some well-known DoS attacks, go to *www.grc.com/freepopular.htm* and look for the Original DDoS Report, which discusses an attack perpetrated on that Web site by a 13-year-old. Read the report and write a synopsis of how the attack was carried out and what could have been done to prevent it.

Case Project 10-2

Using the information on open ports you found with NetInfo in Hands-On Project 10-1, research these ports to determine what their function is and whether it's safe to leave them open. A Google search is a good place to begin your research. Write a summary of what you found and list which open ports pose a security risk.

Case Project 10-3

Search for security policy templates on the Internet. A good place to start is the SANS Institute (*www.sans.org*). Using one or more of the templates you find, develop a security policy for your school or a business. Present the policy to the class. This project can also be assigned to groups of students.

Case Project 10-4

A small research company in Pittsburgh is working to develop a new method of mass storage to replace current hard drive technology. Four engineers and an office manager work there.

The engineers are highly skilled professionals, and the office manager is a capable computer user. The company has an always-on Internet connection because employees must conduct research frequently. The employees have hopes of making a breakthrough and bringing the company public within the next two years. You have been hired as a security consultant to assess the company's needs. Write a paper recommending what type of security policy should be used (open, moderately restrictive, or highly restrictive) and what security technologies should be put in place. On what areas should the security policy focus (physical security, data security, auditing, passwords, and so forth), and what technologies should be used to secure those areas?

Case Project 10-5

An architectural firm of eight employees, each with a networked desktop computer, wants you to develop a security policy for the company. Management has emphasized that ease of use is paramount, and little time is available for training. Working in small groups, each group should write a list of questions aimed at getting enough information for developing the policy. After determining the questions, each group should interview another group, with the other group posing as the architectural firm and answering the list of questions. What level of security should the policy reflect? Use one of the templates you found in Case Project 10-3 to develop the policy based on the answers the other group supplies.

10

11

SUPPORTING A SMALL BUSINESS NETWORK

After reading this chapter and completing the exercises, you will be able to:

♦ Address the needs of a small business network

♦ Identify small business network equipment requirements

♦ Identify small business application requirements

♦ Describe the issues of supporting a small business

Once an overlooked sector of users of information technology, small businesses are spending on information technology at a rapid rate. In the United States, small businesses spent more than $161 billion on IT products and services in 2003 and are expected to increase that amount to $215 billion by 2008. This large market has been overlooked by IT companies and publishers of IT books and certifications. This chapter covers some technology issues small businesses face to give you more insight into addressing a small business's computer and networking needs.

ADDRESSING THE NEEDS OF SMALL BUSINESS NETWORKS

What exactly is a small business? The government has, in typical fashion, multiple definitions, but a small business is often defined as one that's independently owned and operated, does not dominate its field of operation, and has revenues of less than $500,000 and/or fewer than 500 employees. For the purposes of this chapter, a small business can be defined as one that has fewer than 200 computers, only one or two locations, and modest technology needs. Modest technology needs has been included as a characteristic of a small business because this chapter is geared toward the entrepreneur, consultant, or small computer company that can design, install, and support a small business network without having to become an expert in more advanced computing technologies, such as minicomputers and mainframes, complex WAN environments, and so forth.

Small businesses usually have more modest requirements of their computer networks. Most want to share files and printers, have a networked application that applies to their business, and networked Internet access. Most small businesses don't require a complex, highly restrictive security policy, data encryption, or advanced WAN technologies. That being said, there are plenty of exceptions. You should be aware that one size does not fit all, and the most important aspect of being successful in supporting small businesses is to listen to their requirements and design a solution that works for them. Small business owners can be a frugal bunch, and part of the challenge facing a network designer/installer is to provide a solution that gets the job done at a price that's reasonable for a small business.

Data and Application Sharing in a Small Business

One of the first decisions to make before determining how to set up a data-sharing scheme is whether the network should be peer to peer or server based. When possible and when funds allow, a server solution is probably the best way to go, particularly if you'll be supporting the network after it's installed. A peer-to-peer network is fraught with problems, particularly when a user untrained in managing a networked computer is left in control of a computer that's sharing resources. On a peer-to-peer network, users can shut down their computers, unknowingly severing other employees' access to shared files or printers, which can cause data loss and corruption. In addition, a user controlling a network resource might not understand the company's security policy or how to follow it and could make sensitive data available to unauthorized users. If you're forced to use a peer-to-peer scheme, you should limit the number of computers hosting network resources to minimize potential problems.

Whether you're using a server-based or peer-to-peer scheme, the simplest file-sharing solution is usually the best solution. Designate as few computers as possible as file-sharing computers. A common practice is for each user to have a home directory on the server, thereby making backups easier and giving each user a place to save most of his or her files. Depending on the security policy, other users might have read access (but usually not write access) to each other's home directory to facilitate file sharing. If the policy is more stringent, users have access only to their own home directories, with select managers also having access as necessary.

In addition to home directories, a typical practice is having one or more common folders that the entire company has access to or perhaps departmental folders shared among members of a department. Having common folders is a convenient way to distribute master documents without employees having to know which user maintains the document. When changes to a document such as a purchase order form are made, the document developer can post a new version in the common folder. In most operating systems, permissions can be set on individual documents so that the developer can specify that only read access is allowed to that document; in this way, a user can't inadvertently change the master document. Users can copy the file to their own home directories and make changes to the copy, if necessary.

Applications can also be shared across a network. Many applications can be installed on a network file server and be run from workstations via a shortcut installed on the desktop. Some applications have a short installation program that creates the necessary shortcut and sets up any Registry information the application requires, such as the location of data files. In other cases, an application allows sharing data across the network but must be installed in its entirety on each workstation that runs it. In either case, multiple computers having access to the same data is a big advantage compared to storing multiple sets of data or having only one computer with access to the application.

Configuring Simple File Sharing in a Windows XP Network

This section discusses configuring file sharing in a Windows XP peer-to-peer or workgroup environment. As mentioned, designating as few computers as possible to share resources is recommended. Usually, the computers used for sharing resources belong to a manager or competent administrator who can be counted on to follow some simple required procedures.

By default, on a Windows XP Professional computer, file and printer sharing are disabled. You can run the Network Setup Wizard or go to the Sharing tab in a folder's Properties dialog box to enable file and printer sharing. To use the Network Setup Wizard, go to Control Panel, select Network and Internet Connections, and then click the option for Set up or change your home or small office network (see Figure 11-1).

After the Network Setup Wizard starts, you're prompted to select whether and how the computer is connected to the Internet. For most business networks, choose the option "This computer connects to the Internet through a residential gateway or through another computer on my network." (Internet connections are discussed later in this chapter in "Communicating with the Outside World.") The residential gateway usually means a router. Next, you're asked to give the computer a description and name. A unique name and an informative description should be used to identify each computer. In a peer-to-peer environment, you should enter a workgroup name, which should be the same for all computers so that they show up under the workgroup name in a My Network Places browse list.

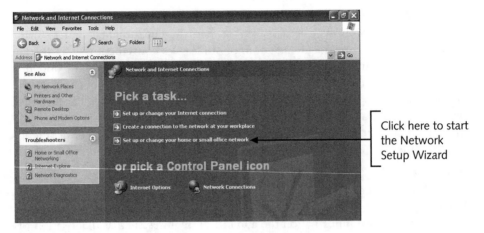

Click here to start the Network Setup Wizard

Figure 11-1   Starting the Network Setup Wizard

At this point, you can make a network setup disk for use on other computers you need to set up. When the wizard is finished, you must restart the computer for changes to take effect. After the computer restarts, My Computer then contains a Shared Documents folder that's shared on the network in simple file-sharing mode. Simple file sharing means you can't specify different levels of access to files or folders. All users have one of two access levels to a shared folder: Users can read files in the folder, or users can read and change the files. Having permission to change files (the default permissions) means network users could also delete the files. To view and change permissions on a shared folder, open My Computer, right-click Shared Documents, and select Sharing and Security to open a dialog box like the one shown in Figure 11-2.

To share additional folders, simply right-click a new or existing folder, select Sharing and Security, and then click the Share this folder on the network check box. Then enter a name that network users can use to access the shared folder, and decide what type of access users should have. If you want to change the default change access to read access, clear the Allow network users to change my files check box.

Simple file sharing is best used in a small peer-to-peer network with a fairly open security policy that requires little network administration. In this setting, there's no need to create user accounts on the computers where file sharing is enabled. You can use this setup when all users must have access to a number of documents created by different users. In this case, you would create two shared folders. One folder allows users to change (and, therefore, create) files, and the other folder allows only read access. A user who creates a document that must be shared (such as a purchase order form) would copy the document to the folder with change permissions. Next, the person who manages the computer where the share is located would move the document to the folder that has only read permissions. This arrangement allows users to get their files to the shared folder easily but doesn't allow other users to make changes to the document.

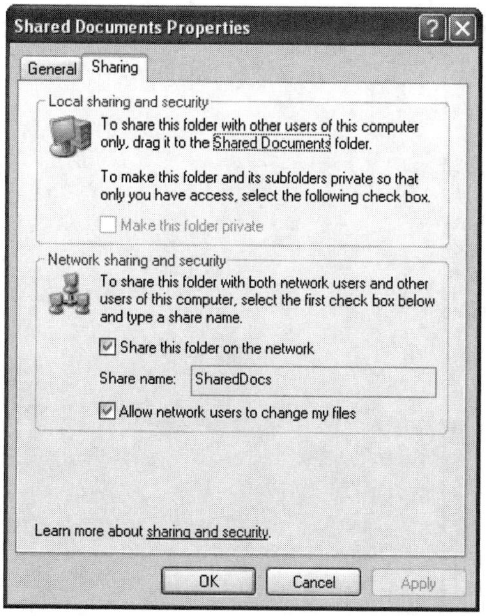

Figure 11-2   A shared folder's properties in simple file-sharing mode

Configuring Advanced File Sharing in a Windows XP Network

Most networks, large or small, often benefit from the advanced file-sharing options available in Windows XP. By disabling simple file sharing, an administrator has more control over users' permissions to files in shared folders. New Windows XP installations have simple file sharing enabled, and it must be disabled to use the more advanced options. To disable it, open Windows Explorer and choose Tools, Folder Options from the menu. Click the View tab, scroll down, and clear the Use simple file sharing check box. After simple file sharing is disabled, the Sharing tab of a folder's Properties dialog box has additional options and the Security tab is added (see Figure 11-3).

In the Sharing tab, click the Share this folder option button, if necessary, and then click the Permissions button to view and change permissions for the share. By default, on new file shares, the Everyone group is assigned permissions. The Everyone group is a special Windows group that specifies all users. Before Windows XP Service Pack 2 (SP2), the Everyone group was assigned the Full Control permission to new shares. Windows XP SP2, Server 2003, and Vista assign Everyone the Read permission to new shares. Sharing permissions can be assigned Full Control, Change, and Read permissions.

If the shared folder is on an NTFS volume, you can use the Security tab to fine-tune permissions more than you can in the Sharing tab. A variety of permissions, including Read, Write, Modify, List Folder Contents, and Full Control, can be assigned to users or groups. Besides controlling access to network users, NTFS permissions enable you to specify access to files and folders when a user is logged on to the computer locally. One caveat when using Sharing and Security permissions: Permissions are combined so that the most restrictive set of permissions applies. For example, Figure 11-4 shows the User One account with Sharing

11

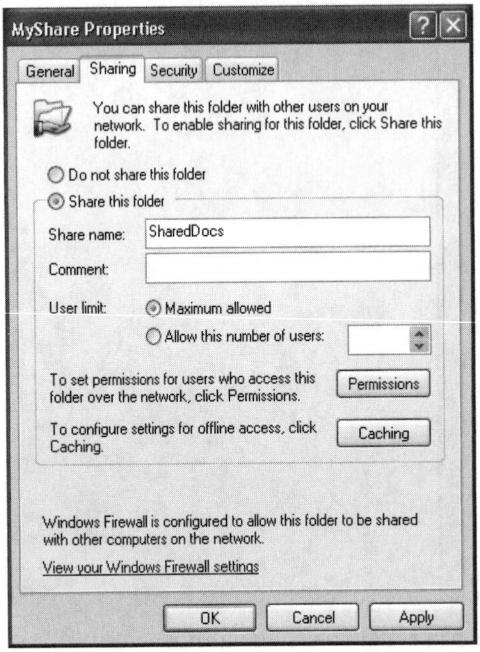

Figure 11-3   The Sharing tab with simple file sharing disabled

permissions of Full Control. Figure 11-5 shows the same account with NTFS permissions of Read. Therefore, User One has only read access to the shared folder's contents because the Read permission is more restrictive than the Full Control permission.

One administrative drawback of using more advanced file-sharing options is that a user account must be created for each user who will have access to the files. For this reason, limiting the number of computers that share files is highly recommended so that you don't have to duplicate the work of creating user accounts on several computers. If more than one computer is required to share files, using a file server with centralized security, as in a Windows domain environment, is highly recommended.

Sharing Files in a Windows Domain Environment

If more than one computer is required to share files, using a file server with a centralized user database is the best way to go. In Windows, this means installing a domain controller. After installing a Windows server configured as a domain controller, user accounts need to be created only on the domain controller. All desktop computers and other servers simply need to be made members of the domain. After user accounts are created, they, along with group accounts, can be used to assign file and folder permissions on any computer throughout the domain. So you can share folders on the domain controller, other servers, and even desktop computers, and permissions can be set by using the accounts created on the domain controller. This centralization of accounts vastly simplifies resource management when resources are spread among two or more computers.

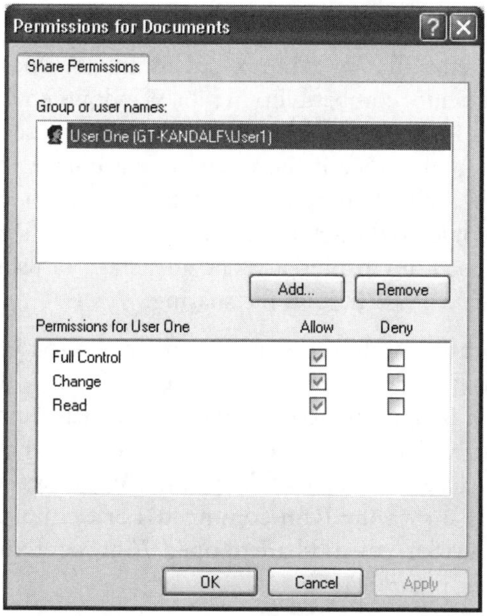

Figure 11-4 Sharing permissions: User One has the Full Control permission

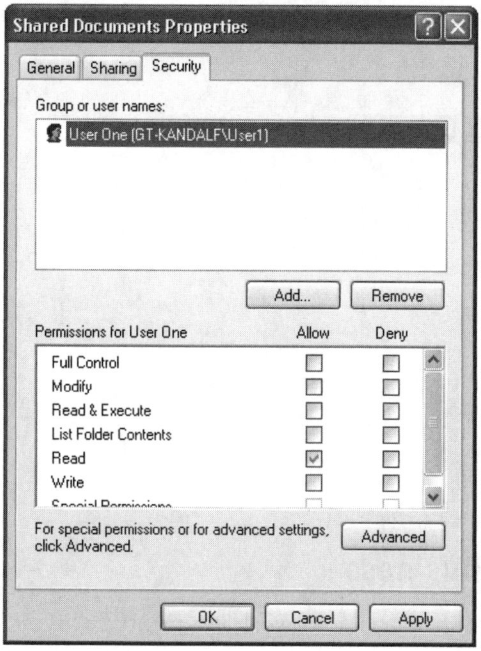

Figure 11-5 NTFS permissions: User One has the Read permission

Sharing Files in a Linux Environment

Typically, you have two choices for sharing files in a Linux environment. One is to use Samba, discussed in Chapter 9, which provides compatibility with a Windows environment. (You worked with Samba in Hands-On Project 9-3.) The other choice is to use Network File System (NFS), which might be a good choice if the environment consists of mostly Linux computers. In both cases, the Linux client computer mounts a shared folder into its own file system and accesses the shared folder as though it were a local resource. Permissions are set in the Linux file system, as discussed in Chapter 10. The advantage of using Samba rather than NFS is Samba's compatibility with Windows file sharing.

Fedora Core 4 Linux comes equipped with a Samba server management application that has a GUI. Using this interface, you can easily share folders and change configuration options. Figure 11-6 shows the Samba Server Configuration program with a new share being added. A Samba share can be made read-only or writable. You use the Access tab to give individual users or everyone access to the share. To access the shared folder from a Windows computer, you can specify the UNC path to the share via the Run command. For example, you can open the Run dialog box and type \\LinuxServer\smbshare to open Windows Explorer and view the contents of the share created in Figure 11-6.

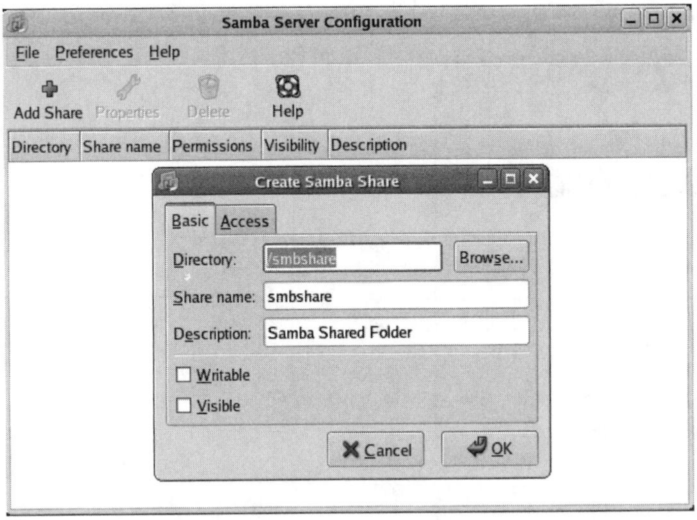

Figure 11-6   Creating a Samba share in Linux

Equipment Sharing in a Small Business

The most common piece of equipment shared in a network is a printer. A typical issue in small businesses is sharing personal printers attached directly to a user computer's parallel or USB port. Sharing printers in this manner presents challenges because the user has control over that printer's operation. The user could shut down the computer, turn off the printer, or take some other action that prevents network users from printing to the shared printer. Nonetheless, printer sharing is an important requirement of most small business networks.

One way to facilitate printer sharing is to connect the printer directly to the network rather than to a user's desktop. Some printers come with a slot to plug in a network interface, thereby allowing you to connect the printer directly to the network. Failing that option, a number of companies make small network print server boxes that plug into the network on one end and plug into the printer via a parallel or USB port. Whether the network interface is built into the printer or is an add-on device, these print servers can be assigned an IP address and be accessed by most OSs.

Scanners can also be shared. Typically, scanners that can be shared on a network come with their own sharing software and can't be shared by using the same method printers use. Hewlett-Packard (HP), for example, has a utility that runs on the computer to which the scanner is attached. This utility shares the scanner and allows you to specify a password if needed. Other computers must have the HP scanning software installed and run the remote scanning software supplied by HP. Because high-end scanners can be expensive and take up a lot of desktop space, sharing them among a number of users makes sense.

Other devices that can be shared on a network include external hard drives that connect via a USB interface and card readers that read secure digital (SD) and compact flash (CF) cards, such as those in digital cameras and PDAs. External hard drives that connect via USB are a good solution for backing up data in lieu of tape or removable media, such as CDs or DVDs. Because hard drives have so much capacity, they can be set to back up data files of many users quickly and easily over the network.

Communicating on a Small Business Network

Aside from data and equipment sharing, one of the big advantages of networking is making it easy for employees to communicate. E-mail is one of the first applications that comes to mind when discussing people communicating over a network. Other communication methods include instant messaging, calendar sharing, whiteboard sharing, and even video conferencing. Many small businesses can afford the equipment and software required for most of these applications. Some communication software is even a free download or comes built into the OS.

E-mail, the most ubiquitous application on a network, is built into every OS, and ISPs give subscribers one or more e-mail accounts as part of their service. Most small businesses are best served by assigning employees e-mail accounts provided by the ISP. This way, the business owner does not need to be concerned with managing and supporting an in-house e-mail system. If the business does want an in-house system, there are a number of ways to go:

- *Microsoft Small Business Server*—This affordable package from Microsoft includes Exchange Server and Office Outlook, which is a complete e-mail and software collaboration solution that includes e-mail, calendaring, and whiteboard applications.

- *Novell's Small Business Suite*—This package comes with GroupWise, an e-mail and calendaring application with features similar to Microsoft Exchange Server.

■ *Linux built-in e-mail server*—Every Linux distribution comes with a built-in e-mail server called sendmail, which might be all a business needs if e-mail is its primary communication concern.

Instant messaging (IM) is a popular application because communication happens in real time, as opposed to e-mail, which requires waiting for recipients to open and respond to messages. Instant messaging can take the place of phone conversations and has the advantage of creating a written record of the conversation. A number of IM applications are available, including Microsoft Messenger, AOL Instant Messenger (AIM), ICQ, and many distributors of the Internet Relay Chat (IRC) standard. Linux Fedora Core 4 comes equipped with a multiprotocol IM application that allows you to communicate with most common IM programs. IM applications are not just for text messaging, however. Voice and video conversations can be held with many IM applications—all you need is a microphone and an inexpensive Web camera.

EQUIPPING SMALL BUSINESS NETWORKS

Most television advertisements for network equipment are aimed at large enterprise network administrators. The equipment required for most small businesses is considerably more modest. A rack full of blade servers is overkill for most small businesses, unless their business is Web hosting. A typical small business environment might consist of one or two servers, some workstations, a few switches, and a router to connect to the Internet.

Servers and Desktops

Most computer manufacturers, such as Dell, Gateway, and Hewlett-Packard, have small business solution centers that focus their offerings on the needs of small businesses. Go to any of these companies' Web sites, and you'll see a link to their small business offerings. Usually, you can purchase a server fully loaded with a small business edition of an OS and features you can choose, such as e-mail, Web server, and database server features. Many companies give you an option of which OS you want preinstalled, or you can install your own. Common choices are Windows Server 2003 Standard Edition, Microsoft Small Business Server 2003, Linux, and Novell NetWare 6.5. Several server manufacturers offer a buying guide listing features and servers that support the features.

A general rule of thumb when purchasing a server for a network is to buy as much hardware as the budget allows that will meet the company's estimated needs for the next two to three years. Buying hardware with expandability features that you can't foresee using in more than two to three years makes little sense because by that time, upgrading to a new computer might make more sense than upgrading the hardware on an existing one—and that assumes you can upgrade. An example of buying too much expandability is purchasing a server with one CPU that can be upgraded to four CPUs. If one CPU meets your needs today, it's unlikely you will need four CPUs in a year or two. In addition, because CPU technologies change so quickly, acquiring the additional CPUs you need to upgrade might be difficult.

Besides, in two to three years, a single CPU will probably be able to do as much work as four older CPUs for less money. That being said, you should consider being able to upgrade to a faster CPU or add a processor because these needs are likely to come up within a year after your initial purchase.

Memory and storage expansion are critical design features to look for in a server. You might think that a server with 1 GB of RAM and 200 GB of hard drive space is enough, but when that simple file and print server turns into a database server and Web server, the OS might be starving for resources.

Another feature to look for on a server is fault-tolerant storage solutions. That usually means a RAID disk system, which makes it possible for the server to continue to operate even if a disk drive fails. A common disk configuration is to use RAID 1 (disk mirroring) on the drives containing the OS and applications and RAID 5 (disk striping with parity) on data drives. Disk mirroring requires two equal-size disk partitions on separate drives because everything written to one disk partition is automatically written to the second disk partition. If one disk partition fails, the other disk partition has a complete up-to-date copy of the system, and the server can continue running as though nothing happened. Disk striping with parity requires at least three disks. When data is written to a RAID 5 disk system, it's spread evenly over two of the disks, and parity information is written to the third disk. With this arrangement, if a disk fails, the data on the failed disk can be reconstructed from the data and parity on the remaining disks.

Desktop computers for a small business usually differ from a typical computer designed for home use in the software installed and some hardware components. Most home computers emphasize multimedia and entertainment components and software, but most business computers emphasize productivity software and manageability. For example, many home computers have Windows XP Home Edition or Windows Media Center Edition (MCE) installed, whereas a business computer is better off with Windows XP Professional. Computers running Windows XP Professional can be part of a Windows domain, and this OS offers more management and security features than does Windows XP Home Edition or MCE.

NOTE   For a feature comparison of Windows XP Professional and Windows XP Home Edition, see *www.microsoft.com/windowsxp/pro/howtobuy/choosing2.mspx*.

Networking Equipment

One of the first decisions to make before you select networking equipment for a small business is where to put the equipment. Most small businesses don't have a large wiring closet made especially for the network, so you might need to get creative. For example, in a business consisting of only eight peer-to-peer computers, an existing cabinet can be used with an eight-port switch bolted to the wall of the cabinet. Care has to be taken to ensure adequate ventilation, but such a small switch doesn't require much. In a small business, the space used for network equipment is often shared with another function, such as telephone and alarm system equipment. Common sense must be used to make sure the space is adequate to the job. Servers and some network switches can generate a lot of heat, so cooling is essential. Hard disks can fail or become corrupted and motherboard components can fail if the system gets too warm.

Making a Wired Connection

In a small network of only a few computers, simply running cable from the back of the computer directly to the hub or switch might be tempting, but don't give into this temptation. The biggest problem with running a single cable from station to switch is that when you move the computer, you might not have enough cable slack. Even if you have only a few computers to connect, you should have network jacks at the work area wired to a patch panel in the wiring closet near the switch. Then make the connection from the jack to the computer's NIC and from the patch panel to the switch using patch cables. This cabling arrangement was shown previously in Figure 3-11. Category 5e or 6 cable should be used, and after it's installed, it should be tested. If you're working with an existing cable plant, test all cable runs before you begin your work, and replace or reterminate any cables that fail or have suspect terminations.

Using hubs is an acceptable solution to connecting a small group of computers, but switches are preferable. Most vendors that sell networking equipment focus on switches. When choosing a switch, you should consider the following choices:

- *Speed of the switch*—100 Mbps Ethernet switches are the norm today. In a server-based environment, an asymmetrical switch is recommended, with most ports being 100 Mbps ports and one or two being Gigabit Ethernet ports. Servers should be attached to the Gigabit Ethernet ports.

- *Managed or unmanaged*—A managed switch has a number of advanced configuration options and can sometimes gather network data on a per-port basis. The extra functionality comes at a price—usually 5 to 10 times that of an unmanaged switch. In most cases, an unmanaged switch suffices. A 24-port 100 Mbps switch with two Gigabit ports can be had for as little as $100 up to $400 or more.

- *Support for multiple media types*—Higher-end switches might have provisions for both copper and fiber-optic connections. In some cases, the fiber-optic connections come as an optional plug-in module. This type of switch is ideal when you have to connect to computers or another switch exceeding the distance limitations of UTP cable or if the cable must pass through an electrically noisy environment, such as a manufacturing floor.

As you plan and install wiring for the network, be sure to keep in mind the company's security policy. Although many small businesses don't have a defined security policy, physical security issues should be discussed before equipment is installed so that the business owner and you can make informed decisions.

Making a Wireless Connection

The availability of wireless equipment at a good price with reasonable performance makes going unwired an attractive option, especially for new installations with a fairly small number of computers. Access point vendors don't typically provide information on the maximum wireless connections an access point can handle, but independent testing has revealed that most consumer products (such as an access point you might find at an office supply store) max out at around 40 nodes. More expensive commercial products, such as those manufactured by Cisco Systems, can likely handle more than 100 connections with little data loss. These restrictions do not mean that you can't use wireless in a larger network; they simply mean that multiple access points might be required, especially if the connecting computers are spread over a large area.

That being said, wired connections are recommended when the environment accommodates running wires and the computers are stationary. If the environment consists primarily of users running around with laptops or handheld computers, a wireless infrastructure is definitely an advantage. Of course, nothing prevents you from using a combination of wired and wireless networking. In fact, a combination is the most common design. A wired infrastructure is used for all desktop computers and servers, and a wireless access point is set up for mobile users. The wireless access point connects to the wired network so that the two networks can communicate with one another, as shown in Figure 11-7.

11

Working with a wireless network involves special considerations not present in a wired network. For example, outside (and unauthorized) people can access the wireless network simply by being close enough to the access point to receive a signal. That security concern is why using the wireless security practices discussed in Chapter 10 is imperative. Using a form of encryption is an absolute necessity when installing a wireless network for a business; otherwise, its data is at risk. Another issue with wireless networks is unique forms of interference. Cordless telephones can use the same frequency as an 802.11 network. If a phone is in use, users can lose connection with the network. This problem might not be too severe in a home network (although it's annoying), but it can grind business to a halt. When designing a wireless network, identify any sources of potential interference, such as cordless phones, microwave ovens, and other radio frequency sources, and be sure they're on different frequencies than the wireless standard you plan to deploy. Also, make sure you test during normal business operations rather than after hours because equipment might be in use during business hours that you would be unaware of after hours.

When selecting wireless equipment, one of the most important considerations is the security standard supported. Whichever security standard (WEP, WPA, 802.11i) the access point supports must also be supported by the wireless NICs you use. Another feature to consider is whether the access point can be bridged to other access points. If your wireless network extends beyond the reach of one access point, multiple access points might be required, and you need to ensure that all access points can communicate with one another.

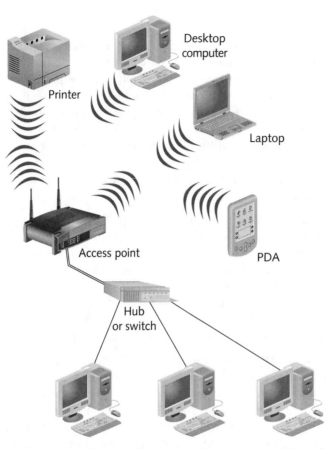

Figure 11-7   Wired and wireless networks coming together

Communicating with the Outside World

Even small businesses need to communicate with the outside world, particularly in accessing the Internet. Besides Internet connections, many businesses need employees to be able to access the company network from home or while away on business. Some issues discussed in this section include Internet access, dial-up connections, and virtual private network connections.

Accessing the Internet

Most small businesses today require Internet access. For 10 to 20 computers, a broadband cable or DSL connection is likely sufficient. A typical setup includes a cable modem or DSL modem connected to a router and the router connected to one of the switches, as shown in Figure 11-8.

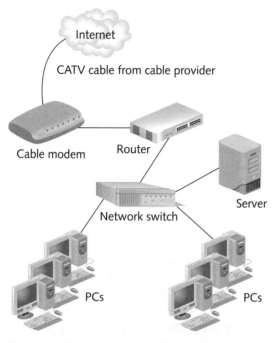

Figure 11-8   A network with a cable modem

In a network setup such as the one in Figure 11-8, the router is usually responsible for being a network firewall as well. However, depending on your security needs, investing in a dedicated firewall that sits between the router and the switch might be worthwhile. In some cases, the router and firewall are the same piece of equipment. The router also usually plays the role of DHCP server and network address translator, handing out private IP addresses to internal computers and translating them via Port Address Translation (PAT) to the address the ISP provides when Internet requests are made. Besides an IP address, the router also gives each workstation a default gateway address (the router's address) and the DNS server addresses that each workstation needs to translate domain names to IP addresses. The router usually acquires DNS server addresses from the ISP. Figure 11-9 is a screen shot of the DHCP configuration page of a typical router used in a small business environment.

The type of router used in this situation is typically an inexpensive device (less than $100) that uses a Web browser interface for configuration. If a wireless network is desired, a router that supports both wired and wireless connections can be used. These devices can be purchased from computer retailers and office supply stores.

The default operation of these devices is to allow all packets through if an internal computer initiates the communication session. However, no unsolicited packets are allowed into the network from the outside. If communication needs to originate from the outside (for example, the business is running its own Web server), the router configuration can be changed to allow this communication. Figure 11-10 shows the configuration page for allowing this type of communication. The configuration option is sometimes referred to as

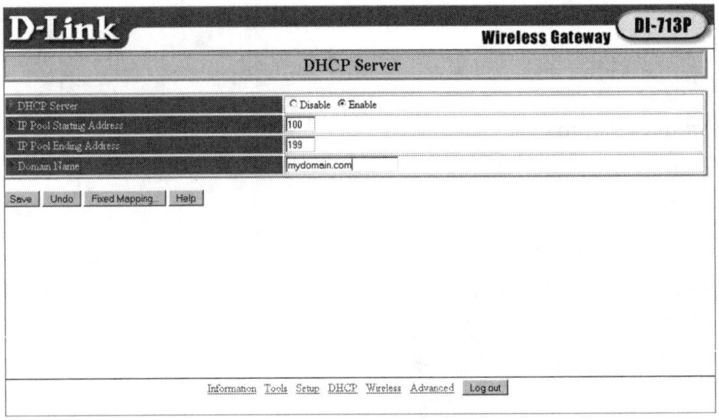

Figure 11-9   DHCP configuration for a router

port forwarding because you're configuring the router to forward requests that apply to only certain TCP communication ports. In Figure 11-10, port 80, which is the port for HTTP or Web communications, is being forwarded to an internal Web server.

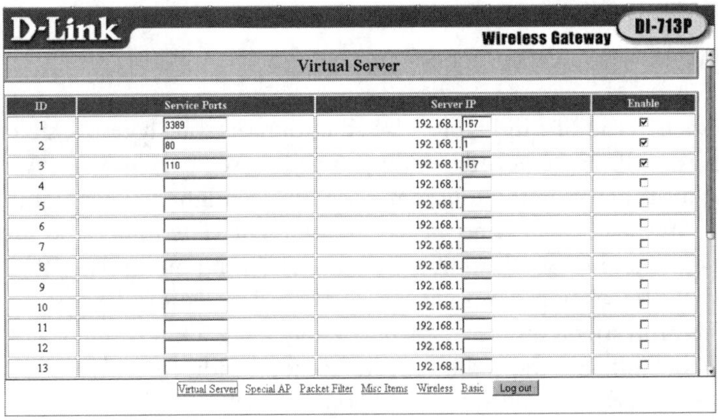

Figure 11-10   Configuring port forwarding on a router

Of course, the company security policy should be taken into account when configuring access to the outside world because that type of connection is where most trouble originates. As soon as an Internet connection is established, equipping all servers and workstations with antivirus and antispyware software is doubly important.

Dial-up Remote Access

If occasional remote access to the company network is required, a dial-up connection using modems and a phone line might be adequate. Windows Server 2003, with Routing and Remote Access Service (RRAS), can serve as a dial-up remote access server and offers a number of advanced features for managing and securing dial-up connections. In a network that doesn't use a server with built-in remote access features, a third-party program can be used. Be aware of the security issues when setting up dial-up connections, however. If an outsider connects to your network via dial-up, this person might as well be connected to one of your switches.

To make dial-up networking secure, the phone number for the connection should be unlisted. User accounts that have access should be limited to only those users who require remote access. These user accounts must have strong passwords, and users should be required to change their passwords periodically. Finally, the dial-up connection should be set to authenticate the user, disconnect, and then automatically call the remote user back at a predefined number. This method ensures that dial-up access can be achieved from only predefined users at predefined locations. An alternative, if your phone system supports it, is to use caller ID to verify the caller. These methods work particularly well for dial-up telecommuters who work from home. Traveling employees might not be able to use these methods because the number they're calling from changes. Also, these methods don't work well if the user is calling from a hotel phone system that doesn't allow calling directly to rooms. Figure 11-11 shows the Dial-in tab of a user account's Properties dialog box in Windows Server 2003.

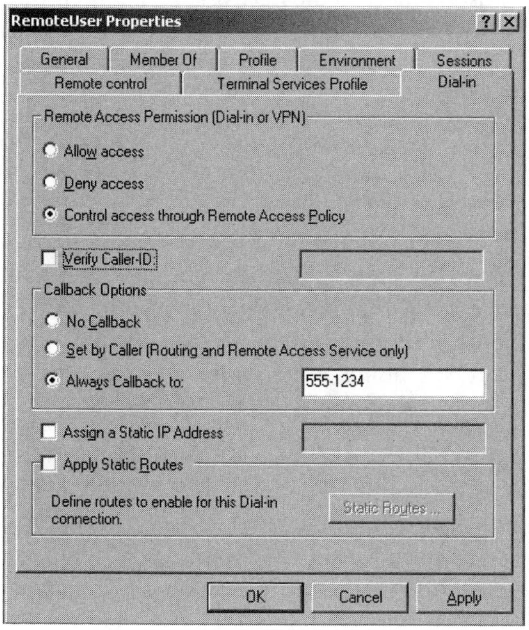

Figure 11-11   The Dial-in tab of a user account in Windows Server 2003

When several employees use remote access frequently, dial-up might not be the best solution. Each dial-up connection requires a separate phone line, which can get expensive. In addition, if users are calling in from out of town regularly, long-distance charges can add up. The solution to both problems is to use a VPN, as discussed in the next section.

VPN Remote Access

A VPN remote access connection can be made as long as both parties are connected to the Internet. Recall from Chapter 10 that a VPN creates a private communication channel between two parties using a nonprivate network, such as the Internet. Two VPN modes are available with most VPN devices:

- *Gateway-to-gateway VPN mode*—Using this mode, a VPN connection is established between two routers that support VPN. No software is required to be installed on the computers using the VPN. This mode is used primarily between offices connected to the Internet through a router that supports VPN. In this setup, all communication between the two offices is private, even though the data travels across the public Internet.

- *Client-to-gateway VPN mode*—This mode establishes a VPN connection between a single client computer and a VPN device. This mode requires VPN client software to be installed on each computer participating in the VPN and a VPN device to which clients connect. This mode is best for providing private communication to the company network for employees working from home or to employees who travel and must connect to the network during their travels. In this setup, users connect to the Internet through their ISPs, and then run the VPN client software to create a private connection with their company network.

A number of small office/home office equipment manufacturers, such as Linksys and D-Link, have fairly inexpensive VPN routers that support either VPN mode. Prices for this equipment range from under $100 for a VPN router that supports eight or fewer VPN connections to under $500 for a VPN router that supports as many as 30 or 40 connections. Be aware of some VPN terminology when purchasing a router for VPN. Some routers claim to support VPN pass-through, which allows a VPN client to connect to a remote VPN device but doesn't actually create a VPN connection. This type of router is best for users who have a small network at home and want to connect to the company network by using client-to-gateway VPN mode. Their home router doesn't participate in the VPN connection; it simply allows the VPN connection to pass through it.

When outfitting your business with a router that supports VPN connections from remote clients, look for one that supports VPN endpoints. The number of endpoints or tunnels the VPN router supports tells you how many VPN connections can be established. In client-to-gateway VPN mode, one VPN endpoint per user connection is required. In gateway-to-gateway VPN mode, where a connection is being made LAN to LAN, one endpoint per LAN connection is required.

IDENTIFYING REQUIREMENTS FOR SMALL BUSINESS APPLICATIONS

The application needs of small businesses range from ho-hum simple to quirky and complex. On the simple side, some businesses need only an office application suite, such as Microsoft Office or WordPerfect Office. On the complex side, a business might use a custom program specifically designed for it with little or no support for networking, which requires the network administrator to be creative in making it work with the office network. This chapter doesn't delve into industry-specific applications; instead, it concentrates on some standard business applications that have a place in many small businesses.

Before discussing specific types of software, two issues for network applications should be addressed. The first is that not all software is designed to operate over a network with multiple users accessing the data. Many applications, such as account and sales management software, sell both single-user and multiuser versions of their programs. It might be possible to network a single-user version, but you're usually limited to one user at a time accessing the data. If you know that multiple users need to access the application simultaneously, you probably need to purchase the multiuser version. The second issue is software licensing. Just because an application has been purchased doesn't necessarily mean it can be installed on the network or on multiple computers. The **end user license agreement (EULA)** should be consulted before purchasing any software for use by multiple users.

Small Business Accounting Software

A number of accounting or bookkeeping applications are tailored to small businesses, such as QuickBooks by Intuit, MYOB's Business Essentials, and Sage Software's Simply Accounting and Peachtree Accounting. Plenty of other choices are available, too. Most of these applications offer a choice of version, depending on the complexity of the company's needs. Most packages come in basic versions to support the most common business needs, such as invoicing, check writing, inventory tracking, and payroll. For more complex needs, many packages have a pro or advanced version that supports multiple users, bill of materials handling, time and billing management, and other advanced features. As a network technician or administrator, typically your job is not to support the function of these applications, but to help ensure that the network is set up to run them adequately and to be sure data is backed up. Some issues facing a network technician in supporting these applications include the following:

- Should the software be accessible by multiple users in the company? If so, should users be able to access the application and make changes to data simultaneously?

- How should the application be secured from users who shouldn't have access?

- Older software packages might not integrate with Windows well or support networking directly. You might need to use mapped drives to specify network locations or use printer redirection to print to network printers.

- How is the software and its data backed up? Some applications have their own backup program for data files. A scheme must be devised to support backing up and restoring data whether you use a third-party backup program or the backup program that came with the application.

These issues are just a few of the many to consider in supporting accounting software. Because accounting is of utmost importance to a business's operation, care must be taken

11

before performing any actions that might corrupt or destroy data. When possible, consult the application vendor's technical support when configuring or troubleshooting these applications.

Sales and Contact Management Software

Although many small business owners are aware of accounting needs and some software that supports accounting, they might not be familiar with sales and contact management software. In many cases, the rolodex or its electronic equivalent is the standby for most businesses. Today's sales and contact management software offers features that are leaps and bounds ahead of a rolodex. Notes on customer conversations can be tracked and accessed by multiple users, promotional mailings can be targeted and automated, and even customer birthdays and their pets' names can be tracked.

Products such as Goldmine from FrontRange Solutions, Maximizer by Maximizer Software, and ACT! by Sage Software have been industry standards in this area for years. These type of packages fall into the category of **customer relationship management (CRM)**. These programs go far beyond simple electronic phone books. Shared calendars and to-do lists, sales forecasting, extensive client history management, and integration with handheld computers are just some of the features these programs support.

CRM software has some of the same support issues you might encounter with accounting software. Again, although you might not want or even need to be an expert in this type of software, a network technician working with small businesses is often expected to be a jack of all trades in computer and network support, including making recommendations for applications and supporting small business applications.

Is Linux a Viable Desktop Alternative to Windows?

Much has been written about Linux in the workplace, and most of it has focused on using Linux as a server OS. However, Linux is making inroads into desktops, too. Using an open-source Linux distribution is certainly less expensive in terms of software cost than a Windows or Mac OS solution. The biggest questions surrounding the use of a Linux desktop are **total cost of ownership (TCO)** and application support. TCO is the cost when you factor in intangibles such as support costs and productivity gain or loss. Linux has come a long way since the early 1990s, when only the savviest computer technician was willing to take on its difficult installation and configuration. Today, Linux installation is no more difficult than a Windows installation for most distributions. Although after-installation configuration still presents challenges, Linux is definitely a viable option as a base OS. In application support, Linux-based Web browsers and e-mail clients are more than satisfactory by most accounts, and a number of powerful (and often free) office application suites are available. KOffice (*www.KOffice.org*) provides a full-featured word processor, a spreadsheet program, presentation software, a database application, and many other add-on applications. KOffice runs on Linux and some versions of UNIX and offers limited Microsoft Office compatibility. OpenOffice.org (*www.openoffice.org*) is an open-source office application suite that runs on Windows, Linux, Sun Solaris, and Mac OS. It's available as a free download and consists of a word processor, a spreadsheet program, presentation software, a database program, and a drawing and diagramming application.

Although Linux has a number of office productivity solutions, support for industry-specific applications is lacking. If a small business simply needs what an office productivity suite includes, Linux is a viable option, particularly if support is available from the business's network technician. However, if the company needs to run industry-specific applications, care must be taken to find out whether Linux is supported. If a business is sold on Linux because of its open-source licensing and improved security over some competitors, there are solutions for running Windows applications in Linux. Windows Emulation (WINE) is one solution that's available free for all Linux distributions where a Windows environment is simulated, allowing an application to run as though it were running on Windows. WINE can be complicated to set up and doesn't work with all applications. VMware (*www.vmware. com*) is a virtualization program that allows one computer to run two or more OSs simultaneously. This software permits an entire Windows OS along with applications to run on a Linux desktop. Of course, if you use VMware, you still need the Windows OS license.

Linux has come a long way, but its suitability for the desktop depends on the expertise of the computer and network technician who sets it up and the compatibility of applications the business needs to run.

11

SUPPORTING A SMALL BUSINESS

The job of supporting small businesses in their IT needs can sometimes be more difficult than supporting a large business because small businesses rarely have specialized expertise. Large businesses might have somebody who specializes in supporting the network infrastructure, another who supports servers, one who supports desktop OS, and still another who supports specialized applications; small businesses usually count on their hired consultant to do it all. This is where you, the entrepreneur, come in.

Entrepreneurs Wanted

Although it's true that many equipment manufacturers have started catering to small businesses, many computer consulting companies still have a large-business mentality. They are used to large jobs with large budgets, and their job is to install the network and leave the rest to the internal staff. Small businesses don't have large budgets or internal staff to support a network after it's installed. If you decide you want to specialize in working with small businesses, you need to understand their needs and be able to enlighten them as to what technology can do for them. That's why it is important to know the choices available to these businesses, be it accounting software, CRM software, or office suites. You also have to understand and respect the way companies do business, yet be able to gently nudge them toward solutions you know will make sense for them when they understand their options.

Working with small businesses can be financially rewarding and create a sense of achievement because you can make a difference in a company's success by helping it use technology to increase and maintain its business. Before you can start working with small businesses, however, you must convince small business owners to place their information technology in your hands.

Getting the Job

Most small business owners who are looking for a computer or network consultant usually request proposals from multiple vendors. If you're called on to develop a proposal, the most important thing you can do is listen to the company's requirements. Find out what kind of business this company is in, how it's currently managing day-to-day information, and where it wants to be in the next several years. Talk not only to the owner or manager, but also to the people actually using the computers (if they are currently computerized), working with customers, handling accounting, and so forth. The more you know about how the business works, the more tailored and detailed you can make your proposal.

Most small businesses are customer friendly, and they expect the same from their vendors. Many small businesses delve into technology cautiously because they don't have internal expertise and are hesitant to place the future of their business in the hands of a consultant. So above all, be responsive when a customer or potential customer calls you. They need to know they can count on you and that you will be available when they need you. Large businesses often don't expect to talk to a live person when they call for support because their own company is automated. If a small business owner gets your voicemail or an automated answering service, you might lose that business as a customer.

When developing a proposal for a consulting job, be detailed about what's included in the price you are quoting. Many businesses want to have choices, so provide multiple quotes when appropriate, and spell out the advantages of the higher-priced option. Each line item of a proposal should specify what need it fills. That way, owners don't have to wonder whether they really need what you're quoting and whether all their needs are addressed adequately.

Securing a Small Business Network

One aspect of your proposal to a small business that you shouldn't neglect is security. Spell out in your proposal how you plan to secure the network and data. First, you need to determine what type of security will work best with the business: an open security policy, for example, or a highly restrictive policy. When discussing a business's needs, be sure to emphasize the trade-offs between an open policy and a more secure policy. A more secure policy better safeguards data but at the expense of more training and perhaps lower productivity. You must factor in how this company currently does business and whether tight security is even a requirement for its business.

Passwords and Backup

Don't automatically assume that every business should have password policies that require frequent changes and complex passwords—or any passwords, for that matter. Some businesses simply do not need or want that level of security. Perhaps all that's required is antivirus and antispyware software and an easy-to-follow backup scheme. It is the consultant's job to make technology work for a business, not against it. As long as you explain the ramifications of an open security policy, and that's what the business wants, you need only carry it out. If, on the other hand, a business does want a secure network, it's your job to know how to construct it. Chapter 10 discusses many of the security issues you should be aware of and the tools available to set up security measures.

Regardless of the security policy, one of the first security-related items on your agenda should be an easy-to-use backup strategy. Every business needs backup, and unless you're going to be available every night to run the backup, the process should be clear and concise so that any one of the business's users can do it. Tape backup is still a favorite method, especially when hundreds or thousands of gigabytes must be backed up regularly. However, in a small business, tape backup might be unnecessary and unnecessarily complicated. Depending on the amount of data to back up, using removable media, such as DVD-RWs, might make sense; if there's more data, USB hard drives can be used. For data on computers, backup of document files can be made to a network hard drive, and that hard drive can be backed up periodically to removable media for offline storage, if necessary. The OS and applications don't usually require regular backup. One convenient method of backing up a user's OS and applications is to create a drive image of the computer's hard drive periodically and back up the image to a network location. Many software packages are available to create an image of a hard disk, such as Symantec Ghost. A hard disk image allows you to recover from hard-drive failure by simply restoring the image to a new disk. The user's computer will be returned to the same state it was in when the image was last recorded.

11

Security from the Outside World

Antivirus and antispyware software, as previously mentioned, are a must for any computer with an Internet connection. Beyond that, a firewall should be in place for most businesses that share a connection to the Internet, such as through cable modem or DSL. If a Windows computer is used to share an Internet connection, Windows Firewall (available starting with Windows XP SP2) can be used, but a dedicated router is probably preferable. A dedicated router offloads the extra traffic from a Windows XP computer and usually has more firewall features.

If a router is used to provide Internet access to multiple computers, it should be equipped with a firewall. Most inexpensive commercial routers are designed to block incoming traffic unless that traffic is part of an existing conversation with an internal computer. However, for more complete protection, opt for a router described as a firewall router. These routers have firewall features that protect a network from external threats, such as DoS attacks and IP spoofing. They can also be set up to filter Web sites based on URL and to block cookies and certain scripting languages that can install spyware on company computers. In addition, these firewalls can be set up to allow Internet access only during certain times of the day and block unproductive bandwidth-intensive content, such as music streaming and peer-to-peer file sharing.

If you're running a wireless network, extra care must be taken to ensure that outside wardrivers can't break into your wireless network and gain free reign of its resources. Many of the wireless security precautions discussed earlier in this chapter and in Chapter 10 should be used. In addition, using an access point that permits adjusting the signal strength might be worthwhile. Some access points allow you to adjust the wireless signal strength so that only devices in close proximity can hear the signal. You can adjust the strength so that all your wireless devices receive the signal but someone walking by outside can't.

Managing a Small Business Network

Unlike a large business with its own IT staff, a set-it-and-forget-it approach doesn't usually work for a small business network. There are hard drives to defragment, virus scanners to update, OS patches to install, and the list goes on. For this reason, working out a maintenance schedule and contract is usually a good idea. Some tasks can be automated, but others, such as software updates and disk cleanup, aren't as easy to automate. Setting up a weekly or monthly visit for maintenance keeps you in front of the small business owner, inspiring confidence as well as making you the prime choice of vendor when more work needs to be done.

In managing a small business network, there's nothing like personal contact. However, sometimes on-site visits are impractical or unnecessary. In these situations, remote access might be the best way to solve a problem quickly and easily. The following list describes some ways to achieve remote access to a network:

- *VPN*—If the business is connected to the Internet through a broadband connection, a VPN is probably the best method for accessing and supporting the network remotely. From wherever you have an Internet connection, you can connect to the company network securely. This secure connection can be used to establish a remote desktop session with servers and workstations or to monitor or update devices on the network. Windows has a built-in remote desktop application that allows remote control of a computer's desktop. Virtual Network Computing (VNC; *www.realvnc.com*) is another remote control/remote desktop application that works across several platforms, including Linux, UNIX, and Windows.

- *Dial-up*—Dial-up access is another, albeit less convenient, option for accessing a network remotely. You can use Windows Server 2003 to configure remote dial-up access to a Windows network or third-party products, such as pcAnywhere, can be used on servers or desktops.

- *Telnet*—Telnet is one way to gain command-line access to a computer or network device. It should be used when a secure connection has already been established, such as through a VPN. Telnet is not a secure protocol, so user names and passwords are sent across the network in plain unencrypted text. Telnet is best used to access Linux or UNIX systems and command-line based routers and switches. In a pinch, Telnet can also be used to manage a Windows system.

- *Windows Remote Assistance*—For user help, Window's built-in Remote Assistance is an option that doesn't require a VPN, as access to the user's computer is by invitation only. In addition, the user must enable remote control.

However remote access to the network is accomplished, it must be done securely. Even if the business has an open security policy, that policy should never apply to remote connections.

The technology needs of small businesses can be varied and complex. Like the people who own the business, each has its own quirks and requirements. Rarely can you devise a one-size-fits-all solution for a small business network, but if you come prepared for something new every time you visit a new business, you will soon have an arsenal of tools, tips, and tricks that make supporting small business networks easier and, at the same time, help make each business you come in contact with more successful.

CHAPTER SUMMARY

- ❑ Most small businesses have modest computer network requirements that don't require advanced WAN technologies, data encryption, or highly restrictive security policies.

- ❑ A server-based solution is often the best solution, but a peer-to-peer network is an option. Either way, it's best to design the simplest file-sharing solution that meets the organization's requirements.

- ❑ By default, on a Windows XP computer, file sharing is disabled, and when it's enabled, simple file sharing is on by default. To gain more control over user permissions, simple file sharing should be disabled.

- ❑ The two most common choices for file sharing in a Linux environment are Samba and NFS. Samba is compatible with Windows file sharing; NFS works best when most computers are Linux or UNIX based.

- ❑ E-mail is the primary communication tool in most networks, but other options include instant messaging, calendar and whiteboard sharing, and videoconferencing. Microsoft Small Business Server, Novell's Small Business Suite, and Linux have built-in e-mail servers.

- ❑ Most computer manufacturers maintain small business solution centers with equipment for sale that focuses on the needs of small businesses. When purchasing servers, buy as much hardware as the budget allows that will meet needs for the next two to three years.

- ❑ When choosing network equipment, you need to decide between a wired and wireless network. In most cases, a wired solution works best for stationary systems, and wireless can be used for laptops and mobile device users.

- ❑ A connection to the Internet and remote access usually require a broadband connection and a router. Some routers can be purchased with built-in VPN capability.

- ❑ Small business application requirements can range from simple and straightforward to very complex. Both single-user and multiuser versions are available for many applications.

11

❏ Some of the most common applications small businesses use include office applications, such as word processors and spreadsheets; accounting software; and sales and contact management software.

❏ Working with small businesses requires excellent communication skills and the ability to make proposals that the business owner can understand. Security should not be neglected, and a reliable backup scheme is a must.

❏ To manage a small business, remote control options should be considered, including Remote Desktop through VPN, dial-up, Telnet, and Windows Remote Assistance.

KEY TERMS

client-to-gateway VPN mode — This VPN mode establishes a VPN connection between a single client computer and a VPN device.

customer relationship management (CRM) — A class of software designed to help businesses manage their customers and prospects.

end user license agreement (EULA) — The license that governs how an application can be used. The EULA specifies how many users are allowed to use an application, how many times it can be installed, and whether the software can be copied, among other things.

gateway-to-gateway VPN mode — This VPN mode establishes a connection between two routers that support VPN.

port forwarding — The process by which a router forwards a request for a particular TCP or UDP port on to a specified computer.

total cost of ownership (TCO) — The cost of a product or service when intangibles such as support costs and productivity gain or loss are factored in.

REVIEW QUESTIONS

1. Which of the following is one of the most important aspects of supporting a small business?
   a. finding the cheapest solution
   b. using a canned solution you can apply to all small businesses
   c. listening to the company's requirements and designing a solution
   d. using your experience to tell the business what it needs

2. Which of the following is a possible problem with a peer-to-peer network solution? (Choose all that apply.)
   a. Users can unknowingly sever access to shared files or printers.
   b. A failure on one computer could cause the network to crash.
   c. Sensitive data could be made available to unauthorized users.
   d. The centralized server could cause security leaks.

3. What does the term residential gateway usually refer to when setting up an Internet connection in Windows XP?

   a. a network switch

   b. a hub

   c. a router

   d. a server

4. What is the limitation of simple file-sharing mode?

   a. You are required to specify permissions for every user.

   b. Only read access is permitted.

   c. Only change access is permitted.

   d. All users have the same level of access to a folder.

5. Simple file sharing is best used in what type of environment?

   a. a small peer-to-peer network with a fairly open security policy

   b. a server-based network with high security

   c. large peer-to-peer networks with more than 50 users

   d. in a setting where permissions must be assigned to individual accounts

6. What are the valid permissions that can be assigned to a share in Windows XP with simple file sharing disabled?

   a. Full Access, Write, Read

   b. Change, Write, Edit

   c. Full Control, Change, Read

   d. Full Access, Write, Delete

7. Which of the following is true about NTFS permissions? (Choose all that apply.)

   a. NTFS permissions control access to files and folders for locally logged-on users.

   b. NTFS permissions control access only to files for network users.

   c. When used with sharing permissions, the most restrictive permissions apply between sharing and NTFS permissions.

   d. NTFS permissions have fewer permission options than sharing permissions.

8. A domain controller simplifies resource management by doing what?

   a. distributing account creation

   b. providing larger hard drives

   c. eliminating the need to log on

   d. centralizing accounts

11

9. What are the two most common options for sharing files in a Linux environment? (Choose two answers.)

   a. NetBIOS

   b. NFS

   c. TCP

   d. Samba

10. A UNC path to a network share is specified as which of the following?

   a. \\share\server

   b. \\server.share

   c. \\server\share

   d. \\share.server

11. What is the built-in e-mail server that comes with most Linux distributions?

   a. mailman

   b. sendmail

   c. sendmessage

   d. mailserve

12. Which of the following is a common fault-tolerant disk configuration for servers?

   a. RAID 0 for the operating system and RAID 1 for the data

   b. RAID 5 for the operating system and RAID 0 for the data

   c. RAID 1 for the operating system and RAID 5 for the data

   d. RAID 1 for the operating system and RAID 0 for the data

13. Which of the following is a consideration when purchasing a switch? (Choose all that apply.)

   a. speed of the switch

   b. support for multiple media types

   c. support for multiple Network layer protocols

   d. whether it's managed or unmanaged

14. Which of the following is a consideration when selecting wireless network equipment? (Choose all that apply.)

   a. support for the 802.5 protocol

   b. Category 6 cable connections for gigabit transfers

   c. security standards supported

   d. interference from other wireless devices

15. To run a Web server on a network protected by a router or firewall, you must enable what feature?
    a. address translation
    b. port forwarding
    c. port filtering
    d. address filtering

16. Which of the following is a VPN mode? (Choose all that apply.)
    a. client-to-endpoint
    b. VPN-to-router
    c. gateway-to-gateway
    d. client-to-gateway

17. What legal document should be read carefully before purchasing software that multiple users will use?
    a. ELAN
    b. EULA
    c. readme
    d. user's manual

18. Which of the following describes the cost of a product when intangibles are factored in?
    a. CRM
    b. VPN
    c. TCO
    d. EULA

19. Which network remote access method provides a secure connection over the Internet?
    a. dial-up
    b. Telnet
    c. UDP
    d. VPN

20. Which of the following is a feature provided by a firewall router? (Choose all that apply.)
    a. protection against DoS attacks
    b. Web site filtering
    c. cookie blocking
    d. IP spoofing protection

11

HANDS-ON PROJECTS

Hands-On Project 11-1

In this project, you set up a pair of file shares on a Windows XP system using simple file sharing. One share allows users to change files, and the other share allows users only to read files.

1. Open Windows Explorer by clicking **Start**, **Run**, typing **explorer**, and clicking **OK**.

2. Verify that simple file sharing is enabled by clicking **Tools**, **Folder Options** from the menu. Click the **View** tab, and then scroll down to the Use simple file sharing (Recommended) option. If the check box is not selected, click it, and then click **OK**.

3. Click the **C:** drive in Windows Explorer and create two new folders called **Change** and **ReadOnly**.

4. Right-click the **Change** folder and click **Sharing and Security**.

5. If necessary, click the **Sharing** tab. In the Network sharing and security section, click to enable the **Share this folder on the network** check box. In the Share name text box, type **NewFiles**. Network users will see the share with the NewFiles name instead of the folder name Change. Verify that the Allow network users to change my files check box is selected, and then click **OK**.

6. Next, right-click the **ReadOnly** folder and click **Sharing and Security**.

7. If necessary, click the **Sharing** tab. In the Network sharing and security section, click to enable the **Share this folder on the network** check box. In the Share name text box, type **BizForms**. Network users will see the share with the BizForms name instead of the folder name ReadOnly. If necessary, click to clear the **Allow network users to change my files** check box, and then click **OK**.

8. You can test your work yourself, or you can access a partner's computer. To check your work yourself, follow the next steps.

9. Click **Start**, **Run**, type *computername***newfiles** (replacing *computername* with the name of your computer), and click **OK** to open a Windows Explorer window.

10. Right-click in the window, point to **New**, and click **Text Document**. A new file should be created called New Text Document. To rename it, type **Phonelist**.

11. Double-click the **Phonelist** file to open it in Notepad. Type some information into the file; for example, you can type your name and a fictitious phone number.

12. Save the file and close Notepad. Close Windows Explorer.

13. Open a Windows Explorer window again, and navigate to the **C:\Change** folder. You should see the file you just created. Right-click the **Phonelist** file and click **Cut**.

14. Next, navigate to the **ReadOnly** folder you created earlier. Right-click in the Windows Explorer window and click **Paste**.

15. Open the BizForms share by click **Start**, **Run**, typing *computername***bizforms** (replacing *computername* with the name of your computer), and clicking **OK** to open a Windows Explorer window.

16. Double-click the **Phonelist** file to open it in Notepad. Make some changes to the file and try to save it. You should get an error indicating that the file can't be created. Click **OK**, and then click **Cancel**. Close Notepad without saving the file. Close all open windows.

HANDS-ON PROJECTS

Hands-On Project 11-2

In this project, you disable simple file sharing to explore some other permissions you can assign to files and folders.

1. Open Windows Explorer.

2. To disable simple file sharing, click **Tools**, **Folder Options** from the menu. Click the **View** tab, scroll down, click to clear the **Use simple file sharing (Recommended)** check box, and then click OK.

3. Click the **C:** drive in Windows Explorer. Right-click the **Change** folder you created earlier and click **Sharing and Security**.

4. Click the **Sharing** tab, if necessary, and notice that the information is different from when simple file sharing was enabled. What are some new options in the Sharing tab that did not exist with simple file sharing?

   _____

   _____

5. Click the **Permissions** button. Who is assigned sharing permissions and with what level of access?

   _____

6. To add a group to the permissions list, click the **Add** button, type **Users** in the Select Users or Groups dialog box, and then click **OK**.

7. To give the Users group the Change permission, make sure Users is selected in the Group or user names list box, and click the **Change** check box under the Allow column.

8. Next, to remove the Everyone group from the permissions list (which is considered a security risk), click **Everyone** in the Group or user names list box, and then click **Remove**.

9. Click **OK**, and then click **OK** again.

11

10. The changes you just made should allow any user with an account on your computer to access the NewFiles share with the Change permission. Explain how this differs from simple file sharing, and then close all open windows.

_____

_____

Hands-On Project 11-3

In this project, you explore NTFS permissions.

1. Open Windows Explorer.

2. Click the **C:** drive, right-click the **Change** folder you created earlier, and click **Sharing and Security**.

3. Click the **Security** tab. The user name you used to log on to the Windows XP system should be included in the list of users and groups. Click your user name to select it.

4. In the Permissions dialog box, click the **Full Control** check box in the Deny column, and then click **OK**. Click **Yes** in the message box that opens.

5. Now try to open the share by clicking **Start**, **Run**, typing *computername***newfiles** (replacing *computername* with the name of your computer), and clicking **OK**. You should see a message stating that access is denied. Click **OK**.

6. Why did you get this message when trying to access the share over the network when the sharing permissions give you change access?

_____

_____

Hands-On Project 11-4

In this project, you use Linux to create a Samba file share. This project requires a working version of Fedora Core 4 with Samba installed on a computer that's on the same network as the classroom computers running Windows XP.

1. Log in to the Linux computer as **root**. (Ask your instructor for the root password.) If your Linux computer doesn't start in the graphical user interface, type **startx** at the command prompt and press **Enter**.

2. Before you can access a Samba share, you must create a user account on the Linux system that will log in to the Samba share. To do this, click **Desktop**, **System Settings**, **Users and Groups**.

3. Click **Add User**. In the User Name text box, type the user account name you use to log on to your Windows XP computer. In the Password and Confirm Password text boxes, enter the password you use to log on to your XP computer, and then click **OK**.

4. Close the User Manager window. Click **Desktop** at the top of the screen, click **System Settings**, **Server Settings**, and then click **Samba**.

5. Click **Add Share**, and then click **Browse**. Click the **/root and select /** drop-down list.

6. Click **New Folder**, type **samba**, and then click **Create**.

7. In the Folders dialog box, double-click **samba**, and then click **OK**.

8. Click to enable the **Writable** and **Visible** check boxes, and then click **OK**. In the message box that opens, click **OK**. Under Only allow access to to specific users, click the **samba1** check box, and then click **OK**.

9. Click **Preferences**, **Samba Users**. Click **Add User**.

10. Click the **Unix Username** list arrow, and click the user you created in Step 3.

11. In the Windows Username text box, type the same user name you just selected.

12. Type a password in the Samba Password and Confirm Samba Password text boxes. You can use the same password you used when you created the user, but using a different password is recommended. Click **OK**, and then click **OK** again.

13. Click the share name, and then click **Properties**. Click the **Access** tab. Click the **Only allow access to specific users** option button, click the check box for the user you just created, and then click **OK**.

14. From a Windows XP computer, click **Start**, **Run**, type *computername*\samba (replacing *computername* with the name of the Linux computer), and click **OK** to open a Windows Explorer window for the Samba share you just created. If you're asked for a user name and password, type the ones you used in Steps 10 through 12.

15. Close all open windows.

CASE PROJECTS

**CASE
PROJECTS**

Case Project 11-1

This project can be done in groups. You're going into business as a computer networking consultant, and you want to be sure that all your potential clients get the same service. Devise a questionnaire that you and your other employees can use when interviewing a client about computer and networking requirements. Be sure to cover as many bases as you can think of, including but not limited to number of users, security, resource sharing, Internet access, applications, budget, existing cabling and equipment, and support needs. Save your questionnaire for use in the next project.

Case Project 11-2

Your instructor will concoct a fictitious small business for the purposes of this project. Each group should use the questionnaire designed in Case Project 11-1 to interview the instructor about the networking requirements of his or her small business. After the interview, each group should develop a proposal to submit to the business. The proposal should specify only solutions to the business's requirements and shouldn't include pricing yet. Each proposal should be presented to the entire class. Groups can revise their proposals based on feedback from the class and the instructor's suggestions. A final proposal should then be submitted to the instructor.

Case Project 11-3

Based on the final proposal submitted in Case Project 11-2, each group should create a detailed quote for services. Good sites to find information on pricing include *www.tigerdirect.com*, *www.newegg.com*, *www.lanshack.com*, and *www.cyberguys.com*, but your group can use other resources to determine costs. Be sure to include labor costs at $50 per hour (to keep labor rates consistent for all proposals). All items in the quote must be tied to part of the proposal submitted in the previous project. All quotes and final proposals should be presented to the class. The instructor will select a vendor based on completeness of the proposal and the price quote.

CHAPTER

12

NETWORK ADMINISTRATION AND SUPPORT

> ## After reading this chapter and completing the exercises, you will be able to:
> ♦ Manage networked accounts
> ♦ Monitor network performance
> ♦ Protect your servers from data loss

N etwork administrators must have a varied skill set. They must have good communication skills, excellent technical skills, and solid managerial skills. Perhaps above all, network administrators must be able to continually learn new technologies and adapt to a changing and often growing network. This chapter focuses on the technical skills an administrator must possess and the tasks of day-to-day network management.

Network administration involves more than simply installing and troubleshooting hardware. After hardware is installed and configured, a network administrator must ensure that the network performs to specifications, verify that users can easily access the resources they're authorized to use, monitor network traffic, and be responsible for security issues. This chapter explains how to set up and manage user accounts and groups, how to monitor network performance, and how to prevent data loss.

MANAGING NETWORKED ACCOUNTS

The main task of network management is basic: Make sure all users can access resources they're allowed to access, and prevent users from accessing resources they don't have permission to access (or shouldn't be allowed to access). This seemingly simple concept isn't always easy to apply, but there are ways to assign users and groups permissions to the resources they need without threatening system security. The following sections discuss how to set up and maintain user and group accounts.

A user account is a collection of information about a user, including an account name, an associated password, and a set of access permissions for network resources. A group, on the other hand, is a named collection of user accounts, usually created for resource sharing specific to that group's needs. For example, the Design group needs access to the ColorLaser1 printer. Instead of adding printer permissions for each user account in the Design Department, you need to create and assign print permission to the Design group only once.

The principles of user management for Windows and Linux systems are similar, but the management utilities are quite different. Windows OSs use graphical interfaces, such as the Local Users and Groups MMC in Windows XP and Vista and the Active Directory Users and Computers utility (in Windows Server 2003 after Active Directory is enabled). In Linux, as in Windows systems, user and group information is stored in specially formatted files somewhere in the file system hierarchy. In Linux, you're more likely to open and operate on these files directly because they are simple text files; in Windows, the files contain binary information, and a graphical interface is used to view and edit them. As you read through the following sections, note that most administrative activities (such as creating and managing users and groups) are common to nearly all network operating systems. The differences, of course, lie in the details, but the principles and practices are largely the same. To simplify the discussion, the focus is on the Windows and Linux OSs.

NOTE

The following discussion assumes that the administrator performing the tasks is logged on to the computer with an Administrator account or its equivalent and for Windows, the Administrative Tools folder is enabled on the Start menu (covered in Hands-On Project 12-1).

Creating User Accounts

Windows Server OSs come with two predefined accounts: the Administrator account, for management duties, and the Guest account, for users who have no personal account in the local domain. All users, however, are discouraged from using either of these accounts. It's unclear who's doing what to a system if everybody with administrative access to a machine uses the default Administrator account. Therefore, employees who have administrator duties should no longer use the Administrator account after they receive their own uniquely named accounts with administrative privileges. After that, if anyone attempts to use the Administrator account, you know that a break-in is probably being attempted.

That being said, assigning the Administrator account a strong password and guarding it carefully are still important. The Administrator account can't be locked out or deleted, but it can be disabled or renamed. Renaming the Administrator account is recommended so that if people try to access the computer, they are foiled if they try to use Administrator as the user name. Disabling the Administrator account is not recommended because if you forget the password to your personal account or your personal account is disabled or locked out, you need to log on to the system with the Administrator account to solve the problem with your personal account.

NOTE

The Guest account provides only limited access to the local domain and is disabled by default in Windows Server 2003.

Before you begin to create accounts, you must make some network administration decisions:

- *User names*—What type of naming convention should be used for user logon names? How many characters should they be? Should the user name be based on the user's real name, or should the administrator create it so that it's hard to guess? Remember, a person trying to break into the system needs both a user name and a password. If the user name is difficult to guess, breaking in is more difficult.

- *Passwords*—Should users be able to change their passwords? How often should passwords be changed? How many characters should the password contain? How often should users be able to reuse passwords? Should failed attempts to log on lead to account lockouts?

- *Logon hours*—Should users be restricted to logging on during certain hours of the day or only on certain days?

- *Auditing*—Should user actions (for example, log on, log off, object access, and policy changes) be tracked? To what degree?

- *Security*—Will all accounts be required to use a secure network protocol, such as IPSec, when connecting to the network?

Some of these account details were discussed in Chapter 10. This section discusses creating and managing user accounts in Windows and Linux and explains some options that can be selected for user accounts.

User Account Creation in Windows

Depending on whether accounts are created on a Windows Professional or Server edition, some details might change. This section explains account creation on a Windows XP Professional computer, but most of the process also applies to creating accounts on a Windows server. To create a new user account, open the Computer Management MMC via Start, Administrative Tools, Computer Management. Expand Local Users and Groups, and

12

then click the Users folder. A list of all the local user accounts defined on that machine is displayed. To create a new user, right-click in the right pane and click New User to open the New User dialog box shown in Figure 12-1.

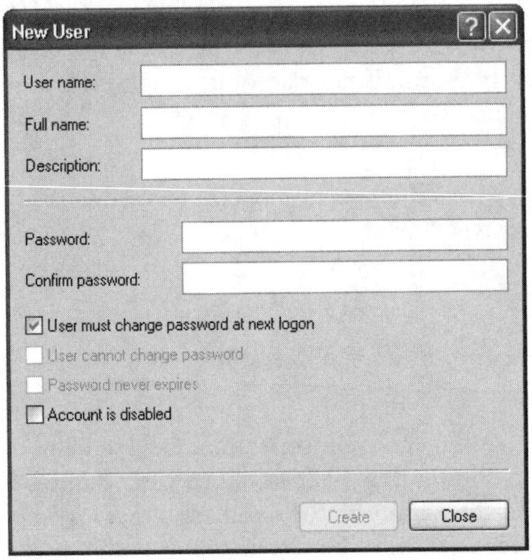

Figure 12-1   The New User dialog box

You enter the new user's logon name in the User name text box. The rest of the fields are optional, including the password fields if blank passwords are permitted. However, you should fill in the Full name text box with the user's real name to better identify the account and fill in the Description text box with identifying information about the user's department and location, for example. If a password is used, you must enter it twice to help prevent typos. Most organizations allow users to create their own passwords according to password policies.

The four check boxes at the bottom are used to control password information and allow you to disable the user account, if necessary:

- *User must change password at next logon*—If this check box is selected, the user is prompted to create a new password the first time he or she logs on.

- *User cannot change password*—Administrators use this option to prevent users from changing the account password. This feature is used when multiple people share an account, such as a generic Sales1 or Support1 account that isn't tied to a particular person.

- *Password never expires*—You use this check box to override password expiration policies for the user. It's enabled only if the User must change password at next logon check box isn't selected.

- *Account is disabled*—You use this check box to disable an account, which is a useful option when a user leaves for an extended period or leaves the company. Instead of deleting a user account when the associated user leaves the company, many administrators prefer to disable the account. This way, if someone is hired in the user's place, the account can be enabled and renamed to reflect the new user's name, and the new user has the same permissions and rights as the previous user.

After an account is created, you can double-click it to open the Properties dialog box and make additional configuration changes to the account. The account's Properties dialog box has three tabs: General, Member Of, and Profile. You use the General tab to modify the Full name and Description text boxes and the four check boxes shown in Figure 12-1. However, the General tab has an additional check box—Account is locked out. This check box is enabled if account lockout policies are in place and the account has been locked out after failed logon attempts. If a user's account becomes locked out for this reason, an administrator can clear the Account is locked out check box to allow the user to try to log on again.

NOTE

Additional tabs are available in the account's Properties dialog box on a Windows Server 2003 computer. These tabs are related primarily to Terminal Services and remote access configuration.

12

The Member Of tab is where an administrator can view and change group memberships. By default, all new user accounts are members of the built-in Users group. Accounts can be made members of additional groups or be removed from the Users group. The Profile tab contains two sections: Profile path and Home folder (see Figure 12-2). In the User profile section, the Profile path and Logon script text boxes are blank by default. To change where a user's profile is stored, enter the information, specified as a UNC path, in the Profile path text box. By default, a user's profile is stored in C:\Documents and Settings*username*. If a profile path that points to a network share is specified, the user has what's called a **roaming profile**. A roaming profile allows a user's settings and files to be applied to any computer he or she logs on to. Administrators can use the Logon script text box to specify a program or batch file that should run every time the user logs on to the computer.

In the Home folder section, the Local path and Connect options are also blank by default, but they can be changed to specify a path other than C:\Documents and Settings*username*\My Documents as the default location for saved document files. If Local path is selected, the administrator can specify a location on the local machine where the home folder should reside. If Connect is selected, a drive letter is assigned to the network location specified in the To text box. Figure 12-2 shows the home folder being stored on the assigned Z: drive that points to a folder on server1.

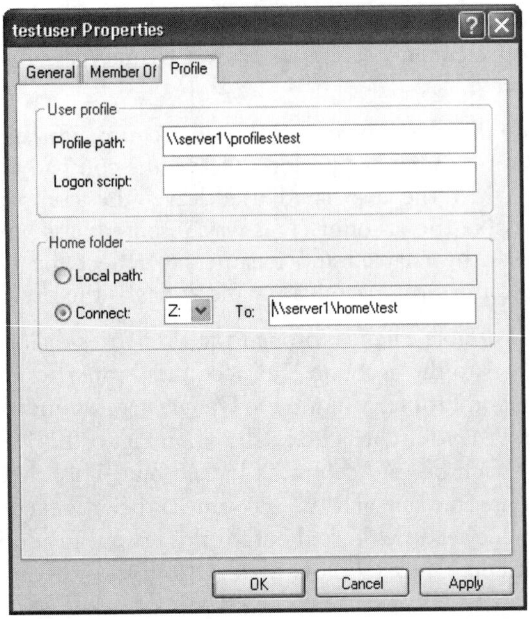

Figure 12-2   The Profile tab for a user account

NOTE

The fields in the Profile tab are of limited use in a Windows workgroup environment and are used mainly with user accounts created on a Windows Server 2003 domain controller.

Here's a time-saving tip when creating new user accounts in a Windows domain environment. If you're creating a number of users who have several similar properties, such as group memberships and profile information, you can create a template user account and then copy it to create all the other users. For each account, you need to change only the user name, full name, and password.

If a user account is deleted in Windows, the account can't be re-created simply by creating an account with the same name. For each user account created, a unique number called a security identifier (SID) is assigned to that account automatically. SIDs can't be reused, and Windows uses the SID to identify a user account. If an account is deleted and a new account is created, the new account has a different SID and, therefore, is treated as a completely different user.

User Account Creation in Linux

Many Linux distributions have a GUI for creating and managing users, but the interface usually differs from distribution to distribution. The tried-and-true method for creating users in Linux is the useradd command-line program. The most basic use of useradd is simply useradd *username* (replacing *username* with the login name of the account you're creating). Most account details on password expiration are taken from the /etc/login.defs and /etc/default/useradd files, as discussed in Chapter 10. After a Linux account is created, it's not enabled until a password is created. You use the passwd command-line program to create a password for a user. For example, if you type "passwd testuser," you're prompted to enter a password for testuser and then asked to enter the password again to verify it. Some options you can use when creating a Linux account with useradd include the following:

- -c *comment*—This option is usually used to specify the user's name and/or a description.

- -d *home_dir*—This option specifies another location for the account's home directory, which is similar to a Windows user's profile path. By default, all users have home directories located in the /home directory.

- -e *expire_date*—This option allows you to specify a date when the account is disabled. This option is useful for creating temporary accounts.

The useradd command has a number of other options. The best way to learn the options for a Linux command is to use **man pages**, which are similar to help files. From the command line, you can get help on the useradd command, for example, by typing man useradd. This command displays a list of options and their descriptions for the useradd command (see Figure 12-3).

12

```
 File  Edit  View  Terminal  Tabs  Help
USERADD(8)                                                    USERADD(8)

NAME
       useradd - Create a new user or update default new user information

SYNOPSIS
       useradd [-c comment] [-d home_dir]
               [-e expire_date] [-f inactive_days]
               [-g initial_group] [-G group[,...]]
               [-m [-k skeleton_dir] | -M] [-n] [-o] [-p passwd] [-r] [-l]
               [-s shell] [-u uid] login

       useradd -D [-g default_group] [-b default_home]
               [-e default_expire_date] [-f default_inactive]
               [-s default_shell]

DESCRIPTION
   Creating New Users
       When  invoked  without  the  -D option, the useradd command creates a new
       user account using the values specified on the  command  line  and  the
       default  values from the system. Depending on command line options, the
       useradd command will update system files and may also  create  the  new
       user's home directory and copy initial files. The version provided with
 :
```

Figure 12-3 Man pages for the useradd command

After a Linux user is created, the user's properties can be changed with the usermod command, and the account can be deleted with the userdel command. As in Windows, a user account in Linux is assigned a numeric ID. Unlike Windows, however, the administrator can assign the ID manually; otherwise, the system assigns the ID automatically. So if a user is deleted in Linux, another user can be created with the same ID. To the Linux system, the new user and deleted user are indistinguishable, which means the new user has permissions to the same files as the deleted user. If a Linux user account must be disabled, the usermod command can be used with the -L option, which inserts "!" at the beginning of the password to indicate a disabled account. You can also add the "!" manually by editing the file containing the user password.

Creating and Managing Groups in Windows

Group accounts are used to assign rights and permissions to several users at one time. Assigning permissions with group accounts rather than user accounts is preferable because group accounts are easier to keep track of. For example, if the six users in the Accounting Department are made part of a group named Accounting, you need to assign file permissions only to the group account, not to each user. If a user leaves the department, you simply remove the user account from the group to remove the associated permissions. If permissions had been assigned to the user account, you would have to locate every place in the network where the user account was assigned permissions and remove the user from those permissions lists manually.

There are no configuration options for groups in a Windows workgroup environment, but there are two methods for adding users to a group. One method is to open the user account's Properties dialog box, select the Member Of tab, and add groups that account should belong to. The second method is to create a group account and add user accounts to the group.

In a Windows Server 2003 domain environment, there are multiple classifications of groups: domain local groups, global groups, and universal groups. **Domain local groups** are used to assign permissions and rights to resources in a particular domain. **Global groups** are used to group users together who require access to similar resources. The users added to global groups are members of the domain in which the global group was created. However, global groups can be assigned permissions to resources in any domain in the Active Directory structure. **Universal groups** can contain users from any domain in the Active Directory structure and be assigned permissions and rights to any resource within Active Directory.

In small single-domain networks, domain local groups might be the only group type needed. However, in large multidomain networks, assigning resource permissions to users throughout Active Directory might be necessary, which requires using global or universal groups. For Windows domains, adhering to the following guidelines for groups is recommended:

- Global groups should include users from the same domain as well as other global groups in the same domain.
- Domain local groups can include users from any domain but should usually contain only global groups or other domain local groups.
- Domain local groups are used to assign rights and permissions to users who are members of global groups.
- Universal groups can contain one or more user accounts or global groups.

For more on using Windows groups, go to *www.microsoft.com* and search for "group scope."

TIP

Aside from the groups you can create to organize users and assign permissions, Windows defines a number of default groups. **Default groups** have preassigned rights that apply to all group members. Table 12-1 shows the most important default domain local groups in Windows Server 2003 running Active Directory and the rights assigned to those groups.

Table 12-1   Some Windows Server 2003 default domain local groups

Group	Rights
Administrators	Has complete control over the computer and domain
Account Operators	Can administer user and group accounts for the local domain
Backup Operators	Can back up and restore files that users normally cannot access
Guests	Is permitted guest access to domain resources
Print Operators	Can add, delete, and manage domain printers
Server Operators	Can administer domain servers
Users	Has default access rights that ordinary user accounts have

12

In addition to domain local groups, Windows Server 2003 has numerous default global groups, including Domain Admins, Domain Users, and Domain Guests. Essentially the same as domain local groups with similar names, these groups apply to entire domains rather than a single machine.

Although assigning rights and permissions via groups is the recommended method of assigning permissions to users, a network administrator does have the option of assigning extra rights or permissions to users on an individual basis. For example, you could add the right to create printers to Carla's account, although as a member of the Users group, ordinarily Carla wouldn't have this right. You can also assign a user to more than one group to extend that user's rights. You could assign Carla to Users and to Print Operators, and she would acquire the rights for both groups. Remember that rights are cumulative; when rights conflict (for example, one group has the right to do something but another group doesn't), the widest-reaching right normally applies. The exception is when No Access is assigned to a group; in that case, No Access overrides any other rights to that resource assigned to the user or group.

In addition to the groups to which you can assign them, users are added to certain groups automatically when they log on, and you can't change these memberships. Microsoft refers to these groups, listed in Table 12-2, as "special identities."

Table 12-2 Windows Server 2000/2003 special identity groups

Group	Membership
Everyone	Everyone currently belonging to the domain
Authenticated Users	All users who logged on to the domain with a valid account and password
Interactive	Everyone logged on to the domain locally
Network	Everyone logged on to the domain through the network

It's important to remember that these special-identity groups exist. For example, members of the Everyone group might have full control over some objects, which means they can add, delete, and change those objects. Sometimes this is exactly what you want, but recall that Everyone's membership includes everyone from the network administrator to the intern who started last week. The default permission for all new shares in Windows 2000 and Windows XP before Service Pack 2 is Full Control for the Everyone group, which could be excessive in many networks. In Windows Server 2003, the default share permission is Read for the Everyone group, which is somewhat better. However, you should still use caution when assigning the Everyone group any level of permission.

Of course, you can add and delete rights for groups just as you can for users, and even create entirely new groups to assign exactly the rights they need. You can even add groups to other groups.

Creating and Managing Groups in Linux

Linux groups are used in much the same way groups are used in Windows. The primary goal is to make assignment of rights and permissions to resources easier. However, unlike Windows, where the list of users and groups that can be assigned permissions to a resource is essentially unlimited, resources in Linux can have permissions assigned to only three entities: the owner, the group, and everybody else (Others). Figure 12-4 shows the permissions assigned to a Linux directory called home.

When a Linux user is created in Red Hat or Fedora Core Linux, by default a new group is created and given the same name as the user. This group is that user's primary group membership, and the new user is the sole member of the new group. You can, however, change this default behavior during user creation. Other distributions of Linux behave differently. For example, in Novell's SUSE Linux, new users are made a member of the Users group by default, and this group becomes the new user's primary group. However it's done, each user in Linux has a primary group membership. Groups can also be created manually with the Linux command groupadd. After a group is created, users can be added to the group when they are created or by using the usermod command.

When a resource such as a file or directory is created in Linux, permissions are assigned to that resource automatically. The user account that created the file or directory is assigned default owner permissions, the user's primary group is assigned default group permissions, and Others (which refers to all other users in the system) is assigned default permissions. The

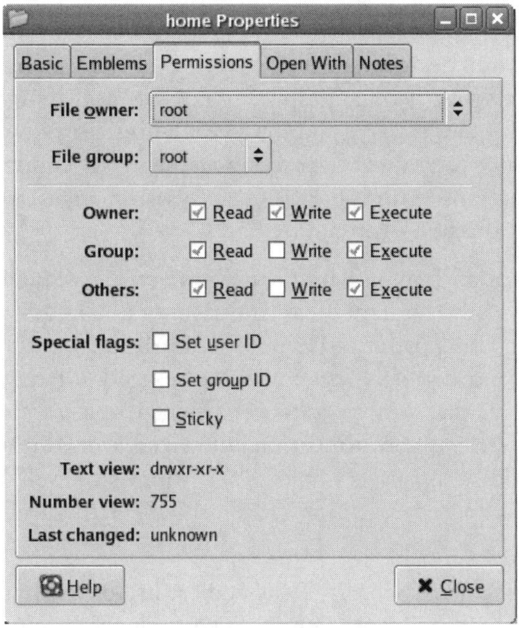

Figure 12-4   The Permissions tab for a Linux directory

actual default permissions assigned to each entity are determined by the system administrator. Naturally, the owner and group of a file or directory can be changed. Figure 12-4 shows two drop-down lists for assigning the file owner and file group. You can also use the chown ("change ownership") command to change both the owner and group of a file or directory or a group of files and directories.

The command-line programs for managing users and groups in Linux are the primary tools for Linux administrators. However, the Linux community has recognized the need for GUI tools for some functions, especially for users coming from the Windows environment. Fedora Core 4 has a GUI program called User Manager, shown in Figure 12-5. Similar programs are available in most current Linux distributions.

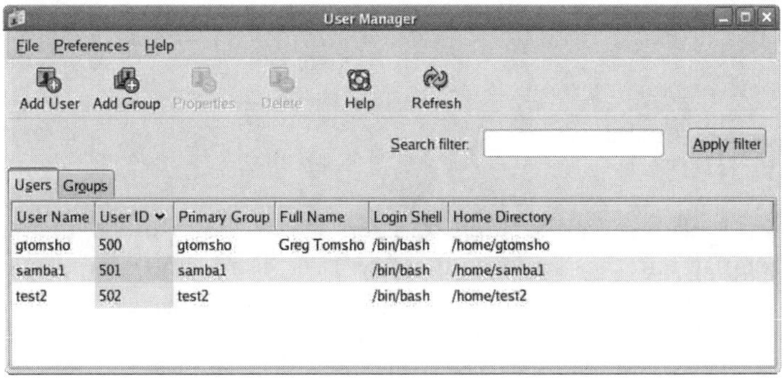

Figure 12-5   User Manager in Linux Fedora Core 4

Auditing

After users have been assigned rights and permissions on a system, monitoring your security scheme might be necessary to make sure no inappropriate access is going on. You can accomplish this in a Windows environment by using auditing. With **auditing**, you can keep track of what's happening on a network (or, more accurately, on a server) by configuring the server so that it records certain actions—such as object accesses, changes to security information, logons and logoffs, and the like—for later review.

How much you should audit depends on how much information you can store efficiently. Although you could conceivably log every activity on the network, a huge volume of information would result. Also, recognizing patterns that point to intrusions or attacks might be difficult amid all the successful (and perfectly legal) activities logged. Often, recording only failed access attempts is enough; that way, you know which people are trying, but failing, to access the network. Of course, if you suspect unauthorized access attempts, you should record successful accesses (at least, for suspect objects or resources) as well. However, you must always use auditing sparingly because it can adversely affect the availability of system resources.

In Windows, auditing is enabled by using the Security Policy editor in Administrative Tools. Logs generated by auditing can be viewed in Event Viewer's Security log. In Linux, a variety of log files are maintained that report on system and user activity, many of which can be found in the /var/log directory. Various open-source products, such as logcheck, can scan these logs automatically to look for security violations. You can find an excellent white paper on Linux auditing at *www.sans.org/rr/whitepapers/auditing/81.php*.

MONITORING NETWORK PERFORMANCE

Obviously, when monitoring a network, you want to ensure that cables are operational and network cards don't conflict, but you need to monitor additional parameters, such as the following:

- Data read from and written to the server each second
- Security errors (errors accessing data)
- Connections currently maintained to other servers (server sessions)
- Network performance parameters

Data Reads and Writes

The number of bytes read from and written to a server provides a useful measure of the server's activity, particularly if these counts increase over time. You can also count the amount of data that can't be read or written. On a Windows network, the server attempts to take large data streams not as sets of packets, but as streams of **raw data** unbroken by header information. The server's refusal to accept many streams of raw data is a possible indication of server memory problems because a certain amount of available memory (called a "buffer") is needed to accept the stream.

Security Errors

Although there might be an innocent explanation, a high rate of failed logons, failed access to objects, or failed changes to security settings could indicate a security risk on your network. An attacker might be attempting to break into the system, or users might be trying to use objects to which they have been denied access. Either way, errors are events to watch for, and auditing helps you see who's causing the errors. A protocol analyzer, which is a combination of hardware and software that can capture network traffic and create reports and graphs from the data it collects, is also useful. It helps you find the source of errors, in case a user is being "spoofed" (for example, when an unauthorized user acts as an authorized user).

Server Sessions

You can draw conclusions about server activity by observing details of **server sessions**, such as connections between network devices and the server, the rate at which connections to the server are made, and how those connections are broken, whether by a normal logoff, an error, or a server timeout. Errors and timeouts can indicate that the server is overloaded and is refusing connections or unable to service them quickly enough. More RAM in the server could solve the problem, or you might need to update other hardware.

Network and System Performance

If your network runs Windows Server 2003, four tools for monitoring your system's performance are included: Event Viewer, Task Manager, Performance Monitor, and Network Monitor. For Linux servers, numerous comparable utilities are available.

Event Viewer

Event Viewer, available in Windows Vista, XP, and Server 2000/2003, enables administrators to view and manage three log files that maintain information on system operation, security, and application activities: System log, Security log, and Application log. Depending on the services that are installed, other logs might also be available. For example, if Active Directory is installed on a server, the Directory Service, DNS Server, and File Replication Service logs are added to Event Viewer. These log files maintain a history of what has occurred on the computer, including user activity, and system and application events, such as a service starting or an error occurring.

However, the System and Security logs are most important to this discussion. The Security log records security events based on the audit filters you configure in the policy setting, so it's the most useful log for getting information about failed attempts to log on or access data.

Be aware that the Security log starts recording information only after auditing has been enabled and configured. In Windows Server 2003, auditing of account logon events is enabled by default, so this log contains information immediately on those systems. The System log records events by Windows system components and, therefore, provides basic information about how OS services are running and whether all hardware works correctly. For example, if a new network card you installed recently isn't working, you can check the System log to see whether it recorded an interrupt conflict. In Event Viewer, you can also see the times when services stopped or started, so you can be sure that all necessary services are running. Figure 12-6 shows Event Viewer in Windows XP.

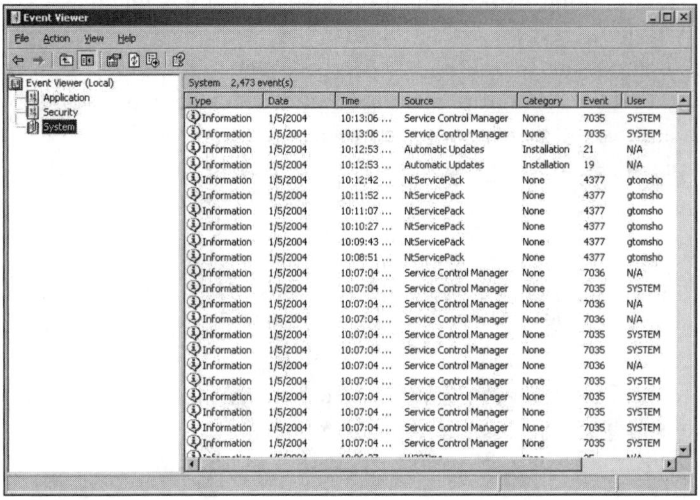

Figure 12-6   Event Viewer in Windows XP

Task Manager

Task Manager can be used to produce a quick summary view of server and network performance. In Windows XP or Windows Server 2003, start it by pressing Ctrl+Alt+Delete or right-clicking the taskbar and clicking Task Manager. Task Manager in Windows XP before Service Pack 2 (SP2) has four tabs: Applications, Processes, Performance, and Networking, as shown in Figure 12-7. A fifth tab, Users, is available in Windows Server 2003, Vista, and Windows XP SP2. The five tabs in Task Manager offer the following information:

> **NOTE**
> In Windows XP, the User tab in Task Manager is available only if Fast User Switching is enabled.

- *Applications*—This tab shows currently running programs along with their status, which is usually Running but might be Not Responding if the application has crashed or become unable to respond to input. In addition, an administrator can terminate a running application and its associated processes, if necessary.

- *Processes*—This tab shows detailed information about each running process. A process might be related to an application shown on the Applications tab, or it might be a program that runs in the background. By default, each process listed shows the amount of CPU time it's currently using and the total amount of CPU time it has used since it was started. In addition, the amount of memory each process is using is displayed. To see other details about each process, choose View, Select Columns from the menu. From this choice, an administrator can terminate a process, assign priority to a process, and select which processors a process can use in a multiprocessor system.

- *Performance*—This tab, shown in Figure 12-7, provides a quick summary of vital system statistics, such as CPU usage, physical memory usage, and virtual memory usage. If your system is acting sluggish, you can look at this screen and see whether your CPU is working overtime or you're using most of your system memory.

- *Networking*—This tab shows the current utilization of the network segment to which the computer is connected. As with the Processes tab, you can select View from the menu and choose a number of different statistics for the Networking tab to display.

- *Users*—This tab, found in Windows Server 2003, Vista, and Windows XP SP2, lists currently logged-on users and allows administrators to disconnect a user or send a user a message.

12

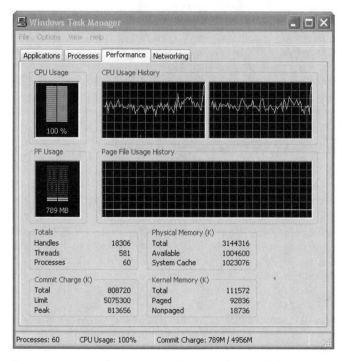

Figure 12-7 Task Manager showing the Performance tab

Performance Monitor

Unlike Event Viewer, which records individual events, **Performance Monitor** is best for recording and viewing trends. In Windows XP, you open this tool via Start, Administrative Tools, Performance.

Performance Monitor keeps track of certain counters for system objects, thereby monitoring performance on a server or workstation. An **object** is any system component or resource that's accessible to a user program in Windows, such as the CPU on a system or the IP protocol. A **counter**, on the other hand, is a certain part of an object that tracks an aspect of its behavior. For example, the Processor object has counters such as % Processor Time and Interrupts/sec, and the IP object has Datagrams sent/sec and Datagrams received/sec counters. Figure 12–8 shows Performance Monitor in Windows XP.

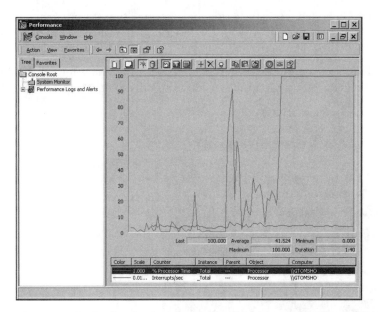

Figure 12-8   Performance Monitor tracking processor time and interrupts per second

For the purpose of monitoring a server, typically you need to collect data for the following system objects:

- Logical or physical disk on the server
- Network interface
- Any of the protocol counters (for example, IP packets per second)
- Redirector
- Server
- Server work queues

Monitoring these types of objects can give you helpful information, such as what hardware needs upgrading and where system bottlenecks occur. When you monitor a system that's behaving normally under normal loads, you produce a snapshot of its behavior known as a system baseline. You can refer to this baseline as changes or errors occur to compare what's normal against what's happening at a specific moment.

NOTE Because running Performance Monitor takes resources that you probably want to save for servicing client requests, it's a good idea to monitor a server remotely, perhaps from a Windows XP Professional machine. Remote monitoring increases network traffic, but the degradation in performance won't be as intrusive as running Performance Monitor directly from the server being monitored. It's the user interface portion of running Performance Monitor that requires resources, not gathering counter data for Performance Monitor objects.

Network Monitor

Unlike Event Viewer and Performance Monitor, **Network Monitor** is not installed automatically during Windows setup; it must be installed separately from Control Panel's Add/Remove Windows Components applet, and then it becomes part of the Administrative Tools menu. Note that Network Monitor is available only in Windows Server operating systems.

Network Monitor is a software-based protocol analyzer for capturing network traffic and creating reports and graphs from the data it collects. It oversees the network data stream by recording the source address, destination address, headers, and data for each packet, as shown in Figure 12-9. Network Monitor can capture as many frames as will fit in physical memory. However, it's best not to fill memory with extraneous data; you can specify filters to select only the data you want. For example, you can filter data packets based on the transport protocol used to transmit them, by source and destination address, or by data pattern, such as looking for specific ASCII or hexadecimal streams in the data at a certain point.

For security reasons, Network Monitor detects other installed instances of Network Monitor agents on the network, showing the name of the computer on which the agent runs, the name of the logged-on account, what the monitor is doing at the moment, the adapter address, and the version number. Some instances of Network Monitor might not be detected if there's a router between those agents and the network where your agent is installed. If other instances can detect you, however, you can detect them. If Network Monitor is being used to get a reading on overall network performance, you must install it on at least one server per network segment so that the overall network picture is represented.

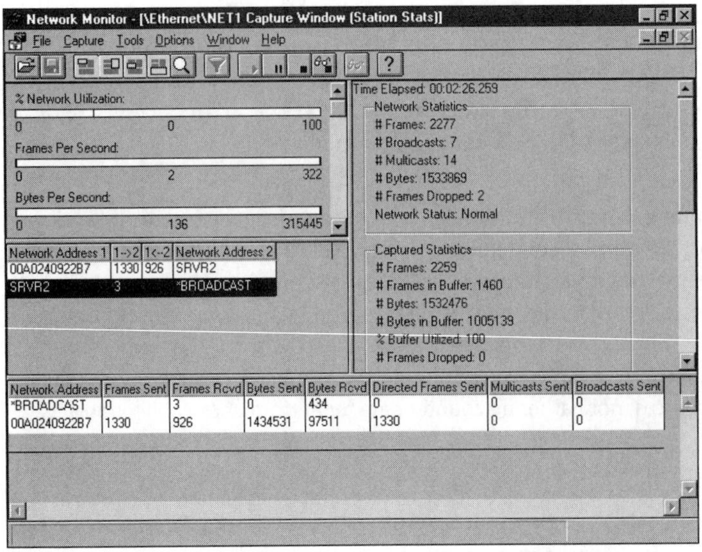

Figure 12-9 Network Monitor displaying network statistics

Total System Management

Although events on the network constitute a major network performance concern, they aren't the only influence. Considering what's happening on the server side in hard drive performance and memory use is also important.

Hard Drive Performance

Of the tools that come with Windows Server 2000/2003, Performance Monitor is most useful for monitoring hard drives on a Windows network. To monitor hard drive performance, look at the following:

- Disk space remaining

- Speed at which requests are serviced (throughput and the amount of data being transferred)

- How often the disk is busy (how often it runs and the average number of queued requests)

When monitoring drives, notice whether you're viewing the physical disk object or the logical disk object—they might not represent the same thing when a physical hard disk consists of only a single disk partition. Also, notice that not all disk-related counters add up precisely to 100%, even if they're totaled on a percentage basis for a single drive. That's because readings for multiple logical drives stored on a single physical drive might add up to more than 100% for the entire physical drive, especially if file compression is used. Sometimes you must average the results across multiple logical or physical drives for more meaningful results.

Memory Use

Another major server issue concerns the amount of memory available to service incoming requests. Windows is designed to page data out of memory (that is, store information in a separate paging file) when it's not in use or when the memory is needed for other, more recently used data. If paged-out data is needed again, a page fault occurs to get the data back in memory. When the server has to page too much data (compared to a baseline performance), consider installing more memory.

There are two kinds of page faults. **Soft page faults** occur when data is removed from a program's **working set** (the set of data actively in use by the process) but moved to another area in physical memory. When that data is needed, getting it back into the working set is a quick operation. **Hard page faults**—when the data has gone unused for so long or there's such a shortage of physical memory that program data is stored on the hard disk—are another matter entirely. Reading data from disk takes considerably longer than reading it from memory, so if too many hard page faults occur, response time slows considerably. Therefore, the best measure of memory shortages is the rate of hard page faults.

CPU Utilization

A computer's CPU is where its real work takes place. That's why monitoring CPU utilization (or the percentage of time the CPU stays busy on average) produces such an important statistic. It's possible to measure CPU utilization at a specific moment or over a longer period. Keep in mind that activities such as starting a program, triggering an event, or fielding an interrupt can cause the CPU to show utilization rates of 100%. Don't let peaks at that level be a cause for alarm.

When evaluating system health, it's best to monitor the % Processor Time counter for the Processor object. This counter provides an average utilization figure over the past second rather than an instantaneous reading. Constant rates of 90% or higher on this counter (along with a queue length of two or more) might indicate that the machine is overloaded. As with any potential bottleneck, you must evaluate other counters, such as Memory pages/sec, to make sure high utilization isn't a secondary symptom of insufficient memory or a device that's generating suspicious interrupts, for example.

Network Statistics

You can monitor network statistics in Performance Monitor or Network Monitor on a Windows system. In Performance Monitor, you should check statistics for the Network Interface object and protocol stack objects; the TCP and IP objects, for example, keep track of statistics for those protocols, and the Network Interface object tracks bytes read from or written to the network. In Network Monitor, you can track the same data, but you can also see error rates and investigate specific packets or errors. (Performance Monitor simply counts events and monitors data rates; it can't capture data, as Network Monitor can.)

Utilization rates can also be meaningful on networks, so monitoring network utilization in Network Monitor or the Bytes Total/Sec counter on the Network Interface object in Performance Monitor can give you a general measure of a network's health. Remember that healthy utilization rates vary with the networking technology. An average 80% utilization over time on a token ring network is perfectly acceptable, but the same utilization on an unswitched Ethernet network is not. (On a hub-based Ethernet network, data collisions frequently occur when utilization creeps past the 56% to 60% range.)

Maintaining a Network History

Both Performance Monitor and Event Viewer can prepare log data you can use to keep long-term records of network performance and events. Long-term records are useful mostly for determining trends or noticing new problems. As with any other form of troubleshooting, to recognize "sick," you must know what "healthy" looks like. The look of a healthy system, in terms of performance statistics, is known as a baseline.

 Be selective about the data you keep. A major error that novice network administrators make is archiving too much data. When it's time to review logs, there's an impossible amount of data to wade through, and the history is useless.

TIP

Avoiding Data Loss

Another aspect of data security involves protecting data from loss or destruction as well as unauthorized access. Protecting data on corporate computer systems should be an administrator's number-one priority. The chances of a hard drive failing are probably higher than the risk of a break-in. This section covers methods for protecting data and reducing the chances of data loss. In most cases, you can best protect data with a three-tiered scheme that reduces the chance of data loss, makes quick recovery from data loss easy, and, if all else fails, allows you to completely rebuild lost or corrupted data.

Tape Backup

Backups are the most obvious form of data security. Tape backups are more popular than other methods, such as optical drives or removable hard drives, because tapes offer a useful combination of respectable speed, high capacity, and cost effectiveness. Although a tape drive can't act as a separate drive, as some backup media can, tape backup is otherwise an excellent backup medium and is widely supported by tape-backup software (such as the backup programs included with most Windows versions).

When making backups on any medium, backing up regularly and often is essential. Typical backup types include the following:

- *Normal backup*—Copies all selected files to tape and marks files as backed up

- *Incremental backup*—Copies all files changed since the last full or incremental backup and marks files as backed up

- *Differential backup*—Copies all files changed since the last normal backup; doesn't mark files as backed up

- *Copy backup*—Copies selected files to tape without marking files as backed up

- *Daily backup*—Copies all files changed the day the backup is made; doesn't mark files as backed up

Of the five types, normal, incremental, and differential backups are most useful as part of a regular backup schedule. A copy backup is good for copying files to a new location, and a daily backup is good for collecting data to work on at home or other off-site locations.

A good model for creating a backup schedule combines a weekly normal backup with daily differential backups so that you can perform backups quickly on a daily basis and restore easily by restoring the contents of two tapes: the normal backup overlaid with the differential backup. You can also use incremental backups for daily backup, but restoration is more difficult because of the number of tapes required to keep a full incremental set.

When creating a backup schedule, posting the schedule and assigning one person to perform the backups and sign off on them each day is a good idea. That way, you can see at a glance when the last backup was done, and train one person to perform backups and care for the tapes.

NOTE

If you maintain a Windows server, be sure to back up System State data daily so that you can restore changes to your system if the Registry or other System State information becomes corrupted. The System State data contains information stored in the Registry, boot files, Active Directory, and so forth.

Another important aspect of a successful backup plan is to make sure you can restore data. Use the "verify data" option that comes with your backup software to ensure that data copied to tape matches data on the drive. Create some test files, back up those files, and then practice restoring the files to the server to check that the restore operation works correctly.

In addition, make sure tapes are stored in a cool, dry, dark place to minimize the risk of damage by heat, moisture, or light. Periodically take a tape off the shelf, and make sure it's readable and its data can be restored *after* the tape has been removed from the machine. For example, a miscalibrated tape drive might accept tapes for backup but refuse to restore their contents—a condition usually discovered only when you need to restore data. Have a policy to rotate tapes so that no single tape set is reused in the same week. In addition, have a policy to remove tapes completely from the set after a predetermined amount of time to avoid worn tapes that might affect performance.

Tape backup is the preferred method for doing regular system backups to ensure data integrity and to allow restoring files that have been corrupted or deleted accidentally. To save an entire disk drive with a particular configuration, you can use drive copying or drive ghosting. Third-party products for this function are available, such as Norton Ghost by Symantec.

Keep in mind that tape backup is most useful for recovering lost or corrupted files, but it isn't a good solution when system failure occurs. When a failure such as crashed drives or malfunctioning motherboard components happens, fault-tolerant systems (discussed later in the "Fault-Tolerant Systems" section) can get you back up and running quickly.

System Repair or Recovery in Windows

Windows systems occasionally fail to boot or exhibit problems or errors after booting that indicate the system is damaged or corrupted and possibly needs repair. Windows network OSs include repair utilities to correct these problems. The repair and recovery tools for Windows systems discussed in this section are Recovery Console, Last Known Good Configuration, System Restore, and Driver Rollback.

Recovery Console

The Recovery Console repair utility in Windows 2000/2003/XP is fairly sophisticated and more powerful than its predecessors. The command-line console supports 27 commands you can use on the system, such as commands for repairing its partition table or replacing specific files and folders. This utility, started from the Windows Setup program, also includes specific commands to replace the Master Boot Record (fixmbr), write a new boot sector (fixboot), format hard disks (format), and even manage disk partitions (diskpart).

Last Known Good Configuration

The Last Known Good Configuration repair utility can fix a Windows 2000/2003/XP system that doesn't boot or is unstable because of the installation of a new device driver. It's very specific in what it restores—the single Registry key HKLM\System\CurrentControlSet. It can't recover from a deleted or corrupt device driver, so the best time to use this utility is right after a new device driver is installed. To use Last Known Good Configuration, start the Windows computer, and press F8 after the system BIOS screen appears. You should see a screen similar to Figure 12-10.

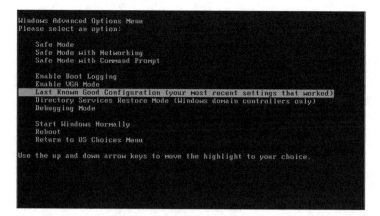

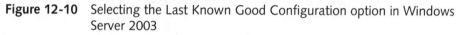

Figure 12-10   Selecting the Last Known Good Configuration option in Windows
Server 2003

System Restore

Windows XP includes System Restore, a handy utility that restores a system to a previous (and, it is hoped, working) state. The System Restore utility monitors all drives and partitions and records changes made to system files, such as the Registry, and some applications. When major changes are made, System Restore creates a restore point so that the computer can be restored to its operating parameters before the changes, in case something goes wrong with a driver installation, application install, or Registry change.

Users can also create their own restore point. For example, if you're about to install a hardware device and several associated applications, you can create a restore point before the install. If the system becomes unstable after the installation, you can restore Windows XP to the point before the installation. System Restore does not delete user files or delete application files that have been installed—you still must run Add/Remove Programs to uninstall applications. However, any system files (such as the Registry) changed by the application setup program are undone. System Restore can run from a regular boot or a Safe Mode boot, in which only basic drivers are loaded. This boot method is used for troubleshooting when you can't boot Windows XP normally.

Driver Rollback

Included in Windows XP and Windows Server 2003, the Driver Rollback feature is used when a new driver installed for an existing device causes a problem with the system. To run this feature, open Device Manager. Double-click the device for which you want to roll the driver back to a previous version, click the Driver tab, and then click the Roll Back Driver button.

12

Uninterruptible Power Supply

Of course, backups help only if they are made, and if you're making daily backups and a thunderstorm knocks out the power—and the server—at 4:00 p.m., you've lost nearly an entire day's data. Sometimes this kind of loss is unavoidable, but power protection can help prevent this mishap.

An **uninterruptible power supply (UPS)** is a device with a built-in battery, power conditioning, and surge protection. You plug the UPS into a wall outlet and the computer (and monitor) into the UPS so that while the AC power from the wall outlet powers the computer, it charges the battery. If the power goes out, the charged battery takes over and keeps the computer running long enough for you to perform an orderly shutdown, which can be important in bringing a server back up after an outage. If users connected to the server have UPSs, they also have a chance to save their data before powering down. The amount of time you have depends on the size of the UPS battery and the amount of power drain on it, but you should plan for at least 10 minutes to shut everything down. Smart UPSs can communicate with a server or workstation and initiate a system shutdown when the UPS is about to lose battery power. When choosing a UPS, explain what you plan to plug into it, and the vendor should be able to help you choose the right one for your needs.

UPSs come in two categories: online and standby. A standby UPS normally supplies power to plugged-in devices by passing the AC power directly from the wall outlet to the device receptacle. In a power outage, a standby UPS detects the power failure and quickly switches to battery power to supply power to the plugged-in devices. Unfortunately, if the switchover doesn't happen quickly enough, the plugged-in devices might lose power long enough to reboot or cause a malfunction. An online UPS supplies power continuously to plugged-in devices through the UPS battery, which is recharged by the wall outlet power. In a power outage, there's no need to switch to battery power because the UPS is already supplying power from the battery. Overall, an online UPS is a far better solution for computer equipment.

CAUTION Never plug a laser printer into a UPS! Laser printers draw an enormous amount of power—some as much as 15 amps (the amount an entire kitchen might require)—and can drain the battery almost immediately.

Battery backup isn't the only advantage of UPSs. In these days of overloaded power grids, power conditioning and surge protection are equally important. **Power conditioning** cleans the power, removing noise caused by other devices on the same circuit (such as a laser printer). **Surge protection** keeps the computer from being affected by sags or spikes in power flow—a condition often occurring during thunderstorms, even if the power doesn't go out, or when there's a drain on power resources, such as on a hot day when air conditioners strain power stations.

Fault-Tolerant Systems

Another method of data protection comes in the form of **fault–tolerant disk configurations**, which can be hardware or software. The two most popular configurations are disk mirroring (or duplexing) and disk striping with parity. These disk structures are based on **redundant array of independent disks (RAID),** so they can be built from standard hard disks using specialized disk controllers to create and manage special features associated with the type of RAID in use. Table 12-3 describes eight variations of RAID arrays, but only RAID 1 and RAID 5 are discussed in more detail because they are the most common types that provide fault tolerance.

Table 12-3   RAID levels

RAID Level	Description and Use Information
RAID 0	Called disk striping, RAID 0 distributes data over two or more disks. RAID 0 has no fault-tolerance capabilities but does enhance disk performance. Available in Windows Server 2000/2003 as well as Linux.
RAID 1	Applies to disk mirroring and disk duplexing, in which two drives are exact copies of each other, and failure of the primary drive causes the secondary drive to take over automatically. Available in Windows Server 2000/2003 as well as Linux.
RAID 2	Uses separate check disks, in which data bits are striped on both data and check disks, to replace information from a damaged data or check disk in the array. Because check data requirements are high and require multiple separate drives for data, this form of RAID is seldom used. Not available for Windows OSs.
RAID 3	Uses a single check disk for parity information (sometimes called a parity disk for that reason) for each group of drives. Because the same size chunk of data is read or written each time the array is accessed, space allocation on these drives isn't efficient, especially for small files. Not available for Windows OSs.
RAID 4	Works much like RAID 3 but uses block or sector striping so that a single block or sector can be accessed at a time, instead of requiring all drives in the set to be accessed. Inefficient for writing data because check writes must occur immediately after data writes. Not available for Windows OSs.
RAID 5	Divides parity data across all drives in the RAID array so that each drive can be reconstructed from parity data stored on all other drives in the set. This array type, also called disk striping with parity, is available for Windows Server 2000/2003.
RAID 10	Combines RAID levels 0 and 1. It uses a RAID 1 mirror set and stripes that set with another set of drives and can survive multiple disk failures in some circumstances.
RAID 0+1	Combines RAID levels 0 and 1 but starts with a stripe set and mirrors a stripe set. RAID 0+1 can withstand only a single drive failure.

12

RAID 1: Disk Mirroring

Disk mirroring requires two disks configured to work in tandem. When data is written to one disk, the same data is written to the second disk, thus creating a constant backup of data. If either disk fails, the other disk contains a complete copy of all data. It's even possible to mirror a system disk so that if the boot disk crashes, the second one can take over.

Normally, disk mirroring involves two hard drives on a single controller. **Disk duplexing** is disk mirroring in which each disk has its own controller, thereby protecting the system from controller failures as well as disk failures. Disk mirroring is simple to set up and makes recovery from disk failures easy. Its main disadvantage is the amount of disk space it requires—twice as much as the amount of data.

RAID 5: Disk Striping with Parity

Disk striping with parity is a more space-efficient solution to the problem of how to create a fault-tolerant disk configuration; in keeping with standard RAID terminology, these disk structures are called RAID 5 volumes in Windows Server 2000/2003. In this configuration, an array of disks—at least three, although Windows Server 2000/2003 supports arrays of up to 32 disks—is treated as a single logical drive. Not all of each disk must be part of an array, but every area on each disk must be the same size. For example, if areas of free space on three disks equal 100 MB, 200 MB, and 150 MB, when those areas are combined to make a stripe set, only 100 MB on each disk is used. That 100 MB section on each disk is divided logically into narrow stripes.

To users, data written to a stripe set looks as though it's simply being sent to a single logical drive. Actually, data along with parity information is written to the stripes on each disk in the array, as shown in Figure 12-11. RAID 5 can recover only from a single failed disk. If more than one disk fails, data must be recovered from backup.

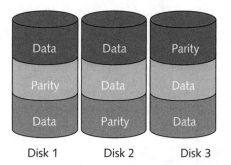

Figure 12-11   Stripe set with parity

Although disk mirroring requires a lower initial investment than disk striping (two disks instead of a minimum of three), disk striping uses space more efficiently, using only $1/n$ (n is the number of disks in the stripe set) for redundancy information instead of half the disk space. Disk mirroring performs better than striping in writing data (all that parity calculation takes extra memory), and striping takes a big performance hit for reading if a disk in the array dies and the data must be regenerated from parity data. Disk mirroring recovers data more quickly than disk striping does because data on the dead disk doesn't need to be regenerated; only the mirror set is broken, so the second disk can function independently of the one it mirrored. In short, both mirroring and striping have advantages, so the choice depends on your situation. For example, if storage space is limited, disk striping is the way to go. If disk space isn't a concern, a disk mirror or duplex is the better choice.

NOTE

Most network operating systems that support RAID configurations support only RAID 0, RAID 1, and RAID 5.

Intellimirror

Another interesting addition introduced in Windows 2000 is **Intellimirror**, a client/server application that runs on Windows Server 2000/2003 machines; a Windows Professional or Windows Server machine can be a client, but a Windows Server OS must be the server. Intellimirror creates a "smart" backup copy of a system on a server. If a user wants to log on to another machine on the network, that user's home desktop can be re-created elsewhere.

With Intellimirror, all files, applications, and customizations on users' home desktops can be accessed on any other Windows machine that can establish a working connection to the Intellimirror server storing their home desktop images. This home desktop image is called a smart backup copy because Intellimirror copies only items to the desktop that the user requests (or that it can predict the user needs, such as basic desktop settings, permanent file share and network printer definitions, and so forth).

Intellimirror is more capable than a system recovery or backup access mechanism because it can deploy, recover, restore, or replace user data, software, and personal settings in a Windows environment. Intellimirror plays an important role in disaster protection and disaster recovery in a Windows environment and reduces the need for and cost of administrative intervention.

CHAPTER SUMMARY

- ❑ The main task of network management is to ensure that all users can access what they are allowed to access but can't access resources they don't have permission to access. Windows Server uses the Active Directory Users and Computers utility to manage users and groups. Windows Professional OSs use the Local Users and Groups snap-in of the Computer Management MMC.

- ❑ Windows groups in a Windows domain can be domain local, global, or universal. Users are added automatically to some groups, such as Everyone, at logon.

❏ Permissions can be granted to user accounts or to groups to control access to objects and resources on the network.

❏ Monitor the performance of a Windows 2000/2003 Server network using Event Viewer, Performance Monitor, Task Manager, and Network Monitor, which include audit logs for system, driver, security, and application event information.

❏ Avoid data loss by making regular data backups, using Intellimirror, and installing fault-tolerant system components.

❏ Windows 2000/2003/XP provide strong repair and recovery tools, such as Recovery Console, Last Known Good Configuration, System Restore, and Driver Rollback. Note that System Restore is available only in Windows XP, and Driver Rollback is available only in Windows XP and Windows Server 2003.

KEY TERMS

auditing — Recording selected events or actions for later review. Audits can help establish patterns and note changes in those patterns that might signal trouble.

copy backup — A backup type that copies all selected files without marking files as backed up.

counter — A certain part of an object that tracks an aspect of its behavior. For example, the Processor object has counters such as % Processor Time and Interrupts/sec. *See also* object.

daily backup — A backup type that copies all files modified on the day of the backup; this type doesn't mark files as backed up.

default groups — Special groups created during installation in a Windows environment that have preassigned rights.

differential backup — A backup type that copies all files modified since the last normal backup; this type doesn't mark files as backed up.

disk duplexing — A fault-tolerant disk configuration in which data is written to two hard drives, each with its own disk controller, so that if one disk or controller fails, the data remains accessible.

disk mirroring — A fault-tolerant disk configuration in which data is written to two hard drives rather than one so that if one disk fails, the data remains accessible.

disk striping with parity — A fault-tolerant disk configuration in which parts of several physical disks are linked in an array, and data and parity information is written to all disks in this array. If one disk fails, the data can be reconstructed from the parity information written on the others.

domain local groups — Groups defined in a Windows domain that are used to assign permissions and rights to resources throughout the domain.

Event Viewer — A Windows Server 2000/2003 tool that records events in three logs based on type of event: Security, System, and Application logs.

fault-tolerant disk configurations — Arrangements of physical or logical disks that ensure data remains accessible, if one disk fails, without requiring a restore from backups.

global groups — Groups meant to be used in more than one domain; used to group users together who require access to similar resources.

hard page faults — Exceptions that occur when a program needs data that must be called back into memory from its storage space on the hard drive. Large numbers of hard page faults slow system performance.

incremental backup — A backup type that copies all files modified since the last full or incremental backup; this type marks files as backed up.

Intellimirror — A Windows Server 2000/2003 client/server application that creates a smart backup copy of a Windows system. Users can access all files, applications, and customizations on their desktops on any other Windows machine that can establish a working connection to the Intellimirror server storing their desktop images.

man pages — Help pages in Linux/UNIX that are available for most commands and applications.

Network Monitor — A Windows NT and Windows 2000/2003 Server network service that you can use to capture network frames based on user-specified criteria, such as a software protocol analyzer.

normal backup — A backup type that copies all selected files and marks files as backed up.

object — A system component or resource that's accessible to a user program in Windows, such as the CPU on a system or the IP protocol. Each component in Windows Server 2000/2003, XP, and Vista is considered an object.

Performance Monitor — A Windows 2000/2003/XP tool used for graphing trends based on performance counters for system objects.

power conditioning — A method of cleaning the power input, removing noise caused by other devices on the same circuit.

raw data — Data streams unbroken by header information.

redundant array of independent disk (RAID) — Two or more drives on a network server that provide fault tolerance (through disk mirroring or disk striping with parity).

roaming profile — A user profile in a Windows environment that's stored on a server and can be accessed from any computer the user logs on to.

server sessions — Connections between a network server and another node.

soft page faults — Exceptions that occur when data must be called back into a program's working set from another location in physical memory. Soft page faults take less time to address than hard page faults. *See also* working set.

surge protection — Power protection that evens out spikes or sags in the main current and prevents them from affecting a computer.

Task Manager — A Windows monitoring tool that provides a quick summary of server and network performance.

uninterruptible power supply (UPS) — A power protection device that includes a battery backup to take over if the main current fails. Usually incorporates power conditioning and surge protection.

universal groups — Groups available in Active Directory that can contain users from any domain in the Active Directory structure and be assigned permissions and rights to any resource in Active Directory.

working set — Data that a program actively uses at any given time. A working set is only a small subset of the total amount of data a program *could* use.

12

REVIEW QUESTIONS

1. Which of the following user accounts is predefined in Windows Server 2000/2003? (Choose all that apply.)

    a. Domain Administrator

    b. Guest

    c. Administrator

    d. Users

2. When an employee leaves an organization, and you want to prevent that account from being used but maintain all rights and permissions so that it can be reactivated, you should _____ the account.

3. Which Windows repair and recovery facility can be run by booting to the installation CD, can replace files, and can manage partitions?

    a. Last Known Good Configuration

    b. Recovery Console

    c. System Restore

    d. Driver Rollback

4. What is the Linux command-line program for creating users?

    a. useradd

    b. newuser

    c. passwd

    d. createuser

5. Which of the following records failed logon attempts?

    a. auditing

    b. Performance Monitor

    c. Network Monitor

    d. none of the above

6. The _____ log in Event Viewer is most useful for determining which drivers have been loaded.

7. To disable an account in Linux Fedora Core 4, you should do which of the following?

    a. Delete the user's password file.

    b. Insert "!" at the beginning of the user's password.

    c. Run DisableUser.

    d. Issue the deluser command.

8. Which of the following is most useful for getting detailed performance information about a server's disks?

   a. Performance Monitor

   b. Event Viewer

   c. System log

   d. Network Monitor

9. Which kind of backup type does not mark files as backed up? (Choose all that apply.)

   a. copy

   b. normal

   c. differential

   d. incremental

10. In a three-disk RAID 5 stripe set, where is the parity information?

    a. on the first disk

    b. on the second disk

    c. on the third disk

    d. on all disks

11. You created a six-disk stripe set with parity. Each disk is 30 GB. How much room do you have in the stripe set for user data?

    a. 180 GB

    b. 150 GB

    c. 30 GB

    d. 60 GB

12. Which RAID level provides enhanced performance but no fault tolerance?

    a. RAID 0

    b. RAID 1

    c. RAID 2

    d. RAID 3

    e. RAID 4

    f. RAID 5

13. You are installing a new server. You want to mirror the partition that the OS will be installed on, and you want the partition to be 100 GB. Which of the following best satisfies these requirements?

    a. one 200 GB drive divided into two 100 GB partitions

    b. two 150 GB drives

    c. one 150 GB drive and one 50 GB drive

    d. four 50 GB drives

14. For security reasons, you should delete the Everyone group. True or False?

15. You have just installed a new device and its driver on a Windows XP computer. When you restart the computer, you get an error and Windows fails to boot. When you restart the computer again, what key should you press to access Last Known Good Configuration to undo the effects of the newly installed driver?

16. You're about to install several devices and applications on your Windows XP computer, but you want to make sure you can bring your system back to its current operating point before the installations, just in case something goes wrong. What should you run?

    a. Recovery Console

    b. System Restore

    c. Driver Rollback

    d. Last Known Good Configuration

17. Which of the following Windows Server 2000/2003 fault-tolerance features enable you to access user settings, data files, and applications from your home desktop on another Windows machine on a network?

    a. disk mirroring

    b. disk duplexing

    c. RAID 5

    d. Intellimirror

18. Which of the following RAID levels is available in Windows Server 2000/2003? (Choose all that apply.)

    a. RAID 0

    b. RAID 1

    c. RAID 2

    d. RAID 3

    e. RAID 4

    f. RAID 5

19. Which RAID level has a striped mirror set?

20. Which backup scheme backs up all files that have changed since the last backup and marks files as backed up?

    a. normal

    b. incremental

    c. differential

    d. copy

    e. daily

21. What user account option must be reset to allow users to log on if they have entered their account passwords incorrectly a defined maximum number of times?

    a. Account is disabled

    b. User must change password at next logon

    c. Account is locked out

    d. Password is expired

22. When a user's profile is stored on a network server, it's called a
    _____ .

    a. server profile

    b. roaming profile

    c. mobile profile

    d. default profile

23. What command allows a user account to be used in Linux after the account is first created?

    a. passwd

    b. useradd

    c. enable user

    d. login

24. Which of the following entities can be assigned file and folder permissions in Linux?

    a. owner, group, everyone

    b. user, group, everyone

    c. owner, group, others

    d. user, group, others

25. Where do you find most Linux log files that report on system and user activity?

    a. /log

    b. /etc/log

    c. /var/log

    d. /bin/log

12

HANDS-ON PROJECTS

Hands-On Project 12-1

To enable the Administrative Tools folder on the Start menu in Windows XP, follow these steps:

1. Log on to Windows XP with an account that's a member of the Administrator group.

2. Right-click **Start** and click **Properties**.

3. Click the **Start Menu** tab and click the **Customize** button.

4. Click the **Advanced** tab. In the Start menu items section, scroll down until you see System Administrative Tools.

5. Click the **Display on the All Programs menu and the Start menu** option button.

6. Click **OK**, and then click **OK** again.

7. Verify that Administrative Tools is on the Start menu by clicking **Start**.

Hands-On Project 12-2

Follow these steps to access the Windows XP Recovery Console:

1. Boot from the Windows XP installation disk. (*Note:* You might have to change your system BIOS to boot from the CD. Ask your instructor how to do this if you don't know.)

2. After some files have been copied, you see the Setup screen. Press **R** to start the Recovery Console.

3. If there is more than one installation of Windows XP on the machine, the Recovery Console asks you to select the one you want to repair. If more than one entry is displayed, ask your instructor which one to select. Select that entry, and then press **Enter**. (If there's only one entry, type **1** and press **Enter**.)

4. Next, you're prompted for the Administrator password. Without that password, you can't run this utility, so type the Administrator password after the prompt, and then press **Enter**.

5. Type **help** and press **Enter**. You see a list of commands that work in the Recovery Console. Notice that you can list, copy, and delete files and perform many other common system administration tasks at the command line, which makes this utility both powerful and dangerous. Scroll through the commands, and then press **Esc** to return to the prompt.

6. Type **exit** and press **Enter** to close the Recovery Console and restart your machine.

Hands-On Project 12-3

In this project, you learn how to create a set of mirrored disks on Windows Server 2003. This project requires two disk drives in addition to the Windows Server 2003 system disk and assumes that the drives have not been initialized.

1. Log on to a Windows Server 2003 computer with an Administrator account.

2. Click **Start**, point to **Administrative Tools**, and click **Computer Management**. Then click the **Disk Management** item under the Storage item. If a wizard starts, cancel it. You should see a window similar to Figure 12-12.

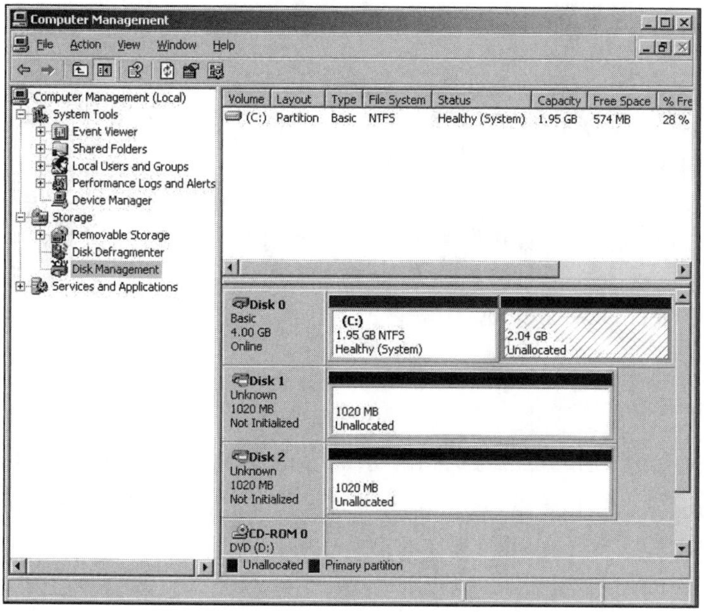

Figure 12-12 Windows Server 2003 Disk Management utility

3. Right-click **Disk1** (or any disk that isn't initialized) and click **Initialize Disk**. A pop-up window with all uninitialized disks selected is displayed. Click **OK**.

4. Right-click a newly initialized disk, and then click **Convert to Dynamic Disk**. A message box is displayed asking which disks should be converted. Select only the disks you initialized in Step 3, and click **OK**.

5. After the disks have been converted to dynamic disks, you can create a new volume. Right-click the first disk you converted, and then click **New Volume** to start the New Volume Wizard. Click **Next**.

6. In the Select Volume Type window, click the **Mirrored** option button, and then click **Next**.

7. In the Select Disks window, select the other dynamic disk listed under Available, click the **Add** button, as shown in Figure 12-13, and then click **Next**.

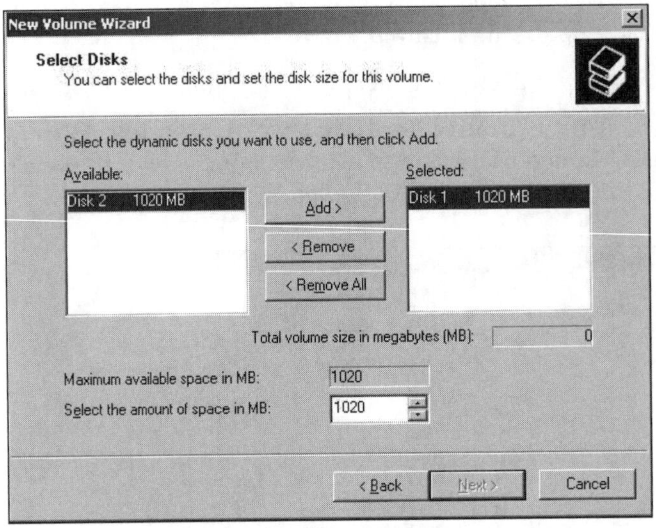

Figure 12-13 The Select Disks window

8. In the Assign Drive Letter or Path window, accept the default choices by clicking **Next**.

9. In the Format Volume window, accept the default choices by clicking **Next**.

10. Click **Finish** and wait while the volumes are formatted. When the formatting is finished, you see a window similar to Figure 12-14.

11. Close the Computer Management window.

Hands-On Project 12-4

In this project, you use Performance Monitor in Windows XP to check CPU performance indicators on your computer.

1. Start Performance Monitor by clicking **Start**, **Control Panel**. If necessary, click **Switch to Classic View**. Double-click **Administrative Tools**, and then double-click **Performance**.

2. Click the **New Counter Set** button, and then click the **+** (plus sign) on the toolbar to open the Add Counters dialog box.

3. If necessary, in the Performance object list box, click **Processor**, and then click the **Select counters from list** option button.

4. If necessary, click **% Processor Time** and then click the **Add** button.

5. Click **Interrupts/sec** and then click the **Add** button.

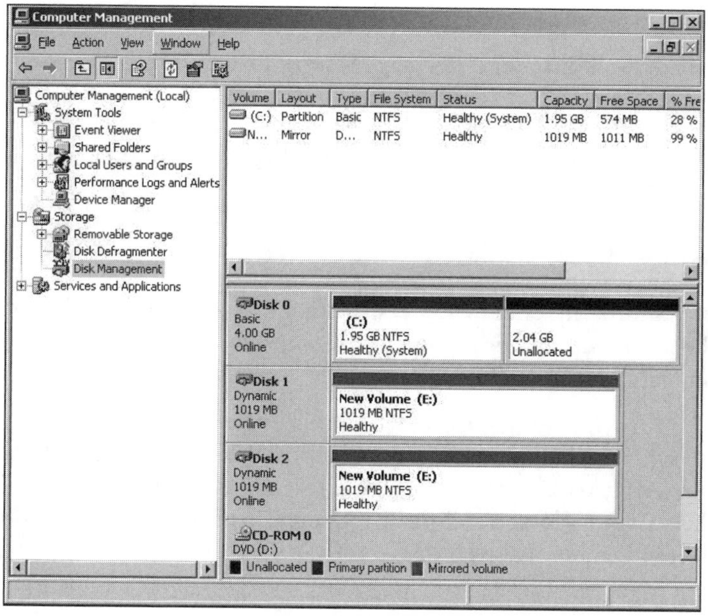

Figure 12-14   Two disks in a mirrored volume appear as a single drive letter

6. Click **Close** to close the Add Counters dialog box. You see a vertical bar cross the graph in Performance Monitor, leaving a line histogram of the % Processor Time and the Interrupts/sec counters (and possibly some other counters that were already added to Performance Monitor). If your machine is fairly idle, you don't see much movement in the histogram. To create some movement, open a Web browser window or Windows Explorer. These actions cause the CPU to work and create interrupts. You can also run an action game such as Pinball to see how this type of activity affects performance.

7. When you finish, close Performance Monitor. Click **No** if you're asked to save console settings.

Hands-On Project 12-5

In this project, you enable auditing on a Windows XP Professional computer and perform some actions that create Security log events. In the next project, you examine event logs. For this project, your Windows XP Professional computer must not be part of a domain.

1. Log on to a Windows XP computer. Click **Start**, **Control Panel**. If necessary, click **Switch to Classic View**. Double-click **Administrative Tools**, and then double-click **Local Security Policy**.

2. Under Security Settings in the left pane, click to expand **Local Policies**.

3. Click **Audit Policy**. In the right pane, double-click **Audit account logon events**.

4. Click the **Failure** check box.

5. Click **OK** and then close the Local Security Settings dialog box.

6. Log off Windows.

7. When you log back on, misspell your password so that your logon fails. Then log on correctly.

Hands-On Project 12-6

In this project, you examine the contents of the System, Security, and Application logs to learn more about their contents and functions. Regular review of these logs is an important part of system maintenance on any Windows machine, especially a server.

1. If necessary, log on to your Windows XP computer with administrative privileges. (Your instructor will supply a password, if needed.) Click **Start**, **Control Panel**. If necessary, click **Switch to Classic View**. Double-click **Administrative Tools**, and then double-click **Event Viewer**. All three logs appear in the left pane, and the contents of the selected log are displayed in the right pane.

2. Click **System** in the left pane. Items in Event Viewer logs use colors and icons to indicate status: A red X or stop sign indicates an error, a yellow triangle indicates a warning, and a blue "i" in a circle indicates an informational message. You can double-click an entry in the log to open an Event Properties dialog box that shows information Event Viewer collected for this item. Select an item of each kind, if available, and double-click it to examine its details.

3. Next, click **Security** in the left pane. You should see the results of the logon auditing you set in Hands-On Project 12-5. Double-click some entries in the Security log to view the details of the logon failure event. If you like, you can also view the Application log.

4. Close Event Viewer.

CASE PROJECTS

Case Project 12-1

You have just purchased a new server, and you need a UPS to maintain the server's power in case the electricity goes out in your server room. The server is a Dell PowerEdge 2800 with the following specifications: rack-mount chassis, four Xeon processors, six Ultra 160 internal hard drives, a tape drive, and a CD-RW drive. The system uses a NEMA 5-20P type power plug. You will not be powering a monitor with the UPS. You want 20 minutes of runtime after a power failure and at least 40% excess power for future expansion. The UPS should mount in a rack. To determine the best UPS for your environment, use APCC's UPS selection program at *www.apcc.com/solutions/index.cfm*. Review the proposed solutions, and write a summary of each solution and its advantages and disadvantages.

Case Project 12-2

Network management involves managing servers, workstations, and network infrastructure and security. Most OSs don't have all the tools (or the best tools) you need to adequately manage all aspects of a large network. Sometimes a third-party add-on product is the way to go. Do a search on the Internet to find one or more network management tools that perform the following functions at a minimum:

❏ Disk imaging for multiple computers

❏ PC configuration management (remotely manage user and system settings)

❏ Server monitoring and management

❏ User account management

❏ Network monitoring (including network device status)

Look for tools for both Windows and Linux environments. This project can be done in groups. Create a list of tools you have found and describe their major functions.

Case Project 12-3

On your network, all network administrators upgraded their machines to Windows XP Professional, and a Windows Server 2003 server with an enormous amount of disk space is available for their use. Explain which Windows Server 2003 fault-tolerant feature they should use to protect their desktop settings, applications, and data files, and describe how it provides this protection.

12

Case Project 12-4

Under normal circumstances, auditing focuses on failures to access rather than successful accesses. Explain why it might be a good idea to audit successful access to files in a directory that contains highly confidential files.

Case Project 12-5

Although Windows Server 2000/2003 supports software RAID arrays for RAID 0 and RAID 5, in practice, hardly anyone uses RAID implemented in software; instead, administrators prefer to buy a hardware RAID controller and let the hardware handle the RAID subsystem. Give three reasons that this decision shows good judgment. (*Hint*: At least two reasons involve performance.)

13

ENTERPRISE AND WIDE AREA NETWORKS

> **After reading this chapter and completing the exercises, you will be able to:**
>
> ♦ Explain how large networks can be implemented with a variety of devices
>
> ♦ Discuss the technologies used in constructing WANs
>
> ♦ Explain some terminology used in implementing WANs
>
> ♦ Configure and describe remote access protocols

Today, few networks are an island. LANs often need to be connected to other LANs or at least to the Internet. To accomplish this connectivity, a number of technologies are typically used. To connect one LAN to another within a building or campus, which forms an internetwork, routers are put into service. To connect one LAN to another distant LAN, which forms a WAN, routers and WAN-specific technologies are used. To connect a remote worker to the company LAN, remote access protocols and technologies are used.

This chapter introduces some devices that allow the expansion of networks locally or across the world. First, you learn about the devices that make it possible to expand a simple LAN into a large internetwork, and then you learn about the technologies used in wide area networking and remote access.

CREATING LARGER NETWORKS

As an organization grows and uses its network more heavily, eventually the network might no longer be as efficient as it should be. Perhaps the network's physical limitations have been reached, or network traffic increases so much that you must find a way to relieve congestion. A time comes in every administrator's life when the network must be changed. There are different ways to stretch or expand network capabilities:

- Physically expanding to support additional computers
- Segmenting the network into smaller pieces to filter and manage network traffic
- Extending the network to connect separate LANs
- Connecting two or more disjointed networking environments

Many devices are available to accomplish these tasks, discussed in more detail in the following sections:

- Repeaters
- Bridges
- Switches
- Routers
- Gateways

Repeaters

A signal that travels along a cable degrades and becomes distorted through attenuation. If the cable is long enough, the signal eventually becomes so degraded that it's unrecognizable. A repeater accepts a signal, cleans it, regenerates it, and sends it down the line, effectively doubling the length of the network. Repeaters operate at the Physical layer (Layer 1) of the OSI model without concern for the type of data being transmitted, the packet address, or the protocol. Repeaters operate only with bits and can't perform any filtering or translation on the actual data.

Although a repeater can't connect different types of network architectures, such as Ethernet and token ring, it can connect different physical media. For example, a repeater running Ethernet over UTP cable might have an additional interface that connects to a fiber-optic cable. This feature can be used to interconnect hubs that are farther apart than UTP allows, as shown in Figure 13-1.

Recall that a hub is simply a multiport repeater, as discussed in Chapter 2. When computers are connected to a hub or repeater, only one computer at a time can transmit because hubs create a shared media environment. Review Simulation 2-1 to see that when a signal is sent to one computer, all computers attached to the hub receive the signal, but only the intended destination processes the information. Furthermore, extending the network by adding more

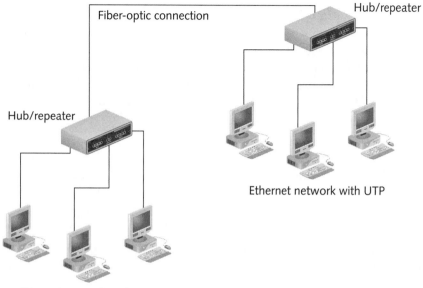

Figure 13-1   Repeaters can connect different physical media

hubs or repeaters increases the chance of a collision because the signal is propagated to all repeaters in the LAN.

Repeaters retransmit data at the same speed as the network. However, a slight delay occurs as the repeater regenerates the signal. Using a number of repeaters in a row can create **propagation delay**, which is the time it takes a signal to travel from the source device to the destination device. Many network architectures limit the number of repeaters because too much delay between the time the transmitting device sends the signal and the time the destination receives the signal can cause data loss. For example, a 10Base2 network can have a maximum of four repeaters connecting five network segments. Hubs or repeaters are useful for quickly and easily extending the reach of your network or adding stations to an existing network. However, because switches are so affordable, do away with many limitations of repeaters, and reduce network congestion, they are the preferred device for connecting multiple computers to a network. Table 13-1 lists the advantages and disadvantages of repeaters.

Table 13-1   Advantages and disadvantages of repeaters

Advantages	Disadvantages
Allow easy expansion of the network	Can't filter frames
Have little propagation delay	Can't connect different network architectures
Allow connections between different media	Create a shared media environment, which reduces bandwidth availability

Bridges

Like repeaters, **bridges** also connect two network segments and can connect dissimilar physical media. However, bridges can also do the following: limit traffic on each segment; reduce bottlenecks; connect different network architectures, such as Ethernet and token ring; and forward frames between network segments. Recall that bridges work with frames as the protocol data unit (PDU). Frames contain physical address information and are defined at the Data Link layer (Layer 2), which is where bridges operate.

A bridge functions primarily to filter traffic between network segments. As a network segment receives a frame, the bridge looks at the frame's physical destination address before forwarding the frame to other segments. If the frame's destination is on another network segment, the bridge retransmits the frame out the correct port. However, if the destination is on the same network segment that receives the frame, the bridge assumes the frame has already reached its destination and discards it. As a result, network traffic is reduced.

How does a bridge know which computers are on which network segments? As mentioned, bridges work at the Data Link layer, which is where source and destination MAC addresses are added to a packet, at which point the packet becomes a frame. Because bridges function at this layer, they have access to this address information. To determine the network segment on which a computer exists, bridges use two methods: transparent bridging and source-routing bridging.

Ethernet networks most often use **transparent bridges** or learning bridges. These bridges build a **bridging table** as they receive frames. When a bridge is powered on, the bridging table is empty. As it receives a frame, the bridge notes the port through which the frame was received as well as the frame's source and destination addresses. By doing this, the bridge builds a comprehensive list of MAC addresses and the port through which each address can be reached.

When the bridge receives a frame, it compares its source and destination addresses to the bridging table. If the two addresses are on the same network segment, the bridge discards the frame. If the bridge finds the MAC address of the frame's destination in its bridging table, it sends the frame out the port where that destination computer can be found. If, however, the destination MAC address isn't in the bridging table, the bridge sends the frame out all its ports except the one that received the frame. This process, called flooding the frame, ensures that the frame reaches its destination.

Source-routing bridges, used primarily in token ring networks, rely on the frame's source to include path information. Bridges of this type require little processing power because the sending computer does most of the work. Source computers use explorer frames to determine the best path to a particular computer. The explorer frame includes this information when it's sent across the network. When a source-routing bridge receives an explorer frame, it notes the path and uses it for future frames sent to that destination.

Regardless of the type of bridge used, bridges are slower than repeaters because they examine each frame's source and destination addresses. However, because they filter traffic and break the network into smaller collision domains, bridges can increase throughput on a network.

Note, however, that bridges don't reduce network traffic caused by broadcast frames (transmissions sent simultaneously to all network devices). Most traffic in a computer network is destined for a particular computer, and a bridge can send the frame to its destination. However, when a computer needs to send information to all other computers on the network, it sends a broadcast frame. When a bridge receives a broadcast frame, it forwards the frame out all its ports (except the port on which the broadcast was received) to ensure that all computers receive the frame.

In many instances, a network benefits from broadcasts. For example, Address Resolution Protocol (ARP, discussed in Chapter 6) depends on broadcasts to determine the MAC address of the computer assigned a particular IP address. Of course, too many broadcast frames cause a network to bog down, especially if a malfunctioning NIC or computer generates the broadcasts. In this situation, the NIC can flood the network rapidly, causing a **broadcast storm**. A broadcast storm occurs when so many broadcast frames are sent on the network that other types of traffic can't be processed. Unfortunately, bridges don't help in this situation and, in fact, might exacerbate it.

As mentioned, bridges, like repeaters, can connect networks of dissimilar media because bridges operate at the Physical layer as well as the Data Link layer. For example, a bridge can connect an Ethernet 10BaseF network to an Ethernet 10BaseT network. Generally speaking, bridges are intended to connect two network segments of the same architecture. However, **translation bridges** can connect different types of networks. For example, a translation bridge can connect an Ethernet network to a token ring network. To Ethernet nodes, these bridges appear as transparent bridges and accept Ethernet frames. To token ring nodes, they appear as source-routing bridges and accept token ring frames. Translation bridges are also available for conversion from Ethernet to Fiber Distributed Data Interface (FDDI). Table 13-2 lists the advantages and disadvantages of bridges.

13

Table 13-2 Advantages and disadvantages of bridges

Advantages	Disadvantages
Easily extend network distances	Slower than repeaters
Filter traffic to ease congestion	Forward broadcast frames
Connect networks with different media	Can be more expensive than repeaters
Can connect different network architectures with translation bridges	

Switches

A switch is really a high-speed multiport bridge, an intelligent device that maintains a switching table and keeps track of which hardware addresses are located on which network segments. Review Simulation 2-2 to see how a switch uses a table to forward frames.

Like bridges, switches operate at the Data Link layer of the OSI model and work with a frame as the PDU. Switches have almost all the features of bridges; the primary difference between them is in implementation details. Whereas a bridge might have only two or three ports permitting only two or three network segments to be connected, a typical switch might have between four and hundreds of ports, which allows many network segments to be interconnected. In the past, switches were too expensive to use to connect all computers to a large corporate network. However, because of falling switch prices and their inherent advantages, they have largely replaced multiport repeaters in corporate networks.

Another primary difference between bridges and switches is the speed at which they perform their tasks. A bridge has a general-purpose CPU running a software program to carry out the bridging function. A switch uses a specialized processor preprogrammed to perform the switching function. Therefore, a bridge performs its functions in software, and a switch performs its functions in hardware.

Like a bridge, a switch sends a frame down only the network segment on which a computer resides, so the network works more efficiently than with a multiport repeater or hub. Each port on a switch provides a separate collision domain. If you use a 24-port hub to connect 24 computers, each computer shares the bandwidth of the medium (in Ethernet, typically 10 Mbps or 100 Mbps) and only one of the 24 computers could transmit at a time without causing a collision. If you replace the hub with a 24-port switch, each computer has access to the medium's full bandwidth, allowing all 24 computers to transmit simultaneously without collisions.

Switches receive a frame on one port and forward it out another port by using a variety of methods. The simplest and fastest is **cut-through switching**, in which the switch reads only enough of the incoming frame (in Ethernet, 12 bytes) to determine the frame's source and destination addresses. After the forwarding location is determined, the frame is switched internally from the incoming port to the outgoing port, and the switch is free to handle additional frames. The benefit of cut-through switching is speed. A typical Ethernet frame can be up to 1518 bytes, whereas a token ring frame can be up to 18,000 bytes. With cut-through switching, the switch reads only a small portion of the total frame before sending the frame on its way. The disadvantage of this switching method is that the switch indiscriminately forwards frames containing errors, so it ties up bandwidth needlessly with frames that will be discarded.

On the other hand, **store-and-forward switching** requires that the switch read the entire frame into its buffers before forwarding it. The switch first examines the frame's frame check sequence (FCS) field to be sure the frame contains no errors before it's forwarded. If an error is found, the switch discards the frame. The store-and-forward switching method has the advantage of conserving bandwidth when many frames contain errors. The disadvantage is that the entire frame must be read, stored in memory, and examined before it can be forwarded. This process takes time and slows the network somewhat. To see an animated representation of cut-through switching and store-and-forward switching, run Simulation 13-1.

Simulation 13-1 Store-and-Forward Switching Versus Cut-Through Switching

A third popular switching method is **fragment-free switching**, which reads enough of the frame to guarantee that the frame is at least the minimum size for the network type. For Ethernet, this minimum frame size is 64 bytes. One type of frame error that can occur in a network is a **frame fragment**, in which the frame is damaged because of a collision or a malfunctioning device, such as a NIC or hub. When this type of damage occurs, the frame might be truncated to less than the minimum allowable size. A switch operating in fragment-free mode detects this problem and discards the frame without forwarding it. For a summary of switching method features, refer to Table 13-3.

Table 13-3   Switching method summary

Switching Method	Switching Performance	Errors Forwarded
Cut-through	Fastest	All errors forwarded
Fragment free	Medium	All errors except frame fragments forwarded
Store-and-forward	Slowest	No error frames forwarded

13

A benefit of switching technology is its capability to dedicate bandwidth to each port on the switch. For example, in an Ethernet 10BaseT environment using a regular hub, all the hub's ports share the maximum throughput of 10 Mbps; so if a repeater or hub has 48 ports, all 48 ports share the 10 Mbps. However, in a switched networking environment, a switch can dedicate 10 Mbps to each port on the switch, which ensures that the maximum bandwidth is available to all computers on the network. In addition, repeaters allow only half-duplex communication, in which a device can send or receive data but can't do both simultaneously. A switch, however, permits full-duplex communications, allowing a connected workstation to send and receive data simultaneously, further increasing throughput.

Another important feature available on switches but not on bridges or repeaters is the capability to segment a network into **virtual local area networks (VLANs)**. VLANs allow network administrators to group users and resources logically instead of by physical location. With conventional networks, a user or resource's location dictates to which network it's assigned. This limitation sometimes makes resource sharing inefficient because, ideally, users are assigned to the same network as the resources they access most often.

A switch that supports VLANs permits any switch port or group of ports to be assigned to a VLAN, which can be a benefit. Suppose you have a group of employees from different departments working on a long-term project. A new server has been allocated for this project, but the employees working on the project are scattered in different buildings. To solve this problem, you can assign the switch port to the same VLAN to which each employee's computer is connected. You can also assign the switch port to the same VLAN to which the server is connected. In this way, these employees and the resources they share, although physically separated, are logically grouped by using VLANs.

Because each VLAN is assigned a unique network number, a router is needed to communicate between VLANs. Figure 13-2 depicts how users and resources from different physical locations can be assigned to the same VLAN. Although the details of implementing VLANs are beyond the scope of this book, you can read a good overview on the subject at *http://computer.howstuffworks.com/lan-switch8.htm.*

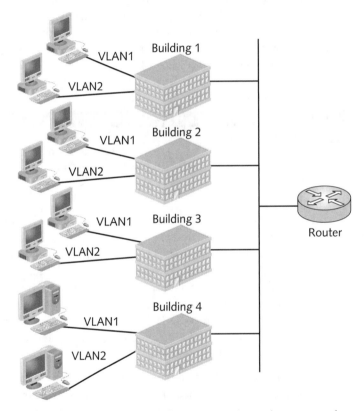

Figure 13-2   VLANs logically group users and resources from different physical locations

Like bridges, switches also forward broadcast frames. In a large, busy network, broadcasts can quickly overwhelm network switches and hosts because every broadcast must be forwarded to every other computer in a network using switches and repeaters. In turn, each computer must process the broadcast frame even if the broadcast is unimportant to that particular computer. At some point, the number of broadcasts takes a toll on the network's overall performance, and the network must be segmented into smaller broadcast domains, which is where a router comes in.

Routers

Routers operate at the Network layer (Layer 3) and work with packets as the PDU. **Routers** are advanced devices that connect separate logical networks to form an internetwork. Connecting two or more independent networks so that they continue to function separately creates an internetwork. A good example is two networks, one in each building of a multibuilding campus. Users on both networks should be able to exchange information, but both networks should continue to function separately. A router can be used to facilitate exchanging data between networks, but frames such as broadcasts are kept in their respective network. Recall that the Internet uses routers to interconnect thousands of networks around the world. If the Internet interconnected networks with bridges or switches, which forward broadcast frames, any broadcast frame generated by any computer connected to the Internet would be forwarded to and processed by every other computer on the Internet. If this were the case, the only traffic flowing on the Internet would be broadcasts!

Like bridges, routers can connect multiple network segments and filter traffic; unlike bridges, routers can be used to form complex networks. As shown in Figure 13-3, routers can connect complex networks with multiple paths between network segments; these multiple paths are commonly used to provide fault tolerance.

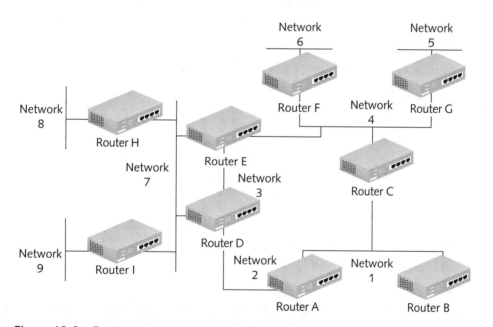

Figure 13-3   Routers can connect networks with many different paths between them

Each network segment, also called a subnetwork (or subnet), is assigned a network address, and each node on a subnet is also assigned an address. To route a packet through the internetwork successfully, a router must determine the packet's path. To do this, it uses only the network portion of a packet's destination address. When the router receives a packet, it analyzes the packet's destination network address and looks up that address in its **routing table** (explained in more detail in the next section). The router then repackages the data and sends it to the next router in the path.

Because routers operate at a higher layer of the OSI model than do bridges and switches, routers can easily send information over different network architectures. For example, routers can send a packet received from a token ring network over an Ethernet network. The router removes the token ring frame, examines the packet to determine the network address, repackages the data into Ethernet frames, and sends the data to the Ethernet network. For instance, as mentioned previously, Ethernet frames have a maximum size of 1518 bytes, whereas token ring frames have a maximum size of 18,000 bytes. So for a single token ring frame at its maximum size, routers must create 12 Ethernet frames. Although routers are very fast, this type of translation affects network speed.

One primary difference between bridges and routers, aside from a router's capability to select the best path, is what routers do with unknown addresses. As mentioned, when a bridge receives a frame with an unknown destination address, it forwards that frame to all connected network segments. When a router receives a packet with an unknown destination network address, however, it discards that packet. This also applies to corrupted packets and broadcasts. A router discards any packet it doesn't understand or for which it has no route to the destination. Simulation 13-2 shows how a packet travels from one network to another through routers.

Simulation 13-2 Routing Packets from One Network to Another

SIMULATION

Routing Tables

The routing tables maintained by routers vary from bridging tables. A bridge keeps track of the hardware address of each device on a network segment, but a routing table contains only network addresses and addresses of the routers that handle those networks. Table 13-4 shows the sample routing table for Router A from Figure 13-3. The table lists the next hop (that is, where transmissions go next) and metric. A **metric** is a value that describes the distance to the destination network. In this example, the metric uses a value of hops. A **hop** is described as a packet traveling through a router on its way to the destination network. The total number of routers data must travel through to get to the destination network is the hop count or metric.

Table 13-4   Router A's routing table

Network	Next Hop	Metric
1	Directly connected	0
2	Directly connected	0
3	Router D	1
4	Router C	1
5	Router C	2
6	Router C	2

Table 13-4 Router A's routing table (continued)

Network	Next Hop	Metric
7	Router D	1
8	Router D	2
9	Router D	2

Notice that there are multiple ways to get to many of the networks. Often, a router keeps only the shortest path to a destination network in its routing table. However, if the shortest path route goes down, the router can use the next shortest path as a backup. In other cases, a router can use two different paths to a network and use load balancing to spread the traffic load over multiple pathways.

Routing tables can be populated in two ways: static routing or dynamic routing. If a router uses **static routing**, the administrator must manually update the routing table, adding each route by entering commands into the router. With static routing, the router always uses the same path to a destination, even if it's not necessarily the shortest or most efficient route. If the table has no route to a particular destination, the router drops the packet.

A router using **dynamic routing** uses a discovery process to find information about available routes. Dynamic routers communicate with each other and constantly receive updated routing tables from other routers. If multiple routes to a particular network are available, the router decides which route is best and enters that route in its routing table.

A router chooses the best path for a packet in two ways:

- Using a **distance-vector algorithm**, the router calculates a particular route's metric based on factors such as the number of routers between the two networks (hop count), the bandwidth of lines between networks, network congestion, and delays. It determines the path a packet takes by identifying the route with the lowest metric. Distance-vector algorithms communicate with each other by periodically exchanging copies of their routing tables. Routing Information Protocol (RIP), used by both TCP/IP and IPX/SPX, is a distance-vector routing protocol.

- When using a **link-state algorithm**, the router relies on speed of the links, referred to as cost, between networks to determine the lowest metric. Routers using link-state algorithms communicate by sending the status of all their interface links to the other routers in the internetwork. This exchange of information takes place only when a change occurs in the network. This type of algorithm requires more processing power but delivers packets more efficiently. Open Shortest Path First (OSPF) is a TCP/IP link-state routing protocol.

Dynamic routers are easier to maintain and provide better route selection than static routers, but the routing table updates and discovery generate additional network traffic. This is especially true of distance-vector protocols such as RIP, which sends its entire routing table across the network every 30 seconds. Table 13-5 shows the advantages and disadvantages of routers.

13

Table 13-5 Advantages and disadvantages of routers

Advantages	Disadvantages
Connect networks of different physical media and network architectures	More expensive and more complex than bridges or repeaters
Choose the best path for a packet through an internetwork	Work only with routable protocols; dynamic routing updates create network traffic
Reduce network traffic by not forwarding broadcasts or corrupt packets	Slower than bridges and switches because they must perform more intricate calculations on packets

Gateways

A **gateway** is an intricate piece of networking equipment that translates information between two dissimilar network architectures or data formats. For example, a gateway can allow network communication between a TCP/IP LAN and an IBM mainframe system by using Systems Network Architecture (SNA). Another example of a gateway is a system that converts Microsoft Mail to Simple Mail Transport Protocol (SMTP) for transmission over the Internet. Although routers work at the Network layer and can route packets of the same protocol (such as TCP/IP) over networks with dissimilar architectures (such as Ethernet to token ring), gateways can route packets over networks with different protocols. Gateways can change the actual format of data, whereas routers only repackage the data into different frame types if necessary.

Gateways often connect PCs to mainframe computers, as in the TCP/IP-to-SNA example. However, many other types of gateways are found in smaller networks. For example, as Chapter 9 discusses, Windows Server operating systems include Services for Macintosh, which allows Windows clients to communicate with Macintosh clients through a Windows server. This gateway software allows Macintosh file servers and printers to appear to Microsoft clients as though they were on Windows networks, and vice versa. The gateway handles all translations between NetBEUI or TCP/IP and AppleTalk.

When packets arrive at a gateway, the software strips all networking information from them, leaving only the raw data. The gateway then translates the data into the new format and sends it back down the OSI layers using the destination system's networking protocols. Because gateways translate data, they generally operate at the upper layers of the OSI model. Usually, this operation takes place at the Application layer, but some gateways can translate at the Network or Session layer.

Generally, gateways are harder to install, slower, and more expensive than other networking equipment. They are usually a separate computer with only one task, such as translating Microsoft Mail to SMTP.

WIDE AREA NETWORK (WAN) TRANSMISSION TECHNOLOGIES

In large, and sometimes even small, businesses, a company often has multiple sites. For example, a company might have sales offices in New York and Los Angeles and a manufacturing plant in Chicago. Facilitating communication among geographically dispersed sites requires a WAN, which is simply an internetwork that spans a large geographical area. In other words, a WAN is organized to allow each segment of a network to be situated in a different building, city, state, or even country. The distances involved in WANs pose intriguing problems for maintaining, administering, and troubleshooting networks.

As far as users are concerned, a WAN looks and operates in the same way as a LAN. Users can access network resources on their LAN or across the country or globe over the WAN. The interface and access methods remain the same. One distinction is the time delay as electronic signals traverse the globe, which can be quite substantial, depending on the quality of the network connection.

WANs are often constructed by linking LANs to improve or increase the level of communication. These connections are established by using communication devices, such as switches and routers, with communication lines from an ISP or telco (telephone company or service provider). Some special communication links to construct WANs include the following:

- Packet-switching networks
- Fiber-optic cable
- Microwave transmitters
- Satellite links
- Cable television coax systems

13

Because these link types are expensive and complex, most organizations lease WAN links from a service provider instead of purchasing, installing, and deploying their own long-distance cable or wireless connections. Another benefit of leasing a communication link is that because transactions often include unlimited use of the link, organizations don't have to pay per-minute charges. Consider how large the phone bill would be to maintain a 24-hour, seven-day telephone link between the United States and Kenya, and then multiply that amount by 10, 100, or even 1000 to get a general idea of WAN link per-minute charges.

A number of WAN technologies are available, each with its own strengths and weaknesses. Organizations choose the best technology for their needs, based on speed, reliability, cost, and availability, and can select a combination of technologies tied together by routers and gateways, if needed. These are the main technologies for communicating between LANs across WAN links, discussed in more detail in the following sections:

- Analog
- Digital
- Packet switching

Analog Connectivity

To establish a WAN link to remote computers and networks, a LAN can use the same telecommunications network you use to talk on the phone. This network is often referred to as **public switched telephone network (PSTN)** or **plain old telephone service (POTS)**. Figure 13-4 shows a simple PSTN connection, which uses analog phone lines and requires modems to convert signals to and from the digital format computers use.

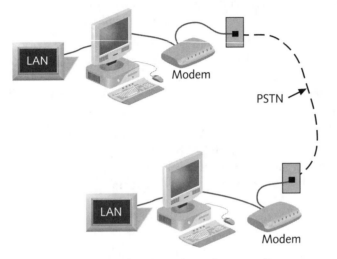

Figure 13-4   A simple PSTN network connection

Unfortunately, the quality of PSTN varies substantially from location to location, depending on the age of the system and the level or quality of installed media. This variation in quality, and the fact that PSTN was originally designed to support voice-only communication, makes PSTN an economical but low-quality choice for most WAN links.

Because PSTN lines require modems to transmit digital computer data over the analog telephone network, data transmission is extremely slow. Also, because PSTN is a circuit-switched network, connection quality is highly inconsistent; a link is only as reliable and fast as the circuits linked to establish the pathway. The greater the distance a connection covers, the more likely it is that the connection is poor or unusable.

 Recently, telcos upgraded some PSTN lines to support data transmission more reliably. They are now installing fiber-optic cable to support the increasing demand for high-bandwidth data communications.

NOTE

One way to improve the quality of a PSTN connection is to lease a dedicated line or circuit instead of relying on the random circuits supplied when you dial in to a PSTN to establish a connection (called "dial on demand"). A dedicated line is more expensive than a dial-on-demand connection but usually guarantees a reliable connection over the circuits and offers higher-quality, more consistent data transmissions. **Line conditioning**, an additional feature available for most dedicated circuits, requires extensive testing and line upgrades for the connection to sustain a consistent transmission rate. This feature improves overall signal quality and reduces interference and noise.

When deciding between a dial-up or dedicated PSTN connection, you need to consider a number of factors:

- Length of connection time required (daily, weekly, monthly)

- Cost of service and usage levels

- Availability of dedicated circuits, conditioning, or other quality improvements

- Assessment of the need for a 24-hour, seven-day connection

If you need infrequent or limited-duration connections, a dial-up line is the most cost-effective solution. However, if you need constant access, a PSTN line might not offer enough speed to support your network activities.

Modems in Network Communications

A **modem** is a device for making an analog connection between computers over a telephone line, effectively making a WAN connection between computers or networks. Because a modem can use existing telephone lines, it remains a popular method to connect remote users to a network or the Internet. A modem converts a digital signal from a computer into an analog signal. This conversion is called modulation. A modem modulates the digital signal into an analog signal, and at the other end of the line, another modem demodulates the analog signal back to digital. Therefore, the term *mo*dulator/*dem*odulator—modem, in its shortened form—is used.

Internal or external modems are available on most computers. Internal modems are added to an expansion slot in the computer. An external modem is a separate box, with its own power supply, that connects to a computer's serial port with the RS-232 communications interface standard or to a USB port. Both types of modems include RJ-11 connectors to allow easy connection to a standard telephone wall jack, using a standard modular phone cable.

Modem speed is measured in the number of bits per second (bps) that can be transmitted. Table 13-6 shows some of the **V-series** standards the International Telecommunications Union (ITU) developed to define modem speed. The table lists standards with the terms "bis" and "ter." These terms don't refer to modem speed; rather, they are the French words for second and third, used to indicate revisions of the original standard. As a point of reference, the V.22bis modem transmits a 1000-word document in 25 seconds, the V.34 modem sends the same document in two seconds, and the V.42bis compression modem sends the document in only one second.

Table 13-6 ITU communications standards

Standard	bps	Year Introduced
V.22bis	2400	1984
V.32	9600	1984
V.32bis	14,400	1991
V.32ter	19,200	1993
V.FastClass (V.FC)	28,800	1993
V.34	33,600	1994
V.42bis	57,600	1995
V.90	56,000	1998

NOTE

The term **baud** is sometimes used to denote modem speed. A baud represents the oscillation of a sound wave that carries one bit of data. For earlier modems, the terms baud and bits per second (bps) are used interchangeably; a 300 bps modem has 300 oscillations of sound waves each second. However, with new compression technologies, the number of bits per second has increased way beyond the number of oscillations per second. For example, a modem that transmits at 28,800 bps might actually be transmitting at 9600 baud.

Types of Modems

Two types of modems are used today: asynchronous and synchronous. Which type you use depends on the type of phone lines and the network requirements. Also, when continuous network connections are needed (as when linking a branch office to a headquarters location), digital technologies such as DSL or cable modems (discussed later in this chapter in "Digital Modems") offer higher bandwidth and better communication capabilities at little or no extra cost.

Asynchronous communication uses regular telephone lines. Asynchronous modems convert each data byte into a stream of 1s and 0s. As shown in Figure 13-5, start and stop bits separate each byte from the next. Both the sending and receiving devices must agree on the start and stop bit sequence.

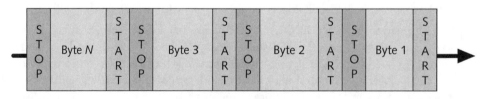

Figure 13-5 Asynchronous modems use start and stop bits

In asynchronous communication, there's no synchronization of communication between two computers, other than the start and stop bits. The sending computer transmits data in a continuous stream, with only the start bit to indicate to the receiving device that data is on the way.

Many modems correct transmission errors as they occur. In addition to start and stop bits, a parity bit is added for each byte of data. The sending computer counts the number of 1s in the data stream. If the number is odd, it sets the parity bit to 1. The receiving computer counts the number of 1s in the data stream, determines whether the number is odd or even, and then compares the result with the parity bit. If the parity bits match, the chances are high that the data arrived intact. If not, the modem requests retransmission of the data packet.

The most common asynchronous modem standard for connecting to the Internet is the V.90 standard. The V.90 standard makes connection speeds up to 56 Kbps possible by eliminating one of the modulation/demodulation steps in traditional modem communication. As shown in Figure 13-6, traditional modem communication converts a computer's digital data into analog data. The analog signal travels over telephone lines until it reaches the telco, where the signal is converted to digital. The telco then must convert the signal back to analog for the receiving modem at the ISP, which, in turn, converts the signal to digital for the Internet. This two-way conversion limits transfer speeds to 33.6 Kbps because each conversion degrades the signal quality.

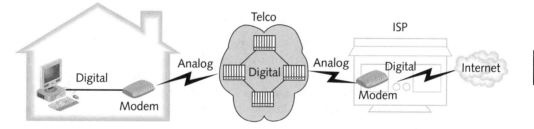

Figure 13-6 Modem communication using two analog-to-digital conversions

V.90 modems assume that the network from the telco to the ISP and then to the Internet is an all-digital network. Therefore, instead of modulating analog data into digital data as it's received from the telco, a V.90 modem uses a technique called **pulse code modulation (PCM)** that digitizes analog signals. It introduces less noise into the signal than traditional modulation/demodulation techniques, so it boosts the total number of bits per second at which data can be transferred. As shown in Figure 13-7, there's only one analog connection—from the home to the telco. From the telco to the ISP and then to the Internet, the signal is all digital.

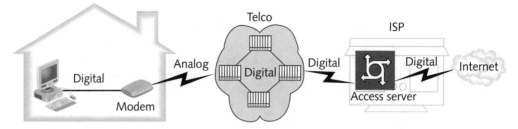

Figure 13-7   Modem communication using the V.90 standard

Two caveats with V.90 communications: There must be only one analog circuit between the modem and the Internet, and 56 Kbps communication works in only one direction—the download direction. This means data from the modem to the ISP travels at only 33.6 Kbps, but data from the ISP to the modem travels at the V.90 speed of 56 Kbps. Data traveling in the download direction at a speed different from the upload direction is known as **asymmetric communication**. Although V.90 technology is capable of data transfer speeds up to 56 Kbps, FCC regulations limit the maximum download speed to 54 Kbps. However, actual transfer rates depend on line conditions.

Asynchronous modems depend on start and stop bits in the data stream to determine where data begins and ends; **synchronous** modems depend on timing. Two devices coordinate this timing scheme to separate groups of bits and transmit them in blocks known as frames. Both modems must be synchronized for communication to occur. Figure 13-8 shows the frame format of data with synchronization (or sync) bits inserted periodically to ensure accurate timing.

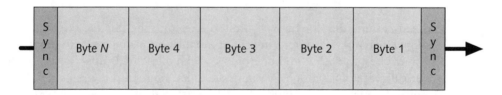

Figure 13-8   Synchronous modems send synchronization bits periodically

If an error occurs, the modem simply requests that the frame be retransmitted. Because synchronous modems have so little overhead in terms of error checking, they are much faster than asynchronous modems. In addition, synchronous protocols provide a number of functions not available in asynchronous communication. They format the data into blocks, add control information, and check the information for errors. There are three primary synchronous communication protocols: **Synchronous Data Link Control (SDLC)**, **High-level Data Link Control (HDLC)**, and **Binary Synchronous (bisync)**.

Synchronous modems were *not* designed for use over regular phone lines; instead, they are generally found in dedicated, leased-line environments. Because of the specialized lines and the more expensive equipment, a synchronous solution for network communication costs much more than asynchronous solutions.

Digital Connectivity

Because computers and LANs transmit data digitally, using digital techniques to connect LANs or computers over long distances to form a WAN makes more sense than introducing a conversion from digital to analog and then back to digital again. In fact, the only real reasons for using analog technologies are cost or availability. Analog phone connections are inexpensive and available almost anywhere, and until the late 1990s, digital connections, particularly for residences and small businesses, were expensive and often hard to come by. All that has changed as digital connections in the form of digital cable and DSL are fast becoming as ubiquitous as analog connections. In addition, more advanced digital connections, such as T1 and T3, can satisfy the bandwidth appetite of all but the hungriest networks.

Digital Data Service (DDS) lines are direct or point-to-point synchronous communication links with 2.4, 4.8, 9.6, or 56 Kbps transmission rates. DDS links provide dedicated digital circuits between both endpoints and guarantee a specified quality and data transmission rate. The most important benefit of digital links is a nearly 99% error-free transmission of data, compared with an error rate up to 40% for a typical PSTN connection. Some DDS line types discussed in this chapter are ISDN, T1, T3, and switched 56K.

13

DDS does not use modems to establish connections because these communications are purely digital. Instead, DDS uses a special communication device called a **Channel Service Unit/Data Service Unit (CSU/DSU)**. A network uses a CSU/DSU to accept data from a bridge or router. That CSU/DSU then sends data over the digital network to a receiving CSU/DSU, which hands it to a bridge or router that delivers data to the remote network (see Figure 13-9).

Digital Modems

Another increasingly prevalent modem type is a **digital modem**. Of course, because a modem translates a signal from digital to analog, the term "digital modem" isn't technically accurate and most often refers to the interface for Integrated Services Digital Network (ISDN, described in "Integrated Services Digital Network" later in this chapter). The interface for ISDN is sometimes referred to as a digital modem. However, the adapters for ISDN consist of a network termination (NT) device and terminal adapter (TA) equipment. Because most users are familiar with the term modem, however, manufacturers of these NT/TA devices often use it. Since 1998, cable TV operators and telecommunications companies have offered higher-speed digital connections that supplanted ISDN and conventional asynchronous modems for small office/home office (SOHO) use. In both cases, the term modem is often used, even though these technologies might require no digital-to-analog and analog-to-digital demodulation.

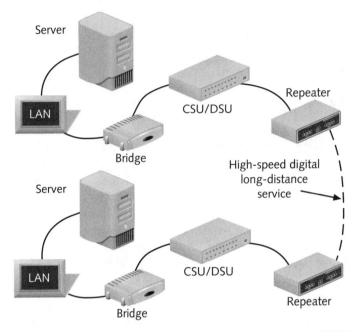
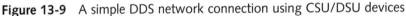

Figure 13-9   A simple DDS network connection using CSU/DSU devices

Cable modems take advantage of the high bandwidth of broadband CATV cables and the wide availability of this infrastructure to transmit signals to and from Internet points of presence. The devices that attach to a NIC on a computer typically feature a BNC connector, where the CATV coaxial cable attaches, and an RJ-45 connector that attaches through a modular cable to a computer's NIC. Some CATV systems do indeed use analog signaling, so the term "cable modem" is correct in these cases. However, most cable companies have switched to digital cable, which retains broadband's use of multiple channels on a single cable but switches from analog to digital signaling methods on a per-channel basis. In these cases, cable modems aren't really modulator/demodulators, but the term indicates that the devices (which customers usually rent from the cable company) make it possible for a computer to attach to the Internet through the CATV infrastructure.

Cable modems provide bandwidth to users as a form of shared media access. That is, all users on a CATV cable segment (usually part of a neighborhood or large building, for example) share the available bandwidth. Therefore, more users (or more traffic per user) means less bandwidth per user because access is shared. Maximum bandwidth for most CATV cable segments is about 10 Mbps (roughly equivalent to a T1 connection). One powerful advantage of cable modem access, however, is that distance limitations don't govern functionality. As long as users have access to cable TV and the cable company offers Internet access on the local cable segment, users can install a cable modem and access the Internet for as little as $30 to $50 per month.

Aside from performance issues caused by shared access media in cable modem networks, security was a concern in early cable networks because users who shared the same cable segment could eavesdrop on others' communication sessions. However, networks that comply with the DOCSIS cable modem standard use a strong 56-bit encryption key for each user connection, which provides some privacy and security.

Telecommunications carriers offer a competing digital technology called digital subscriber line (DSL). (Typically, these companies include local phone companies and their competitors, such as long-distance companies, local-exchange carriers, and digital-only carriers, such as Covad and Qwest.) To deliver digital services, DSL uses the same twisted-pair phone lines that deliver voice services. Unlike cable modem connections, DSL connections are not shared, so they offer subscribers guaranteed bandwidth. Because bandwidth is guaranteed, however, upstream (communications from the user to the remote side of the connection) and downstream (communications from the remote side of the connection to the user) data rates are metered. Users must pay more for higher bandwidth connections. Nevertheless, DSL is a great SOHO technology because it costs less than ISDN and usually offers considerably higher upstream and downstream bandwidth than does ISDN. As with cable modems, most DSL connections top out at around 1.5 Mbps bandwidth. (Even so, they usually cost less than a T1 line.)

DSL's primary disadvantage is its distance limitation (measured as the wire runs) between the user's location and the nearest central office (CO), where a copper-to-fiber interface device links to the telecommunication carrier's digital backbone. Depending on which vendor's equipment is used, this distance limitation varies between 17,500 feet (3.31 miles or 5.33 km) and 23,000 feet (4.36 miles or 7.01 km). Therefore, it's important to measure how far a connection point is from the local CO to determine whether DSL is a viable network option.

Although there are many types of DSL, the two most common are **Asymmetric Digital Subscriber Line (ADSL)** and **Symmetric Digital Subscriber Line (SDSL)**. Upload and download speeds differ for these types of DSL. ADSL supports speeds up to 8 Mbps in the download direction and up to 1 Mbps in the upload direction, but typical connection speeds are less than 1.5 Mbps for download and less than 1 Mbps for upload. The upload and download speeds are equivalent in SDSL. This technology is often chosen for businesses operating a Web site because the amount of traffic uploaded and downloaded is likely to be similar.

NOTE

ADSL is ideal for home Internet users because the bulk of traffic in these connections travels in the download direction.

DSL and cable modems both share one important advantage over asynchronous modems—they are "always on." Both technologies maintain constant connections to a remote server on the other side of the connection, so there's never a delay to establish a connection, as with a conventional modem. Given the higher bandwidth, faster access, and relatively low cost of digital connections, it's no wonder that droves of users are switching from modems to digital alternatives for SOHO connections. However, because mobile users (those who want to dial in to the Internet or a private network from a laptop while traveling) will remain part of the remote user base, conventional modems are still used. Other digital technologies aren't widely available to mobile users yet, but conventional telephone lines are.

 TIP

For more information on DSL technology, see *www.dslreports.com.*

T1

One of the most widely used high-speed digital lines is the **T1**, a DDS technology that uses two two-wire pairs to transmit full-duplex data signals at a maximum rate of 1.544 Mbps. One pair of wires transmits, and the other pair receives. T1 can adequately support data, voice, and narrowband video for a moderate number of senders and receivers.

T1 is a fairly expensive digital link that organizations usually purchase or lease if they can't sustain productive WAN network activity over a lower-quality line. Because a T1 line consists of 24 separate channels, each with a data rate of 64 Kbps, subscribing to one or more channels instead of an entire T1 is possible with a service called **fractional T1**. In some countries (mostly European, but also many in the Pacific Rim), the E1 digital carrier technology is used. An E1 line supports a signal rate of 2.048 Mbps. Table 13-7 lists E class characteristics and data rates.

Table 13-7   E channels and data rates

Voice Channels	Carrier	E1s	Data Rate (Mbps)
30	E1	1	2.048
120	E2	4	8.448
480	E3	16	34.368

Multiplexing, or "muxing," enables several communication streams to travel simultaneously over the same cable segment. Bell Labs developed this technology years ago to allow a single telephone line to carry a number of concurrent conversations. Through multiplexing, Bell Labs established a T-carrier network that expanded its capabilities to support simultaneous communication links over the same set of cables. T1 uses multiplexing to combine data transmissions from several sources and deliver them over a single cable. After it's received, a transmission is decoded into its original form before being sent to its final destination.

As mentioned previously, each channel in a T1 link supports 64 Kbps data transmission. Each channel takes a data sample 8000 times per second, and each data sample consists of 8 bits; this combination produces the per-channel data rate of 64 Kbps. This rate of data transmission is known as DS-0. The rate of a full T1 using all 24 channels is known as a DS-1. The "DS" specifications categorize DDS lines. Table 13-8 lists DS rate levels, their corresponding T designations, and their specifications.

Table 13-8   DS channels and data rates

DS Level	Carrier	T1s	Channels	Data Rate (Mbps)
DS-0	N/A	N/A	1	.064
DS-1	T1	1	24	1.544
DS-1C	T1C	2	48	3.152
DS-2	T2	4	96	6.312
DS-3	T3	28	672	44.736
DS-4	T4	168	4032	274.760

Multiplexing can increase DS-1 rates up to DS-4 speeds. Standard copper wires can support transmission rates of T1 and T2 lines, but T3 and T4 lines require microwave or fiber-optic technologies.

T3

A **T3** line has 28 T1s or 672 channels and supports a data rate of 44.736 Mbps. Many large service providers offer both T3 and fractional T3 leased lines with transmission rates of 6 Mbps and up. A single T3 commonly replaces several T1 lines.

13

Switched 56K

Switched 56K leased lines are an older, digital, point-to-point communication link offered by local and long-distance telcos. Before recent advances in fiber-optic and multiplexing technologies, the 56K digital network offered the best alternative to PSTN connections, particularly given its on-demand structure. A circuit was not dedicated to a single customer; rather, each time a customer required a connection, a pathway was established. When the transmission ceased, so did the link. Therefore, lease terms were based on per-minute use charges, not on 24-hour, seven-day dedicated circuit allocation. Today, with the ready availability of cable modems and DSL, switched 56K service is used only when multiple 56 Kbps channels are aggregated for frame relay services or when other specialized dedicated digital leased lines are needed (and when bandwidth requirements exceed T1).

Integrated Services Digital Network

Integrated Services Digital Network (ISDN) is a digital communications technology developed in 1984 to replace the analog telephone system. Not as widely deployed as expected, it's available in many metropolitan areas of the United States as well as most of Western Europe. The ISDN specification defines single-channel links of 64 Kbps. With the 10 Mbps LANs of the 1980s, this was more than sufficient, but with today's 100 Mbps or faster networks, ISDN offers no major benefits. If not for private and SOHO use to establish

Internet connections, ISDN might never have been deployed. One application for which ISDN still enjoys some popularity in corporate WANs is as a backup line. Because ISDN charges are often based on connect time, a company can use ISDN in standby mode, so that the WAN connection is established only if the primary connection fails.

ISDN offers speeds two to four times that of a standard POTS modem—not an overwhelming increase in speed, but a vast improvement for SOHO users when faster technologies such as DSL or cable modem aren't available. The cost of ISDN is reasonable (perhaps twice that of a regular phone connection yet providing both voice and data connections).

ISDN is available in two formats or rates:

- *Basic Rate Interface (BRI)*—Consists of two B-channels (64 Kbps) and a D-channel (16 Kbps). Each B-channel can transmit and receive voice or data independently of the other, or bonded together, for a speed of 128 Kbps. The D-channel is used for call setup and control.

- *Primary Rate Interface (PRI)*—Consists of 23 B-channels and a D-channel. Each B-channel can be used independently or aggregated. A PRI offers the same bandwidth as a T1 line but uses different equipment at the endpoints and vastly different signaling techniques. As with BRI, the B-channels in a PRI are 64 Kbps channels, but the D-channel is also 64 Kbps, compared to only 16 Kbps in a BRI.

Broadband ISDN (B-ISDN) is an ISDN variation that supports much higher data rates than standard ISDN and works with other technologies, such as Asynchronous Transfer Mode (ATM), Synchronous Optical Network (SONET), and frame relay. The bandwidth of B-ISDN varies according to the application requirements. Although the range is not yet fixed, B-ISDN is expected to operate from as low as 64 Kbps to more than 100 Mbps. B-ISDN is designed to work over fiber-optic media and is targeting applications such as video telephone, audio, and high-definition television.

NOTE

ATM and SONET were discussed in Chapter 7. Frame relay is discussed later in this chapter.

Packet-Switching Networks

Packet-switching networks are often used to communicate data over short and long distances. They provide fast, efficient, and highly reliable technology. The first part of the name refers to how the technology breaks data into small packages—packets. Switching refers to the delivery and transmission methods to move these packets over various pathways to a single destination. The Internet is a prime example of a packet-switching network.

A packet-switching network handles data in the following manner:

1. The original data is segmented into packets.

2. Each packet is labeled with a sequence order and a destination address (also known as the header).

3. Each packet is sent separately on the network toward the destination.

4. As a host receives the packet, it reads its header. If the host is the packet's destination, the host keeps the packet. If the host is not the destination, the host attempts to send the packet to the destination by the fastest, shortest, or most logical route available at the moment of transmission.

5. After the destination machine receives all packets, it uses the sequence information in the packets' headers to reconstruct the original data. It also requests retransmission of any missing or damaged packets.

A key benefit of a packet-switching network is that data delivery doesn't depend on any single pathway between the origin and the destination. In fact, no two packets are required to take the same route to reach the destination. The sequential information in each packet header is, therefore, important because packets commonly arrive out of order, and the destination computer must rearrange them before extracting the original data. In addition, packets are small, so if any packet fails to arrive at its destination, the resulting retransmission request can be serviced with minimal time loss. The small size also reduces the time each switch or host needs to receive, analyze, and retransmit packets.

13

Virtual Circuits

Many packet-switching networks use **virtual circuits** to provide temporarily "dedicated" pathways between two points. No real cable exists between the two endpoints; instead, a virtual circuit consists of a logical sequence of connections with bandwidth allocated for a specific transmission pathway. This pathway between sender and receiver is created after devices at both ends of the connection agree on bandwidth requirements and request a pathway. To improve transmission quality and ensure successful communication, virtual circuits incorporate communication parameters that govern receipt acknowledgements, flow control, and error control.

There are two types of virtual circuits: switched and permanent. **Switched virtual circuits (SVCs)** are established when needed and then terminated when the transmission is completed. The path between two communication points is maintained only as long as it's in active use. **Permanent virtual circuits (PVCs)** are similar to leased lines, in that the pathway between two communication points is established as a permanent logical connection; therefore, the pathway exists even when it's not in use.

X.25

Developed in the mid-1970s, the **X.25** specification provided an interface between public packet-switching networks and their customers. Used most often to connect remote terminals with centralized mainframes, X.25 defines how devices communicate over an internetwork. X.25 networks are SVC networks, meaning they create the best available pathway for transmission *at the time of* transmission.

Early X.25 networks used standard telephone lines as communication links, which resulted in numerous errors and lost data. Adding error checking and retransmission schemes improved the success of X.25 transmissions but severely dampened speed. With its extensive level of error control, X.25 could deliver only 64 Kbps transmission rates. A 1992 specification revision improved the maximum throughput of X.25 to 2 Mbps per connection, but this new version was not widely deployed.

X.25 is usually associated with **public data networks (PDNs)** instead of public or private networks. AT&T, General Electric, Tymnet, and other large commercial service providers offer PDN service. X.25 is also popular outside North America, where the availability of digital communications from service providers is much lower and more expensive than in the United States and Canada. Using data terminal equipment (DTE) and data circuit-terminating equipment (DCE), explained later in "WAN Implementation Basics," connecting to an X.25 network can be accomplished with one of three different methods:

- An X.25 NIC in a computer
- A **packet assembler/disassembler (PAD)** that supports X.25 communications for low-speed, character-based terminals
- A LAN/WAN X.25 gateway

Even though X.25 networks offer reliable and error-free communications, use of this technology is declining because of its speed limitations and the development of other higher-speed technologies, such as frame relay and ATM.

Frame Relay

Frame relay is a point-to-point PVC technology that offers WAN communications over a fast, reliable, digital packet-switching network. It was developed from X.25 and ISDN technology. Because frame relay doesn't use error checking, overall throughput is improved. Error checking is not required on the digital fiber-optic links most frame relay connections use. Instead, the devices on each end of the communication perform error checking. Frame relay also uses variable-length packets or frames for data transmission at the Data Link layer.

Frame relay uses a PVC between communication points, so the same pathway carries all communications, which ensures correct delivery and higher bandwidth rates. A PVC is similar to a dedicated line, in that communication devices aren't concerned with route management and error checking. Instead, all the resources of devices are dedicated to moving data. This is why frame relay technology can maintain transmission rates of 56 Kbps to 1.544 Mbps (T1 speed); T1 multiples are also available.

Frame relay services have quickly grown in popularity. They are inexpensive (compared to other solutions, such as ATM) and allow customers to specify the bandwidth needed. Charges depend on the PVC's bandwidth allocation, also known as its **Committed Information Rate (CIR)**. CIR is the guaranteed minimum transmission rate that the service provider offers. Customers can purchase frame relay services in CIR increments of 64 Kbps. Because customers can pay for a customized bandwidth solution, frame relay is sometimes preferred to T1 because it's generally less expensive.

A frame relay connection is established by using a pair of CSU/DSUs—as with T1 lines—with a router or bridge at each end to direct traffic on and off the WAN link. An important difference between a frame relay connection and a T1 connection is that T1 is a point-to-point link, which means a T1 customer gets full-time bandwidth to the destination (usually an ISP). However, frame relay connections are virtual circuits that go through a switch. This arrangement makes it possible to reach multiple destinations with a single frame relay connection. Therefore, a corporate customer can, for example, have a frame relay link to each of its several branch offices as well as a frame relay link to the Internet yet require only a single frame relay connection. Figure 13-10 shows a simplified depiction of this arrangement.

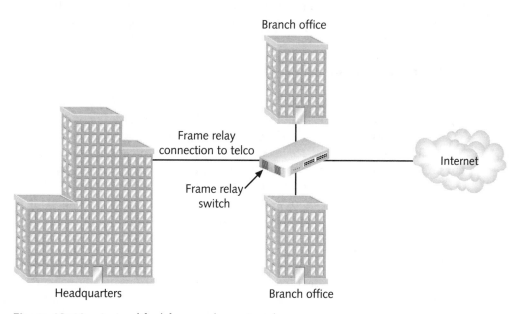

Figure 13-10   A simplified frame relay network

WAN Implementation Basics

You have already learned some terms for the technologies that make WANs work, such as POTS, ISDN, and frame relay. This section discusses how WANs are implemented.

Customer Equipment

When an organization must build a WAN to connect geographically dispersed resources, some equipment is the organization's responsibility and some is the provider's responsibility. The organization building the WAN is always referred to as the customer, and the equipment at the customer site that's usually the responsibility of the customer is called the **customer premises equipment (CPE)**. The customer might own or lease the equipment from the provider. CPE usually includes devices such as routers, modems, and CSU/DSUs. Modems are needed when some type of analog connectivity is involved, and CSU/DSUs are required for digital circuits.

Every WAN has a connection from the customer equipment (usually a cable from the CSU/DSU or modem) to a junction panel called the **demarcation point**. The demarcation point is the point at which the CPE ends and the provider's responsibility begins. This junction is where the physical WAN connection is made from the customer to the telco or ISP (the provider).

Provider Equipment

As mentioned, the provider location nearest the customer site is often referred to as the central office (CO). A cable runs from the customer site demarcation point to the CO of the WAN service provider. This cable is usually copper or fiber-optic and is the provider's responsibility. For a wireless connection to the provider, no cables are used, but a wireless transmitter is usually mounted on the customer's building. The connection between the demarcation point and the CO is called the **local loop** or **last mile**. The equipment specific to the WAN technology usually resides at the CO. This equipment might be a frame relay switch, an X.25 switch, or any other WAN device.

Going the Last Mile

The CPE must be able to send data in the correct format onto the connection that makes up the local loop and receive data coming from that connection. That is where the CSU/DSU or modem comes in. The device that sends data to (and receives data from) the local loop is called **data circuit-terminating equipment (DCE)** or sometimes "data communications equipment." The CSU/DSU or modem is called the DCE device. The device that passes data from the customer LAN to the DCE is called the **data terminal equipment (DTE)**. A typical DTE is a router or bridge that has one connection to the customer LAN and another connection to the DCE that makes the WAN connection. Figure 13-11 illustrates this arrangement.

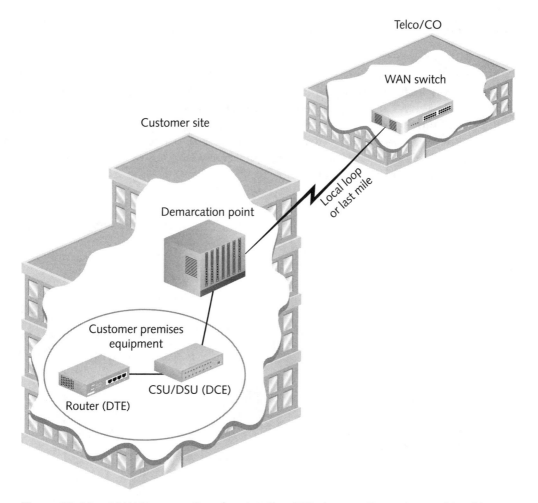

Telco/CO

WAN switch

Customer site

Local loop
or last mile

Demarcation point

Customer premises
equipment

CSU/DSU (DCE)

Router (DTE)

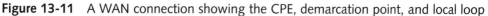

Figure 13-11 A WAN connection showing the CPE, demarcation point, and local loop

As you can see, getting all these definitions and acronyms straight is half the struggle of understanding how to specify, design, and support these technologies. For more information on installing and configuring WANs, refer to *A Guide to Designing and Implementing Local And Wide Area Networks, Second Edition* (Bruce Sinclair and Michael Palmer, Course Technology, ISBN 0-619-12122-X).

REMOTE ACCESS NETWORKING

For your network to be even more effective, you might need to allow users dial-in access from their homes, remote sites, or hotel rooms. A simple way to do this in a Windows Server network is to use Routing and Remote Access Service (RRAS). Loaded on Windows servers, RRAS allows up to 256 remote clients to dial in if the hardware is available. Figure 13-12 shows how Windows RRAS might interact with a LAN to provide remote access. RRAS includes routing software that permits a server to function as a low-end routing device. It also offers local area routing services as well as the capability to route between one or more remote or local connections.

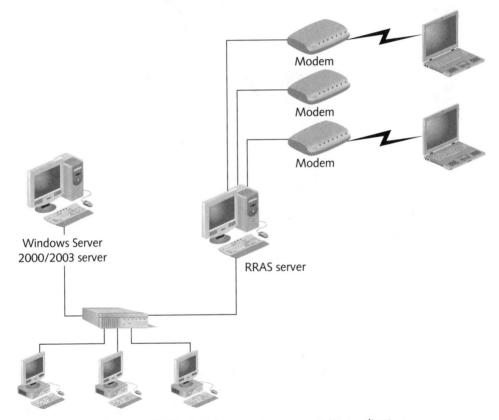

Figure 13-12 Windows RRAS provides remote connectivity to clients

Using RRAS to connect to a network, users can dial in over general-use telephone lines or cable lines. After the connection is established, the remotely connected computer acts exactly as though it were connected directly to the network, albeit more slowly. In addition, RRAS also supports virtual private network (VPN) connections across the Internet. (Virtual private networks were covered in Chapter 10.) Users need only connect to a local ISP and establish a VPN connection to a remote access server also attached to the Internet.

NOTE

The option for users to dial in to a Windows remote access server is disabled by default for security reasons. This feature must be enabled in a user's account information.

All versions of Windows, starting with Windows 95, include **Dial-Up Networking (DUN)** software to make an RRAS connection. The DUN client also connects computers to ISPs. Two protocols, discussed in the following sections, are available for remote access: Serial Line Internet Protocol (SLIP) and Point-to-Point Protocol (PPP).

Serial Line Internet Protocol (SLIP)

Serial Line Internet Protocol (SLIP) is an older protocol used primarily by PCs to connect to the Internet via a modem. A Data Link layer protocol, it provides connectivity across telephone lines and no error correction. SLIP, which relies on hardware for error checking and correction, supports connections only for TCP/IP and requires no addressing because a connection is made only between two machines. Standard implementations of SLIP provide no compression, but a version called compressed SLIP (CSLIP) does support this option. SLIP is still supported but not used much in today's environment.

Point-to-Point Protocol (PPP)

Point-to-Point Protocol (PPP) provides a more dynamic connection between computers than does SLIP. The major difference between SLIP and PPP is that PPP provides both Physical and Data Link layer services, which effectively turn a modem into a NIC. Therefore, PPP supports multiple protocols, including IP, IPX, and NetBEUI. In addition, PPP inherently supports compression and error checking, which makes it faster and more reliable than SLIP.

Although both SLIP and PPP allow connectivity through TCP/IP, PPP supports dynamic assignment of IP addresses. This feature allows administrators to assign a block of addresses to RRAS modems. Because it's more robust and allows more flexibility, PPP has replaced SLIP as the remote protocol of choice for TCP/IP connections. In fact, although using a Windows computer to dial in to a remote connection using SLIP is possible, the only dial-up connections that RRAS supports require PPP (or a direct Internet connection for VPN connections).

CHAPTER SUMMARY

❑ Repeaters, bridges, switches, and routers can be used to expand a network. Repeaters work at the Physical layer and, therefore, have little propagation delay, but always forward data to all destinations. Switches and bridges work at the Data Link layer and can filter traffic based on MAC addresses. However, bridges and switches always forward broadcast frames. Routers work at the Network layer and are the slowest of these devices. Routers filter by network address and do not forward broadcasts.

- A repeater increases the length of your network by eliminating the effect of attenuation on the signal. Repeaters can connect two different media types.

- A bridge installed between two network segments filters traffic according to hardware destination addresses. By placing computers that communicate most often on the same side of the bridge, you can reduce network traffic. You can also use a bridge to connect networks of different physical media, such as 10BaseT and fiber-optic networks.

- Switches are similar to bridges, but the advanced technology allows them to handle more network segments and switch frames much faster than bridges. Three primary switching methods are cut-through, store-and-forward, and fragment-free.

- A router connects several independent networks to form a complex internetwork. It's capable of connecting networks with different physical media, as a bridge can, but a router can also connect networks using the same protocols but different network architectures, such as Ethernet and token ring. In a network with multiple paths, a router can determine the best path for a packet to take to reach its destination.

- Analog WAN connections use conventional PSTN phone lines and offer little reliability or speed. Digital WAN connections offer high-speed connections and more reliable communication. Digital links range from 56 Kbps to 274 Mbps. A CSU/DSU is required to connect to higher-bandwidth digital media, such as frame relay, T1, and T3.

- Low-cost, medium-bandwidth technologies, such as DSL and cable modem, are taking over for SOHO connections, where users always connect from the same location and seek better price and bandwidth than analog modems or ISDN can provide. Users also avoid paying the additional costs for CSU/DSU equipment and bandwidth required by frame relay, T1, T3, and so on.

- T1 and similar lines are not single cables but collections of pairs of cables, so fractions of these links can be leased. Multiplexing is the process of combining and delivering several transmissions on a single cable segment.

- Packet-switching networks are fast, efficient, and reliable WAN connection technologies. This process segments data into packets and adds a header containing destination and sequence details. Each packet takes a unique route to its destination, where it's reassembled into its original form.

- Frame relay is a WAN technology that offers transmission rates of 56 Kbps to 1.544 Mbps and no error checking. Frame relay uses a switched connection, unlike other high-speed technologies such as T1. This switched connection permits multiple destinations from a single frame relay connection.

- Equipment at the WAN customer site is referred to as the customer premise equipment (CPE). The demarcation point is where a customer's responsibility ends and the provider's responsibility begins. The data terminal equipment (DTE) passes data to the data circuit-terminating equipment (DCE), which, in turn, passes data onto the local loop that connects to the provider's equipment.

- Windows Routing and Remote Access Service (RRAS) enables up to 256 remote clients to dial in if the hardware is available. Two protocols are available for remote access: Serial Line Internet Protocol (SLIP) and Point-to-Point Protocol (PPP).

KEY TERMS

asymmetric communication — Communication in which data travels in the download direction at a speed different from the speed of the upload direction.

Asymmetric Digital Subscriber Line (ADSL) — A digital telecommunications technology that uses different speeds for downloading and uploading data.

asynchronous — A communication method that sends data in a stream with start and stop bits that indicate where data begins and ends.

Basic Rate Interface (BRI) — An ISDN version that provides two 64 Kbps B-channels. Generally used for remote connections.

baud — A measurement of modem speed that describes the number of state transitions occurring per second on an analog phone line.

Binary Synchronous (bisync) — One of the primary synchronous communication protocols.

bridges — Networking devices that work at the Data Link layer of the OSI model. They filter traffic according to a packet's hardware destination address.

bridging table — A reference table created by a bridge to track hardware addresses and to track on which network segment each address is located.

Broadband ISDN (B-ISDN) — An ISDN variation that supports much higher data rates than standard ISDN and works with other technologies, such as ATM, SONET, and frame relay.

broadcast storm — A phenomenon that occurs when a network device malfunctions and floods the network with broadcast packets.

Channel Service Unit/Data Service Unit (CSU/DSU) — A device that links a computer or network to a DDS communications link.

Committed Information Rate (CIR) — A guaranteed minimum transmission rate offered by the service provider.

customer premises equipment (CPE) — The equipment at the customer site that's usually the responsibility of the customer.

cut-through switching — The fastest switching method, in which the switch reads only enough of the incoming frame to determine where to forward the frame.

data circuit-terminating equipment (DCE) — The device that sends data to (and receives data from) the local loop, usually a CSU/DSU or modem.

data terminal equipment (DTE) — The device that passes data from the customer LAN to the DCE, usually a router.

demarcation point — The point at which the CPE ends and the provider's equipment responsibility begins.

Dial-Up Networking (DUN) — The Windows program (beginning with Windows 95) that allows connectivity to servers running RAS or RRAS.

Digital Data Service (DDS) — A type of point-to-point synchronous communication link offering 2.4, 4.8, 9.6, or 56 Kbps transmission rates.

digital modem — A hardware device used to transmit digital signals across an ISDN link.

13

distance-vector algorithm — One method of determining the best route available for a packet. Distance-vector protocols count the number of routers (hops) between the source and destination. The best path has the least number of hops.

dynamic routing — The process by which routers dynamically learn from each other the available paths.

fractional T1 — One or more of the 24 channels (but not all) of a T1 connection.

fragment-free switching — A switching method in which the switch reads in enough of the frame to guarantee that the frame is not less than the minimum frame size allowed for the network type.

frame fragment — A frame error that occurs because the frame is less than the allowable minimum size for the network type. A frame fragment usually occurs because of a collision or a device malfunction.

frame relay — A point-to-point permanent virtual circuit (PVC) technology that offers WAN communications over a fast, reliable, digital packet-switching network

gateway — A networking device that translates information between protocols or between completely different networks, such as from TCP/IP to SNA.

High-level Data Link Control (HDLC) — One of the primary synchronous communication protocols.

hop — A packet traveling through a router on its way to the destination network.

Integrated Services Digital Network (ISDN) — A WAN technology that offers increments of 64 Kbps connections, most often used by SOHO (small office/home office) users.

last mile — The connection between a WAN's demarcation point and the central office (CO). *See also* local loop.

line conditioning — A feature that sustains a consistent transmission rate, improves overall quality, and reduces interference noise levels.

link-state algorithm — A method used by routers to determine a packet's best path. In addition to the number of routers involved, routers using link-state algorithms take network traffic and link speed into account to determine the best path.

local loop — The connection between a WAN's demarcation point and the central office (CO). *See also* last mile.

metric — A value that describes the distance to the destination network.

modem — A device computers use to convert digital signals to analog signals for transmission over telephone lines. The receiving computer then converts the analog signals to digital signals.

multiplexing — A technology that enables several communication streams to travel simultaneously over the same cable segment

packet assembler/disassembler (PAD) — A device that supports X.25 communications for low-speed, character-based terminals.

permanent virtual circuits (PVCs) — Pathways between two communication points that are established as permanent logical connections; therefore, the pathway exists even when it's not in use.

plain old telephone service (POTS) — Also known as PSTN, the normal telephone communications system. *See also* public switched telephone network (PTSN).

Point-to-Point Protocol (PPP) — A remote access protocol that supports many protocols, including IP, NetBEUI, and IPX.

Primary Rate Interface (PRI) — An ISDN version that provides 23 64-Kbps B-channels.

propagation delay — Signal delay created when a number of repeaters connect in a line. To prevent this, many network architectures limit the number of repeaters on a network.

public data networks (PDNs) — WAN services, usually provided by private companies, for the purpose of enabling WAN technologies, such as X.25.

public switched telephone network (PSTN) — Another term for the public telephone system.

pulse code modulation (PCM) — A technique for digitizing analog signals. PCM introduces less noise into the signal than traditional modulation/demodulation techniques, thus boosting the total number of bits per second.

routers — Networking devices that operate at the Network layer of the OSI model. A router connects networks with different physical media and translates between different network architectures, such as token ring and Ethernet.

routing table — A reference table that includes network information and the next router in line for a particular path.

Serial Line Internet Protocol (SLIP) — The dial-up protocol originally used to connect PCs directly to the Internet.

source-routing bridges — A type of bridge used in IBM token ring networks that learns its bridging information from information in the frame's structure.

static routing — A type of routing in which the router is configured manually with all possible routes.

store-and-forward switching — A switching method in which the switch reads the entire frame to check for errors before forwarding the frame.

switched 56K — Digital point-to-point leased communication links offered by local and long-distance telcos. Lease terms are based on per-minute use charges, not on 24-hour, seven-day dedicated circuits.

switched virtual circuits (SVCs) — A communication circuit that's established when needed and then terminated when the transmission is completed.

Symmetric Digital Subscriber Line (SDSL) — A digital telecommunications technology that uses equivalent speeds for downloading and uploading data.

synchronous — A communication method in which computers rely on exact timing and sync bits to maintain data synchronization.

Synchronous Data Link Control (SDLC) — One of the primary synchronous communication protocols.

T1 — A DDS technology that uses two two-wire pairs to transmit full-duplex data signals at a maximum rate of 1.544 Mbps.

T3 — A communication line that has 28 T1s or 672 channels and supports a data rate of 44.736 Mbps.

13

translation bridges — A type of bridge that can translate between network architectures.

transparent bridges — Generally used in Ethernet networks, these bridges build their bridging tables automatically as they receive packets.

virtual circuits — A logical sequence of connections with bandwidth allocated for a specific transmission pathway.

virtual local area networks (VLANs) — A feature of switches that allows network administrators to group users and resources logically, regardless of their physical location.

V-series — The ITU standards that specify how data communication takes place over the telephone network.

X.25 — A WAN protocol that defines how devices communicate over an internetwork. X.25 networks are SVC networks, meaning they create the best available pathway for transmission *at the time of* transmission.

REVIEW QUESTIONS

1. A router using a _____ algorithm sends updates to other routers only when the network status changes.

   a. spanning tree

   b. distance-vector

   c. link-state

   d. triggered-vector

2. Which of the following devices allows only one computer at a time to transmit and create a shared media environment?

   a. router

   b. hub or repeater

   c. switch

   d. distance vector

3. Which of the following operates at the Physical layer of the OSI model and effectively doubles the length of the network?

   a. repeater

   b. gateway

   c. router

   d. switch

4. The time it takes for a signal to travel from the source device to the destination device is called _____ .

5. When a switch sends a frame out all ports except the one on which it was received, it's called which of the following?

   a. repeating

   b. filtering

   c. flooding

   d. forwarding

6. Bridges and switches do not forward broadcast frames. True or False?

7. At which layer of the OSI model do switches operate?

   a. Physical

   b. Network

   c. Transport

   d. Data Link

8. A switch performs its functions in _____, whereas a bridge performs its functions in _____ .

   a. hardware, software

   b. software, hardware

   c. RAM, ROM

   d. ROM, RAM

9. Which is the fastest method of switching?

   a. store-and-forward

   b. broadcast

   c. fragment-free

   d. cut-through

10. A router using a _____ algorithm periodically exchanges its entire routing table with other routers.

    a. spanning tree

    b. distance-vector

    c. link-state

    d. triggered-vector

11. Which of the following converts digital signals to analog signals and back again?

    a. bridge

    b. router

    c. modem

    d. gateway

13

12. Which of these benefits apply to a router? (Choose all that apply.)

    a. can connect networks of different physical media

    b. filters by MAC addresses

    c. does not forward broadcasts

    d. faster than bridges and switches

13. Which of the following networking devices causes the least propagation delay?

    a. router

    b. repeater

    c. switch

    d. gateway

14. A manually configured router uses _____ routing.

    a. static

    b. dynamic

    c. predefined

    d. spanning

15. Which of the following limitations applies to cable-based access to network services?

    a. A connection is possible only within 17,500 to 23,000 feet of the local point of presence.

    b. All users on the local CATV cable segment share the bandwidth.

    c. Only one user can access the network at a time.

    d. Service is scarce and extremely expensive.

16. Which of the following limitations applies to DSL-based access to network services?

    a. A connection is possible only within 17,500 to 23,000 feet of the local point of presence.

    b. All users on the local CATV cable segment share the bandwidth.

    c. Only one user can access the network at a time.

    d. Service is scarce and extremely expensive.

17. Which of the following statements best describes frame relay?

    a. It transmits fixed-length packets at the Physical layer through the most cost-effective path.

    b. It transmits variable-length packets at the Data Link layer through the most cost-effective path.

    c. It transmits variable-length packets at the Physical layer through the most cost-effective path.

    d. It transmits fixed-length packets at the Data Link layer through the most cost-effective path.

18. What type of device is required to connect to a dedicated digital communication line?

    a. modem

    b. NIC

    c. CSU/DSU

    d. digital recorder

19. Which term describes the place in a WAN connection where the customer's responsibility ends and the provider's responsibility begins?

    a. data circuit-terminating point

    b. demarcation point

    c. CPE

    d. central office

20. Which of the following places data on the local loop?

    a. DCE

    b. DTE

    c. router

    d. DMZ

21. Which WAN technology was designed specifically to replace the analog telephone system?

    a. ATM

    b. ISDN

    c. frame relay

    d. SONET

22. Why is a nondedicated PSTN line such a poor choice for WAN connections? (Choose all that apply.)

    a. limited bandwidth

    b. inconsistent quality of equipment

    c. too expensive

    d. originally designed for voice-only communication

23. A DDS line offers point-to-point synchronous communication links at what transmission rate? (Choose all that apply.)

    a. 2.4 Kbps

    b. 4.8 Kbps

    c. 9.6 Kbps

    d. 56 Kbps

    e. 64 Kbps

13

24. Which of the following is a characteristic of a T1 line? (Choose all that apply.)

    a. 1.544 Mbps transmission rate

    b. full-duplex communications

    c. supports data, voice, and video

    d. consists of 24 channels

25. Which statement best describes multiplexing technology?

    a. It combines multiple communication lines in a single aggregated pipeline.

    b. It gives users multiple phone numbers.

    c. It enables multiple communications to travel simultaneously over the same cable segment.

HANDS-ON PROJECTS

HANDS-ON PROJECTS

Hands-On Project 13-1

In this project, you enable and configure RRAS on Windows Server 2003. This project requires a server with at least two network connections.

1. Log on to the Windows server using an account with administrator access.

2. Click **Start**, point to **All Programs**, point to **Administrative Tools**, and click **Routing and Remote Access**.

3. Click the name of the server in the left pane.

4. Click **Action, Configure and Enable Routing and Remote Access** from the menu.

5. When the Routing and Remote Access Server Setup Wizard starts, click **Next**.

6. You see the list of options for configuring the server. Click the **Remote access (dial-up or VPN)** option button, and then click **Next**.

7. Click to select the **VPN** and **Dial-up** check boxes, and then click **Next**.

8. Choose which interface is connected to the Internet, and then click **Next**.

9. Click the **Automatically** option button, and then click **Next**.

10. Click the **No** option button, and then click **Next**.

11. Click **Finish**. If prompted, click **OK** in the window describing the DHCP Relay Agent.

12. You have successfully configured RRAS to accept incoming connections. To disable RRAS, click **Action, Disable Routing and Remote Access** from the menu. Click **Yes** when prompted.

Hands-On Project 13-2

For this project, you need a Windows XP Professional computer with a modem already installed. To add a dial-up networking client to a Windows XP Professional computer, follow these steps:

1. Click **Start**, **Control Panel**. If necessary, click **Switch to Classic View**, and then double-click **Network Connections**.

2. Under Network Tasks at the left, click **Create a new connection**. (If a dialog box opens prompting you to enter your area code, do so, and then click **OK** twice.)

3. When the New Connection Wizard starts, click **Next**.

4. Click the **Connect to the Internet** option button, and then click **Next**.

5. Click **Set up my connection manually**, and then click **Next**.

6. Click the **Connect using a dial-up modem** option button, and then click **Next**.

7. Enter a name for your ISP, and then click **Next**.

8. Enter the phone number for your ISP, and then click **Next**. (If you don't plan to actually dial an ISP, you can enter any phone number you want.)

9. Enter the user name and password (you need to enter the password twice) for your ISP account. (Again, if you don't plan to actually dial an ISP, enter anything you like.) Click **Next**.

10. Click **Finish**. Congratulations! You have just added a dial-up connection to Windows XP.

11. Click **Cancel** in the Connect dialog box, and close the Network Connections window.

Hands-On Project 13-3

In this project, you set up a VPN connection using a Windows XP computer.

1. Click **Start**, **Control Panel**. If necessary, click **Switch to Classic View**, and then double-click **Network Connections**.

2. Under Network Tasks at the left, click **Create a new connection**. (If a dialog box opens prompting you to enter your area code, do so, and then click **OK** twice.)

3. When the New Connection Wizard starts, click **Next**.

4. Click the **Connect to the network at my workplace** option button, and then click **Next**.

5. Click the **Virtual Private Network connection** option, and then click **Next**.

6. Type a descriptive name for this connection, and then click **Next**. If necessary, click the **Do not dial the initial connection** option button, and then click **Next**.

13

7. Type the name or IP address of the VPN server, and then click **Next**. (If you don't have an actual VPN server to connect to, ask your instructor for an address to enter.)

8. Click **Finish**.

9. The VPN client then attempts to connect to the VPN server. If you have a VPN server set up, ask your instructor for the user name and password, and then click **Connect**; if not, click **Cancel**.

10. Close the Network Connections window.

Hands-On Project 13-4

In this project, you visit a Web site that sends data to your browser and measures the delivery time required to determine the effective bandwidth or throughput—that is, the actual speed at which your connection works.

1. Start your Web browser. Type **http://performance.toast.net** in the Address text box, and then press **Enter**.

2. In the Select Speed Test Type section, click one of the first five selections.

3. Next, in the Select Speed Test Host section, click any of the available hosts.

4. Click the **Run Test** button.

5. Your results are displayed along with a comparison to major ISPs. Try different hosts to see whether the results change. Why do you think your results varied with each test?

_____

_____

6. Close your Web browser.

Hands-On Project 13-5

In this project, you use the Trace Route (Tracert) command to determine the router hops between you and another network. Your network firewall must not block ICMP, the protocol that Tracert uses, for this project to work.

1. Open a command prompt window.

2. Type **tracert www.yahoo.com** and press **Enter**.

3. Note the number of hops it takes to reach *www.yahoo.com*. Note the names of the routers displayed. You can use this information to determine which ISPs your data travels through to get to a destination.

4. Try a few other common Web sites to see how the results vary.

5. If you're moving on to the next project, leave the command prompt window open; otherwise, type **exit** and press **Enter**.

Hands-On Project 13-6

In this project, you view the routing table that Windows XP maintains internally. Even though Windows XP is not configured as a router, it maintains a routing table that's used primarily when more than one network interface is installed.

1. Open a command prompt window, if necessary.

2. Type **route print** and press **Enter**.

3. Inspect the table of data displayed in your command prompt window. It should resemble Figure 13-13.

```
C:\Documents and Settings\user1>cd \

C:\>route print
===========================================================================
Interface List
0x1 ........................... MS TCP Loopback interface
0x2 ...00 0c 29 be 3a f2 ...... AMD PCNET Family PCI Ethernet Adapter - Packet S
cheduler Miniport
===========================================================================
===========================================================================
Active Routes:
Network Destination        Netmask          Gateway       Interface  Metric
        0.0.0.0          0.0.0.0      172.31.1.250    172.31.1.22      10
      127.0.0.0        255.0.0.0       127.0.0.1      127.0.0.1       1
     172.31.0.0    255.255.0.0      172.31.1.22    172.31.1.22      10
    172.31.1.22  255.255.255.255     127.0.0.1      127.0.0.1      10
 172.31.255.255  255.255.255.255   172.31.1.22    172.31.1.22      10
      224.0.0.0      240.0.0.0      172.31.1.22    172.31.1.22      10
255.255.255.255  255.255.255.255   172.31.1.22    172.31.1.22       1
Default Gateway:      172.31.1.250
===========================================================================
Persistent Routes:
  None

C:\>
```

Figure 13-13   Results of the Route Print command

4. Here's how to interpret the information, starting with the headings:

   ❐ *Network Destination (or Network Address)*—A network that the current network can reach

   ❐ *Netmask*—The IP subnet mask that applies to that network

   ❐ *Gateway (or Gateway Address)*—The IP address of the router that connects to that network

   ❐ *Interface*—The IP address of the interface on your computer that connects to that network

   ❐ *Metric*—The distance to the destination network; smaller numbers usually indicate a better route to the destination

5. Here's how to interpret the information in the rows (the IP address information on your screen will be different):

   ❐ *0.0.0.0*—The default network. 0.0.0.0 is the notation that indicates the default place where all packets are sent if there's no entry in the routing table for the specific destination. In this case, the default network, or default gateway, is 172.31.1.250, which can be found by sending packets out the 172.31.1.22 interface.

13

❏ *127.0.0.0*—The Class A network address for loopback and testing purposes; it uses a Class A netmask of 255.0.0.0 and the only valid loopback address, 127.0.0.1, for the gateway and interface addresses (which are virtual in this case, not actual).

❏ *172.31.0.0*—The private Class B IP network address where this computer resides. All packets destined for this network are sent out the 172.31.1.22 interface.

❏ *172.31.1.22*—The address of the local machine. Notice that the netmask is 255.255.255.255, which indicates a host route—not really a network destination but the address of the host itself.

❏ *172.31.255.255*—The local broadcast address for the 172.31.0.0 network. All broadcasts for this network are sent out the 172.31.1.22 interface.

❏ *224.0.0.0*—The default network address for multicasting RIPv2 routing table updates to an IP router, based on the RFC that governs RIPv2; if this computer were acting as a dynamic RIPv2 router, it would have to listen on this network address to obtain routing table updates.

❏ *255.255.255.255*—The general broadcast address for all IP network addresses; included in the routing table to ensure that broadcasts are sent out the 172.31.1.22 interface.

❏ *Default Gateway*—The address of the router to which this computer sends all packets destined for nonlocal networks.

6. Type **exit** and press **Enter** to close the command prompt window.

Case Projects

Case Project 13-1

As network administrator for a growing company, you are asked to solve a remote access dilemma. The 12 employees who work out of their homes complain about not being connected to the network except by e-mail. The company also has a number of employees who travel and would benefit from dial-up network connections. The director of marketing is responsible for part of the cost and wants only the best solution. Currently, you run a Windows Server 2003 network, and the users want access to all systems. Develop a plan to connect your remote users. Your solution can involve more than one remote access type. Describe your plan for remote access.

Case Project 13-2

Recently, you connected two departments' 10BaseT hub-based networks by connecting the two hubs with a 10BaseT cable. Now workers on both networks complain that the network is too slow. You're running a Windows server with Windows XP clients using TCP/IP, and users now need access to the file servers on both LANs.

Why has network performance degraded? Develop a plan to ease traffic on the network, including any additional hardware requirements. Describe your plan.

Case Project 13-3

Your company is considering connecting its mainframe to the PC network. The mainframe currently connects only to terminals, but management wants to be able to access it from desktops. You run a token ring network. The mainframe manufacturer supports Ethernet but not token ring. Develop an outline of possible solutions for making this connection, including hardware options and possible reconfiguration of the mainframe.

Case Project 13-4

You are the administrator of a LAN that has increased the number of users by a factor of three over the past couple of years. You have been adding users by increasing the number of switches and switch ports on the network. Now users are complaining that network response is slowing and even their computers seem slower. You monitor the network for a few days and find that broadcast frames constitute a high percentage of your network traffic. What can you do to contain the broadcasts? What network reconfiguration might you have to do?

13

Case Project 13-5

XYZ Corporation wants an affordable way to establish remote connections for its sales force, who log on from customer sites all over the country, and its three branch offices. The company's headquarters is in Washington, D.C., and its branch offices are in Santa Monica, CA, Des Moines, IA, and New York, NY. Explain what kind of connections the sales force and branch offices should use and what kinds of services should be installed on the headquarters network to keep communication costs to a minimum.

SOLVING NETWORK PROBLEMS

After reading this chapter and completing the exercises, you will be able to:

♦ Describe the benefits of network management and planning

♦ Explain different approaches to network troubleshooting

♦ List the steps of the problem-solving process

♦ Explain the types of specialized equipment and other resources for troubleshooting

♦ Describe some measures to take in common troubleshooting situations

The role of a network administrator encompasses many areas of responsibility. Typical tasks include server configuration, user connectivity and management, data protection, and network planning and monitoring. This chapter covers two of the most important aspects of network management—preventing problems and dealing with those that do occur.

This chapter describes how to prevent problems through planning and documentation and how to monitor and troubleshoot your network. This chapter also outlines a method for troubleshooting networks, describes related tools and resources, and concludes with a survey of common network problems and ideas on how to troubleshoot them.

PREVENTING PROBLEMS WITH PLANNING AND DOCUMENTATION

In a perfect world, networks would always work smoothly and users would be blissfully unaware of network administration. In the real world, however, problems can and do occur. Typically, you solve network problems in one of two ways: preventing problems through planning and management (called **preemptive troubleshooting**) or repairing and controlling existing damage (called **troubleshooting**). This section covers prevention through planning and management. Later sections discuss damage control.

Network management and troubleshooting should combine to form an overall network plan. As a network administrator, you need to outline this plan in a comprehensive document that evolves with the network. A network plan, an extension of the network diagram discussed in Chapter 2, should include cable diagrams, cable layouts, network capacity information, a list of all protocols and network standards in use, and documentation on computer and network device configurations, software, and important files.

You should establish the policies and procedures that apply to your network during its planning stages and continue throughout the network's life. These policies should include backup methods, security, hardware and software standards, upgrade guidelines, and documentation. Through careful planning, you can minimize the damage from most predictable events and control and manage their impact on your organization.

Backing Up Network Data

A comprehensive backup program can prevent major data loss. Any backup plan is an important part of a network plan and should be revised as your needs—and your data and applications—change. To formulate any backup plan, consider the following guidelines:

- Determine what data should be backed up and how often. Some files, such as program executables and configuration files, seldom change and might require backup only weekly or monthly.

- Develop a schedule for backing up your data that includes the type of backup to be performed, how often, and at what time of day. Chapter 12 reviews the most common backup methods.

- Identify the people responsible for performing backups.

- Test your backup system regularly. The person responsible for backups should perform these tests, which include backing up data and restoring it. After a backup system is in place, conduct periodic tests to ensure data integrity.

- Maintain a backup log listing what data was backed up, when the backup took place, who performed the backup, and which tapes were involved. The automatic log that most tape-backup systems create can often augment this backup log.

■ Develop a plan for storing data after it has been backed up to tape (or whatever backup medium you use). This plan should include on-site storage, perhaps in a fireproof safe, and off-site storage in the event of a catastrophe. For both on-site and off-site storage, ensure that only authorized personnel have access to the backup medium.

Setting Hardware and Software Standards

As an administrator, you are at least partially responsible for supporting the network, so you should also be involved in deciding what hardware and software components to use on it. To make hardware and software easier to manage, all network components should follow established standards. When you define standards for desktop computers, establish configurations for several levels of users. For example, a user in the Accounting Department might need a more powerful system than an administrative assistant in manufacturing. These standards should cover hardware (for example, processor, NIC, memory, and monitor) and software configurations (for example, OSs and applications).

You must also establish standards for networking devices, including supported hardware manufacturers and OSs (and versions), and indicate which networking protocols and services should be used. In addition, you must define standards for server configurations, document current server configurations, and establish guidelines for new server installations. Servers are sometimes installed haphazardly, as are desktop computers. An official standard can eliminate the problems of having a hodgepodge of server manufacturers and hardware and make purchasing new servers easier.

When establishing hardware and software standards, bear in mind the pace of industry change. To keep up, you must evaluate standards often—ideally, once per quarter. Regular evaluations help ensure that your network doesn't become outdated, even if you don't make purchases every time standards are updated. This task might seem unduly time consuming, but a solid set of standards makes the review process simple and painless.

Your hardware and software standards should be documented and available to all IT personnel; even better, create a Web document of these standards that's available to your entire company so that everybody can refer to it when a software or hardware purchase is under consideration. This standards document is likely to be a fluid document to keep pace with changing technology, so design it so that changes and updates are easy to maintain.

Establishing Upgrade Guidelines

As an extension of hardware and software standards, you must also establish guidelines for upgrades. Vendors often upgrade products and introduce new ones. If you establish guidelines in advance, you can handle upgrades more easily. To help ease the upgrade process, always give your users advance notice so that they know changes will take place and can prepare for them. In addition, disruptive upgrades shouldn't be carried out during normal working hours. It's also a good idea to "pilot" new upgrades with a small group of

14

technically astute network users. By using this method, you can work through any problems that come up without affecting all network users.

When performing upgrades, always formulate a plan to undo the installation, if needed. This plan is called a **rollback plan**. Sometimes, it's best to cut your losses and return the system or network to its preupgrade state. If this happens, reevaluating the upgrade and conducting more testing are advisable.

Upgrades are a fact of life in any network environment. Better computers, peripherals, and software are constantly being developed, and an organization's (or user's) needs can change. Through careful planning and testing, you can make the upgrade process go more smoothly.

Maintaining Documentation

As mentioned earlier, complete, up-to-date network documentation is an invaluable reference when training or troubleshooting. When a problem occurs, concise network documentation provides helpful information about the network's configuration and the location of troubleshooting resources. This documentation shouldn't be limited to LAN information and configuration; it must include WAN connections, too, if applicable.

If your networking environment encompasses multiple LANs, each LAN should have its own set of documentation with the same level of detail. The following list outlines a set of documents you should include in any network plan:

- *Network address list*—This list is especially useful in a network with protocols that use arbitrary addresses, such as TCP/IP. However, you should create a complete list that defines all addresses on a network, including the hardware addresses for specific computers. For example, an ideal list includes the MAC address of each computer's NIC, its IP address, its physical location, and the identity of its primary user. Documenting TCP/IP and MAC addresses helps you locate a computer when error packets or excessive traffic is coming from a single address in your network.

- *Cable map*—This document gives a more detailed outline of the cable installation for your network. For example, a cable map for a twisted-pair network includes cable type (for example, Category 5 or 6 UTP), wall-jack numbers and office locations, and the corresponding ports on the patch panel or concentrator. It also includes the cable's maximum speed and the speed at which it's used, if the two rates differ.

- *Contact list*—Sometimes called an escalation procedure, this document should include people to be informed during a network problem or failure. The list encompasses not only network administrators, but also vendor contacts, phone numbers, and information such as circuit numbers for WAN links.

- *Equipment list*—This list must include the date equipment was purchased and serial numbers, vendor information, and warranty information. In many cases, network administrators keep separate lists for computers and for other equipment.

- *Network history*—This single comprehensive document outlines all upgrades applied to the network, including what problems have occurred along with their symptoms, solutions, dates, contacts, procedures, and results.

- *Network map*—A comprehensive network map includes hardware locations and cabling.

- *Networking hardware configuration*—Configuration information includes a hard copy of each server's, router's, or other networking device's configuration files and protocol information.

- *Policies and procedures*—This document describes all tasks the network administrator performs. Established policies for user and group configuration and naming conventions are prime examples. It should also include procedures for setting up or deleting network users, performing backups, and restoring files. Update this information when necessary. These documentation tasks might seem time consuming, but they pay off by easing the training process when new people join the network. If the network administrator is unavailable, an accurate set of procedures ensures that company productivity isn't affected.

- *Server configuration*—A separate document for each server should list the hardware configuration of installed software (including version number), the type of data stored (file server, database server, e-mail server, and so on), and the schedule and location of backups.

- *Software configuration*—This configuration document defines the software installed on each network node and its configuration data, such as the type of drivers installed, the settings in configuration files, and exceptions to standard configurations.

- *Software licensing*—This document lists each software product used on your network as well as licensing information for those products, including the number of user licenses and the license numbers. This document must be kept up to date.

- *User administration*—This document outlines the types of users defined on the network, naming conventions, and network resource assignment for users.

Keep documentation in hard copy and electronic form so that it's readily accessible. Complete, accurate, up-to-date documentation helps you troubleshoot your network, train new employees, and plan for growth.

Performing Preemptive Troubleshooting

Although preemptive troubleshooting might seem costly in the short term, it saves time when problems do come up, prevents equipment problems, and ensures data security. Also, a preemptive approach can prevent additional expense and reduce frustration when trying to identify the causes of failures. For example, if network monitoring shows a steadily increasing number of broadcast messages on your network, making design and/or protocol

14

changes on your network to reduce broadcast activity or contain broadcasts to a smaller area is prudent. This way, you can solve the problem before it becomes a noticeable performance degradation.

The International Organization for Standardization (ISO) identifies five preemptive troubleshooting network management categories:

- *Accounting management*—Record and report use of network resources
- *Configuration management*—Define and control network component configurations and parameters
- *Fault management*—Detect and isolate network problems
- *Performance management*—Monitor, analyze, and control network data production
- *Security management*—Monitor and control access to network resources

Do your best to cover all these categories by gathering information for each type of management before problems happen. You'll be better equipped to handle trouble if and when it does occur.

Practicing Good Customer-Relation Skills

Technical training programs often place too little emphasis on customer relations. As a network administrator, help desk operator, or network technician, all network users are your customers, and your customers are the best source of information when something goes wrong with your network. After all, users are the reason you have a job.

Build a relationship with your users so that they trust you and are more likely to give you pertinent information when there's a problem. Establish a special relationship with technically adept users in the organization. These key users are an excellent source of troubleshooting information, and they can often help you with minor user issues.

All IT Departments should have guidelines that instruct personnel how to interact with users. These guidelines should include what questions to ask users, how to respond to irate users, how to respond to user questions, and how to follow general user communication etiquette guidelines. Following good communication practices with users helps them have more patience when network or computer problems happen. Furthermore, remember that your users are a key source of information when a problem occurs. If users feel comfortable talking to technicians, they are more likely to divulge details, such as applications or hardware they might have installed, that can help with the troubleshooting process.

Using Network-Monitoring Utilities

Many network-monitoring programs are available to help identify conditions that can lead to problems, prevent network failures, and troubleshoot problems when they occur. Network-monitoring utilities are long-term troubleshooting tools. As a network administrator, you must learn which statistics to monitor. In addition, you must collect data over a period of time to develop an idea of typical network performance. After you establish a baseline for network performance, you can monitor the network for changes that could indicate potential problems. You must establish what's "normal" for your network to recognize "abnormal" conditions when they occur. OSs, such as Windows Server 2003 and Linux, include many network-monitoring utilities. In addition, third-party products are available to perform these functions or to augment monitors included with OSs.

Network-monitoring utilities gather the following types of information:

- *Events*—Include errors, resource access, security settings changes, and other significant occurrences, such as the failure of a program to load or the failure of a service to start.

- *System use statistics*—Indicate who accesses resources and how they use those resources.

- *System performance statistics*—Indicate processor and memory use, server throughput, and other indicators of system activity and behavior.

The information that network monitors gather enables network administrators to take a proactive role when making network decisions. This information can help with the following tasks:

- Identify network devices that create bottlenecks.

- Provide information for forecasting growth and planning capacity requirements.

- Develop plans to improve network performance.

- Monitor events caused by software or hardware changes.

- Monitor trends in network traffic and utilization.

As you learned in Chapter 12, the Windows Performance Monitor utility monitors and tracks many different areas of server performance and can monitor many events concurrently. Using Performance Monitor, you can analyze network operations, identify trends and bottlenecks, determine system capacity, notify administrators when thresholds are exceeded, track performance of devices, and monitor both local and remote computers.

Creating a Network Baseline

To use network monitoring effectively as a preemptive troubleshooting tool, you must establish a baseline for network performance. As explained in Chapter 12, a baseline defines a point of reference for measuring network performance and behavior when problems occur. A baseline is exceptionally helpful for identifying daily network utilization patterns, possible network bottlenecks, heavy use patterns, and protocol traffic patterns. Using Performance Monitor and a network performance baseline, you can often avoid potential network problems. A baseline can indicate whether a network needs partitioning, more file servers, or the increased speed of upgraded NICs and networking equipment.

14

You must establish a baseline for network performance over a period when no problems are evident on the network. After you create a baseline, you can then compare all network performance to it as part of your ongoing network management and troubleshooting activities. For instance, if utilization levels on a 10 Mbps hub-based Ethernet network are routinely 60% or higher, it's time to segment the network using switches to distribute the load or move to a higher-speed technology. Observing utilization levels over time with Performance Monitor helps you determine whether high utilization is an occasional condition or a chronic circumstance. This information helps you determine how best to upgrade the network or whether an upgrade is even necessary.

A baseline is not a "do it once and forget it" process. Baselines must be taken periodically so that you can recognize trends as they occur, such as steadily increasing bandwidth use or an increase in the number of error packets. In addition, baselines must be established whenever you make major changes to your network, such as adding segments, servers, or equipment.

Monitoring with Simple Network Management Protocol

Simple Network Management Protocol (SNMP), part of the TCP/IP protocol suite used for network management, is an industry-standard protocol that most networking equipment manufacturers support. In a Windows environment, SNMP management can be installed through the Add/Remove Programs applet in Control Panel.

A network environment has **software agents** loaded on each network device that SNMP manages. Each agent monitors network traffic and device status and stores information in a **management information base (MIB)**. To use the information gathered by software agents, a computer with an SNMP management program must be on the network. This management station communicates with software agents and collects data stored in the MIBs on network devices. Then it combines information from all networking devices and generates statistics or charts of current network conditions. With most SNMP managers, you can set thresholds for generating alert messages to network administrators when those thresholds are exceeded.

In addition, you can manage many network components with SNMP. Through their software agents, you can configure networking devices and, in some cases, reset them from the management station. SNMP can manage network devices, such as hubs, switches, and routers, and important network resources, such as servers. An SNMP management program can query these devices and even make configuration changes remotely to help managers control networks from a single application.

Using Remote Monitoring for Advanced Monitoring

Remote Monitoring (RMON) is an advanced networking monitoring protocol that extends the capabilities of SNMP. RMON comes in two versions: RMON1 and RMON2. SNMP defines a single MIB type to collect network data, but RMON1 defines nine additional MIB types, called RMON groups, to provide a more comprehensive set of data about network use. RMON-capable devices, such as hubs, routers, and switches, contain software agents called probes that collect data and communicate with a management station by using SNMP.

RMON1 is designed to capture data and collect statistics at the Data Link and Physical layers. RMON2 can collect and analyze traffic at the Network layer and higher layers, which makes detailed analysis of enterprise-wide network and application software operation possible. RMON-capable devices are not inexpensive, but the ability to monitor networks and solve network or application problems before they become serious is well worth the expense, considering the benefit of increased productivity for organizations. For more information, you can find an excellent paper on RMON and RMON2 at *www.cisco.com/univercd/cc/td/doc/cisintwk/ito_doc/rmon.htm*.

APPROACHES TO NETWORK TROUBLESHOOTING

Tackling different problems requires different approaches. Sometimes it makes sense to just try a solution and see whether it works. Sometimes you can use a similar system as a working model, or you might have to buckle down and research the problem thoroughly. In this section, you learn about different methods and circumstances in which some methods work and others do not. This knowledge enables you to try a variety of approaches for your environment.

Trial and Error

The trial-and-error approach to network problem solving is not very scientific, and technical purists often frown on it. Nevertheless, it does have its place in everyday practice and is a method that few network specialists can deny having used. There's a time and place for it, however, and you shouldn't rely on this method exclusively because you can do more harm than good in some situations.

As the name suggests, the trial-and-error method requires an assessment of the problem, an educated guess as to the solution, an implementation of the solution, and a test of the results. You repeat the process until the problem is solved. This approach can be used under the following conditions:

- The system is being newly configured, so no data can be lost.
- The system is not attached to a live network, so no other users are affected by changes.
- You can undo changes easily.
- Other approaches would take considerably more time than a few trial-and-error attempts.

14

- There are few possible causes of the problem, which makes your educated guess at the solution a good bet.

- No documentation and other resources are available to draw on to arrive at a solution more scientifically.

As mentioned, it's not always wise to just try something and see whether it works. Changes made to one system on a network can affect other nodes or make an existing problem worse. The trial-and-error method isn't advisable under these conditions:

- A server or internetworking device is live on the network.

- The problem is being discussed over the phone and you're instructing an untrained user.

- You aren't sure of the consequences of the solutions you propose.

- You have no sure way to undo the changes after they're made.

- Other approaches will take about the same amount of time as the trial-and-error approach.

If you determine that trial and error is the right approach for your problem, however, you should follow some guidelines:

- Make only one change at a time before testing the results. That way, if the problem is solved, you know which change is the solution. You can add this information to your network support documentation for future use.

- Avoid making changes that might affect the operation of a live network. For example, if you suspect an incorrect TCP/IP address, don't change the address without first verifying that the new address is available to be used. Using an address that's not available could cause another device to stop working.

- Document the original settings of hardware and software before making changes so that you can put the system back to its original state.

- Avoid making a change that can destroy user data unless a known good backup exists.

- If possible, avoid making a change that you can't undo.

The following examples help you determine under what circumstances this troubleshooting method is appropriate.

You are called to solve a problem on a client/server network of about 100 computers, and employees access the Internet. The problem is that a workstation running Windows XP can't access the Internet. You sit down at the workstation and open Control Panel to check the settings. You find that TCP/IP is installed, so you check the address settings. TCP/IP is configured to use Dynamic Host Configuration Protocol (DHCP). You know that DHCP isn't used on this network, so it must be the problem. You recall from an earlier visit that the network address is 206.17.44.0. You decide to configure the computer with an address that you randomly select from that network to see whether this step solves the problem.

Should you use trial and error to solve this problem? Absolutely not. Although you might have happened on the cause of the problem, simply choosing an address without knowing whether it's already in use can cause a conflict with another machine. The correct course of action is to consult the network documentation that lists all IP addresses in use. This document should also have other settings, such as DNS server addresses and the default gateway address. You must carefully consider the effect that changes you make have on the rest of the network. If you're unsure, play it safe and consult the documentation.

In the second example, you have been asked to troubleshoot a new PC running Windows XP on a client's network. The network is small, has only seven PCs, has access to the Internet through a cable modem and router, and is set up in a workgroup environment. An employee in the company has already done some of the work, such as assigning a computer and workgroup name, but the new PC still can't communicate with other PCs on the network or access the Internet. You find that the protocol installed is IPX/SPX. You suspect that the protocol in use on the network is TCP/IP, and addresses are assigned via DHCP by the router. Unfortunately, this PC is all the way at the other end of the plant, so there's no way to verify this information quickly. You decide to install TCP/IP and configure it to get an address via DHCP.

Would trial and error be a safe, effective troubleshooting method in this situation? If you said yes, that's correct. Installing a network protocol such as TCP/IP is a reversible action and probably wouldn't cause problems. Setting the IP client to get an address via DHCP is safe because there's no chance of conflicting with another station. If it works, you have solved the problem. If not, no harm done.

In the third example, you receive a call from a client having intermittent problems with a subnet. The client tells you that when employees try to access a server on a different subnet, sometimes it works, but sometimes the connection times out. The network has four subnets, all connected through one router. None of the other subnets is having problems. You have seen a similar problem at other networks, and resetting the router seemed to solve the problem. You tell the client to power down the router, wait 10 seconds, and power it back up.

Is this a reasonable way to go about solving this problem? By powering down the router, you affect all four subnets. This action could cause loss of data, time, and possibly even money. Additionally, you don't know whether the router configuration has been saved, so powering down the router could cause even worse problems after the router restarts. Finally, you should never instruct a user to perform a procedure when you have no way to make sure the person is performing it correctly.

Sometimes using trial and error to solve problems is quicker and easier. In fact, this option might be your only way of solving some problems in a timely manner. However, you must be careful not to make matters worse if your proposed solution can affect other systems or cause data loss.

14

Solve by Example

Solving by example is the process of comparing something that doesn't work with something that does, and then making modifications to the nonfunctioning item until it performs like the functioning one. Solving by example is one of the easiest and fastest ways to solve a problem because it requires no special knowledge or problem-solving skills. When most organizations purchase new computers, they purchase similar models and set them up the same way as the old ones. You simply take advantage of this fact when confronted with a problem on a machine.

Some problems can be difficult to troubleshoot, particularly when they involve an OS configuration. In addition, hunting down the problem and fixing it could take considerable time. If you have a working example of a device that's nearly identical, however, you can copy the configuration, or parts of the configuration, from a working machine. This effort might involve checking Control Panel for installed components, copying system files such as device drivers, copying configuration files, or even making a copy of an entire disk.

To see how this process works, take a look at an example. Bill, a networking consultant, has been called into a client's office because two of the firm's 20 computers lock up periodically when accessing a network database program on a Novell NetWare 4.11 server. Bill checks Control Panel on the two computers, and everything seems to be in order. Bill sees IPX/SPX and Microsoft Client for NetWare Networks loaded. The two computers can access the network, but when the database program runs, the machines invariably lock up within a half hour of use. Bill asks whether other computers run the same software and is told yes. He takes a look at one of the computers that's not locking up. This computer also has IPX/SPX loaded, but the client is Novell Client32. Bill checks a few other computers and finds they are using Novell Client32, too. He decides to install this client on the two machines that are locking up. After several hours of testing, no lockups occur and Bill calls it a day.

What is your analysis of the situation? Bill certainly could have pulled out his network analyzer and captured network packets to try to determine what the problem was, or he could have played trial and error with different network settings to see whether he could correct the lockups. However, with several working examples nearby and one obvious difference between the working machines and the faulty ones, Bill did the smart thing by taking what works and applying it to what didn't work.

As with the trial-and-error method, there are some caveats to using the solve-by-example method. Here are some general rules to follow:

- Use the solve-by-example approach only when the working sample has a similar environment as the problem machine. For example, don't compare a machine having problems accessing Windows NT with one accessing NetWare.

- Don't make configuration changes that will cause conflicts. For example, don't change the TCP/IP address of a nonworking machine to the same address as a working machine.

- Don't make any changes that could destroy data that cannot be restored.

In another example, Terry is fairly new to networking but has been asked to connect some new computers to a stack of switches. A similar stack of switches already exists, and she is supposed to make these connections in a similar fashion. Armed with a box of patch cables, Terry starts plugging the computers into the switches. When she gets to the last switch port, she realizes that she must save that port to connect to the next switch. She connects the two switches with a patch cable but doesn't see a link light indicating that the connection is good. She tries another patch cable with the same result.

Not sure what to try next, Terry examines the similar stack of switches and recognizes a button next to one of the ports. It's a two-position button with the positions marked as Normal or Uplink. The button is set to the Uplink position on the existing switches. Because the switches she's setting up are the same, Terry compares her switches with the working switches. The button is set to the Normal position on her switches, so she changes it to the Uplink position on all switches. The link light indicator comes on, and Terry finishes her job.

Is the solve-by-example method appropriate in this situation? Because Terry had an example in an environment similar to the one she was having trouble with, she was able to make these changes with confidence. The switches weren't being used on the live network yet, so her changes wouldn't cause any problems.

The Replacement Method

The replacement method of problem solving is a favorite among PC technicians. It requires narrowing down possible sources of the problem and having known working replacement parts on hand so that they can be swapped out. Sounds simple, and it is—at least after the source of the problem has been identified. That's where the difficulty and the skill come in. The replacement method is effective only if the source of the problem can be determined, and the source of the problem is a defective part. A lot of time and money can be wasted in replacing parts that aren't defective, so you need to apply your troubleshooting skills before you show off your installation skills.

Follow these rules in order when using the replacement method:

1. Narrow the list of potentially defective parts down to one or two possibilities.

2. Make sure you have the correct part replacement on hand.

3. Replace only one part at a time.

4. If your first replacement doesn't fix the problem, reinstall the original part before replacing another part.

Step by Step with the OSI Model

The step-by-step method of troubleshooting involves using the OSI model. In this approach, you test a problem starting at the Application layer and keep testing at each layer until you have a successful test or you reach the Physical layer. This method of problem solving is what most people think of as network support. To use this approach, you must understand how networks work and where you should use troubleshooting tools. Networks are complex, multilayered systems. When confronted by a problem for which there's no obvious fix, remembering the layered approach to network systems can be helpful. If you reconceptualize the problem following the seven layers of the OSI model, you can take a step-by-step approach to solving the problem. To see how this approach works, start by reviewing the simple network diagram in Figure 14-1.

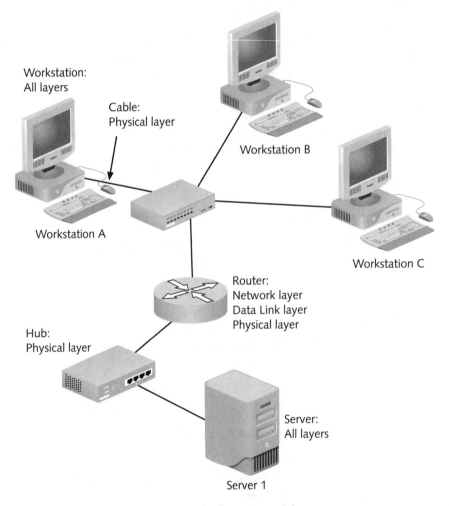

Figure 14-1   Troubleshooting with the OSI model

Suppose the user on Workstation A complains that an error occurs when she tries to access files on Server 1. Users at Workstations B and C aren't having similar problems. No more information is available. When you arrive on the scene, you see that Workstation A is running Windows 98. First, you open Network Neighborhood to view network resources.

As expected, no resources are available. This step involves the upper layers of the OSI model. Now that you have determined these functions aren't working correctly, you can start looking at the lower layers. Your goal is to find the lowest layer at which there's functionality.

You check the network documentation and see that TCP/IP is the protocol being used. You then verify that TCP/IP is installed correctly on this computer, so you know you have functionality in Layers 3 and 4. Time to keep moving down the OSI model. A common tool for troubleshooting TCP/IP is the Ping command-line utility. Referring to the network documentation, you try to ping Server 1. No success. Look at the diagram in Figure 14-1 again. If you can communicate with the router but not the server, you can narrow your search. Try pinging the router. Again, no success.

Which layers remain to be tested? The Data Link and Physical layers. Data Link layer problems most often affect the entire network, or the problem lies with a single computer's NIC drivers. Unless you have reason to believe there's a problem with the drivers, it's best to leave them for later. Most network technicians would move on to the Physical layer because this layer is where problems restricted to one station are most likely to occur. After a brief investigation, you find that the patch cable from the jack to the workstation has gone bad, and you replace the cable. Problem solved.

Many network technicians approach a problem by starting with the Physical layer and then working their way up. The approach you take depends on your experience and information you have learned from interviewing users. What's important is that you understand everything required for the network connection to work, which allows you to test and check all components involved with the tools available to you.

14

THE PROBLEM-SOLVING PROCESS

One of the most difficult aspects of network problem solving is deciding where to begin. What's described next is a general framework for approaching problems that you can apply in almost any situation. The specific actions you take depend on the situation. The process described in this section can be applied to a variety of problems, both in your networking environment and in everyday life. These are the steps of the problem-solving process:

1. Determine the problem definition and scope.

2. Gather information.

3. Consider possible causes.

4. Devise a solution.

5. Implement the solution.

6. Test the solution.

7. Document the solution.

8. Devise preventive measures.

Several steps in this process must be repeated. For example, if Step 6 doesn't lead to a solution for the problem, you probably need to repeat Steps 2 through 6 until you do have a solution. Each step might also require several substeps (explained in the following sections) before you can move on to the next step. For example, Step 4 might require setting up a test environment to duplicate the problem and test possible solutions before implementing a solution on a live network. Figure 14-2 is a flowchart of the basic process.

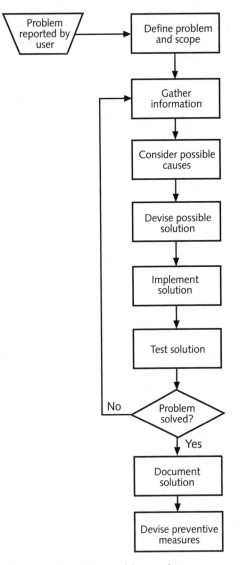

Figure 14-2   The problem-solving process

Step 1: Determine the Problem Definition and Scope

Before a problem can be solved, it must be defined. "Mary's computer doesn't work" does not define the problem well enough to create a plan of action. "Mary can't run WordPerfect because an illegal operation occurs every time she tries to run it" is much better. A problem definition should also describe what does work and what doesn't work. If Mary can't run WordPerfect, stating whether she can run her e-mail program or other applications should be included in the problem definition.

You need to know who and what are affected by the problem. You take a vastly different approach if an entire floor rather than a single user is affected by a network problem. Is the problem related to a single application—for example, e-mail—or are all functions affected? If you're working with routers, is only one router exhibiting problems, or are several routers affected? Determining the scope of a problem is important not only for deciding where to start your troubleshooting process, but also for deciding what priority to assign to the problem. The malfunction of an entire network switch or server demands a higher priority than a problem affecting one user. Determining the scope quickly and accurately, therefore, is not only part of the first step, but also an essential step of the troubleshooting process.

Most network problems come to the network administrator's attention by way of a user phone call or e-mail. This communication is your first opportunity to learn more about the problem. Although this part of the troubleshooting process is more art than technical skill, there are some questions you can ask to start you on your way:

- Is anyone else near you having the same problem?
- What about other areas of the building?
- Is the problem occurring with all applications or just one?
- If you move to a different computer, does the problem occur there as well?

The goal of your questions is to determine a problem definition and scope. If a solution comes about as a result of this interview, all the better, but that's not the goal of this step, nor is it a goal to determine the cause of the problem. Rather, the goal is to define the problem in detail and accurately determine the scope of the problem. Examples of a problem definition and scope include the following:

- Jim can't access the e-mail server. Other servers are available to Jim, and no one else reports the problem.
- Third-floor users can't log on to the network, but all other floors can.
- Sherry can't print to the new LaserJet printer on the fourth floor. She has tried several applications. No other users have tried to print to this printer.
- Bill reports that the network is slow while accessing his home directory. Access to the Internet and other resources seem to work with normal performance.

After you define the problem and understand its scope, you can assign a priority to the problem. Assigning priorities takes a little experience and some political savvy. You must

14

have a clear understanding of what areas the organization deems most critical to its business functions. Creating a document to show management in which order problems are solved when there's a backlog is helpful.

Most IT Departments are understaffed, so backlogs usually are the norm. Besides prioritizing according to business functions, prioritizing according to who reports the problem or who it affects is common. If the president of the company can't check e-mail, giving that problem a number-one priority can be a double-edged sword. On the one hand, if you solve the problem right away, you curry favor with the boss. On the other hand, if you solve the problem right away, you must not have much else to do, so why are you always complaining that you're understaffed? In any event, after you have prioritized the problem, you can assign the support person who's best equipped to solve the problem. After the problem is ready to be tackled, you can move to the next step: gathering information that can help you solve the problem.

Step 2: Gather Information

This step is where your user interview skills can really shine. Most of the initial information you get about a problem comes from users. Knowing what questions to ask and how to ask them can mean the difference between a quick fix and an all-nighter.

Did It Ever Work?

Strangely enough, this question is often overlooked. There's a big difference between something that worked once and then stopped working and something that never worked at all. Users often don't volunteer this information, so it pays to ask. If something worked once and now doesn't, you can assume something has broken the process. If it never worked at all, there's a good chance it was not set up correctly in the first place. In the former situation, you go into troubleshooting mode and continue with the interview. In the latter situation, you go into installation mode and look at it as just another task to put on the to-do list.

To illustrate this principle, consider the following example. Karen receives a call from user Jim. Jim tells Karen that he can't print to the printer down the hall. After determining that Jim is the only one having the problem as far as he knows, Karen goes into the information-gathering step. She asks Jim if he could ever print to that printer, and he replies that he could not. Karen can go into installation mode at this point. This problem has just become a simple printer installation that isn't really a problem at all. Had Karen never asked that question, she might have gone into troubleshooting mode, continuing to ask questions, checking printer queues, determining printer permissions, and investing time in a host of other time-wasting activities.

When Did It Stop Working?

Assuming that the problem being reported was a function that used to work and has now stopped or changed in some way, you need to find out when the change occurred. The purpose of this question is not only to get a sense of the problem's time and date of occurrence, but also to determine what else might be going on at that time to cause the problem. For example, is another application running when the problem occurs, or does the air conditioner kick on about the time the problem occurs? This line of questioning can also give you a sense of urgency. If the user has lived with the problem for two weeks and is just now reporting it, and you have bigger and hotter fires to put out, you might be able to put this one on the back burner. A good support technician must acquire the ability to listen to customers and understand their sense of urgency or frustration.

You might also want to ask the following:

- Does the problem occur all the time or only intermittently?
- Are there particular times of the day when the problem occurs?
- Are other applications running when the problem occurs?

Has Anything Changed?

You have to be careful with this question when you're talking to users about workstation problems. If users think you're implying that they might have caused the problem, they are likely to clam up. Their answers are essential pieces of information. New applications on workstations, new hardware devices, and updates to existing applications or drivers can all cause problems. While you're asking users this question, you need to ask yourself as well. Were any changes made to the network that could cause the problem? Were any upgrades made to servers or were new router configurations implemented?

Never Ignore the Obvious

Sometimes it's easy to get caught up in a problem, pull out the network analyzer, and start some serious troubleshooting. One of the most common problems, which thankfully has one of the easiest solutions, is an unplugged cable. Don't assume that your users will have checked this possibility. Experience suggests that a good 10% of network problems involve an unplugged cable. Maybe the culprit was the cleaning crew, or maybe one of your technicians did it while installing a new sound card or working on a server or router.

Sometimes, you can discover the obvious when you realize that people have their own unique perceptions of a problem. For instance, descriptions such as "slow network response" are subjective; what seems normal to one person might be considered a problem by another. Suppose an employee has been on the night shift for the past year and has recently taken a shift during the day. This employee reports that server response is very slow, but you have had no complaints from other users. Because the night shift works half-staffed, this employee has probably become accustomed to a server operating with a lighter load during the night, which results in quick response times. His idea of slow response might simply be a normal response time for the day shift.

14

Define How It's Supposed to Work

Gathering solid facts about a problem is difficult if you don't have a good definition of how things are supposed to work. Having good documentation and a clear baseline of your network pays off. Periodic baselines are compared with previous baselines to spot trends that indicate problems ahead. For example, if average network utilization increases 2% to 3% per month for several months, you can prepare for a performance upgrade that will no doubt be required before too long.

A baseline of your network should include network utilization statistics; utilization statistics on server CPUs, memory, hard drives, and other resources; and normal traffic patterns. This information can be compared with statistics you gather during the troubleshooting process. It can help you determine whether reports of slow response time are valid and point you in the direction of the problem's source if they are indeed valid. It can also help you know when it's time to upgrade the network infrastructure or servers.

Step 3: Consider Possible Causes

In this step, based on symptoms and other information you have gathered, you consider what could possibly be the cause of the problem. Experience is invaluable in this step, as the more problems you have seen, the more likely you are to recognize symptoms of a particular problem. As you proceed through this step, you'll probably gather more information.

Your goal in this step is to create a checklist of possible things that could have gone wrong to cause the problem. For example, an entire area of a building has lost connection with the network, but no other areas are affected. Without knowing anything else, you could construct the following list of possible causes:

- The connection in the main wiring closet to the rest of the network has failed.
- The hub or switch to which all workstations are connected has lost power or completely failed in some way.
- All workstations have acquired a virus through the network, and the virus affects their network connection.
- A major upgrade has been performed recently on all workstations in that area, and an incorrect network protocol was installed.

You could create quite a list if you put your mind to it. Of course, during Step 2, you would probably have eliminated all but a few of the possible causes. If you find yourself with a long list of possible causes, you likely need to go back to Step 2 and gather more information. After you have created a list of possible causes, you can investigate each one and rule out or confirm it. In the previous example, you would probably check the wiring closet to see the status of devices there, or if you had a network management program, you could verify the health of wiring closet devices remotely.

Step 4: Devise a Solution

After determining a likely cause, you can devise a solution. In the example discussed in Step 3, assuming the cause of the problem is a failed hub, devising the solution is easy: Replace the hub. Suppose, however, that many users have reported a periodic loss of connection to certain resources. After you have gathered information and considered possible causes, you find that several routers become overutilized periodically and start dropping packets. This problem is not so simple. You don't want to rush in and replace the problem routers with bigger, stronger, faster routers because that solution could affect other routers or other network components. Is the problem with the routers, or are the dropped packets simply another symptom of the problem? You don't really know.

Before devising a solution, it's important to consider the following:

- Is the identified cause of the problem truly the cause, or is it just another symptom of the problem's true cause?

- Is there a way to adequately test the proposed solution?

- What results should the proposed solution produce?

- What are the ramifications of the proposed solution for the rest of the network?

- Do you need additional help to answer some of these questions?

The last question is a sore point for many network professionals. However, being an expert in everything is impossible, and some network problems can be too complex or the equipment needed to answer questions is too expensive for many IT Departments. A broken network that results in reduced productivity and, therefore, lost money can be more expensive than calling in experts occasionally.

After you have the solution, it's time to carry it out immediately, right? Wrong. Before you implement the solution, you must be prepared for the possibility that it could make things worse than the existing problem. Whether your problem and proposed solution affect an entire network or just a few users, you must devise a rollback plan so that you can return things to their original state if the solution doesn't work. Depending on the scope of the problem and solution, you might need to do the following:

- Save all network device configuration files.

- Document and back up workstation configurations.

- Document wiring closet configurations, including device locations and patch cable connections.

- Conduct a final baseline to compare new and old results if a rollback becomes necessary.

14

Step 5: Implement the Solution

If you have done a good job with the first four steps, the implementation step should go fairly smoothly. During this step, you create opportunities for intermediate testing and inform users of your intentions. Then you put the plan into action.

Create Intermediate Testing Opportunities

You need to design the implementation so that you can stop and test it at critical points, instead of testing the completed solution only to find that something doesn't work. Testing small steps in which a limited number of things could go wrong is far easier than testing a complex solution with dozens or hundreds of problem areas.

Suppose your solution is to add a network segment to your internetwork to alleviate broadcast problems. You have purchased a new router and a switch to accommodate the workstations that will form the new segment. One way to go about this solution is to hook up all the equipment, configure the router and switch, assign new addresses to workstations, plug in all the cables, and then hope for the best. When that method doesn't work, however, where do you start looking? Is the problem the router configuration or the switches? Is your addressing scheme incorrect? You don't know.

A better way to tackle this solution is to have a step-by-step plan that allows intermediate testing. For example, you could use the following steps that alternate between implementing and testing to test the new router and switch:

1. Configure the router.
2. Verify its standalone operation by pinging each interface.
3. Attach the router to the rest of the network.
4. Verify that all parts of the network can be reached by pinging.
5. Use the Trace Route command-line utility to verify the path selection.
6. Install and configure the switch.
7. Configure workstation addresses for the new network.
8. Cable workstations to the new switch.
9. Verify connectivity within the network.
10. Connect the router to the switch.
11. Verify that you can ping the router interface from workstations.
12. Verify that you can reach other networks from workstations.
13. Create a baseline of the new network segment.

A carefully planned implementation of your solution with testing along the way allows you to catch unforeseen results at a stage when they are easy to see and easy to fix.

Inform Your Users

When your action plan affects other parts of the network and, therefore, other users, you need to inform your users of the possible disruption to some network services while work is progressing. Give your users plenty of time to schedule downtime of the network. Nothing can take the wind out of your sails more quickly than getting a frantic call from a boss who needs the network for a big presentation just as you are halfway through a day-long network upgrade.

Put the Plan into Action

After you have your checklist of actions and intermediate testing ready and have informed your users, it's time to take action. Provided you have done everything correctly up to now, this step is the easy part. You have your list of actions; now is the time to carry them out.

 Remember that making only one testable change at a time is crucial.

TIP

Take notes about every change you make to the network or servers. For example, document the upgrade of a driver or the change to an IP address. This way, you know the current state of your network when your changes are completed. A well-documented network is easier to troubleshoot and upgrade in the future.

14

Step 6: Test the Solution

It's 3:00 a.m. and you're finished with the upgrade. Time to go home, right? Wrong. It's time to test your implementation as a whole. If the issue is a simple workstation connectivity problem, you verify that the station can access the resources assigned to it. If it's a major network or server overhaul, however, the testing is more involved. In either case, if you have done intermediate testing during the implementation step, the testing step should be fairly straightforward.

Your testing should attempt to emulate a real-world situation as closely as possible. If you're testing a workstation problem, verification that the workstation can ping a server is not enough. If possible, you should attempt to log on to the network as a user with similar privileges as the workstation's main user. Next, attempt to access applications that would likely be run from the workstation. Take notes about what you learned and saw.

If you're testing a major network upgrade, you have probably already tested end-to-end connectivity during implementation. Now you need to put some stress on the network. Start some workstations on the upgraded part of the network, if possible, with the help of some assistants, and run some network-intensive applications. Access the Internet, if Internet access is included in your network. All the while, you should be gathering information about how the network behaves while you're working it. Compare your results to the results you saw before the changes were carried out. Again, take notes about the results of your testing. When you have tested everything possible, go home and get some sleep; tomorrow will be the real test, when your users begin using your new solution.

Step 7: Document the Solution

If you have made it this far, congratulations—you have solved a problem! It's time to take all the handwritten notes made during the implementation and testing steps and turn them into a cohesive document. This step is as important as any of the previous steps. No matter how big or small the problem was, a similar problem will likely happen in the future. If you took notes about the problem and the solution, you have this documentation available as a valuable resource for solving the next problem of its kind. Your documentation should include everything pertinent to the problem, such as the problem definition, the solution, the implementation, and the testing. If necessary, you should be able to reproduce both the problem and the solution from your documentation. If the problem and its solution have implications for the entire network, including this information in your overall network plan is advisable.

Step 8: Devise Preventive Measures

After you have solved a problem and documented it, you should do everything you can to prevent that problem or similar problems from recurring. For example, if your problem was the result of a virus that spread throughout your network and caused considerable damage before it was found, you can install virus protection programs on your network and tighten policies for software and e-mail downloads. The preventive measure is obvious and reasonably simple to implement.

Suppose, however, that your problem is a degenerative one, in which your network gradually becomes slower and less responsive. Preventing this problem is not as simple as installing some software and sending a policy memo. There are some measures you can take, however. For instance, you can devise certain rules for the operation of your network. For example, you can specify that no more than 50 workstations be installed on a network segment, or stipulate that your Linux servers can have no more than 200 simultaneous logins before adding a new server or adding a new CPU to the server. These types of rules help prevent performance problems in the future. In addition, if those in charge of the budget approve these rules, you have instant justification for an upgrade when the time comes.

Devising preventive measures is proactive rather than reactive network management. If you let the problem come to you, it's always far more serious than if you had nipped it in the bud before it caused serious productivity issues. You might be tempted to pat yourself on the back and rest on your laurels after solving a difficult problem, but coming up with methods to prevent the problems in the first place is wiser.

MAKING USE OF PROBLEM-SOLVING TOOLS

This section covers tools available for troubleshooting, monitoring, and documenting your network. Each tool has its place; experience will tell you what's appropriate for different situations.

Experience

Your most effective weapon in supporting your network and diagnosing and solving problems is your own experience. Unfortunately, people often don't make effective use of their experience. Whether you have been limited to working on computers in the classroom and at home or have been working on a large multiplatform network, there are plenty of opportunities to expand and enhance your experience.

Make the Most of Your Experience

Few people have photographic memories. They see something, say they are going to remember it for future use, and then promptly forget it. Sometimes people remember generalities but forget the details, which is easy to do with computer networks because so much changes constantly.

Take notes about what you see and learn. This advice applies even if you have been in the computing world for years, but it's particularly pertinent when you are first starting out and your experiences are limited. Keep a journal of your experiences. Even if you never read it again, the act of writing information down helps preserve it in your memory for future use. Say you're upgrading a system with a DVD-RW device. After several jumper changes, cable swaps, and driver installations, you finally get it to work. If you write down the type of system, the type of DVD-RW, what worked, and what didn't work, you have a reference for the next time you have to perform a similar upgrade.

An electronic journal is helpful because you can file your entries alphabetically and search for them when needed. Of course, a printout is also useful when your network crashes and electronic documentation is unavailable.

If It Happened Once, It Will Happen Again

One mistake technicians make is thinking that a problem is so obscure that it's not worth the time and effort to make a note of it. However, hardware and software are standardized today, and millions of people use the same or similar components in their computers and networks. So if you're seeing a problem now, you will likely see it again. Make a note of it, and the next time the problem occurs to you or one of your colleagues, you can be the hero by already having the solution in hand.

14

Colleagues' Experience

One of the most overlooked resources for solving problems is your colleagues and classmates. Use the people you know as a resource. They will appreciate your coming to them for possible answers and, in turn, they will come to you in the future. Some people build up a network of colleagues and put them on an e-mail distribution list. When faced with a difficult question or problem, they can easily send an e-mail to several knowledgeable people. There's a good chance one of them has faced a similar problem in the past and can steer the problem-solving process in the right direction.

Experience from Manufacturers' Technical Support

Sometimes there's nothing left to do but call for help. Every time you install a new piece of hardware or a new application, one of the first things you should do (besides reading the installation manual) is enter the manufacturer's technical support number in your database of important phone numbers.

The best time to call technical support is when you have a specific error number or message that you can report to the manufacturer. Be prepared to have a lot of other information at the ready as well. The more prepared you are, the more responsive the support person is likely to be. Information you are likely to need includes the software's version number or the hardware's serial number, the OS and version, whether it's an application problem, and, for a router or switch problem, the firmware revision number. You need to be as detailed as possible in giving the circumstances of the problem or error so that the manufacturer can reproduce it if necessary. Gather all the pertinent information before you call technical support; if you don't have the necessary information, you'll have to call back a second time.

In addition, use some of the troubleshooting methods discussed earlier to rule out obvious problems, such as a defective part. If you have another part handy, use the replacement method so that you can tell technical support you have already tried swapping parts. You can also try the suspect part or application on a different system so that you can report that information to technical support. Again, the more prepared you are, the better results you'll get. In addition, if you have tried all the obvious troubleshooting techniques and can report this fact to technical support, you are likely to have your problem transferred to a more knowledgeable person or to have tech support send a replacement part.

The World Wide Web

If you can describe the problem with a few words or an error message or number, the Web is the first place to look for answers. Most manufacturers put considerable time and effort into building databases of problems and solutions so that their customers can research the problem themselves without calling the technical support line.

The Web is one of the best resources for computer and networking professionals. What used to take days or weeks to accomplish via phone calls and driver updates on floppy disks sent by mail can be accomplished in minutes by using the Web. You can't install a new network card on the new version of Windows you just installed? Get on the Web and download the latest driver. Every time you try to send an e-mail, you get error number 3744? Go to the manufacturer's Web site and enter the error number into a search, and you might get a response explaining how to solve the problem.

Most manufacturers store their technical support problems and solutions in a database called a knowledge base or a **frequently asked questions (FAQ)** document. A knowledge base is a searchable database containing descriptions of problems and errors along with known solutions, if any. It can also contain installation notes and compatibility information. A FAQ is more like a text document with two parts to each entry. The first part is a question the manufacturer has anticipated or actually received from customers; the second part is an answer to that question. A FAQ is more helpful for general installation and configuration help, although it can have information about error messages, solutions, and compatibility issues.

Using a Knowledge Base

The old adage of "garbage in, garbage out" applies perfectly to using a knowledge base. You have to provide a database search program with the right words, phrases, or error numbers to find the information you want. Even then, finding what you're looking for can take several attempts, and you might have to sift through several entries before you find the information that will help with your particular problem.

When you're researching a problem, you should be as specific as possible. If you have error numbers or messages, enter them. With error messages, you get the best results if you enclose them in quotation marks. For example, if the error message says "Too many open files," enter that exact phrase enclosed by quotation marks to get the best and fewest search results. Enter as many keywords or phrases as possible to limit the number of results returned; you can get hundreds or thousands of results if the keywords you enter are too general. If your first search returns no results, cut back on the specificity of the search and try again. After a while, you'll get a feel for the type and amount of information to enter.

Finding Drivers and Updates

When installing a new piece of hardware, a new OS, or a new networking device, one of the first things you should do is check whether bug fixes, driver updates, or new firmware revisions are available. Before you call a manufacturer's technical support line, make sure you have the latest versions, or the support person will likely tell you to call back if the problem persists after you have installed the new version.

Most manufacturers devote a section of their Web sites to the latest fixes and drivers you can download. A word of caution: Read the installation guide or Readme.txt file before installing OS updates because you might need to be aware of special preinstallation items before you start the update.

14

Consulting Online Support Services and Newsgroups

Many online support services are dedicated to technical subjects such as networking. You can use these services to tap into the knowledge of experienced networking professionals by posting questions. One excellent source for finding solutions to problems is Experts Exchange (*www.experts-exchange.com*). This Web site is a subscription pay service, but you can earn points toward your subscription by answering questions posted by members. In addition, many companies use user communities to their best advantage by creating newsgroups or support forums that users of their products can go to exchange experiences and help one another.

Researching Online Periodicals

Given rapid industry change, periodicals that deal specifically with computers and networking can be the best sources of information on new products, trends, and techniques. Many periodicals are available on the Internet, and some offer free subscriptions to networking professionals. Some of the most popular networking journals include *LAN Magazine*, *LAN Times*, *Communications Week International*, *InfoWorld*, *eWeek*, and *Network Computing*. There also are several publications that focus on Windows, such as *Windows IT Pro Magazine* (*www.windowsitpro.com*), or Linux, such as the *Linux Journal* (*www.linuxjournal.com*) and *Linux World* (*www.linuxworld.com*).

Network Documentation

Many network administrators dislike the task of network documentation, but it's one of the best resources for knowing what's happening with a network and what needs to be done to fix a problem. Good network documentation can mean the difference between a five-minute fix and hours, or even days, of troubleshooting.

As mentioned, you should document everything that's important to installing, maintaining, and troubleshooting the network. Your documentation should read like a user's manual for network administrators. You know it's complete when you feel as though you could leave your network in a stranger's hands for a month, and everything would still be working fine when you come back. In a strong documentation packet, you should have information in at least two categories: network topology and internetworking devices. This classification is a general guideline; your network might have many more categories and subcategories. If your documentation is weak in either area, you should set aside time to improve it.

Network Topology

A picture is worth a thousand words, and that statement is certainly true for a network. Your documentation should include a network diagram showing the logical topology and another diagram showing the physical aspects of your network, such as buildings and floors. Complete documentation shows a level of detail down to the floor plan and location of jacks. Figure 14-3 shows a logical topology, and Figure 14-4 shows a physical topology.

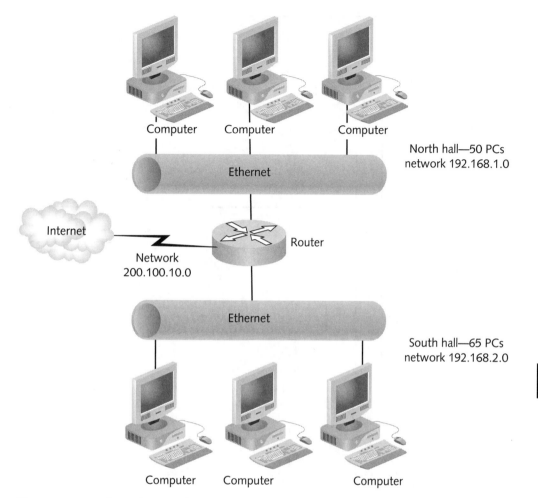

Figure 14-3   A logical network topology

14

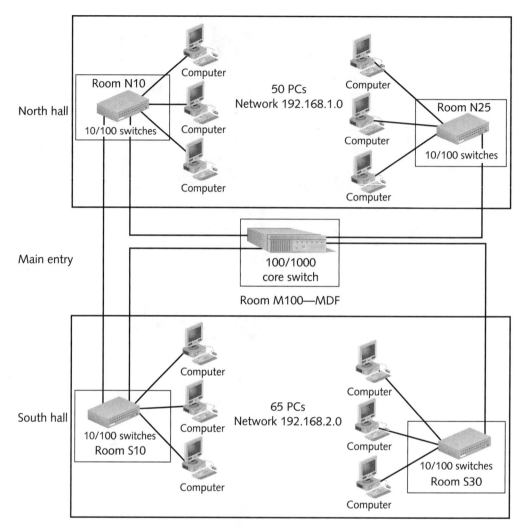

Figure 14-4 A physical network topology

Internetworking Devices

Internetworking devices require different levels of documentation, depending on the type of equipment. Simple hubs require the least information, for example, whereas routers normally require the most. Besides depicting internetworking devices in your network diagrams, you should list them in tabular form, as shown in Table 14-1's example. A similar table should be created for all types of devices so that they can be located and identified easily when necessary. This information also helps with expansion plans because you have the number of free ports available where you can add new workstations and other devices.

Table 14-1 Network equipment list: switches

Switch Model/ Serial #	Location	IP Address	MAC Address	# Ports/# Free
Cisco 2950/ 2117760	Room N10	192.168.1.240/24	00000cab3546	24/0
Cisco 2950/ 2117761	Room N25	192.168.1.241/24	00000cab3547	24/0
Bay 28115	Room S10	192.168.2.240/24	000003f25567	24/4

Additional Tools for Network Troubleshooting

Experience, colleagues, the Web, phone support, and documentation are all fine resources for network support and troubleshooting. Sometimes, however, the only place you can get the information you need is from your own network. Many networking problems occur at lower layers of the OSI model, where they are often difficult to troubleshoot. Fortunately, there are tools for diagnosing these problems. The next sections discuss some of the most common tools and their possible uses on a network.

Digital Voltmeter (DVM)

A **digital voltmeter (DVM)**, also called a volt-ohm meter (VOM), is the most basic electrical measuring device. As used in network troubleshooting, it measures a cable's resistance and determines whether a cable break occurred. When you connect the test leads for a DVM to either end of a cable and send a small current through it, the DVM measures the resistance. If it finds none or finds resistance to be within the cable's rated tolerance, the current is flowing properly and the cable is intact. However, if the DVM shows infinite resistance, there might be a break in the cable that doesn't let the current flow; similarly, higher than normal resistance could indicate an overly long or overloaded cable.

Another application for a DVM in a coaxial cable environment is to connect one lead to the central core of a cable and one lead to the shielding. In this case, if there's no resistance, the shielding is in contact with the core at some point, most often at some connector. Called a **short circuit** (or short), this condition prevents network traffic from traversing the cable and requires repair or replacement of that cable.

Time-Domain Reflectometer (TDR)

You can use a **time-domain reflectometer (TDR)** to determine whether there's a break or short in a cable, just as you can use a DVM to detect a break. Unlike a DVM, however, a TDR can pinpoint how far from the device the break is located by sending an electrical pulse down the cable that reflects back when it encounters a break or short. The TDR measures the time it takes for the signal to return and, based on the type of cable tested, estimates how far down the cable the fault is located. A high-quality TDR can determine the location of a break within a few inches. TDRs are available for fiber-optic as well as electrical cables.

14

Although cable installers use them most often, TDRs can be invaluable diagnostic tools for network administrators as well. When installing any new cables, ask your cable installer to use a TDR to document actual lengths of all cables. Rent a TDR (or hire someone who owns one) to measure any cables on your network whose lengths are not documented already. The TDR function is standard in most advanced cable testers. Remember, each medium has distance limitations, so running a TDR scan on each cable segment is critical in documenting your Physical layer installation.

Basic Cable Testers

You can purchase basic **cable testers** for less than $100. Typically, these testers test only the correct termination of a twisted-pair cable or the continuity of a coaxial cable. They are excellent tools for checking patch cables and testing for correct termination of a cable at the patch panel and jack. However, these testers can only verify that the cable wires are terminated in the correct order or that there are no breaks in the cable. These low-priced testers can't check a cable for attenuation, noise, or other possible performance problems in your cable run.

Advanced Cable Testers

More expensive than DVMs or TDRs, advanced cable testers not only measure where a break is located in a cable, but can also gather other information, including a cable's impedance, resistance, and attenuation characteristics. These testers function at both the Physical and Data Link layers of the OSI model. With this information, advanced cable testers can measure message frame counts, collisions, congestion errors, and beaconing information or broadcast storms. Therefore, they combine the characteristics of a DVM, a TDR, and a protocol analyzer (discussed later in this section).

Oscilloscopes

Oscilloscopes are advanced pieces of electronic equipment that measure signal voltage over time. When used with a TDR, an oscilloscope can help identify shorts, sharp bends or crimps in a cable, cable breaks, and attenuation problems.

Network Monitors

Network monitors are software packages that can track all or part of the network traffic. By examining the packets sent across the network, a network monitor can track information such as packet type, errors, and traffic to and from each computer. These network monitors can collect this data and generate reports and graphs. Windows Server 2000/2003 includes Network Monitor, a scaled-down version of a full-blown network monitor that can monitor network traffic coming into and going out of the machine on which it's installed. Microsoft also produces an advanced version of Network Monitor that can measure traffic on the entire network segment, but this product ships only with Systems Management Server (SMS).

Other common network monitors for Windows networks include WildPacket's EtherPeek, Network Instruments Analyst/Probe, and Information Systems Manager Inc.'s PerfMan. Many of these programs, such as EtherPeek, also capture and decode network traffic, which allows them to qualify as software-only protocol analyzers.

Protocol Analyzers

Perhaps the most advanced network troubleshooting device available, a protocol analyzer evaluates the network's overall health by monitoring all traffic. This tool not only monitors the traffic in real time, but also captures traffic and decodes received packets. Protocol analyzers can look inside received packets to determine the cause of the problem. Because they can generate statistics based on network traffic, they provide a good indication of network cabling, software, file server operations, workstation operations, and NICs. For instance, you could use Network Monitor in Windows Server 2003 to track down a network problem in which virtual machines running on the network are receiving duplicate IP addresses. After capturing the packets generated by DHCP, you could determine that the virtual machines have duplicate MAC addresses, which causes DHCP to send the same IP address to each machine. You could then configure the software to eliminate the reason for the duplicate MAC addresses and solve the problem.

The most advanced protocol analyzers combine hardware and software in a self-contained unit. These analyzers sometimes include a built-in TDR to help determine the network's status. Some examples of protocol analyzers include the following:

14

- *Network General Sniffer*—The Sniffer product line ranges from software solutions to help analyze traffic on a small LAN or LAN segment to hardware-based products that can help troubleshoot a large enterprise network. Sniffer is often considered the performance standard in the industry for protocol analysis and network troubleshooting. You can read more about Sniffer products at *www.networkgeneral.com*.

- *WildPacket EtherPeek*—EtherPeek is an outstanding software-only protocol analyzer that handles all major networking protocols. For more information, visit *www.wildpackets.com*.

- *Fluke Network Protocol Inspector*—Protocol Inspector is another software-based protocol analyzer that handles AppleTalk, TCP/IP, IPX/SPX, SMB, and Application-layer protocols for a wide range of applications. You can use Protocol Inspector in a distributed fashion by loading remote agents on computers throughout your network. These agents then forward captured data to a computer running the console software that decodes and displays the data. For more information, visit *www.flukenetworks.com*.

- *Ethereal*—This popular free protocol analyzer is available for both Windows and Linux/UNIX environments. It supports all major protocols and a number of lesser-known protocols as well. For more information and to download this software, visit *www.ethereal.com*.

Most experienced network administrators rely on protocol analyzers to establish baselines for network performance and to troubleshoot their networks, especially when they suspect software problems or when network (Layer 3) devices appear to be responsible for network problems.

COMMON TROUBLESHOOTING SITUATIONS

Consider the following problem on a network: 10 Mbps hubs were being replaced with 100 Mbps switches. It was confirmed that all NICs could support 100 Mbps, but certain stations simply wouldn't communicate on the network. After some investigation, it was determined that the NIC driver software was set to force the NIC to communicate at 10 Mbps in half-duplex mode, whereas the switch was set to communicate only at 100 Mbps in full-duplex mode. A quick change in the NIC configuration solved the problem.

Using the structured problem-solving approach to network troubleshooting described earlier, you can eventually solve networking problems such as this one. To help get you started with this sometimes arduous exercise, this section outlines some common network problems and possible solutions.

Cabling and Related Components

As mentioned earlier, the majority of networking problems occur at the Physical layer and include problems with cables, connectors, and NICs. The first step in troubleshooting these problems is to determine whether the problem lies with the cable or the computer. One easy way to do this is to connect another computer—ideally, a portable PC—to the cable. If the portable PC functions normally, you can conclude that the problem lies with the original computer. If the portable PC exhibits the same symptoms, first check the cable, and then check the hub or whatever device it connects to, and so forth.

After you determine that the cable is the likeliest culprit, check that it's connected to the computer correctly, and verify that it's the right type of cable for the connection. Make sure you use the same type of UTP cable throughout the network. Double-check cable lengths to make sure you don't exceed the maximum length limitation for that medium. By using a TDR or DVM, you can identify and correct these types of problems quickly.

If you suspect a faulty or misconfigured NIC, check the back of the card. As discussed earlier, the NIC might have light indicators to show whether it's functioning and its network connection is active. If the NIC lacks these indicators, you must replace the suspect NIC with a known working NIC—in much the same way you replace a suspect computer with a known working one to determine whether the network or the computer is the cause of the problem.

If the NIC seems functional and you're using TCP/IP, try using the Ping utility to check connectivity to other computers. (Hands-On Project 14-5 shows how to use the Ping utility.) If the NIC works but the computer still can't access the network, you might have more serious hardware problems (for example, a faulty bus slot), or NIC configuration settings could be invalid. Either way, you must conduct further troubleshooting.

Power Fluctuations

Power fluctuations in a building—caused by an electrical storm or power failure, for example—can affect computers adversely. First, verify that servers are up and functioning. When possible, remind users that it takes a few minutes for servers to come back online after a power outage.

One way to eliminate the effects of power fluctuations, especially on servers, is to connect them to uninterruptible power supplies (UPSs). UPS systems provide battery power to computers so that they can be shut down without data loss. Some available packages perform shutdowns automatically, thereby eliminating the need for human intervention when power failures or severe power fluctuations occur.

Upgrades

Because networking technology changes constantly, frequent upgrades of equipment and software, such as the file server's OS, are necessary. During these upgrades, it's common for some equipment to run on an old OS and some to run on a new one. When you perform network upgrades, remember three important points:

14

- Ignoring upgrades to new software releases and new hardware can lead to a situation in which a complete network overhaul is necessary because many upgrades build on top of others. If administrators don't keep current, they might need to do an overwhelming amount of research and endure a lack of technical support for older software or hardware. Keep current and do one upgrade at a time to make your life easier.

- Test any upgrade before deploying it on your production network. Ideally, use a test laboratory where you can try all upgrades and work out any problems. If a test lab isn't an option, select a small part of your network—one department or a few users—and perform the upgrade. This method gives you an opportunity to work through possible issues before imposing changes (and the problems that sometimes go with them) on the entire network.

- Don't forget to tell users about upgrades. A well-informed user is an understanding user. Everyone who might be affected by an upgrade must be informed when it will occur, what is involved, and what to expect.

Poor Network Performance

If all goes well, the network monitoring and planning you do ensures that the network performs optimally. However, you might notice that your network slows down; this problem can happen quickly, or it might be a gradual deterioration. Whether performance problems manifest themselves slowly or suddenly and acutely, answering the following questions should help pinpoint the causes:

- What has changed since the last time the network functioned normally?

- Has new equipment been added to the network?

- Have new applications been added to computers on the network?

- Is someone playing electronic games across the network? (You would be surprised at the amount of traffic networked games can generate.)

- Are there new users on the network? How many?

- Could any other new equipment, such as a generator, cause interference near the network?

If new users, added equipment, or newly introduced applications seem to degrade network performance, it might be time to consider expanding your network and adding equipment to limit or contain network traffic. Higher-speed backbones, network partitions, additional servers, bridges, and routers are alternatives worth considering when you must increase capacity to accommodate usage levels that have grown beyond your network's current capabilities.

CHAPTER SUMMARY

- A key part of network management is planning and documentation, which includes setting backup schedules and guidelines, security guidelines, hardware and software standards, and upgrade guidelines. Be sure to create written plans, policies, and procedures to cover these topics.

- You should also maintain a complete set of network documentation that includes a network map, a cable map, an equipment list, a server configuration document, a software configuration document, an address list, a user administration document, a software licensing document, a contact list, a network hardware configuration document, a network history, and a comprehensive list of policies and procedures.

- Preemptive troubleshooting and customer-relation skills often aren't emphasized enough in managing a network. Preventing problems before they start and having a good relationship with network users make network management and troubleshooting considerably easier.

- Many programs are available to assist with network monitoring. Using these tools to monitor your network, you can establish a network-performance baseline against which to identify anomalies. Performance Monitor, included with Windows XP and Windows Server 2000/2003, is a valuable network-monitoring tool for establishing a baseline and tracking network performance. SNMP is a specialized TCP/IP protocol for network monitoring and management. With an SNMP manager program, you can manage and monitor most network devices. RMON software probes can provide detailed network and application information. RMON1 works at the Data Link and Physical layers, and RMON2 can analyze data from the Network layer to the Application layer.

❏ A number of approaches can be taken when troubleshooting a problem, and each has its place in the troubleshooting process. Care must be taken that the right approach is used for a given circumstance.

❏ The problem-solving process involves eight steps, some of which must be repeated if a solution is hard to devise. One of the most difficult but important steps is gathering accurate and relevant information, which is where a good relationship with users is important. The last step, devising preventive measures, is proactive network management.

❏ Many tools and resources are available to help you troubleshoot your network. In addition to hardware specially designed for network troubleshooting, software and Internet resources are available. With these resources, you can tap into a vast amount of knowledge amassed by networking professionals. Don't forget to use the knowledge you have gained from your own and your colleagues' experience.

❏ Network documentation is an indispensable tool that can help with network troubleshooting and facilitate upgrades and expansion.

❏ Change is the most common cause of network problems. When problems occur, always try to identify what's changed recently to help you decide whether the change might be causing the problem. Common sources of problem-causing changes include adding new equipment or software, upgrading existing software or equipment, and workload or workplace behavior that manifests in increased network traffic or use.

14

KEY TERMS

cable testers — Network troubleshooting devices that can test for cable defects, monitor network collisions, and monitor network congestion.

digital voltmeter (DVM) — A network troubleshooting tool that measures voltage, amperage, and resistance on a cable or other conductive element.

frequently asked questions (FAQ) — A Web document with two parts to each entry. The first part is a question the manufacturer has anticipated or received from customers; the second part is an answer to that question.

management information base (MIB) — A set of objects containing information about a networking device that SNMP uses to manage that device.

network monitors — Software that monitors network traffic and gathers information about packet types, errors, and packet traffic to and from each computer.

oscilloscopes — Network troubleshooting devices that measure the signal voltage per amount of time. When used with a TDR, they can help define cable problems. *See also* time-domain reflectometer (TDR).

preemptive troubleshooting — A method of forestalling network problems by planning in advance and performing regular network maintenance.

Remote Monitoring (RMON) — Specialized software that gathers network data and provides statistics to a network management console.

rollback plan — Part of an upgrade plan that provides instructions on how to undo the upgrade if problems happen during the upgrade.

short circuit — A condition that occurs when conductors that are normally insulated from one another establish a connection. In a coaxial cable, if the shield and the internal conductor become connected, the cable stops functioning because the short circuit blocks all network traffic; the same condition can occur in twisted-pair cable if two or more of the paired wires become connected.

software agents — Part of the SNMP structure loaded on to each device to be monitored.

time-domain reflectometer (TDR) — A network troubleshooting device that can determine whether there's a break or short in the cable and, if so, approximately how far down the cable it's located.

troubleshooting — The process of detecting problems, identifying causes or contributing factors, and applying necessary workarounds or repairs to eliminate their effects.

REVIEW QUESTIONS

1. A(n) _____ can determine whether a cable break or short exists and approximately how far down the cable it's located.

   a. oscilloscope

   b. volt-ohm meter

   c. time-domain reflectometer

   d. protocol analyzer

2. At what level of the OSI model do most networking problems occur?

   a. Physical

   b. Network

   c. Transport

   d. Session

3. A(n) _____ is a simple network troubleshooting device that measures voltage, resistance, and current flow on a cable.

   a. oscilloscope

   b. digital voltmeter

   c. time-domain reflectometer

   d. protocol analyzer

4. What categories of network management does ISO define? (Choose all that apply.)

   a. accounting management

   b. configuration management

   c. application management

   d. performance management

   e. user management

   f. security management

   g. fault management

5. Which type of plan facilitates returning a network to its preupgrade state?

   a. backup plan

   b. rollback plan

   c. upgrade plan

   d. downgrade plan

6. Based on the eight-step problem-solving process discussed in this chapter, what is the first step in network troubleshooting?

   a. Devise a solution.

   b. Consider possible causes.

   c. Test the cables.

   d. Determine the problem definition and scope.

7. Which problem-solving approach requires a solid understanding of how networks work?

   a. trial and error

   b. step by step with the OSI model

   c. solve by example

   d. the replacement method

8. Under which conditions is using the trial-and-error approach not advisable? (Choose all that apply.)

   a. You can undo changes easily.

   b. A server or network device is live on the network.

   c. You can't undo changes easily.

   d. No data can be lost.

9. The _____ method of problem solving requires having known working replacement parts.

10. The _____ layer is where problems restricted to one station are likely to occur.

   a. Data Link

   b. Transport

   c. Physical

   d. Presentation

14

11. After implementing a solution, what is the next step?

    a. Document the solution.

    b. Test the solution.

    c. Devise preventive measures.

    d. Consider possible causes.

12. List in order the eight steps of the problem-solving process described in this chapter.

13. What is the most common network problem you're likely to encounter?

    a. application problems

    b. system problems

    c. cabling problems

    d. protocol problems

14. Which of the following can be used to prevent data loss during a power fluctuation or failure?

    a. TDR

    b. UPS

    c. DVM

    d. VOM

15. Which of the following is an element of the information-gathering step in the problem-solving process? (Choose all that apply.)

    a. Find out whether the function ever worked.

    b. Determine whether something has changed.

    c. Compare the current operation to a baseline.

    d. Consider possible causes.

16. When measuring network performance, what do you need as a point of reference?

17. _____ is the TCP/IP protocol used to configure and watch network resources.

    a. ICMP

    b. SNMP

    c. DHCP

    d. SMTP

18. A logical topology includes jack locations and room numbers. True or False?

19. What condition occurred if the resistance between the shielding and the conductive core of coaxial cable reads zero?

    a. open circuit

    b. cable break

    c. short circuit

    d. nothing (condition is normal)

20. What utility can test whether two stations can communicate through TCP/IP?

21. What tool does its job by measuring the amount of time it takes for a signal to travel the length of the cable and back?

22. What is an advanced network-monitoring protocol that has more capabilities than SNMP?

    a. SNMP-2

    b. RMON

    c. TDR

    d. DVM

23. For which of the following network conditions must you use a protocol analyzer or network monitor for further diagnosis? (Choose all that apply.)

    a. cable break

    b. cable short

    c. slow network performance

    d. high rate of transmission errors

24. At what layer of the OSI model does a DVM operate?

    a. Layer 1, Physical

    b. Layer 2, Data Link

    c. Layer 3, Network

    d. Layer 4, Transport

25. At what layers of the OSI model does a protocol analyzer operate?

14

Hands-On Projects

In these projects, you outline and describe the current status of your documentation, and use Network Monitor in Windows Server 2003 to check network functions. You also install SNMP in Windows Server 2003 and troubleshoot IP network access from Windows XP. In addition, you download and install a free protocol analyzer called Ethereal.

Hands-On Project 14-1

To document your current network configuration, follow these steps:

1. On a blank page, outline the documentation you know currently exists for your network.

2. List the diagrams, standards, policies, and procedures you must still develop.

3. Create a draft for one of the missing standards.

Hands-On Project 14-2

In this project, you learn how to install Network Monitor on Windows Server 2003.

You must have access to a computer with Windows Server 2003 with TCP/IP installed and a connection to the Internet or a local TCP/IP-based network.

NOTE

Network Monitor consists of two components: the monitor interface tools and a monitoring agent. You can install the agent only or both the tools and agent. If you install the agent only, you can't configure or view data captures unless you use Network Monitor tools from Systems Management Server (SMS), which also includes remote monitoring capabilities. By installing tools and agent both, you can configure and view data captures locally.

To install Network Monitor on Windows Server 2003, follow these steps:

1. Click **Start**, **Control Panel**, and then click the **Add or Remove Programs** link.

2. Click the **Add/Remove Windows Components** icon at the left.

3. In the Windows Components Wizard, scroll down until you find the Management and Monitoring Tools item. Click to highlight it, but don't click to select the check box.

4. Click the **Details** button to open the Management and Monitoring Tools dialog box.

5. Click to select the **Network Monitor Tools** check box, and click **OK**.

6. Click **Next**. If prompted, direct setup to the location of the distribution files (you might need the Windows Server 2003 installation CD), and then click **OK**.

7. Click **Finish** when the installation is completed, and then close all open windows.

Hands-On Project 14-3

In this project, you learn to use Network Monitor on Windows Server 2003.

NOTE

You must have access to a computer with Windows Server 2003 with TCP/IP installed and a connection to the Internet or a local TCP/IP-based network with Network Monitor installed.

1. Click **Start**, point to **All Programs**, point to **Administrative Tools**, and click **Network Monitor**. You might see a message asking you to specify on which network you want to capture data. Click **OK**. If this message is not displayed, skip to Step 3.

2. In the Select a network dialog box, click the **+** (plus sign) next to Local Computer, and then click **Local Area Connection**. Click **OK**.

3. Click **Capture**, **Start** from the menu. This step instructs Network Monitor to begin capturing information. In the next steps, you cause some network activity.

4. Minimize Network Monitor. Create some traffic by starting a Web browser and navigating to a Web site.

5. Close your Web browser and restore Network Monitor from the taskbar.

6. Click **Capture**, **Stop** from the menu.

7. Click **Capture**, **Display Captured Data** from the menu.

8. Double-click any listed frame to see more details about it. When you finish reviewing the details, close the window.

9. Click **Capture**, **Addresses** from the menu to open the Address Database dialog box, which shows all network names and addresses stored in the current database. When you finish, close the dialog box.

10. Click **Capture**, **Filter** from the menu. If a warning message is displayed, click **OK**. The Capture Filter dialog box displays a capture filter decision tree. You can edit and manipulate this tree by using the buttons on the right. When you finish examining this information, close the Capture Filter dialog box.

11. Click **Capture**, **Trigger** from the menu. You use the Capture Trigger dialog box to control the triggers that initiate an action while Network Monitor is running and that halt data capture if detected. Examine the information, and then close this dialog box.

12. Close Network Monitor.

14

Hands-On Project 14-4

To install SNMP support on Windows Server 2003, follow these steps:

1. Click **Start**, **Control Panel**. Right-click **Network Connections**, and click **Open**.

2. Click **Advanced**, **Optional Networking Components** from the menu to start the Windows Optional Networking Components Wizard.

3. Click the **Management and Monitoring Tools** item, and then click the **Details** button to open the Management and Monitoring Tools dialog box.

4. Click to select the **Simple Network Management Protocol** check box, and then click **OK**.

5. Click **Next**. If you're asked to insert the Windows Server 2003 CD, do so, and then click **OK**.

6. Click **File**, **Close** from the menu to close the Network Connections window.

Hands-On Project 14-5

When working in an IP environment, users occasionally report difficulties in accessing some remote hosts. Sometimes they even report problems accessing any remote networks at all. This project steps you through some handy IP-based troubleshooting steps from a command-line interface to pinpoint where difficulties might be happening.

This project assumes you can reach a network host. If the hosts listed aren't present or you can't reach them from your computer, ask your instructor to supply a different host name or IP address.

NOTE

To troubleshoot IP network access on Windows XP, follow these steps:

1. Open a command prompt window.

2. To document your machine's IP address and default gateway, type **ipconfig** and press **Enter**. Record the values for IP address and default gateway here:

_____

3. Next, you use the Ping command to check connectivity from the IP stack (localhost) to the local workstation (*IPaddress*), to the default gateway, and to a remote host. The first two Ping commands make sure the local machine is networking correctly, the third one checks the gateway to all remote networks, and the fourth one makes sure a well-known remote host is accessible (that is, the gateway is working to reach external networks). Type the following commands, pressing **Enter** after each one. For *IPaddress* and *gateway*, substitute the values you recorded in Step 2. For *remote host*, substitute **ftp.course.com** or another name your instructor supplies.

```
PING localhost
PING IPaddress
```

```
PING gateway
PING remote host
```

4. Next, type **tracert ftp.course.com** and press **Enter**. Record the resulting data. If a printer is available in your lab, you can print the results by typing **tracert ftp. course.com >> traces.txt**, pressing **Enter**, typing **print traces.txt**, and pressing **Enter** again. (When you're finished, you might want to delete this file by typing **del traces.txt** and pressing **Enter**.)

 Now you can systematically ping all intermediate routers in the path from your machine to the remote machine. This is how you could investigate performance problems (long round-trip times or timeouts) or reachability issues (host unreachable errors) when troubleshooting access problems outside your own network.

5. Type **exit** and press **Enter** to close the command prompt window.

Hands-On Project 14-6

In this project, you download Ethereal, a freeware protocol analyzer, and install it in Windows XP.

1. Start a Web browser, type **www.ethereal.com** in the Address text box, and press **Enter**.

2. Click the **Download Now** button. In the Official Releases section of the page, click the **Download Now** button next to Windows. Click **OK** when prompted to save the file to disk.

3. Close your Web browser. Open Windows Explorer and navigate to the folder where you saved the file.

4. Install Ethereal by double-clicking the Ethereal setup file you downloaded in Step 2. Accept the default installation options by clicking **Next** in each window. When you get to the window about installing Winpcap, make sure both check boxes are selected, and then click **Next**. When the installation is completed, click **Finish**.

14

Hands-On Project 14-7

In this project, you run the Ethereal program you downloaded in Hands-On Project 14-6.

1. To run Ethereal in Windows XP, click **Start**, point to **All Programs**, point to **Ethereal**, and click the **Ethereal** program icon.

2. To start a capture, click the **Start a new live capture** icon on the toolbar (see Figure 14-5).

3. If a message pops up asking you to select a capture interface, click **Capture**, **Options** from the menu, and then select an interface in the Interface drop-down list box. (Your instructor can tell you which interface to choose if there's more than one.) Then click **Start**.

Start a new live capture

Figure 14-5 Starting a new live capture in Ethereal

4. If the Captured Packets counters don't increase in a short time, open a Web browser and go to a Web site to create some traffic.

5. When at least 10 packets have been captured, click the **Stop** button. You should see a window like the one in Figure 14-6.

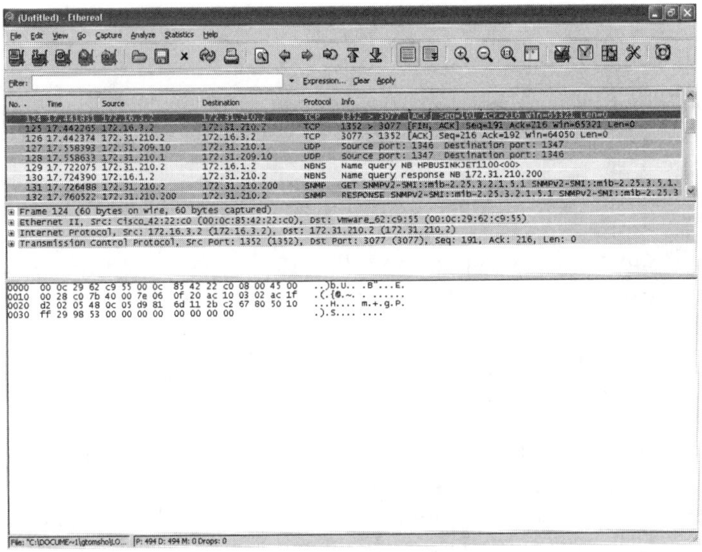

Figure 14-6 The Ethereal packet capture window

6. The top pane shows a summary of captured packets, with each line representing a packet. The middle pane shows details for the selected packet, including frame headers, Network layer headers, and Transport layer headers. Click the **+** (plus sign) next to each entry in the middle pane to view each header. What do you think the bottom pane shows you about the packet?

_____

_____

7. Close the Ethereal program. Click **Continue without saving** when prompted to save the capture.

CASE PROJECTS

Case Project 14-1

A user calls to report that she's unable to log on to e-mail. You respond with a couple of quick questions. Because you know that no one else is using the network right now, you can't determine whether the problem is unique to her machine or affects the entire network. Probing further, you learn that she's also unable to print. You decide this problem is probably easier to troubleshoot from the user's computer.

Using the eight-step problem-solving process covered in this chapter, outline the items you must check and the questions you must ask when you arrive at the user's office. Based on the possible responses to your questions, describe the actions you will take to correct the potential causes of the problem.

Case Project 14-2

Determine the speed and duplex mode of the NIC on your workstation. Examine the light indicators (if any) on the faceplate of your NIC, and describe what information you were able to determine from this examination.

Case Project 14-3

Document the computers, servers, and network equipment in your classroom. Design a form for gathering this information, including space for items such as model number, serial number, NIC card type, MAC address, logical address, location, patch-panel port connections, and hub/switch port connections. What other information might be important?

14

Case Project 14-4

Describe two network problems that can be solved by replacing 10 Mbps hubs and NICs with 100 Mbps switches and NICs.

Case Project 14-5

Describe the types of problems for which you might want to use a protocol analyzer, such as Network Monitor or Ethereal.

A

COMMON NETWORKING STANDARDS AND OLDER TECHNOLOGIES

The discussions and examples in this book and your own experiences in assembling new networks or working with existing ones have demonstrated that a network is built of many parts. These components include the networking media (cabled or wireless), network interfaces and supporting equipment, computers, connections, and many types of hardware. Other network parts include software drivers, networking protocols, networking services, application interfaces, and network-related programs. Given the complexity of assembling a network, it might seem miraculous that networks function at all.

What ensures their functioning is networking standards. At every level of the OSI reference model, network standards enable NIC developers to build NICs that attach to standard cables with standard connectors. Standards also permit e-mail vendors to count on basic delivery services built on the TCP/IP-based Simple Mail Transport Protocol (SMTP) and to get support for attachments of many kinds from Multipurpose Internet Mail Extensions (MIME).

If not for standards, networks couldn't work together effectively because vendors would have to work out the details of managing communication at many levels each time they try to solve a networking problem. Standards enable vendors to make simplifying assumptions about the way things behave, connect, and communicate on networks. This appendix examines the major networking standards, from the Physical layer all the way up to the Application layer, and gives pointers for additional information.

STANDARDS-MAKING PROCESS

Committees create most standards because making standards involves many groups, each with its own special interests and agendas. Therefore, standards invariably involve compromises and alternatives that exceed practicality and technology. Nevertheless, it's possible to describe the general standards-making process. Most standards setting occurs within the framework of standards-setting bodies, industry associations, trade groups, or other organizations that consist primarily of unpaid volunteers, with a small core of paid professionals. As general members propose "hot topics" or specific networking needs germane to the umbrella group, or if ideas come from other possible channels, special interest groups (SIGs) form. SIGs include representatives from governments, the vendor community, academia, the consulting community, and user groups (especially large and well-funded ones that can afford staff to participate in this endeavor). Sometimes representatives from particular factions play pivotal roles in these groups.

Within a SIG, working groups coalesce around certain topics. Each group selects a chairperson and appoints members of the working group, who then address the problems related to that working group's focus and discuss ideas related to the topic. In a working group, constituencies usually propose ideas, which invariably start out based on proprietary technologies or idiosyncratic viewpoints. As a proposal takes shape, it broadens as members of different constituencies work to ensure that their viewpoints are addressed. Over time, these groups work hard to achieve consensus, which emerges from a long series of rough draft proposals that are amended until the SIG is ready to submit a rough draft for outside review. This process can—and sometimes does—take years, but three to nine months is typical. Even so, many rough drafts never go beyond this step because the groups can't reach consensus or because newer technologies emerge and supplant their proposals.

The rough draft is submitted to the SIG for further discussion and approval. Another series of drafts and rewrites occurs. Perhaps the entire SIG reaches consensus that the proposal is worthy of draft status; otherwise, the proposal is abandoned. Again, three to nine months is a normal transit time for this process. The SIG then submits the draft to its parent group or to the body of the entire organization, depending on the organization, for more discussion and another approval process, which results in acceptance or rejection. This process takes another three to six months. If the entire membership accepts a proposal, it's published as an official standard for that group, when designated members of the working group submit it in a final, approved form for publication. This step can take anywhere from several weeks to several months, depending on the size of the proposal document and the remaining work it requires.

Official standards must be reviewed on a regular cycle and amended as needed. Champions or key proponents from the original working group usually take stewardship of standards and perform the tasks needed to maintain their currency and accuracy. Typically, reviews occur yearly or twice yearly (if the membership doesn't call for earlier review) and can take from one or two months to half a year to complete.

A standard becomes obsolete when the organization designates it as such. This designation usually means the organization approved a newer standard to take its place or a subsequent revision involves so much change that the preceding version becomes obsolete, and its replacement is designated as the new official standard.

Clearly, this process is complex and labor intensive. The delay inherent in any consensual process explains why proprietary technologies and approaches to networking (among other fields) continue to play an important role in business and industry. New and improved proprietary technologies keep the pressure on standards makers to deliver usable results as quickly as possible and provide a neverending stream of alternatives. Among the hundreds of industry consortia, trade groups, professional associations and societies, and SIGs in the networking community, only a small number manages the standards with the most influence on networking hardware and software. The following sections describe the most important standards makers in networking.

IMPORTANT STANDARDS BODIES

Standards come from many sources, some more influential than others. Most of the standards bodies discussed here exert considerable influence around the world. Some focus more on hardware and signaling issues; others are concerned more with software. Be aware that many more standards bodies exist than are covered in this appendix. Familiarize yourself, at a minimum, with the main groups and their networking standards and technologies. For an outstanding online reference on all kinds of networking standards, visit *www.cmpcmm.com/cc/standards.html*.

Here's a list of the most important standards-setting bodies, described in more detail in the following sections:

- American National Standards Institute (ANSI)
- Comité Consultatif International Téléphonique et Télégraphique (CCITT)
- Electronic Industries Alliance (EIA)
- Internet Architecture Board (IAB)
- Institute of Electrical and Electronics Engineers, Inc. (IEEE)
- International Organization for Standardization (ISO)
- Object Management Group (OMG)
- The Open Group (TOG)
- World Wide Web Consortium (W3C)
- Internet Corporation for Assigned Names and Numbers (ICANN)

American National Standards Institute (ANSI)

ANSI creates and publishes standards for programming languages, communication methods and techniques, and networking technologies. ANSI is also the U.S. representative to ISO, the preeminent international standards-setting body for networking and wireless communications, and to the CCITT, the main international standards-setting body for telephony and long-haul digital communications.

ANSI programming languages include C, COBOL, and FORTRAN as well as a version of Structured Query Language (SQL) commonly used in database access and programming. ANSI standards also cover the Small Computer Systems Interface (SCSI) used for high-speed, high-capacity disk drives and other microcomputer peripheral devices. A standard PC device driver, Ansi.sys, used to drive character-mode screen displays in DOS (and DOS emulation modes), is a file commonly found on PCs.

The following are among the major ANSI specifications:

- *ANSI 802.1-1985/IEEE 802.5*—Token ring access, protocols, wiring, and interfaces
- *ANSI/IEEE 802.3*—Coaxial cable standards, CSMA/CD definition for Ethernet
- *ANSI X3.135*—SQL database query methods for client/server database access
- *ANSI X3.92*—Privacy/security encryption algorithm for network use
- *ANSI X3T9.5*—FDDI specification for voice and data transmission
- *SONET*—Fiber-optic specification for transmitting computer and time-sensitive data (such as real-time video) across a global network

For more information about ANSI standards, visit ANSI's Web site at *www.ansi.org*.

Comité Consultatif International Téléphonique et Télégraphique (CCITT)

CCITT (in English, the Consultative Committee for International Telegraphy and Telephony) is a permanent subcommittee of the International Telecommunications Union (ITU), an organization that operates under the auspices of the United Nations. This committee's parent body includes representatives from 160 countries, primarily from national Postal, Telephone, and Telegraph (PTT) services. The CCITT is responsible for many standards that apply to communications, telecommunications, and networking, including X.25 packet-switched networks, X.400 electronic messaging systems, X.500 directory services, encryption and security, the V.nn standards for modems, and the I.nnn standards for ISDN. (In these generic standards designators, nn and nnn stand for sequences of two or three digits.)

Because the CCITT works closely with ISO, many standards carry designations from both groups. CCITT recommendations appear once every four years, most recently in 2004. In March 1993, the CCITT was officially renamed the International Telecommunication

Standardization Sector (ITU-T, sometimes called ITU-TS or ITU-TSS), but nearly all resources still refer to this organization by its original name. The CCITT includes the following study groups:

- *A, B*—Working terms, definitions, and procedures
- *D, E*—Tariffs
- *F*—Telegraph, telemetric, and mobile services
- *G, H*—Transmissions
- *I*—ISDN
- *J*—Television transmission
- *K, L*—Facilities protection
- *M, N*—Maintenance
- *P*—Telephone transmission
- *R–U*—Terminal and telegraph services
- *V*—Telephone-based data communications
- *X*—Data communication networks

The V-series modem and teledata communication standards are as follows:

- *V.22*—1200 bps full-duplex modem
- *V.22bis*—2400 bps full-duplex modem
- *V.27*—Fax/modem communications
- *V.28*—RS-232 interface circuits
- *V.32*—Asynchronous and synchronous 4800/9600 bps
- *V.32bis*—Asynchronous and synchronous up to 14.4 Kbps
- *V.35*—High data-rate communications across combined circuits
- *V.42*—Error checking
- *V.42bis*—Lempel-Ziv data compression for modems
- *V.90*—Modem standard for 56 Kbps downstream, 33.6 Kbps upstream

The X-series standards, which overlap with OSI standards, include the following:

- *X.200 (ISO 7498)*—OSI reference model
- *X.25 (ISO 7776)*—Packet-switching network interface
- *X.400 (ISO 10021)*—Message handling
- *X.500 (ISO 9594)*—Directory services, security, and encryption
- *X.700 (ISO 9595)*—Common Management Information Protocol (CMIP)

For more information about CCITT standards, visit *www.itu.int/home/index.html.*

Electronic Industries Alliance (EIA)

The EIA (*www.eia.org*) is an industry trade organization founded in the 1920s of U.S. manufacturers of electronic components, parts, and equipment. The EIA supports a large library of technical documents (many available online), including standards for interfaces between computers and communications equipment. The EIA works closely with other standards organizations, including ANSI and CCITT. Many EIA standards have CCITT counterparts, so EIA RS-232 is the same as CCITT V.24. The EIA's best-known standards are those for serial interface connections, particularly connections between computers and modems:

- *RS-232*—Defines serial connections for modems, including DB-9 and DB-25 connectors

- *RS-422*—Defines a balanced multipoint interface, commonly used for data acquisition

- *RS-423*—Defines an unbalanced digital interface, also used for data acquisition

- *RS-449*—Defines a serial data interface with DB-37 connectors that specifies RS-422 and RS-423 as subsets of its capabilities

Internet Architecture Board (IAB)

The IAB is the board governing the Internet and the parent body for the many other boards overseeing Internet protocols, technologies, research, and development. IAB can be considered the primary controlling authority over Internet standards, but no single body controls the Internet. The IAB is part of the Internet Society, a general membership organization for people interested in Internet technologies and related social issues. (Visit *www.isoc.org* for information on joining.) The following are some important IAB constituent bodies:

- *Internet Engineering Task Force (IETF)*—The group under the IAB that develops, approves, and maintains standards defining valid Internet protocols, services, and related information. The IETF manages a collection of RFC documents defining draft, experimental, proposed, historical, and official Internet standards. Its Web site is at *www.ietf.org*.

- *Internet Network Information Center (InterNIC)*—Responsible for providing information on Internet domain registration services. InterNIC currently contracts this function to third parties worldwide. The InterNIC Web site (*www.internic.net*) has a database you can check to see whether another party already has the name you want to register, a form to report a problem with a registrar, and a FAQ with answers about domain registration.

- *Internet Corporation for Assigned Names and Numbers (ICANN)*—Responsible for managing the Internet's IP address space as well as related domains and domain names. It's also responsible for doling out IP addresses—typically to ISPs, who then allocate them to customers. ICANN took over responsibility for the Internet Assigned Numbers Authority (IANA). Its Web site is at *www.icann.org*, but you can still find information at IANA's Web site (*www.iana.org*).

- *Internet Engineering Steering Group (IESG)*—Executive group that guides activities of the IETF's many constituent elements.

- *Internet Research Task Force (IRTF)*—Works on long-term research proposals, new technologies, privacy and security issues, and other aspects of proposed Internet technologies with social as well as technical implications.

The number and nature of Internet standards is too vast a subject for this appendix. One RFC provides a map to all other current, valid RFCs. At this writing, it's RFC 2500. Titled "Internet Official Protocol Standards," it summarizes all the current official Internet standards. A Web-based version of this document is available at *www.cis.ohio-state.edu/rfc/rfc2500.txt*. You can also search for the most recent version with the RFC-Full Text Search engine at *www.faqs.org/faqs/*. If you search for RFC 2500, you should be able to find any older versions because new RFCs always list obsolete versions of the RFCs they replaced.

Institute of Electrical and Electronics Engineers, Inc. (IEEE)

The IEEE (*www.ieee.org*) is a U.S.-based professional society that publishes many technical standards, including networking-related standards. The IEEE's 802 Committee, discussed in Chapter 5, developed some of the most important LAN standards in use today. After the IEEE finishes work on a standard, it usually shares that work with ANSI, which might then forward it to the ISO. This process explains why several elements of the IEEE 802 standards family are also ANSI and ISO standards.

Several working committees were formed as part of the 802 project at the IEEE because no single group was capable of handling the many topics involved in this mammoth undertaking. The following committees were created to cover the full range of topics in the 802 project:

- 802.1: Internetworking

- 802.2: Logical Link Control (LLC)

- 802.3: CSMA/CD Network (Ethernet)

- 802.4: Token Bus Network

- 802.5: Token Ring Network

- 802.6: Metropolitan Area Network (MAN)

- 802.7: Broadband Technical Advisory Group

- 802.8: Fiber-optic Technical Advisory Group

- 802.9: Integrated Voice/Data Networks

- 802.10: Network Security

- 802.11: Wireless Networks

- 802.12: High-Speed Networking

- 802.13: Unused

- 802.14: A now-defunct working group that specified data transports over cable TV

- 802.15: Wireless PAN (covers emerging standards for wireless personal area networks)

- 802.16: Wireless MAN (covers wireless MANs)

- 802.17: Resilient Packet Ring (covers emerging standards for very high-speed, ring-based LANs and MANs)

- 802.18: Wireless Advisory Group (monitors radio-based wireless standards)

- 802.19: Coexistence Advisory Group (addresses issues of coexistence with current and developing standards)

- 802.20: Mobile Broadband Wireless (addresses always-on multivendor mobile broadband wireless access)

International Organization for Standardization (ISO)

The ISO, sometimes referred to as the International Standards Organization, focuses on defining global-level standards. Member countries are represented by government bodies or their premier standards-setting bodies. (For example, ANSI represents the United States, and the British Standards Institute represents Great Britain.) The ISO also includes representatives from businesses, educational institutions, research and development organizations, and other international standards bodies, such as the CCITT. ISO's overall charter is broad—to establish international standards for all services and manufactured goods and products.

For computing, ISO seeks to establish global standards for data communication and information exchange. These standards are intended to promote interoperability across networking environments worldwide and to allow mixing vendor systems and products without regard to system type or country of origin. The ISO's primary efforts in interoperability are directed at the Open Systems Interconnection initiative (OSI or ISO/OSI). You can find an overview of important OSI standards at *www.iso.org/iso/en/ISOOnline.frontpage*.

Object Management Group (OMG)

The OMG (*www.omg.org*) represents a federation of more than 700 member organizations from business, industry, government, and academia involved in devising a set of tools to permit system vendors to create platform- and OS-neutral applications. The OMG's efforts extend to programming and scripting languages, application and data-conversion interfaces, and protocols. For a fee, the OMG offers certification services to indicate that products conform to standards and specifications agreed on by OMG member organizations.

The cornerstone of the OMG's efforts is its Object Management Architecture (OMA), which defines a common model for object-oriented applications and runtime environments. A key element of the OMG's efforts focuses on Common Object Request Broker Architecture

A

(CORBA), a set of standard interfaces and access methods that permit interchanging objects and data across a wide variety of platforms and OSs. In addition, The Open Group (described in the next section) incorporates the OMG's architecture in its Distributed Computing Environment and Distributed Management Environment.

The Open Group (TOG)

The Open Group (*www.opengroup.org*) formed in February 1996 by consolidating two leading open systems consortia—the X/Open Company Limited (X/Open) and the Open Software Foundation (OSF). Under the TOG umbrella, OSF and X/Open work together to deliver technology innovations and promote wide-scale adoption of open systems specifications. Founded in 1988, the OSF hosts industry-wide, collaborative software research and development for the distributed computing environment. Founded in 1984, X/Open's brand is recognized worldwide as a guarantee of compliance to open systems specifications and now includes ownership of the UNIX trade name.

TOG is devoted to defining and elaborating vendor-neutral computing and development environments with a special emphasis on user interfaces. TOG's legacy from the OSF includes the following main elements:

- *Distributed Computing Environment (DCE)*—Simplifies development of software for use in heterogeneous networked environments.

- *Distributed Management Environment (DME)*—Defines tools to manage systems in distributed, heterogeneous computing environments.

- *Single UNIX Specification*—Defines a common reference model for an advanced UNIX implementation, with support for SMP, enhanced security, and dynamic configuration.

- *X-Window System*—Provides a well-recognized industry standard model for a platform-neutral GUI.

- *Motif Toolkit API*—A well-recognized industry standard for a common user interface definition that recognizes IBM's Common User Access (CUA) model.

- *Network File System (NFS)*—Defines a well-accepted standard model for a UPD/IP-based distributed file system.

- *Common Desktop Environment (CDE)*—Offers a set of tools for building client-side application front ends. Its current release integrates the Motif 2.0 GUI, the X-Window System, and a set of common application interfaces for standardizing application displays across distributed multiplatform environments.

- *Baseline Security Services (XBSS) and Secure Communication Services (GSS-API)*—XBSS defines a base set of security-related functions to be provided by open systems with recommended default settings for security-related parameters; GSS-API is an application programming interface that ensures secure communication when interacting with peer applications across a network.

- *Structured Query Language (SQL) Definitions and Services*—Defines application access to relational databases using SQL embedded in C and/or COBOL. TOG's XPG4 SQL includes dynamic SQL, which corresponds to ISO/IEC 9075:1992. XPG4 SQL also includes specifications developed with the SQL Access Group that allow portability of applications to distributed environments.

The World Wide Web Consortium (W3C)

Founded in the early 1990s in the wake of CERN's decision to release its work on HTML and HTTP to the public, the W3C is the standards-setting body for Web-related markup languages, specifications, accessibility guidelines, and more. Organizations such as Massachusetts Institute of Technology (MIT) in the United States and INRIA (Institut National de Recherché en Informatique et en Automatique, the French National Institute for Research in Computer Science and Control) are involved in staffing and housing this organization.

At first, a Web-oriented standards group might not seem to have much to do with networking, but the importance of the Web in finding networking information can't be overstated. Web-based services are also essential for in-house networks (intranets) and the public Internet. Savvy network administrators must know how to use the Web, and many must also be able to manage Web servers on their networks. Key W3C standards include the following:

- *HTML and Extensible HTML (XHTML)*—Used to create most Web pages
- *Extensible Markup Language (XML)*—The basis for XHTML and numerous other XML-based applications
- *HTTP*—Transports Web page requests from clients to servers and responses from servers to clients
- *Accessibility guidelines*—Explain how to make the Web equally available to all users, regardless of visual or reading disabilities
- *Cascading Style Sheets (CSS)*—Provide detailed instructions on how to display content from HTML and XML documents
- *XML-based applications*—More than 30 additional XML-based applications for everything from mathematical notation to wireless telephone access to Web data

For more information on these and other standards, tools, and best practices, visit the W3C's Web site at *www.w3.org*.

Internet Corporation for Assigned Names and Numbers (ICANN)

ICANN is less a standards body and more a controlling and organizing body for the names (domain names) and numbers (IP addresses and port numbers) used to access Internet resources. ICANN oversees distribution of top-level domains (such as .com, .org, and .net) and helps manage the distributed DNS system, which works to ensure that Internet resources can be located by using names rather than numbers. ICANN is also responsible for the distribution and management of the IP address space and the assignment of TCP and UDP port numbers used to identify Application layer protocols. As mentioned, ICANN has taken over the responsibilities of IANA. You can read more about ICANN and IANA at *www.icann.org* and *www.iana.org*.

A

OLD OR OBSOLETE TECHNOLOGIES

This section contains information on older or obsolete technologies that were included in previous editions of this book. Details of these technologies were removed in chapter coverage to make room for current topics but might still be important for some readers.

Thinwire Ethernet (Thinnet)

Thinwire Ethernet is a thin, flexible cable approximately 0.25 inches (0.64 cm) in diameter. Thinwire cabling is easy to work with and fairly inexpensive to build or buy. (Prefabricated cables in many lengths are widely available.) Thinwire is especially well suited for small or constantly changing networks. Using BNC T-connectors, thinwire cables attach more or less directly to networking devices and to each computer's network adapter card.

Working with the U.S. military, cable manufacturers designated Radio Government (RG) specifications for various types of cable, including many varieties of coax. Thinnet belongs to the RG-58 family and has a characteristic impedance of 50 ohms. (Impedance, measured in ohms, is the electrical resistance to current flowing in this type of cable.) The main differences among the members of the RG-58 family lie in the center conductor. For some members, this conductor is solid wire; in others, it has a braided core. Table A-1 compares some members of the RG cable family.

Table A-1 Well-known types of RG cable

Designation	Type	Impedance	Description
RG-58/U	Thinwire	50 ohms	Solid copper core (U stands for utility grade; not recognized as valid thinwire cable by IEEE 802.3)
RG-58 A/U	Thinwire	50 ohms	Stranded copper core (A/U indicates a tinned copper braid as the center conductor with foam dielectric insulator)
RG-58 C/U	Thinwire	50 ohms	Military version of RG-58 A/U (uses a solid dielectric insulator)
RG-59	CATV	75 ohms	Broadband cable; used for cable TV and sometimes for ARCnet
RG-6	Broadband	75 ohms	Larger diameter and higher bandwidth than RG-59; used as CATV drop cable
RG-62	Baseband	93 ohms	Used for ARCnet and IBM 3270 terminals
RG-8	Thickwire	50 ohms	Solid core; approximately 0.4 inches in diameter
RG-11	Thickwire	75 ohms	Stranded core; approximately 0.4 inches in diameter; used for CATV trunk lines

Table A-2 summarizes the key characteristics of thinwire Ethernet cable.

Table A-2   Thinwire Ethernet characteristics

Characteristic	Value
Maximum cable length	185 m (607 ft.)
Bandwidth	10 Mbps
Bend radius	360 degrees/ft.
Installation/maintenance	Easy to install and reroute; flexible
Cost	Cheapest form of coax cable; prefabricated cables average $1/ft.
Connector type	British Naval Connector (BNC)
Security	Susceptible to eavesdropping
Interference rating	Good: lower than thicknet, higher than TP

NOTE   Research shows numerous names for the BNC acronym for thinwire Ethernet and thicknet connectors, including British Naval Connector (preferred Microsoft use), bayonet nut connector, bayonet navy connector, and bayonet Neill-Concelman.

Thickwire Ethernet (Thicknet)

Thickwire Ethernet is a rigid coaxial cable about 0.4 inches (approximately 1 cm) in diameter. It often has a bright-yellow Teflon coating and is commonly described as "frozen yellow garden hose," which accurately conveys its rigidity. Thicknet is sometimes described as Standard Ethernet because it was the first type of cable used for this networking technology. However, its expense and lack of ductility, or flexibility, have made it the least commonly used type of Ethernet cable.

Thickwire's increased diameter does offer some advantages: better resistance to interference and better conductivity. This means a longer maximum cable segment length and an increase in the number of devices that can be attached to a single segment. Thickwire's capability to carry signals over longer distances, coupled with its superior interference resistance, help explain why this cable is most commonly used for backbones—heavy-duty, long-run cables—that interconnect smaller thinnet- or TP-based network segments.

Thinwire Ethernet cables connect directly to network interfaces, but attaching to thickwire Ethernet takes a different approach. For thickwire, a device called a "vampire tap" is usually used to attach a device to the cable, which in turn attaches to a transceiver. The tap must be installed carefully because a hole must be drilled into the wire, which can result in a short. The transceiver then attaches to a drop or transceiver cable that plugs into an attachment unit interface (AUI) on the computer's NIC or on other devices to be attached to the network.

Transceiver cables can be up to 50 meters long (approximately 164 feet), so there can be some latitude when running thickwire cable; its path doesn't have to snake from system to system. Thinwire, however, must go from system to system because the network cable attaches directly to the network interface on the computer or other device. As long as the

A

distance between the cable and the computer remains under 50 meters, thickwire Ethernet requires less network cable than thinwire. On the other hand, the necessary transceivers and transceiver cables make thickwire more expensive than thinwire. The increased expense of using thickwire, its larger diameter, and its lack of flexibility explain why it's rarely used now for new network installations. Table A-3 summarizes the characteristics of thickwire.

Table A-3   Thickwire Ethernet characteristics

Characteristic	Value
Maximum cable length	500 m (1640 ft.)
Bandwidth	10 Mbps
Bend radius	30 degrees/ft.
Installation/maintenance	Hard to install and reroute; rigid
Cost	More expensive than thinwire; cheaper than fiber
Connector type	BNC
Security	Susceptible to eavesdropping
Interference rating	Good: lowest of all electrical cable types

All types of Ethernet coaxial cable have an additional requirement to create a working network. A connector (a female BNC for thinwire and thickwire) must cap each end of a cable, and a terminator must screw into each end connector. Terminators "soak up" signals that arrive at the end of the cable; otherwise, they would bounce and reflect up the cable, interfering with network traffic. Without proper termination, a coax-based Ethernet network can't work.

The two features that make coaxial cable an attractive medium are its capability to carry signals a long distance and its resistance to interference. However, its relatively low bandwidth capability, coupled with its expense, make coaxial cable obsolete in LAN applications. Twisted-pair, fiber-optic, and wireless media rule in most of today's networks.

The IPX/SPX Protocol Suite

Open Data-link Interface (ODI) is similar to the Microsoft Network Device Interface Specification (NDIS) discussed in Chapter 4. It allows a single network driver to support multiple protocols, thereby enabling a computer to use multiple protocols for network communications through a single network interface card.

Internetwork Packet Exchange (IPX) is a Transport and Network layer protocol that handles all addressing and routing on a network. Workstations use the NIC's hardware (MAC) address for identification. IPX is a connectionless protocol that provides fast but unreliable services.

IPX Routing Information Protocol (IPX RIP) is used by servers and routers to exchange information about network addresses and topology. IPX RIP is a distance-vector protocol that uses the number of hops between points to determine the best path for a packet to take from sender to receiver. In addition to hops, IPX RIP uses ticks, a value based on the expected delay between routers, to determine the best path. Chapter 13 discusses RIP and other routing protocols in more detail.

Sequenced Packet Exchange (SPX) works with IPX to provide connection-oriented services. As with all connection-oriented protocols, transmission is slower but more reliable than with a similar connection-oriented protocol.

NetWare Core Protocol (NCP) functions at the Transport layer and all upper layers (Session, Presentation, and Application) to provide a broad range of client/server functions. NCP handles client redirection through IPX/SPX or NWLink, including printing and file sharing.

Service Advertising Protocol (SAP) is used by file and print servers to advertise their services to computers on the network. Broadcast periodically (usually every 60 seconds), SAP packets ensure that all computers know the services available and the addresses of those servers. Newer NetWare implementations avoid SAP and instead use Novell eDirectory and related protocols because SAP's once-per-minute update interval can cause problems on large networks with many service advertisers.

Service Lookup Protocol (SLP) is a new IP-based NetWare protocol that applies when clients want to look up the services available on an IP-only network. SLP packets locate the nearest identifiable directory tree and ensure that all directory-enabled computers can easily inquire about available network services.

10Base5 Ethernet

10Base5 uses transceivers attached to thicknet by a vampire tap. When vampire taps are installed, a special jig fixture is used to drill through the covering and mesh. The tap makes contact only with the center conductor. A vampire tap has small teeth that keep the tap/transceiver from moving after it's installed. A drop cable connects the transceiver to the NIC's AUI or DIX port (standard Ethernet connectors). Each computer connected to the thicknet cable must have a transceiver and drop cable.

The distance limitations for 10Base5 Ethernet are more stringent than for other Ethernet implementations. Transceivers must be at least 2.5 meters (about 8 feet) apart. Each cable segment can be a maximum length of 500 meters (1640 feet). Up to five cable segments can be attached using repeaters, creating a network with a total length of 2500 meters; the drop cable connecting the computer to the transceiver must be less than 50 meters (164 feet). However, the length of the drop cables isn't figured into the total network length.

All coaxial Ethernet networks (10Base5 and 10Base2) are subject to the 5-4-3 rule, which states that a coaxial Ethernet network can consist of a maximum of five segments, with four repeaters, with devices attached to three of the segments. This configuration prevents signal loss caused by attenuation. Note that the 5-4-3 rule is an "end to end" rule, not a "total population" rule. The difference has to do with how many segments and repeaters exist between any two machines, instead of stipulating the total number of elements in an entire network. This rule applies only to individual pairs of segments, when a node on one segment seeks to transmit data to a node on another segment. Therefore, the 5-4-3 rule doesn't mean a 10Base5 or 10Base2 network can have only five segments, four repeaters, and so forth in total; this rule applies only when tracing a route from a node on one segment to a node on another segment. Plenty of networks with hundreds of segments and numerous repeaters don't violate the 5-4-3 rule because they are designed not to.

As mentioned, 10Base5 networks represent the original Ethernet architecture. However, 10Base5's limitations and the difficulties of working with thicknet cable have eliminated it as an option for new installations in most networking environments. Table A-4 lists the specifics for 10Base5 Ethernet.

Table A-4   10Base5 Ethernet summary

Category	Specification
IEEE specification	802.3
Advantages	Long maximum cable length
Disadvantages	Difficult to install; cost
Topology	Linear bus
Cable type	50 ohm thicknet
Channel access method	CSMA/CD
Transceiver location	Connected to cable at vampire tap
Maximum cable segment length	500 m (1640 ft.)
Maximum total network length	2500 m (8200 ft.)
Maximum drop cable length	50 m (164 ft.)
Minimum distance between transceivers	2.5 m (8 ft.)
Maximum number of segments	Five connected by four repeaters
Maximum number of populated segments	Three
Maximum devices per segment	100
Maximum devices per network	1024
Transmission speed	10 Mbps

10Base2 Ethernet

10Base2 was the second version of Ethernet. Following the IEEE naming convention, you would think 10Base2 could support a single 200-meter cable segment. The original IEEE specification for 10Base2 did permit a 200-meter cable segment, but that distance was shortened to 185 meters to improve performance and to account for patch cables. Like 10Base5, 10Base2 uses coaxial cable, but instead of thicknet, it uses thinnet, which is flexible and easier to manipulate. Also, unlike 10Base5, the transceiver is part of the NIC, so the cable attaches directly to the device. 10Base2 uses a BNC connector to connect the NIC to the cable and uses the bus topology with terminators at each end of the cable segment. The minimum cable length for 10Base2 is .5 meters (about 20 inches).

Although thinnet cable looks remarkably like the coaxial cable used for television, they aren't interchangeable. The IEEE specification states that thinnet must use RG-58A/U or RG-58C/U. Thinnet uses 50 ohm coaxial cable; the cable used for cable TV is 75 ohm cable. In addition, other RG-58 cable types (RG-58U, for example) can't support Ethernet 10Base2.

Like its 10Base5 predecessor, 10Base2 follows the 5-4-3 rule. The 10Base2 limitations on cable length from end to end on a network allow for five 185-meter segments connected by four repeaters, with three segments populated. This creates a maximum total network length of 925 meters from any one end to any other end of the network. In each of those five cable segments, a BNC barrel connector can be used to connect two shorter thinnet cables. Its use should be limited, however, because each barrel connector degrades the signal as it travels across the network. 10Base2 supports up to 30 devices per cable segment.

Because of its ease of installation and lower price, thinnet rapidly replaced thicknet as the preferred network medium. As new Ethernet standards developed, thinnet, too, was eventually replaced but has not disappeared entirely. It's still being used in networks installed in the late 1980s and early 1990s, and you can still purchase NICs and cabling that support thinnet. However, its use is strongly discouraged for new installations. Table A-5 summarizes the 10Base2 Ethernet standard.

Table A-5   10Base2 Ethernet summary

Category	Specification
IEEE specification	802.3
Advantages	Inexpensive; easy to install and configure
Disadvantages	Difficult to troubleshoot
Topology	Linear bus
Cable type	50 ohm thinnet (RG-58A/U or RG-58C/U)
Channel access method	CSMA/CD
Transceiver location	On NIC
Maximum cable segment length	185 m (607 ft.)
Maximum total network length, end to end	925 m (3035 ft.)
Minimum distance between devices	.5 m (20 in.)
Maximum number of segments	Five connected by four repeaters
Maximum number of populated segments	Three
Maximum devices per segment	30
Maximum devices per network	1024
Transmission speed	10 Mbps

100VG-AnyLAN

The Ethernet Standard 100VG-AnyLAN—also called 100BaseVG, 100VG, VG, or AnyLAN—was developed by Hewlett-Packard and AT&T. It combines elements of Ethernet and token ring architectures and uses a demand priority channel access method in which intelligent hubs control network communication. When a computer has data to transmit, it sends a demand packet to the hub, which then tells the computer when the channel is free to send its data. These hubs can cascade, much like 10BaseT, creating a star topology network. A root hub or parent hub connects to multiple hubs, each of which can connect to other hubs.

100VG-AnyLAN is designed to run over any data-grade UTP cable and can be used with Category 3 or higher. In older facilities, it's an attractive option because existing cabling can be reused. However, one caveat is that 100VG requires all four pairs or wires in a typical UTP cable (two to transmit and two to receive), whereas 10BaseT uses only two pairs. In some existing 10BaseT installations, two pairs of wires can be used for data, and the other two pairs on the same cable can be used for voice. In this case, the cabling must be upgraded before 100VG-AnyLAN can work. (It might make even more sense to use a different, less expensive 100 Mbps Ethernet technology.)

The biggest limitation of 100VG-AnyLAN is its cost. The requirements for special NICs and hubs for demand priority channel access and for all four pairs of wires in UTP make costs much higher than those of other 100 Mbps Ethernet implementations. Because of these disadvantages, 100VG-AnyLAN is a networking technology that came and went without making much impact on the networking world. Table A-6 summarizes the 100VG-AnyLAN standard.

Table A-6 100VG-AnyLAN summary

Category	Summary
IEEE specification	802.12
Advantages	Fast; easy to configure and troubleshoot; supports token ring and Ethernet packets
Disadvantages	High cost; limited distance over UTP
Topology	Star
Cable type	Category 3 or higher UTP and STP, fiber-optic
Channel access method	Demand priority
Transceiver location	On NIC
Maximum cable segment length	100 m (328 ft.) Category 3 UTP; 150 m (492 ft.) Category 5 UTP; 2000 m (6561 ft.) fiber-optic
Maximum number of segments	1023
Maximum devices per segment	One
Maximum devices per network	1024
Transmission speed	100 Mbps

B

PLANNING AND IMPLEMENTING NETWORKS

This appendix provides a "virtual blueprint" to help you plan, install, and implement a network. Most experts divide the network-planning process into the following phases, which are covered in more detail in this appendix:

- Assessing and justifying needs
- Creating a network plan
- Implementing the network plan
- Planning for network extensions or expansions
- Obtaining post-sales technical support and information

NEEDS ASSESSMENT AND JUSTIFICATION

Before you plan a network, you must have management support in terms of resources and backing. Resources must include funding, personnel, and time to do the job; these resources can be difficult to obtain and require working within an organization's budgetary restrictions and funding requirements. More intangible and, therefore, more difficult to assess, backing should include at least an enthusiastic endorsement from some member of an organization's executive staff, if not an outright champion for the process. In most organizations, beginning a network plan without both forms of support is pointless.

Establish the Need for a Network

After analyzing your organization's information-processing and communication needs, you might realize that a network is not necessary. Especially in small organizations, the added cost and complexity of a network sometimes negate its benefits. When seeking funding—a key ingredient for any network installation—the only way to justify a network is to prove that its benefits outweigh its costs. The best way to do that is to demonstrate that the return on investment (ROI) is greater than a network's initial and ongoing costs.

Many organizations use formal methods to measure ROI. Before you can tackle this issue, therefore, you need to investigate how your organization calculates ROI. However, determining ROI typically involves only two activities:

- Establish a budget for the planned network that includes all potential sources of cost. In addition to the costs of cabling, equipment, and installation, don't forget to assess costs for employee time (including costs for time spent on design, installation, configuration, and management for IT staff as well as costs for time spent training employees), consultants, and periods of lost productivity, which often occur when changing systems from an old approach to a new one.

- Assign dollar values to the benefits of the network after it's in place. This calculation often requires estimating productivity increases and then using those figures as a multiplier of current employee productivity to estimate increases in the organization's revenue or employee output.

The good news is that the numbers seldom lie. If you can make a case that productivity benefits will repay the network's costs, support for its planning and deployment is seldom disputed beyond some checks to make sure the assumptions behind the numbers are valid.

One of the best techniques to help justify a network and quantify its potential ROI is to document its potential uses and then try to assign each a dollar value. For most new networks, at least some of the following features apply:

- Improved communication
- Automated information sharing
- Improved information delivery

- Easier sharing of work assignments

- Improved sharing of data across multiple types of computers

- Access to legacy systems and applications (mainframes and minicomputers)

- Improved systems management

- Ability to back up all systems

- Improved security and access controls for sensitive data

- Departments or other organizational units taking custody of their own data resources

Be sure to examine these possibilities and consider other potential benefits when assessing the basis for your network's possible ROI. After you get the necessary backing for your project, it's time to proceed to the next step—planning your network's design and deployment.

NETWORK PLAN

Planning a network involves more than simply mapping the cable layout, planning equipment purchases, and selecting the necessary software tools. Because adding a network to any organization involves changing the way people work, considering those people is especially important. Any network plan must include the following elements:

- Training administrators and users to work (and think) in new ways

- Documenting the system and providing key information, such as administrator accounts/passwords and contact information for vendor and technical support

- Procedures for management and maintenance

- A transition scheme to help users switch from their former way of doing things to the networked way of doing things (which might mean calling on extra temporary technical support during the transition)

Working with Consultants

For all but the smallest of networks, unless you're an experienced networker, consider enlisting the services of a qualified network consultant in planning and implementing your network. Remember that consultants deliver what you ask for, however; the more specific and detailed your requests, the better the results. An important step before engaging a consultant is to create an initial statement of requirements for your network and to assess your organization's information-processing and networking needs. This information helps you tell the consultant what you want and ensures that your organization's networking needs are fully met. Many networking consultants or network equipment vendors provide planning questionnaires that you complete to determine your hardware, software, installation, training, and support needs. Always inquire about these tools, and use them if they're available.

You might be tempted to turn your network over to a consultant for design and implementation and devote yourself to other activities in the interim. However, you should schedule regular meetings and ask for explanations during each step toward network deployment, including at least a detailed plan, a schedule of activities, a list of purchases, and a phased implementation of the network's hardware and software components. Doing so ensures that you understand what's happening at each step and provides important opportunities for feedback in both directions to make sure the network meets your organization's needs.

Identifying and Involving Network Staff

Building a network usually requires the efforts of multiple people. Depending on your organization's structure, this effort might involve members of a centralized MIS group as well as MIS specialists from others departments or organizational units. The key to a successful network plan—and its deployment—is to identify and involve these people in the planning process as soon as possible. For larger networks, you probably need the additional help anyway. Appointing a project leader who can delegate planning tasks to team members as needed is helpful.

Knowing Your Organization

The human impact of adding a network to an organization is often the most difficult aspect to manage, despite the many hardware and software elements involved in constructing a network. It's essential to analyze and understand a network's potential impact on an organization and to do the best possible job of matching the network to the organization it must serve. This means you need to understand the following components of organizational culture to create a network plan that employees embrace and welcome rather than fear:

- How well does your organization deal with change? Some organizations thrive on it; others seldom deal with it and require extra support. For change-oriented organizations, adapting to a network probably seems like an adventure; for change-resistant organizations, it's wise to plan for extra support during initial deployment phases.

- How quickly does your organization grow? Some companies plan for growth rates in excess of 100% yearly, whereas others grow at more modest rates, if at all. Whatever type of network you deploy must accommodate and keep pace with organizational growth; otherwise, the organization might see the network as a bottleneck rather than a benefit.

- What kind of technical resources and support are available? Organizations with well-defined IT groups and support mechanisms can add networks to their mix of tools and technologies more quickly and easily than organizations that lack these assets. Either way, access to technical resources and support must be made available.

In the final analysis, successful network deployment is more likely if you work within existing policies and procedures and fit your network to your organization's prevailing mindset.

B

Starting to Plan

Planning for a network is like planning for any other complex system. It requires assessing your needs against available technologies and picking the solutions that best fit your needs. It also requires weighing solution options against available monetary and staff resources so that the solution you pick fits within these all-important constraints. This effort can require a high investment in time and energy and be quite expensive. If it's undertaken in a vacuum, there's no guarantee that this process can deliver the best possible network.

That's why most networking experts usually start their planning efforts from a set of well-known, standard network blueprints rather than from scratch. Drawing on the collective wisdom and experience of the networking industry makes it possible to shortcut a complete analysis of all the possibilities so that you can concentrate on a smaller group of possibilities. Of course, standard blueprints must be customized to meet an organization's requirements, but they can certainly accelerate developing a network plan if they're used as a point of departure. Table B-1 shows the most typical LAN configuration. It works well for networks with up to 50 users; the next step up appears in the third column.

Table B-1 Typical LAN configuration

Component	Implementation	Step Up To
Topology	Switched	Switched high-speed backbone
Cable	Category 5/5E/6 UTP	Fiber-optic for backbone
NICs	Ethernet 10/100BaseT	Ethernet 10/100BaseT for workstations, 1000BaseT for servers
Hubs	Ethernet 10/100BaseT switches	Gigabit Ethernet for servers
Resource sharing	Servers and peer-to-peer	Pure server-based
Printer sharing	Server/workstation-attached printers	Network-attached printers
Other services	Fax, e-mail, dial-up, database management system (DBMS)	VPN, groupware

This configuration is an excellent place to start planning almost any network because it addresses needs at a local level quite effectively. Even extremely large networks can include this kind of configuration for local use, no matter what kind of backbone or WAN links are also required. Because technology changes quickly, however, this recommendation might become dated sooner than you think. That's why all networking professionals should keep abreast of current technology so that they can adjust these recommendations to incorporate whatever version of this configuration makes sense in the future.

Many factors might cause you to adjust this basic LAN configuration and make changes in wiring layouts, equipment, network interfaces, and planned network uses. Typically, these factors include the following:

- *Bandwidth requirements*—For real-time video, high-speed data transfers or intensely interactive applications (such as 3-D modeling), 10 Mbps Ethernet is not enough. Be prepared to step up to 100 Mbps or 1000 Mbps Ethernet or even faster technologies as they become available.

- *Security*—For extremely sensitive data or high-security operations, fiber-optic cable might make sense because it's nearly impossible to tap without detection. Tight security also dictates pure client/server environments with beefed-up authentication and encryption software.

- *Size/scale*—As networks grow larger and more complex, they might need more infrastructure, which can involve WAN links, routers, backbones, and server farms, for example. Be prepared for more complexity, higher-speed requirements, and more equipment as networks grow to serve hundreds to thousands of users.

- *Specialized software requirements*—Some mission-critical applications require specialized hardware or networking attachments; as these systems become more prevalent, complexity and integration issues often become extremely important.

Using a Network Map for Planning

As you make hardware selections and decide on cable types and ancillary equipment, you should adjust the basic network model to meet your circumstances and draw a map of your network. The best way to begin constructing a map is to get a set of architectural plans for the space where the network is to be laid out. Next, incorporate whatever information you can find about existing electrical wiring, HVAC, firewalls, and other site improvements that you must contend with when laying cable or situating equipment. If you take this approach to designing your layout and keep it up to date during installation, you create a permanent record of your network's wiring and layout. It will be an invaluable aid when you need to troubleshoot wiring or extend the network to accommodate growth.

Creating Network Questionnaires

Your instructor can furnish an electronic version of a questionnaire prepared to help you understand your organization's needs and pick the network elements that can help satisfy those needs. You must answer questions on several topics, including the following:

- Network type (peer-to-peer, client/server, or a combination)
- Network technology (size, speed, and scale requirements)
- Network cabling
- Network interfaces
- Network protocols
- Printer requirements
- E-mail requirements
- Data and network security requirements
- Network performance requirements
- Compatibility requirements

Your answers should help you make most of the hard decisions about a network and lead you through the selection process for hardware and software needed to construct a viable network for your organization.

IMPLEMENTATION PLAN

When you decide what network components go where and how to run the cable, it's time to get ready to put your plans to work. In the process of building your network map, you should have diagrammed the wiring layout and location of equipment. You can then address the other factors of devising a working network:

- Plan the order of installation and the steps to connect users to the network.

- Observe the daily routine in the workplace to figure out how to minimize disruptions caused by a network installation.

- Consider the advantages and disadvantages of installing the network over a three-day weekend.

- Test along the way to make sure all parts work correctly.

- Arrange a fallback plan, in case any part of the network installation fails or is subject to delay.

- Learn how to locate and arrange for technical support in a crisis.

- Prepare for things to go wrong (for example, failed installations, incompatibilities, and user errors).

No matter how small or simple a network installation might seem, the chances of encountering obstacles are better than 50%, especially for first-timers. Even experienced networking professionals take time to plan carefully before the real work starts. An installation plan acts as an invaluable road map through the process.

Good Plans Produce the Best Results

A well-run network is staged like a museum or a theme park, in that the users notice only the network's capabilities and services; they don't notice all the underpinnings that make it work. "Staging" means deciding what must take place for the network to be installed and then determining the order in which events must occur to install the network most efficiently. Staging is as important to a successful network installation as selecting the elements, items, and tasks to create the network. As you become more familiar with networking, you learn to appreciate the benefits of obscurity—in other words, networks tend to be noticed most when they're not working correctly. Good staging helps keep your efforts unobtrusive and well coordinated so that you don't attract any more notoriety than necessary.

A typical order for installing a network is as follows:

1. Lay out the entire network on paper, including cabling, network equipment, servers, connections, and other required elements. Usually, you record this information on a network map.

2. Consult building plans, electrical plans, and other wiring plans (for example, telephone, cable TV, and so forth) to check the planned layout.

3. Perform a site inspection to double-check these plans and investigate traditional problem areas, such as elevator shafts, firewalls, and potential sources of interference.

4. Revise the network layout to reflect what you learned during the inspection process.

5. Calculate cable run lengths and determine overall wiring requirements, including the exact types of cable to be used. You must check them against applicable building codes and revise if needed. Then determine the type and number of spools, establish connector types and counts, and establish and order any special items for ancillary equipment (for example, punchdown blocks for TP wiring).

6. Specify equipment needs in detail, including network gear such as switches, hubs, routers, and network servers. Configuration requirements are particularly important for servers, which can contain several internal and external peripherals and add-ons.

7. Draft a bid list or request for proposal (RFP). These documents specify everything you have documented to give vendors a chance to compete for your business. Be sure to ask for installation charges if you're seeking a third party to do this work or issue a separate bid request or RFP for this aspect of the installation, if necessary.

8. Do-it-yourselfers should order any special-purpose tools they might need, such as cable construction tools, and rent or purchase test equipment to check newly installed cabling.

9. Evaluate responses to the bid lists or RFPs—and choose one or more vendors to provide the equipment and perhaps undertake the installation work as well.

10. Do-it-yourselfers should construct an installation plan for wiring that includes the order of installation of cables and equipment and establish labeling conventions for cables (and purchase labels or tags).

11. Install, label, test, and measure wiring or cables. Update your network map, if needed.

12. Install and test equipment. Update your network map, if needed.

13. Test the network as cable segments and ancillary equipment come online. At this point, you should also install and test client software so that users can access the network. Until this point, you have tested only components; this stage represents the first test of the network's capability to permit devices to communicate.

14. Advertise the network to its users and begin training. The network can finally be used regularly.

As this list indicates, you must do a lot of preparatory work before any real installation work begins. The installation plan is nothing more than a document that records all the steps just outlined, with all the essential details included. Experience indicates that the better the plan, the higher the odds of a successful installation.

Working Around Users

No matter how good your installation plan is, you can still run into problems unless you understand the necessity of working around your users. Crawling in the ceiling over their desks or installing conduit when they're trying to do their jobs can lead to users' frustration and irritation. This leads to a sad but necessary fact of life for network administrators: Because your job is to help other people do their jobs, you often find yourself working when nobody else is around. Nevertheless, you must still be available while they work because you're an important link in the chain to solving network problems.

The best way to work around co-workers is to work around their schedules, which means you should schedule the most disruptive activities for evenings or weekends, when other workers are less likely to be interrupted by what's happening. If you hire a third-party installation crew, this means paying overtime and pleading for special treatment. If you can't afford to do this or the vendor can't oblige your request for off-hours service, schedule installation during a company holiday or an off-site meeting or at a slow time of the year (for example, between Christmas and New Year's) to minimize the impact on employee productivity.

A bad experience during installation can sour employees on the network before they even have a chance to use it. If you schedule your activities so that they disrupt work as little as possible, you're less likely to create a bad impression before the network becomes part of the work environment. This effort also improves the chances of a successful network deployment.

Importance of Fallbacks

No matter how carefully you plan an installation and perform the work, it's always possible that something can go wrong during the installation process. An incorrect measurement, an unforeseen obstacle, late delivery of critical materials, or a key technician's illness can cause serious delays. How does this conventional wisdom apply to network installation? Here are some ways to guard against delays:

- Order 20% more materials than you need for installation in case something is defective or to compensate for minor mistakes when estimating quantity. It's almost always better to have too much and not need it than to not have enough to complete the job, especially if you plan to build your own cables.

- Make sure your supplier has additional stock on hand or can get additional stock on short notice. This precaution should cover you if you discover major material defects or your estimates are seriously short.

- Test all equipment as it's unpacked from the box. If it doesn't appear to work, don't try to use it; call the vendor and arrange for an immediate replacement. If you have to return equipment by mail or overnight service, ask the vendor for a return merchandise authorization (RMA) number or return code. Also, ask the vendor to "cross-ship" the replacement, which means the replacement is shipped the same day you ship the defective part. Other alternatives are to purchase a pool of spares or ask your vendor to stock spares for you, should any problems occur with delivered units. The larger your order, the more helpful and supportive your vendor should be.

- Set up a test installation of the network in a test lab or separate room to test network software for servers and clients. (You should have one of each type of client and server you plan to use on the production network.) Build short cables to hook everything together, and then use this environment to became familiar with the software and hardware you'll use on the production network.

- Build an "installation notebook" as you work with cables, equipment, and software. Record all the details and workarounds you discover as you learn how to make this collection of components work, especially any information the installation guides don't include. When you repeat a task, use the notebook to help you shortcut the installation process as much as possible.

If you're ready to deal with shortages, failures, or missing elements, you're also prepared to solve most installation problems you might encounter.

Access to Emergency Expertise

Occasionally, you might find yourself stumped by something that crops up during installation. That's when it's a good idea to bring in a professional. If you're determined to build your own cables, do yourself a favor and find a cable installer in the Yellow Pages before you begin. Call the installer to learn hours and rates before you begin, and ask how to reach a technician in an emergency. If things get out of control, you have a place to turn for help.

The same guideline holds true for network equipment and software installation. Whether you work with a local user group, a network reseller, or a networking consultant, establish a contact list of experienced networkers in your vicinity. You can get free advice before you start, but it's usually worth the money to pay a consultant to review your network installation plan and network map before you start installing. A consultant can point out potential problems you overlooked or even find outright mistakes. The same expert who can bail you out of a jam charges less to steer you clear of it. Regardless, make sure you have a list of names and numbers of potential sources of expert assistance before you install anything yourself.

Transitioning Users onto the Network

Planning a network deployment also means planning to bring users on board and equip them with the knowledge and skills they need to take advantage of the network's capabilities. When planning a transition, your contact with users should include one or more of the following:

- *Orientation sessions*—Show users what they have and how to use it, and answer any questions that come up.

- *Training sessions*—Users often need detailed coverage of new software, tools, and techniques. You might want to schedule some classroom training with equipment, exercises, and opportunities to interact with experts in what employees must learn.

- *Job aids*—Quick reference cards, manuals, keyboard shortcuts, and anything else you can give employees to help them learn and make them more productive are helpful. Check any materials on a group of power users before using them with the general population.

- *Technical support information*—Even when orientation and training ends (and especially if it's minimal or not offered), users need access to sources of help and information. Make sure each user receives a list of Web pages, online documents, and phone numbers for technical support.

The better you prepare users to deal with the networked environment, the less work you will have. A little knowledge might be a dangerous thing, so try to equip users with the right amount of knowledge to handle routine tasks and with the resources to extend their knowledge base as their needs and interest levels dictate.

PLANNING FOR NETWORK EXTENSIONS OR EXPANSIONS

To some degree, expanding a network beyond local confines means incorporating WAN technologies and WAN links. To that end, a WAN questionnaire has been prepared that you can use to assess your needs in this area. (Feel free to skip the parts that don't apply to your situation.) The questionnaire is available in electronic form from your instructor and can help you deal with issues such as the following:

- Dial-in/dial-out connectivity

- Needs assessment for ancillary network equipment (repeaters, bridges, routers, gateways, and so forth)

- WAN link requirements, bandwidth assessment, and link selection

The questionnaire should help you determine what kinds and levels of services you need and select the corresponding equipment or service arrangements. Remember to research and incorporate cost information as well as technical requirements, especially for higher-bandwidth WAN services. Costs can rise out of sight faster than you might realize.

OBTAINING POST-SALES SUPPORT AND INFORMATION

To get help with your network or the software running on it, you must take the right steps. Getting whatever support vendors supply shouldn't be too difficult, as long as you know how to ask for and get the answers you need. This section explains how best to interact with technical support organizations. You can work most effectively with them if you prepare to meet their needs and know how to work with them so that they can answer your questions. It also helps if you understand what kind of help and how much help you can expect from vendor technical support.

Build a List and Check It Twice!

If you followed the recommendations outlined in this appendix, you maintained a complete list of network equipment and configuration information during network construction and maintenance. You should also have an up-to-date map showing the location of cables and networking components. It's important to have a complete picture of what's on your network. You can compile a list of network assets with a variety of network inventory packages, but paper and pencil work, too. Compiling a network inventory can be tedious, but it's essential. Without a network inventory, you might find yourself in a situation similar to trying to collect insurance after your house burns down with no list of what was inside. Record each NIC on your LAN, what type of file servers you use, information about each workstation, and which applications each user runs. The following list shows the kinds of equipment and software to inventory:

- Cable plant (type, length, location, end labels)
- Disk storage
- File servers
- Software running on each workstation
- Backup devices
- Workstations

Be Familiar with the Assets Under Your Control

You must record each file server's vital statistics: how much RAM, how much disk space, the type of NICs and disk controllers, and the kind of display it uses. Save the information so that you can find it when you need it. Next, record the same kind of information for each workstation on the LAN. While you're at it, add the contents of workstations' configuration files.

After you finish these lists, you should document the software configuration of the LAN. You should record your server's services configuration, build emergency boot disks for servers, and capture repair and configuration information for all your servers. List the following items:

- User names on the LAN and their network addresses
- Groups on the LAN

- File and directory attributes and permissions for each user and group
- Application structure
- Server directory structure
- Drive assignments for workstations

When you encounter a problem, write down what happened before the problem appeared. List any changes made to files or hardware right before the problem occurred, and record any error messages. Write down what application was running or what task was being performed when the problem occurred. When you call a technical support line, you need to supply all this information, so you might as well have it ready.

Ready for Action

After you record this information, you're fully prepared to work with a vendor's technical support staff when something goes wrong. When you place a call, have your information ready. Don't expect immediate gratification; instead, prepare for these possible outcomes:

- You sit on hold, waiting for what seems like forever for a response. When you do get through, you can only leave voicemail and hope that someone calls back before the end of the year.
- You are told it's an "operator error," a term technical support people use when someone makes a mistake. However, the term also seems to come up when they don't want to deal with a question or don't know the answer.
- You might be told "no one has ever done anything this dumb." Even if someone is a pioneer in new realms of the unlikely, the technical support person should still help you.
- The person you contact might not have an answer but will have someone else who can solve the problem get back to you.
- A polite and knowledgeable person helps you solve the problem.

Before you call, gather your information. Better yet, get close to the PC or network device exhibiting problems so that you can step the technical support person through whatever error messages show up (for example, when trying to duplicate the problem).

Escalation

If it seems as though your technical support person doesn't want to help you, take the same steps you follow when you contest a bill. Ask for a supervisor (in technical support, this step is called "escalating"). After all, you paid for the product and you deserve help—especially if, as is so often the case with technical support, you're paying extra for the help you're not getting.

The same rule applies to people who don't call back in a reasonable amount of time; one full working day after a call is as long as you should wait. Call again and leave a message. Record the day and time of each technical support call. Record how long it takes for a callback, and make sure you keep good records. This is another time that documentation comes in handy.

Some vendors offer 24-hour technical support. When you buy products, find out about the vendor's technical support line. It might be worth paying more for a product to have access to good support later. Some vendors charge extra for access to telephone support (and might have a variety of yearly contract options); the more important the network component, the more willing you and your organization should be to pay for support. Twenty-four-hour support is critical for network hardware. No reasonable network administrator takes down a network during normal working hours to insert a new NIC in the server. That's why it's important that support be available when you're supposed to be working on your systems—during nonpeak working hours—so that troubleshooting and repairs don't interrupt your users.

NETWORK
TROUBLESHOOTING GUIDE

This appendix lists basic questions you can ask when you approach network problems. Guidelines for troubleshooting specific areas of networking technology are also included.

GENERAL QUESTIONS FOR TROUBLESHOOTING

When troubleshooting, the first question you should ask is "Has this piece of equipment or procedure ever worked correctly?" If it did in fact work once, your next question should be "Since then, what has changed?" The following is a list of other useful questions:

- Was only one user affected, or were many users affected?
- Were users affected randomly or all at once?
- Is only one computer down, or is the whole network down?
- Does this problem happen all the time, or does it happen only during specific times?
- Does this problem affect only one application, more than one, or all applications?
- Does this problem resemble any past problems?
- Have you added any users to the network?
- Have you added any new equipment to the network?
- Did you install a new application just before the problem occurred?
- Have you moved any equipment recently?
- Are any vendor products involved in this problem? If yes, who are the vendors?
- Does this problem occur in components, such as disk drives, hubs, application software, cards, or network operating software?
- Has anyone else attempted to remedy this problem?
- Can the computer having the problem function as a standalone computer if it's not functioning on the network?
- If the computer can't function on the network, have you checked its network adapter card? Is it working?
- Is the amount of traffic on the network normal?

The following sections list questions that are helpful when troubleshooting specific components of your network.

Cabling Problems

If you suspect a problem with cabling, check the following items:

- Missing or loose connections
- Frayed or broken sections
- Correct length
- Cable and connectors match (Cat 5E cable and Cat 5E connectors, for example)
- Network adapter card specifications

- Crimped or bent cables
- Location of the cable routing near a transformer, large electric motor, or air conditioner
- Correct termination at jacks and patch panels

Problems with Adapter Cards

Here are some things to check with adapter cards (NICs):

- Do the settings of your adapter cards match the network OS settings?
- Are there any I/O address conflicts?
- Are there any interrupt conflicts?
- Are there any memory conflicts?
- Are you using the correct interface (such as AUI, RJ-45, or BNC)?
- Is the network speed setting correct?
- Are you using the right kind of network card for the network (Ethernet card in an Ethernet network, for example)?
- Are there any setting conflicts if you have more than one NIC in a computer?
- Are the type (half- or full-duplex) and signaling speed (for example, 10 Mbps, 100 Mbps, 1000 Mbps) set correctly?
- In a wireless environment, are the SSID and encryption key set correctly?

Driver Problems

Check the following to isolate driver problems:

- How old is the equipment?
- Have any changes been made to the equipment since it was working correctly?
- Has anyone moved any hardware?
- Has software been installed recently?
- Are old drivers being used with new equipment?
- Have you checked the manufacturer's Web site for the newest drivers?

Problems with Network Operations

Here is a checklist to follow for network operation problems:

1. Inspect the hardware in your server and verify the following:
   - It's on the OS vendor's compatibility list.
   - It has the correct, most current drivers installed.

- It contains enough memory for the network operations you currently perform.

- It has adequate hard drive space for the amount of information stored on it.

- It has plenty of processing power to support your network.

2. Check all your network bindings to make sure they are correct and the most used bindings are listed first.

3. Double-check your client computers to verify that they have the correct client software (redirectors) installed.

4. Check that the installed protocol matches the protocol already in use on the network.

5. In a wireless network, make sure matching standards are in use; for example, ensure that all devices use 802.11b, 802.11a, or 802.11g as appropriate.

6. In a wireless network, check that all clients have a strong enough signal from the access point.

Problems with Network Printing and Fax Services

Check the following if there's a problem with network printing or faxing:

- Is the shared fax's or printer's power on?

- Is the selected shared printer or fax machine the correct one for the client computer's driver?

- Are the permissions correct for the shared printer or fax that users and printer/fax managers are using?

- Are the cables used by the shared printer or fax in good condition and connected correctly?

Problems with Network Applications

Check the following for problems with network applications:

- Is the configuration of all users' scheduling programs and e-mail appropriate?

- Are all messaging gateways configured correctly and working properly?

Problems in a Multivendor Environment

Answer the following questions to isolate problems with products from multiple vendors in a single networking environment:

- Have redirectors been configured for every type of server OS the client computer needs?

- Are all shells or redirectors configured correctly and in working order?

- Are the network services clients need configured correctly and working on servers?
- Are the gateway computers that permit access between environments configured correctly and working?

Problems with Client/Server Computing

Check the following for problems with clients or servers in a client/server environment:

- Is the client front end configured correctly and working?
- Is the server software configured correctly and working?
- Is the network application doing what it's supposed to?
- Does the server running the network application have enough RAM, space on its shared disk, and processing power?
- Have users received training in using the network application, and are they using the correct methods to get the most out of it?

Problems with Network Accounts

Check the following if a user can't log on with a certain account:

- Is the person entering the correct user name?
- Is the name of the domain (if logging on to a Windows domain) correct?
- Is the user typing the correct password? Remember that passwords are case sensitive.
- Has the user account been disabled or locked out?

Problems with Data Security

Use the following checklist if you suspect problems with data security:

1. If a user can access a resource that should be unavailable or can't access a resource that should be available, check the following:

   - Does the user have the correct permissions to the resource?
   - Does the user belong to a group that has the correct access to the resource?
   - Do any trustee assignments to the resource conflict? (Check share-level permissions versus user-level permissions.)

2. Check whether the user belongs to any group assigned the No Access permission.

3. If the user can access previously secured data or there's a problem with data theft, alteration, or contamination, check the following:

   - Who has access to the server if it's in a locked room?
   - Are any computers being left on as logged on, and then left unattended?

- Are any passwords written on paper and left in obvious places, such as on the monitor, in a desk drawer, or under the keyboard?

- Are any users using obvious passwords, such as names of children, pets, or spouses?

- Are any users using the same password with a revision number (that is, Dawn1, Dawn2, Dawn3, and so on)?

- Do any users have a regular logon name equivalent to a superuser (administrator)?

- Are any users storing confidential data on their local hard drives?

- Do any users have their OSs configured to log them on automatically, bypassing the user name and password process?

Problems with Large Network Communications

To start, you troubleshoot a WAN in the same way you do a LAN. However, some considerations are specific to WANs. These types of problems usually require the assistance of vendors or service providers. Here's a set of questions related to WAN troubleshooting:

1. Did any vendor replace, add, or remove anything from the WAN?

2. Is the power to the following components turned on, and are the components themselves turned on?

   - Bridge

   - Router

   - Repeater

   - Gateway

   - Modem

   - CSU/DSU

3. For the same components, check the following:

   - Are all cables connected properly and in good condition?

   - Is the component compatible with the communication medium and the communication device at the other end of the link?

   - Is the software configured correctly, and does it match the configuration of the connected communication equipment?

D

NETWORKING RESOURCES, ONLINE AND OFFLINE

Numerous resources are available to help you find information you need to implement a network successfully. This appendix identifies many valuable networking resources. In addition to the resources listed here, you can locate good networking information via an Internet search engine or by visiting the Web sites listed in the "Online/Electronic Materials" section.

Printed Materials

Ciampa, Mark. *Security+ Guide to Networking Security Fundamentals, Second Edition.* Course Technology, Boston: 2004 (ISBN 0-619-21566-6).

DiNicolo, Dan and Brian McCann. *70-290: MCSE Guide to Managing a Microsoft Windows Server 2003 Environment, Enhanced Edition.* Course Technology, Boston: 2006 (ISBN 0-619-21752-9).

Eckert, Jason W. and M. John Schitka. *Linux+ Guide to Linux Certification, Second Edition.* Course Technology, Boston: 2006 (ISBN 0-619-21621-2).

Feibel, Werner. *Encyclopedia of Networking (Network Press).* Sybex Books, Alameda, CA: 2000 (ISBN 0-7821-2255-8).

Green, James Harry. *The Irwin Handbook of Telecommunications, Fourth Edition.* McGraw-Hill, Englewood Cliffs, NJ: 2000 (ISBN 0-07-135554-5).

McCann, Brian, Jason Eckert, and M. John Schitka. *70-291: MCSE Guide to Managing a Microsoft Windows Server 2003 Network, Enhanced Edition.* Course Technology, Boston: 2005 (ISBN 0-619-21753-7).

Tomsho, Greg. *Guide to Network Support and Troubleshooting.* Course Technology, Boston: 2002 (ISBN 0-619-03551-X).

Tulloch, Ingrid and Mitch Tulloch. *Microsoft Encyclopedia of Networking.* Microsoft Press, Redmond, WA: 2002 (ISBN 0-735-61378-8).

Online/Electronic Materials

Acronym Finder (*www.acronymfinder.com*)

Dan Kegel's repository of ISDN pointers and information (*www.alumni.caltech.edu/~dank/isdn/*)

Gigabit Ethernet Resources (*www.ethermanage.com/ethernet/gigabit.html*)

How StuffWorks: A great Web site to learn how just about anything works, from networks to yo-yos (*www.howstuffworks.com/*)

IEEE Local and Metropolitan Area Network Standards: The place to find information on all IEEE networking standards, purchase the standards, or download the 802 standard in PDF format (*http://standards.ieee.org/catalog/olis/lanman.html*)

Internet Access Tutorial (*www.iec.org/online/tutorials/int_acc/*)

Overview of Cable Modem Technology and Services (*www.cabledatacomnews.com/cmic/cmic1.html*)

Protocols.com: A great reference for reviewing packet structure and header fields of all networking protocols (*www.protocols.com*)

TechFest Networking tutorials (*www.techfest.com*)

TechNet online version: Also available monthly on CD from Microsoft by subscription, starting at $349 per year (*http://technet.microsoft.com/en-us/default.aspx*)

TechWeb Online Encyclopedia (*www.techweb.com/encyclopedia*)

Wi-Fi News: A Web site dedicated to the 802.11b wireless networking standard (*www.wi-fiplanet.com*)

O'Reilly Safari Bookshelf: A subscription service to hundreds of current information technology books you can read online (*http://safari.oreilly.com*)

D

Glossary

1000BaseT — 1000 Mbps Ethernet (1 Gbps) over twisted-pair cabling; defined by IEEE standard 802.3ab.

100BaseFX — 100 Mbps Ethernet over two-strand fiber-optic cable.

100BaseT4 — 100 Mbps Ethernet over four-pair Category 3 or higher UTP.

100BaseTX — 100 Mbps Ethernet over two-pair Category 5 or higher UTP.

10Base2 — A designation for 802.3 Ethernet thin coaxial cable (also called thinnet, thinwire, or cheapernet). The 10 indicates a bandwidth of 10 Mbps, the Base indicates it's a baseband transmission technology, and the 2 indicates a maximum segment length of 185 meters (originally 200, hence the "2") for this cable type.

10Base5 — A designation for 802.3 Ethernet thick coaxial cable (also called thicknet or thickwire). The 10 indicates a bandwidth of 10 Mbps, the Base indicates it's a baseband transmission technology, and the 5 indicates a maximum segment length of 500 meters for this cable type.

10BaseF — The 10 Mbps Ethernet standard that defines Ethernet over fiber-optic cable.

10BaseT — A designation for 802.3 Ethernet twisted-pair cable. The 10 indicates a bandwidth of 10 Mbps, the Base indicates it's a baseband transmission technology, and the T indicates that the medium is twisted-pair. (Maximum segment length is around 100 meters, or 328 feet, but the precise measurement depends on the manufacturer's testing results for the cable.)

802.11 — The IEEE specification in Project 802 for wireless networks.

802.11 Wireless Networking Standard — An IEEE standard for wireless networking. A version of the 802.11 standard appeared late in 1997.

802.11i — A security extension to 802.11 and a successor to Wi-Fi Protected Access that is the currently accepted best security protocol for wireless networks.

802.15 — The IEEE specification that covers emerging standards for wireless personal area networks (PANs).

802.16 — The IEEE specification that covers wireless metropolitan area networks (MANs).

802.2 — The IEEE specification in Project 802 for the Logical Link Control (LLC) sublayer of the OSI model's Data Link layer.

802.3 — The IEEE specification in Project 802 for Carrier Sense Multiple Access/Collision Detection (CSMA/CD) networks (more commonly called "Ethernet"). Ethernet users can attempt to access the medium any time it's perceived as "quiet," but they must back off and try to transmit again if they detect any collisions after transmission begins.

802.5 — The IEEE specification in Project 802 for token ring LANs, which map a circulating ring structure onto a physical star and circulate a token to control access to the medium.

access control — In the context of the Network layer and routing, the process whereby a router consults a list of rules before forwarding an incoming packet. The rules determine whether a packet meeting certain criteria (such as source and destination address) should be permitted to reach the intended destination.

access control lists — Sets of rules defined by an administrator that determine which packets should be allowed and which should be denied.

access controls — Methods for imposing controls that allow or deny users access to network resources, usually based on a user's account or a group to which the user belongs.

access point (AP) — The central device, or hub, through which signals pass in a wireless network.

access point device — The device that bridges wireless networking components and a wired network. It moves traffic between the wired and wireless sides as needed.

account names — Strings of letters, numbers, or other characters that identify a user's account on a network.

Active Directory — The directory service environment for Windows Server 2000/2003. Active Directory includes enough information about users, groups, organizational units, and other kinds of management domains to represent a complete digital model of the network.

active hubs — Network devices that regenerate received signals and send them along the network.

active monitor — A computer in a token ring network responsible for guaranteeing the network's status.

active topology — A network topology in which computers are responsible for sending data along the network.

ad hoc topology — A wireless communication scheme by which devices communicate directly with one another without using a central hub.

adapter slot — The sockets built into a PC motherboard that are designed to accommodate add-on cards, such as NICs. *See also* Industry Standard Architecture (ISA) and Peripheral Component Interface (PCI). (Both are specific types of adapter slots.)

Address Resolution Protocol (ARP) — A protocol in the TCP/IP suite used to resolve logical IP addresses to physical MAC addresses.

American National Standards Institute (ANSI) — The U.S. representative in the International Organization for Standardization (ISO), a worldwide standards-making body. ANSI creates and publishes standards for networking, communications, and programming languages.

amplifiers — Hardware devices that increase the power of electrical signals to maintain their original strength when transmitted across a large network.

analog — The method of signal transmission used on broadband networks. Creating analog waveforms from computer-based digital data requires a special device called a digital-to-analog (d-to-a) converter; reversing the conversion requires an analog-to-digital (a-to-d) converter. Broadband networking equipment must include both kinds of devices to work.

antenna — A tuned electromagnetic device that can send and receive broadcast signals at particular frequencies. In wireless networking devices, an antenna is an important part of a device's sending and receiving circuitry.

AppleTalk File Protocol (AFP) — The Macintosh remote file-management protocol.

Application layer — Layer 7 in the OSI reference model provides interfaces that enable applications to request and receive network services. *See also* OSI reference model.

application protocol — A type of protocol that works in the upper layers of the OSI model to provide application-to-application interaction.

application server — A specialized network server with the job of providing access to a client/server application and sometimes to the data belonging to that application.

application service providers (ASPs) — Companies that specialize in providing customers with access to applications and file services through a Web browser over the Internet.

asymmetric communication — Communication in which data travels in the download direction at a speed different from the speed of the upload direction.

Asymmetric Digital Subscriber Line (ADSL) — A digital telecommunications technology that uses different speeds for downloading and uploading data.

asynchronous — A communication method that sends data in a stream with start and stop bits that indicate where data begins and ends.

Asynchronous Transfer Mode (ATM) — A high-speed network technology designed for both LAN and WAN use. ATM uses connection-oriented switches to allow senders and receivers to communicate over a network.

attached resource computing network (ARCnet) — A 2.5 Mbps LAN technology created by DataPoint Corporation in the late 1970s. ARCnet uses token-based networking technology and runs over several kinds of coaxial cable, twisted-pair, and fiber-optic cable.

attenuation — The weakening of a signal as it travels the length of a medium, which eventually causes the signal to be unreadable.

auditing — Recording selected events or actions for later review. Audits can help establish patterns and note changes in those patterns that might signal trouble.

authentication — A security feature that allows an administrator to control who has access to the network.

authorization — A security feature that allows an administrator to control what a user can do and which resources can be accessed after the user is authenticated to the network.

automatic link aggregation — A feature of some NICs that adds the bandwidth of two installed NICs together, resulting in a higher aggregate bandwidth.

automatic private IP addressing (APIPA) — A special range of addresses that starts with 169.254 and is used by a computer when no DHCP server responds to a DHCP request. *See also* Dynamic Host Configuration Protocol (DHCP).

autonegotiation — The process by which a NIC driver automatically selects an operating mode (speed and duplex mode). To make this selection, the NIC driver negotiates the optimal connection type with the device the NIC is connected to.

back end — A server in a client/server networking environment.

backbone — A single cable segment used in a bus topology to connect computers in a straight line.

backbone cabling — The part of the cable plant that interconnects telecommunications closets and equipment rooms. Backbone cabling runs between floors or wings of a building and between buildings to carry network traffic destined for devices outside the work area.

backdoor — A program installed on a computer that permits access to the computer, thus bypassing the normal authentication process.

bandwidth — The range of frequencies that a communications medium can carry. For baseband networking media, the bandwidth also indicates the theoretical maximum amount of data that the medium can transfer. For broadband networking media, the bandwidth is measured by the variations that any single carrier frequency can carry, minus the analog-to-digital conversion overhead.

baseband transmission — A technology that uses digital signals sent over a cable without modulation. It sends binary values (0s and 1s) as pulses of different voltage levels.

Basic Rate Interface (BRI) — An ISDN version that provides two 64-Kbps B-channels. Generally used for remote connections.

baud — A measurement of modem speed that describes the number of state transitions occurring per second on an analog phone line.

beaconing — The signal transmitted on a token ring network to inform networked computers that token passing has stopped because of an error.

bend radius — For network cabling, the maximum arc that a segment of cable can be bent over some unit length (typically, one foot or one meter) without incurring damage.

Binary Synchronous (bisync) — One of the primary synchronous communication protocols.

binding — The OS-level association of NICs, protocols, and services to fine-tune network operation and performance.

Boot PROM — A special programmable chip that includes enough software to permit a computer to boot sufficiently and access the network. From there, it can download an operating system to finish the boot process. Also known as PXE compliant.

boot up — The process a computer goes through when starting; also called booting.

bridges — Networking devices that work at the Data Link layer of the OSI model. They filter traffic according to a packet's hardware destination address.

bridging table — A reference table created by a bridge to track hardware addresses and to track on which network segment each address is located.

Broadband ISBN (B-ISBN) — An ISDN variation that supports much higher data rates than standard ISDN and works with other technologies, such as ATM, SONET, and frame relay.

broadband optical telepoint networks — An implementation of infrared wireless networking that supports broadband services equal to those a cabled network provides.

broadband transmission — An analog transmission technique that can use multiple communication channels simultaneously. Each data channel is represented by modulation on a particular frequency band, and sending or receiving equipment must be tuned to that band.

broadcast domain — The extent to which a broadcast frame is forwarded from device to device without going through a router. An IP network or subnet is also referred to as a broadcast domain.

broadcast frames — Data frames with destination addresses that specify that all computers on a network must read and process these frames.

broadcast storm — A phenomenon that occurs when a network device malfunctions and floods the network with broadcast packets.

buffer — A temporary storage area that a device uses to contain incoming data before it can be processed for input or to contain outgoing data before it can be sent as output.

bus — A network topology in which the computers connect to a backbone cable segment to form a straight line.

bus mastering — The capability of an adapter card's circuitry to take possession of a computer's bus and coordinate data transfers without requiring any service from the computer's CPU.

bus width — The number of parallel lines that make up a type of bus. For example, ISA supports 8- and 16-bit bus widths, and PCI supports 32- and 64-bit bus widths.

cable modem — A special-purpose networking device that permits a computer to send and receive networking signals, primarily for Internet access, by using two data channels on a broadband CATV network (one to send outgoing data, the other to receive incoming data). Cable modems can support bandwidth up to 1.544 Mbps, but upstream traffic (from computer to network) between 100 and 300 Kbps and downstream traffic (from network to computer) between 300 and 600 Kbps are more typical.

cable plant — The combination of installed network cables, connectors, patch panels, wall jacks, and other media components.

cable testers — Network troubleshooting devices that can test for cable defects, monitor network collisions, and monitor network congestion.

Cardbus — A credit-card-size expansion card used primarily to add functionality to laptop computers. Cardbus provides data transfer rates up to 132 MBps. *See also* ExpressCard.

Carrier Sense Multiple Access with Collision Avoidance (CSMA/CA) — A contention-based channel access method in which computers avoid collisions by broadcasting their intent to send data.

Carrier Sense Multiple Access with Collision Detection (CSMA/CD) — A contention-based channel access method in which computers avoid collisions by listening to the network before sending data. If a computer senses data on the network, it waits and tries to send its data later.

central processing unit (CPU) — The collection of circuitry (a single chip on most PCs) that supplies the "brains" for most computers.

centralized computing — A computing environment in which all processing takes place on a mainframe or central computer.

channel access methods — Rules that determine when a computer can access the cable or data channel for the purposes of sending data.

Channel Service Unit/Data Service Unit (CSU/DSU) — A device that links a computer or network to a DDS communications link.

chips — Fixed-sized elements of data broadcast over a single frequency by using direct-sequence modulation. *See also* direct-sequence modulation.

cladding — A nontransparent layer of plastic or glass material inside fiber-optic cable; cladding surrounds the inner core of glass or plastic fibers. Cladding provides rigidity, strength, and a manageable outer diameter for fiber-optic cables.

Classless Interdomain Routing (CIDR) — An IP addressing method in which address classes no longer dictate the part of an IP address designated as the network portion. With CIDR, a network administrator can assign however many bits are appropriate to the network design.

client — A computer on a network that requests resources or services from another computer.

client network software — A type of software designed for workstations that enables the use of network resources.

client-based multivendor solution — In this environment, when multiple redirectors are loaded on a client, the client can communicate with servers from different vendors.

client/server — A model for computing in which some computers (clients) request services and other computers (servers) respond to requests for services. Applications are sometimes divided across the network so that a client-side component runs on the user's machine and supplies request and display services, and a server-side component runs on an application server and handles data processing or other computation-intensive services on the user's behalf.

client/server computing — A computing environment in which processing is divided between the client and server.

client-to-gateway VPN mode — This VPN mode establishes a VPN connection between a single client computer and a VPN device.

coaxial cable — A type of cable that uses a center conductor, wrapped by an insulating layer and surrounded by a braided wire mesh and an outer jacket or sheath, to carry high-bandwidth signals, such as network traffic or broadcast television frequencies. "Coax" is often used as a shortened form of "coaxial cable."

collision — The result of two or more devices sending a signal along the same channel at the same time.

collision domain — The extent to which signals are propagated on an Ethernet network.

Committed Information Rate (CIR) — A guaranteed minimum transmission rate offered by the service provider.

Common Internet File System (CIFS) — The Windows method of accessing files across a network; this method is a newer version of Server Message Block.

communication server — A specialized network server that provides access to resources for users not directly attached to the network or enables network users to access external resources not directly attached to the network.

communications carrier — A company that provides communications services for other organizations, such as a local phone company and long-distance telephone carriers. Most mobile computing technologies rely on the services of a communications carrier to handle wireless traffic from mobile units to a centralized wired network.

computer bus — A specialized collection of parallel lines in a PC used to transfer data between the CPU and peripheral devices and occasionally from one peripheral device to another.

concentrators — Devices used in an FDDI network to connect computers at a central point. Most concentrators connect to both available rings.

conduit — Plastic or metal pipe laid specifically to provide a protected enclosure for cabling of any kind.

connectionless — A type of protocol that sends data across the network to its destination without guaranteeing receipt.

connection-oriented — A type of protocol that establishes a formal connection between two computers, guaranteeing that data will reach its destination.

contention — A channel access method in which computers vie for time on the network.

cooperative multitasking — A form of multitasking in which each process controls the length of time it maintains exclusive control over the CPU.

copy backup — A backup type that copies all selected files without marking files as backed up.

counter — A certain part of an object that tracks an aspect of its behavior. For example, the Processor object has counters such as Processor Time and Interrupts/sec. *See also* object.

cracker — Someone who attempts to compromise a network or computer system for the purposes of personal gain or to cause harm.

crosstalk — A phenomenon that occurs when two wires lay against each other in parallel. Signals traveling down one wire can interfere with signals traveling down the other, and vice versa.

customer premises equipment (CPE) — The equipment at the customer site that's usually the responsibility of the customer.

customer relationship management (CRM) — A class of software designed to help businesses manage their customers and prospects.

cut-through switching — The fastest switching method, in which the switch reads only enough of the incoming frame to determine where to forward the frame.

Cyclical Redundancy Check (CRC) — A mathematical recipe that generates a specific value, called a checksum, based on a frame's contents. The CRC is calculated before frame transmission and then included with the frame; on receipt, the CRC is recalculated and compared to the sent value. If the two agree, it's assumed that the data frame was delivered intact; if they disagree, the frame must be retransmitted.

daily backup — A backup type that copies all files modified on the day of the backup; this type doesn't mark files as backed up.

data circuit-terminating equipment (DCE) — The device that sends data to (and receives data from) the local loop, usually a CSU/DSU or modem.

Data Link layer — Layer 2 in the OSI reference model is responsible for managing access to the networking medium and ensuring error-free delivery of data frames from sender to receiver. *See also* OSI reference model.

Data Over Cable Service Interface Specification (DOCSIS) — The official standard governing cable modem operation.

data section — The frame component that's the actual data being sent across a network. The size of this section can vary from less than 50 bytes to 16 KB, depending on the network type.

data terminal equipment (DTE) — The device that passes data from the customer LAN to the DCE, usually a router.

database management systems (DBMSs) — Client/server computing environments that use SQL to retrieve data from the server. *See also* Structured Query Language (SQL).

datagrade — A designation for cabling of any kind; datagrade indicates that cabling is suitable for transporting digital data. When applied to twisted-pair cabling, "datagrade" indicates that the cable is suitable for voice or data traffic.

decapsulation — The process of stripping the header from a PDU as it makes its way up the communication layers before being passed to the next higher layer. *See also* protocol data unit (PDU).

dedicated circuit — An ongoing (but possibly transient) link between two end systems.

dedicated server — A network server that acts only as a server and is not intended for regular use as a client machine.

default groups — Special groups created during installation in a Windows environment that have preassigned rights.

demand priority — A high-speed channel access method used by 100VG-AnyLAN in a star hub topology.

demand signal — A signal sent by a computer in a demand priority network that informs the controlling hub it has data to send.

demarcation point — The point at which the CPE ends and the provider's equipment responsibility begins.

denial-of-service (DoS) attack — An attempt to tie up network bandwidth or services so that network resources are rendered useless to legitimate users.

designator — This NOS software component aids in network resource interaction and drive mapping. Working in coordination with a redirector, it exchanges the locally mapped drive letter with the correct network address of a directory share inside a resource request.

device driver — A software program that mediates communication between an operating system and a device for the purpose of sending and receiving input and output from that device. These drivers are operating system dependent. They also need to be kept up to date per information on the manufacturer's Web site.

device sharing — A primary purpose of networking: permitting users to share access to devices of all kinds, including servers and peripherals such as printers or scanners.

diagnostic software — Specialized programs that can probe and monitor a system (or system component) to determine whether it works and, if not, try to establish the cause of the problem.

Dial-Up Networking (DUN) — The Windows program (beginning with Windows 95) that allows connectivity to servers running RAS or RRAS.

differential backup — A backup type that copies all files modified since the last normal backup; this type doesn't mark files as backed up.

differential signal — The use of two wires to carry a signal, where one wire carries a positive voltage signal and the other carries a negative voltage signal. Differential signals help mitigate the effects of noise and crosstalk. *See also* electromagnetic interference (EMI) *and* crosstalk.

Digital Data Service (DDS) — A type of point-to-point synchronous communication link offering 2.4, 4.8, 9.6, or 56 Kbps transmission rates.

digital modem — A hardware device used to transmit digital signals across an ISDN link.

digital subscriber line (DSL) — A broadband-based technology that delivers Internet data over existing phone lines.

digital voltmeter (DVM) — A network troubleshooting tool that measures voltage, amperage, and resistance on a cable or other conductive element.

direct memory access (DMA) — A technique for addressing memory on some other device as though it were local memory directly available to the device accessing that memory. This technique lets a CPU gain immediate access to the buffers on any NIC that supports DMA.

directory server — A specialized server with the job of responding to requests for specific resources, services, users, groups, and so on. This kind of server is more commonly called a domain controller in Windows Server 2000/2003 networking environments.

directory service — A comprehensive network service that manages information about network services, resources, users, groups, and other objects, so that users can access resources and services by browsing for them, or asking for them by type, along with maintaining and enforcing access control information for directory objects.

direct-sequence modulation — The form of spread-spectrum data transmission that breaks data into fixed-length segments called chips and transmits the data on multiple frequencies.

disk duplexing — A fault-tolerant disk configuration in which data is written to two hard drives, each with its own disk controller, so that if one disk or controller fails, the data remains accessible.

disk mirroring — A fault-tolerant disk configuration in which data is written to two hard drives rather than one so that if one disk fails, the data remains accessible.

disk striping with parity — A fault-tolerant disk configuration in which parts of several physical disks are linked in an array, and data and parity information is written to all disks in this array. If one disk fails, the data can be reconstructed from the parity information written on the others.

diskless workstations — Network computers that require a special type of ROM because they have no built-in disk drives.

distance-vector algorithm — One method of determining the best route available for a packet. Distance-vector protocols count the number of routers (hops) between the source and destination. The best path has the least number of hops.

domain — A uniquely named collection of user accounts and resources that share a common security database.

domain controller — On Windows Server 2000/2003 networks, a directory server that also provides access controls over users, accounts, groups, computers, and other network resources.

domain local groups — Groups defined in a Windows domain that are used to assign permissions and rights to resources throughout the domain.

domain model — A network based on a Windows server operating system with security and access controls residing in a domain controller.

Domain Name System (DNS) — A TCP/IP protocol used to associate a computer's IP address with a name.

dotted decimal — The format of an IP address, expressed as four decimal numbers separated by a period.

drive mapping — The convention of associating a local drive letter with a network directory share to simplify access to the remote resource.

dual attachment station (DAS) — A type of NIC connected to both rings in an FDDI network.

dual-cable broadband — A broadband technique in which two cables are used; one is for transmitting, and one is for receiving.

Dynamic Host Configuration Protocol (DHCP) — A TCP/IP protocol that allows automatic IP address and subnet mask assignment.

dynamic routing — The process by which routers dynamically learn from each other the available paths.

electromagnetic interference (EMI) — A form of interference, also referred to as "noise," caused by emissions from external devices, such as transformers or electrical motors, that can disrupt network transmissions over an electrical medium.

electronic eavesdropping — The capability to "listen" to signals passing through a communications media by detecting its emissions. Eavesdropping on many wireless networking technologies is especially easy because they broadcast data into the atmosphere.

Electronic Industries Alliance (EIA) — An industry trade group of electronics and networking manufacturers that collaborates on standards for wiring, connectors, and other common components.

electronic mail (e-mail) — A networked application that enables users to send and receive text messages, with or without file attachments.

encapsulation — The process of adding header information to a PDU as it makes its way down the communication layers before being passed to the next lower layer. *See also* protocol data unit (PDU).

encoding — The representation of 0s and 1s as a physical signal, such as electrical voltage or a light pulse.

Encrypting File System (EFS) — A feature available on Windows operating systems that allows file contents to be encrypted on the disk. These files can be opened only by the file creator or designated agents.

encryption — A technology used to make data unusable and unreadable to anybody except authorized users of the data.

end user license agreement (EULA) — The license that governs how an application can be used. The EULA specifies how many users are allowed to use an application, how many times it can be installed, and whether the software can be copied, among other things.

entrance facility — The location of the cabling and equipment that connects a corporate network to a third-party telecommunications provider.

equipment room — An area that serves as a connection point for backbone cabling running between telecommunications closets; also houses servers, routers, switches, and other major network equipment.

Ethernet — A network architecture developed by Digital, Intel, and Xerox that uses CSMA/CD as its channel access method.

Ethernet 802.2 — An Ethernet frame type used by IPX/SPX on Novell NetWare 3.12 and 4.x networks.

Ethernet 802.3 — An Ethernet frame type generally used by IPX/SPX on Novell NetWare 2.x and 3.x networks; also called Ethernet raw.

Ethernet II — An Ethernet frame type used by TCP/IP.

Ethernet SubNetwork Address Protocol (SNAP) — An Ethernet frame type used in Apple's EtherTalk environment.

EtherTalk — The standard for sending AppleTalk over Ethernet cabling.

Event Viewer — A Windows Server 2000/2003 tool that records events in three logs based on type of event: Security, System, and Application logs.

ExpressCard — A credit-card-size expansion card used primarily to add functionality to laptop computers. ExpressCard provides data transfer rates up to 500 MBps. *See also* Cardbus.

extended LANs — Microsoft's name for the networks resulting from certain wireless bridges' capability to expand the span of a LAN up to 25 miles.

extended star — Sometimes referred to as a hierarchical star topology, in which devices are connected in a star of stars. A central device, usually a switch, sits in the middle of the topology. Instead of attached computers forming the arms of the star, other switches (or hubs) are connected to the central switch's ports. Computers and peripherals are then attached to these switches or hubs, forming additional stars.

fast Ethernet — The 100 Mbps implementation of standard Ethernet, also called 100BaseT.

fault tolerance — A feature that allows a system to continue working after an unexpected hardware or software failure.

fault-tolerant disk configurations — Arrangements of physical or logical disks that ensure data remains accessible, if one disk fails, without requiring a restore from backups.

fax server — A specialized network server that can send and receive faxes via phone lines and direct them to users across the network.

Federal Communications Commission (FCC) — Among other responsibilities, the FCC regulates access to broadcast frequencies throughout the electromagnetic spectrum, including those used for mobile computing and microwave transmissions. When these signals cover any distance (more than half a mile) and require exclusive use of a frequency, FCC requires a broadcast license. Many wireless networking technologies make use of unregulated frequencies set aside by the FCC. These frequencies don't require licensing, but they must be shared with others.

Fiber Distributed Data Interface (FDDI) — A networking architecture that uses a token-passing channel access method and is defined to run at 100 Mbps over fiber-optic cable.

fiber-optic — A cabling technology that uses pulses of light sent along a light-conducting fiber at the heart of the cable to transfer information from sender to receiver. Fiber-optic cable can send data in only one direction, so two cables are required to permit network devices to exchange data in both directions.

file and print server — The most common type of network server (not considered a specialized server). It provides file storage and retrieval services across the network and handles print jobs for users.

file system — The method by which an operating system stores, organizes, and manages access to files on a mass storage device, such as a hard drive.

File Transfer Protocol (FTP) — A TCP/IP protocol used for file transfer and manipulation services.

firewall — A hardware device or software program that inspects packets going into or out of a network or computer and then discards or forwards those packets based on a set of rules.

FireWire — A high-speed, external serial bus that supports bandwidths up to 400 Mbps and can connect up to 63 devices; also known as IEEE 1394. FireWire is used for streaming video and multimedia, networking, and attaching video devices to computers.

flow control — A process designed to regulate information transfer between a sender and a receiver. Flow control is often necessary when there's a speed differential between sender and receiver.

fractional T1 — One or more of the 24 channels (but not all) of a T1 connection.

fragment-free switching — A switching method in which the switch reads in enough of the frame to guarantee that the frame is not less than the minimum frame size allowed for the network type.

frame — The basic unit for network traffic as it travels across the medium. Data is broken into these smaller, more manageable pieces for faster, more efficient delivery.

frame fragment — A frame error that occurs because the frame is less than the allowable minimum size for the network type. A frame fragment usually occurs because of a collision or a device malfunction.

frame header — Information added to the beginning of data being sent, which contains, among other things, addressing and sequencing information.

frame relay — A point-to-point permanent virtual circuit (PVC) technology that offers WAN communications over a fast, reliable, digital packet-switching network.

frame trailer — Information added to the end of the data being sent in a frame; it generally contains error-checking information, such as the CRC.

frame types — A standard that defines the structure of an Ethernet packet: Ethernet 802.3, Ethernet 802.2, Ethernet SNAP, or Ethernet II.

frequency hopping — The type of spread-spectrum data transmission that switches data across a range of frequencies over time. Frequency-hopping transmitters and receivers must be synchronized to hop at the same time to the same frequencies.

frequently asked questions (FAQ) — A Web document with two parts to each entry. The first part is a question the manufacturer has anticipated or received from customers; the second part is an answer to that question.

front end — A client in a client/server networking environment.

full-duplex communication — In this type of communication, a computer can send and receive data simultaneously.

gateway — A networking device that translates information between protocols or between completely different networks, such as from TCP/IP to SNA.

gateway-to-gateway VPN mode — This VPN mode establishes a connection between two routers that support VPN.

geosynchronous — An orbital position relative to Earth where a satellite orbits at the same speed as Earth rotates. This orbit permits satellites to maintain a constant fixed position in relation to Earth stations and represents the positioning technique used for microwave satellites.

Gigabit Ethernet — An IEEE standard (802.3z) that allows for 1000 Mbps transmission using CSMA/CD and Ethernet frames.

global groups — Groups meant to be used in more than one domain; used to group users together who require access to similar resources.

groups — Named collections of user accounts, usually created for a specific purpose. For example, the Accounting group might be the only users permitted to use a bookkeeping application.

groupware — A type of network application in which multiple users can simultaneously interact with each other and with data files.

hacker — Sometimes a derogatory term to describe an unskilled or undisciplined programmer. Hacker can also mean someone who is highly skilled with computer systems and programs and is able to use some of the same tools crackers use to poke around networks or systems, but not for evil purposes.

half-duplex communication — In this type of communication, a computer can send data and receive data, but can't send and receive simultaneously.

hard page faults — Exceptions that occur when a program needs data that must be called back into memory from its storage space on the hard drive. Large numbers of hard page faults slow system performance.

hertz (Hz) — A measure of broadcast frequencies in cycles per second; named after Heinrich Hertz, one of the inventors of radio communications.

hexadecimal — A mathematical notation for representing numbers in base 16. The numbers 10 through 15 are expressed as A through F; 10h or 0x10 (both notations indicate the number is hexadecimal) equals 16.

High Performance Parallel Interface (HIPPI) — A high-speed parallel communication interface originally developed to serve supercomputers and high-end workstations.

High-level Data Link Control (HDLC) — One of the primary synchronous communication protocols.

hoax virus — A type of virus that's not really a virus but simply an e-mail announcement of a made-up virus. Its harm lies in people believing the announcement and forwarding the message on to others.

hop — A packet traveling through a router on its way to the destination network.

horizontal wiring — Network cabling that runs from the work area's wall jack to the telecommunications closet and is usually terminated at a patch panel.

hot spots — A term used in wireless networking for areas in which wireless access to a network or the Internet is possible. Often these areas are in nontraditional locations, such as outside cafes or college campus courtyards.

hub — The central point of connection of a star network.

hybrid network — A network in which elements of a server-based network and a peer-to-peer network are in use. Small workgroups can share files, printers, and other devices with one another in a peer-to-peer fashion, and all network users log on to and access network-wide resources provided by the servers in a server-based arrangement.

Hypertext Transfer Protocol (HTTP) — The protocol used to transfer Web pages from a Web server to a Web browser.

incremental backup — A backup type that copies all files modified since the last full or incremental backup; this type marks files as backed up.

Industry Standard Architecture (ISA) — Originally an 8-bit PC bus architecture, but upgraded to 16-bit with the introduction of the IBM PC/AT in 1984.

infrared — The portion of the electromagnetic spectrum immediately below visible light. Infrared frequencies are popular for short- to medium-range (10 m to 40 m) point-to-point network connections.

infrastructure mode — The mode of wireless communication in which wireless devices are configured to use an access point.

insertion loss — The weakening of signals that occurs on a cable segment each time a network device is attached. Necessary restrictions on the maximum number of devices keep the signals that traverse the network clean and strong enough to remain intelligible to all devices.

Institute of Electrical and Electronics Engineers (IEEE) — An engineering organization that issues standards for electrical and electronic devices, including network interfaces, cabling, and connectors.

Integrated Services Digital Network (ISDN) — A WAN technology that offers increments of 64 Kbps connections, most often used by SOHO (small office/home office) users.

Intellimirror — A Windows Server 2000/2003 client/server application that creates a smart backup copy of a Windows system. Users can access all files, applications, and customizations on their desktops on any other Windows machine that can establish a working connection to the Intellimirror server storing their desktop images.

International Organization for Standardization (ISO) — The international standards-setting body based in Geneva, Switzerland, that sets worldwide technology standards.

Internet — A vast public wide area internetwork that makes it possible for any computer in the world to communicate with any other computer in the world using standard technologies and protocols.

Internet Control Message Protocol (ICMP) — A TCP/IP protocol used to send information and error messages.

Internet Message Access Protocol (IMAP) — An Internet e-mail standard that might replace POP3 because of its advanced message controls and fault-tolerance features. The appeal of IMAP (a more modern client message transfer protocol) is that it permits clients to read and manage messages locally while leaving them stored on the server.

Internet Protocol version 4 (IPv4) — TCP/IP's primary network protocol; it provides addressing and routing information.

Internet Protocol version 6 (IPv6) — An updated version of IPv4 created to solve some problems inherent in that protocol, such as a somewhat limiting 32-bit address space, lack of built-in security, a sometimes complicated setup, and a lack of built-in Quality of Service.

internetwork — A network of networks that consists of two or more physical networks. Unlike a WAN, an internetwork resides in only a single location. Because it includes too many computers or spans too much distance, an internetwork can't fit within the scope of a single LAN.

Internetwork Packet Exchange/Sequenced Packet Exchange (IPX/SPX) — IPX is Novell's protocol for packet routing and forwarding. In this protocol suite, IPX serves many of the same functions that IP does in the TCP/IP suite. SPX is Novell's connection-oriented protocol that supplements IPX by providing reliable transport.

interrupt request (IRQ) line — Any of 16 unique signal lines between the CPU and bus slots on a PC. IRQs define the mechanism whereby a peripheral device of any kind, including a network adapter, can stake a claim on a PC's attention. This claim is called an "interrupt," so the lines carrying this information are called "interrupt request lines."

intranet — An in-house TCP/IP-based network for use within a company.

intrusion detection system (IDS) — Usually a component of a firewall, an IDS detects an attempted security breach and notifies the network administrator. An IDS can also take countermeasures to stop an attack in progress.

IP Security (IPSec) — An extension to the IP protocol suite that creates an encrypted and secure conversation between two hosts.

IrDA devices — Devices that are compliant with the Infrared Device Association's specifications for infrared components and devices.

jack couplers — The female receptacles into which modular TP cables plug.

keycode — A string of characters that a user must supply to wireless NIC software so that the computer can decrypt communications on a wireless LAN, therefore allowing the client to access the LAN.

knowledge base — A searchable online database containing problems and errors, along with their solutions, related to a manufacturer's product.

last mile — The connection between a WAN's demarcation point and the central office (CO). *See also* local loop.

latency — The amount of time a signal takes to travel from one end of a cable to the other.

layers — The functional subdivisions of the OSI reference model. *See also* OSI reference model.

light-emitting diodes (LEDs) — A lower-powered alternative for emitting data at optical frequencies. LEDs are sometimes used for wireless LANs and for short-haul, fiber-optic-based data transmissions.

line conditioning — A feature that sustains a consistent transmission rate, improves overall quality, and reduces interference noise levels.

line-of-sight networks — Networks that require an unobstructed view, or clear line of sight, between the transmitter and receiver. Narrowband tight-beam transmitters and receivers must have an unobstructed path between them.

link-state algorithm — A method used by routers to determine a packet's best path. In addition to the number of routers involved, routers using link-state algorithms take network traffic and link speed into account to determine the best path.

local area network (LAN) — A collection of computers and other networked devices that fits within the scope of a single physical network and provides a building block for internetworks and WANs.

local loop — The connection between a WAN's demarcation point and the central office (CO). *See also* last mile.

localhost — A special DNS host name that refers to whatever IP address is assigned to the machine where this name is referenced. (Think of it as a special way to access the current IP address on any computer.)

LocalTalk — The cabling system used by Macintosh computers. Support for LocalTalk is built into every Macintosh.

locking connection (LC) — A type of fiber-optic connector that pushes on and pulls off using an RJ-45 style latching mechanism.

Logical Link Control (LLC) — The upper sublayer of the IEEE Project 802 model for the Data Link layer of the OSI model. It handles error-free delivery and controls the flow of frames between sender and receiver across a network.

logical topology — The path that data travels between computers on a network.

loopback address — A special DNS host name that refers to the reserved Class A address 127.0.0.1, used to confirm that a computer's IP configuration works.

MAC address filtering — A security method often used in wireless networks, whereby only devices with MAC addresses specified by the administrator can gain access to the wireless network.

mail server — A specialized server that manages the flow of e-mail messages for network users.

malware — Any software designed to cause harm or disruption to a computer system or otherwise perform activities on a computer without the consent of the computer's owner.

man pages — Help pages in Linux/UNIX that are available for most commands and applications.

management information base (MIB) — A set of objects containing information about a networking device that SNMP uses to manage that device.

maximum segment length — The longest cable segment that a particular networking technology permits. This limitation helps network designers and installers make sure the entire network can send and receive signals properly.

mechanical transfer registered jack (MT-RJ) — A fiber-optic connector that provides a high-density connection using two fiber-optic cables.

Media Access Control (MAC) — The lower sublayer of the IEEE Project 802 model for the Data Link layer of the OSI model. It handles access to network media and mapping between logical and physical network addresses for NICs.

Media Access Control (MAC) address — The number that identifies the physical address of a network computer. This address is burned into the computer's NIC in the form of data programmed on to the interface's ROM.

medium interface connector (MIC) — One of a number of fiber-optic cable connector types. MIC connectors feature a separate physical connector for each cable in a typical fiber-optic cable pair.

member server — Any server on a Windows NT or Server 2000/2003 network that's not responsible for user authentication.

mesh — A hybrid network topology in which all computers connect to each other; this topology is used for fault tolerance.

Message Handling System (MHS) — A Novell-developed standard that's similar to X.400.

metric — A value that describes the distance to the destination network.

metropolitan area network (MAN) — A type of network that uses WAN technologies to interconnect LANs within a specific geographic region, such as a county or a city. In most cases, however, a municipality or a communications carrier operates a MAN; organizations must sign up for service and establish connections to use a MAN.

mid-split broadband — A broadband technique in which two channels on different frequencies are used to transmit and receive signals via a single cable.

mobile computing — A form of wireless networking that uses common carrier frequencies to permit networked devices to be moved freely within the broadcast coverage area yet remain connected to the network.

modem — A device computers use to convert digital signals to analog signals for transmission over telephone lines. The receiving computer then converts the analog signals to digital signals.

mount point — The local directory in a UNIX or Linux file system in which an NFS volume is made accessible. *See also* Network File System (NFS).

multicast frames — Frames that use a special destination address so that any computer listening for this address can read and process the frame's data.

multiplexing — A technology that enables several communication streams to travel simultaneously over the same cable segment

multiport repeater — A device used in a star topology that takes a signal coming in on one port, cleans it up, strengthens it, and then sends the regenerated signal out all other ports. *See also* active hubs.

multistation access unit (MSAU) — An active hub in a token ring network.

multitasking — A mode of CPU operation in which a computer processes more than one task at a time. In most instances, multitasking is an illusion created through the use of time slicing.

naming convention — A predetermined schema for naming objects within network space. It simplifies the location and identification of objects.

narrowband radio — A type of broadcast-based networking technology that uses a single specific radio frequency to send and receive data. Low-powered, narrowband implementations don't usually require FCC approval but are limited to a 250-foot or so range; high-powered narrowband implementations do require FCC approval and licensing. Also called "single-frequency radio."

Nearest Active Downstream Neighbor (NADN) — The computer in a token ring environment to which another computer sends the token.

Nearest Active Upstream Neighbor (NAUN) — The computer in a token ring environment from which a computer receives the token.

NetBIOS Extended User Interface (NetBEUI) — A network protocol developed by IBM and Microsoft specifically to provide transport services for NetBIOS. NetBEUI is not routable. In addition, it's nearly obsolete and is no longer supported on current Windows operating systems.

NetWare Core Protocol (NCP) — Novell's upper-layer protocol that provides all client/server functions.

Network Address Translation (NAT) — A process by which an organization can assign private IP addresses to workstations; those addresses are translated to public IP addresses when accessing the Internet.

network administrator — The person responsible for installing, configuring, and maintaining a network, usually a server-based network such as Windows Server 2003 or Novell NetWare.

network applications — Enhanced software programs made possible through the communication system of a network. Examples include e-mail, scheduling, and groupware.

Network Basic Input/Output System (NetBIOS) — A protocol that establishes and manages communications between computers and provides naming services.

Network Device Interface Specification (NDIS) — A driver standard for providing an interface between a network interface card and the network medium; this standard enables a NIC to use multiple protocols.

Network File System (NFS) — A distributed file system originally developed at Sun Microsystems. It supports network-based file and printer sharing using TCP/IP-based network protocols and is the native file-sharing protocol for Linux/UNIX systems.

Network Information Service (NIS) — A service available on the Linux operating system that provides a central database for user names and passwords, which controls user access to network resources.

network interface card (NIC) — The hardware device that mediates communication between a computer and the networking medium.

Network layer — Layer 3 of the OSI reference model handles addressing and routing PDUs across internetworks in which sender and receiver must traverse multiple networks. *See also* protocol data unit (PDU) *and* OSI reference model.

network medium — A term that usually refers to the material (metallic or fiber-optic cable) that links computers on a network. Because wireless networking is possible, it can also describe the type of wireless communications that allow computers to exchange data via a wireless transmission frequency.

Network Monitor — A Windows NT and Windows Server 2000/2003 network service that you can use to capture network frames based on user-specified criteria, such as a software protocol analyzer.

network monitors — Software that monitors network traffic and gathers information about packet types, errors, and packet traffic to and from each computer.

network operating system (NOS) — A specialized collection of software that enables a computer to communicate over a network and take advantage of a broad range of networking services. Windows Server 2003, Novell NetWare, and Linux are examples of network operating systems.

network protocols — Sets of rules for communicating across a network. To communicate across a network successfully, computers must share a common protocol.

network resource — Any kind of device, information, or service available across a network. A network resource could be a set of files, an application or a service, or a network-accessible peripheral device.

network services — Resources offered by a network that aren't normally found in a standalone OS.

NFS volume — A portion of a UNIX or Linux file system that has been exported and made available to NFS clients.

nonroutable — A protocol that doesn't include Network layer or network address information.

normal backup — A backup type that copies all selected files and marks files as backed up.

Novell eDirectory — The centralized database of user, group, and resource information that enables NetWare servers to handle network logins and resource access requests and to manage resource information for an entire network.

NTFS permissions — Permissions assigned to files or folders on an NTFS-formatted volume in a Windows system. NTFS permissions affect user access to resources whether the user is logged on locally or over the network.

NWLink — The Microsoft implementation of the IPX/SPX protocol suite. *See also* Internetwork Packet Exchange/Sequenced Packet Exchange (IPX/SPX).

object — A system component or resource that's accessible to a user program in Windows, such as the CPU on a system or the IP protocol. Each component in Windows Server 2000/2003, XP, and Vista is considered an object.

octet — A grouping of eight binary digits or bits ("oct" means eight), usually expressed as a decimal number. An octet is one of the four decimal values that make up an IP address.

on-board co-processor — A special- or general-purpose microprocessor on an adapter card, usually for offloading data from a computer's CPU. Typically, NICs with on-board co-processors use the special-purpose variety.

on-board NIC — The electronics that make up a network interface integrated directly onto a computer motherboard.

Open Data-link Interface (ODI) — A specification developed by Apple Computer and Novell that simplifies driver development and enables a single NIC to use multiple protocols.

open source — A term describing software that's always available at no charge, even after modifications to its source code.

Open Systems Interconnection (OSI) — The family of ISO standards developed in the 1970s to facilitate functionality of networking services among dissimilar computers on a global scale. The OSI initiative was unsuccessful, owing to a fatal combination of an all-inclusive standards-setting effort and a failure to develop standard protocol interfaces to help developers implement its manifold requirements.

oscilloscopes — Network troubleshooting devices that measure the signal voltage per amount of time. When used with a TDR, they can help define cable problems. *See also* time-domain reflectometer (TDR).

OSI reference model — ISO standard 7498 defines a frame of reference for understanding networks by dividing the process of network communication into seven layers. Each layer is defined in terms of the services and data it handles on behalf of the layer directly above it and the services and data it needs from the layer directly below it. The OSI reference model remains the OSI initiative's most enduring legacy.

packet assembler/disassembler (PAD) — A device that supports X.25 communications for low-speed, character-based terminals.

parallel transmission — The technique of spreading bits of data across multiple parallel data lines to transmit them simultaneously, instead of according to an ordinal and temporal sequence.

partition — A logical separation of disk space that is viewed as a separate logical drive.

passive hub — A central connection point through which signals pass without regeneration.

passive topology — A network topology in which computers listen to the data signals being sent but do not participate in network communications.

passwords — Strings of letters, numbers, and other characters intended to be kept private (and hard to guess) and used to identify a user or to control access to protected resources.

patch cable — A short length (1 to 20 feet) of network cable used to connect a computer's network interface card to a jack in the work area or to connect from a patch panel to a hub or switch in the wiring closet.

patch panels — Elements of a wiring center in which separate cable runs are brought together. By making connections between any two points on the patch panel, the physical path of wires can be controlled and the sequence of wires managed.

PCI Express — A high-speed bus standard that relies on serial communications arranged in lanes to provide communications up to 8 GBps.

PCI-X — A high-speed bus standard that supports 64 bits at 66 MHz up to 533 MHz for .5 GBps to more than 4 GBps data transfer rates.

PCMCIA cards — Credit-card-size expansion cards used primarily to add functionality to laptop computers. Two standards are in common use: *See also* Cardbus and ExpressCard.

peer-to-peer — A type of networking in which each computer can be a client to other computers and also act as a server.

penetration tester — A term used to describe a security consultant who is able to detect holes in a system's security for the purpose of correcting these vulnerabilities.

Performance Monitor — A Windows 2000/2003/XP tool used for graphing trends based on performance counters for system objects.

Peripheral Component Interconnect (PCI) — The 32- and 64-bit PC bus architecture that currently prevails as the best and fastest of all available bus types, operating at 33 and 66 MHz.

peripheral device — Any hardware component on a computer that's not the CPU. In a networking context, it usually refers to some kind of device, such as a printer, that users can share across the network.

permanent virtual circuits (PVCs) — Pathways between two communication points that are established as permanent logical connections; therefore, the pathway exists even when it's not in use.

personal digital assistants (PDAs) — Handheld computers used for personal organization tasks, such as appointment and address book management.

Physical layer — Layer 1, the bottom layer of the OSI reference model, transmits and receives signals and specifies the physical details of cables, adapter cards, connectors, and hardware behavior. *See also* OSI reference model.

physical topology — The arrangement of the cabling that interconnects network devices.

ping scanner — An automated method for pinging a range of IP addresses.

plain old telephone service (POTS) — Also known as PSTN, the normal telephone communications system. *See also* public switched telephone network (PTSN).

plenum-rated — Cable that has been burn-tested to make sure it doesn't emit toxic fumes or large amounts of smoke when incinerated. Most building and fire codes require this designation for any cable to be run in plenum space.

Plug and Play (PnP) — The Microsoft requirements for PC motherboards, buses, adapter cards, and operating systems that enable a PC to detect and configure hardware on a system automatically. For PnP to work, all system components must conform rigorously to its specifications; currently, Windows 9x, 2000, XP, 2003, and Vista support this architecture.

Pluggable Authentication Modules (PAM) — A software service used on many Linux distributions for authenticating users. PAM is extensible so that new authentication features can be added as needed.

Point-to-Point Protocol (PPP) — A remote access protocol that supports many protocols, including IP, NetBEUI, and IPX.

polling — A channel access method in which a primary device asks secondary devices in sequence whether they have data to send.

port forwarding — The process by which a router forwards a request for a particular TCP or UDP port on to a specified computer.

port scanner — Software that determines which TCP and UDP ports are available on a computer or device.

Post Office Protocol version 3 (POP3) — An Internet message transfer protocol that e-mail clients use to copy messages from an e-mail server to a client machine to be read and managed on the local desktop.

power conditioning — A method of cleaning the power input, removing noise caused by other devices on the same circuit.

power-on self test (POST) — The set of internal diagnostic and status-checking routines a PC and its peripheral devices run each time the computer is powered on.

preemptive multitasking — A form of multitasking in which the NOS or OS retains control over the length of time each process can maintain exclusive use of the CPU.

preemptive troubleshooting — A method of forestalling network problems by planning in advance and performing regular network maintenance.

Presentation layer — At Layer 6 of the OSI reference model, data can be encrypted and/or compressed to facilitate delivery. Platform-specific application formats are translated into generic data formats for transmission or from generic data formats into platform-specific application formats for delivery to the Application layer. *See also* OSI reference model.

Primary Rate Interface (PRI) — An ISDN version that provides 23 64-Kbps B-channels.

primary ring — The FDDI ring around which data is transmitted.

Project 802 — The IEEE effort that produced the collection of 802 networking specifications and standards.

propagation delay — Signal delay created when a number of repeaters connect in a line. To prevent this, many network architectures limit the number of repeaters on a network.

protocol analyzers — Programs or devices that can capture packets traversing a network and display packet contents in a form useful to the user.

protocol data unit (PDU) — A unit of information passed as a self-contained data structure from one layer to another on its way up or down the network protocol stack.

protocol stack — An ordered collection of networking protocols that together provide end-to-end networked communications between a sender and a receiver.

protocol suite — A family of related protocols in which higher-layer protocols provide application services and request handling facilities, and lower-layer protocols manage the intricacies of Layers 1 to 4 in the OSI reference model.

protocol type field — A field used in the Ethernet SNAP and Ethernet II frames to indicate the network protocol being used.

protocols — The rules and procedures for communicating.

public data networks — WAN services, usually provided by private companies, for the purpose of enabling WAN technologies, such as X.25.

public switched telephone network (PSTN) — Another term for the public telephone system.

pulse code modulation (PCM) — A technique for digitizing analog signals. PCM introduces less noise into the signal than traditional modulation/demodulation techniques, thus boosting the total number of bits per second.

Quality of Service (QoS) — A networking term that specifies a guaranteed level of service when applied to applications requiring high bandwidth.

radio frequency interference (RFI) — Any interference caused by signals operating in the radio frequency range. This term has become generic for interference caused by broadcast signals of any kind.

RAM buffering — A memory-access technique that permits an adapter to use a computer's main memory as though it were local buffer space.

random access memory (RAM) — The memory cards or chips on a PC that provide working space for the CPU to use when running applications, providing network services, and so on. Where RAM on a server is concerned, more is usually better.

raw data — Data streams unbroken by header information.

redirector — A software component that intercepts requests for service from a computer and redirects requests that can't be handled locally across the network to a networked resource that can handle the request.

redundant array of independent disks (RAID) — Two or more drives on a network server that provide fault tolerance (through disk mirroring or disk striping with parity).

reflective wireless networks — An infrared wireless networking technology that uses a central optical transceiver to relay signals between end stations. All network devices must have an unobstructed view of this central transceiver, which explains why they're usually mounted on the ceiling.

registered jack 45 (RJ-45) — The eight-wire modular jack used for TP networking cables and PBX-based telephone systems.

Remote Monitoring (RMON) — Specialized software that gathers network data and provides statistics to a network management console.

repeaters — Networking devices used to strengthen a signal suffering from attenuation. *See also* attenuation.

request-response — A description of how the client/server relationship works: A request from a client leads to some kind of response from a server. (Usually, the response is the service or data requested, but sometimes it's an error message or a denial of service based on security.)

ring — A network topology consisting of computers connected in a circle, forming a closed ring.

RJ-11 — The four-wire modular jack commonly used for home telephone handsets.

roaming profile — A user profile in a Windows environment that's stored on a server and can be accessed from any computer the user logs on to.

rollback plan — Part of an upgrade plan that provides instructions on how to undo the upgrade if problems happen during the upgrade.

rootkits — Forms of Trojan programs that can monitor traffic to and from a computer, monitor keystrokes, and capture passwords. They are among the most insidious form of Trojan software because they can mask that the system has been compromised by altering system files and drivers required for normal computer operation.

routable — A protocol that includes Network layer information and can be forwarded by a router.

routers — Networking devices that operate at the Network layer of the OSI model. A router connects networks with different physical media and translates between different network architectures, such as token ring and Ethernet.

routing — A Network-layer service that determines how to deliver an outgoing packet of data from sender to receiver. Routing entails several methods for managing delivery and requires error and status reporting so that senders can determine whether packets are reaching the receivers.

Routing and Remote Access Service (RRAS) — A software component bundled in Windows Server 2000/2003 that combines Remote Access Service (RAS) and Multi-Protocol Routing, in addition to packet filtering, demand-dial routing, and support for Open Shortest Path First (OSPF).

routing table — A reference table that includes network information and the next router in line for a particular path.

Samba — An open-source software suite that makes Linux servers look and act like Windows servers. It permits DOS or Windows clients to access Linux- or UNIX-based file systems and services without special software on the client end.

satellite microwave — A microwave transmission system that uses geosynchronous satellites to send and relay signals between sender and receiver. Most companies that use satellite microwave lease access to the satellites for an exorbitant fee. *See also* geosynchronous.

scatter infrared networks — An infrared LAN technology that uses flat reflective surfaces, such as walls and ceilings, to bounce wireless transmissions between sender and receiver. Because bouncing introduces delays and attenuation, this variety of wireless LAN is the slowest and supports the narrowest bandwidth of any infrared technology.

secondary ring — An FDDI ring used for the sole purpose of handling traffic in the event of a cable failure.

Serial Line Internet Protocol (SLIP) — The dial-up protocol originally used to connect PCs directly to the Internet.

serial transmission — A technique for transmitting data signals that sends each bit's worth of data (or its analog equivalent) one at a time, one after another, in sequence.

server — A computer with the job of responding to requests for services or resources from clients on a network.

Server Message Block (SMB) — The message format used by DOS and Windows to share files, directories, and devices. SMB file sharing is also supported by most Linux and UNIX operating systems.

server network software — A type of software designed for a server computer; this software enables the hosting of resources for clients to access.

server sessions — Connections between a network server and another node.

server-based — A type or model of networking that requires a server to provide services and resources and to manage and control access to those services and resources.

server-based multivendor solution — A server, such as one running Windows Server 2003, that can readily communicate with clients from multiple vendors.

Service Access Points (SAPs) — Logical interface points used to transfer information from the LLC sublayer to the upper OSI layers. *See also* Logical Link Control (LLC).

service set identifier (SSID) — The name assigned to a wireless LAN.

Session layer — Layer 5 of the OSI reference model is responsible for setting up, maintaining, and ending ongoing sequences of communications (called sessions) across a network. *See also* OSI reference model.

shadow passwords — A secure method of storing user passwords on a Linux system.

share — A network resource made available for remote access by clients.

shared adapter memory — A technique for a computer's CPU to address memory on an adapter as though it were the computer's own main memory.

shared system memory — A technique for an adapter to address a computer's main memory as though it resided on the adapter.

sharing — One of the fundamental justifications for networking. In the Microsoft lexicon, this term refers to the way in which resources are made available to a network.

sharing permissions — A list of permissions that can be assigned to users and groups and applied to Windows shared folders. Sharing permissions don't affect access to files and folders by users logged on locally to the system hosting the files.

sheath — The outer layer of coating on a cable; sometimes also called a jacket.

shielded twisted-pair (STP) — A variety of TP cable in which a foil wrap encloses each of one or more pairs of wires for additional shielding, and a wire braid or an additional layer of foil might enclose the entire cable for further shielding.

shielding — Any layer of material included in cable to mitigate the effects of interference on the signal-carrying cables it encloses.

short circuit — A condition that occurs when conductors that are normally insulated from one another establish a connection. In a coaxial cable, if the shield and the internal conductor become connected, the cable stops functioning because the short circuit blocks all network traffic; the same condition can occur in twisted-pair cable if two or more of the paired wires become connected.

signal bounce — A phenomenon that occurs when a bus is not terminated and signals continue to traverse the network.

signal propagation — Signals traveling across a medium until they weaken or are absorbed.

Simple Mail Transport Protocol (SMTP) — A TCP/IP protocol used to send mail messages across a network. SMTP is the basis for e-mail on the Internet.

Simple Network Management Protocol (SNMP) — A TCP/IP protocol used to monitor and manage network devices.

single attachment station (SAS) — A type of NIC that's connected only to the primary ring in an FDDI network.

smart multistation access unit (SMAU) — An active hub in a token ring network.

sneakernet — A metaphorical description of a non-networked data exchange method: A person, presumably wearing sneakers, copies files on a disk at one computer and then hand-carries the disk to another computer.

soft page faults — Exceptions that occur when data must be called back into a program's working set from another location in physical memory. Soft page faults take less time to address than hard page faults. *See also* working set.

software agents — Part of the SNMP structure loaded on to each device to be monitored.

source-routing bridges — A type of bridge used in IBM token ring networks that learns its bridging information from information in the frame's structure.

spam — Unsolicited e-mail. The harm in spam is the loss of productivity when people receive dozens or hundreds of spam messages daily and the use of resources to receive and store spam on e-mail servers.

specialized server — Any special-function server—an application server, a communications server, a directory server or domain controller, a fax server, an e-mail server, or a Web server, among others.

spoofed address — A source address inserted into a packet that is not the actual address of the sending station.

spread-spectrum radio — A form of wireless networking technology that passes data by using multiple frequencies simultaneously.

spyware — A type of malware that monitors or in some way controls part of your computer at the expense of your privacy and to the gain of some third party.

standalone computer — A computer that's not attached to a network.

standby monitors — Computers in a token ring network that monitor the network status and wait for a signal from the active monitor. *See also* active monitor.

star — A network topology in which computers connect through a central connecting point, usually a hub.

start frame delimiter (SFD) — A field in the Ethernet 802.3 frame that defines the beginning of the packet.

stateful packet inspection (SPI) — A filtering method used in a firewall, whereby packets are not simply filtered based on packet properties but also the context in which packets are being transmitted. If a packet is not part of a legitimate ongoing data conversation, it's denied.

static routing — A type of routing in which the router is configured manually with all possible routes.

store-and-forward switching — A switching method in which the switch reads the entire frame to check for errors before forwarding the frame.

straight connection (SC) — A type of one-piece fiber-optic connector that's pushed on yet makes a strong and solid contact with emitters and sensors.

straight tip (ST) — The most common type of fiber-optic connector used in Ethernet networks with fiber backbones. These connectors come in pairs, one for each fiber-optic cable.

structured cabling — A specification for how network media should be installed to maximize performance and efficiency.

Structured Query Language (SQL) — The standard database query language designed by IBM.

subminiature type A (SMA) — Another fiber-optic connector that twists on and comes in pairs.

subnet mask — A 32-bit dotted decimal number used to signify which part of an IP address is the network portion and which part is the host portion. The subnet mask consists of a string of binary 1s followed by a string of binary 0s. The binary 0s mask the host portion of an IP address. A binary 1 signifies that the corresponding bit in the IP address belongs to the network portion of the IP address, and a binary 0 signifies that the corresponding bit in the IP address belongs to the host portion.

subnetting — The process whereby a single network address is divided into two or more subnetwork addresses, each with fewer available host IDs than the original network address.

supernetting — The operation of "borrowing" bits from the network portion of an IP address to combine a group of contiguous IP addresses. For supernetting to work, the group of IP addresses must be contiguous.

surge protection — Power protection that evens out spikes or sags in the main current and prevents them from affecting a computer.

switch — A special device that manages connections between any pair of star-wired devices on a network.

switched 56K — Digital point-to-point leased communication links offered by local and long-distance telcos. Lease terms are based on per-minute use charges, not on 24-hour, seven-day dedicated circuits.

switched virtual circuits (SVCs) — A communication circuit that's established when needed and then terminated when the transmission is completed.

switching — A media access method whereby all devices connect to a network switch, and the switch controls access to the medium. With switching, each device connected to the switch has access to the full media bandwidth.

Symmetric Digital Subscriber Line (SDSL) — A digital telecommunications technology that uses equivalent speeds for downloading and uploading data.

synchronous — A communication method in which computers rely on exact timing and sync bits to maintain data synchronization.

Synchronous Data Link Control (SDLC) — One of the primary synchronous communication protocols.

Synchronous Optical Network (SONET) — A high-speed, baseband digital networking standard that specifies incrementally increasing data rates across fiber-optic links.

T1 — A DDS technology that uses two two-wire pairs to transmit full-duplex data signals at a maximum rate of 1.544 Mbps.

T3 — A communication line that has 28 T1s or 672 channels and supports a data rate of 44.736 Mbps.

Task Manager — A Windows monitoring tool that provides a quick summary of server and network performance.

telecommunications closet (TC) — A small room or area housing equipment (such as patch panels, hubs, and switches) that provides connectivity to computer equipment in the nearby work area.

Telecommunications Industries Association (TIA) —An industry consortium of telephone equipment, cabling, and communications companies that formulates hardware standards for equipment, cabling, and connectors used in phone systems and on networks.

Telnet — A TCP/IP protocol that provides remote terminal emulation.

Terminal Services — A software subsystem for Windows NT and Windows 2000 Server that permits clients to run large or complex applications on computers with minimal processing power by transferring the burden of client processing to the server.

terminator — A hardware device used to absorb signals as they reach the end of a bus, thus freeing the network for new communications.

terrestrial microwave — A wireless microwave networking technology that uses line-of-sight communications between pairs of Earth-based transmitters and receivers to relay information. The large distances the signals must extend requires positioning microwave transmitters and receivers well above ground level on towers, on mountaintops, or atop tall buildings. This equipment is usually expensive.

thicknet — A form of coaxial Ethernet that uses a rigid cable about 0.4 inches in diameter. Because of its common jacket color and its rigidity, this cable is sometimes called "frozen yellow garden hose." Also known as thickwire and 10Base5.

thin client — A networked computer with a keyboard, a pointing device (mouse), a display device, a network interface, and enough processing power to access terminal services or a mainframe, where the real application processing occurs.

thinnet — A form of coaxial Ethernet that uses a thin, flexible cable about 0.2 inches in diameter. Also known as thinwire, 10Base2, and cheapernet.

time slicing — A method of granting CPU cycles to different processes by limiting the amount of time each process has exclusive use of the CPU.

time-domain reflectometer (TDR) — A network troubleshooting device that can determine whether there's a break or short in the cable and, if so, approximately how far down the cable it's located.

token — A small data packet used in some ring topology networks to ensure fair communications between all computers.

token passing — A method of passing data around a ring network.

token ring — A network architecture developed by IBM that's physically wired as a star but uses token passing in a logical ring topology.

TokenTalk — The standard for sending AppleTalk over token ring cabling.

topology — The basic physical layout of a network and the way in which network components communicate with each other. *See also* logical topology *and* physical topology.

total cost of ownership (TCO) — The cost of a product or service when intangibles such as support costs and productivity gain or loss are factored in.

traffic management — In terms of NICs, features that improve network accessibility for remote users, especially those using applications that require higher bandwidth, such as streaming video or multimedia.

transceiver — A compound word made from the words "transmitter" and "receiver" to describe a device that combines the functions of a transmitter and a receiver and integrates into a single device the circuitry needed to emit and receive signals on a medium.

translation bridges — A type of bridge that can translate between network architectures.

Transmission Control Protocol (TCP) — The core of the TCP/IP suite. TCP is a connection-oriented protocol responsible for reformatting data into packets and reliably delivering those packets.

Transmission Control Protocol/Internet Protocol (TCP/IP) — A protocol suite that supports communication between heterogeneous systems. TCP/IP has become the standard communications protocol for the Internet.

transparent bridges — Generally used in Ethernet networks, these bridges build their bridging tables automatically as they receive packets.

Transport layer — Layer 4 of the OSI reference model is responsible for fragmenting large PDUs from the Session layer for delivery across the network, inserting integrity controls, and managing delivery mechanisms to allow for error-free reassembly on the receiving end of a network transmission. *See also* OSI reference model *and* protocol data unit (PDU).

transport protocol — A protocol type responsible for providing reliable communication sessions between two computers.

Trojan program — A program that appears to be something useful, such as a free utility you can use on your computer, but in reality contains some type of malware.

troubleshooting — The process of detecting problems, identifying causes or contributing factors, and applying necessary workarounds or repairs to eliminate their effects.

twisted-pair (TP) — A type of cabling in which two copper wires, each enclosed in some kind of sheath, are wrapped around each other. The twisting permits narrow-gauge wire, otherwise extraordinarily sensitive to crosstalk and interference, to carry higher-bandwidth signals over longer distances than is traditionally possible with straight wires. TP cabling is used for voice telephone circuits as well as networking.

unicast frame — A data frame addressed to a single recipient.

uninterruptible power supply (UPS) — A power protection device that includes a battery backup to take over if the main current fails. Usually incorporates power conditioning and surge protection.

universal groups — Groups available in Active Directory that can contain users from any domain in the Active Directory structure and be assigned permissions and rights to any resource in Active Directory.

Universal Naming Convention (UNC) — A standard method for naming network resources; it takes the form *servername**sharename*.

Universal Serial Bus (USB) — A hot-pluggable Plug and Play serial interface; USB ports support peripheral devices, such as mouses and keyboards, in addition to some printers, scanners, telephony equipment, and monitors. USB 1.0 operates at a maximum data transfer rate of 12 Mbps; USB 2.0 supports up to 480 Mbps.

unshielded twisted-pair (UTP) — A form of TP cable that includes no additional shielding material in the cable composition. This cable encloses one or more pairs of twisted wires inside an outer jacket.

User Datagram Protocol (UDP) — A connectionless TCP/IP protocol that provides fast data transport.

users — People who use computers as standalone systems or to access a network.

virtual circuits — A logical sequence of connections with bandwidth allocated for a specific transmission pathway.

virtual docking — One of numerous point-to-point wireless infrared technologies that enable portable computing devices to exchange data with desktop machines or allow data exchange between a computer and a handheld device or a printer. The "virtual" term is used because this capability replaces a cable between the two devices.

virtual local area networks (VLANs) — A feature of switches that allows network administrators to group users and resources logically, regardless of their physical location.

virtual private networks (VPNs) — Temporary or permanent connections across a public network that use encryption technology to transmit and receive data.

virus — A malicious program that spreads by replicating itself into other programs or documents. A virus usually aims to disrupt computer or network functions by deleting and corrupting files.

voicegrade — A designation for cable (usually TP) that indicates it's rated to carry only telephone traffic. Voicegrade cable is not recommended for network use.

V-series — The ITU standards that specify how data communication takes place over the telephone network.

wall plates — A modular plate used to accommodate numerous outlets used for networking and voice applications.

wardrivers — Attackers who drive around with a laptop or PDA looking for wireless LANs to access.

Web server — The combination of hardware and software that stores information accessible over the Internet via the World Wide Web (WWW).

wide area network (WAN) — An internetwork that connects multiple sites; a third-party communications provider, such as a public or private telephone company, that carries network traffic from one location to another.

Wi-Fi Protected Access (WPA) — A wireless security protocol that is the successor to Wired Equivalency Protocol. WPA has enhancements that make cracking the encryption code more difficult.

Win32 Driver Model (WDM) — A unified driver standard that allows a single driver to be written for any 32-bit version of Windows (those since Windows 98).

Wired Equivalency Protocol (WEP) — A form of wireless security that encrypts data so that unauthorized people receiving wireless network signals can't interpret the data easily.

wireless — A network connection that depends on transmission at an electromagnetic frequency through the atmosphere to carry data transmissions from one networked device to another.

wireless bridges — A pair of devices, typically narrowband and tight beam, that relay network traffic from one location to another. Wireless bridges that use spread-spectrum radio, infrared, and laser technologies are available and can span distances from hundreds of meters up to 25 miles.

Wireless Fidelity (Wi-Fi) — A term used to indicate wireless networking, usually using one of the 802.11 wireless networking standards.

wireless personal area network (WPAN) — A short-range wireless networking technology used to connect a user's handheld or wearable computing devices.

wiring center — A set of racks with associated equipment that generally includes hubs, patch panels, backbone access units, and other network-management equipment, which brings TP-wired network cables together for routing, management, and control.

work area — The space in a facility or office where computer workstations and other user devices are located.

workgroup model — The Windows name for a peer-to-peer network that includes one or more Windows-based computers.

working set — Data that a program actively uses at any given time. A working set is only a small subset of the total amount of data a program *could* use.

World Wide Web (WWW) — This most well-known aspect of the Internet is made up of millions of documents that can be interlinked by using hyperlinks. Being able to view and retrieve documents with the click of a mouse makes the Internet's resources available to just about anyone.

Worldwide Interoperability for Microwave Access (WiMax) — A wireless technology designed for wireless metropolitan area networks defined in standards 802.16-2004 and 802.16e.

worm — A self-replicating program, similar to a virus, that uses network services such as e-mail to spread to other systems.

X.400 — A hardware- and software-independent message-handling protocol.

X.500 — An improved message-handling protocol that can communicate across networks and maintain a global database of addresses.

Index